Also available: *The Bible of Peckham Vols. 1 & 2*
The Only Fools and Horses Story

BBC WORLDWIDE
Series producers: Ray Butt and Gareth Gwenlan

First published 2001
Only Fools and Horses format and scripts © John Sullivan 2001
Additional material by Steve Clark
The moral right of the author has been asserted.

ISBN 0 563 53745 0

Published by BBC Worldwide Limited,
Woodlands, 80 Wood Lane, London W12 0TT

Commissioning Editor: Ben Dunn
Project Editor: Barnaby Harsent
Art Director: Linda Blakemore
Designed@Peacock

Photographs: © BBC

Set in Frutiger and Dom Casual by Keystroke, Jacaranda Lodge.

The Random House Group Limited supports The Forest Stewardship
Council® (FSC®), the leading international forest-certification organisation.
Our books carrying the FSC label are printed on FSC®-certified paper.
FSC is the only forest-certification scheme supported by the leading
environmental organisations, including Greenpeace. Our
paper procurement policy can be found at
www.randomhouse.co.uk/environment

Printed and bound in Great Britain by Clays Ltd, St Ives plc

The Bible of Peckham

Volume 3

The Feature-length Episodes 1986-96

Written & Created by

★★★ JOHN ★★★

SULLIVAN

Starring
★ DAVID ★
JASON

and
★NICHOLAS★
LYNDHURST

and
★ TESSA ★
PEAKE-JONES

and ★ GWYNETH ★ STRONG

CONTENTS

 14

A Royal Flush

EXT. DAY. THE MARKET.

Such is the temperature of today's sales items that Del has discarded the trestle table and is using the suitcase alone. As Del spiels, Rodney is standing behind him on the very kerbstones keeping a very wary eye out. Del is holding open a vinyl case which contains a canteen of cutlery. The suitcase, which contains many more of the cases, lies open on the pavement. A small crowd has gathered.

Del I mean, just look at the quality! I mean, that's the Titmus test innit, the quality? These are hand-made from Indonesian steel. They've got ivory-effect handles and they come in a genuine synthetic-leather case.

We see Rodney surveying the area and doing his job well for once.

Now these canteens of cutlery are a very exclusive line. The only other places you can buy 'em are Harrods, Libertys and Patel's Multi-Mart!

Now, as Rodney surveys the area, his attention is drawn to something on the opposite side of street. We cut to see one of the smaller, aluminium framed stalls containing paintings and sketches (all unframed). Seated on a camp stool, and reading a book, we see Vicky. She is in her early twenties, casually to scruffily dressed but attractive, without being stunning. She looks up from her book, scans area for potential customers, and then notices Rodney looking across at her. Rodney smiles – just polite and friendly. Vicky returns the smile and goes back to her book. Over these shots we can hear Del's spiel continuing.

Del *(OOV)* Now look at this, what can't speak can't lie. See that price tag? What does it say? I'll tell you what it says. It says; 'Manufacturers' recommended retail price, forty two pounds, ninety nine pence!'

We cut back to Del just as a man (middle-aged) starts arguing with Del.

Man You could have printed them yourself!

Del Do me a favour pal! Do I look like Rupert Maxwell? Now, I'm not asking you good people …

Man *(Cuts in)* There are two Ms in 'recommended!'

Del *(Checks price tag)* That is the Indonesian spelling, you plonker! Now I'm not asking you for forty two pounds, ninety-nine pence! I ain't

come here to stripe you. I ain't even asking for a score. If I said a tenner you'd think you'd had a right result.

We cut to Vicky. She looks up from her book, directly across at Rodney and smiles. She returns to her book. Rodney is stunned. The girl is actually showing out. Over these shots Del's spiel continues.

Del *(OOV)* But I don't want a tenner! Before I tell you my price, I must warn anyone of an excitable nature to move along a bit lively.

We cut back to Del.

A thirty six piece canteen of hand-made cutlery, normally priced at forty two pounds, ninety nine pence – to you, three pounds fifty! Go'n, nick 'em off me! Don't let me see 'em go, you know it hurts!

The crowd do not share Del's enthusiasm. Rodney now begins his move across to Vicky. Del has his back to Rodney and so doesn't notice him leave. As Rodney moves across street, we see (at least some) of the argument Del has with the man in background.

Del Come along ladies and gentlemen, what d'you want, jam on it?

Man They can't be top quality, they're too cheap!

Del How can anything be *too* cheap, you plonker?

Man Listen, I'm not a plonker!

Del No? So what you doing, an impression?

Rodney is now at Vicky's stall. She looks up from her book. In background and OOV the argument continues over.

Vicky Hello.

Rodney Hi. Your first day in the market?

Vicky *(She speaks with a softer, less grating, Sloane Ranger accent)* Hmm, first day.

Rodney Thought I hadn't seen you here before.

Rodney examines some of the sketches. In background we can hear:

Man I bet we don't get a guarantee with 'em!

Del *(OOV)* All you're gonna get is a smack in the mooey me old cocker! Now go and annoy someone else for a month or two!

Rodney Is this all your own work?

Vicky Yes, I'm afraid so!

Rodney Oh no, no! They're very good.

Vicky D'you really think so? Oh that's very sweet of you, thank you.

Del *(OOV)* These are not just bargains, they're investments! You can't go wrong with knives and forks!

Rodney I'm an artist. I went away to college, for a while.

Vicky *(Delighted to find a kindred spirit)* Really? I was at the Chelsea School of Art for two years, then I had a spell at the Sorbonne. Where were you?

Rodney Basingstoke.

Vicky Basingstoke? I don't think I've heard of it?

Rodney It's a big town in Hampshire!

Vicky I mean I haven't heard of the Basingstoke College of Art.

Rodney Oh it's famous! Well, round Basingstoke it is! By the way, my name's Rodney.

Vicky Victoria. Well, Vicky.

Cut back to Del, we see Trigger arriving with council dust barrow and broom.

Del Come along now ladies, make the neighbours jealous. Only the finest steel goes into the making of this premier cutlery.

Man Yeah, but how do *we* know that??

Del *(Removes a knife)* Run your wrist gently down the blade, you'll soon find out!

Trigger Alright Del boy?

Del Alright? I'd rather have shingles than these knives and forks. You can get rid of shingles! How's things with you, Trigger?

Trigger Known it worse!

Del *(To crowd)* Alright, I'll tell you what I'll do for you, I'll let 'em go at three quid each. Now you know it makes sense!

Trigger Three quid? Here, I'll have one of them Del!

Del *(Pulls Trigger to one side)* What d'you mean, you'll have one?

Trigger Well at three pounds they're a bargain!

Del Trigger, these are the ones you sold me last week for a nicker each!

Trigger No, they ain't the same. *(Indicates the £42.99 price tag)* Mine didn't have them on.

Del I don't believe him! Look, just hang around Trigger, I'll go'n give Miss Dianna a bell!

At this point Del notices a uniformed policeman. He hasn't noticed Del yet, but he's getting too close for comfort.

Del *(To the crowd)* Go on, away you all go 'fore you get your collars felt!

The crowd disperse.

Del now spots Rodney on the opposite side of street chatting merrily away to Vicky.

Del Look at that stupid little dipstick!

Del quickly closes his case locked and is about to move off away from the policeman. He

reacts as we see a uniformed police woman on the opposite side of Del. She is giving directions to someone.

I'm surrounded! I know how Custer felt now! Listen, do exactly as I say Trigger!

Cut to policeman. The sudden disappearance of the small crowd has aroused his suspicions. He moves through the shoppers towards Del and Trigger. As he arrives so Del has his suitcase in hand and is wearing his dark glasses.

Trigger *(Talking to Del in a slow and deliberate manner as if Del is foreign)* You are looking for the Hilton Hotel?

Del Si! Heelton 'otel!

Trigger Okay. Turn *left* at the top of the road.

Del *(Aware of the policeman standing close by and observing it all with a knowing look)* Si!

Trigger And you'll see a bus stop! Big red bus!

Del Si!

Trigger Get a 159 to Park Lane and that is where the Hilton Hotel is!

Del Si! Danke schon. Bonjour.

Del moves off quickly following Trigger's direction.

Trigger Don't get many tourists round this way, eh officer?

PC No. Especially tourists that speak three different languages – all at once!

Trigger just smiles at PC.

We cut to Rodney and Vicky.

Rodney So how's business? You selling much?

Vicky Not a sausage, it's been absolutely awful. I've only hired the stall for one day, just to see how it went. I want to be a *real working* artist. Someone who survives by their own efforts. I find it rather tiresome and belittling to continually live off allowances from Daddy! D'you know what I mean?

Rodney Yes! I wouldn't worry too much Vicky. You get good days and bad days down the market. *(Examining a sketch)* Maybe I could be your very first customer. How much is this?

Vicky That's fifty pounds.

Rodney Oh ..! *(Picks up another one)* How about this?

Vicky That's eighty five.

Rodney I see! D'you mind if I give you a word of advice Vicky? You see, people round here don't pay eighty five pounds for a painting! People round here don't pay eighty five pounds for a car!

Vicky Oh but surely, everyone has paintings in their homes!

Rodney Yeah, but these people don't get their

A Royal Flush

painting from galleries and what 'ave you. They get 'em from British Home Stores and Prize Bingo! You've got the wrong market Vicky. You should try Portobello Road, you might be in with a shout then.

Vicky Hmm, possibly you're right. Oh well, nothing ventured, eh? Would you be an absolute love and help me carry some of this back to the car?

Rodney I'd like to help Victoria, but I'm afraid I'm very busy. I'm working with my bro … *(Sees Del has gone)* Oh! He must have sold out early and gone for a bit of grub. Well in that case, I'm at your service Miss.

Vicky Oh that's very sweet of you. I'm sorry ..?

Rodney Rodney.

Trigger *(Calls across)* Wotchyer Dave.

Rodney *(To Vicky)* No. My name is Rodney, he's just very thick!

Vicky I see.

EXT. DAY. SIDE ROAD. LEADING OFF MARKET.

Rodney and Vicky, carrying all the paintings, sketches etc. are walking along.

Vicky What line of business are you in, Rodney?

Rodney I am a partner in a … in a partnership. Me and my brother. We buy and sell – this and that.

Vicky You don't specialise?

Rodney Em – no!

Vicky I envy you. It must be wonderful to work in the market every day. I find it so stimulating. All the hustle and bustle, and those lovely, lovely characters one meets. I know they're not all lovely! Did you spot that noisy little person selling the tatty cutlery?

Rodney Yeah! That's my brother!

Vicky Oh! I'm frightfully sorry! When I said noisy I didn't mean any …

Rodney *(Cuts in)* No that's alright. He is noisy! He's always been noisy! But he's as good as gold really. I sort of, look after him.

Vicky Oh I see. I have no brothers or sisters.

Rodney D'you want him?

Rodney *(Laughing)* No thank you. Well, here's the old crate.

Rodney reacts. We see a gleaming car parked at kerb. Vicky opens the boot and they place the paintings etc. inside.

Rodney Nice car!

Vicky It was a birthday present.

Rodney Oh! I got a Nick Kershaw L.P! Right then, I'm gonna get something to eat. See you around Vicky.

Vicky Where do you lunch?

Rodney Lunch? Oh, I usually go down to the Greasy Thumb.

Vicky The Greasy Thumb?

Rodney No, it's Sid's caff really, we just call it the Greasy Thumb. Out of affection.

Vicky May I join you for lunch?

Rodney You? In the Greasy Thumb? Oh I don't think you'd like it Victoria! It's all steam and bacteria – it's 'orrible!

Vicky I get the feeling you're an inverted snob, Rodney. Come on, jump in. I'll chauffeur you down there.

Rodney *(Climbing into passenger seat)* But you won't like it Victoria! *I* don't even like it and I'm a regular! Look, there's a McDonalds round the corner!

The car pulls away in a cloud of burning rubber.

INT. DAY. SID'S CAFE.

It is packed with market workers, building site labourers, punks, skinheads, rastas etc. A jukebox is playing loudly. The windows are steamed up. We see cigarette smoke and hear all the sounds of a workman's cafe. The sounds of a pinball machine, arguments and Sid calling out for people to come and collect their meals and shouting orders through a serving hatch to the kitchen.

The first shot is of Sid's hand holding a plate of sausage, egg and baked beans. His thumb is in the bean juice, as he hands the plate to customer we see the greasy thumb print it leaves on the side of plate.

Sid *(Shouting for customers to collect) (cigarette still between lips)* Sausage, egg, beans! Bacon, egg and toms twice! Egg, bubble and beans twice!

1st man *(Cockney labourer)* Egg and chips! Egg, sausage and chips! Egg, sausage, beans and chips!

Sid *(Shouts through hatch as two plates containing pie and chips, and pie, chips and peas are handed out to him)* Egg and chips! Egg, sausage and chips! Egg, sausage, beans and chips! *(Now calls for customer to collect)* Pie and chips! Pie, chips and peas!

Rodney arrives at counter (He and Vicky are already seated in cafe)

Rodney The egg, bubble and beans twice.

Sid *(Hands him the two plates)* There you go Rodney. Don't forget your tea, son. *(Collects from hatch. Calls)* Two of dripping toast! Bacon, egg and one slice!

 17

Rodney returns to table cautiously winding his way through some of the big labourers who are standing round the one-armed bandit. Rodney holds both plates in one hand and the two mugs of tea in the other.

Rodney 'Scuse me … Sorry … Thanks a lot.
He arrives at table, places food and tea down and sits. Seated next to Rodney and asleep on the table is an old dosser.

Rodney There you are, Vicky.

Vicky Thank you. I think it's lovely in here.

Rodney Yeah, it's er, it's good innit?

Vicky Is this the bubble and squeak?

Rodney Yeah, that's the bubble.

Vicky And what is it actually?

Rodney It's sort of, em, greens and, er, and sort of potatoes, and you mix it all up and, em, and fry it.

Vicky *(Tastes some)* Mmmh! It's absolutely munchy!

During all this we hear in the background

2nd man *(OOV)* This machine's broke again Sid!

Sid *(OOV)* If you don't keep tilting the sodding thing it wouldn't break, would it? Burger, chips and peas! Chicken, chips and beans. *(Etc)*

Rodney You're not from round Peckham way, are you?

Vicky No, I was born and raised in Berkshire. I moved up to London about three months ago. Have you always lived here?

Rodney Yeah, always.

Vicky I've been wanting to live in London for ages. Berkshire's so boring. Boring Berkshire I call it. *(She laughs loudly)*

Rodney laughs politely and wonders what the hell she is laughing at.

Vicky I wanted to be near the art galleries. I suppose you're always in them?

Rodney Well not really. Although I went up to the National Gallery a couple of weeks back. I suddenly realised – and I'm ashamed to admit it – but in all the years it's been housed there I'd never actually seen the Da Vinci cartoon.

Vicky Well I'm ashamed to admit but I haven't seen it either. What did you think of it?

Rodney Em, well actually they were closed! But I'm gonna try again.

Vicky Why don't we go together?

Rodney Yeah, cushty!

Vicky Cushty?

Rodney It means – wonderful, t'riffic.

Vicky Oh I see, how frightfully Albert Square! So shall we say tomorrow at noon?

Rodney Tomorrow? I don't know if I'll be able to get time off work.

Vicky I though you said you were a partner?

Rodney Yeah, I am a partner but … Yeah, alright then, I'll give myself the day off! Tomorrow at noon.

Vicky Cushty! Do you like the opera Rodney? Of course you do, I can tell!

Rodney Yeah!

Vicky There's a new production of *Carmen* opening at the Royal Opera House next week. I've tried *everywhere* to get tickets but it's absolutely impossible!

Rodney Yeah, I couldn't get any either. Vicky, I hope you don't mind me saying this, but I didn't think Peckham would be your scene!

Vicky Oh no, I absolutely adore this area. It' a so rough and raw and vibrant! I saw a woman spit yesterday! You see, I was brought up in a tiny community in the wilds of boring Berkshire. My world was one of nannies, live-in tutors, gymkhanas and village fetes. The first time I left there was when I was eleven, and that was only to Roedean. Then I went on to a Swiss finishing school. Mine was a very insular existence. I didn't realise there was a *real* world – until I decided to make art my life. I suppose that's why I like it round here – it must be the artist in me. My mother was a painter. She had some of her work exhibited at the Royal Academy.

Rodney *(Very impressed)* No? Oh Mega! The Royal Academy! Does she still paint?

Vicky *(Saddened to speak of this)* No.

Rodney Have I said something wrong?

Vicky No. You see my mother died when I was twelve. A skiing accident in Austria.

Rodney Oh I'm very sorry Vicky! I know how much it must have hurt you!

Vicky I doubt it Rodney.

Rodney Oh I know exactly how you felt. The same thing happened to me when I was only five.

Vicky Oh poor Rodney. How awful for you! *(Squeezes his hand)* Where was your mother skiing?

Rodney No – no, my mum weren't skiing! All in all, according to what the rest of the family tell me, my mum didn't do a lot of skiing! She just had something wrong with her, that's all.

Vicky Oh I see … Sorry! *(Checks watch)* Lord, look at the time! I must fly otherwise they start worrying.

Rodney Who do?

Vicky Special Branch.

Rodney S … s … Sorry! Special Branch?

Vicky Oh, it's all incredibly tedious! They protect us you see. Well, Daddy mainly.

A Royal Flush

Rodney Why, what is he, a supergrass?

Vicky *(Laughing)* No! Silly! He's … oh it's so boring! My father is the Duke of Maylebury.

Rodney was about to eat some bubble'n'squeak. It falls off the fork and onto his lap.

Rodney The … The Duke of Maylebury?

Vicky I told you it was boring. Well, I must dash. See you tomorrow at the National?

Rodney *(Weakly)* Yeah!

Vicky Cushty! Ciao! *(She exits)*

Rodney remains seated and totally dumbfounded. He picks up mug of tea and sips it. The old dosser wakes.

Dosser Oi, that's my tea!

Rodney *(Still in trance)* Sorry … *(Now reacts)* Eerghh – you dirty old bark!

INT. DAY. THE TROTTERS' LOUNGE.

Rodney is seated on the settee still wearing his market clothes and his big Doc Martin boots. He is reading Burke's Peerage. He looks up from book, stunned.

He now picks up a magazine (Country Life) and opens it to a black and white picture. It is a photo of Princess Anne at a horse trials. She wears riding gear and has a number pinned to her. Standing next to her, also in riding gear and number (but minus a riding hat) we see Vicky. They are both smiling (posing) for camera. Rodney puts mag down and stares blankly into space. We now hear the ront door open and Del and Albert's voices.

Albert *(OOV)* I don't know why you couldn't of left it till tomorrow!

Del *(OOV)* Will you give it a rest Albert? You've done more bleedin' whining than a spin-dryer!

Albert enters, he is exhausted and wiping sweat from his brow with a hankie.

Albert Rodney's back Del boy, someone must have paid the ransom!

Del enters, he too is wiping sweat from his brow. He gives Rodney a glare and then moves to the drinks cabinet.

Rodney What's up?

Albert What's up? Where you been all afternoon?

Rodney I went down the library.

Albert What for?

Rodney See if me shoes were done! What d'you think I went to the library for? To get a book! *(Holds book up)*

Del Burke's? What is it – a teach-yourself book?

Rodney It is a genealogical and heraldic history of the British peerage!

Albert Yeah, well while you've been wasting yer time down the library I've had to help Del collect a consignment of computers *and* stack 'em in the garage!

Rodney Well, a bit of hard work won't hurt you Unc!

Del And how the hell would you know?

Rodney I don't bel … Alright, so I had this afternoon off, is that such a big deal?

Del I ain't concerned with this afternoon Rodney. What I'd like to know is what the bleedin' hell were you doing this morning?

Rodney You know what I was doing this morning! I was on look-out in the market.

Del Oh you was on look-out alright, but it weren't for the Old Bill, was it! I almost got a tug from the local gendarmerie while you were chatting that little tart up!

Rodney Well, I didn't see any coppers!

Del Of course you didn't 'cos you had your nose buried in her etchings! I've been grafting all day long to make us a few bob, and all I've seen of you was a fleeting glimpse as you went into the landscape department!

Rodney *(Maintaining his pride)* Alright! Sorry! I'll pay more attention in future!

Del Make sure you do, otherwise you'll be going down the road!

Rodney This might not be the right time to ask, but can I have tomorrow off?

Del Can you ..? I don't believe you said that Rodney!

Rodney It's important Del! I've gotta go somewhere. It really is important – honest!

Albert *(Concerned)* You alright son?

Del *(Equally concerned)* Yeah, you gotta go to the hospital or something?

Rodney No. I have to go to the National Art Gallery!

Albert Oh it's an emergency then?

Rodney In certain respects, yes! I'm an artist!

Albert So was Hitler!

Rodney Why don't you keep your nose out of it Albert?

Albert It's none of my business son! I'm saying nothing on the matter! If Del don't mind you taking the rise out of him, that's fine by me! I'll make some tea. *(Exits to kitchen)*

Rodney Look – that girl who was selling the paintings down the market, Vicky, well neither of us has ever seen the Leonardo Da Vinci cartoon!

Del I've never seen the pyramids but I don't have a day off sick for it! Alright Rodders, take Vicky, or whatever her name is, up to the National Gallery. And while you're mooching

around discussing the brush strokes and pretty colours, you tell her that your big brother ain't giving you no wages this week!

Rodney Oh come on Del, that ain't fair!

Del Ain't fair? Because of you and your dopey paintings I came within three yards of a sudden summons this morning! That ain't fair Rodney!

Rodney Well, thanks a bunch! Thanks a great big bunch Del! That is – that is just cosmic!! I'm supposed to take her out tomorrow and I'm potless! It'll be right embarrassing. Specially with her coming from a money background.

Del (Reading newspaper) It's a tough old world innit … (Without taking his eyes from paper) What d'you mean, a money background?

Rodney Her old man's very wealthy.

Del Why? What game's he in?

Rodney I've gotta tell someone Del. But promise me this will go no further?

Del Righto, it's just between us.

Rodney Have you ever heard of the Duke of Maylebury?

Del The Duke of ..! Give over, you twonk!

Rodney It's the God's honest truth, Del!

Del No!

Rodney Del, I cross my heart and hope to die in a cellarful of rats! It's the truth!

Del What that little girl ..? Her Daddy ..?

Rodney Honest, it's for real!

Del Bloody hell!

Rodney It's our secret, alright?

Del Yeah, yeah, course it is!

Albert enters from kitchen.

Del D'you hear that Albert?

Rodney reacts.

Del D'you know that little sort Rodney's knocking around with?

Albert What about her?

Del Her father – only owns a pub!

Albert Go'n, you're pulling me leg!

Del No, he owns the Duke of Maylebury. It's over Nunhead Way, innit Rodney?

Rodney No! No listen! He don't *own* the Duke of Maylebury! He *is* the Duke of Maylebury! He's nobility! He's a peer of the realm!

Del and Albert stare at him, now they both burst out laughing.

Del Leave it out Rodders! I've seen a picture of the real Duke of Maylebury in the *Sporting Life*. He owns that horse, Hanover Canaan, second favourite for next year's Derby. That little bird looks nothing like him! She's no more nobility than you!

Rodney (Shows them the photo from Country Life) No? Have a look at that!

Del I don't believe it! That's the girl from the market!

Albert Which one?

Del Her there, with the long hair. She's with Princess Anne at a rodeo or something!

Rodney (Referring to Burke's) They're in here as well. Her father's sort of second cousin to the Queen!

Del and Albert, mouths open in disbelief, just stare at Rodney.

Rodney Vicky's in here as well. (Finds page) Here are. Her full title is 'Lady Victoria Marsh Hales'. Only child of Sir Henry Marsham, K.G.B. G.L.C. B.O. and Bar. Fourteenth Duke of Maylebury! Family home; Covington House, Upper Stanameer, Berkshire.

Del and Albert look at each other.

Del (Angrily to Rodney) You ain't had a go at her, have you?

Rodney No I aint!

Del Well you keep your mucky mits off her! Otherwise we'll have her mother throwing royal prerogatives all over the shop!

Rodney I doubt it, her mother died nine years ago in a skiing accident!

Albert Alright then, answer me this. If she is a titled lady what's she going out with *him* for?

Rodney reacts offended.

Del Listen Albert, Rodney has got a lot of qualities. She might have been smitten by his rakish charms and boyish good looks! Then again she might be a posh tart who fancies a bit of scrag! You never can tell. Tel Aviv as the French say!

Rodney Look, Vicky and I just happen to relate to each other well. We've got a lot in common.

Albert No, son, she's got a lot and you're just common!

Rodney He's giving me the right 'ump, Del!

Del Hold on a minute! Albert might have cracked it! I think I know what this is all about! Listen to me. It is a well known fact that every two or three hundred years or so, the aristocracy have to bring a bit of common stock into the family to water the old blue blood down a bit.

Albert (Indicating Rodney) What, and they can't do better than that? Do me a favour!

Rodney I'm gonna whack him right round the ear'ole in a minute!

Del Well, why shouldn't it be Rodney? I mean, Mark Phillips was a commoner!

Albert But there's a common and there's a common! Mark Phillips was a wealthy man and well known in the Royal Courts. Rodney's polo mint and well known in the magistrate's courts!

A Royal Flush

Del Well, I don't care what you say. I reckon Lady Victoria Marsham-Hales has been instructed to sort herself out an old man from the lower classes. And Rodney's in the frame! Rodney, ask her to marry you!

Rodney Mar … I don't wanna get married!

Del Listen to me you dipstick! Don't you see what this could all lead to? Vicky is the sole heiress to the Maylebury fortunes! She's got no brothers or sisters and the old gel popped her clogs half way down the giant slalom! So when the old duke finally says bonsoir to this mortal curl, she becomes the Duchess! And you know what that means?

Rodney What?

Del Albert, I want you to remember this moment. We could be looking at – the future Duke of Maylebury! *(Bows to Rodney)*
We see Rodney lounging back in the armchair. He has a roll-up between his lips. One foot is resting on the knee of the other leg so we can see his big boots.

Albert He don't look like a peer of the realm!

Del Not at the moment, no. But a coronet, bit of ermine, get rid of them boots and he'll be a dead ringer!

Rodney I don't want to be a Duke!

Del Don't give me all that Tony Benn cobblers! Think of all the advantages! You'll be a member of the House of Lords!

Albert Yeah … we'll be able to watch you on the telly having a kip.

Rodney Del Boy, so far all I have done is buy Victoria a plate of egg and bubble at Sid's caff! That is hardly the basis for a marriage proposal!

Del *(Horrified)* You took one of the Queen's relatives to the Greasy Thumb? What is the matter with you Rodney? The poor little mare'll be up all night with the thrupenny-bits! Their palates are different from ours. They can't eat egg and bubble!

Rodney Well Sid didn't have any venison on the menu today! I am not asking her to marry me! In a few weeks I might not even like her!

Del I don't care if you chuck up at the very sight of her, Rodney!

Albert Del ain't asking you to like her – just marry her! Get your plimsoles under that old Chippendale and you'll never look back! You'll be a titled person.

Rodney Dracula's a titled person!

Del He's only a Count. Anyway, he ain't real!

Rodney I'm beginning to wonder if you are! Del, Victoria and I are like … well, we're more like mates than anything! We have just one mutual interest – art! Other than that we're worlds apart! I mean, she wants us to go to places like … well, the opera.

Albert Why, what's on?

Rodney An opera!

Albert I mean what opera?

Rodney I don't know! *Carmen* or something!

Del That's one of my favourites. *(Sings)* Figaro, Figaro, Figaro, Figaro!

Rodney Hear that Unc? He knows all the words! Listen, I don't know the first thing about operas? And besides, it's impossible to get tickets for the opening night.

Del If you want tickets for the opening night, you shall have tickets for the opening night, Cinders.

Rodney How?

Del How'd you think? Limpy Lionel the tout! He can get tickets for anything!

Albert Gonna cost, Del?

Del What does money matter compared with little Rodney's happiness? When you see that little tar … her ladyship, tell her you've got tickets for the opening night! And it's my treat Rodney.

Rodney Oh cheers Del Boy! You are a pal! You are a *real* pal!

Del *(Produces a wad of money)* And I want you to pay for her to get into that art gallery tomorrow.

Rodney No, art galleries are f … cheers Del!
Takes the money.

Del Then I want you to take her for a right slap up meal. Steak, wine, the works. I mean don't get her Oliver Twist or nothing! We don't want a scandal!

Rodney *(Takes the rest of the money)* Leave it to me, Del.

Del And when you see that Leonardo Da Vinci cartoon – *you laugh!*

Rodney Why?

Albert Let her know you get the joke!

Rodney Oh of course! *(Counting the money)* Well, don't you worry. I'll be laughing alright! I'm gonna whip down the pawn shop and liberate me evening suit. See you later.
Rodney exits through hall door.

Albert Well, that's a turn up for the book, Del! Young Rodney marrying into the Royal family. How'd you think the Queen'll feel about it?

Del Dunno really. I s'ppose when she first hears the news she'll be a bit gutted. But once she meets him I think she'll like him. I mean, he's a nice boy. Friendly, polite, respectful. He'll have to knock them roll-ups on the head. You can't

waltz round a garden party with a packet of Green Rizla sticking out of yer morning suit!

Albert Here, we might be able to wangle ourselves a winter cruise on the old Britannia!

Del No Albert, no! We're not gonna ponce off 'em! That sort of thing causes family rifts. And another thing, let's not count our chickens before we've crossed 'em? I'm starting to get a funny feeling.

Albert What, something might go wrong?

Del If we leave it in Rodney's hands it's a guarantee! He ain't got a clue when it comes to women! That boy's been blown-out more times than a wind-sock! Sometimes you have to help Rodney to help himself.

Albert Yeah but what can we do?

Del We can help him make the right impression! That is the all important thing – the *impression!* He's gotta prove that he appreciates the finer things of life. Show that he's au fait *(fate)* with gracious living.

Albert *(Surveys the debris of the flat)* How's he gonna do that?

Del *(Shakes his head in a superior, smug way)* This is where I come in! Simply to add that element of good breeding. A little touch of refinement, a sprinkle of sophistication! *(Checks watch)* Right, I'd better phone Limpy Lionel and sort these tickets out.

EXT. NIGHT. ONE OF THE LONDON BRIDGES.

The lights of the embankment and the reflection from the river give us a sense of sophistication as we see a sleek, chauffeur-driven limousine glide past. Seated in the back of the limo we see Vicky, dressed beautifully for the opening night (seated on driver's side) and Rodney wearing a white dinner-jacket, black bow-tie (seated near-side back).

Since managing the impossible and getting two tickets for the opening night, Rodney is a lot more confident in her company.

Vicky I still don't understand how you managed it! Even *Daddy* couldn't get tickets for the opening night, and he tried everywhere!

Rodney Oh it was nothing really! I have – let's just say – contacts!

We see the chauffeur (Eric) eyeing Rodney in the rear view mirror – he knows Rodney's bullshitting. Rodney sees the eyes reflected in the mirror and reacts embarrassed.

Vicky But they must have cost the earth!

Rodney I didn't ask – I just told my man,

'Get them!'

We see Eric's reaction. He sighs and shakes his head. He looks in the mirror again. Rodney sees his reflection in the mirror. He looks from the window sheepishly.

EXT. NIGHT. THE ROYAL OPERA HOUSE.

We see the limousine pull up outside. Eric alights and opens the back door for Vicky.

Eric Have a nice evening miss.

Vicky Thank you Eric, I'm sure we will.

Vicky moves towards pavement. Rodney, who assumes Eric will open his door, is still seated back. Eric leans into the car.

Eric Oi, out!

Rodney Oh, right! *(Opens door himself and alights)*

He and Vicky ascend steps to Opera House.

INT. NIGHT. FOYER OF OPERA HOUSE.

Rodney and Vicky enter the packed foyer and begin to make their way towards the person taking the tickets. Rodney produces the two tickets from his inside pocket.

Vicky *(Purely as a joke)* I hope they're not forgeries! *(Laughs)*

Rodney laughs, now stops suddenly, his face frozen. He realises how right she may be. As they move across the foyer a few people nod and smile to Vicky. Rodney is oblivious to it all, he is like a zombie gripped with fear.

Ticket Collector Good evening Lady Victoria.

Vicky Hello.

Ticket Collector *(Takes tickets from Rodney)* Thank you, sir.

Rodney has a manic grin. The ticket collector checks tickets. Looks up to Rodney. We see his silly grin. The ticket collector now smiles at Rodney, tears tickets in half and hands him the stubs.

Ticket Collector Thank you sir, have a nice evening.

Rodney *(His voice even sounds idiotic with nerves)* What?

Ticket Collector I said, have a nice evening sir.

Rodney Oh! Thank you. Thank you very much.

Rodney and Vicky move away.

Vicky Is there anything wrong?

Rodney No, I'm fine! I'll get us a programme.

Moves to programme seller.

Rodney Two programmes please.

Prog. Seller *(Before handing him the programmes)* That's eight pounds sir.

Rodney No, I said *two* programmes!

Prog. Seller They're four pounds each, sir.

A Royal Flush

Rodney Oh … Right! *(Pays for programmes)*
Rodney and Vicky continue on their way towards bar.

Vicky Rodney. I know you'll think me a frightful old bore, but you know you'd invited me to a soccer match on Saturday? Well, I'm afraid I'll have to cancel.

Rodney *(Thinks he's getting the brush off)* Oh! Well, that's no problem Vicky.

Vicky I have to go home you see, Daddy's invited a few friends down to the estate for the weekend – a shoot and then dinner – and I simply *have* to be there, I'm the lady of the house these days.

Rodney No, that's alright. I understand.

Vicky Would you like to join us, as my guest?

Rodney Oh, em … well …

Vicky You could stay overnight and then on Sunday I'll take you for the most wonderful lunch at our little local.

Rodney Well … thank you Vicky, I'd love to!

Vicky Oh that's super!

INT. NIGHT. THE BAR. OPERA HOUSE.

Rodney Can I get you a drink?

Vicky A *very* dry white wine and soda please.

Rodney Right. Shan't be a moment.
Rodney moves through the crowds to the bar.

Rodney *(To barman)* Excuse me! Could I have two *very* dry white wines and soda, thank you.
We now hear, from the very back of the bar.

Del *(OOV) (A high, shrill whistle)* Rodders!
Rodney is frozen. He is the only one who doesn't turn and look in the direction of the noise. Rodney is shaking his head in disbelief as Del, in his flash mohair evening suit, arrives at his shoulder.

Del Alright bruv? *(Indicating watch)* I was getting a bit worried, the old time was creeping on! *(To an elderly lady who is staring at him)* Alright darling? They reckon it's a good 'un tonight! *(Shouts down to the barman who is serving Rodney)* Oi John, when you've finished yer dinner break, any chance of some service?

Rodney He is already serving me!

Del Well, that's alright then! Get us a cubra libre, Rodney.

Rodney What the bloody hell are you doing here?

Del Oh charming, after all I've done for you! There were *four* tickets up for grab! And you know me, I love a bit of opera!

Rodney You? The only opera you've ever seen was *Tommy*, and that was on video! You've never been to an opera in your life!

Del I've never milked a cow in me life but I still like a bit of cheese! *(Vicky joins them)* Good evening, Victoria. May I say you are looking particularly lovely?

Vicky Thank you. I didn't realise you'd be joining us tonight.

Del Yes, there were four tickets available, you see.

Rodney *(Quickly)* And I bought 'em all!

Del Eh? Yes, and Rodney bought them all! He's like that, generous to a fault!
We cut to another part of the bar. Exiting from ladies room we see June. Her dress is too low, too short and too tight. A slit up the side of the dress reveals even more of her fishnet tights. She wears silver stiletto shoes. She is heavily made up and wears a lot of junk jewellery. She carries a handbag which is more like a kit bag.
Rodney, being the tallest, spots June over the heads of the crowd. He doesn't recognise her immediately.

Rodney I don't believe it!

Vicky You don't believe what?

Rodney This is the Royal Opera House and someone's ordered a Kissogram!

Del Never! Where?
Del peers through the bodies and spots June.

Del *(To Rodney)* You saucy little … That's my bird!

Rodney *(Horrified)* No! Please Del, it's not!

Del It's Junie! You remember June! Lives over in Zimbabwe House!

Rodney *(Feels like crying)* Del, I used to go out with her daughter.

Del Don't worry. She won't say a word.
June joins them. Due to the tightness of her dress and height of her heels, she doesn't actually 'walk'. She kind of totters. She has a glass of Benedictine and lemonade.
Throughout the evening Del treats her warmly and almost affectionately.

June I weren't sure where you'd got to! Them karseys ain't half posh.

Del You only go to the best places with me, sweetheart! Allow me to introduce you. Lady Victoria, I'd like you to meet June Snell.

Vicky Good evening, June.

June Hello, you alright?

Del *(Nudges her)* Oi! It's *Lady* Victoria! Remember?

June Oh yeah! *(Curtsys as Del has trained her to)* It's a great pleasure to meet you, m'am.

Vicky *(Embarrassed)* Please, it really isn't necessary.

Del Oh no, Victoria. June likes to keep herself in perspective, don't you girl?

June Yeah, I think it's best!

Del You remember Rodney.

June Wotchyer.

Rodney Wotchyer.

June *(To Vicky. referring to Rodney)* He used to go out with my daughter Debby!

Rodney reacts

June *(To Rodney)* She's living with a Cypriot geezer now!

Rodney T'riffic!

Vicky *(Changing the subject to save Rodney's embarrassment)* So you're an opera buff as well, are you, June?

June I saw one once. It was on BBC2. Our telly had gone up the wall and that was the only channel we could get. You came round that night Del, remember? Well you'd just delivered the telly, hadn't you?

Del That's right. *(To Vicky)* Just needed a little adjustment, that's all.

June There was that world famous foreign bloke singing, weren't there?

Del Yes. Wonderful voice!

June Oh yes, he was very talented. Great big fat git, weren't he?

Del Mmmh, but couldn't he put a song across? *(To Vicky)* Of course, this is my most favourite opera, *Carmen. (Begins singing)* Figaro, Figaro Figaro Figaro Figaro!

Vicky That's from *The Barber of Seville.*

Del Eh?

Vicky It's not from *Carmen*, it's from *The Barber of Seville.*

Rodney *(Like an expert)* Yes, definitely *The Barber of Seville.*

Del Of course it is! Of course it is! I don't know what's the matter with me. I *always* get *Carmen* and *The Barber of Seville* mixed up!

June Well, *Carmen* is a hair-dryer innit?

Del Of course, that's it!

The bell that warns the show is about to start rings.

Del *(Checks watch)* Blimey, he's rung that one early ain't he?

Rodney Well, hurry up, we might get another one in! So it's white wine and soda. June?

June I'm on Benedictine and lemonade.

Vicky Excuse me. The bell is simply to warn the audience that the performance is about to begin.

Del and Rodney look at each other, they both feel right prats.

Del Yes, we know that!

Rodney Yeah, we know that, we just thought

we might have time for a quick one!

Vicky I don't think so. We really ought to be taking our seats.

Rodney Yes of course! *(Proffers his arm)* May I?

Vicky Thank you. *(Places her hand on his arm)*

Rodney and Vicky move towards exit.

Del *(With a gesture of the head to June)* Come on then.

June How come she's got a programme and I ain't?

Del She can read!

June *(Accepting the explanation)* Oh!

Del struts towards exit. June totters after him.

INT. NIGHT. THE AUDITORIUM.

On stage the production is in full flow.

We see a section of the audience where, in the centre of a row we see June, then Del, then Rodney, then Vicky. Del is mouthing along with the song although we can tell that he doesn't have a clue what the words are. He moves his hands passionately and contorts his face emotionally. June is sucking on the straw of a plastic canister of orange juice which she most probably bought in the foyer. Vicky is enthralled with the performance. Rodney is feigning interest but is also concerned about Del's behaviour.

June reaches the end of her orange juice. We hear that awful slurping sound of liquid and air. A few people in audience turn slightly at noise Vicky is too spellbound to hear it. Rodney is embarrassed. Del ignores it, he's used to these sort of noises. June drops the empty carton on floor.

Del *(To June)* Blinding opera innit?

June It's alright I suppose. It don't get going, does it?

Del It's not s'pposed to get going! This is culture! See, you don't come to an opera to enjoy it, you come because it's there!

June Oh, I didn't know that! I like Vince Hill.

Del *(In total agreement)* Yeah, yeah, I like Vince Hill as well. He's almost culture. Not quite, but almost.

OOV Sssshhhh!

Del *(Looks for the culprit)* What's that about?

June Dunno. Maybe there's someone talking somewhere.

Del Yeah maybe. Some people have got no protocol.

June Na. *(She searches round her big handbag. She produces a squashed and already open box of liquorice allsorts)* I've got a few liquorice allsorts left.

A Royal Flush

Del You got one with the hundreds and thousands on it?

June *(Picks one out)* Only one. *(She eats it herself)*

Del takes the packet.

Del *(Nudges Rodney)* Rodney.

Rodney What?

Del Wanna liquorice allsort?

Rodney No.

Del Vicky … Vicky!

A man in audience turns.

1st Man Ssshhh!

Del He having a pop at me?

Rodney No he's not! Just be quiet, Del!

Del Alright, alright … Vicky!

Vicky D'you wanna liquorice allsort?

Vicky No thank you.

Del Oh, alright. *(Sits back. To June)* There's only a couple left, might as well finish 'em off.

He and June eat the last two sweets. Del crunches box up and drops it on floor. We see it land next to the empty carton of orange. Rodney breathes a sigh of relief that it is all over and the sweets have gone. We stay on Rodney. OOV We hear the rustling of paper.

Del *(Nudges him)* Rodney.

Rodney What?

Del D'you wanna crisp?

Rodney No!

Del Vicky …

Man Ssshhhh!

Del Don't you shush me, pal!

Rodney Del, please!

Del Well … Vicky …

Vicky Yes?

Del Fancy a crisp?

Vicky Oh, no thank you.

Del sits back in seat. Stay on Rodney who is once more relieved that that little episode is over. We hear (OOV) the heavy crunching of crisps from Del and June. Other members of the audience turn and look. One of the performers hears the noise and looks up into the audience.

Del *(Nudges Rodney)* Rodney.

Rodney What?

Del *(Referring to Vicky)* Put your arm round her

Rodney Eh?

Del Put your arm round her shoulder.

Rodney I don't bel … Del, this is not the Odeon!

OOV Ssssshhh!

Rodney Sorry.

Del Don't you 'sorry' him! *(To man)* Just keep on pal, see what you get!

Del sits back and takes the packet of crisps from June.

Del *(Finding the packet almost empty)* You've had all of them!

June No I ain't, you had some!

Del takes the last crisp and lets the packet drop to floor. We see it land next to the carton and the empty box.

INT. NIGHT. THE AUDITORIUM.

Del's seat is empty. June is now eating a packet of dry-roasted peanuts, she drops the empty packet. We see it land next to the empty carton etc.

Rodney *(To June)* Where's Del gone?

June He went out to the ice-cream lady.

Rodney *(Worried)* Oh!

We cut to stage and stay with performance for a while. We now cut to the dark aisle where we see Del, eating a choc-ice and holding three others, looking for his place.

Del *(Calls as quietly as possible)* Rodney! We see a couple of people in aisle seats react.

Del Rodney!

Rodney hears him and tries to wave as discreetly as possible. Del doesn't see him.

Del Rodders!

Woman Will you please be quiet?

Del I can't find my place! Rodney!

June stands and calls.

June We're over here, Del!

Del moves to his row.

Del Excuse me, please.

The people in the row have to stand. We hear lots of moaning and groaning from them and the people sitting behind.

Del Thank you very much … thank you … oh sorry, was that your toe?

He now squeezes past June. As he does so we see the floor (the box of allsorts, the packet of crisps, the packet of dry-roasted peanuts and the empty orange carton. We see Del's foot land on the empty orange carton. Cut to the auditorium/stage. We hear a mighty 'pop' as the carton explodes. We see the singer, in fact the entire cast, react and look out into audience. They now manage to pick the song up and continue. We cut back to our section of audience. A great, confused, hushed row ensues. It is very confused with people talking and shouting over each other.

1st man For God's sake, how long do we have to put up with this?

Del I didn't know there was an empty carton on the floor! *(To June)* What d'you drop it on the floor for?

June Well how was I to know you were gonna tread on it?

Woman Are you going to continue making this noise throughout the entire performance?

Del I don't know, I might let you off for the second half!

Rodney Del, please, sit down.

2nd Man I am trying to listen!

Del Well shut up then!

1st Man Will you please be quiet?

Del I'll come down there and smack you in the eye if you keep on!

There should be lots of other complaining voices which are lost in a general buzz of sound. At some point in this sequence we cut to stage and see the cast's reaction.
Del sits, things begin to calm.

Rodney Just take it easy, please!

Del Well he's giving me the 'ump Rodney!
Pause as Del eats away at his choc-ice. He hands a choc-ice to June. Without looking at Rodney, Del nudges him with the hand which is holding the choc-ice. A small dab of chocolate is left on the lapel of Rodney's white dinner jacket. No-one notices this except us.

Del Rodney.

Rodney What?

Del Wanna choc-ice?

Rodney No!

Del But I bought you one.

Rodney I don't want it!
Pause.

Del Vicky … Vicky!

Vicky Yes?

Del I got you a choc-ice.

Vicky No thank you, I never eat ice-cream.

Del But I bought it for you.

Rodney She doesn't eat ice-cream!

Vicky I've never ever liked ice-cream.

Del Oh … What am I supposed to do with these?

Rodney You can stick 'em where the sun don't shine as far as I'm concerned. Just shut up!

Del Well thank you, bruv! Thank you very much.
He drops the two choc-ices down on the floor next to the now busted carton, the crisp wrapper, the peanut packet, the allsorts box and the piece of choc-ice wrapping that June tore off and threw away
Now all is calm. All that can be heard, besides the singing on stage, is the smacking of lips

and licking of choc-ice from Del and June. June finishes her choc-ice, screws up what's left of the foil wrapping and throws it on floor. Del finishes his and just lets the paper fall to floor. The Habanera begins.

Del Oh I love this one!
Del begins whistling along with the song. People are now turning round again.
We see the singer's reaction as she hears someone in the audience whistling along with her.

Rodney *(Nudges Del)* Del!

Del Sshh Rodney, I'm whistling!
As Del continues we pan to June who is obviously beginning to feel quite sick.

EXT. NIGHT. THE ROYAL OPERA HOUSE.
From inside the theatre we can hear the Toreador song. The foyer and the street are deserted. Now a fuming Rodney walks out through foyer and exits to top of steps. He breathes a great lungful of the cold night air in an attempt to calm himself down. He has the small chocolate stain on his lapel. Vicky now joins him.

Rodney I am sorry! I am so, so sorry!

Vicky It wasn't your fault Rodney! I'm not blaming you and you shouldn't blame yourself!

Rodney I know, but … Oh God!
We now see Del, a sick looking June and a St Johns ambulance man exit to top of steps. The ambulanceman has his hand on June's elbow by way of assistance. Del is just walking along beside them, his camel hair coat draped over his shoulders and smoking a Castella.

S.J. A'man A breath of fresh air, madam, and you'll feel as right as rain.

June Thank you very much, doctor.
The ambulanceman returns to theatre. Del and June join Rodney and Vicky.

Del *(Referring to June)* Well, the Phantom of the Opera strikes again! Still, I shouldn't imagine that's the first time someone's been sick in there, eh Victoria?

Vicky I honestly don't know, I haven't read the full history of the building.
She gestures to Eric who is parked a short way up the road.

Del *(To Rodney)* D'you fancy a bite to eat?

Rodney *(Angrily)* No!

Vicky I'm really not very hungry.
The limo pulls up. Eric opens the door for Vicky.

Eric Everything alright Miss?

A Royal Flush

Vicky Not really Eric, but not to worry.

Del *(To Rodney)* If you're taking her back to her flat, behave yourself!

Rodney And what exactly is that supposed to mean?

Del Listen to me Rodney. The last thing we need at this delicate stage of development, is for you to go tubbing her! Now we've made a good impression tonight.

Rodney A good impression?

Del We was doing alright up until June's psychedelic yodel!

Rodney Just go away from me, will you? Just leave me alone!

Rodney climbs into car and they pull away. Del and June are the only people around.

Del Come on then June, let's get you home. *They now wander away from camera. We hold this shot until they turn out of vision. There is something sad about them, two misfits, totally out of their depth, misunderstanding everything they've seen. Del is slightly in front of June. He strolls slowly and confidently, his head bathed in cigar smoke. June totters along behind him, never quite catching him up.*

June I'm sorry about tonight, Del Boy. I don't know what come over me!

Del Nor did that woman in front of you! I mean be fair June, it's your own fault. Just think what you've been shoving down your gullet tonight. Benedictines and lemonades, fizzy orange juice, bacon flavoured crisps, dry-roasted peanuts.

June Liquorice allsorts.

Del Liquorice allsorts *and* the choc-ice! I mean that's enough to turn a warthog over!

June Before I come out tonight I had a blancmange.

Del Oh that's what it was?

June I reckon the milk in the blancmange was on the turn.

Del The only thing that's on the turn round here is you, girl! Don't you be Tom and Dick in my van.

June No I won't Del, honest.

Del Well, you get in the back, you ain't sitting next to me.

They turn corner and out of sight.

INT. DAY. THE VAN.

Del, Rodney and Albert are driving along London roads. Albert is in the back. Del is driving, Rodney is in passenger seat with the window open and his head held almost entirely out.

Del You can't smell it now, Rodney! Albert spent two hours scrubbing this van out with disinfectant!

Albert They could perform an operation on the floor of this van.

Rodney That's what's making me feel ill, the pong of that disinfectant! It's like being a Dettol delivery man!

We see the van drive past in a great cloud of exhaust fumes.

Rodney Disinfectant and exhaust fumes! When we gonna get rid of this van?

Del Why what's wrong with it?

Rodney What's wrong wi ... Look in your mirror? The Fire of London couldn't have made that much smoke?

Albert It's just burning off a bit of carbon, Rodney.

Rodney Leave off! Half the estate's suffering with bronchitis 'cos of this van!

Del This is the thoroughbred of three-wheelers. There's a highly tuned machine under that bonnet!

Rodney *(Obviously reference to last night)* This van is like one of your birds! It drinks too much, makes funny noises and is old enough to know better!

EXT. A GENTLEMAN'S OUTFITTERS.

This is one of those old, South Moulton street-type establishments that sell shooting, fishing and riding gear to the gentry. The van pulls up outside of shop. The Trotters alight. At this point Rodney is unaware that this is the shop where they will be buying his weekend clothes. He now reacts.

Rodney *(Horrified)* Is that the shop you were talking about?

Del Er, yeah!

Rodney I am not going in there and that's final!

Del Listen to me, will you?

Rodney No! When you said we'd buy some clothes for my weekend I thought you meant we'd pop down to Sol bros. in Balham for an 'airy shirt or something! I didn't realise I'd have to get dressed up like a free-range wally!

Del But this ain't *just* a weekend, is it? It's a weekend with the aristocracy! They'll all be there – Earls, Barons, Viscounts, the lot! *(Del pronounces Viscount as in discounts)* You've gotta dress like them otherwise you'll be different!

Rodney Del, it doesn't matter what I wear, I cannot be anything else but *me!*

Albert This is no time for defeatist talk, Rodney!

Rodney Shuddup!

Del Look Rodney, you can't go to Covington House decked out as a Bob Geldof look-alike! Have a butchers at yourself! I've seen wounds dressed better than you! Now I'm not gonna have *anyone* looking down on you! You're as good as them and I want them to see you are!

Rodney I appreciate that Del, and thank you, but a pair of green wellies will not turn me into the Arch-Duke Ferdinand! I'll be Rodney Trotter in a pair of green wellies!

Del But you'll be proving something to them!

Albert Look Rodney, this ain't just a weekend away! This is your interview!

Del Interview?

Albert Of course. The old Duke wants to give you the once over! He wants to see whether you can fit in.

Del And clothes maketh the man!

Rodney But I might not want to fit in!

Del Of course you do, Rodney, I've given this a lot of thought for you. Listen to me. I don't know if I've told you this before – but Mum said to me on her deathbed …

Rodney *(Cuts in)* Let's go in the shop Del.

Del That's the spirit Rodders, you know it makes sense.

> *They walk towards shop door. Rodney sees a few double-barrel shotguns in window.*

Rodney That's another thing. They're having a shooting party. I disagree with blood sports!

Del Do me a favour. You'll never hit one of them grouse things, they're fast!

Albert Tell 'em you've got a wart on your trigger finger.

INT. DAY. THE GENTS OUTFITTERS.

> *The manager (Mr Dow, a Guardian-reading snob of the first order) is behind the counter on telephone, as the Trotters enter.*

Dow *(On phone)* Of course, Sir Alan. The boy will be round this afternoon to collect it.

Del He ain't saying nothing about warts, Albert! The old Duke'll love that. His only child marrying someone who's covered in warts! You say nothing about warts, Rodney.

> *Dow reacts, he's never had anything like this in his shop before.*

Dow *(On phone)* I'm terribly sorry, Sir Alan, I have to go, 'something's' come in … I mean up! Goodbye. *(Replaces receiver. To the Trotters)* Good afternoon gentlemen. May I help you?

Del Well, I do hope so. We wanna buy a bit of gear.

Dow I see. And what is sir's pleasure?

Del Well, birds and curry I s'ppose, but I didn't

come here for all this chit chat. *(Indicates Rodney)* I want you to tog him out for a weekend in the country, 'acking jacket, stout brogues, all the X's *(Lays a wad of notes on counter)* There's a monkey there – that should cover it!

Dow *(Taken aback)* Em, yes, yes of course. If you'd like to come this way, sir.

Del Come on Rodders, let's sort you out. He's got some very strange measurements!

> *Del and Rodney follow Dow towards a door which we assume leads to a fitting room.*

Albert *(Calls)* Don't you worry Rodney, by the time he's finished with you you'll look just like one of them!

Rodney That's what I'm frightened of!

> *Del, Rodney and Dow exit.*

EXT. DAY. COVINGTON HOUSE AND GROUNDS.

> *We are out in the fields with Covington House in the distance. To one side of us, and reasonably close, we have a few old out-houses or barns and a small lane or track. We should have a few open backed Land-Rovers, which we assume have driven the guests up here, and a new-ish Range Rover. We have about twenty guests, ages ranging from late teens to early seventies.*
>
> *We see Victoria and her father, Henry Duke of Maylebury (mid 50's), Rodney, Patterson, the butler (60), Carter, the footman (25), and a couple of women in maids' uniforms who, at the moment, are helping lay out the buffet on a long trestle table.*
>
> *The 'shoot' is in fact clay-pigeons and so we also have the man who controls the machine that fires the clay discs (the loader).*
>
> *We come up on machine. We hear Henry in background.*

Henry *(OOV)* Pull!

> *The loader fires the machine.*
>
> *We see the two discs fly through air, and then shatter as they are both hit.*
>
> *Guests applaud politely. Henry is standing with the still smoking gun, pleased with his effort.*

Patterson *(The butler)* Good shot, your Grace.

Henry Yes, I was quite pleased with that myself, Patterson.

> *One of Henry's friends (Charles) a man of about Henry's age, steps forward with his gun.*

Charles Pure luck Henry, pure luck!

Henry Thank you Charles, I thought you might

A Royal Flush

clear up the mystery. Let's see you do better.

Charles Stand back old boy and watch a real marksman! Pull!

We cut to big close up of Rodney. The screen is filled with his face, we cannot see what he is wearing. His eyes follow the trajectory of the discs. We hear the reports from the gun. We hear mild applause from the other guests.

Rodney Good shot sir.

We now cut back to show Rodney in all his glory. He wears a hacking jacket, a deerstalker, a pair of those plus-fours type trousers tucked into knee-length brown woollen socks and a pair of stout walking brogues. (This is Del's vision of the country gentleman)

Rodney applauds genteely. Vicky approaches.

Vicky Are you hungry?

Rodney No, I'm fine, thank you.

Vicky (Gestures to buffet) There's plenty to eat.

Rodney I'll have something in a moment. Thank you.

Vicky Well, what do you think of it so far?

Rodney Oh it's very interesting. I'm enjoying myself, thank you.

Vicky Rodney, you keep saying 'thank you'!

Rodney Do I?

Vicky Yes, I just thought I'd mention it. I hope you don't mind?

Rodney No. Thank you … Sorry!

Vicky (Laughing) Don't mention it!

Rodney Thank you … I said that one on purpose.

Vicky I know you did! Have you ever used a double-barrelled before?

Rodney A doub … Oh no, I had an airgun when I was a kid.

Vicky Would you like to try?

Rodney No, that's alright Vicky, I'll just watch.

Vicky Come on, don't be such an old stick in the mud! (Calls) Daddy, d'you have a gun there for Rodney?

Henry Yes of course, darling! Patterson, would you load the Purdie.

Patterson Yes, your Grace.

Henry Have you done this sort of thing before Rodney?

Rodney No. I'll just watch if you like.

Henry Nonsense! There's nothing to it. Just be aware of the kick, keep it pointed up, that sort of thing. (Hands Rodney gun)

Rodney Thank you your Grace.

Henry Henry, please.

Rodney Henry. Thank you.

Vicky (Hands him a pair of ear-protectors)

Would you like these?

Rodney Thank you.

Rodney steps up to the firing mark. He felt a big enough prat before. But now he knows all eyes are on him, he feels an even bigger one. He holds the gun pointing directly in front of him. He looks across to the loader. The loader is waiting for his instructions. There is a pause.

Rodney now turns round to Henry, Vicky and any others who happen to be behind him. He still has the gun pointing directly in front of him (at them).

Rodney What do I say to him?

Everyone reacts, they turn away, crouch, put their hands up in front of them.

Everyone in firing line shouts in unison.

All No!

Vicky (Gesturing with her hands) Down Rodney! Put it down!

Rodney (Cannot hear with the ear protectors) What?

Henry Down Rodney! Down!

Rodney, misunderstanding all the gestures, crouches – gun still pointing at them.

Henry No, the barrel Rodney! Down!

Rodney now realises and lowers the barrel. There is a great unified sigh of relief.

Henry Sorry old boy, but one never, never points the gun …

Rodney (Cuts in) Yes I realise what I did! I'm very sorry.

Henry That's alright, my fault, I should have told you … When you're ready you just shout 'pull'!

Rodney Okay then! Thank you … (Prepares himself. Calls) Pull!

We cut to a shot from Rodney's POV. In the distance we can see loader and machine. Further behind him we can see a couple of the barns. As he pulls firing handle, we have the briefest of glimpses of a little yellow van with an iffy exhaust, pulling its way up the lane.

The discs fire into the air.

Rodney moves his head with the discs but now looks back in horror. Both barrels blast blindly into the air. Henry and the others are all puzzled by the fact that Rodney wan't even looking at the targets which have flown merrily on and landed somewhere in the field.

Henry (To Vicky) Is he of a nervous disposition?

Vicky Not as far as I know!

Rodney is staring hungrily, maniacally out into the countryside. From his POV we can see the

loader, who is also looking puzzled by what he has just witnessed. But behind him there is no sign of the little yellow van.

Patterson *(Referring to gun)* Would you like me to take that for you, sir?

Rodney What? Oh thank you. *(He removes the ear protectors)*

Henry That was a … em … jolly good try Rodney.

Rodney Thank you.

Rodney moves away still staring out to where he thought he'd seen the van. Vicky concerned, follows him.

Vicky Are you alright?

Rodney Yes, thank you.

Vicky You seem somewhat – shocked! It wasn't the gun was it?

Rodney No, no, I'm fine.

Vicky I'll get you a drink. *(She moves off towards buffet table)*

Rodney *He is now eyeing the countryside like a hunter. He knows his prey is out there, he's seen it, but where is it now?*

(Mumbles to himself) Come on, where are you? I know you're out there somewhere, you three wheeled yellow *(mouths the next word)* bastard!

We see shots from his POV. The countryside is tranquil. Birds are singing, the sun is shining. Rodney turns away in the opposite direction. He takes a couple of steps forward then suddenly turns and leaps back to his original position, as if trying to catch the van out. We see Carter (the footman) and the two maids watching him incredulously from buffet. Vicky is pouring a drink at buffet and has her back to all this.

From Rodney's POV everything is tranquil. Rodney now begins doubting his own eyes and, indeed, sanity.

Rodney *(Mumbling)* I'm sure it was there! I saw it!

He shakes his head and turns away.
Now, from a distance, he hears the dreaded call.

Del *(OOV calling)* Tally ho Rodders!

Rodney closes his eyes.
We see the yellow van bouncing its way over the grass towards him, Del shouting from the open window, Albert is seated next to him. Everyone at the shoot stops to witness this. Del alights, he wears the camelhair coat, three piece suit and smokes the Castella. Albert, who is in a really grumpy mood, alights from passenger side, in duffle coat etc.

Del *(Calling to some of the guests)* Good

morning. Tally ho there. *(Referring to the weather)* You couldn't ask for better than this, could you!

Rodney Go away!!

Vicky arrives with Rodney's drink.

Vicky *(Just politely)* Hello – again! I didn't think we'd see you here.

Del *I* didn't think *I'd* see me here!

Albert I didn't think I'd see me here either! I was supposed to be playing in a crib championship down at the Legion. 'Stead of that he drags me all the way out to bloody Berkshire!

Del *(Takes the drink from Vicky)* Thank you darling, I needed this. Let me explain. I was having a little clear up back at the flat, and what did I find in one of the wardrobes? *(Indicates Rodney)* His evening suit! He'd left it at home! So I thought he can't sit down to dinner dressed like that! So I had no option but to drive his evening suit all the way out here.

Vicky Oh I see! Well that's very nice of you Derek. Isn't it, Rodney?

Rodney *(Sharply, clenched teeth)* Yeah!

Vicky Daddy … *(Moves away)*

Rodney You bloody liar! I packed my evening suit! *I, I, me* I packed it myself, personally!

Del You couldn't have packed it, Rodney, otherwise how's it get in the wardrobe?

Rodney You took it out of my suitcase after I'd packed it!

Del Now why would I do a thing like that?

Rodney So you could bloody well get down here!

Vicky and Henry approach.

Vicky Daddy, this is Rodney's brother, Derek Trotter. Derek, I'd like you to meet …

Del *(Cuts in)* No introductions necessary, recognize you from your photo in the *Sporting Life*. How is Hansome Samson? Over that fetlock sprain?

Henry Yes, he's coming along nicely, thank you.

Del And what about next year's Derby. Will he be trying?

Henry Trying? It's the Derby, Mr. Trotter. Everyone's trying!

Del Just as long as I know where to put me money, your Grace.

Henry Yes! Victoria tells me you've driven all the way up from London with Rodney's evening suit! Jolly decent of you. You must be exhausted.

Del I'm cream crackered your Grace! I'll just mooch around awhile until I feel strong enough to make the long journey home.

Henry Yes please, make yourself at home. If you're still around later I'm sure cook will provide

A Royal Flush

something to eat.

Del Oh you mean dinner? Well as luck has it, as I was pulling *his* evening suit out of the wardrobe, *mine* came out with it! So I've got all me gear with me!

Henry *(Taken aback)* Oh! Em, yes! Er, well … Patterson. Could you set another place at the table tonight?

Patterson For this, em, gentleman?

Henry Yes.

Patterson Of course your Grace.

Del Well that is jolly civil of you, thank you very much! Your Grace, would you mind awfully if I had a little pot-shot?

Henry Pot sh … Oh, no of course not. Patterson, a gun for Mr. Trotter.

Del That's perfectly alright your Grace, I have my own weapon. Albert, would you mind?

Del gestures towards the van.
Albert walks to the back of the van moaning to himself.

Albert Albert, would you mind! He couldn't care bloody less whether I minded or not! Fight for your country, go down in shark-infested seas, and what thanks do you get, even from your own relatives? They turn you into a gun wallah! *(From the back of van Albert produces a hard gun case. He brings it back to Del)* Here you are, and don't ask for nothing else.

Del Thank you my good man, you may retire.

Albert I thought I'd done that bloody years ago!

Del *(To Henry, embarrassed)* He's been with us for years! … Bit like income tax!

Del moves to the firing area with the gun case. Charles offers Del the ear protectors.

Charles Would you like these?

Del No, thank you. I can't concentrate on music when I'm shooting!

He takes the gun from case and stands. All we see of gun is the wooden butt which is just above his waist.

Del *(Calls to loader)* Ready when you are, John!

Loader *(Calls back)* Do you mean 'pull?'

Del Sorry, Paul! In your own time, son!

The loader shrugs and pulls firing handle.
We see the discs fly through the air.
Del now brings the gun up for us to see. It is a sawn-off, single barrel, pump action shotgun.
He fires from the hip, pumps and fires again. We see the two discs, they do not merely shatter, they explode. We hear the triple-echo resounding across the countryside.
Debris is falling everywhere. We see the

guests ducking from it.
Now silence falls all around. Everyone except Del, is left open-mouthed by what they have just witnessed.
Del has the still smoking gun resting on his hip, man with no name fashion.

Del *(Brings the gun up to lips and blows the smoke away. To Henry)* You wait 'till I get my eye in!

Del wanders away, feeling very proud of himself. He passes the incredulous Rodney.

Rodney Where d'you get that gun from?

Del I borrowed it off Iggy Higgins.

Rodney Iggy Higgins? But Iggy Higgins robs banks!

Del I know! But it's Saturday!

Del wanders away towards buffet. Rodney is frozen to the spot.

INT. NIGHT. THE MAIN HALL COVINGTON HALL.

A large staircase sweeps down into hall. Most of the guests from the shoot (now dressed for dinner) are in hall being served sherry by Carter. Some of the guests are spending the weekend at Covington House, others, who live locally are arriving back at the house. Patterson is attending to the door and their coats etc.
Rodney and Del, both dressed as per opera, (the small chocolate stain still on Rodney's lapel), appear on landing, gallery or at top of stairs.
Del, with a freshly lit Castella, appears confident and obviously looking forward to the evening. Rodney appears unnerved at the sight of the massed nobility.

Del *(Referring to all the guests)* What a sight, eh Rodney? Makes you proud to be British, dunnit? They know a cucumber sandwich from an egg on toast, this lot! … *(To someone downstairs in hall)* Alright? Splendid.

Rodney Del … Derek, listen to me. I was nervous enough about this weekend, and that was *without* you being here! But you arrived! And your presence alarms me! Please Del, please, behave yourself!

Del Well of course I'll behave myself! What sort of bloke d'you think I am? I am here simply to help *you* make an impression!

Rodney But I don't want to make an impression! I just wanna sit quietly and hope no-one notices me!

Del That's no good, Rodders! You've gotta project your image!

Rodney I ain't got a bloody image!

Del Well, you will have before this evening's over! And you can cut that language out for a start! This is the creme de la menthe of British nobility. Look at 'em, there ain't one of 'em lower than a Dowager! *(Rhymes with dagger)*. We don't want them thinking we're oi polloi or nothing! We've gotta be on our bestest behaviour tonight, Rodney!

Rodney Good – we are in agreement then!

Del Right ... *(From their POV we see one of the female guests wearing a low-cut dress which reveals a lot of her ample cleavage)* Cor! Lungs on that!

Rodney reacts. Del descends stairs nodding to and greeting a few people as if they are life-long friends. He helps himself to a sherry from the footman's tray.

One of the paintings on wall should be a Pissarro

Del *(To the Duke)* Alright 'Enry?

Hen What! Oh yes, good evening, Trotter.

Del *(Referring to painting)* Is that a Da Vinci?

Henry No it's not a Da Vinci!

Del Shame. He's my favourite. Have you seen that cartoon of his! Laugh! I tell you, my old ribs were aching for days. And he did the Mona Lisa as well you know.

Henry Did he really?

Del Her with the energetic smile. You're not quite sure whether she's about to grin or she's sucking a sweet.

Henry That's a Pissarro.

Del Oh I don't know, I've seen worse.

Henry Dear God! It's by Camille Pissarro! He was a 19th century Impressionist!

Del What, like Mike Yarwood?

Henry *(Realises there is no point continuing the conversation)* Yes that's right, just like Mike Yarwood.

Del What, and he did a bit of painting an' all?

Henry Yes!

A Royal Flush

Del Well, you live and learn, don't you?

Henry Do you? *(To someone out of vision)* Philip, how nice to see you.

Henry moves out of shot

Del takes another sherry from footman's tray.

INT. NIGHT. THE KITCHEN COVINGTON HOUSE.

The cook, Mrs Miles, and the two maids are busily preparing the dinner – placing meat, vegetables etc in silver tureens and serving dishes which are then placed on a large serving trolley. Mrs Miles is in her mid-fifties – one of them 'comfortable' women who like to fatten men up. Albert is seated at table with a dinner in front of him.

Mrs Miles *(To one of the girls)* Keep your eye on those peas, Shirley.

Hands a cup of tea to Albert.

There you are Albert, three sugars.

Albert Thank you very much Mrs Miles. I'll give you a word of warning. Don't give Mr Trotter any peas, they go everywhere.

Mrs Miles I'll tell Mr Patterson. Who are your people, Albert?

Albert They're not people, they're my nephews.

Mrs Miles Oh, they're not of noble birth then?

Albert Noble? Nearest them two have got to nobility was their great Uncle Jack, he was a tobacco baron! No, the noisy one's a fly-pitcher and the young one's his apprentice.

Mrs Miles You mean that's what you lot do, sell things on street corners?

Albert Not me madam! I was a career man. I was in the navy for thirty years, man and boy. I've been round the world more times than a satellite. I fought in the battle of the Atlantic, battle of the convoys – you name it, I was there!

Mrs Miles I bet you could tell a tale or two, eh Albert?

Albert *(Shakes his head emphatically.)* I never talk about it!

Mrs Miles I understand. I suppose it brings back too many memories?

Albert That's right! I remember once, we was out in the South China Sea.

Carter the footman enters.

Albert We knew there were mines around, so we was on …

Carter *(Comes straight in and interrupts Albert, much to Albert's surprise and annoyance)* That little fella out there is really knocking sherry back! He's had almost a whole bottle of Amontillado to himself already. He keeps talking about Leonardo Da Vinci, it's like he knew him!

Mrs Miles Tell Mr Patterson. He might be able to discreetly suggest that the gentleman moderates his drinking.

Albert Anyway, as I was saying I never talk about it.

Mrs Miles Never talk about what?

Albert About my days in the navy, the battles end everything. But this particular day in the South China Sea, the old captain came to us …

Patterson enters and interrupts Albert.

Patterson Are we nearly ready to serve, Mrs Miles?

Mrs Miles Yes Mr Patterson, ready when you are.

Patterson Good, I want to get Leonardo Da Vinci's best friend sat down before he falls down. *(To Albert)* He's some relation of yours, isn't he?

Albert Who, Leonardo Da Vinci?

Patterson No, the gentleman out there who thinks the stuffed olives are pickled grapes?

Albert Yeah, yeah sort of.

Carter *(Referring to Del)* Is he an ex-navy man as well, Albert?

Albert Him? You must be joking. He thinks a clipper's something you do your hair with! No, I'm the only one in our family who ever went to sea. I tell a lie. My Grandmother's brother was safety officer on the *Titanic*.

All the others are busy with serving dishes etc. They now all stop and look at Albert as they realise what he has said.

Albert But I never talk about it.

INT. NIGHT. THE DINING HALL.

The meal is over and all the guests are engaged in conversation. The room is heavy with cigar smoke. The maids and Patterson are clearing away the remaining crockery. Henry is sat at the top table. Vicky, is at opposite end. To one side of her sits Rodney, to the other side sits a slightly merry Del. The room is filled with conversation, the sound of glasses, lots of laughter.

Charles is seated close to Henry.

Charles Henry, who's the young chap with Victoria?

Henry He's just a friend. Someone she met in some street market. She's going through a 'working artist' stage – her mother, was the same, God bless her. It's just a phase. She's often bringing 'colourful characters' down for the weekend. D'you remember that gypsy-type – arrived with the bull-terrier and a stolen Escort?

Charles Oh yes. Beat Patterson up in the Library?

Henry That's the one. This chap, Roland or Rodney, something like that, he's an artist as well.

Charles And the other fella, his brother?

Henry Yes. He appears to be the biggest artist of them all!

Del *(OOV)* 'Enry, is that a Da Vinci?

Henry *(Without even looking.)* No.

Del *(OOV)* Nice, though.

Henry *(To Charles)* As I say, it's just a phase.

We now see Patterson passing Del. On the floor around Del's chair we have a dozen or so peas. Patterson treads through them as he passes.

Del *(Holds out empty glass)* Patterson. Giss a topperooni, pal.

Patterson reluctantly fills Del's glass. Rodney leans back and calls Del. This conversation takes place behind Vicky's back.

Rodney Will you leave that wine alone? You ain't in the Star of Bengal now!

Del What are you on about? I'm enjoying myself!

Rodney But when you enjoy yourself no one else does!

Del Just trust me Rodney. We're coming to the stage of the evening when we are about to project you.

Rodney I do not want to be projected, got it? I want to remain extremely un-projected!

Del *(Referring to Vicky)* Hold her hand.

Rodney Shuddup!

They break from conversation.

Vicky *(Referring to Del)* I think he's a little drunk.

Rodney He's always been a little drunk!

Del *(To the woman seated next to him)* Thar was a blinging meal yer Ladyship, weren't it?

Lady Yes, excellent.

Del What did you have? The pheasant?

Lady Yes, pheasant.

Del I had the quails, with greens and gravy.

Her ladyship looks at Del's stained serviette which is still tucked in his shirt.

Lady So you did! Tell me — it's Trotter, isn't it?

Del Yes m'lady, but friends call me Del.

Lady I see. Tell me Trotter, how do you come to know Henry?

Del Well, you see his daughter Victoria is getting engaged to my younger brother Rodney

Lady *(Incredulous)* Engaged?

Del Ssh! Keep it under your tiara, we don't want the media getting hold of this. You know what it was like for Andrew and Fergie — couldn't fart without a news flash, could they?

Patterson has been placing decanters of port on table. One decanter to every four people. He places one in front of Del.

Del *(Cont)* *(To her ladyship)* Cor, he's given you a blank your Ladyship! Still perhaps he'll bring your carafe in a minute.

Del pours himself a port.

INT. NIGHT. THE KITCHENS.

The cook and the maids are now busy washing up. Albert and the footman are still at table. The footman rests his head on his hand and is looking bored and sleepy as Albert's saga continues.

Albert I was in the liferaft about twenty yards away from him. The current was so strong I couldn't reach him! Then I saw it! A long black shape, a white foaming line behind it, hurtling straight towards him! I shouted 'Watch out Tommy, there's a torpedo heading straight for you!' Then I realised that I was wrong! I said 'It's alright Tommy, it aint a torpedo, it's a shark!'

Carter I bet that come as a great relief to him!

Albert It was awful! That story will haunt me to the day I die!

Carter I know the feeling!

INT. NIGHT. THE DINING HALL.

Some of the guests have side plates containing fruit – grapes, segments of orange. There are glasses of port, brandy etc. We pan round table and see the guests chatting, laughing, drinking etc, all in a very relaxed, civilised manner. We see quite a few of the guests actually eating the fruits (small fruits, grapes etc) they are using antique silver fruit knives.

As we continue the pan we pass Del whose elasticated tie is hanging at an obtuse angle, a couple of buttons of shirt are undone revealing evidence of a string vest beneath. He is well gone and eating a banana. The decanter of port is almost empty. The tablecloth around him is covered in port stains and cigar ash.

We continue the pan leaving him behind and seeing more of the civilized guests. We now hear a high-pitched whine.

The whole table stops and looks in Del's direction. We see Del is running his finger round the rim of one of the crystal goblets.

Del *(To Henry)* That's how you can tell they're public crystal!

Henry Really? Thank you.

Charles I don't want to worry you Henry, but he

A Royal Flush

threw his banana skin in your Ch'ein Lung jardiniere.

Henry Good grief!

Cut to Vicky's end of table.

Del *(Still examining the glass)* These are lovely Victoria. What are they, Ravenhead or something?

Vicky No it's Stowbridge Crystal. They've been in the family for generations.

Rodney Put it down!

Del Alright! *(Picks up silver fruit knife)* Look at the craftsmanship in that. *(Calls up table)* 'Enry, this knife.

Henry No, it's not a Da Vinci!

Del Pure silver though, I'd wager.

Henry Yes. They were made by William Cawdill in 1648.

Del Really? They've come up well, ain't they?

He now bangs the blade of the knife three times across the rim of the priceless crystal and listens to the tone. Everyone in the room holds their breath.

The glass doesn't smash.

Del Hear that tone? Makes you proud to be British dunnit? Me and Rodney are involved in cutlery. Canteens par excellence. I've got some in the van, it won't take me a minute.

Rodney Del. Just — just leave it will you?

Del Well maybe later.

Giles *(One of the younger set)* Which part of London are you from, Rodney?

Rodney Em – Peckham. Peckham, er, Peckham, London.

Giles Really? Not too far from me, I have a flat in Chelsea.

Vicky Rodney's taking me to Stamford Bridge to see someone play soccer.

Giles Oh you're one of the Faithful! I'm a blues fan myself. Have you taken a box?

Del He don't need a box, he's tall enough to see ain't he?

Giles No, I meant a private box in the new stand!

Rodney No, I'm usually in the Shed.

Giles Yes, I've often seen the chaps in the Shed. Looks great fun! I'm a great Dixon fan.

Del Which Dixon you talking about?

Giles Well, Dixon of Chelsea!

Del Him? I'd rather play Dixon of Dock Green! I mean, he can't dribble like Jimmy Greaves could!

Giles Well maybe not, but he's still a fine player. I mean, he's good in the air!

Del So was Biggles! *(Indicating Rodney)* Of course, he had a great future as an athlete.

Rodney is horrified by this, he's never even won a sack race.

Henry That's jolly interesting, Rodney. Which area of athletics?

Rodney Em ... er, well ...

Del All sorts, weren't it, Rodney? Running and jumping over things – chucking things, all sorts! The headmaster at his university wanted him to go in for the Olympics. But he said no! He gave it all up to concentrate on business. And that's where his true talent lies. He's a future whiz-kid. This time next year he'll be a millionaire.

Henry That's nice to hear. Which university were you at?

Rodney It wasn't actually a university, sir.

Vicky Rodney was at an art college, Daddy. In Basingstoke.

Henry Basingst ...! Yes, yes, I've heard very good things about it?

Charles How long were you there old chap?

Rodney Th ... three weeks.

Charles Three *weeks*?

Rodney I left for ... em, personal reasons.

Del It weren't his fault.

Rodney *(A plea)* Del!

Del No, it's important these good people know the truth! They weren't his drugs what he was found in possession of!

Everyone is stunned by this. Rodney lowers his head. Vicky looks at him with disappointment.

Del It was the Chinese tart! He only went down to her room to borrow a box of chalk. She said have a puff of this Rodney and then SGB burst in. Caught him bang to rights with the reefer *al dente*! He was two mile away in a black Maria. before he even said man! So I just want you all to know, in case the drugs conviction is ever brought up by the gutter press, he was done up like a kipper!

There is now total silence around the table except for the sound of Del pouring himself yet another brandy.

Del Anyway, let's liven things up a bit! Here you are, a little recitation entitled, 'Don't worry mother your son will soon be back, he's only sailing round the world in a Grimsby fishing smack'! Here we go.

Throughout this we see Rodney slowly dying. Most of the other guests have their heads lowered in embarrassment.

Del The boy stood on the burning deck, the water shone like glass. A burning ember flew down his neck, and burnt him on the ... ankle!

Del collapses in great guffaws of uproarious laughter. He is banging the table, glasses

rattling together. There is an embarrassed, pathetic silence from all the others

INT. NIGHT. THE KITCHEN.

From the dining hall we can hear Del's laughter. Patterson, Carter, Mrs Miles and the maids are looking in the direction of the laughter.
Albert is seated at table. He closes his eyes and shakes his head sadly.

INT. NIGHT. THE DINING HALL.

Del continues laughing
Del Oh dear me ... You all thought I was gonna say arse, didn't you? ... Did you hear the one about the Irish bloke on a skiing holiday?
Everyone looks up, horrified that anybody could tell a skiing joke in Covington House.
Del See, this Irish fella wins a skiing holiday in a contest of some sort. This is a killer!
People round the table react.

INT. NIGHT. KITCHEN.

Everyone is there as before.
Albert, realising their weekend is now finished, is putting his duffle coat on, finishing his mug of tea.

INT. NIGHT. DINING HALL.

Del ... and his wife said, 'That's not my Paddy's ear, he had a fag behind his!' *(Laughs uproariously)*
Henry *(Screams down the table at him)* Trotter! I want a word with you! Outside – now!
Del and Henry move towards doors.
Vicky *(To Rodney)* Are you still staying overnight? Or ... or *not?*
Rodney No, I think I'd better get myself off home.
Vicky Fine ... It was ... Yes.

INT. NIGHT. THE MAIN HALL.

Henry Listen carefully Trotter. I want you and all your kith and kin out of my house and off my land right now!
Del Don't you wanna discuss the arrangements first?
Henry Arrangements? What arrangements?
Del *(Quietly)* Rodney and Victoria's wedding!
Henry W ... W ... Wha ... what do you mean – wedding?
Del Oh no! They haven't told you, have they? I hope I haven't spoilt a wonderful surprise!
Henry A wonderful surprise? For whom?
Del Well, for youm! I thought we'd place the

announcements in *The Times, Country Life* and the *Peckham Echo*. What d'you think?
Henry I do not believe I'm hearing this! My daughter is marrying no one! In two months time she leaves for America. She's taking a year's course at the New York School of Art!
Del That's most probably part of their honeymoon! Two months eh? We'd better book a cathedral a bit lively!
Henry The only thing you'll be booking is a bed in intensive care! Your brother is *not*, I repeat *not* marrying my daughter.
Del Look Henry, we're not yippidy yoys you know. We know how to conduct ourselves. In fact, there is a rumour that we are related to the Surrey Trotters!
Henry I don't care if you're related to the Surrey Trotters, the Berkshire Trotters or the Harlem bloody Globe Trotters! I want that young man out of my daughter's life!
Del Well I don't know how you're gonna do that! Your Vicky's stuck on him.
Henry Well I'll find a way of unsticking her, have no fear of that!
Del Well it's not gonna be easy. I know Rodney too well. I can't think of anything that would make, him leave her ... Well, there might be *one* thing?
Henry And what's that?
Del Why don't we talk about it in your study over a brandy?
Henry *(Indicates door)* Through there.
They exit.
Del *(OOV)* What is that one?
Henry *(OOV)* That's a Da Vinci.

INT. DAY. TROTTERS' LOUNGE.

Very early, Sunday morning. From outside we can hear the sound of the Muezzin calling the faithful to worship. Rodney is alone in the lounge. He sits in an armchair vengefully trance-like, still wearing his stained evening jacket (minus the tie) He has not slept and is unshaven and weary.
Albert exits from his bedroom wearing pyjamas and dressing gown.
Albert *(Referring to Muezzin)* Ali's started early this morning ain't he? Can't understand it, Del Boy flogged him a new watch last week ... You're up early an all son. Or ain't you been to bed?
Rodney just shakes his head.
Come on Rodney. You need your kip, boy. I know that last night didn't go as well as you'd hoped for, but ... well, try'n look for the silver lining.

A Royal Flush

Rodney Silver lining?? He called the Earl of Stanton a dipstick! He showed them his scar! He was so drunk he couldn't even order his nightcap of rum and black – he asked for a bum and rack! So where's the silver lining, Unc?

Albert Well … It's lucky he didn't fancy a Bucks Fizz innit? *(He moves towards kitchen. Now stops. Referring to Muezzin)* Ali's still at it. You ever heard him do the Yellow Rose of Texas?

Rodney gives the tiniest of smiles. Del enters from the bedroom area. He is dressed in his casual clothes and is very hung-over.

Del Oh my gawd! Someone's put an 'ampster in my mouth! I feel really sick! Do us a sausage sandwich with brown sauce, Unc. I've gotta have something inside me.

Rodney *(Quietly to himself)* How about a dum-dum bullet?

Del *(Hasn't heard this)* I don't know why we come home so early from 'Enry's drum. I mean we was all having a good time!

Rodney No, Del! *You* was having a good time! Everyone else was praying for their appendix to burst! I'm going outside. I'm gonna try and rationalise the nightmare of yesterday evening! And when I've thought the whole thing through and got my head straight and regained my composure, I'm gonna come back in here and kill you! *(He exits through hall door)*

Del *(To Albert)* Have I upset him or something?

Albert Upset him? I don't know how the boy's managed to keep his hands off you! Last night you drank one and 'alf litres of vintage port, you mixed coca-cola with their one hundred year old cognac, then I heard you took some diabolical liberties with a priceless punch-bowl! I don't know what you did but the maid said she'll never drink Sangria again!

Del Ain't it marvellous, eh? I try and help someone but my good nature always rebounds on me! *(Calls from window)* Ali, give it a rest, son!

INT. DAY. THE LIFT FOYER OF BLOCK.
This is up on the 14th floor. The Muezzin has now stopped. Rodney is standing at window looking out over Peckham.
Del enters foyer.

Del Rodney … Come on Rodders, I was only trying to make an impression.

Rodney And you *made* an impression, Del! It was similar to the impression the Americans made on Nagasaki! Why can't you stay out of my life? For as long as I can remember it's always been the same – you sticking your oar into everything I did! I remember the time I joined the army cadets. I used to enjoy that! Going away for weekends – climbing things. Then you discovered that the boy I shared a tent with had a relative who was a big noise in show-business. That was

the end of my military career weren't it? I was now gonna be a child-star! I was demobbed and straight into a tap-dancing school before I could say, 'Who goes there?'

Del They said you had natural rythmn, it was just your legs.

Rodney It was just an embarrassment – like last night! I was the only kid in that school who didn't have proper tap-dancing shoes.

Del That was because your army boots made more noise!

Rodney Oh they made more noise alright! I used to make 'Zippidy Doo Dah' sound like the advance on Leningrad! Even that painting competition at school – I could have won that if it hadn't been for you! The art teacher wrote that my 'Marble Arch at Dusk' was like a masterpiece!

Del No, he said it was like a mantlepiece, Rodney!

Rodney He said masterpiece.

Del It looked nothing like Marble Arch!

Rodney That's 'cos it weren't the bloody Marble Arch! It was the Arc de Triomphe but none of us could spell Arc de Triomphe, so you said paint a trolley bus in front of it and no-one will be any wiser!

> *In pure frustration he punches the metal dust chute cover with his right hand.*

You see, you *had* to interfere! And now you've interfered again between me and Victoria. You humiliated and destroyed me in front of all them people. You smashed my chances of getting an occasional break from this concrete mess! And you've ruined my opportunity of sharing a warm and friendly relationship with someone I respected. And on top of that Del. On top of *all* that – I think I've broken my hand!!

Del Let's have a look!

Rodney Get away from me! You went everywhere with us! You came to the Theatre Royal and put British Culture back ten years! You called Puccini a wally-Frog! And what you did to that antique punchbowl was little short of criminal!

Del I admit I might have got a bit merry!

Rodney Merry? *(Pokes Del in chest with index finger of right hand)* You ... aargghh?

Del You wanna get that hand looked at!

Rodney Shuddup? *(Pokes him in chest with index finger of left-hand)* You even told the joke

about the Irish bloke on a skiing holiday!

Del No!

Rodney Yes you did! The whole room fell silent!

Del Don't keep on about it Rodney.

Rodney That's when he decided to chuck us all out? D'you know what the most painful incident of the entire evening was? His Grace asked me to join him in his study for a little chat. He said he wanted me to stop seeing Victoria. He wanted me out of her life – now, and for good! Couldn't risk the scandal see. A peer of the realm's daughter getting mixed up with someone like me ... He offered me money!

Del *(Feigning innocence)* No?

Rodney Yeah. You can imagine how I felt!

Del Oh 'orrible Rodney, 'orrible! I'd have told him what to do with his money.

Rodney I did.

Del Good b ... What? You said nito to a grand?

Rodney Yes I did! I still had a little bit of my self-esteem left intact! A thousand pounds don't buy me, Del!

Del Well it could buy me!

Rodney A free-estimate could buy you! *(Reacts)* How did you know he offered me a grand?

Del Eh?

Rodney How did you know he offered me a thousand pounds?

Del Well, that's about the going rate for getting a plonker out your daughter's life!

Rodney You arranged it didn't you?

Del No, no, I didn't actually arrange it! Look Rodney, them sort of people are looked after by Special Branch and MI6. Don't you think they would have run your name through a computer and found out about your conviction? Then, if you refused to get out of Vicky's life they'd have sent a hit team after you. The next peer you'd of seen was that one at Southend as they rowed you out on the midnight tide!

Rodney *(A bit concerned at this)* Course not!

Del No? What would they have said to the old Duke then? Don't worry your Grace, you ain't losing a daughter, you're gaining a pot-head! You'd have been brown bread, Rodney. So I thought, a grand on the hip's better than a poisoned umbrella up the jacksy! But you, you dipstick, turned it down!

Rodney Yes I did!

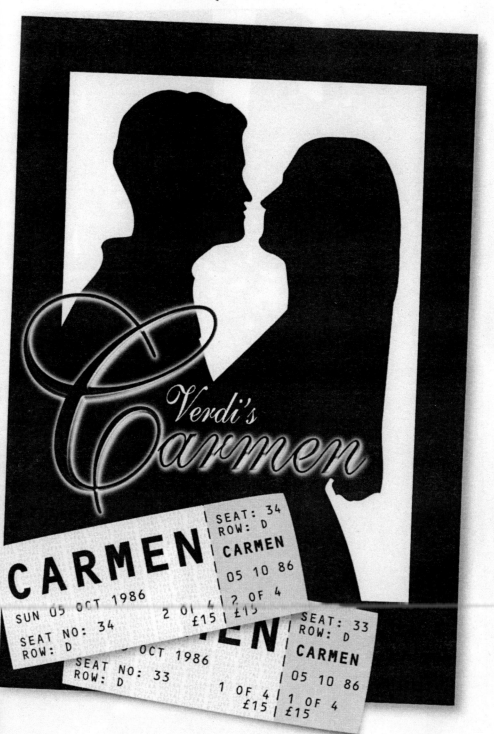

The Frog's Legacy

STUDIO. INT. NIGHT. NAG'S HEAD.

Del and Rodney are at the counter. Albert is seated at nearby table. Trigger is chatting to him.

Del *(Calls)* Michael – Mike.

Mike *(Bored with Del's efforts to sell him something – anything)* What is it now?

Del This is your lucky night. *(Produces brochure of Rajah computer)* What about that for a portable computer, eh, Mike? It's got 64K, UHF output, a megabite disc-drive, it's got ROM, it's got RAM, it's got them, red and green lights, everything!

Mike What do I want with a computer?

Del What does he want with a computer? Everyone's got a computer these days!

Mike Have you got one?

Del Have I got one?

Rodney He's got twenty five!

Del Yes, thank you, Rodney! Michael, this particular model retails at three hundred and ninety nine pounds of the realm. I'm *giving* it to you for one hundred and fifty, I'll even chuck a joystick in. See? You can process all your data.

Mike And what exactly does that mean?

Del Well it means you can … you can … tell him what it means, Rodney. *(To Mike)* He's taken a course in this, he came top of his class.

Rodney Well, in 'layman's' terms it means you can, em, well, you er, you can record all your business deals.

Mike I spend half my life trying to *hide* my business deals. So the last thing I want is to have 'em all recorded on a floppy bloody disc! I'm not interested. Ask Trigger.

Rodney Trigger? With a computer? Do me a favour, he's still struggling with light switches.

Trigger sips his beer (a full pint) and reacts to its weakness.

Trigger Try that, Albert.

Albert *(Sips beer)* Last time I tasted something like that was when I was in Egypt.

Trigger Yeah? What was it a local brew?

Albert No, I fell in the Nile.

Trigger Here, Mike, I ordered *beer*!

Mike Don't try'n be funny with me, Trigger. I'll tell you this much, I've had certificates for my beer.

Trigger Yeah, I've had a few days off work with

it as well!

Del and Rodney move to table.

Del Bloody computers. I bought thirty of the things, I've only sold five.

Trigger Well that's not too bad Del.

Del Not too bad? I've had 'em a year and a half!

Rodney Our sales campaign suffered badly when the local office of fair trading announced to the press that they don't work.

Del They do work, Rodney! You've just gotta fiddle around with 'em a bit.

Rodney They don't work properly!

Trigger You know about this sort of thing, Dave?

Rodney As it happens I do. Recently I took a computer course at the adult education centre.

Albert And failed.

Rodney I didn't fail!

Trigger What, you passed?

Rodney No, I didn't actually pass either. The man in charge said – in not so many words – that I should concentrate more on the theoretical side than the actual keyboard area.

Del: What he actually said was, 'Keep your bloody hands off my machine!'

Rodney Thanks for being so encouraging, Del! If I could pass that course and get my diploma I might be able to get a *real* job, working as a *real* company employee, instead of hanging round with the deadly duo, you and the suitcase!

To Albert and Trigger.

D'you know what he's had me doing today?

Produces one of the inframax massagers.

This is an infra-red massager, cures rheumatics and all that. He's had me hobbling through the market like I've got bad lumbago. Then 'Healing Hands Trotter' spots me and cures with his ray-gun in front of all the punters. He used to be a cowboy now he's a medicine man!

Del Oh shut up you tart! You're just narked cos you had a hole in your vest! *(Checks watch)* Anyway I can't hang around. You know that chop-suey house down by the station? The one we decorated? *(Stands)* They've gone bust and they're auctioning all their gear tonight, so I'll see you later.

Del moves towards the entrance, as he does so we see Mr Jahan enter. He wears a blazer and old school tie. He scans the bar, obviously looking for someone.

Del *(Spots Jahan)* Oh my God!
Del turns and starts to walk in opposite direction.
Mr Jahan *(Calls)* Mr. Trotter!
Del *(Delighted)* Mr Jahan! What a pleasant surprise. What brings you in?
Mr Jahan That computer you sold me last month is still not working.
We see Mike react.
Del *(Trying to quieten Mr Jahan)* No, no, I'm sure there must be a simple explanation. *(Leading him to table)* Let's discuss it over a drink. What can I get you, Mr Jahan?
Mr Jahan Something non-alcoholic.
Del *(Calls)* Pint of your best bitter, please, Mike.
Mr Jahan I have a business to run, Mr Trotter. I bought the computer, at your suggestion, in order to streamline my business. So far your computer has managed to destroy my accounts, wipe out my entire annual stock records and set fire to my curtains.
Del You must be pressing the wrong button. You see Mr Jahan, it's as important for the computer to get used to you as for you to get used to the computer.
Mr Jahan Are you suggesting there is a personality clash?
Del No, no. What I mean is we are talking outer-limits hi-tech. That computer was used in the American space shuttle.
Mr Jahan But it blew up!
Del I don't mean it was the *same* computer. Although that would explain why it's not working too well! Trust me, Mr Jahan. Give it a bit of time and I guarantee you that one of these days you'll wonder how you ever managed without it.
Mr Jahan I'll give it one week then I'll be back to see you.
Del That's the spirit, you know it makes sense. *(Mike brings drinks)* Thank you Michael. Anyway, I thought that young fella who works for you was a computer boffin.
Mr Jahan Oh he has resigned. Said the work did not agree with him.
Del They don't know they're born half of 'em, do they?
Mr Jahan I have placed ads in the local paper and at the job centre, but all to no avail. It's not a difficult job and I pay good wages.
Del turns and looks in Rodney's direction.
Del Yeah, it's not gonna be easy, Mr Jahan. I mean you're looking for a young man with plenty of drive and enthusiasm.
Mr Jahan Not really.

Del A couple of GCEs wouldn't go amiss though, would they?
Mr Jahan It is not a necessity. Basically I am looking for someone who can walk.
Del That's what I mean, you're talking top-notch. Most people of that calibre have gone off with the brain-drain. No, it's gonna be difficult ... Pot pourri, pot pourri! This is your lucky night, Mr Jahan. I may have the perfect person for you.
Mr Jahan Really? Who?
Del My very own younger brother. Enthusiastic, and he's got GCEs in maths and art. Since he left Cambridge he's spent most of his time wheeling and dealing in the commodities market. All the headhunters have been after him from the Bank of England to ICI but he fancies something a bit more local.
Mr Jahan Can he walk?
Del *(Motions with hands as if dodging round tables)* Dashes about all over the place.
Mr Jahan Would he like to discuss it with me?
Del No, no, I'll do that for him. How much you offering?
We cut to the table of Rodney, Albert and Trigger. Mike has now arrived at Rodney's table.
Mike Del Boy's got something going over there.
Rodney That means someone's gonna suffer. *(Smiles at the fate of this anonymous person.)*
Trigger Talking of suffering, my niece is getting married next Saturday. *(To Rodney)* You remember little Lisa, don't you? She came up last year. She was the one who arranged for Del Boy to have a go on the hang-glider.
Rodney Oh yeah, I liked her.
Trigger Well she's invited you all down to Hampshire for the wedding.
Mike Well that's very nice of her, Trigger. Tell her I'd be delighted.
Trigger *(To Albert and Rodney)* You two are coming, Del's accepted for you.
Rodney He's accep ... He's something else ain't he ... Hold on, I thought Lisa was getting married last year?
Trigger *(Slightly embarrassed)* Yeah, she was. Then she found she wasn't.
Mike and Albert *(Catch on after a tiny pause)* Oh!
Rodney Wasn't what?
Albert You got a pencil and a bit of paper, Mike?
Rodney *(Now catches on. Does pregnant gesture)* Oh!
Trigger Yeah. Well now she's found she is again. Should be good though. A day down by the coast, nice little drink afterwards. Talking of

The Frog's Legacy

drinks, I'll get these in.

Trigger moves to bar. We see Mr Jahan leaving. Del arrives at Rodney's table.

Del Rodders, this is your lucky night! I've only been and got you a job.

Rodney *(Without hesitation)* I don't want it!

Albert What d'you mean you don't want it? You only just said that you'd like to get a job.

Rodney Yes, but not from *him*! I've had some of his little 'jobs' in the past and I am here to tell you that he's no Brook Street Bureau!

Del That's charming innit? After all my time and effort that's the thanks I get! This wasn't just a job, Rodney, it was a career move!

Rodney But I haven't got a career.

Del But you could have had one! And it'd been moving! And it would have been some wages coming into the flat. We are brassic at the moment.

Rodney Yeah, some of your novel, money-saving devices are in evidence – again! So what's this job?

Del Well you're not interested, Rodney, so it's purely epidemic innit?

Albert What sort of job was it, Del?

Del He would have been a trainee computer programmer! Eventually. It was mentioned that the successful candidate would – with endeavour – attain executive status.

Rodney Well … I thought, sort of, well I thought I'd be humping boxes round and all that. I didn't know it was trainee executive.

Del He mentioned your CV. How bad's that eh? Nice little Citroen.

Rodney No, I think he might have been referring to my curriculum vitae.

Albert Well that's no problem, there's no heavy lifting involved.

Del Well, he'd have to start at the bottom of course.

Rodney Of course. Doing what?

Del Well, em, basically it's kind of … em, kind of delivering! Only to begin with though! And it's ninety pound a week in your hand, no tax, no nonsense!

Rodney But if I'm working for cash in hand I'm not a real employee!

Del It's only for a trial period! So what do you say?

Rodney Where will I be working?

Del D'you know that new office block in Wilmot Road, the one with all the smoked glass and lairy cars?

Albert Where all them young birds come out of at lunchtime?

Del That's the one.

Rodney *(Head filled with leather chairs and mini skirts)* Yeah I know it!

Del Well, right opposite it there's an alley.

Rodney *(The balloon deflating)* An alley?

Del Between the undertakers and the Light of Nepal restaurant. Well, at the bottom of the alley there's a yard. Pop your head in there Monday morning and ask for Mr Jahan and he'll give you your duties and uniform. Is that the time? Gotta get down the Chinkies before the auction finishes. See you in the morning. *(He is gone)*

Pause on Albert and Rodney.

Rodney Why would a trainee computer programmer need a uniform?

Albert Dunno, son … *(Albert starts laughing at Rodney. One of those slow burn laughs.)*

Rodney I don't know what you're laughing at, Unc. Don't you see what this means? You've just been promoted to the bloke in the market with the bad back!

Albert's laugh dies.

INT. DAY. FOYER OF RECEPTION HALL.

A set of open doors lead through to the main hall. All we can see of the main hall is the end of a dining table with a waitress putting the final touches to flowers, glasses etc. (This is purely background to suggest where the wedding breakfast will be held). Coming off the foyer is a corridor leading to an entrance or some kind of cloak area where a semi-private conversation could be held.

We also have a set of french windows overlooking open countryside. (We must emphasise we are in the country)

We have two tables joined together and bearing a pile of presents. Two presents are placed apart from the rest. The first present is very neatly wrapped in tasteful and expensive wrapping paper and complemented by a large silk bow. (This is the Boyces' present) The second present is wrapped in a rather cheap paper and is very untidy, as if a heavy handed man has wrapped it. (This is the Trotters' present)

Andy, the groom, and his male relatives are wearing morning suits. Lisa's male relatives are wearing Burtons' suits.

As we come up on scene Lisa (in wedding dress) and Andy are receiving their guests who are in a queue. Most of the guests have been received and are standing around sipping sherry and awaiting permission to enter main hall.

*We see Albert staring out of the window
The vicar goes to greet Andy and Lisa.*

Vicar Congratulations, Lisa, and you too Andrew. My *very* best wishes for your future happiness.

Lisa Oh, thank you Reverend.

Andy Yes, thank you very much, sir. It was a lovely service.

Vicar Why, thank you. And who knows, in a year or two from now we could all be back in church celebrating the christening of your first born.

Lisa and Andy look at each other.

Lisa *(Quietly to vicar)* Actually, my Mother wants to talk to you about that.

Vicar *(Reacts)* Oh … Oh yes … I see. *(Wanders away)*

We see Del exiting from main hall eating a piece of brown bread and butter he has just taken from one of the tables.

Del *(Calls, as if he's addressing a life-long mate)* Vicar!

Vicar *(Reacts alarmed at the sound of Del's voice. He would have liked to have avoided him)* Ah, Mr Trotter, how nice. Thank you once again for the lift.

Del Oh bain-marie, bain-marie, it's the least I could do. I'm sorry it was a bit bumpy, but, there again, we didn't have far to go. By the way, that computer I was talking to you about earlier. I left it in your vestry.

Vicar *(Reacts. He didn't want the computer)* You left it in my vestry?

Del Oh, please, it was no problem! I mean I had to clear it out the back of the van to make room for you! Now remember, in case the Bishop asks, they retail at three ninety nine, it's yours for one an' a half and a score off for cash. I can't say fairer.

Vicar But I'm not sure I have need of a computer!

Del You can have it on two weeks approval. I mean, if I can't trust you then who can I trust? Ask and it shall be given, that's my motto *(To someone out of vision)* Hello there, turned out nice, didn't it?

Del moves out of shot leaving a bewildered vicar.

We cut to Albert at window. Rodney joins him and hands him a sherry. It's been a nice day and Rodney is feeling particularly benevolent and so there is a nice 'family' atmosphere between him and Albert.

Albert *(Takes sherry)* Thanks, Rodney.

Rodney What you doing over here on your own?

Albert Just reminiscing *(Gesturing to countryside)* This used to be my old stamping ground. Portsmouth's only a couple of miles up the road there.

Rodney Bet you had some laughs round here, eh?

Albert Not half! The warning used to go out, 'Lock up your daughters, Trotter's back in port!'

We cut away to bride, groom and queue. Trigger and Mike are chatting to the happy couple.

Trigger *(To Lisa)* You remember Mike, don't you? He's the water-diviner from the Nag's Head.

Lisa *(Kisses Mike)* Of course I do. Hello, Mike, it's lovely to see you again. This is Andy, my husband.

Mike *(To Andy)* Congratulations, son. You will never regret what you did today! I should know, I've been married eighteen years.

Andy Thanks a lot. Is your wife here?

Mike No, we broke up in '73. Anyway, well done.

Cut back to Albert and Rodney.

Albert Finally the skipper said; 'I know, we'll try and hide in one of the fjords.' So …

Rodney *(Cuts in)* Albert, I think I might have heard this story. Did you sink?

Albert Yeah.

Rodney I've heard it! *(Walks away)*

Del is standing a couple of yards away next to the table bearing the presents. He has heard the tag-end of Albert's story and is chuckling at Rodney.

Del Why do you listen to him?

Rodney I don't know – a moment of weakness I suppose.

Boycie and Marlene approach.

Marlene *(Referring to reception)* It's all a bit up-market, innit, Del?

Boycie Mmmh, I was surprised to see you here.

Del I am at home in all walks of life, Boycie. *(To Marlene)* Anyway, how are you, sweetheart? *(Touches her up)* Woh!

Del and Marlene laugh.

Boycie I don't believe it! Will you behave yourselves! This is only an hyphen or two off a society wedding and you're acting like you're on a charabang trip to the lights!

Marlene Oh shut up you snobby git!

Boycie I am merely trying to conduct myself with a bit of decorum! *(Does double-take on the Trotters' present)* I assume that 'bundle' is from you?

Rodney *(Offended by his tone)* Yeah, that's our present.

The Frog's Legacy

Boycie God, it looks like the bomb squad have had a go at it! And what have you bought the unlucky couple?

Del It's a thirteen piece dinner service!

Marlene *(Worried about the clash of presents)* But we've bought 'em a dinner service as well!

Boycie I shouldn't worry, Marlene, they'll be no comparison. *(Touching or patting their present)* We got ours from Royal Doulton, they most probably got their's from *Dalton's Weekly*.

Del *(To Rodney)* He's something else, ain't he? He's got more front than Southend.

Marlene No, but it is a lovely dinner service, Del. It's got a hand-painted pattern depicting the changing seasons of the English countryside.

Boycie He's most probably given 'em that old crockery he bought at the Chinese auction.

Del and Rodney react deeply offended. Rodney's expression now changes as he remembers the strong oriental influence of the crockery.

Del *(To Boycie)* How dare you! What sort of bloke d'you think I am?

Boycie Well I wouldn't put it past you. Shall we circulate, Marlene?

As they walk away we hear Marlene in background.

Marlene Bloody 'ell, Boycie, we've been round more times than a break dancer!

Rodney Did our dinner service come from the bankrupt Chinkies?

Del No it didn't! I swear to you on my life!

Rodney Well those plates had an awful lot of Pandas and Pagodas on 'em!

Del Alright, they did come from the Chinese take-away. Look, we've been a bit strapped for money recently! Anyway, they're very nice Pagodas.

Rodney No they're not, they look more like prisoner-of-war camps! I mean how is it gonna make us look? Boycie and Marlene's service depicts the changing seasons and ours contains scenes from *Tenko*!

Del Yeah, I suppose you've got a point ... Hang on a minute.

Del now removes his carnation and deliberately drops it to floor. He bends down to pick up and is now at eye-level with the two presents. Taped to the front of both presents are small envelopes containing congratulations cards. Del removes the two cards and swaps them. He now stands and surveys room making sure nobody has seen. Rodney has witnessed it and is terrified that they have been seen. Del nudges him.

Del *(Quietly)* He who dares wins, Rodders.

Del wanders off into room saying hello to a few total strangers.

INT. NIGHT. THE FOYER OF RECEPTION HALL.

The doors to main hall are still open but the dining tables have gone and been replaced by dancing guests and the sounds and lights of a disco.

The wedding presents have disappeared and been replaced by a couple of long trellis tables which act as a bar complete with optics stand.

Mike is behind bar serving. Rodney, Trigger and Boycie are standing around bar chatting. Trigger's Auntie Reen appears from corridor or wherever. She is about 60 and a cockney. Jovial, good natured, good hearted and went through the entire blitz without spilling a drop of gin.

Trigger *(Calls her)* Aunt Reen. D'you wanna drink?

Reen I'll have a port and lemon. Better make it a small one, I've had my orders from young Lisa, I mustn't get Oliver Twist in front of 'his' family. I don't know who she thinks they are, big hats and no drawers most of 'em!

Albert exits from main hall.

Trigger *(To Reen, referring to Albert)* Here's a face from the past.

Albert recognises her immediately and smiles. Reen squints at him before recognition.

Reen Albert Trotter? I don't believe it!

Albert Hello, Reeny girl, how you going?

Reen I thought you went down with the Lusitania!

Rodney *(Quietly to Mike)* Fiver says he did!

Albert No, they tried but they couldn't get me. How long you been living out this way?

Reen I moved from Peckham in 1965. I couldn't stand that estate anymore. It's nice and peaceful out here *and* I don't have to save up to get to the seaside. You must be retired now.

Albert Yeah. I'm living back with the family, Joannie's kids.

Reen *(As if it is too much to hope for)* Del Boy's not here is he?

Albert Yeah, he's in there having a dance. He'll be out soon, he ain't had a drink for four minutes. And little Rodney's here as well!

Rodney *(With a dread)* Oh no!

Reen Rodney's here? Oh the little love!

Albert *(Indicating the group at bar)* He's over there.

Reen walks towards group at bar.

Reen The last time I saw you you were still in your pram.

She now kisses an unsuspecting Boycie on the cheek, accompanied by a big hug.

Boycie Who the bloody hell is this woman?

Rodney *(To Reen)* No, no. I'm Rodney.

Reen You're little Rodney? Ain't you got big? *(Gives Rodney a big kiss)* You don't remember me, do you, darling?

Rodney No.

Albert This is Trigger's Aunt Reeny. She used to be your mum's best friend.

Reen Oh yeah, me and Joannie, the terrible twins. D'you remember when your mum had that cleaning job at the town hall?

Rodney No.

Reen I used to look after you while she was at work – bath you and everything.

Rodney is cringing with embarrassment. Mike is enjoying Rodney's discomfort.

Reen D'you remember when I took you shopping that day in Woolworths?

Rodney No.

Reen As I was pushing you round you were picking things up off the counters and I didn't know! When I got home and took you out the pram I found three bottles of scent, a packet of Weights and a Helen Shapiro record! *(Laughs)* So the next day I took you up Selfridges! *(Laughs even louder)*

As her laughter fades she begins to study Rodney critically.

Reen *(Quietly to Albert but referring to Rodney)* I reckon the rumours were true, don't you Albert? Joannie was never a hundred percent sure, but you can see the likeness, can't you?

Rodney is puzzled by this. Albert is embarrassed.

Albert D'you fancy a dance, Reen? I can still cut a rug with the best of 'em.

Reen You keep your hands to yourself though, *(To Rodney)* see you later, love.

Albert and Reen move to main hall.

Rodney *(To Mike)* What was that all about?

Mike Gawd knows.

Boycie I remember her from years ago, she's never been the full ten bob.

Rodney closes his eyes in embarrassment for Trigger.

Trigger Oi, she's my Auntie!

Mike It must be a family trait then!

As Albert and Reen reach the doors to main hall so they virtually bump into Del as he exits. Del is jacketless and sweating from dancing. He is tucking his shirt flap back into his trousers.

Del Be careful in there, Albert. Marlene is pulling all the blokes' shirt flaps out.

We see Boycie's reaction to this news. Del now spots Reen.

Del No … No, it's not! Reeny Turpin!

They embrace.

Reen Remember me, do you?

Del Remember you, I'm still having nightmares about you! How are you, sweetheart? You keeping well?

Reen I'm smashing, Del. *(Referring to gold chains and rings)* I must say you're looking very prosperous.

Del Well, life has been good to us, innit, Rodney?

Rodney Oh yeah, a non-stop Mardi Gras.

Del Let's have a sit down, eh? I'm feeling a bit cream-crackered after that dancing.

Del and Reen move to chairs.

Albert *(To Rodney)* She used to be a right little raver in her younger days.

Rodney *(Smiles at this)* Yeah?

Trigger is a couple of feet behind Rodney.

Albert They reckon during the war she had more yanks than Eisenhower.

Rodney and Albert laugh. Upon hearing the laughter Trigger turns and smiles as if he wants to be in on the joke.

Albert *(Looking in Reen's direction and so not spotting Trigger)* I heard the Normandy landings started from her scullery.

Rodney and Albert laugh again.

Trigger *(At Rodney's shoulder and smiling)* Who you talking about?

Rodney Trigger's Aunt. *(Reacts)*

We cut away to Del and Reen.

Del So how long is it since I last saw you?

Reen I moved from Peckham in '65, so that's nearly twenty three years! You said you'd pop down and see me.

Del I've been a bit tied-up, Reen, you know how it is, business and what have you.

Reen He seems a nice kid, little Rodney.

Del That boy has got a diamond where other people have got hearts. Clever kid an all, GCEs the lot.

Reen But he's had you there to guide him, Del. He wouldn't be in the position he's in today if it hadn't been for you.

Del *(Modestly)* Well, you know, I've done my best by him. Kept my promise to Mum.

Reen She would have been so proud of you two. I think that's why I moved down here. The old place changed after your mum went. I lost the best friend I ever had.

The Frog's Legacy

Del Yeah, she was a lovely lady.

Reen If things had worked out a bit better you and Rodney could have been millionaires by now. I remember visiting your mum in hospital and her saying to me; 'If only I knew where he'd hidden it, Reen. My boys could be set for life!'

Del *(Nods in agreement. Now reacts)* Hidden? Hidden what?

Reen *(Now quieter. Assuming Del knows)* You know, the gold!

Del What gold?

Reen 'His' gold!

Del Who's 'he'?

Reen Freddy the Frog!

Del Freddy the Frog? Who's Freddy the Frog?

Reen *(Reacts as she realises Del knew nothing)* You mean your mum never told you? Oh my Gawd, me and my mouth! Forget I said anything Del.

Del How can I forget it? You might as well tell me, Reen, otherwise I'll get it out of someone else.

Reen It all happened a long time ago. She met him in about 1959.

Del Met who?

Reen Freddy Robdal.

The vicar is collecting his coat. Upon hearing the name Robdal he turns as if recognising the name. He then exits.

Del Who's Freddy Robdal?

Reen That was Freddy the Frog's real name. He was a villain from Rotherhyde, he wasn't a nasty-type though, no guns or violence. He was a gentleman thief. Bit of a dandy was Freddy, loved french wine and paintings and what have you. He had a little holiday chalet down this way. They reckon when the police broke in the walls were covered with Monets and other originals.

Del Yeah, yeah, but what's this got to do with my mum?

Reen Well, she, sort of, 'befriended' him.

Del Yeah, well, she was a friendly lady, weren't she? Help anyone out.

Reen Yeah. Well, she used to help Freddy the Frog out. Anyway, one day in August 1963 Freddy and a little gang broke into the vaults of a bank up in the city. They got away with over a quarter of a million pound in gold bullion. The rest of the gang got caught but Freddy – and the gold – got away. Well, a short time afterwards, while still on the run, he was tragically killed in a freak accident. When they opened his will he'd left everything he owned to your mum.

Del What, including the Monets and originals?

Reen Oh no, they had to be returned to their rightful owners. The same went for the gold except no-one knew where Freddy had hidden it. Then your mum left all her worldly possessions to you and Rodney – including the lost gold.

Del If it was valued at a quarter of a million in 1963 it's gotta be worth at least a million now! Maybe two! And it's mine!

Reen Yours and Rodney's.

Del Same thing! I'm a millionaire.

Reen Yeah. Bloody shame no one knows where it is, innit?

Del Yeah, it is a bit of a choker. *(Takes her glass)* I'll get us a re-fill.

As he moves to bar he passes Rodney.

Del Rodders, I know you may find this hard to believe and it may come as a bit of a shock to you, but – you and me are millionaires!

Rodney Oh good, perhaps we can take the magnet off the electric meter now.

Nods his head as he realises that nothing has changed, they are still skint.

EXT. DAY. THE MARKET.

We are at (or give the impression of being at) the far end of the market where the road joins a T-junction. Del is on corner of Market Road and the more residential road. He has the trellis table open with the suitcase on top. He is trying to flog infra-red, hand-held massagers.

Del *(Spieling to a small crowd. Indicating his back)* Now in the past if the old Cilla Black was playing you up you'd have to stagger down to the quack's to pay a two pound fifty prescription for a three bob tube of Algipan. But those days are over thanks to this revolutionary device – The Inframax deep-penetration massager. *(We hear a few giggles from a group of girls in the crowd)* No, no, you're miles off. This is an osteopeadic machine which emits soothing infra-red rays right into the muscles and warms your pains away. Now if you tried to buy one of these up Harley Street they'd nip you for seventy to eighty pounds, but thanks to free-enterprise, bulk buying and a mate of mine who does a bit of smuggling, I can offer it to you good people for a mere fifteen quid. *(There is little reaction from the crowd)* Come along now, I can't be any fairer. You be glad you sprained your ankle with one of these. *(At this point Albert appears round corner as part of the act. He is stooped with mock back pains as he hobbles through the crowd)* Alright, fourteen quid, that's what I paid for 'em, snatch it off me. *(To Albert)* Excuse me sir, could you hurry along please, I'm tryna do

some business.

Albert Sorry, son.

Del *(To crowd and ignoring Albert)* I don't care if you've got back-ache, neck-ache, ear-ache or any other ache, this little thing will cure it.

A woman in crowd calls out to Del. Her tone is not accusing or suspicious but jovial and all part of the fun and interplay that builds between a good market spieler and his audience.

Woman *(Referring to Albert)* Try it on him then.

Del Eh?

Man in crowd Try it on the old fella.

Del No, no, I don't wanna do the batteries up. *(We now hear light-hearted jeering from the crowd. 'Go away' and 'Get off home' etc.) (Referring to Albert)* That might not be back-ache. For all you know it could be body-language.

Albert No, it's rheumatics, son. Suffered with it for years.

Woman Try your massager on him.

Del *(Defiantly)* Alright, I will.

Albert *(Indicating massage machine)* That soppy little thing won't do me no good. My back's been under experts! Confounded the medical world, my back has.

Del Well, at least let me try, sir. It can't do any harm. Let's get your coat off. Nice and easy.

He gently removes Albert's duffle coat. Albert flinches a few times in pain.

(Referring to Albert's medals) I see you're a naval war hero.

Albert Forty years before the mast fighting for King and country. *(Snaps to attention and salutes)*

Del *(Quietly to himself)* He aint real! *(Whispers to Albert)* Groan, you daft old git!

Albert Eh? Oh yeah. *(Groans loudly and clutches the small of his back)* Oh Gawd, my back!

Del No sudden movements, sir. Not until I have applied the healing rays of the Inframax deep-penetration massager.

Del switches the machine on. Displays the machine to crowd like a magician starting a trick. He now begins to rub the machine gently over Albert's lower back.

Del Can you feel the relaxing warmth soothing the tension and pain from your lumbar region?

Albert Yeah, that's very theraputic that is. I've never had this done to me before.

Del Coming from an old sailor that's saying something, innit?

Albert *(Referring to the warming rays on his back)* Oh, that's lovely. My back feels better already. *(Begins straightening up)* Look at that, I can stand up straight! I haven't been able to stand up straight for years!

To emphasise his new found mobility Albert goes right over the top and does a little tap-dance routine. Del turns away in disbelief.

Del I don't believe him! What is he doing to me?

The crowd is now laughing and dispersing.

Man *(To his mate, referring to Albert)* He's just a stooge!

Woman He's part of the act!

Del No he ain't! We've never met before, have we, sir?

Albert Never, Del. *(Del hurls the massage machine to ground in anger. The crowd disperses and drifts away. Albert approaches the fuming Del.)* You told me to 'get better' in front of the crowd.

Del Yes, but I didn't ask you to do the third act of 'Singing in the Rain'! You came round that corner looking like Old Father Time. One rub of me massager and you turned into Wayne Sleep!

Albert Well, I'm not used to all this market spieling. Why didn't you get Rodney to do it?

Del Because Rodney started his new job this morning. He can't be in two places at once. *(Indicating suitcase, table etc.)* Right, clear this all up will you?

Albert *(Reluctantly and mumbling to himself)* Innit bloody fair, eh? I fought a war for the younger generation.

Del Yeah, but whose side was you on?

Albert begins closing suitcase, folding table etc. We see Trigger and his dust cart appear in background, he is sweeping round the corner of the T-junction.

Trigger Del Boy, Albert.

Del Wotchyer, Trigger.

Trigger Good wedding weren't it?

Del Yeah mustard.

Trigger Lisa and Andy were double pleased with that dinner service you bought 'em. Must have cost a fortune?

Del It was nothing Trigger. Anything to help the young couple.

(We hear the bip of a car horn. We see Boycie pulling up in his mercedes. He wears dark glasses and has a large cigar between his fingers (really flash). He stops car in centre of the more residential road and prepares to reverse into space on corner of T junction.) Here comes money!

Trigger *(Referring to Boycie)* D'you see the

The Frog's Legacy

crappy present he bought 'em?

Del No, no I didn't catch that, Trigger.

Trigger Load of cheap old plates. Kind of thing you'd get in a bad Chinese restaurant.

Del Well, that's how he got rich, through being tight.

Trigger Yeah, he's always been tight, ain't he?

Del He's the kind of bloke who'd buy a tin of baked beans on Tuesday 'cos he fancied a bubble bath Wednesday.

Trigger nods in agreement. Boycie reverses into space and alights.

Boycie Good morning, gentlemen. Another fine day in Gotham City. The wedding seemed to go well, Trigger, all things considered.

Trigger Yeah it was alright, weren't it?

Boycie Did Lisa and what'shisname find time to look at my present?

Trigger Yeah they looked at it – not for long though.

Boycie *(Bemused by Trigger's last remark. Now referring to Del)* And what about 'his' little gift?

Trigger They put Del's present straight in their display cabinet.

Boycie *(Horrified)* Peasants!

Del Talking of the wedding, there's something I wanted to ask you two. Think back to the early sixties. Do either of you remember – Freddy The Frog?

Albert, who is a yard or two behind them, turns sharply upon hearing the name 'Freddy the Frog'. Making it obvious to the audience that he knows the name and is alarmed upon hearing it after all these years.

Trigger Freddy The Frog? No, don't ring a bell. I remember Torchy the Battery Boy.

Boycie Yeah, and what about Twizzle? (Does the stretching, growing motions of Twizzle)

Del This is something else! They're from another planet!

Trigger now spots something in distance.

Trigger *(Respectful tone)* Hold up lads, hats off.

Del and Trigger remove their hats.

We cut to see a hearse carrying a flower covered coffin moving slowly along the road. We are at an angle whereby we cannot see the driver of hearse, or front seat passenger, at this point.

Boycie Albert, your mini-cab's arrived.

Albert gives him a sneer.

We cut to see the funeral cortege. Behind the hearse (we still cannot see the driver or passenger) comes one official funeral car, behind this comes an old Renault and then a Cortina, both containing mourners.

We cut back to see Del, Albert, Trigger and Boycie (and a few other locals who have stopped to show their last respects). Trigger now zeros in on something at the very front of cortege.

Trigger *(To Del)* Is that Dave?

Del *(Sheepishly)* Yeah.

We cut to see Rodney walking slowly and mournfully in front of the hearse wearing the long-tailed coat and uniform of the official chief mourner (he carries his black top hat in hand); he is obviously feeling very self-conscious.

We now cut to the hearse where we see a white driver and Mr Jahan sitting next to him. They are both dressed in smart black undertakers' suits. We cut back to Rodney who does a quick double-take as he spies Del in the crowd.

Rodney *(Seething and loathing. He tries to hiss the word under his breath but his anger is so powerful he cannot contain it)* You git! You rotten git!! *(Del holds a finger to his lips and indicates the cortege – reminding Rodney of his duties) (Shouting across the street at Del)* You didn't tell me my new job was a chief mourner!

Del Have some respect, Rodney!

Cut to interior of hearse.

Mr Jahan *(Referring to Rodney) (To driver)* What's he doing?

Driver shakes his head. Cut back to street. Rodney is walking on in middle of road but is looking in Del's direction.

Rodney I'll get you for this, you bloody well see if I don't!

Del Behave yourself, Rodney. You're in a responsible position now!

Rodney You just wait, Del! You just wait!

Rodney turns to the front and walks on a few paces. He now stops as he realises he has led the cortege into a no-entry street. He holds his hand out for cortege to stop. We see the cars all pull to an abrupt halt, not actually crashing into each other but getting too close for comfort. We hear a couple of tiny screeches of tyres.

Mr Jahan *(Opens passenger window of hearse and calls)* Why are you taking us down there, Rodney? It's a no-entry!

Rodney Yes, sorry, Mr Jahan, I was talking to my brother and I ... Sorry! *(Calls to car at back of cortege)* If you could back up a little bit, please.

We cut to Del.

The last car in the cortege (the Cortina) has stalled and as the driver tries to re-start

engine we can hear the battery running down.

Rodney is running up towards the car.

Rodney Would you mind backing up a bit, please? *(To driver)* What's the trouble?

Del I can't stand it any more. What a plonker! *He turns and disappears into crowd.*

Boycie Yes, I'm finding this very upsetting as well.

Trigger D'you know the bloke in the hearse then?

Boycie No, but I know the bloke in the Cortina, I sold it to him last week.

We cut to cortege. Rodney is now calling to the occupants of the official mourners' car and the old Renault.

Rodney Would you mind giving us a push, please? It won't take a moment. *(Calls down towards hearse)* Sorry, Mr Jahan!

STUDIO. INT. NIGHT TROTTERS' LOUNGE.

Albert is alone in lounge and reading newspaper. From the bedroom area we can hear Del and Rodney arguing.

Rodney (OOV) You're a liar, Del!

Del (OOV) Rodney, I swear to you I didn't know what your duties would be, Mr Jahan never told me!

Rodney (OOV) Didn't know, my arse! You just set me up for that job so that I could bring some money into the flat.

Del enters.

Del Well every little helps, Rodders. Anyway that black suit looks really good on you.

Rodney *(Enters)* No it doesn't! I saw my reflection in a shop window and I looked like a wand! You said I'd be a trainee computer programmer!

Del And are you not programming his computer?

Rodney Oh yeah, I'm programming the computer. I'm also an apprentice pall-bearer, a fully-fledged chief mourner *and* I have to go and get the sandwiches!

Albert Long as you've got job-satisfaction, that's the main thing.

Rodney No, I have not got job-satisfaction! To be honest, I'm thinking of resigning!

Del Well, I'd hurry up before he sacks you!

Rodney That big traffic jam was not my fault! Alright, name one person who blamed me!

Del Mr Jahan did.

Albert The grieving relatives did.

Del The Flying Eye did.

Rodney I can't help it if the differential on that

Cortina seized up! I had to call the RAC, and they had to call for a tow truck which couldn't get through.

Albert Why?

Rodney 'Cos of the big traffic jam. Anyway it all went off alright in the end.

Del Yeah, and you could have set a trend. Floodlit funerals could be all the rage! Anyway, I don't want to talk about it anymore, I've got far more important things on my mind.

Rodney Oh, we're not going back to Freddy the bleedin' Frog again, are we?

Del Yes we are, Rodney. There's a million quids worth of gold bullion out there, and it's ours!

Rodney You're something else, you are. Some drunken old woman spins you a cock 'n' bull story and you fall for it.

Del Reeny might have been a good time girl who likes the occasional Tizer, but she was never a liar. Besides, I've been and seen a few faces this afternoon and they've confirmed it. The robbery – the gold never being found – the lot.

Rodney But how can you be certain it hasn't been found? I mean at some time or another, every policeman and underworld figure in the country must have been searching for that gold.

Del And what would they have done with it? They'd either have put it through a fence, which meant it became public knowledge within the month, or they'd have to smelt it down and sell it themselves, and that amount of bullion coming on the market causes ripples, the kind of ripples that'd be remembered for a long time!

Albert And what if the police found it?

Del I'm talking about the police! The chaps haven't found it either. I had a chat with the Driscoll brothers.

Rodney *(A chill down the spine)* You went and saw the Driscoll brothers?

Albert Why what they like?

Rodney Smashing blokes, Unc. It's like bumping into the two Ronnies – Biggs and Kray! They didn't catch on why you were asking questions?

Del No. You know what they're like. A couple of years back some Guru said the world would end in a month. Danny Driscoll bet a grand it would. And he's the *brains* of the outfit. Trouble was I had to keep referring to him as Freddy the Frog, I couldn't remember his surname. It was Robson or something.

Albert Robdal.

Del That's it, Robdal! I've been tryna think of that all day lo ... Did you know him?

Albert Vaguely!

Del Why didn't you say?

The Frog's Legacy

Albert Well, the first time I met him he was just a kid – eighteen, nineteen, a different age group from me. Then over the years I'd bump into him every so often, usually in one of the pubs near the docks. He was a likeable fella, always knew the latest jokes, and a generous bloke. He was very tall and handsome. Everyone liked him, specially the women. Used to fall over themselves for Freddy.

Del Yes, yes, yes, but what about the gold bullion?

Albert Well they robbed a bank in the city …

Del Yes, yes I know all about that! I mean what happened *after* the robbery.

Albert About a week after, Freddy and an explosives expert, bloke called Jelly Kelly, broke into a sub post office in Plumstead. Apparently they'd wired the explosives up and everything was going well, when – and no-one knows why – but Freddy the Frog sat on the detonator. They eventually found him on the roof … of a building across the road.

Del And what about the other mush, Jelly Kelly?

Albert Well, he was holding the nitroglycerine when Freddy sat down.

Del So obviously he didn't survive either.

Rodney Well, if he did he'd be no good in a Mexican Wave.

Del Wherever I go it's the same story – Freddy took the secret with him.

Albert Maybe he shipped the gold abroad.

Rodney There wouldn't have been time. There was only a week between him doing the job and hitting the snooze-button.

Del There's something else that's confusing me as well. If he was having an affair with a married woman on this estate, why did he leave all his money to our mum?
  Rodney and Albert just stare at Del in disbelief.

Albert *(Shakes his head)* It's a mystery, innit?

Rodney I'll make some tea. *(Exits to kitchen)*

Del I was talking to one of the Driscoll heavies. He said he'd heard that Freddy had a son by this woman.
  We cut to kitchen and see Rodney's reaction. Cut back to lounge.

Albert *(Nervously eyes kitchen door, fearing Rodney might have heard).* Just rumours, Del. I'd take no notice of rumours.

Del No. But if it were true the boy would be in his mid-twenties by now. Still, he don't know who his real Dad is so he can't make a claim on the fortune.
  Rodney enters from the kitchen.

Del Bloody good, innit, bruv? Here we are, millionaires, and we're getting threatening letters from the milkman! *(Holds up note from Express Dairies)*

Rodney *(To Albert)* This er, this Freddy Robdal. Did he have any hobbies or pastimes?

Del Hobbies or pastimes? We're searching for his gold, not his tennis racket!

Rodney No, I thought the more you know about him the more you'll know how his mind works.

Del Yes, good thinking, Rodney. He was a bit of an artist weren't he, Albert?
  Rodney reacts.

Albert *(Very aware of Rodney)* Yeah, good artist. They reckon if he hadn't been a tea-leaf he could have made a very good forger.

Del Well that's got us a lot closer. It's almost solved. I'm gonna sleep on it. I'll see you two in the morning.
  Del exits to the bedroom area. 'Goodnights' are exchanged. A long look is exchanged between Rodney and Albert.

Rodney Did Mum ever …

Albert They're rumours, Rodney. That's all, rumours. Goodnight son. *(Exits to bedroom)*
  Rodney sits alone considering it all.

Del *(OOV)* Rodney. Don't forget, you've gotta be down the morgue by half nine.
  Rodney closes his eyes.

INT. DAY. NAG'S HEAD.

Del We'll finish this then we'll pop down the market and have another go with the massagers. And this time, when I've finished operating on you, no tap-dancing! Just straighten up slowly like it's a miracle.
  Rodney in chief mourner's gear appears from entrance on far side of bar.

Rodney *(Calls excitedly)* Del! Got it!
  Rodney is holding a piece of paper which is some kind of printed form with biro handwriting on it.

Del *(As Rodney makes his way round bar, to Albert)* What's that about?

Albert Dunno. It looked like 'peace in our time!'
  Rodney arrives at table.

Rodney This morning Mr Jahan asked me to transfer all his old paper files onto the computer.

Del *(Horrified)* What, my computer?

Rodney Yeah. *(Hands him paper)* Have a read of that.

Del *(Refused to touch paper)* No. No! What is it, a summons?

Rodney No. It's one of Mr Jahan's order forms

from July 1963. Look who ordered a coffin to be specially made. One Frederick Robdal. It was ordered five weeks *before* the robbery, six weeks before he blew himself up. D'you see what it means?

Albert He had a premonition.

Rodney You berk!

Del (*Reading the paper*) No, Freddy only paid for it, it was made for some bloke called Alfred Broderick. Who was Alfred Broderick?

Rodney No, look at the two names closely. It's an anagram.

Del Oh yeah, yeah, I can see that. But who was he?

Rodney No – bloody 'ell – look, if you transpose – you know, mix up – all the letters in Frederick Robdal it turns into Alfred Broderick. In other words Alfred Broderick never existed, it's just one of Freddie's aliases.

Del and Albert study the paper

Albert He's right an' all.

Del So he put …

Rodney … the bullion …

Del in the coffin and then got the Co-op to hide it for him or in this case, Mr Jahan.

Rodney Right. It was all above board and out in the open. It was most probably paraded through these streets.

Del I'll bet the old Bill stopped the traffic for it.

Rodney Yeah. Then it was buried with all the usual honours. All Freddy had to do was bide his time, then come back for it.

Albert You two seem to be forgetting something. This isn't a family pet we're talking about. If what you're suggesting is right he'd have needed permission from the authorities – he'd have needed official documentation – and lots and lots of it! So where's he get all that?

Del and Rodney look at each other. They have no answer.

Rodney He always has to spoil things, don't he?

Del Wait a minute, I think I've cracked it. Back in the early sixties when you was a nipper, Mum used to work at the town hall as a … secretary.

Rodney A secretary?

Del Yeah. Well, part of her duties was hoovering out the Registrar's department. Don't you see, she could have got her hands on every document he needed and marked it with the official stamp!

Mr Jahan in his funeral director's suit, enters.

Mr Jahan Rodney, what are you doing here? You're supposed to be helping me with the embalming.

Rodney Yeah, sorry, Mr Jahan. I just took an early lunch.

Del Sit down Mr Jahan. I want to have a chat with you. Now, Mr Jahan, Rodney found this in your files. (*Shows him paperwork*)

Mr Jahan But this is confidential material.

Del It just shows you how enthusiastic he is. He's even taking homework to lunch with him. Do you happen to remember this gentleman, Mr Frederick Robdal?

Mr Jahan Oh yes I remember him very well, a most charming man. My father had only just bought the business and Mr Robdal was one of our very first clients. The other reason it sticks out in my mind is because Mr Robdal ordered an extra-large casket to be made.

Del (*Smiling as it all clicks into place*) Did he now? Well, I suppose his friend, Mr Broderick, must have been an extra-large chap.

Mr Jahan I wouldn't know, we didn't handle the funeral.

Del (*The smile fades*) What?

Mr Jahan We simply supplied the casket. Mr Robdal collected it in a van one night.

Del You mean it was a take-away?

Mr Jahan Mr Robdal told us it was to be a very private affair. We didn't question his decision – we did not wish to intrude upon his grief and we needed the business. (*He stands*)

Del (*Pulling him back down*) So you don't know where it was buried?

Mr Jahan I have no idea, as I say, it was a private affair. Now, I must return. Rodney, how long will you be? (*Stands*)

Rodney Back soon, Mr Jahan. (*Jahan exits. Del sits at table, trance-like and socked*) Well, that's the end of that.

Albert You'll never find it now, son.

Del Yes we will!

Rodney Del, the gold has been missing for twenty four years. The last thing anyone saw of Freddy the Frog was on a radar screen, so what chance have we got?

Del He must have buried it somewhere local. I mean he'd stick to an area he knew well. I tell you what we're gonna do. I'm gonna see the flower man in the market and get us a codgel of tulips on sale or return. You're gonna visit every graveyard and cemetery in the district and check the name on every headstone. Leave a flower on each one as if you're a relative.

Albert But there's thousands of 'em!

Del If anyone asks tell 'em you're from a big family! You do the same thing on your travels, Rodders. It'll be like a busman's holiday to you. In the meantime I'm gonna check a few records

The Frog's Legacy

at the town hall, churches, stonemason's yards, that sort of thing. We'll find it! You mark my words.

Rodney Derek, I don't want to be the prophet of doom or nothing, but I just get the feeling we're wasting our time. Time that should be spent in more practical pursuits, like earning some money and paying some bills. We owe two months rent, we're drinking tea without milk and the electricity board are calling round to see why their meter is going backwards.

Del There's food in the cupboard, ain't there?

Albert Yeah, thanks to my pension and Rodney's wages. It wouldn't be a bad idea for you to drive down to Hampshire and pick up that computer money off the vicar.

Del Listen to me, that gold is here somewhere. It can't just have disappeared, this is Peckham not the Bermuda Triangle. And for me to drive all the way down to Hampshire to collect a piddling hundred and twenty quid would be like admitting defeat. A sign that I'd given up all hope of ever finding my birthright. And that is not my style. When Del Trotter says he's gonna do something, Del Trotter does it!

STUDIO. INT. DAY. CHURCH VESTRY.

The computer is on the table and plugged in. The screen shows lots of fizzy lines like interference. The vicar enters followed by Del.

Vicar *(Indicating screen)* You see what I mean Mr Trotter, I've tried everything but it simply refuses to work.

Del Hmm, I see. Has the machine received a knock of any kind?

Vicar Oh no, I can assure you.

Del Oh. *(Del now gives a heavy thump with the side of his fist. The screen clears and appears to be in working order.)* There you are, that's all it needed.

Vicar Yes! Well, I'm not as technically minded as you, Mr Trotter.

Del Sometimes these hi-tech advancements need a bit of encouragement. So, if you've got the money vicar, I'll bid you farewell.

Vicar I'm afraid I shan't be needing the computer, Mr Trotter.

Del What?

Vicar As I said to you at the wedding, I honestly couldn't see what part a computer could play in the daily running of a small parish such as this. And my words have been borne out.

Del Oh yeah, but if it had been working properly you might have seen the benefits.

Vicar I'm very sorry, Mr Trotter and I'm very grateful to you for giving me two weeks approval on the machine, but I simply have no need of it.

Del *(Becoming increasingly desperate. Closes door)* I can't take it back now, it's been used.

Vicar Well, of course it's been used! You told me to use it!

Del Yeah, but it's been taken out of its protective wrapping. *(Pointing to a spot on computer – the spot where he hit it.)* And it's had a whack on the side as well.

Vicar But you just did that!

Del Yes but I'm not a technician, I'm just the salesman. So what do I tell my head office? You've taken the protective wrapping off, messed about with it, let an unqualified wally repair it and now you wanna elbow it! I mean that was in lovely condition when I loaned it to you, but now it's second hand … Look, I'll be fair with you. Even though you were the one who naused it up I'll let you have it at a second hand price. Gimme hundred notes and we'll say no more on the matter.

Vicar I don't want the computer!

Del But this machine is the top of the range, this is the Silver Cloud of computers. And just think, there are thousands of people pouring out of London to live in new housing estates in this Parish. Your flock is increasing daily, you're gonna need something to keep a check on 'em all!

Vicar I only wish it were true. Unfortunately few of them seem to need the spiritual services of this church. It's a pity more of them couldn't be like our mutual friend Mr Robdal.

Del What?

Vicar I apologise, but I couldn't help overhearing you and Mrs Turpin discussing Mr Robdal at the wedding.

Del You knew Freddy the Frog?

Vicar I'm sorry?

Del Freddy Robdal. You knew him?

Vicar Many years ago when I first came here to St Mary's. He had a holiday home just a few miles from here. He'd always call in when he was down this way. A charming and very generous man. He donated the stained-glass windows. In fact he loved this church so much he had his parents buried here.

Del Did you ever meet Freddy's mate? Bloke called Broderick.

Vicar *Alfred* Broderick? Yes, well I didn't actually 'meet' him, not in the conventional sense. It was my sad duty to lay the poor man to rest. He must have been a rather large man, it took eight of us to carry him from the hearse.

Del Yeah, he was an anagram! Could you tell me where you buried it – him? I'd like to pay my last respects.

Vicar Why, of course. I'll check the records. *(Begins checking a giant ledger)* He must have been very close to Mr Robdal. I'll never forget the way he constantly patted the coffin and contained his grief behind a smile.

Del Yeah. We was all a bit choked. You found it yet?

Vicar Ah, here it is.

Del shoves vicar out of the way and reads the page of ledger.

Vicar About the computer?

Del Don't worry about the computer. Give it to the jumble sale, it's a load of junk anyway!.

EXT. DAY. THE CHURCH.

Rodney is reading. A puff of smoke drifts past his face. He looks at Albert.

Rodney What do you put in that thing?

Albert It's me own recipe. Dutch tobacco. Navy shag and a spoonful of rum to keep it moist.

Rodney is revolted.

Albert *(Takes a deep, deep breath)* Smell the salt, Rodney?

Rodney You put condiments in it as well?

Albert I mean the ozones in the air. Takes me back. Funny how a smell can start the mind turning.

Rodney *(Looking at pipe)* Not to mention the stomach.

Del now rushes from the church doors and towards the van. He has a quick, purposeful step. He is alive and raring to go. We should not be able to tell whether his mood is one of anger, determination or greed.

Del Rodney! I know where it's buried!

Rodney What, you mean – here?

Del Yes, here! Come on. *(Indicating back of van)* Albert, fetch that shovel!

Del moves off quickly along path leading to graveyard. Rodney gives chase but never quite catches Del. Albert follows with shovel.

Rodney *(Calling after Del in a kind of hushed shout)* Del, you can't go digging up a grave in broad daylight!

EXT. DAY. AREA OF GRAVEYARD.

Del marches towards us with Rodney some yards behind and Albertert further back carrying the spade.

Rodney I mean. I know there's nothing actually in it – except for gold bullion, but if anyone saw us doing it they might not understand!

Del Come on!

EXT. DAY. ANOTHER AREA OF GRAVEYARD.

This is the edge of the graveyard and the perimeter is marked by a small fence (two foot high).

Del *(Steps over fence)* Over here.

Rodney and Albert follow.

EXT. DAY. AREA OF OPEN GRASSLAND WHICH LIES BEHIND GRAVEYARD.

Del walks out into the centre of the grassy area and stops. Rodney and Albert now join him.

Del *(A nod of the head which indicates nowhere in particular)* This is it. This is where he buried it!

Rodney *(Surveys grassland)* Where?

Del *(Points straight ahead)* There!

Rodney turns in that direction.

We pan to find ourselves looking out to sea. If possible it should be wide open ocean – no islands, headlands, piers or ships to mar the view – just miles and miles of sea.

We are in fact upon a clifftop or high point.

Rodney *(Incredulously)* A burial at sea? But why? How did he ever hope to get the gold back?

Del There are a few minor things our dear Uncle forgot to inform of us, Rodney. He told us he met Freddy the Frog but he didn't tell us where and how.

Albert I met him when he was doing his national service in the navy.

Rodney closes his eyes as things begin to click into place.

Del Yes, he was a sailor! And he also omitted to tell us why he was nicknamed Freddy the Frog. We assumed it was because of his love of all things French.

Albert No, it was 'cos he was a frogman.

Rodney closes his eyes again and lets out a low moan.

Del Yeah, I know that now, the vicar's just given me the full SP.

Rodney *(To Albert)* Why didn't you tell us?

Albert Well, you know me. I never talk about my days at sea.

Rodney Look, we knew that Freddy had a chalet down here by the coast. If we'd have also known that he was an ex-sailor *and* a deep sea diver we could have put two and two together.

Del And saved ourselves a fortnight of creeping round every cemetery and churchyard in South London!

The Frog's Legacy

Albert Well, if you knew he was buried at sea why'd you ask me to bring this shovel?

Del *(Grabs shovel)* To whack you on the bloody head with!

As Del lifts shovel in air, Rodney grabs it and stops him.

Rodney Del, take it easy!

Del Well, he's given me the 'ump, Rodney, he's given me the right steaming 'ump! *(Staring out to sea)* I mean, it's beautiful, innit? He had all the kosher paperwork, a pukka ceremony with an authentic vicar. He even got two off-duty policemen to help carry the coffin to the boat!

Rodney All he had to do was wait for the dust to settle, then come back with his frogman gear and dive down and get it. He must have known these waters well, most probably been diving here for years.

Del It's out there, Rodney, our legacy!

Albert Nothing you can do about it now, Del.

Del I'm not leaving it there! The sea shall not have it! *I* will bring it back to the surface! *We* can do it! I've got faith in *you*, Rodney!

Rodney But how are we gonna ... *Me*? What d'you mean you've got faith in me?

Del I'll get you all the equipment, flippers, goggles, the works. You're the only one in the family who can swim, Rodders.

Rodney All I ever got was a fifty yard certificate at school.

Del You've only gotta swim fifty yards – down!

Rodney On your bike!

Albert *(To Del)* Where you gonna start searching? You're looking at five hundred square miles of ocean! It took 'em seventy years to find the Titanic so what chance we got with an outsize coffin?

Del *(Becoming almost hysterical in his frustration and greed)* There's gotta be a way! He who dares wins! There's a million quidsworth of gold out there – *our* gold! We can't just say Bonjour to it!

Del storms away from them leaving Albert and Rodney alone. Albert and Rodney stare out to sea. (Slight pause)

Rodney Do I look like him?

Albert It was just a rumour, son.

Rodney Do I look like him?

Albert Bit.

Rodney I always felt as if I was different from the rest of the family. A bit of a cuckoo.

Albert It was just a rumour! *(Walks away leaving Rodney alone)*

Rodney looks out to sea

Rodney Freddy the Frog! Killed himself by sitting on someone else's detonator! The last thing anyone saw of my Dad was on a radar screen! *(He smiles to himself)*

Rodney looks up to the sky. We see a seagull gliding above. To Rodney, the artist, it represents the free-spirit.

Rodney smiles to himself. He now feels completely at one with the world and himself. He turns and walks back past Del.

Rodney Come on, let's talk about it over a pint.

Del Yeah, alright, bruv. *(Points at the sea as if threatening it)* But in the words of General MacArthur, 'I shall be back soon!'

They walk towards us. Rodney steps over the small fence, followed by Albert. Del is following them.

Del I am not leaving our birthright down there in Davey Smith's locker. No way. I tell you Rodders. This time next year we'll be millionaires.

They turn and walk to the car.

Dates

INT. NIGHT. TROTTERS' LOUNGE.

Rodney is seated at the table working something out with the help of a calculator and many grubby receipts, etc. Del is seated watching TV. He is wearing a silk dressing gown and matching silk pyjamas. He smokes a big cigar and sips an exotic cocktail.

His air of civility suggests he is at one with the world, in other words they've been earning recently.

Rodney Have you any idea how much money we've made recently?

Del Loads of bunce, Rodders, loads of bunce.

Rodney We've made nearly two thousand pounds in the last month!

Del Am I a genius or just a miracle worker?

Rodney We've sold over four hundred of those ladies electric razors.

Del I told you they'd sell, didn't I?

Rodney You'd never guess there was that much hair about, would you?

Del Oi, you chuck all those receipts and bills down the chute. I don't want no evidence left in the flat.

Albert enters from his bedroom. He is carrying a battered old black tin box.

Rodney *(Referring to box)* What's that dirty looking thing?

Del That is your Uncle, Rodney, please show a bit more respect!

Del and Rodney laugh.

Help yourself to a drink, we're celebrating.

Albert Yeah thanks, son. This is from my old days, Rodney. All those years ago when I used to sail the seven seas.

Rodney What is it, treasure?

Albert has opened the box and produces a bundle of tattered and brown letters and photographs, etc.

Albert No, just a few old photos and letters from my days in the navy. It's nothing much – just my memories!

Del Don't worry. Rodney's chucking a whole load of gear down the chute in a minute, he'll get rid of it for you.

Albert This is a history of my life!!

Del That's why I thought you'd wanna get rid of it!

Rodney *(Has picked up one of the photos)* Is that you?

Albert Yeah. That's when I first joined the navy. Seventeen I was.

Rodney You ain't changed, Unc.

Del What d'you mean, he had a big white beard then?

Rodney No, I mean he's wearing the same clothes!

Del and Rodney laugh

Albert What's the matter with you two daft sods?

Del We've had a blinding month. *(Picks up a photo)* What's this one? '1941. My birthday party on board HMS *Peerless*.' Cor, they look a bunch of toerags, Albert!

Albert Yeah. That's me and some of me mates when we was serving out in the South China Sea. They were brave lads, Del. Look at 'em, like steely-eyed young lions.

Del Yeah. You look more like Clarence the cross-eyed lion!

Albert Well, I'd just been out to a nightclub celebrating me birthday.

Rodney Who's the bloke with the G-string and the ruby in his belly-button?

Albert That's one of the dancing girls from the nightclub. We'd sneaked her back to 'show her round HMS *Peerless*!' *(A licentious laugh)*

Del You dirty old goat!

Albert The captain used to call it *(Posh voice)* 'A submarine hunter'. But she was nothing more than an old tug.

Del *(Studying photo)* Yeah, she looks like a rough and ready girl.

Albert I'm talking about HMS *Peerless*!

Del Oh sorry!

Albert Just a few hours after that photo was taken we was in action.

Rodney *(Studying photo)* I'm surprised it took you that long!

Albert A Japanese sub was spotted in the area.

Del That's all you need, innit?

Albert There was an American aircraft carrier, anchored off-shore. The USS *Pittsburgh*. It was our job to protect her. Well, we'd only been sailing for about an hour and we crashed right into her. Cor, didn't half make a noise!

Del *(Incredulous)* You went and whacked into the boat that you were going out to protect?

Albert Yeah. It was a good job she was there actually, she picked up most of the survivors.

Rodney Was your ship badly damaged?
Albert We couldn't tell, Rodney, it sunk. Course, they tried to put the blame on me.
Del Sounds fair.
Albert Just 'cos I was on watch at the time. I had me excuses ready.
Rodney What, you were drunk?
Albert Don't be silly! The American vessel was at battle stations and was showing no light. You weren't allowed, there was a war on.
Del Course there was.
Albert So then they tried to get me on naval technicalities, like it happened in broad daylight.
Rodney You didn't see an aircraft carrier?
Del Forty-two thousand tons of steel!
Rodney In broad daylight!
Albert Well, I wasn't close enough!
Rodney You must have been reasonably close, Unc, you hit it!
Del They'd have stood more chance with Ray Charles in the crow's nest!
Albert Well, I mean I wasn't up on deck. I was in the radar room watching the screen. I couldn't make head nor tail of it. It was all blibs and blobs. Still, the Japanese sub had it away a bit lively.
Rodney I suppose it didn't feel needed with you around. Did you get into trouble for it?
Albert Court-martial. The papers were sent to naval headquarters, Singapore.
Rodney You were court-martialled?
Albert No. As luck would have it, before my trial the Japanese invaded! And I never heard another word about it. And the blokes in my lifeboat used to say I was unlucky!
Del That was a bit strong, trying to court-martial him.
Rodney He had just ruined a perfectly good aircraft-carrier.
Del Yeah, but it was his birthday!
Rodney Oh yeah, I forgot! *(Looks at photo)* But not for long though! This picture was taken at his birthday party in 1941 right. You seen the date.
Del That's about a fortnight's time, innit?
Rodney Yeah. You don't think the ancient mariner was trying to let us know so that we'd arrange a birthday treat, do you?
Del Wash your mouth out with soap and water, Rodney. Your Uncle Albert is not a crafty person! He's as cunning as a lighthouse rat! The sly old git! Right, he wants a surprise for his birthday does he?
Rodney What you gonna do?
Del Dunno yet, but I'll think of something to

pull him up a bit lively!
Rodney Let's give him one of them electric razors!
They both break down laughing.

INT. DAY. NAG'S HEAD PUB.
This is lunchtime. We can hear piano music. Boycie is at bar wearing his usual wide-awake clothes. Mike is leaning on bar and looking grimly in direction of piano. We see Albert at piano. He is playing an off-key middle eight to some mysterious song.
Mike and Boycie cringe at his efforts.
After eight or nine seconds of this, Albert picks up the final chords of song.
Albert *(Sings)* I'm in the mood for love.
Albert runs to take his ovation.
Mike *(To Boycie)* Why does he keep doing it, eh?
Boycie Gawd knows. I suppose at some time in his life someone told him he could play the piano.
Mike Yeah, but I'd like to meet the git who told him he could sing!
Boycie He's a Trotter! What more can you say about the man? A couple of years ago I went down the local library and read some ancient manuscripts written by the Elders of Peckham. Did you know, five hundred years ago this was a green and peaceful area? The old Earl of Peckham had a castle where the Kwik-Fit exhaust centre now stands. Flaxen-haired maidens used to dance round the village maypole of an evening. And then one fateful medieval day, the Trotter clan arrived in a stolen Zephyr. Before you knew it the flaxen-haired maidens were up the spout, the old Earl had been sold some hooky armour and someone nicked the maypole! A hundred years after that the Black Death arrived in England. The people of Peckham thought their luck had changed.
Mike nudges Boycie and gestures towards entrance door.
Mike 'Ere, talk of changing luck, look at this!
We see Trigger has just entered. He is wearing a brown two-piece suit, a purple shirt, orange tie covered with a colourful V-neck jumper and he is carrying a small spray of flowers.
Trigger Alright Boycie?
Boycie Well, I was!
Mike *(Places drink on counter)* There you go Trig, there's a scotch, mate.
Boycie How did you know I wanted a scotch!
Mike 'Cos if I was dressed like that, I'd want a scotch.

Dates

Boycie Er, is this something to do with a new religion?

Trigger I'm taking a lady out to lunch.

Mike and Boycie *(Incredulously)* You sure?

Trigger Yeah, positive. I've booked us a table at that little Italian *(pronounced Eye-talian)* place opposite. I thought I'd better try an' make an impression.

Boycie Well you'll certainly do that Trig, no worries.

Trigger Thanks, Boycie.

Del Good morning, Michael. *(Calls as he walks towards bar)* Same again for Boycie, a non-alcoholic lager-top for Rodney, a Malibu and cherryade for moi, and one for yourself. *(Looks at Trigger)*. Is it Comic Relief Day again? It only seems a little while ago.

Mike *(Interrupts him)* No, it ain't Comic Relief Day.

Trigger I've got a date.

Rodney You wanna watch them stones, 'cos Del got one caught in his throat last Christmas.

Trigger No, Dave. I mean I've got a lunch date with a lady.

Del and Rodney You sure?

Trigger Yeah! I've gotta meet her in a couple of minutes. I just popped in for some Dutch courage.

Del So who is it? Anyone we know?

Trigger You don't know her. Come to that, I don't know her either.

Mike How d'you mean?

Trigger *(Produces some paperwork)* These people arranged it for me.

All 'The Technomatch Friendship and Matrimonial Agency'!

Del You've been to a computerised dating firm?

Trigger Yeah. They've just opened up down the High Street, so I thought I'd have twenty-five quids worth, see what occurs.

Boycie So what's this bird look like?

Trigger I dunno, they don't show you pictures of each other.

Mike That's a bit risky, innit?

Del *(Defending Trigger)* Well, that's her problem!

Trigger They fed all my information into a computer and it came out with a woman who was compatible with me. *(There are fearful reactions as to what this woman might look like)* That's what I like about this agency, you know where you stand with 'em – they insist on honesty.

Boycie So you told 'em you're a roadsweeper?

Trigger No, I told 'em I was a bus inspector.

Rodney Why?

Trigger To add a bit of glamour!

Rodney Oh yeah, good idea.

Trigger *(Downs his whisky in one gulp)* Right then, here goes. I'll see you later.

Boycie Well, rather him than me. He's walking straight into the unknown.

Mike moves down the bar to serve.

Rodney It's a bit like that television programme, innit?

Boycie Yeah.

Rodney You know, *Blind Date*.

Boycie Oh, I thought you meant *That's My Dog*! *(Laughs)* Marlene and Duke sit and watch that – soppy as sacks the two of 'em – Duke gets more questions right than her.

(Del moves down the bar to Mike)

Del Mike, can I have a word about Albert?

Mike Well, there's a coincidence Del, I wanted to have a word with you about him as well.

Del He's not still singing here of an evening, is he?

Mike Oh no, no, no, no. He's doing matinees now! My pie sales have fallen!

Del I'll have a word with him, Mike. Look, listen, I wanted to ask a favour. It's Albert's birthday in a couple of weeks' time and I wanted to throw a little party for him.

Mike What, in here?

Del Well, yeah, yeah a few drinks, a bit of grub, that sort of thing. I'll stick a hundred and fifty across the counter to cover it.

Mike You can have the pub on one condition – he doesn't sing!

Del Fair enough, Mike.

Mike He doesn't use no bad language in front of the ladies.

Del Righto, Mike.

Mike And he doesn't dance!

Del Gotcher, Mike.

Mike He tells no rude jokes.

Del Goes without saying, Michael.

Mike And he don't drink too much.

Del Perish the thought.

Mike He just sits down quietly and soberly and enjoys himself.

Del He's gonna be really looking forward to this, Mike. Thanks for everything.

Del returns to Rodney and Boycie.

He makes up more rules than the common market that bloke! Be honest, he's ruining this pub ain't he?

Boycie I honestly wouldn't know, Del Boy, I'm very rarely in here these days. I spend most of my free time down at the lodge.

Rodney Oh of course, the lodge. What is it you've become, a Buffalo?

Boycie I am not a Buffalo! I am a pukka mason, secret handshakes, initiation ceremonies, the works!

Del What d' you wanna join that bunch of dipsticks for?

Boycie It is a great honour to be chosen! It is not something you turn down lightly, Derek. Oh no, it's changed my life. I'm involved in a lot of charity work. I'm helping the local needy and underprivileged. It's got its good side as well. Us masons vow to help each other in business whenever humanly possible.

Rodney It sounds like a load of old snobs trying to clone another load of old snobs.

Boycie We're not snobs! Anyone can join. We come from all walks of life, right across the social spectrum. We've got estate agents, a judge, a commissioner of police, the mayor. We've got all sorts!

Rodney Yeah, so's Bertie Bassett! That is not all walks of life, Boycie!

Boycie We got, a … er, we got … a … got a television director!

Rodney Yeah, what's he do? Film the secret handshakes in case you wallies forget?

Del is creased up with laughter.

Rodney Listen, I'm gonna have a chat with Mickey and Jevon.

Mickey and Jevon Rodney!

Del I'm popping down the betting shop. I'll pick you up later alright?

Rodney moves over to where Mickey Pearce and Jevon are standing.

Boycie What is the matter with that boy? He's all social conscience!

Del He's one of life's carers, ain't he? He reminds me a bit of my mum, don't he you?

Del exits.

Boycie Yeah. *(To himself)* Standing in the corner of a pub with two geezers!

EXT. DAY. ITALIAN RESTAURANT.

This could be the Nag's Head car park. Del exits from the pub and moves towards the van. He now does a double-take on something he has seen on the opposite side of the road.
From Del's point of view we see Trigger, still carrying the spray of flowers, and his date entering the Italian restaurant. His date is a woman in her mid-thirties. She is slim, smartly-dressed and attractive.

Del I don't believe it! That's a woman!

He watches as the waiter shows them to a window table. Trigger hands her the spray. She smiles and thanks him politely. Del turns and walks to the van, shaking his head in confusion.

INT. DAY. NAGS HEAD PUB.

We are in the bar.
Rodney is in the background still talking to Micky and the immaculate Jevon.
We see Nerys. She is an attractive and shapely nineteen-year-old. Although she speaks with a south London accent and her clothes are geared to accentuate her figure, she is not a tart. She is in fact a rather nervous and neurotic type although she hides this rather well.
Rodney moves up behind her.

Rodney Wotchyer, Nerys.

Nerys *(Jumps)* Oooh! You made me jump!

Rodney It's only me. Can I get you a drink?

Nerys I've got one.

Rodney Oh. Nerys, I was wondering, maybe if you'd quite like to go out somewhere during the week.

Nerys Where?

Rodney I don't know, anywhere.

Nerys Who with?

Rodney Well … me.

Nerys Yeah, alright then. But I work at night so have to be during the day.

Rodney Oh, I'll have to see if I can get a day off.

Nerys But you told me you run the business.

Rodney Well, yeah, yeah I do. I do run the business but y'know I don't like leaving Del in charge, he mucks me system up. I'll phone you on it.

Nerys Alright then. I'll see you in the week.

Rodney Right.

Now we see Mickey and Jevon whispering to each other. They are obviously plotting some wind-up.

Jevon *(Quietly to Mickey)* Go'n then, go'n!

Mickey You come with me!

The two approach Rodney.

Mickey Alright, Rodney? How did you get on with Nerys?

Rodney Okay.

Jevon I'll bet you didn't get a date with her!

Rodney Save your money, Jevon my man. I'm taking her out next week.

Jevon How did you manage that? I've been trying to date her for ages and bear in mind who's talking here. I've had to employ a secretary to handle all my dates!

Dates

Mickey Rodney has got something you haven't got, Jevon. It's a thing called Machismo! I've told you before, Nerys is turned on by macho-men! *(Rodney reacts curiously to this)* I have known Rodney a lot longer than you and he can be a right hard nut when he wants to be!

Rodney *(Shrugs modestly)* Well!

Mickey And that is what Nerys goes for. Muscle and sweat!

Jevon Yeah, but Rodney's no Master of the Universe.

Mickey But he has the aura of inner strength!

Rodney I'm wirey, see.

Mickey Nerys likes guys who live their lives a hundred miles an hour. And they reckon when she's hot she is hot! The only guy who could put her out is Red Adair and he's too expensive!

Jevon Yeah well I think you should treat a chick with consideration.

Mickey And that's why you'll never get a date with Nerys. She prefers a bunch of fives to a bunch of flowers. But if my main man here plays his cards right … See you big guy!

Rodney *(Mentally he is already king of the Bronx)* Hey.

Jevon Take care.

Rodney *(Slaps hands with Jevon)* Yo.

Jevon *(Another slap)* Bro.

Rodney & Jevon *(Another slap)* Woh!
The last slap hurts Rodney's palm.
Rodney walks towards the exit. It is more of a strut! A pimp roll. We cut back to Mickey and Jevon who are creased with laughter. One of the other young guys (Chris) enters and approaches them.

Chris What's happening?

Mickey Rodney Trotter's just got himself a date.

Jevon And we've convinced him she likes really tough, macho-men!

Chris Who's the bird then?

Jevon Nerys.

Chris What, Nervous Nerys?

Mickey and Jevon Yes!
The three of them are now laughing uproariously.

EXT. DAY. FILM. BUSY LONDON HIGH STREET.
We are in elevated position.
Opposite us we see the three-wheeled van at a parking bay with an out-of-order bag over the meter. The van is parked outside a shop which has been converted into an office and has frosted glass windows to give privacy to his clients.

Across the frosted glass is printed 'Technomatch Friendship and Matrimonial gency'.

INT. DAY. TECHNOMATCH AGENCY.
It is a light and pleasant modern office.
The agent is a smartly-dressed man in his mid-thirties. He has a computer and screen in front of him into which he prints information from Del's answers.

Agent So can you tell me, what kind of person are you looking for?

Del Well … a bird?

Agent Yes. But are there any particular requirements?

Del A local bird if possible, I don't want too much of that driving lark.

Agent So you're not looking for a special type of person?

Del Well, she's gotta be a bit of a sort!

Agent A bit of a sort?

Del Well, everything in the right place, you know. She must be a bit refined.

Agent Must she?

Del Oh yes. I don't want you lumbering me with some old bow-wow who don't know the difference between a Liebfraumilk and a can of Tizer!
The agent's expression tells us that he has never met anyone like Del before.

Agent Quite!

Del I'm a bit of a culture vulture meself you see.

Agent Ah, a man of the arts.

Del Oh yes, you can't whack it. And you can tell the lucky lady she is guaranteed a steak meal.

Agent *(Fazed)* A steak meal?

Del Guaranteed! Do you wanna put that on your floppy disc, or what?

Agent Yes, I'll make a note. A steak meal. Now please don't feel pressurised by this next question. We're not trying to force you into any decision or commitment. The question is simply asked to protect our clients.

Del Fire away. I've got nothing to hide.

Agent What exactly do you seek from this proposed introduction. Is it simply friendship?

Del Yeah, that'll do.

Agent What I'm getting at is: do you see this leading to a more permanent relationship or even marriage?

Del Slow down John. Blimey, you ain't even sorted me one out yet! Let's leave it at friendship for the time being eh?

Agent Yes, of course. Fine, well, let's see what surprises the computer has in store for you. I'll

61

just feed your information into our main computer.

We hear computer noises. Now data flashes upon the screen.

Ah, now there's a lady here who may suit. Obviously a refined lady, she's on the board of governors of an arts fund committee. Thirty-eight years old.

Del Knocking on a bit.

Agent She's widowed. *(Del is not that interested)* Her late husband was a stockbroker. *(Del is now interested)* No, I don't think you're right for each other.

Del Let's not jump the gun. I'll give it a bash if she will.

Agent I don't think so. She's a rather – em – sensitive person.

Del Well, that's right up my street, innit?

Agent Yes! But she's specified a non-smoker.

Del Well, win some lose some.

The agent presses a key and more data appears on screen.

Agent This looks more promising. A young lady, thirty years old, something of a career woman.

Del Go on.

Agent She's an actress.

Del Yeah? Is she famous?

Agent I wouldn't have thought so, would you?

Del No, I suppose not.

Agent It might be a nice introduction seeing as you share a common interest.

Del What's that?

Agent Why the arts.

Del Of course! Perfect. So where would we meet and how would we recognise each other – assuming of course she fancies the idea – what d'you say her name again was?

Agent Miss Turner. Raquel Turner.

Del D'you know that Raquel is my most favourite name?

Agent How fortunate. In the present social climate we recommend that the first meeting is during the day – a lunch appointment. After that it's entirely up to the two clients. A good meeting place is under the main clock at Waterloo station. It's rather traditional and in its way quite romantic. It evokes memories of Trevor Howard and Celia Johnson. We suggest that the gentleman carries a bunch of flowers as a point of recognition and as a gift for the lady.

Del Will do ... did they hit it off alright?

Agent Who?

Del Well, this Trevor and the Celia sort.

Agent Yes!

Del Cushty. Right, well you get on the blower and give Raquel the old SP. Oh and tell her to be on her toes, 'cos the last girl I met at Waterloo station got mugged on the escalator.

Agent Yes, I'll tell her. When, or indeed if, you and Miss Turner should meet, we do emphasise the importance of complete honesty. There is very little future in fabrication or deceit.

Del I agree. We've gotta be right up front with each other.

Agent Good. Now I'm afraid I'll have to trouble you for the twenty-five pounds membership fee.

Del peels some notes off a massive wad.

Agent I'm sorry I've forgotten, is there an E on the end of your name?

Del No, E. It's Duval. Derek Duval. It's from the French side of my family.

INT. DAY. TROTTERS' LOUNGE

This is a week later. Albert is seated watching television.

Del enters from bedroom area. He is wearing his very best suit and jewellery. He moves to mirror and checks his appearance (makes sure his fly is done up).

Albert You going out?

Del No, I'm gonna bleed the brakes on the van. Course I'm going out.

Albert What is it, a special occasion?

Del It might be Albert, you never can tell.

Albert Oh. I didn't know if it was one of your mates' birthdays or something?

Del No, no nothing like that. I'm taking a lady out to lunch.

Albert When I was a lad, I had some smashing birthday parties. But when you get to my age nobody bothers.

Del No, it's a bark innit, eh?

Albert *(Sadly)* Yeah. So who's the bird?

Del She's not a bird Unc, she's an actress.

Albert Yeah? Who?

Del Raquel Turner.

Albert Name don't ring a bell. What's she been in?

Del Oooh lots. I can't remember 'em all off the top of me head.

Albert What's she look like?

Del *(Hasn't got a clue)* Em, it's difficult to describe her.

Albert Well is she tall, short, fair, dark, fat, thin?

Del She's an actress, she changes her appearance.

Albert How you gonna recognise her then?

Del I'll recognise her! Don't keep going on about it.

Dates

Albert If you've got anything for the launderette go and get it now.

Del Why, it's not your washing day today is it?

Albert No, but Rodney's going out as well. I don't wanna sit in this flat on me own.

Exits to kitchen. Del now practises meeting Raquel.

Del Miss Turner, how lovely – no, no, *Muzz*! Muzz Turner, how lovely to meet you. I've admired your work for many years. May I call you Raquel? Do you know that Raquel is my most favourite name? *(Chuckles confidently to himself)* My old *joie de vivre* will knock her bandy. A little livener before we go.

Del moves to cocktail cabinet.

The door from bedroom area opens and a hesitant Rodney peers into room as if checking that the coast is clear. As Del is behind the door, or at least out of Rodney's eye-shot, he thinks he is alone in the room. He is wearing his macho gear. A pair of dirty jeans with a large silver buckled belt, a grubby armless T-shirt and a thick leather wrist band. He is unshaven and his hair is greased back. He strides confidently towards the mirror. He practises his meanest look in the mirror. Del coughs. Rodney spins round and tries to act as casual and normal as possible.

Rodney Oh, you're still here then?

Del Yeah, just about. I thought you were taking that Nerys bird out?

Rodney I am.

Del Well, you better get ready or you'll be late.

Rodney I am ready!

Del You're going out like that?

Rodney What's wrong with me?

Del Well, you look like an 'ooligan!

Rodney It is the fashion. Haven't you read about it? It's called the James Dean look.

Del Yes, but when they say the James Dean look, they mean *before* the crash. I can't see you getting very far with young Nerys dressed like that, Rodney.

Rodney *(Tapping his nose)* Will you just keep it out? Let me lead my own life!

Del I won't say another word. Maybe she goes for blokes who look like Barney Rubble.

Albert enters from kitchen with a washing bag.

Albert I thought you were going out?

Rodney I am going out.

Albert Well, hurry up and change, I'll take those clothes down the laundrette for you.

Rodney I am wearing these clothes!!

Albert Yeah? Where you taking her then, scrumping? *(Laughs)* Del Boy's going out to lunch with a world famous actress!

Rodney *(Totally unmoved)* Yeah? You got my socks and pants in there?

Albert Yeah, I've got 'em, boy. I'll see you later.

Rodney So who is it then, Meryl Streep?

Del No. Raquel Turner.

Rodney Are you kidding me?

Del No, straight up.

Rodney What, *the* Raquel Turner?

Del Well yeah, have you heard of her?

Rodney No. *(Laughs)* She been in anything?

Del Yes, loads of things but nothing that you would have seen her in, Rodney.

Rodney What's that mean?

Del It means she has not been on *Top of the Pops* or repeats of *Batman*.

Rodney So where you taking her?

Del I am meeting her at Waterloo station and I have booked a table for lunch at the Hilton in Park Lane.

Rodney You taking the van?

Del No, I am not taking the van!

Rodney Where would *you* meet an actress?

Del Em, a friend of mine in show business introduced us.

Rodney *(As if he's catching on to the truth)* Wait a minute. The other day Albert took a call for you. It was some agency.

Del *(Closes his eyes as the embarrassing truth is about to be revealed)* Oh yeah, was it?

Rodney *(Now his lovely innocence)* Is your mate an agent?

Del *(Can't believe his luck)* Eh? Yeah, he's a show business agent. Yeah, that's it.

Rodney Bloody 'ell, Del. You wait till I tell the others! Hey, any chance of an autograph?

Del Yeah, no problem. I'll get you hers as well.

Del walks to the mirror and smothers himself in after-shave from a nearby bottle of Brut.

Rodney *(Worrying)* Del, you don't think you are being a bit ostentatious?

Del *(Studying his mirrored image)* Well maybe, but I can afford it.

Rodney No, what I meant was *(Gesturing at clothes, but too frightened to say)* – well you know the Hilton and all that; Don't you think you're being a teensy-weensy bit over the top? After all she's an actress and she's bound to be very cool and laid back.

Del Rodney, give me credit for having some savvy. I do know that a woman like Raquel appreciates the *subtle* approach. I have played the game before. I know what I'm doing.

Rodney Yeah of course you do! Well best of luck.

Del Cheers bruv.
From kitchen, Del produces a gigantic bouquet of flowers, complete with a large, pink satin bow. Open the door for us, Rodders.

Del, and the bouquet, exit.

EXT. DAY. WATERLOO STATION.
We see Del (in his camel hair coat) and the bouquet waiting beneath the clock in the main concourse of the station. He paces a small area nervously.
He checks the clock which stands at 12.30. He checks this against his watch. Now rechecks his watch and taps it a few times as if it has gone wrong. We see a policeman patrolling the station. He observes Del (not suspiciously at this point) more out of interest, he's never seen such a large bouquet. Del smiles nervously to the policeman.

EXT. DAY. CORNER OF URBAN ROAD.
Nerys is standing on corner waiting for Rodney. We see the van pulling up behind her with Rodney, in his James Dean look, driving. Rodney bips the hooter. This makes the nervous Nerys jump. Rodney opens the passenger door from the inside and then lounges back in the driver's seat, all muscle and machismo. He has a newly-lit roll-up between his lips (maybe a pair of shades). Nerys studies the van critically.
Rodney Hi.
He pats the passenger seat. Nerys climbs in.
Nerys Is this a three-wheeled van?
Rodney Well it was the last time I counted!
Nerys I've never been in a three-wheeled van before.
Rodney Well then you have never really lived!
Nerys It's sort of – oh what's the word? Smelly.
Rodney That is the odour of honest toil and

Dates

sweat, Nerys. So, where'd you fancy going?

Nerys I don't mind.

Rodney Just name your destination.

Nerys I don't care.

Rodney So there's nowhere special?

Nerys No, anywhere.

Rodney Shall we take in a movie?

Nerys I don't fancy the pictures.

Rodney Well, how about a drink?

Nerys Na. The pubs round here are 'orrible.

Rodney D'you fancy a hamburger?

Nerys No, I've just had me dinner.

Rodney Where'd you wanna go then?

Nerys I don't mind, anywhere.

Rodney Well, that's cool, Nerys. We'll just cruise.

Nerys What, in a three-wheeled van?

Rodney Yes! This will be an experience you will never forget, Nerys.

Rodney very coolly takes the cigarette from his lips and flicks it out of the window. The cigarette hits the glass of the window which Rodney had forgotten to wind down.

Oh shit!

Nerys You didn't wind your window down!

Rodney I know I didn't! Get out quick before it catches fire!

Nerys alights from van. Rodney alights from van. We leave them with Nerys standing on the pavement and Rodney down on his hands and knees at the open driver's door, searching for the dog end.

EXT. DAY. WATERLOO STATION.

Del is waiting anxiously. He looks up at the clock which now stands at 12.35. Del reacts as he sees there is a woman standing beneath the clock just a few yards from him. She has her back to Del. From the back she appears to be a slender and sophisticatedly dressed woman. Del takes a deep breath and approaches.

Del (*Nervously*) Hello.

Sonia Hello, love.

Del Blimey! You're not Raquel, are you?

Sonia I can be anyone you want, darling.

Del No, no, I mean you're not an actress, are you?

Sonia Well, I've played a few demanding roles in me time. There's a very nice little hotel round the corner, why don't we go and discuss it there?

Del No, that's alright, there's been a bit of a mistake. My fault entirely.

Sonia (*Becoming annoyed with him*) Oh you're

one of those who just likes to 'talk' aren't you?

Del No, really. It was a genuine mistake. I'm waiting for someone and I thought you … Look, I'm starting to lose my rag, sweetheart. I'll count to ten then I'll shove these flowers …

We don't hear Del's next words as they are drowned by the sound of a train's klaxon. We don't even see Del say the words as we cut to the policeman who is watching the argument with growing suspicion. We cut back to Sonia who appears surprised at what Del has just said.

Sonia You realise that will be extra.

Del Oh God.

Sonia (*Spots the policeman*) Oh hell – the filth! See you darling.

She exits.

Del gives the policeman an embarrassed smile.

EXT. DAY. DOWNTOWN STREETS.

We see the three-wheeled van approaching with Rambo Rodney at the wheel.

Now we see a beat-up Cortina waiting to turn out of a side road. There are five really tough-looking yobs inside the car (usual thing, radios blaring, lots of verbal).

The Cortina now screeches out of the side turning and cuts right across the path of the oncoming van (in other words it is now going in opposite direction to van).

Rodney screeches to a halt. Nerys lets out a nervous yelp of fear. The yobs (without stopping) scream a load of abuse at Rodney ('Out of the way, pus-head' 'Get that heap of shit off the road') As the Cortina roars away, Rodney sticks his finger in the air and calls after them.

Rodney Swivel on that, camel-breath!

(*Rodney smiles confidently to the nervous-looking Nerys*)

Cut to interior of van

Nerys Weren't you frightened?

Rodney What, of them punks? Nooo way!

EXT. DAY. WATERLOO STATION.

The clock stands at 12.45. Del has got fed up carrying the bouquet and now reacts and puts flowers on the floor.

Del checks his watch and then the station clock.

Now let us see Raquel approaching the clock. We should know it's her by her nervous hurry. Raquel is in her early thirties. She is attractive, has a good figure and studies her

65

appearance. Her clothes are smart but not designer stuff. She is a working class girl (from any part of the country) and has to watch the pennies.

We shall discover that she has been hurt in her life, and when this happens people react in one of two ways. They either become hard and distance themselves from any possible further harm, or they try even harder to please others in the hope that someone will like them. Raquel is of the latter persuasion. She is a very nice, warm and friendly lady.

At this point, like Del, she is nervous. She looks at the clock and reacts to being so late. She now sees Del who has his back to her.

Raquel *(Tentatively)* Hello.

Del turns and looks her up and down quickly. He doesn't realise at first that it is Raquel. To Del actresses are either the war-paint and cleavage brigade or the trendy bohemian type. Raquel doesn't fit his picture.

Del Just now he nearly nicked one of your mates, so I'd have it away on your toes if I was you.

Raquel *(Bewildered)* Is it Derek?

Del Raquel?

Raquel Yes. Hi.

Del Hello. I'm sorry about that.

Raquel No, I should apologise for being so late. You know what these trains are like. Have you been waiting long?

Del Well, since about ten o'clock this morning, y'know. No, not really, just joking. *(Picks up bouquet)* This is for you.

Raquel Is it? You shouldn't have gone to all this expense.

Del Mais oui, mais oui. Well, I've booked a table at my favourite restaurant – if that is alright with you?

Raquel Oh yes, sounds lovely.

Del *(Gesturing towards cab rank)* Your carriage awaits.

Raquel Thank you. *(They walk away from camera)* This is a bit like *Brief Encounter*, isn't it?

Del You reckon?

Raquel That's my favourite film.

Del Mine as well.

Raquel Really?

Del Yes. I loved the bit at the end when the big space ship comes down and all the little Martians come out. *(Thinks about it)*

Raquel That's *Close Encounters*.

Del Yeah. Loved it.

EXT. DAY. DOWNTOWN STREETS.

The three-wheeled van passes us.
Cut to interior of van.
Rambo Rodney has his window open and is gorilla-gripping the roof with his right hand and steering with the left.

Nerys I always thought you were such a quiet person.

Rodney They're the ones you've gotta watch, Nerys.

Nerys But just now you were so ... well, tough.
This is a complaint from Nerys, but Rodney doesn't understand.

Rodney Huh – I get by. I've lived in these streets too long to be frightened.
Gesturing back to the incident with the yobs. Those punks back there, they're used to people running scared from 'em. They don't scare me Nerys. This is my jungle and I'm at the top of the tree.
Rodney has a confident, unflinching smile as he casually checks the mirror. He does a horrified double-take. We see in the wing mirror that the yobs in the Cortina have turned round and are now right behind the van. They are hanging from the windows, brandishing weapons and screaming death-threats and other abuse.

Rodney *(He has never been so terrified)* Oh my ... !

Nerys *(Slightly alarmed by Rodney)* What's wrong, Rodney?

Rodney Nothing!
With a great crunch of cogs, Rodney hurls the van into third gear. The van roars past with the Cortina in hot pursuit.

Nerys Why are we going so fast?

Rodney I love speed!

Nerys You said we were gonna cruise!

Rodney Yeah, but I like to cruise quickly.

INT. DAY. HILTON RESTAURANT.

The bouquet is in evidence. We see Raquel seated alone at a table with her untouched starter. She sips her white wine nervously and obviously is feeling slightly out of her depth. We see Del standing just outside entrance to restaurant area. He is talking quietly to the head waiter (Charles). Charles seems rather concerned at Del's request, but his attitude alters as Del slips a twenty-pound note into his palm. Charles smiles and nods in a 'a pleasure, sir' manner. Del now walks to the table.

Del Sorry about that. I had to get a message to

Dates

an old friend.

Raquel Oh that's okay.

Del *(Referring to the starter)* Well go on get stuck in, don't wait for me.

(They both eat)

Raquel This is wonderful.

Del Well, you can't go wrong here. I hope you don't mind me saying this, Raquel, but well I'm very surprised to find that someone like you – attractive and talented – at a computer dating agency.

Raquel Well, I might say the same about you. A successful person – managing director of his own import–export business. Why did you go to them?

Del Dunno really.

Raquel I suppose I was grabbing at straws really. I've been married before and that was a disaster, and I've had – you know – relationships with men which have always ended unhappily. Maybe it's been the same for you?

Del No, blokes don't do a lot for me.

Raquel You know what I mean! I found I used to take my relationships seriously – used to plan and stupid things like that. But they were just playing a game. Anyway, when I saw the agency's advertisement I thought; why not? At least I knew I'd be meeting someone who wanted me to be there. Was it the same for you?

Del Yeah, exactly. I just thought y'know that you being an actress you'd meet lots of people – on the film sets and that sort of thing.

Raquel *(Embarrassed)* Look, I've got to be honest with you. The agency asked me what I did for a living, so I said I was an actress. Well I suppose that's what I am. I'm a member of the union, at least. I had one line in a *Doctor Who* about ten years ago. I was a lizard person. I've done fringe theatre and that sort of thing, but I never got the chance to – 'make it'. I gave it all up for nine years while I was married. My husband was one of those old-fashioned types who thought there should be only one bread winner.

Del Yeah, my Dad was like that. He used to get up at six every morning to make sure my Mum got to work.

(A disbelieving look from Raquel)

No, straight up.

Raquel Anyway, recently I've tried to pick up my career – for what it was. But I can't see me ever doing anything.

Del Au contraire Raquel. This time next year you'll be a star!

Raquel Oh come on.

Del She who dares wins. That is my motto. No matter what has happened in our lives I've always said that to my kid brother, 'Rodney, this time next year we'll be millionaires!'

Raquel And look at you now.

Del Yeah! Look at me now. The secret is never giving in, if you want something bad enough, you'll get it, as long as you don't stop believing!

Raquel *(Smiles at him)* This is nice ... There's a lovely feeling of ... I don't know – honesty.

Del Yeah ... well ... that's what it's all about, innit?

She nods in agreement.

The head waiter approaches

Charles Mr Duval.

Del Yes.

Charles I'm terribly sorry to bother you, sir there's an important call from your New York office.

Del Oh thank you very much, Charles. *(To Raquel)* I'm sorry about this.

Raquel Please, it's no problem.

(Del stands and takes a step forward. Now a change of mind.)

Del Charles. You tell them I'm busy.

Charles Of course, sir.

Raquel Please, don't do this for me.

Del No, no. I'm enjoying the company and I'm not gonna have it spoilt by some soppy problem in New York. These yanks have gotta learn to make decisions for themselves. *(Raises his glass)* To success.

EXT. DAY. DOWNTOWN STREETS.

We see Trigger in his roadsweeper's donkey jacket sweeping a gutter. He reacts as he hears the sound of racing engines. The three-wheeled van now roars past him in a cloud of exhaust fumes.

Trigger Wotchya, Dave.

Now the Cortina roars past him.

Trigger smiles to himself. He thinks it's the lads out having a laugh.

INT. DAY. THE HILTON RESTAURANT.

Del and Raquel are now on their coffees. Del lights a cigar.

Raquel When the agency phoned and mentioned you I was really excited. They said you were a man of the arts, and it's not that often that you meet a man who's interested in the theatre.

Del Oh yeah, I love it.

Raquel Going into a theatre is so exhilarating. Just the 'feel' of the place.

Del Yeah, gets me going as well. You can't whack a good play, can you?

Raquel Did you see the RSC's production of Moliere's *Le Misanthrope*?

Del E ... m ... No, I was out.

Raquel *(Puzzled at first)* Oh, you mean out of the country.

Del Yes. Away on business.

Raquel Oh you missed something wonderful!

Del Yeah, I was gutted. That's the sort of thing you like, is it?

Raquel Not really. I like *anything* to do with entertainment. When I was a kid my Mum used to send me to tap-dancing lessons. I loved it. And when I was about seventeen another girl and me formed a pop-duo. 'Double Cream' we called ourselves – we were rotten! But, that's what I mean, I like anything – pop music to heavy drama. I don't know about you, but I just love the works of Shaw.

Del Oh yeah! *(Sings)* 'Like a puppet on a string ...'

Raquel You! You're just putting me on!

Del *(Doesn't understand, but laughs)* No, no I really do like it! *(Waiter arrives with the bill)* Oh thank you, Charles.

He reads the bill and is horrified, but cannot show it. He turns to one side and coughs gently. He now takes a great wad of notes from his pocket and peels a few off.

Raquel Thank you. I've really enjoyed this afternoon.

Del Ah so have I. Em ... d'you fancy going out Saturday night?

Raquel Saturday? No I can't make Saturday.

Del *(Thinking he's getting the brush-off)* Oh that's alright. ?No y'know just thought I'd ask.

Raquel Let me explain. I'm always busy on Friday and Saturday nights at drama class.

Del Oh, drama class?

Raquel I teach.

Del Oh I see. Well how about Monday night?

Raquel I'd love to.

Del Great. Where shall I meet you?

Raquel Why don't you come round the flat?

Del Okay then. And you've got no worries about letting me into your flat, I'm not a pervo or nothing.

Raquel I figured that one out! I feel terrible, I've kept you away from your business.

Del That's alright. My brother handles things when I'm not there.

Cut to Rodney still being pursued by the Cortina.

Rodney Oh no! Aaaaaaagggggghhhhh! Aaaaagggggghhhhhh!

EXT. DAY. DOWNTOWN STREETS.

We are looking at the brow of a hill.

The van now races over the top of the hill. There is smoke belching from its exhaust. The Cortina comes over the brow of the hill a few seconds later.

The two vehicles should appear to be doing 70mph.

Cut to interior of van.

Rodney, eyes wide with fear and not blinking, is holding the steering wheel in a white-knuckled death-grip. There is a small cloud of fumes wafting around inside the van. We do not see Nerys.

From Rodney's point of view we see that at the bottom of the hill there is a set of traffic lights at a crossroads. Let us see the lights facing Rodney turn to amber. He puts his foot on the gas in an attempt to beat the lights. The lights turn red.

Realising that even if he had wanted to stop he wouldn't be able to, Rodney puts his life in the hands of the gods.

In anticipation of the imminent holocaust Rodney lets out a long cry of alarm.

Rodney Aaaaaaagggggggghhhhhhh!

We see the lights for the waiting traffic turn green. The traffic begins to move forward. Now, to a symphony of screaming tyres, blaring horns and breaking glass, the van roars through the small gap in the traffic. (Lots of exhaust smoke and Rodney's continuing scream.)

Rodney *(OOV)* Aaaaagggggghhhhhhhh.

The van disappears into the distance. We see that a Metro police car has crashed into the back of another car. We see the occupants – a young, rather flash and aggressive PC and an attractive and quite shapely WPC alight from the metro, angrily.

PC Well get his number! I don't believe it! *(Referring to his car)* They only gave me this yesterday! *(To the returning WPC)* Did you get it?

WPC No, he was going too fast. But there can't be too many yellow three-wheeled vans round here.

PC That's right! I'll get him! You see if I don't!

The PC now zeros in on the yobs in the American car which is parked at the lights. The yobs smile and wave at him.

The PC is desperate for revenge. He turns to the other driver. He wants to nick him but he can't.

You ... I ... I ... Don't ever do that again!

Dates

EXT. DAY. QUIETER SUBURBAN ROAD.

The three-wheeled van screeches round corner and pulls to a halt in a cloud of smoke (we still don't see Nerys).

Cut to interior of van.

Rodney collapses across the wheel, sucking in air in the kind of heart-pounding exhaustion that abject fear brings. He opens the window and checks that he is safe. He slumps back in seat with relief.

Now from the passenger seat we hear the sound of whimpering. We see Nerys sobbing uncontrollably. Tears are running down her face and she takes great gulps of air between each sob.

Rodney *(Concerned)* What's wrong, Nerys? Nerys?

INT. NIGHT. RAQUEL'S FLAT.

It's a clean and pleasant lounge. The furnishings are early B&Q. Two doors lead off: one to hallway, bathroom and bedroom, etc (we never see this), the second door leads to kitchen. As we come on scene, the kitchen door is open. On the dining table we have a few plates, cups, etc. from a recently finished meal.

Del is at the table alone. His jacket has been removed and his tie loosened. He puffs his cigar and sips brandy. He now stands and moves to settee.

Raquel enters from kitchen and collects the plates, etc. from table.

Raquel D'you want another brandy?

Del No, I'm fine, thank you.

Raquel Sit down.

Del Oh right, 'ere listen … You didn't have to go to all this trouble – cooking a meal and what'avyer. I told you I was gonna take you out.

Raquel And I told you, it's my way of saying thank you for the other lunchtime.

Del Well, it was really lovely, thank you.

Raquel D'you think your car'll be alright out there? We get a lot of vandalism round here.

Del That's why I didn't bring the car. I mean you leave a Ferrari out there and see what you come back to.

Raquel Oh good.

Exits to kitchen.

In a vase on a table there are the flowers that Del had given Raquel at their lunch date. They are now dead and drooping all over the place.

Del I say, these flowers are lasting well, ain't they?

Raquel I'm not throwing them away. They're

my memories of a lovely day.

Del is chuffed and moved by this silly gesture on her part.

INT. NIGHT. RAQUEL'S KITCHEN.

It's a small but clean kitchen. On one wall there is a damp patch of crumbling, rotten plaster. Raquel is putting the crockery in the sink.

Del enters.

Raquel D'you want a coffee?

Del Yes please.

Del is trying to say something important but is struggling to find a way.

Raquel.

Raquel Mmmnnn?

Del I like you.

Raquel I like you.

Del Oh Good … Erm.

Raquel *(Frightened by what he might ask)* Look at the state of this wall!

Del Yeah, it's 'orrible innit? Yeah, listen I wanted to ask you something.

Raquel Del. Wait a while, eh? See how we feel in …

Del *(Cuts in)* No, it's not that! Cor blimey! No, no it's just that I had this idea that might help you. I thought I'd better talk to you about it. You see, a friend of mine is a mason.

Raquel *(Referring to wall)* Oh I don't need a mason, a plasterer can do that.

Del No, not a stone-mason, I mean a masonic mason. Look, come and sit down.

INT. NIGHT. RAQUEL'S LOUNGE.

Del leads Raquel in by the hand and sits her on the settee.

Del The way I see it is this – you're a talented actress.

Raquel Says who?

Del Says me. I can tell these things. But life has never given you a decent break, and it doesn't matter how clever you are, you can never prove yourself until someone gives you that break. Right?

Raquel Yeah.

Del Right, well. One of my friend's fellow masons is a television director, right? So if I become a mason I can get him to give you that break. Put you in a show.

Raquel But why would he do that? He doesn't even know me.

Del He doesn't have to. You see masons *have* to do each other favours. He couldn't refuse to help me.

Raquel But what favour would you do him?

Del Well I don't know. I'll drop him a monkey or something, look don't worry, he'll be sweet as a nut.

Raquel You'd actually join the masons just to help me?

Del Yeah. *(Raquel kisses him)* Well, I mean it's no hardship is it? It's the masons not like the moonies. They chuck a lovely dinner 'n' dance an' all you know.

Raquel But I'd be cheating, wouldn't I?

Del No, of course you wouldn't be cheating! I'll do all that for you.

Raquel No, I mean I'd be using inside influence to further my career.

Del Well, it's the name of the game, innit? It's who you know. You can't hang about for another three years waiting to be discovered! You've gotta get in now before you're past your sell-by date.

Raquel Oh thanks!

Del You know what I mean. This is your first opportunity – it could be your last. You're gotta now get in while the going's good. She Who Dares Wins!

Raquel Well I ... I'll leave it up to you, Del. Whatever you think is best.

Del Alright. You do the coffee and I'll do the bizzo.

Del picks up the telephone receiver and begins pushing the buttons.

Raquel D'you think it'll work?

Del Yeah, course it will. It'll be a piece of cake. They've been begging me to join their lodge for ages, but I always give 'em a blank.

Raquel exits to the kitchen.

NIGHT. INTERCUT BETWEEN HALL OF BOYCIE'S HOUSE/RAQUEL'S LOUNGE.

Boycie's hall is very grand and ornate and totally over the top. The phone begins ringing on the telephone table. We hear the deep, dark brown barking of Duke.
We hear Marlene's voice.

Marlene Get out of there, Duke. Get out! Daddy will be cross!

Marlene enters hall, checks her appearance in the mirror before answering the phone.

Boycie *(Screams)* Marlene! That dog is in my aquarium again!

Marlene *(Screams back)* I've told him to get out but he don't take any notice!

Boycie He'll take some bloody notice when I put piranha in there!

Marlene *(Screams)* You're the master of the

house, you get him out! *(Picks up receiver, now quiet, sweet and posh)* Hello, this is Boyce House.

Del Hello, Marlene? It's Del Boy, how are you sweetheart?

Marlene Oh hello, Del. How's tricks?

Del Never been better. Is the old man about?

Marlene Yeah, unfortunately. I'll get him for you. Oh Del, when you've finished don't put the receiver down, I want to have a word with you about a birthday present for Albert. Hang on.

Del Oh Gawd, I forgot all about that. It's this Friday, innit? Raquel, we're going out for a celebration Friday night, d'you fancy it?

Raquel Not Friday. I'm at drama class.

Del Oh yeah. Couldn't you knock it on the head, for this week?.I wanted you to meet the family.

Raquel Honest I can't, we're in the final rehearsal. Anyway, I'm no good at meeting families, I always say something stupid.

Exits to kitchen.

Del *(To himself)* You don't know my family.

Boycie Hello.

Del Hello Boycie – Del Boy. Yeah listen, I want you to do me a very big favour. I want you to recommend me for membership to your masonic lodge.

Boycie *(Roars with laughter)* What's the matter Del, has someone slipped some angel dust in your piña colada? Only the most respected members of our society can join my lodge.

Del You said they take anyone!

Boycie Yes, well, it wouldn't stretch to you. You'd be black-balled at the first go.

Del No, it'll be a doddle. My best friend's a member.

Boycie Who?

Del You!

Boycie Oh no! No Del! I couldn't even consider proposing someone like you.

Del I could be a very good mason. In fact I'll prove it to you. Masons are supposed to do each other favours, right? Well you do me the favour of proposing me and I'll do one for you.

Boycie And what might that be?

Del I won't tell Marlene about that little bird in Sheffield.

Boycie *(Surveys the hall as if Marlene might have heard)* You wouldn't

Del Try me!

Boycie No, you may be many things Del, no but you're not a grass. I don't think we have anything else to say to each other. Bye for now.

Marlene enters hall.

Dates

Marlene Don't put that phone down, I wanna talk to him about Albert's birthday. *(Takes receiver)* Del, What d' you think he'd like for a present?

Del *(Rejected)* I don't know darling, honest I don't. *(Now has bright idea)* Oh there is one thing. He loves a bit of fishing and he was talking about getting himself a proper angler's knife. But it must be made of Sheffield steel.

Marlene Sheffield?

Boycie Giss that phone!

Del *(From Del's reaction we get the impression that Boycie is giving him a real roasting)* Yes! Yeah alright, Boycie! I know, I know ... Yeah right!

> *Del replaces the receiver. Raquel enters from kitchen.*

INT. NIGHT. NAG'S HEAD PUB.

> *This is Albert's birthday party.*
> *There are happy birthday signs and balloons on the walls.*
> *Albert is on stage playing the piano and signing a song to the tune of 'Lilly Marlene'.*

Albert *(Singing)* 'Driving across the desert, sixty miles an hour. We are the eighth battalion and what a bloody shower. We can't speed up, we can't slow down, the gear-box is in upside-down. We are the eighth battalion. Royal Engineers.'

Del Look at that daft old twonk!

Rodney Be thankful for small mercies. The Queen has *two* birthdays a year!

Del That's true!

> *(Mike approaches)*

Mike 'Ere Del you promised me!

Del What can I do Michael, you've given him too much to drink, haven't you?

Mike He's started to slur his words. He's almost offended some of the ladies.

Rodney How d'you mean?

Mike Well, he wanted a rum and black, he ordered a bum and rack!

Del Yeah, well cross your fingers he don't fancy a Bucks Fizz, Michael!

Rodney So come on tell us, what happened down at Boycie's masonic lodge last night?

Del Oh yeah, I had to meet a few of the committee members – try and make an impression, you know.

Rodney Yeah, so are you a mason now?

Del No, the committee are discussing me this evening. But as Boycie said, there's always the chance that I could be black-balled.

Rodney What's that, part of the initiation ceremony?

Del No, no. You see, each committee member has one white ball and one black ball. And to vote they have to put one of the balls in a bag.

Rodney *(Still puzzled. Then realises)* You mean snooker balls?

Del Yeah.

Rodney Gotchyer.

Del And if, when they empty the bag, all the balls are white – you're in. But if there is one black ball – just one – you're out.

Rodney And you're doing all of this for Raquel?

Del Yep. Yeah she's worth it.

Rodney I can't wait to meet her. Is she coming tonight?

Del No, she's rehearsing.

Rodney Yeah, what in?

Del A rehearsal room I suppose.

Rodney No, I mean what play is she doing?

Del I don't know but it's bound to be deep and meaningful. One of them Russian jobs most probably.

Rodney What, the ones we don't watch on BBC2? Chekhov, that sorta thing?

Del No, no those are the ones I never used to watch. That was because in them days I wasn't esoteric.

Rodney No?

Del No. But Raquel has taught me what's what. I mean these days, you stick me in front of a telly with a singapore sling, an 'am sandwich and a bit of Chekhov and I'm as happy as a sand-boy! She's good news, Rodney. She's so lovely! She's caring and beautiful and talented. Got a good pair of lungs on her as well.

Rodney *(A filthy grin)* Yeah?

Del *(Offended)* I mean she's got a good singing voice! She sounds like Kiri Tikwinana with a little touch of Whitney Houston.

Rodney Lovely, just what the doctor ordered!

> *Boycie enters.*

Del Oi, Boycie. Boycie over here, over here. Sit yourself down Boycie. Have the committee come to a decision yet?

Boycie Yes, it's Derek, and it is bad news, well bad news for you at least. You were black-balled.

Del Oh no someone put a black ball in the bag? Who?

Boycie When they emptied the bag there was more than one black ball.

Del How many?

Boycie Well, let's put it like this. Have you ever seen the bottom of a rabbit's hutch? Sorry, Derek, I did me best.

71

Boycie moves to the bar.

Del What am I gonna tell Raquel now?

Rodney Oh look, if she's as talented as you say she is, she don't need you bribing some television director. Her talent will win through.

Del You're right, Rodney. She's gonna be a star one day 'cos she's got talent.

Albert is up on stage again.

Albert All together now!

Del Which is more than you can say for that soppy old git!

Albert Altogether now, 'Ooooooooooh. I put me finger in the woodpecker's hole and the woodpecker said "God bless my soul, take it out, take it out, wiggle it about remove it"'.

Mike Albert! That is enough! Del, can't you chuck him in the back of the van and drive him home?

Del What, with that engine, you must be joking. It needed a walking frame to get down here tonight.

Rodney, remembering his 'Bullit' style chase turns away.

Trigger Well, it was going alright the other day.

Del Oh yeah, when was that?

Trigger I saw Dave driving it. Some of his mates were following him.

Del Oh yeah?

Rodney Well, yes, and the engine was well lumpy then, Del.

Trigger Yeah, but it was going a fair old lick though, weren't it?

Rodney Yes, well yes, but it was making a terrible racket.

Trigger *(Gesturing towards door)* 'Ere, hang on what's all this about?

A tall naval officer aged about 40 and carrying a naval officer's topcoat, and a wren have entered. The two naval officers talk to one of the regulars who points in Albert's direction.

The two begin to make their way through the crowd. They are stern and officious.

Albert hasn't noticed the naval officers.

Albert All together now, Oohhh!

Naval Officer *(Posh voice)* Albert Trotter?

Albert Aye, sir, ma'am.

Naval Officer Able Seaman Albert Trotter, late of Her Majesty's ship *Peerless*?

Albert Aye, sir

Naval Officer I'm placing you under arrest.

There is a shocked murmur from the crowd.

Del They're only nicking him, look!

Rodney What's goin' on?

Naval Officer You will be taken to the naval stockade, Portsmouth, where you will await court martial.

Naval Officer Dereliction of duty. November 19th 1941. While serving the Royal Pacific fleet. You did wantonly abandon your watch duties. Thus causing the sinking of HMS *Peerless* and causing considerable damage to the American vessel USS *Pittsburgh*.

Albert But ... but ... that was nearly 50 years ago!

Naval Officer The original papers have only just been discovered in the vaults of Admiralty Headquarters, Singapore.

Albert I couldn't understand the radar, it's was all blibs and blobs.

Naval Officer Read the charges, petty officer.

Wren Aye, aye, sir. *(Produces some official looking paperwork)* Able Seaman Albert Trotter. You are hereby ordered by her Majesty the Queen, by the high Lords of the Admiralty and by all your friends and relatives to have a very happy birthday.

Albert reacts. The shirt and tie that the wren is wearing are false and only cover the visible area. She now tears it off and unbuttons her tunic to reveal a skimpy black bra. At the same time she begins singing.

(Sings) I'd like to get you on a slow boat to China, all to myself alone.

Obviously by now everyone knows it's a set-up and are laughing and winding Albert up. We cut away to Del and Rodney who are on the periphery of the crowd and so haven't seen everything clearly.

Rodney Is this your birthday surprise?

Del *(Can hardly talk with laughter)* Yeah. I saw the strippergram in the local paper. I've done him up like a kipper. Look at the old sod's face.

Wren *(Removing skirt to reveal stockings and suspenders)* Leave all your worries on a far away shore.

Albert You wait! I'll get you back for this, you toerag!

As the crowd part slightly, Del is still roaring with laughter. His laughter begins to die as, for the first time, he sees the wren clearly. As she turns towards camera we see that, despite the wig, it is indeed Raquel.

Wren All to myself alone. Yes I'd like to get you ...

Del Raquel?

Raquel just shakes her head. The crowd are murmuring

Boycie Raquel! Is this the 'actress' you've been telling us about Del?

Dates

Roars with laughter. Other people are now laughing as well.

Rodney *(To Del)* That's your Raquel?

Rodney also starts to laugh.

Del cannot answer. He is hurt, deeply hurt. He is filled with rage and embarrassment but above all disappointment. He stares at her. He'd like to cry, he'd like to die. He turns and exits to a backcloth of laughter and derision. Rodney's laughter dies instantly as he realises the seriousness of the situation.

EXT. NIGHT. NAG'S HEAD CAR PARK.

This is at the rear of the pub. Del storms out of the rear doors and towards the van. He pauses and looks up to the heavens. He wants to punch, he wants to kill, he wants to burst into tears and melt into the tarmac. He moves to the van. He punches the van and kicks the tyre. He now falls against the van (facing it), exhausted with anger and frustration.

We now see that Rodney has followed him out and is standing a few yards behind. Rodney doesn't know how to handle the situation or what to say, but his loyalty makes him stay.

Del becomes aware of someone's presence. He turns with killer eyes towards Rodney.

Rodney *(His nervousness makes his greeting over-cheerful)* Alright?

Del *(Shakes his head)* Oddly enough, I am not alright.

Rodney Look, Del. Don't get out your pram over it.

Del Don't get out my pram? Don't get out of my pram! She just humiliated me in front of my friends!

Rodney But you booked her.

Del No, Rodney. I booked a strippergram. I did not know it was her because I did not know she did that for a living! I thought she was an actress. That is what she said she was. Instead, she goes round pubs dressed in stockings and suspender belts flashing her thru'penny bits at blokes!

Rodney I shouldn't worry about it, Del. I don't think many of 'em were taking much notice. *(Del's glare kills that theory)* Anyway, what about a few years ago, when you used to go out with that bird Monique. Now she used to go around in public wearing next to nothing on.

Del She was a lifeguard!

Rodney Yeah, alright.

Del climbs into the van. We now see Raquel

rush from the pub and into the car park. She is wearing the naval officer's topcoat. She is crying and the coat, being miles too big for her, makes her look all the more pathetic.

Raquel Del! Wait a minute.

Rodney *(Rodney stops her)* I wouldn't talk to him yet, love. Just leave him, he'll calm down in a … year or so.

Del *(Screams from van window)* You lied to me!

Raquel No I didn't! I never told you I wasn't a stripper! And anyway, that's the pot calling the kettle black. I've just found out your name is Trotter. You told me you were called Derek Duval!

Rodney Derek Duval!

Del That was just a slip of the tongue!

Raquel And you didn't tell me you were a market trader! *(Referring to van)* And I suppose this is the Ferrari?

Del Alright, so I might occasionally tell the odd porkie or two, but I tell you something I don't do. I, I don't go round pubs dressed in stocking and suspenders flashing me boobs at geezers! Do I, Rodney?

Rodney No, he's never done anything like that.

Del Thank you.

Raquel Oh Del, please listen to me. I just do this a couple of evenings a week to pay for my drama lessons! I mean, where did you think I found the money to live on?

Del I don't know … I thought you were on the old rock'n'roll, didn't I?

Raquel No, I'm not on the dole. I pay for my own way in this world! I'm sorry you don't like what I do for a living. This may come as a surprise to you but I don't bloody like it either! Anyway, you said you wanted me to meet your family.

Del Yes, but I meant with your bloody clothes on! I got black balled for you!

Raquel I'm sorry! But before you start moralising too much, just remember one thing; you booked me for this evening.

Del But I didn't know it would be you!

Raquel Oh, so it would have been alright for you and your mates to leer and lust over a stranger.

Del Yes … No … Oh I don't know!

Raquel Look, this is probably a daft question, but, do you want to see me anymore?

Del Yes of course I want to see you again, sweetheart. But next time I'll pay at the door like all the other punters.

She turns and walks away. Rodney moves hesitantly towards Del.

Dates

Rodney There was no need to say that to her, Del.

Del I know there wasn't, now I wish I hadn't. But it's like most things in my life, it's too bloody late.

Del climbs into the van and turns engine. After a couple of turns there is a clanking sound – and oil and steam gush out from beneath the van. Del alights from the van calmly.

I fancied a bit of a walk, anyway.

Del walks off into the night in the opposite direction to Raquel.

INT. DAY. MARKET CAFE.

Sid is behind the counter, fag in mouth, serving a customer. We find Del, morose and still hurting from the events of a few nights ago, seated at table reading his newspaper. He looks up from his paper unable to concentrate. Sid approaches and starts wiping down the table..

Sid Is that true?

Del Is what true?

Sid All these rumours I've been hearing about you falling in love with some stripper.

Del *(Jack the lad again)* Oh leave it out, Sid. I wasn't in love with her, I was *(winks)*, knocking about with her, you know what I mean?

Sid That's what I thought. I told 'em, Del Boy wouldn't get serious over some tart.

It's like a knife going through him, but he has to play the part.

Del That's right. What do you think I am – some sort of wally?

Rodney enters.

Rodney Cup of tea please, Sid. Alright? Oh what's up with you now? Is it the hundred and seventy-five quid repairs to the van – is it her?

Del Her?

Rodney Raquel.

Del I've never known anyone called Raquel.

Rodney No, right *(Desperately thinking of something to cheer him up)* … you coming down the Coach and Horses tonight, they've got a strip … comedian on.

Del No, I think I'll stay in, bruv, and watch a bit of telly. There's one of them Chekhov plays on BBC2 … load of old cobblers.

Rodney moves to counter and picks up his tea. As he returns so door opens and Raquel enters. Raquel and Rodney look at each other for an embarrassing moment.

Rodney Raquel, what a lovely surprise! Look who's here, Del. *(Del looks up and then back to his paper.)* Have you got time for cup of tea?

Raquel I don't know. *(To Del)* Have I got time

for a cup of tea?

Del Well, it's a free country, innit?

Rodney There you are see, I told you he'd mellow after a bit. Well, I've gotta go somewhere to … somewhere. Here, have my tea.

Rodney hands his tea to Raquel and then exits. Raquel sits at table. She and Del look at each other. Del looks back to his paper. Over this we hear outside:

Mrs Sansom. *(OOV)* Oi, Rodney!

Rodney *(OOV)* Oh hello, Mrs Sansom.

Mrs Sansom *(OOV)* What did you do to my Nerys? She come in shaking like a leaf! White as a sheet she was!

Rodney *(OOV)* No, it wasn't me, Mrs Sansom, it was some yobs.

Raquel What sort of a week have you had?

Del *(All bluff)* Blinding! You?

Raquel Rotten!

Del It's a tough old world, innit?

Raquel Tougher than I ever imagined … I've, em, I've resigned from the strippergram agency.

Del Oh good.

Raquel I've signed on the dole.

Del It's a step up the ladder innit? Why didn't you tell me what you did? Why did you let me find out like that?

Raquel You don't think I wanted you to find out in that way, do you? That night I took a job to give birthday greetings to someone called Albert Trotter. It had been paid for by someone called Derek Trotter. Now if I had known your real name I would have realised it was you and not taken the job!

Del You still didn't tell me what you did for a living.

Raquel I was hoping there'd be no need to. After I met you and I realised we were becoming close, I'd planned to pack the whole strippergram business in. Then you'd have been none the wiser. It didn't work out that way.

Del I thought I knew you! I knew nothing. You were all disguises and secrets!

Raquel I'm sorry … I'm going on a tour.

Del Yeah? I bet it's a mystery one.

Raquel No, it's no mystery. An agent called me a couple of days ago. It could be helpful to my career.

Del Cushty …

Raquel You won't have to worry about bumping into me. It's a tour of the Middle East.

Del The Middle East? I didn't know they went in for all that *Uncle Vanya* and *Run for your Wife*, stuff.

Raquel No, it's not a play. It's a revue, dancing,

that sort of thing.

Del Oh use your noddle, Raquel! You read about that sort of thing in the Sunday papers. You'll end up as an hostess in some topless dive in the Kasbah!

Raquel No, it's an official tour, all above board.

Del You could be kidnapped and end up in a harlem!

Raquel Don't be silly.

Del Oh, alright then. If that's what you want.

Raquel It's not what I want. It's the next best thing … it's a shame the two of us couldn't have been more honest with each other.

Del I was straight with you … alright, alright, so I called myself Duval. That's nothing, is it? Just a joke. I didn't tell you any other lies!

Sid Del.

Gestures for him to come to the counter.

Del What's he want?

Raquel Maybe it's another call from your New York office.

Del smiles at this. Raquel returns his smile and the situation has now softened. Del moves to the counter and Sid hands him his breakfast. Del returns to table with breakfast (bacon, egg, tomatoes and fried bread).

Del, I just wanna say thanks.

Del What for?

Raquel For a lot of things. For being the only man I've met who wanted me to keep my clothes on! For getting yourself black-balled for me and for – I don't know – giving me back some self-esteem. I used to wake up in the morning and look in the mirror and think, 'Oh, you again!' But after I met you I used to wake up and think, 'Great, another day, you're gonna be somebody!' … 'This time next year I'll be famous.' Thanks for that.

Del is moved by this. Looks into her eyes.

Del Raquel … would you like a piece of my fried bread?

Raquel Thanks.

Takes half of his fried bread.

Del When are you leaving?

Raquel Tomorrow afternoon. Gotta cab coming at twelve. It's taking me to Waterloo station. That's ironic isn't it? It doesn't have to be the end. We could still go on seeing each other.

Del Yeah, I'll pop over to Addis Ababa and catch the show.

Raquel I mean, I don't have to go.

Del You said you'd already agreed to it.

Raquel If I'm not there, I'm not there. They'll have to find a replacement. That shouldn't be that difficult, thousands of girls are begging for a chance like this.

Del I don't know what to say sweetheart. It's taken me a bit by surprise.

Raquel I've done all my thinking and I know what I want. If you want me to stay, then I will. And I'm not talking about any heavy commitment like marriage or even living together. We could just – be there for each other. Think about it, won't you?

Del Yeah, of course I will.

Raquel If you like the idea just be at my flat tomorrow. If not, I'll understand.

Del Yeah, just gimme a bit of time, that's all.

Raquel Okay. Thanks for the fried bread. I'll see you … maybe?

Del nods. Raquel exits. Del moves to counter.

Del I can't eat the breakfast, Sid, I've lost my appetite.

Sid Here, was that the stripper?

Del No, Sid. That lady is an up and coming young actress.

Sid Don't recognise her.

Del But you will. This time next year she'll be famous!

INT. DAY. NAG'S HEAD PUB.

Rodney is leaning on the counter. This is Sunday so he is wearing his better Sunday clothes. There are a few other blokes hanging around the counter.

Mike *(Laughing)* You gotta be honest, Rodney, it was funny at the time.

Rodney Del didn't seem to think so.

Mike No, well, he wouldn't, would he? *(Laughs)*
Rodney is feeling angry and uncomfortable at having his brother rubbished.

Rodney Del's been taking it all very well as it happens.

Mike Yeah, we'll have to take your word for that Rodney. 'Cos he ain't been in here since.
More laughter.

Rodney He's been busy.

Mike I thought he would have been in here last night. He's never missed a Saturday session.

Rodney Yeah, well he had a bit of thinking to do last night. He's got a sort of decision to make.

Mike What's that. Whether to pay the bill from the strippergram agency?
There is more laughter. Now the laughter dies. The pub lulls silent, Albert stops playing. We see that Del is in the pub. He has been standing there listening to them. Del has a grim expression. Now he gives them all a big grin.

Del Morning all! *(There are a few half-hearted replies)* Same again for Rodney, a Singapore

Dates

Sling for me and a small rum for Elton John over there. And have one yourself, Michael.

Mike Cheers, Del.

(Mike moves away to get the drinks)

Rodney So, what are you doing?

Del I've been thinking about her all night, last night, Rodney. She's had a tough old life, you know. Her old man was a right roughouse. All the other blokes that she's known before that were no better. You know she's had nothing but bad luck. Then she met me.

Rodney Bloody 'ell. Life's a bitch innit?

Del That is when her luck changed, Rodney!

Rodney Oh well yeah, yeah, that's what I meant.

Del See, I've always been bad luck to women.

Rodney No you ain't.

Mike hands them their drinks.

Del No I have, I have. Last night I was thinking back to all the birds that I've known, I've always left 'em with nothing but aggro … I'm a bit like that Little Joe.

Rodney Little Joe?

Del In *Bonanza* – Little Joe.

Rodney You ain't Del, you're nothing like him.

Del I don't mean in looks Rodney, he's an ugly git. What I mean is if you watch an episode of *Bonanza*, and Little Joe falls in love with a woman, you know she is gonna die! The moment he starts stronging it with a sort you can guarantee that she's either gonna catch the fever, get trampled underfoot in a stampede or the Indians are gonna have her!

Rodney But that won't happen to Raquel.

Del No, I know it won't! She came after me, Rodney. She had to swallow her pride, that took a lot of doing. In my book that makes her a bit special.

Rodney Very special, I'd say.

Del Right. So, I said to myself last night; whatever happens Raquel will not end up full of arrows. I'm gonna have a swift livener then I'm going round her flat.

Rodney Yeah, well done, Del. Stuff what the others think, eh?

Del That's right bruv, that's right. Thank you Rodney, you stood by me, you are a diamond.

Rodney Oh leave off, will you?

Del No, you are and I'll never forget that! You did laugh at the time though.

Rodney I didn't know who it was! So this is all serious stuff then is it?

Del Well, no. We're not talking about marriage or even moving in together. We're just gonna be there for each other. Cheers, Rodney.

Rodney All the best Del.

Del Cheers.

EXT. DAY. URBAN ROAD.

A street of Victorian houses.
We pan up the first floor window of one of the houses. Raquel pulls curtain back and surveys the street looking for Del. She checks her watch. She now lets curtain fall back into place.

INT. DAY.NAG'S HEAD PUB.

Now the atmosphere is one of music and laughter. Mike, Rodney and Del are at the bar laughing.

Del You can imagine how I felt, can't you? I felt like a right dipstick.

Mike Listen, Del, I know we all had a laugh at you, but no offence was meant, mate.

Del I know that, Mike. It's all forgotten about now. No hard feelings.

Mike I thought Albert took it well. Although he did threaten to get even with you.

Rodney Oh yeah, well, Del ain't eaten a thing Albert's cooked ever since.

Del 'Ere, talking about Albert, take that rum over for him, will you Rodney? What's the time? Caw look at the time, I'm supposed to be round Raquel's by noon!

Mike Give her my best, Del. Tell her to pop in for a drink one night.

Del Yeah, I will Mike, cheers.

Rodney *(Hands Albert the rum)* There you go Albert.

Albert So has he reached a decision?

Rodney Yeah, he's going round to her flat in a minute.

Albert Good. She wouldn't have been happy touring round the Middle East. I never liked it over there. Did I tell you about that time I was in Cairo?

Rodney Yes, you must have, Albert, you must have!

Rodney turns. As he does he looks from the window. He looks horrified.

EXT. DAY. NAG'S HEAD PUB.

We see the three-wheeled van.
Parked next to it is a damaged police metro. The young PC and the attractive WPC who were involved in the crash during Rodney's chase sequence, are examining the van.

INT. DAY. NAG'S HEAD PUB.

Rodney Oh God!

Albert What's up, Rodney?

Rodney I gotta go, right, I gotta go!

Del Blimey Mike, you wanna clean your pipes out a bit. It's gone right through him.

We now see the PC and the WPC enter. They have a word with one of the locals who indicates towards Del.

Del Right I'm off. See you all.

PC Is your name Trotter?

Del That's me.

WPC Is that your yellow van out there?

Del What, the one with Trotter written on it? Yes that's mine.

PC Well, a couple of weeks ago a yellow three-wheeled van, very similar to yours, shot the lights between Lewisham Hill and Woodford Lane. We're in the process of questioning the owners of all such vehicles.

Del Oh well, look no further officers. It was me, it's a fair cop, I done it!

Smiles and shakes his head at Albert.

You disappoint me, Uncle.

WPC Mr. Trotter. Either you're not taking this very seriously or you don't understand the full implications of your last statement.

Del Look, I'm a bit pushed for time so, can we get a move on. Come on darling, hurry up.

WPC What d'you mean?

Del takes hold of the buttons on her tunic and pulls it open – shirt as well.

Del Come on, get 'em off, get 'em off!

The WPC covers herself as best she can. The PC is just too stunned to move.

I would have thought you would have come up with something a bit more original than this, Albert.

Albert It's got nothing to do with me, son!

Del Oh leave it out! If you didn't send 'em who did ..? Oh my God!

Now looking out of the window he can clearly see the police car.

Del I'm sorry.

PC Not as sorry as you're gonna be, my old cocker.

WPC Nick him!

Del Wait a minute! It's a mistake! I didn't realise you were police officers.

PC (Gesturing to their uniforms) What d' you think all this is? Plain clothes?

Del No, you see I thought she was a stripper.

WPC That's it! I'm doing him for assault *and* abusive language!

EXT. DAY. RAQUEL'S ROAD.

We see Raquel exit from the front door of the house. She carries her case out to pavement where she awaits the arrival of her cab. She checks her watch and surveys the street despairingly looking for Del.

EXT. DAY. NAG'S HEAD PUB.

Del is now in handcuffs and is being led from the pub by the police officers.

Del Please! Please listen to me. I'm supposed to meet someone at noon.

PC And you're gonna meet someone at noon – our desk sergeant – a very nice man, I'm sure you'll get on like a house on fire!

Del Listen. In my pocket. Money. In my pocket!

WPC What did he say?

Del The old doe ray me's in my pocket! You could have a policeman's ball on it.

WPC Lovely. Now we've got you for attempted bribery as well!

Del Oh please! Give us a break.

EXT. DAY. RAQUEL'S ROAD.

The taxi has now arrived. Raquel places her case in back. She takes one last, sad and longing look for Del. She climbs into cab and slams door.

EXT. DAY. NAG'S HEAD PUB.

The door on Metro slams and it pulls away from camera. We hear Del over.

Del Look, can you take me round to Herrington Road, I gotta see someone. It's left up here.

The Metro turns right.

Del (Cont) Thanks.

EXT. DAY. WATERLOO STATION.

We see the clock which stands at 12.25. Raquel walks past the clock towards the trains. She struggles with her heavy case.

EXT. DAY. URBAN POLICE STATION.

The Metro is parked outside.

The police officers are assisting Del into the station.

Del Can I at least use your phone?

PC You're allowed one phone call.

Del Thank you. What's the time?

WPC Twenty to one.

Del (Deflated) T'riffic! You don't know the code for Addis Ababa do you?

TECHNOMATCH DATING AGENCY

SEARCH FOR:
Derek Duval (no E - French side of family)

A local bird if possible (not too much driving lark)... bit of a sort... everything in the right place... a bit refined - (no old bow-wow)... must know difference between Liebfraumilk and Tizer... guaranteed a steak meal!

SEARCH FOUND:
Raquel Turner

Non-smoker... Actress... nice, warm, friendly...

The Jolly Boys' Outing

EXT. DAY. MARKET.

Del is spieling to a small and indifferent crowd. He is holding a car/radio cassette. We see quite clearly the manufacturer's brand name across radio 'Musta F80'.

The markings on the radio should be very distinctive so that we will recognise it immediately when we see it again in a later scene.

In the background we can see the three-wheeled van and Albert lounging against it. Behind Del is a large-ish cardboard box which has printed across it: 'Musta F80 radio cassette'. We assume that the rest of the radio cassettes are in the box.

Del Now come on, listen to this. I've come here to sell my wares. I haven't come here to be laughed at, chaffed at or generally mucked about. I've come to sell my wares and they're guaranteed. Guaranteed to cure hard core, soft core and pimples on the tongue. Right, now, what we got here today, I tell you what we're doing, we've got the Musta F80 in-car radio cassette player as recommended by Nigel Mansell.

Laughter from crowd.

Del *(Cont)* No no no, straight up. I wouldn't wind you up would I, on something as important as this? This is solid state of the arts technology this, and this is none of your Japanese or German rubbish – no sir, this is actually made in Albania. Listen, let me show you, let me point out some of the advantages of this wonderful machine. It's got multiple pre-sets, synthesised tuners, digital-scan, auto-reverse graphic equalisers. *(A deep breath before continuing)* It's got MW, FM, VHF, LCD, RMS, B&Q and ICI and it comes complete with *two*, not one, two, count them, one … *two* quadraphonic speakers! And I am also giving away free with this technological miracle one Kylie Minogue LP. Wait a minute. Only ten ninety-nine.

We see a marked lack of enthusiasm from the crowd. Some begin wandering away.

Del *(cont)* No, listen, don't walk away, you could regret this for the rest of your life … I tell you what I'm gonna do. Forget the Kylie Minogue LP. Right, ten quid … ten quid, first come, first served.

We cut away to where a bored Albert is lounging against van. We see Cassandra approaching. She is on her lunch break.

Cassandra Hello, Albert.

Albert Oh, hello, love.

Cassandra What are you up to?

Albert I am Trotters Independent Traders' executive look-out. The day Rodney went to work for your Dad I got promotion.

Cassandra Yeah? Wish it was that easy for me.

Albert What, have the bank said something about your new job?

Cassandra No. I had to sit an interview yesterday. Uh … my boss said he'll speak on my behalf, so it's fingers crossed.

Albert You'll get your promotion, Cassandra, I can feel it in me bones. It'll make a lovely anniversary present for you. Talking of anniversary presents, I know what Del's got for you. But, you know me, I ain't saying nothing – yeah, don't wanna spoil the surprise.

Cassandra Oh go on, spoil it.

Albert Alright then. *(Quietly)* It's a car radio.

Cassandra A car ra ..! I've already got a radio in my car.

Albert Have you? It'll do for Rodney then.

Cassandra Oh yeah, it'll look really good on his bike, won't it?

Albert Well, maybe Del's looking for the future. When you get your new job you and Rodney'll become a two car family.

Cassandra I think it'll be a long time before Rodney and I become a two car family.

Albert No, but you've only been married a year, first two or three are always a struggle. It was the same with me and my wife – yeah, she used to write and say me how tough it was.

Cassandra What do you mean, she used to write?

Albert Well, I was away at sea – there was a war on. *(Opens his duffel coat. We see pinned to his jacket is a single medal)* Look, I found this this morning at the bottom of my duffel bag. I ain't seen it for years, I thought I'd lost it.

Cassandra *(Appealing)* Look, Uncle Albert, I've only got one hour for my lunch!

Albert *(Unmoved by her pleas)* It was midnight as we sailed in to this little harbour on board this Greek herring trawler – that was our cover, see.

Del now joins them carrying the box containing the rest of the radios.

Del *(To Albert)* Oi, what is it your game? You're supposed to be on look-out! I haven't seen you look at anything! The entire massed bands of the Metropolitan Police force could march through here playing 'I Shot the Sheriff' and you wouldn't see nothing!

Albert It was Cassandra, she wanted to know where I won me medal.

Cassandra Yeah, it was my fault, Del. I'm sorry. Anyway, I'd better be going, I've got to get some shopping in.

Del Oh yeah, what's that for, tomorrow night's anniversary dinner, eh? What time d'you want us there?

Cassandra *(Reacts – as far as she knew Del and Albert weren't invited)* I thought Rodney said we'd take you and Albert out to a restaurant at a later date.

Del Yes, I know and I told Rodney that that was far too expensive. No, you gotta look after your pennies now, sweetheart.

Cassandra Thing is, Del, um … it's not so much an anniversary dinner, it's more business – I've invited a couple of people along from the bank. I'm worried you'll get bored.

Del No, you don't have to worry about *us*! This is *your* night, and we don't want to let you down – you're family now. Alright?

Cassandra *(Knows she can't win)* Yeah. Eight o'clock okay?

Del Yeah, lovely jubbly!

As Cassandra is about to leave so Marlene appears with her new baby in its pram. We can hear the baby crying.

Marlene Hello Del, hello darling.

Cassandra Hi, Marlene. *(Referring to baby)* Can I look?

Marlene Yeah, if you want, but I warn you he ain't at his best, miserable little git. He's missing his morning nap, ain't you darling?

Cassandra Oh he's most probably got wind. Ah, look at him.

Del *(Looking into pram)* Mm … he's a little cracker, ain't he, eh? Does remind me of Boycie.

Marlene Yeah, what, the eyes?

Del No, no, the wind.

Del and Marlene laugh.

Cassandra What have you named him?

Marlene We've called him Tyler.

Cassandra *(Half-hearted)* Tyler … Nice!

Del Of course, if it had been a girl they would have called it Ruth … then it would have been know as Ruth Tyler … tiler … geddit?

Cassandra *(Uncertain whether to believe him)* Really?

Del No, it's only … *(Referring to Cassandra and Marlene)* What's up with you two?

Marlene approaches Albert.

Marlene Oh hello, Albert? Cor blimey, that's not *another* medal, is it?

Albert Yeah, an act of bravery in the Aegean Sea. I was on this Greek herring trawler, when suddenly out of the darkness come this German torpedo boat!

Marlene *(Interrupts him. She's fed up with his sagas as well)* Albert, you must have come back with more medals than the Russian Olympic squad!

Marlene leaves him and returns to Del, Cassandra and the crying baby. This hurts Albert. Nobody wants to listen to him. He was a hero. He didn't ask to be a hero. His only crime is talking about it.

Albert *(Sadly)* Oh I didn't ask for 'em! They kept giving 'em to me.

We cut to Del, Cassandra and Marlene at pram.

Marlene *(To the crying baby)* Oh, shut up, Tyler!

Albert *(Referring to baby)* Giss him here. Giss him here. I'm a natural with kids.

Albert wheels the pram away a few yards.

Cassandra Alright everyone. I'm off then. Nice to see you.

Del Yes alright Cassandra. Ta-ta now love. Bye.

Cassandra exits.

During the next few speeches the baby's crying in background ceases.

Marlene Bye. That Cassandra's a nice girl, ain't she? Rodney was really lucky marrying her.

Del Yeah, and I was lumbered with the old man of the sea!

Marlene Hey, talking of sea! Boycie's just told me you lot are off on a beano to Margate!

Del Oh what, the Jolly Boys Outing? Yeah, well we go every couple of years. I organise it.

Marlene If he gets up to anything with a bird in Margate I am holding you responsible!

Del Oh he won't get up to nothing! We'll only be there a couple of hours.

Marlene He don't need a couple of hours! Thirty seconds does him!

We cut to Albert who is sitting on a box and talking quietly into the pram. Intercut shots of the baby smiling and cooing and making baby sounds – as if the baby is reacting and answering Albert's questions.

Albert So there I was at the wheel of this Greek herring trawler sailing into the unknown.

Shot of baby.

Albert *(Cont)* It was twenty three hundred

The Jolly Boys' Outing

hours and the night was blacker than a bailiff's heart.

We cut away to Del and Marlene.

Marlene So where's Rodney working now?

Del Mm? Oh he's working with uh ... Alan – you know, Cassandra's Dad – down at the printing works.

Marlene What, what – he managed to keep that job?

Del Oh yeah! And he's doing very nicely. Oh yeah. Works in the computer section.

Marlene Oh.

Del They had a trainee start last month – showing him all the ropes.

Marlene Yeah, Rodney'll soon pick it up.

Del No, no, Rodney's showing the trainee all the ropes!

Marlene Oh.

Cut back to Albert at pram. We don't see the baby now until the end of this sequence. Albert isn't actually looking at the baby anymore. He is staring wistfully into distance.

Albert Then out the darkness came this German torpedo boat. Quick as a flash – and without giving a second's thought to me own safety or anyone else's – I swung the wheel to port and sent the trawler right across the German boat's bow! We were slightly damaged but Jerry sunk within a minute ... That's why they gave me this medal. One day, if you're lucky, you might win one of these. *(Thinks about his last statement)* But then again – hopefully not.

We now see the baby is sound asleep. Albert smiles.

Cut away to Del and Marlene.

Del No, what you've gotta understand, Marlene, is that Rodney's in charge of the *whole* computer section! The *entire* thing! I don't know where that firm would be without Rodney!

INT. DAY. RODNEY'S OFFICE/PRINTERS.

The 'office' is in fact a ten by ten room which has been partitioned off by perspex from a large workshop. Outside the office we can see printing machines and people in protective clothing working them. There are a couple of computers and consoles and one or two computer printers.

As Rodney is in charge of this area, the place is quite messy, paper everywhere.

We find Rodney in shirtsleeves, tie loosened and sleeves rolled up, looking harassed.

We cut from Del's last speech to a computer console screen. The screen is filled with information. Now we hear a 'beep' as a key is touched and the screen goes blank. We hear Rodney's voice.

Rodney (OOV) Shit!

Now we cut to see Rodney looking at the blank screen.

Rodney *(Cont)* That's the second time I've done that today!

Alan opens door and enters. As he opens the door we hear the noise of the busy workshop.

Alan How's it going, Rodney?

Rodney *(Cool and in control)* Oh, fine.

Alan You got those print-outs ready for the bank yet?

Rodney Shouldn't be long, Alan.

Alan *(Chuckling)* I'd be very careful if I was you, you've wiped them off once today already.

Rodney and Alan laugh at this.

Rodney Oh. *(Laughs)* No problem.

Alan So, what have you bought Cassandra for your anniversary then?

Rodney *(Embarrassed)* Oh it was ... clothing.

Alan Clothing, lovely. Well I expect I'll see it tomorrow night, she's bound to wear it at the dinner.

Rodney I don't think she will, Alan.

Alan Well why not? *(Catches on that this is 'personal' clothing)* Oh ... Oh ... Uh ... well I uh ... I really am looking forward to your anniversary dinner.

Rodney Yeah, well, so was I till I found out she's invited that Stephen and Joanne.

Alan Oh no, you gotta be fair son, you know. Stephen is the assistant head of the bank's overseas investment bureau. He's Cassy's boss! She's applied for promotion so she's gotta stay on his good side.

Rodney I know! But he's such a yuppy! It's all that, *(mimics Stephen)* 'Oh yeah, for sure'. And all that, 'Okay, can I just run this past you' Prat!

Alan Yeah, yeah. I can't stand him either. But he's the sort of man that might do the company some good one of these days. I'd rather have him inside the tent spitting out than outside the tent spitting in! Understand?

Rodney Yeah, course I do.

Alan Look, Uh ... if Cassy is lucky enough to get this promotion, one of her jobs and uh ... one of her duties is going to be entertaining at home. So she's uh ... invited Stephen and his wife along to prove that she can throw a good dinner party.

Round about this point a young trainee enters and sits at the second computer.

Rodney *(To Alan)* Yeah, I know. Look, take no notice of me, right, I'm just overreacting.

Alan Well, we'll all be on our best behaviour, make a good impression for our little Cassy, eh? *Moves towards the door.*

Rodney Yeah. *(His face suddenly filled with horror)* Alan! I've invited Del and Albert!

Alan You've what?

Rodney Well, I had to, well, they're family!

Alan *(Thinks about it for a moment)* Oh well, I don't suppose she'd have been very happy in her new job anyway.

Rodney wears a sick grin.

Trainee *(To Rodney)* Excuse me, sir.

Rodney *(Looks behind him then realises the trainee means him)* Oh! What?

Trainee It's just all that data you had on your screen, it's on my one now!

We see that the data which Rodney wiped out is now on second screen.

Rodney *(Bewildered, now acts the boss)* Well, of course it is! *(Shakes his head and smiles at Alan)* They don't know they're born, do they?

Alan exits, smiling at the naivety of the trainee.

INT. NIGHT. RODNEY AND CASSANDRA'S LOUNGE/DINER.

It is a recently built flat and the decor furnishing is modern and tasteful.

On one wall and in amongst all the modern works of art is a print of 'bubbles' (the little boy blowing bubbles) in a rather crappy, ornate gold frame.

The dining table is a six-seater so we should have another two non-matching dining chairs in evidence to make up the numbers.

In the lounge area we have a three-seater settee and two armchairs (or maybe another settee – two-seater and one armchair).

We also have a cocktail cabinet or drinks table. Rodney, Cassandra, Del, Alan, Stephen and his wife Joanne are seated at dining table. At this point Pam is in the kitchen.

Rodney, Alan, Cassandra, Stephen and Joanne are dressed smartly but casually. Del is done up to kill in three-piece and tie, his gold 'D' hanging outside shirt, a gold and ruby tie-pin, his tortoiseshell cigar-holder and his filofax laid on table.

Albert is wearing his finest including medals. Pam, we shall discover, is also slightly over-dressed.

Stephen is in his early thirties and good-looking. He is a twenty four carat 'gold blend' yuppy – although he hates being called that. He is ultra-confident verging on the smug and

has an irritating habit of virtually ignoring those he considers beneath him (this, naturally, includes Del and Albert). His conversation is littered with modern American cliches and jargon from the financial world. Joanne is in her late twenties and is another yuppy. They think similarly.

Their attitudes to him:

Cassy He is her immediate boss and he can help her achieve her ambitions, plus he seems to know what he's talking about. She realises that he's a bit of a pain but she treats him with great politeness.

Pam She thinks Stephen is wonderful and secretly wishes Cassy had married someone like him.

Joanne She also thinks Stephen is wonderful.

Del He admires Stephen's energy and drive but sees him as a 'fellow yuppy'. He feels he has to impress Stephen with his own 'insider knowledge'.

Alan He suffers Stephen because his company is expanding and Stephen is helping arrange a large bank loan. But deep inside he suspects Stephen is a prat.

Rodney He doesn't like the close working relationship Stephen has with Cassy. He's almost convinced Stephen's a prat.

Albert He *knows* Stephen's a prat.

Dinner has finished and plates, etc. cleared away. Everyone is finishing their wine before coffee and liqueur is served.

Albert is seated in armchair. In front of him is a low coffee table upon which is spread a Trivial Pursuits board and accessories.

He is reading answers from the back of cards. We come up on the table, guests in mid-topic. There is laughter and smiles, it's a happy occasion and even Stephen can smile. Laughter.

Stephen Alright, at first glance it may appear to be slightly off the wall. But the word in the city is big bucksville.

Alan Right, so what is this big secret then?

Cassandra Stephen's about to tell you if you give him half a chance.

Stephen Alan, this is no stock market secret or insider information. It is merely my humble opinion – for what it's worth. Okay, let me run this one past you. Try and get your heads round this. I'm going to say one word – but bear in mind I am talking 'future' – long term invest-ment, yeah?

Joanne It's 'hang in there' time.

Stephen Yeah, for sure. Okay, this is the

The Jolly Boys' Outing

bottom line, take it on board if you wish. The word is – Africa!

Del Africa! Africa! I'll make a note of that in my Filofax, if I may, Stephen. You got a pen?

Stephen No. The two main ladies in my life, Joanne and Cassy, know where I'm coming from on this one.

Rodney reacts to this.

Cassandra Stephen was telling me about the projected world growth areas the other day over brunch.

Stephen And Africa is where it's at. Recently Joanne and I spent a little time down in Afrique sur-mer. *(Chuckles at this)*

All the others at table, except for Rodney, chuckle politely.

Del *(To Stephen)* Fabrique belgique.

Stephen This is it. *(Looks at Del and wonders what the hell 'Fabrique belgique' meant. He now continues)* Fruit produce, yeah? With the introduction of new technology we could be talking returns of left-field proportions. Take the banana crop alone, we are into mega-growth.

Del Well, you can't go wrong, Stephen. The bigger the banana the better, ha ha, that's my motto.

Stephen For sure. And statistically we are talking … *(To Del)* What?

Del Well, what I mean is that, uh … it's easier to sell bigger bananas than little 'uns! Ain't it Rodney, eh?

Alan Uh, Del, I think when uh … Stephen talks about 'growth' he's talking about financial investment, not about the uh – well, the actual size of the banana.

Del Oh yeah. No … yeah … no it's … I just wasn't sure.

Pam enters from kitchen pushing a trolley containing coffee things.

Pam Coffee, everyone?

Del Ah, lovely jubbly.

Cassandra Mummy, I was about to do that.

Pam That's alright, darling. You were talking with Stephen, so I thought I might as well make myself useful.

Joanne It's a lovely little flat, Cassandra, everything is so … well, so well coordinated.

Cassandra Thanks.

Del *(To Joanne)* That's 'cos Rodney has got a GCE in Art.

Cassandra *(Desperate to change the subject)* Liqueurs, anyone? Dad?

Alan Oh yeah, yeah, I'll have a scotch, please love.

Pam gives him a warning glance.

Alan *(Cont)* Uh, no, make that a small port please.

Cassandra Roddy?

Del Roddy! *(Laughs, now to Albert)* Roddy! Oi Albert, she only calls him Roddy, look.

Albert laughs.

Rodney *(Embarrassed)* I'll have a lager.

Pam Derek?

Del Mm … brandy, please, Pamela.

Pam Armagnac?

Del Yeah, that'll do if you're out of brandy.

Albert I'll have a rum, dear.

Pam Yes, we know!

Joanne I'll stay with the wine.

Stephen Yeah, same here. I've gotta be up early in the morning, playing baseball.

Del Oh, baseball! Yeah! No … I love it. I always watch it on Channel Four.

Rodney You don't like baseball! You've always called it silly boys rounders!

Del Yeah, that was before that I knew it was 'in'! Nowadays it's the sort of game that guys like uh, me and Stephen enjoy.

Stephen How d'you mean? Guys like me and Stephen?

Del Well, you know, yuppies.

Stephen Yup … *(An embarrassed grin to the others)* Derek, I am not a yuppy.

Del thinks being called a yuppy is one of the greatest honours a man can have bestowed upon him. He now reassures Stephen.

Del You *are*, Stephen, you are! *Guaranteed.*

Stephen No, no, really …

Del *(Interrupts him)* Take it from me, son. You are!

Del gives him a reassuring 'you're one of us' wink. We see Rodney and Alan are hiding their smiles.

Stephen *(Quickly changes subject. Lots of false cheerfulness)* Okay, well, are you gonna give me the chance to wipe the floor with you at Trivial Pursuit or not?

Joanne Oh yeah, brill …

Stephen, Joanne, Cassandra and Pam move to game. Del, Rodney and Alan are a bit slower.

Del *(To Rodney. Rubbing his hands together)* All right, yeah! Trivial Pursuits, eh? Heheh! Lovely Jubbly! *(To Rodney)* How d'you play it?

Rodney *(Fearing the questions may be above Del, he is concerned for his brother's feelings)* The thing is, Del Boy, it's all about general knowledge – you know, it's a bit intellectual.

Del Oh yeah?

Alan *(Also concerned for Del)* Yeah. Some of the questions are, you know, really difficult. It

could be a bit embarrassing.

Del *(To Rodney and Alan)* Don't worry, I'll help you two out Alright?

Rodney and Alan share a look as Del moves towards game. Alan and Rodney follow. Everybody is seated or finding seats. During the following speeches everybody takes a turn at throwing the dice to see who starts the game.

Albert So ... so what part of Africa did you go to?

Del *(To Rodney)* I bet he's been there!

Joanne Well, the trip ended at Dar Es Salaam.

Albert I've been there.

Stephen Okay! Look, this is really boring. We left Nairobi then went south to Moshi, across the Serengeti to Musoma then the long trek east to the coast.

Del *(Quietly mimicking Albert)* During the war.

Albert During the war we pursued a German battleship down the eastern coast and right the way through the Zanzibar Channel. Three days and nights we chased it.

Joanne Did you catch it?

Albert Yeah, worse luck, it sunk us.

Joanne We'll have to find that holiday brochure for Cassandra.

Stephen Yeah, for sure. Right! Try and get your heads round this, okay? Imagine the sun setting on the vast waters of Lake Victoria ... A hundred thousand wildebeest grazing on the Masai Steppe, yeah?

Joanne Oh yeah, wonderful.

Stephen *(Especially to Cassandra)* A misty, sleepy dawn rises to reveal Kilimanjaro in all its hypnotic majesty.

Cassandra Oh, it sounds great!

A pause.

Del We're all going on a beano to Margate next Saturday, Stephen. D'you fancy coming?

Stephen Me? Oh, em, yeah it sounds great but it's bank holiday weekend and uh ... Joanne and I always spend them together.

Joanne No, I'm going away to Mummy and Daddy's next Saturday, remember.

Stephen gives her a look that could kill.

Cassandra It's better than being on your own, Stephen. It'll get you out of the old routine.

Stephen No, I mean, I ... I wouldn't know anyone.

Albert Course you will. Rodney's going.

Rodney and Cassandra react.

He wanted to tell Cassandra himself and she's not best pleased at finding out this way.

Cassandra *(To Rodney)* You're going?

Rodney Yeah. Well, it's tradition. You know, it's the Jolly Boys' Outing.

Cassandra The *what*?

Del It's the Jolly Boys Outing. We've been going on 'em for years.

Pam *(To Cassandra)* Oh you can't stop Rodney from going, darling. After all, it's only a day out. It'll do him good.

Del Yeah. Anyway, your Dad'll be there to keep an eye on him, won't you?

Alan closes his eyes as Pam explodes.

Pam *(To Alan)* You're off on a bloody beano?

Alan Well, Del mentioned it. I thought ... uh, you know, a bit of sea air, do me good.

Pam You're going to get drunk, aren't you? And make yourself ill on jellied eels!

Alan I'm not gonna drink anything and I'm not gonna eat! I'm just gonna – enjoy myself!

Stephen Okay, well, who threw the highest number? Was it me?

Rodney No, Del did.

Del Ah! Yeah! I think it's me

Stephen Well fine. Roll again, Derek, and uh ... I'll ask the questions.

Del rolls the dice and then moves his counter the appropriate number of squares.

Del Alright, there we go. Four. What do I do now? This me, yeah? That one. Look, one, two, three, four.

Stephen Oh, S&N.

Del S&N, ha ha! What's S&N?

Stephen Science and Nature.

Del Oh right.

Stephen *(Takes card and looks at question)* Oh God! It's so simple! *(Reads to Del)* 'What is a female swan called'?

Del What is em ... female swan called?

Stephen *(Incredulously)* You don't know?

Del No no no no. I do, I do. It's just that it's at the back of me uh ... me brain there. Um ... Oh! Can you giss a clue.

Albert Three ... three letters.

Stephen Oh come on now! There's nothing in the rules about clues!

Del Ah, it's a fe ... Female swan. Three letters. Um ...

We now see Rodney has produced a ball-point pen – one of the cheap, see-through type. He is attracting Del's attention by tapping the pen. Del spots this.

Del Um, wait a minute, uh ... got it. It's a Pen!

Stephen reacts. Del picks up the dice and rolls again.

We are off and running!

The Jolly Boys' Outing

INT. DAY. TRAVELLING COACH.

We see the coach's radio and establish that it is a 'Musta F80'. At this moment the radio is working perfectly (no smoke). Music is playing – 'Help' by Bananarama.

We establish the faces – some singing along, others chatting. The two faces we shouldn't see at this time are the driver's and Alan's. We see Albert is asleep. Mickey Pearce sings into Albert's ear.

Mickey *(High pitched)* Won't you please, please help me? Help me …!

Albert *(Wakes with a start)* Get out you noisy little git!

Mickey You miserable old sod! You're on a beano, you're supposed to be enjoying yourself.

Albert I haven't had my full quota of sleep, and I'm starving hungry. Why'd we have to leave before breakfast?

Jevon Don't you read the papers, Albert? The railways are on strike.

Albert So?

Jevon And it's a bank holiday weekend. *(Now as if he is talking to a child)* Which means the roads are gonna be choc-a-bloc, that's why we left early. Now repeat that back to me, I want to make sure you understand.

Albert I'll give you a clump round the ear in a minute.

Jevon and Mickey laugh.

Del is passing up the aisle.

Albert *(Cont)* Del, d'you reckon I could get something to eat?

Del Yeah, 'course you can, unc, Denzil's in charge of the sandwiches. Tell you what, you sit there, and I'll go an' get some for you, alright? Lazy old git!

Del moves towards back of coach.

Jevon You've gotta give Del his dues, ain't ya? He did all the catering by himself.

Mickey Oh leave off, Jevon, can you see Del Boy standing in a kitchen cutting up all them loaves? He probably got some idiot to do it for him.

Trigger No, I made 'em for him.

See Rodney's reaction.

Cut to a seat towards back of coach.
We see Denzil seated at aisle seat.
On the window seat is a large cardboard box filled with cellophane wrapped sandwiches. He produces a small plastic drum of pills. As he pops a couple in his mouth he reacts. He is behaving suspiciously.
We see Del is standing there and has witnessed this.

Del *(Disgusted with him, hands him a can of beer)* Here y'are, want some bitter to wash them down with? Denzil, what's your game? Don't you realise the damage that stuff does to you?

Denzil They're antibiotics!

Del What?

Denzil Antibiotics, the doctor prescribed 'em. *(Hands can of beer back)* And I don't need that, I'm not supposed to drink with 'em … I've got this infection.

Del *(Assuming it's the clap or worse)* Oh have you?

Denzil It's in the ear.

Del How's it get there then?

Denzil That's where you normally get ear infections.

Del Oh.

Denzil Listen Del, you won't tell the others about this, will you? I mean, these days people get the wrong idea about this sort of thing.

Del Oh come on, don't be silly, Denzil. Course I won't.

Denzil It's just an ear infection, that's all.

Del Oi, oi, oi, Denzil! You don't have to prove yourself to me, do you? I'm your mate.

Denzil Cheers, Del.

Del That's alright. Oh by the way, there's been a change in plan. You're no longer in charge of the sandwiches.

Del picks up the box of sandwiches and moves towards front of coach, leaving Denzil flabbergasted.

Del *(Calls towards front of coach)* Michael, your luck's changed. You're in charge of the grub.

Sid has a fag hanging from his lips and looks his usual scruffy self. He calls Del.

Sid Oi, I wanna word with you.

Del Yeah? What is it, Sid?

Sid I own a cafe, right?

Del Yeah, right, so what?

Sid So, why didn't you ask me to make the sandwiches?

Del Well, the explanation is simple. We intend to eat them!

Sid Oh … alright, then.

Del Right then. *(Moves away)* Alright lads, only another ten minutes, then we'll be at the half-way house, that's when the serious stuff begins.

A cheer from the Jolly Boys.

Jevon Make those lagers long and cool.

Rodney Oh yes! Look out Margate, and lock up your daughters. Hey? *(Looks to one side and reacts)* Alright, Alan?

We see Alan sitting at window seat.

Alan Yeah, I'm alright, son …

Mike is moving down the coach, handing out the sandwiches.

Mike Salad … there's cheese for you Tone. Um … there you go Denzil.

Mike hands something to Denzil. We don't see what is is at this point. Denzil, who is looking out of the window, automatically takes it. We hear a bell tinkle.

He now looks to see that Mike has given him the brass bell he calls time with in the pub. The whole coach is now laughing.

Denzil *(Reacts angrily)* Where is he?

Denzil stands and searches for Del. We see Del standing at the front of the coach.

Denzil *(Cont)* You promised you wouldn't say anything!

Del *(Can hardly talk through laughter)* Sorry, Denzil, it just sorta slipped out!

We hear others calling 'eurghhh' and 'unclean!' etc. Denzil sits and smiles – he knows all the jibes are good natured. Del, still laughing, moves to the very front seat. His attention is drawn to something in the driving console of the cab. We now see that the 'Musta F80' radio is smouldering ever so slightly. He ponders the phenomenon until his concentration is broken by Rodney's voice.

Rodney *(Pointing out of front window)* Hey Del. Here y'are mate. It's the halfway house.

Del Ah! Hey! Lovely Jubbly! *(Laughs)*

EXT. DAY. HALFWAY HOUSE PUB.

We see the halfway house with a few empty coaches already parked there. From inside we can hear the sound of pop music. We see the Jolly Boys' coach pull off the road and stop.

INT. DAY. LOBBY OF HALFWAY HOUSE PUB.

Two sets of double doors and one single door lead off from the lobby.

We give the impression that the two sets of swing doors lead to two separate bars. Through the frosted glass of these doors we should see bodies crammed against them to give the impression of a packed pub.

A sign above the single door reads simply 'Toilets'. Heavy music is playing over. Albert and Sid are standing in lobby sipping their almost-finished halves of bitter.

Mike enters from one of the bars.

Mike *(Urgency in his voice)* Oi! You seen Del boy around!

Sid He was here just now. Why? What's up?

Mike I think old Harry's had too much to drink –

he's fallen over twice. Now he's tryin' to juggle with pickled eggs.

Albert So what's that gotta do with Del?

Mike Well, Del organised this outing so it's his responsibility. I'll try the other bar.

As Mike is about to enter the second bar so Eddie Chambers exits from it.

Eddie is about the same age as Mike. He's an East End landlord.

They almost pass each other.

Mike Sorry mate.

Eddie Oi, Mike! It is you, innit?

Mike I don't believe it! Eddie Chambers! 'Ere, I heard you'd emigrated.

Eddie That's right, yeah, I had a pub on the Isle of Wight. So, you still in the trade?

Mike Yeah, yeah, got a lovely little pub down in Peckham. *(Indicating Albert and Sid)* There's two of my satisfied regulars over there.

Sid and Albert look behind them to see who he's talking about.

Mike *(Cont)* You uh … around for a while, then Eddie?

Eddie Yeah, 'bout another half hour.

Mike Oh, I'll catch up with you. We'll … we'll have a right old chat. I've gotta dash. A bit of business. See you later.

Eddie Ah right, yeah!

Mike exits to second bar. Eddie exits to toilets.

Albert Panic over the slightest little thing these days. Wouldn't have done in the war, Sid.

Sid I wouldn't really know, Albert. I spent most of my time in a German prisoner of war camp. Got captured on this little island called Siros – in the Dodecanese – just off the Greek coast.

Albert No chance of escape from there I suppose.

Sid Well, a few of us tried it one night. Got right down to the harbour, over-powered some German sailors and nicked their boat – fast bugger it was as well. We'd almost made it to the open sea and this poxy Greek fishing trawler cut right across our path! Got fished out by the Germans and spent the rest of the war in a stalag.

Albert *(Indicating Sid's empty glass)* Fancy another one, Sid?

Sid Yeah, why not?

Albert takes glass and exits to bar.

INT. DAY. GENTS TOILETS OF HALFWAY HOUSE PUB.

Del is washing his hands at basin. Eddie is at urinals. Del is being very fastidious about washing and drying his hands. He is just

The Jolly Boys' Outing

about to leave when Mike enters.

Mike Oh there you are! Del. Listen, we've got a bit of a problem out in the main bar.

Del Why, what's happened now?

Eddie 'Ere, gotta stop meeting like this, Michael!

Mike Talk about a bad penny! Del, I'd like you to meet an old mate of mine. Eddie Chambers – Del Trotter.

Eddie zips his flies and shakes hands with Del.

Eddie Nice to meet you, Del.

Del And you, Eddie.

Eddie moves to basins. Del now looks at his polluted right hand and then joins Eddie at the basins.

Mike Eddie and I used to be rivals over in the East End, we had pubs almost opposite each other.

Del Yeah?

Eddie Yeah, except mine was better than yours.

Mike You must be joking! Del, you know how I run a pub, don't you?

Del Yeah, that's right. His must have been better than yours, Mike.

Mike Oh thank you very much! *(To Eddie)* You still doing it then, Eddie?

Eddie No, no, I got out the pub game years ago. I own a club now in Margate – the Mardi Gras. We do a decent meal, we gotta resident cabaret, you know, a singer, a magic act, a good comedian, I mean … what more'd you want for a fiver?

Del Well that sounds fair enough to me, Eddie. Here, we're on a beano to Margate as it happens. Here, I tell you what, I just had an idea!

Mike looks at Del with an expression of, 'Oh no! another scheme'.

Del *(Cont)* Why don't you give us some complimentary tickets, like, you know – just to get the ball rolling – and we'll bring the rest of the coach party down to your place to pay at the door? We could pack your place out.

Eddie *(Gives it a moment's consideration)* Yeah, I'll have some of that.

Del Good man. *(Winks at Mike)*

Eddie *(Hand Mike and Del some tickets)* Tell you what, look. Two for you, two for you Del.

Del There you are, you see, you know it makes sense.

Eddie Yeah. Maybe I'll see you later then mate.

Del Yeah, see you later then Eddie.

Mike Yeah … good luck. Cheers Eddie.

Eddie Thank you Mike.

Eddie exits.

Mike *(To Del)* What do we want complimentary tickets for a night- club for, Del? We've gotta be out of Margate by seven!

Del Oh look. Thank you very much. Use your brains, will you Michael? We might be able to flog 'em to the holiday-makers, eh? Make ourselves a few bob. You know what I mean?

Mike Don't you ever stop?

Del No. Yuppies never switch off, Michael. It's all or nothing with us! Right, now, what's this problem?

Mike I think you'd better come and have a look at old Harry.

Del What? Hey? Cor …

They exit.

EXT. DAY. HALFWAY HOUSE PUB.

Rodney, Mickey, Jevon and Denzil are having a very gentle kick-around with a plastic football. They're really passing the ball between them.

We now see Del and Albert exit from pub and hold the double doors open for someone who is following. Harry, who appears to be paralytic, exits being supported on either side by Mike and Trigger. Boycie, Alan and Sid exit behind them.

Del Alright, Harry, you'll be alright, mate. You'll be alright.

Cut back to Rodney, Micky, Jevon and Denzil.

Rodney Look at the state of him!

Jevon And it's only eleven o'clock!

Sid *(To Alan, referring to Harry)* This is good news, innit?

Alan It's no problem. You just chuck him on the back seat, let him sleep it off.

Boycie Chuck him on the back seat? He's the driver!

Alan The dri … Oh bloody 'ell!

Boycie, Alan and Sid join Del and Albert as Mike and Trigger help Harry towards the coach.

Albert So what we gonna do now?

Del I don't know yet. I mean, there's bound to be a way out of it. There's always a way.

Albert Here, young Denzil's a long distance lorry driver.

Boycie That's right, he could handle that coach, no problem.

Alan No, he's just got a Heavy Goods Licence. To drive that coach he'd need a Public Service Licence.

Sid He's got one of them an' all, he used to drive on the buses with me years ago.

Del Well that's it then, innit, eh? We're saved. *(Calls)* Oi, Denzil! Come over here. This is your

lucky day.

Denzil *(Emphatically)* No!

Del No? What d'you mean, 'no'?

Denzil I am not driving that coach! I've been driving all week and this is my day off!

Boycie If you don't drive it we'll have to wait here until Harry sobers up.

Albert And by the look of him that could take about a fortnight!

Denzil Well Sid used to be on the buses, he can drive it.

Sid I'd love to, Denzil, but I've had a couple of drinks.

Denzil Yeah, so have I, you see.

Del No you haven't. You're not allowed to drink. You're on antibiotics because of your disease.

Denzil I have not got a disease! I have got an ear infection!

Cut away to coach where Mike and Trigger are helping Harry up the steps.

Mike Get your left foot up, Harry. Come on.

Trigger What d'you think's wrong with him?

Mike What do I think? Well, snow-blindness would be my bet, Trig.

Trigger Yeah? I thought he was pissed.

We now see two policemen sitting in a panda car about twenty or so yards away. They watch with interest as the hapless Harry is assisted into the coach. They smile to themselves as they feel a nick coming on. They alight from the panda car.

We cut away to Del and co. Del, Boycie, Alan, Albert and Sid are pleading with Denzil.

Denzil Alright! Alright! I'll drive it on one condition – Harry drives it home.

Del Good boy, Denzil, you know it makes sense. That's it, good lad. Go on then, get on there.

They move towards the coach. Rodney, Mickey and Jevon are still having a kick-about. Del, who is now standing at the coach, calls to them.

Del *(Cont)* Right, come on then you lot, come on. Let's get on board. Hurry up! Oi! You three! Get on the coach, we're ready for the off now. Rodney, give me that ball.

Rodney *(Throws the ball in the air)* Ruud Gullit – nowhere!

As the ball drops Rodney gives it a powerful volley in Del's direction. We cut away to Del. The policeman steps into shot.

Policeman *(To Del)* Excuse me sir.

The ball now smacks the policeman in the side of head knocking his hat off and sending him flying out of shot. We see Rodney's

horrified reaction to this. He looks like a drunk. We see Del helping the policeman up.*

Del *(To policeman)* 'Ere, what happened? Hey?

The policeman looks to where Rodney is standing.

Policeman You! You're under arrest!

Rodney I couldn't help it!

Del *(Does gentle throwing motion)* Yeah, he's right, officer. He's right. He just … He just, you know, he just 'threw' the ball back to me, like that.

Policeman *(To Rodney)* I don't know how much you had to drink, son, but it's too much! In the car!

Rodney *(Does the gentle throwing motion)* No, I just 'threw' the ball back at him!

Policeman You can tell me all about it – at the station!

The policeman is now leading Rodney towards the panda car.

EXT. DAY. POLICE STATION.

The coach with everyone on board except Rodney, Del and Alan, is parked outside the police station. We see Boycie at window of coach. He checks his watch and sighs heavily. We now see Del, Rodney and Alan exit from station.

Rodney What's Cassandra gonna say about this?

Alan There's no need for Cassandra to know anything about it.

Rodney And what happens when the summons arrives?

Del Oh summons, what summons? They're not proceeding with the case!

Rodney Del, that copper has just charged me and taken a statement! He's keeping the ball as Exhibit A!

Del He also reckoned the Chief Inspector wouldn't take it any further. They'll let you off with a warning!

Rodney Yeah, but say they don't?

Alan We'll cross that bridge when we come to it. I think you're in the clear, in fact I'm sure you are. Come on, let's get on the coach.

Rodney Alright.

Del Come on, that's the spirit, you know it makes sense.

They climb on to the coach.

Del *(Cont)* Right, come on then Denzil. Full ahead folks, we're off to Margate!

EXT. DAY. MARGATE.

Montage of travelling shots and arrival of

The Jolly Boys' Outing

coach in Margate.
Shots on seafront, beach, funfair.

EXT. DAY. JETTY.
*The music 'Everybody's Talking at Me' fades
and we find Del and Rodney sitting on an
upturned boat. It is now six in the evening
and they are both looking tired and ragged.*

Del Phew! Ooh !

Rodney Well, the coach leaves in an hour.
Hasn't been a bad day though, has it?

Del No, it's bin alright, bruv, it's been alright.
I've really enjoyed meself ... I'm feeling a bit
cream-crackered now, though. I think I might
have a touch of that yuppy-flu, you know.

Rodney Yeah? Couldn't have something to do
with the lobster vindaloo and fourteen pina
coladas, could it?

Del Well, it might have slowed me down a bit,
yeah. I went down the cemetery yesterday – put
some flowers on Mum's grave.

Rodney *(Embarrassed)* I ain't been down there
lately, Del – there's ... there's always something
to do, you know.

Del No, no, it's alright Rodders. She
understands. She knows that you still think

about her.

Rodney Yeah, 'course I do.

Del Yeah, I just, you know, I was ... um ... I just
sat there, you know, I was like chatting and that
– just letting her know what's been happening
... I bet she was well pleased. Yeah. D'you know
your Cassandra, she reminds me a bit of Mum,
you know.

Rodney *(At first he has a worried expression as
he thinks of Mum's reputation)* Oh – good.

Del She's got drive, ain't she? You know. That's
one thing Mum had, yeah, Mum had a lot of
drive.

Rodney *(Half-hearted, almost hollow praise)*
Yeah, Cassandra's *very* ambitious.

Del That's good, innit?

Rodney Mmmh ... Nothing gets in the way of
her career, no doubt about that.

Del You must be well pleased.

Rodney Yeah.

Del 'Cos she's an achiever!

Rodney Yeah.

Del Yeah, she's a bit like me in many ways.

Rodney Yeah, I s'ppose so.

Del Mm ... I've always been an achiever. I've
never actually achieved nothing mind you, but

I've always been in with a shout. *(Gestures to the sea)* You know, this … this reminds me of the time me and Jumbo Mills set up a seafood stall outside the Nag's Head. 'Eels on Wheels' we called it. We was gonna build empires, you know. You know, every pub in London was gonna have a seafood stall outside called Eels on Wheels … D'you know what I said to him the night that we came up with the scheme?

Rodney *(Quietly)* This time next year we'll be millionaires.

Del *(Hasn't heard it)* I said, 'This time next year we'll be millionaires'. And we could have been, Rodney. We could have been. You know what killed off Eels on Wheels, don't you? It was television!

Rodney What, *The Cook Report*?

Del No, no, no. It was the television started humanising fish.

Rodney What you going on about?

Del They did. They started to make fish human! You know, first of all there was that shark thing, Flipper – he had more GCEs than you. Then there was Squidly Diddly, the octopus, he used to play the drums. There was Michael Fish!

Rodney And that put you out of business?

Del Yes, it's true, I'm telling you. Mothers used to come round

complaining that their kids refused to eat our homemade fish fingers in case they was related to *The Man from Atlantis*! And that report from the council health inspector didn't help none either. I could have made it though, bruv! I could have!

Rodney smiles at him. He loves him and his silly dreams.

Rodney You will, Del, you will.

Del Never stop believing, eh, Bruv?

Rodney Never stop believing …

Del Yeah.

Rodney *(Checks his watch)* Come on Andy, time to go home.

Del Yeah.

They stand and walk away.

EXT. DAY. MARGATE COACH PARK.
We cut away to an area where we see the Jolly Boys congregating around their coach. To one side of area we have a BT telephone kiosk (one of those see-through ones). Here we see Rodney pressing out a number. We now see Denzil at coach door.

Greetings from Margate

The Jolly Boys' Outing

Denzil Are we all here now, Del?

Del No, we're just waiting for Rodney, he's reporting in to headquarters.

Denzil sighs at Rodney's plight and then goes back inside coach.

We now inter-cut between Rodney in kiosk and Cassandra in hall of their flat.

Rodney *(On phone)* Hi, Cass? It's me.

Cassandra *(Acts over-surprised and over-friendly, as if she knows something and is leading him into a trap)* Roddy! I've been waiting for your call all day.

Rodney *(Reacts)* Have you?

Cassandra Mmh! So how are you?

Rodney Oh, we're fine. Listen, we're at the coach park, we'll be off in a couple of minutes.

We cut away to Denzil in driver's seat. There is a tiny haze of smoke wafting around the driving area. Denzil sniffs the air and then searches for the source. We cut away to Del and Harry (the original driver). Harry is sitting on an upturned crate and nursing his aching head.

Harry 'Ere, you won't tell my guv'nor what happened, will you Del? I'd get the bullet if he found out about this.

Del Leave it out, Harry, what sorta bloke d'you think I am?

Harry I had one glass of lemonade in that pub! I don't know what happened. Oh ... I felt strange – it was as if I'd been overcome by fumes or something.

Del Yeah, well, whatever it was, it's lucky we had Denzil about, weren't it, eh?

Harry Don't I know it. He's a good bloke, that Denzil.

Del Good bloke! He's one of the best – one of the very best.

Denzil calls from the coach.

Denzil *(Calls)* Del!

Del What does that dipstick want now?

Denzil *(Calls)* There's smoke coming from the radio.

Del *(Calls)* Well you must have pressed the wrong button or something. Oh look, I'll come and sort it out.

Cut away to phone conversation between Rodney and Cassandra.

Rodney So how's your day been?

Cassandra Oh, usual sort of thing. Oh, Stephen phoned this morning.

Rodney *(Shows his dislike for Stephen)* Did he?

Cassandra Yeah. He'd found that holiday brochure he'd been telling us about. Mummy called round to see if I'd like to have some lunch

with her, then the Kent Police Constabulary phoned to confirm that you lived at this address.

Rodney Oh! That was nice of them, wasn't it?

Del and Denzil are studying the smouldering radio.

Denzil I mean, it's not s'pposed to do that, is it?

Del Well, no, well it wasn't in the brochure at least. *(Calls)* Oi! Boycie! Boycie, here! Come here a minute.

Boycie Yes, what is it?

Rodney Look, you see, Del said 'Give me the ball'.

Cassandra *(Breaks in)* Oh! I might have guessed Del would be behind it somewhere!

Rodney No, he didn't mean to get me into trouble!

Cassandra Well, he never does, does he? Yet it seems every time Del's around you something goes wrong and you're at the sticky end of it!

Rodney *(Defending Del)* Not every time!

Del What're we supposed to do about it?

Mike Well, I'd switch it off if I was you, Del. The main petrol line runs right underneath there.

Del Blimey!

Del switches radio off. As he does so flames shoot out of radio and continue burning. There is a mild-ish panic amongst the observers.

Del Gordon Bennett!

Denzil We gotta do something about this!

Boycie Someone get some water.

Del Yes, good idea. Water, we need loads of water.

Trigger Ain't this coach fitted with a fire distinguisher?

Del *(Gets out)* Abandon ship! Come on, get off there.

Cassandra *(In mid-flight and all fired up)* ...and what about that time he entered one of your paintings in a competition and you won first prize? In the under-fifteen category!

Rodney Yes, I do seem to recollect it. But I don't think he ...

Cassandra *(Breaks in)* ... and I had to spend a week in Majorca posing as your common-law step-mother!

Del is organising the evacuation.

Del Come on then everybody. Hurry up. Look lively.

Rodney Alright, look, I agree that Del gets a bit out of hand, but I think it's unfair to say that everything he touches goes wrong!

Rodney's speech is interrupted by an explosion as a ball of flame erupts twenty or so yards behind him. We see the flames'

*reflection on the glass of the kiosk. Rodney
turns to see that the entire front half of the
coach is engulfed in flame.*

*We have a shot in which we establish that all
the Jolly Boys are safe.*

Rodney *(On phone)* Cass? You still there? Our
coach has just blown up!

*We see Harry looking aghast at his burning
vehicle.*

Del *(Spots Harry)* Don't worry, Harry, I won't tell
your guv'nor about it!

EXT. NIGHT. MARGATE RAILWAY STATION.

We don't see the station at this point.
*We see the Jolly Boys marching down the
road.*

*They march with determination and in silence
– we get the impression that there's been a
few rows as everyone has blamed everyone
else for the fire. They arrive at the railway
station to find the entrance is shuttered. A
board outside reads:*

'Station closed due to industrial action. BR
regret any inconvenience to passengers.'

Del I don't believe it! There's only a bloody train
strike!

Boycie Uh … my son is being christened in
three weeks' time!

Sid What about my cafe?

Mike I've got a pub to run, Del!

Jevon I was supposed to meet a bird at nine!

Trigger And I lost my dolphin!

Del Well, just shut up? I've just about had
enough of the lot of you!

Denzil *(Indicates Green Line bus stop)* What
about a Green Line? There's a bus stop over
there.

Rodney Yes. Good idea, Denzil!

They move to bus stop and check timetable.

Del That's it … that's uh uh … there you are,
look. The next bus to London is at twenty
hundred hours! Haha! What's that mean,
Rodney?

Rodney Eight o'clock. So we got half hour wait.

Del Ah well, that's not too bad.

Alan No, wait a minute, wait a minute. That's
the normal schedule … that's the normal
schedule. *(Points further down timetable)* Look
here … uh … Bank holidays, Christmas, last bus
goes at 19.20. We missed it by ten minutes.

Micky So when's the next one then?

Alan Ten past eight tomorrow morning.

Boycie Wonderful! Absolutely wonderful!

Trigger We could hitch-hike.

Mike What, twenty-seven of us?

Trigger Oh yeah.

Albert I remember once just after the war.

Rodney Oh don't start, Unc!

Mickey We've had enough of your stupid
stories for one day, Albert!

Del Oi, oi, oi! Watch it! He's a war hero, he's
got a right to speak!

Albert I fought for free speech!

Del *(To Albert)* Shuddup!

Mickey So why does he have to keep saying
such stupid things then?

Del Look, you keep on Mickey, and the back of
my hand is gonna have a quiet word with your
ear'ole!

Denzil Oh that's it! Let's all have a punch-up in
the middle of the street – that'd put the cherry
on the cake, wouldn't it? *(To Del)* And this is the
last time I come out on a beano with you!

Del And that's the last time I'm gonna invite
you! And I tell you another thing…

Alan Look, calm down, calm down. You'll get
nowhere arguing. Now, let's look at the facts.
What we got here is Hobson's Choice. We can't
get a train, the last bus has gone, our own
vehicle is somewhat out of action. The coach
company has promised to send down a
replacement vehicle – tomorrow morning at nine
o'clock. So there you have it, gentlemen.

*We hear moans and groans of acceptance –
they don't like it but they realise Alan is right.*

Trigger *(To Alan)* So what you saying?

Alan What I'm saying is, we're gonna have to
spend the night here. We book into a hotel, a
bed and breakfast – it's only for one night.

Sid You seem to be forgetting something. This
is a bank holiday. This town is full to the rafters
with holiday-makers. Where are we gonna find a
room?

Alan There's bound to be a couple of them still
vacant.

Boycie Yes, but there's twenty-seven of us!

*Now the eyes are filled with a new-found
alertness. They all realise that rooms are at a
premium and it's first come, first served. They
have to be swift and find a bed before the
others but they have to do it casually so as
not to alert the rest.*

Jevon Er, me and Micky are gonna take a little
walk on the sea front.

Del Yeah, well, we feel like … um … you know,
stretching our legs.

Boycie I quite fancy taking the night air. How
about you, Michael?

*Slowly and casually the Jolly Boys start
dispersing in groups of twos and threes in*

The Jolly Boys' Outing

different directions. They are all keeping their
eyes on each other waiting to see who makes
the first move. It is Jevon, Mickey and Denzil
who start running first. Now Del, Rodney and
Albert break into a gallop. Boycie, Mike and
Alan follow their example.

*We see the Jolly Boys rushing away from the
station in various directions.*

*The only one who is left is Trigger, who
doesn't understand what all the rush is about.
He dithers, not sure who to follow. Del has
gone off to his left, Boycie to his right.
He now exits shot left.*

*We pause on shot. Trigger reappears, still
dithering. He now exits right, close to camera.
Trigger reappears, still dithering.
He now exits shot right.*

EXT. NIGHT. MRS BAKER'S HOUSE.

*This is one of those roads where virtually
every house is a B&B guest house.*

*We see the Trotters walking towards us
checking each window hoping to find a
'Vacancies' sign.*

Rodney We've been down this road once
already, ain't we?

Albert We've been every bloody where! We've
walked further than the Jarrow Marchers.

Del Yeah and they were all out of work and
starving and I bet they didn't moan as much as
you two! Gordon Bennett!

*We see 'Sorry, No Vacancies' signs in a few
windows. They wrap their coats up tight
round their necks to indicate a night chill
setting in.*

*Now we see a 'Vacancies' sign in a window
This is Mrs Baker's house.*

Del Here, hang about! Look at that! I told you
something'd turn up, didn't I? Look! Look,
'vacancies'. Hey? Hey? Come on. Lovely jubbly!

*The house is very pretty and cosy-looking.
White walled with mock swiss-chalet style
shutters either side of the windows. Roses
grow in the garden and pretty, floral design
curtains hang at the windows which are
filled with a welcoming light.*

*The Trotters' hearts are lifted by the vision.
They approach the front door and ring the
bell which has a chime straight out of Miss
Marple.*

*The door is opened by the maid, Helen. She
is about thirty and a very pleasant
wholesome person with a warm and
welcoming smile.*

They go inside.

INT. NIGHT. MRS BAKER'S HOUSE.

*The interior reflects the same style of pristine
olde Englishness as the exterior. Helen leads
the Trotters into the hall. Laying on one of the
steps of the stairs is a very fluffy, pure white
cat.*

Helen If you'd just like to wait here please.

Del Oh right, thank you.

Helen *(Calls)* Mrs Baker.

*Helen now exits towards the kitchen.
Albert is stroking the cat who purrs with
pleasure.*

Del *(Sniffs the air)* Smell that, Rodney. Can you
smell that? That's … that's roast potatoes, innit?

Rodney Yeah, and gravy.

Albert And steak and kidney pie unless I'm
mistaken.

Del We've fallen on our feet here, haven't we?

Rodney Yeah, and I am starving!

Del I know, so am I.

Albert Ain't he a beautiful cat, eh? And he likes
me.

Del Yeah, most probably in love with that
beard. Oh!

*The three laugh again – it's that kind of joyful
mood. Mrs Baker appears. She is a small
rounded lady in her middle sixties. She looks
like everyone's favourite granny. She has grey
to white hair and wears a clean floral pinny.
She evokes an image of home-made crusty
bread and hot buttered muffins. She is a very
sweet lady with a smile straight out of a cake
recipe.*

Mrs Baker Good evening.

Del Good evening. Uh … anyway … look, um
… we'd like a room for the night, you know, you
can chuck in an evening meal, bit of brekkers,
you know, that sort of thing.

Mrs Baker Oh what a shame. I let the last of my
rooms out about an hour ago.

*We see the devastated reaction of the
Trotters.*

Rodney No, you got a sign in the window
saying 'Vacancies'.

Mrs Baker Is the sign still there? Oh that silly
girl. I told her to take it down

*Helen now approaches from kitchen. She
carries a tray upon which we see three plates
containing steak and kidney pie, roast
potatoes, carrots and peas. The food looks
mouth-wateringly appetising.*

Helen Excuse me please.

*We see the frustration on the Trotters' faces
as they study the food.*

Mrs Baker Helen, you forgot to take the sign

out of the window.

Helen Oh I'm sorry, Mrs Baker. I'll just serve dinner then I'll see to it.

Helen exits to dining room leaving the door slightly open.

Mrs Baker I am sorry, gentlemen.

Albert Couldn't we kip down in your front room?

Rodney Yeah, or on the landing.

Del Yeah, or in the airing cupboard, you know, anywhere.

Mrs Baker I'd love to help but it's the regulations, you see.

Rodney Well, is there anywhere round here we can get a room for the night?

Mrs Baker Well, it's difficult. It's a bank holiday weekend you see, and this rail strike doesn't make things any better. You could try … oh no, maybe not.

Del No, please, where?

Mrs Baker *(Loath to say it)* Well, you could try Mrs Creswell's. She's at the Villa Bella just across the square. She's *always* got vacancies.

The Trotters react to the dire portent suggested in Mrs Baker's last words.

Del *(Half-heartedly)* Oh right. Well, thank you, we'll go and knock her up then. Yes. Thanks very much.

As they turn to leave they catch a glimpse inside the dining room. Here we see Mickey Pearce, Jevon and Denzil seated at the table and getting stuck into the steak and kidney pie. A blazing log fire burns in the hearth. They are laughing about the incident in the coach park.

Denzil And the next thing you know – whoosh, up it went!

Mickey Did you see Del Boy's face?

Jevon Oh I wish I'd had my video camera with me.

Mickey *(Spots the Trotters)* Oh, look who's here. It's the Coachbusters!

More laughter.

Jevon Are you staying here as well?

Del No, no, we're … no we're not, no.

Denzil Oh that's a shame, 'cos you would have liked it here.

Mickey Yeah, we've had a lovely hot bath each.

Jevon Nice warm room.

Denzil And the food's great. You would have really liked it here.

Rodney *(Proudly defiant)* Yeah well, we don't care 'cos we got somewhere even better to go.

Del Yeah, yeah. That's right, yeah.

Mickey 'Ere, you're not going to the Villa Bella, are you?

Del Um … no, no, we're not, no, no …

Rodney *(Stumped)* No, no, we're no … We're going down the … it's a secret!

Denzil Well that's a relief. I was beginning to feel guilty 'cos it's so nice here.

Del How's your disease, Denzil?

Denzil *(This kills his laugh)* I have not got a disease! It's an ear infection!

Del *(To Mrs Baker)* Yeah. Mrs Baker, would you make sure that he takes his tablets. Only the doctors down at the clinic for iffy diseases did say that it's not contagious. Well, at least they said they *hope* it wasn't. *(To Denzil, Micky and Jevon)* Bon appetite, gits!

As the Trotters troop up the hallway towards the front door Albert thrusts a hand out towards the cat (not touching it – just frightening it).

Albert *(To cat)* Gertchyer!

We hear the cat meow in alarm.

EXT. NIGHT. MRS CRESWELL'S HOUSE.

The Trotters exit from Mrs Baker's house.

Del Oh look! There it is, look. Villa Bella.

The Trotters walk out of frame leaving us looking at Mrs Baker's lovely little white house. We have a shot as if we are in the doorway of number sixty-seven and looking out at the road. The Trotters arrive and look at the house.

We take their reactions.

Now we cut to see what they are looking at. We see that no. 67 is a dark, brooding house with an overgrown front garden. The window sills and front door are painted brown and are decaying. An eerie, pale light glows in the downstairs window.

Here we see a 'Vacancies' sign. (We could accompany this shot with a flash of lightning and a clap of thunder.)

Del *(Putting a brave face on it)* Oh well. There you are, don't look too bad.

Rodney Don't look too bad? Look at it! It looks like the Munsters' weekend place! Oh come on Del, let's find somewhere else.

Del Oh Rodney, where? We've been everywhere in the town, ain't we, eh? And look at it, it's gonna start chucking it down again in a minute and then we're gonna get soaked and frozen. Now come on, this is our last chance. You never know, it might be rather nice inside.

Albert Well, I'm game!

Del There you are, that's the spirit, Uncle. See? He who dares wins. Hey, go on … go and ring

The Jolly Boys' Outing

the bell. Go and ring the bell. Hurry up.

They approach front door, a sign above which reads: 'Villa Beach' Albert presses doorbell which gives a sudden deep and rasping ring. This makes them jump slightly. They hear heavy, clumping footsteps on an uncarpeted floor approaching door.

The door is opened by Mrs Cresswell. She is a tall, heavy set woman of about fifty-five. She has a hard, unsmiling face. We see the Trotters' reaction.

Mrs Creswell *(London accent)* Yes?

Del *(Reacts)* Blimey! *(Composes himself)* Are you Mrs Creswell?

Mrs. Creswell Yes.

Del Oh! It's just that the lady down the road – Mrs Baker – she uh … recommended us to you. Said you might have a room for the night.

Mrs Creswell looks them up and down critically.

Mrs Creswell Come in.

The Trotters follow her into the house.

INT. NIGHT. MRS CRESWELL'S HOUSE.

Again, the interior reflects the exterior. The house is in fact clean but badly maintained and decorated. It is all browns and other drab colours. A forty-watt light bulb illuminates the hall. The Trotters follow Mrs Creswell to a small table with a visitors book. On the wall is another sign which reads 'Villa Bella.'

Albert *(To Mrs Creswell)* Are you Bella?

Mrs Creswell No. Bella died ten years ago.

Rodney *(Quietly to Del)* I hope they've buried her!

Del It's cold, innit?

Mrs Creswell That's the weather.

Del Oh is it? I do … I don't know, I'm a stranger round here.

Mrs Creswell I've got a three-bedded room vacant. It's ten pounds a night each and that includes a traditional English breakfast.

Del Oh well, that's uh … that sounds just the ticket, Mrs…. uh … Creswell.

Mrs Creswell That'll be thirty pounds in advance. Sign the book.

Del Oh.

We now see Inga approaching from the kitchen. She is a short, stocky girl of about twenty-five. She has short cropped hair and a surly manner. She is Irish but looks Bulgarian. She carries two plates in her hands. The plates contain steamed fish, jacket potato and peas.

Mrs Creswell Inga, show these gentlemen up to the Blue Room.

Inga Can't you see I'm serving dinner? I've only got the one pair of hands!

Mrs Creswell *(Angrily)* Well, show them up after you've served dinner!

Inga *(Mumbling under her breath)* You do everything your bloody self round here!

Inga kicks door to dining room open. A sign above dining room door reads: The Semprini Room.

Mrs Creswell *(Referring to Inga)* I'm training her.

Del She's coming on a bundle, ain't she?

Mrs Creswell The front door is locked at 11pm and not opened again until 9am

Del Mrs Creswell, thank you.

Inga exits from the Semprini room, sucking particles of food from her thumbs.

Inga *(To Rodney and Albert)* Come on, it's up here. Would you ever come on?

The Trotters follow Inga upstairs. Mrs Creswell follows them. Del tries to sign the register.

INT. NIGHT. THE BLUE ROOM.

It is nearly two hours later. The room is in darkness. There is just enough light to make out the two beds and that there are bodies in them but we can't tell who's sleeping where. Now we hear Rodney and Albert's voices coming from the double bed.

Albert Move over a bit!

Rodney You've got most of the bed!

Albert You're pulling the covers off me!

Now we hear Del from the single bed.

Del Leave it out you two! You gonna carry on like this all night?

Albert *(To Del)* Tell him to stop pulling the covers off me!

Del Rodney, stop pulling the covers off Albert!

Rodney Well, tell him to get over to his own side of the bed.

Del Albert, will you get over to your own side … Well, this is like spending a long weekend with Zippy and Bungle!

Rodney God knows what Cassandra would say if she was here!

Del Oh, she'd most probably say 'Roddy, what's your uncle doing in bed with us?'

Rodney It's alright for you, Derek, this happens to be my first night away from Cassandra for a whole year!

Del Oh.

Albert I bet she ain't half glad!

Rodney What's that supposed to mean?

Albert Is this the way you carry on when you're in bed with her?

Rodney Well, of course it's not!

Albert So why are you giving me all this aggro?

Rodney Beca ... because there is a great deal of difference between sleeping with Cassandra and kipping with *you*!

Albert Like what?

Rodney Like ... Alright, like she smells nice! Like, she wears ... *(Realises he's said the wrong thing)* ... things!

Del Oi, oi, oi! Woh back! Woh back!

Rodney And like she hasn't got a dopey white beard that keeps tickling me!

We hear thumping on the wall.

Rodney See, you've woken somebody up now!

Del Rodney, look, come on, it's only quarter past ten. Let's whip down the old Mardi Gras, eh? Have a couple of ... a couple of jars, you know, scampi supper, eh? What d'you reckon? What d'you reckon?

Rodney *(Obviously tempted)* No. Look. I promised Cassandra I wouldn't go out and I intend to keep that promise.

Pause.

Albert D'you reckon she believed you?

Rodney About what?

Albert When you said you wouldn't go out on the town.

Rodney Well of course she believed me ... Why?

Albert Nothing.

Del Uncle, you're not trying to suggest that if Cassandra thought that Rodney was going out on the razzle that she would go out on the razzle as well, are you?

Albert What, you mean what's good for the goose is good for the gander?

Del Yeah.

Albert No.

Del Oh.

Rodney Cassandra wouldn't have gone out.

Albert How'd you know that?

Rodney Because *I* haven't gone out.

Del Yeah, but how does she know that?

Rodney Beca ... She just does, right? Our marriage is based on trust.

Del Yeah, he's right. Cassandra wouldn't go out enjoying herself.

Rodney Thank you.

Del She wouldn't have to, she's got that flat to herself.

Rodney So what?

Del No, hey, I ... I just meant if she felt a bit 'lonely' – she could invite someone round.

Albert Yeah, like that couple at your anniversary – Stephen and his wife.

Rodney So what's wrong with that?

Del Nothing. Nothing. No, it'll be a bit of company for Cassandra.

Albert She seemed to get on well with that Stephen.

Rodney Oh c ... of course they get on well. They work together at the bank, he's a colleague. In fact he's more than a colleague, he's on top ... he's her immediate superior.

Pause.

Rodney *(Now remembers)* No, anyway, she couldn't have invited them two round, 'cos Stephen's wife's gone away for the weekend, d'you remember?

Del Oh yeah.

Pause.

Now Rodney sits bolt upright in bed.

Rodney *(Very confused)* ... If that Stephen's been round my flat I'll kill him!

Del What? Oh! What put that idea in your head?

Rodney I don't know! It's ... it's just something that's been bugging me!

Del Well, what d'you wanna do? You wanna, you know, pop out for a drink and sort of talk about it, hmm?

Albert Yeah, it might make you feel better Rodney.

Rodney Yeah, well, I suppose I could manage a ... *(Now eyes the two of them angrily as he realises what has been happening)* This is a conspiracy, innit? You two are in league with each other, ain't ya! *(To Del)* You just want me to come to the night-club with you. *(To Albert)* And you want the bed to yourself Well it ain't gonna work! I promised Cassandra I would not go out and I am not going out! Alright?

Del Alright, alright, keep your hair on. No, we was only geeing you up. We didn't mean any harm.

Rodney Alright. Well let's shut up about it and get some sleep.

The three lay down.

Del Do with an extra blanket, I'm freezing in here.

Rodney Yeah, it is a bit cold, innit?

Albert Cold? You bits of kids don't know the meaning of the word. You should have been with me on the Russian convoys. One night it was so cold the flame on my lighter froze.

Rodney *(To Del)* Come on then, just one quick light ale.

INT. NIGHT. MARDI GRAS NIGHTCLUB.

As we join scene Del and Rodney are seated

The Jolly Boys' Outing

at a table eating scampi in a basket.
Their table is situated very close to the stage
where a singer is performing.

Del Blinding bit of scampi, innit, eh? It's fresh an' all, you know. Straight out of the sea into your basket.

Rodney You don't get scampi off this coast!

Del Of course you do! It's the sea, innit?

Rodney Yeah, but it's *Margate*!

Del Yeah I know, but the scampi don't know that, do they?

Rodney No, I s'ppose not.

Del 'Ere, what was that starter that ... um ... Cassandra made us last week?

Rodney Moules Mariniere.

Del Mmm! That's it. They were lovely moules, an' all, weren't they, eh? 'Cos she's got style, see. I mean, that Cassandra is a classy lady.

Rodney I suppose so.

Del No, no suppose so about it. I mean, a lot of people – you know, cheapos – would have used mussels – not Cassandra.

Rodney *(As if trying to broach a very delicate subject)* We get on well.

Del Mmm? Yeah, of course we do! Blimey!

Rodney No, I meant me and Cassandra.

Del Oh, I see. Well that's good, Because I mean, your missus should be more than just your wife, you know. She should be your best mate an' all.

Rodney Yeah. It's just ... sometimes you get the feeling ... I don't know how to explain it ... Have you ever read a book ... *(Realises that Del has never read a book)* ... Well have you ever seen the *film* where someone marries beneath themselves?

Del Oh, don't start that, Rodney! You have not married beneath yourself! Cassandra comes from a very lovely family! Your problem is you're letting her rule you. I mean, that cobblers tonight – you know, she wouldn't let you out! I mean, what are you, a man or a mouse? You've gotta learn to assert yourself. I mean, I may sound old-fashioned, but you take my word for it, in the end a man likes a woman to be a woman! And a bird likes a bloke to be a bloke!

Rodney *(New-found pride and determination)* D'you know, you're right!

Del Mmm, that is Bonnet de Douche, as they say in the Basque region.

Rodney *(Emphatic agreement)* Absolutely!

Del Yeah, that's it. Oh, 'ere, come on. Drink up, we'll have another one ... Look who's here, the three Musketeers. *(Calls)* Oi Boycie! Boycie, over here!

We see Boycie, Mike and Trigger have arrived.

Boycie Hello Del.
They move to the Trotters' table.

Del *(Loudly – at least above the music)* It's good here, innit eh?

Boycie Stunning.

Del Yeah, they got a magician, a singer and a comedian. The singer'll be on in a minute!
The singer sings a few more words then reacts to Del's line, continues singing.

Boycie So where are you staying?

Del Oh, we got a *lovely* little bed and breakfast, ain't we, Rodney?

Rodney Yeah, it's *really* good!

Boycie Yes, well, me, Mike and Alan booked into a hotel, down on the front.

Trigger I got a room in a motel. They don't know I ain't got a car! *(Winks in a 'fooled 'em' way)*

Mike I'd keep quiet about that if I was you, Trig.

Trigger Not half.

The singer ends her act. Applause. Eddie enters stage. Now as Eddie introduces the next act, the Jolly Boys' splinter group go into conversation. We may just about be able to hear the introduction.

Eddie *(Over the Jolly Boys' dialogue)* And now the Margate Mardi Gras is very proud to introduce to you one of Europe's greatest magicians. Ladies and gentlemen, will you give a big Mardi Gras welcome to the Great Ramondo and Raquel.

The Great Ramondo and Raquel are on stage in background. There is a board on an easel which tell us it is indeed: The Great Ramondo and Raquel. Ramondo goes into his act with a gentle trick – turning several scarves into a big silk scarf.
Raquel is prancing around Debbie Maghee fashion with the fixed smile of the synchronised swimmer.

Rodney *(Over the above introduction and entrance)* Oi! Where's Alan?

Boycie Oh of course, you wouldn't have heard about that, would you? Well, you know how much Alan loves shellfish? Well he ate half the ocean bed today. Until at some time or another, he copped an unfortunate whelk!

Trigger *(Has noticed Raquel)* Where have I seen that bird before?
They all look to stage.

Mike It's that sort, wossername? *(To Del)* The one you went out with for a while, Del.

Boycie It's Raquel, the strippagram!

Del No, it is not!

Rodney It is, Del.

Del Mmm?

Rodney You look at the board: The Great Ramondo and Raquel!

Del Blimey! It is her!

On stage Ramondo is in the process of turning a scarf into a dove.
As he does so we see Del stand.

Del *(To Raquel)* Pssstt.

Ramondo doesn't hear this and produces the dove to rapturous applause. He guides the dove gently in Raquel's direction. The dove flies onto her outstretched arm. Ramondo now starts producing another dove.

Del Pssttt!

This time Ramondo hears the noise. He looks down inside his jacket, worried that his 'balloon trick' may have started too early. He produces the second dove and it flies to Raquel's arm. Ramondo is now producing the third dove.

Del Raquel!

We see that Raquel has heard someone call her. She squints out through the stage lights to the audience. As Ramondo produces the third glove and guides it in Raquel's direction, so Raquel spots Del.

Raquel *(Delighted and excited at seeing him)* Del?

At this point she drops her arm. The two doves sitting on her arm fly off, leaving a few feathers floating. The third dove, finding nowhere to land, joins his two friends in flying all around the room.
We see them flying over the heads of the guests. We see Ramondo's reaction. He has feathers floating down in front of his face and his highly trained doves are whizzing all over the shop.

Del *(To Raquel)* Alright?

Raquel now tries to regain her professional composure. The audience is hushed, embarrassed by the performers' embarrassment. But Del, who doesn't know a good performance from a bad one and is in love with Raquel, applauds.

Del Ah! Ha ha! Bloody clever that, innit eh? Marvellous!

INT. NIGHT. MARDI GRAS NIGHTCLUB.

We find Del and Raquel seated at the bar. Raquel is wearing a silk dressing gown as if to suggest that she is still in costume and is due back on stage.

Raquel So I got back to England about six months ago. I wasn't sure what to do with myself – I haven't got any family, except a brother in Milton Keynes, but we haven't spoken for years. So I saw my agent and she tied me in with Ray.

Del Ray? Oh yeah.

Raquel He was working in a holiday camp down in Devon – his last assistant had walked out on him – well, he's a bit of a pig. Anyway, after that we got a three- month contract here. Oh, it's not much but it's a job, it keeps a roof over my head.

Del Yeah … I didn't mean to let you down, you know. I was on my way round to see you and I was … um … unexpectedly arrested.

Raquel I know, it's alright, you've already explained.

Del Why didn't you write to me?

Raquel Write to you? I thought you'd dumped me! I've got pride, Del! I've never written to the other blokes who've dumped me and I wasn't starting with you!

Del D'you want another drink?

Raquel No, I'm back on stage in a little while … there's been no one else. I mean, since we split up – I haven't – you know – I've not been interested.

Del *(Lying through his teeth)* No, no, nor me.
Raquel knows he's lying and grins at him.

Del No, no, honest!

Raquel Yeah, alright, I believe you.

Del Anyway, what you gonna do … uh … when this contract's finished?

Raquel Oh, I'm leaving the act. I can't stand Ray anymore. He's got a temper, sometimes he frightens me. Don't know where I'll go.

Del Peckham's very nice this time of year.

Raquel Is it?

Del I know a lovely little flat you could stay at, an' all.

Raquel Oh, maybe I'll try Peckham then. Thanks.

Del Raquel, would you give me your autograph?

Raquel Get away!

Del No, I mean it, straight. Honest.

Raquel I've never given an autograph before.

Del Well look, it's easy. *(Hands her a beer mat from the bar)* All you got to do, look, is just write your name … and your address and your telephone number.

She smiles and writes.
As she is doing this we see an angry Ramondo approaching. He is still in costume.

Del *(To Ramondo)* Alright? Get your pigeons back alright?

Ramondo Yes, I did! Raquel, I don't know what

The Jolly Boys' Outing

the hell you were playing at on that stage, but don't you ever let that happen again!

Raquel I'm sorry, Ray. I was distracted.

Ramondo Oh! Professionals are not distracted, love! You either get your act together or you find somewhere else! There's plenty more where you came from. We're on in ten minutes!

Raquel Alright, Ray, I'm coming.

Ramondo exits.

Del *(Seething)* D'you want me to whack him for you? Eh?

Raquel Del, please, please! Stay out of it! My contract hasn't long to run so all I want to do is keep him sweet. Besides, he's right, it was unprofessional of me.

Del Oh well.

Raquel I'll see you then.

Del Yeah. You've still got my address, haven't you?

Raquel Yeah.

Del Yeah, well, you know, you can write to me or phone me, you know, if you like. You won't forget, will you?

Raquel Oh, I'll never forget you, Del.

She kisses him and then exits.

Del watches her departure, love beaming from his eyes.

EXT. NIGHT. MRS CRESWELL'S HOUSE.

It is now the early hours of Sunday morning. We see Del and Rodney returning from the nightclub. Rodney is tired and ready for bed. Del is alive with the joys of having met Raquel again.

Del *(Sings)* The most beautiful sound I ever heard.

Rodney Will you keep your noise down?

Del *(Continues singing)* Raq … ue … l!

Rodney People are tryin' to sleep!

Del She's lovely though, ain't she, Rodney? Eh? She's lovely isn't she?

Rodney Yeah she's lovely, now shut up!

They arrive at Mrs Creswell's house..

They approach the front door.

Del *(Produces front door key)* Sshhh!

He turns key in lock but the door doesn't open.

Del It's locked!

Rodney It's what?

Del It's locked.

Rodney Oh, that's right, she said she locks it at eleven! What time is it now?

Del It's twenty to two. I'll just have to ring the bell.

Rodney You can't ring the bell, you'll get Mrs Creswell out of her coffin!

Del Well what we gonna do then, eh? We can't hang round here till the morning, can we?

Rodney Del, if you wake her up she'll sink her teeth into our necks before you can say, 'wooden stake'!

Del You're frightened of her, ain't you?

Rodney *(Shakes his head emphatically)* Yes!

Del Well, I'm not!

Rodney Well, *you* ring the bell! I'm gonna hide behind the wall.

Rodney creeps round to the front of the house. Del determinedly turns to the house. A cold fear now grips his stomach.

Del Alright, maybe there's another way out of this.

Del joins Rodney. They survey the upstairs windows.

In one window we see the glow from a bedside lamp.

Del That's our room, innit? That one?

Rodney Yeah, I think so.

Del Right! *(Calls up to window in hushed tones)* Albert!

Rodney Albert! Abandon ship!

There is no response.

Rodney Throw something up at the window.

Del Yeah, alright.

Del reaches into the darkness. He now throws something at window (we don't see what he throws).

We now hear an almighty crash of breaking glass – not a tinkle – it's as if a sledgehammer has just gone through the window. Del and Rodney protect their heads from the danger of falling glass.

Del You wally, Rodney, now look what you've gone and done!

Rodney Me?

Del Yeah. You were the one that said go on throw something up at the window!

Rodney I meant a little pebble, you just chucked half a paving stone through it!

Del Sssh.

We now hear voices coming from inside the house.

Inga *(OOV)* Mrs Creswell! One of our windows has just been smashed!

Mrs Creswell *(OOV)* I heard it! Phone the police, Inga.

Rodney Oh, that's all I need, innit? I'm gonna get nicked twice in one day!

Del Look alive, Rodney, look alive. Just get out of here. Come on, let's get out, let's get out.

Rodney and Del dash off down street.

INT. NIGHT. RAQUEL'S HALLWAY.

The hallway is in darkness. On the wall is an intercom device.

As we join scene the intercom is buzzing. It stops. Now starts buzzing again.

Door to lounge opens and Raquel enters hallway. She is wearing a dressing gown over her nightdress and is still half-asleep. She presses intercom.

Raquel Hello?

We now hear Del's distorted voice over intercom.

Del *(OOV)* Hello, Raquel? It's Del Boy.

Raquel Del? What d'you want? It's two o'clock in the morning!

Del *(OOV)* Yeah I know. I'm sorry to disturb you, sweetheart, but Rodney's been and got us into a bit of trouble.

We now hear Rodney's distorted voice – his voice is slightly more distant than Del's – as if he is standing behind Del.

Rodney *(OOV)* I didn't get us into this!

Del *(OOV)* Yeah you did! It was your bright idea, weren't it, eh?

Rodney *(OOV)* You chucked the bloody thing!

Del *(OOV)* I know but you said …

Raquel *(Interrupts)* Yeah, look, look, look, look, wait! What's wrong?

Del *(OOV)* Oh, we've been locked out of our digs and we've got nowhere to kip for the night. We was wondering if you could put us up till the morning.

Raquel *(Agonises for a moment)* It's a bit awkward, Del.

Del *(OOV)* Oh Raquel. It's freezing out here! We've just bumped into a brass monkey crying his eyes out.

Raquel Oh, alright then. *(Presses button on intercom)* Push the door and come up.

Del *(OOV)* Oh good girl. You know it makes sense.

Raquel opens the front door a few inches and then exits to lounge.

INT. NIGHT. RAQUEL'S LOUNGE.

Four doors lead off lounge. One is the entry door from the hallway. One is the entry door to kitchen, another is the door to the first bedroom and the fourth one is the door to the second bedroom. Raquel enters from the hall.

She goes immediately to the wall mirror and starts brushing her hair and checking her face and clothes in an effort to smarten herself up. Del and Rodney now enter the lounge from

the hallway, their collars turned up against the cold.

Del *(Referring to the warmth of the lounge)* Oh, that's better. Cor, it's 'taters out there.

Rodney Oh, sorry about this, Raquel.

Raquel Oh, that's okay. So what happened?

Del Well, the old girl where we were staying, she locks her doors at eleven. Well, I mean, we didn't leave your nightclub till gone one, did we?

Raquel *(Gesturing to the furniture)* Well, I'm afraid an armchair and a settee is the best I can offer you.

Del No, no, that's … that's great. Go on. No, that's … that'll be lovely, Raquel. Yeah. It's alright, look, we'll be away first thing in the morning – 'cos our new coach comes about nine o'clock. Listen, sweetheart, you can't give us something to warm the old cockles, can you?

Raquel Yeah, ok. I'll make you a coffee.

Del *(Disappointed)* Oh yeah. Cushty. Cushty.

Raquel exits to kitchen.

Del She's a blinding bird, ain't she, Rodney, eh?

Rodney What, Raquel? Yes. T'riffic, Del.

Del She's got a radiant smile, have you noticed that?

Rodney What, her radiant smile?

Del Yeah.

Rodney Yeah.

Del Yeah, well, you can't miss it can you? I mean, you know … I mean when she walks in she … well she lights up a room.

Rodney Yeah. Most of your birds walk in and light up a fag. *(Laughs. But the laugh soon dies)*

Del *(At first he looks offended. Now he smiles)* Yeah! Yeah, and she's as straight as a die, you know, straight as a die. She don't mess around with other blokes, you know.

Rodney *(Turns on Del venomously as his Freudian slip shows)* What, you're saying Cassandra does?

Del *(Deeply offended at the accusation)* No! No, course not. No, I've got nothing against the girl!

Rodney That's alright then. 'Cos if I thought you … Sorry.

Del You're a touchy little git sometimes, ain't you, eh? All I was just saying was, that since Raquel met me she hasn't been out with any other blokes.

Rodney Well she only met you two hours ago!

Del No, I don't mean this time! I mean like the first time!

Rodney Oh, right.

Del Yeah, she has been true unto me.

Del smiles towards kitchen in a child-like, almost angelic manner. Now the door to the

The Jolly Boys' Outing

first bedroom opens and the great Ramondo enters the lounge. He is wearing pyjamas, a dressing-gown and carpet slippers. His hair is in a 'just woke up' state and he is yawning. We see Del and Rodney's reactions.

Ramondo *(Doesn't spot the Trotters immediately, calls towards the kitchen)* Raquel, what's all the noise?

Del The Great Ramondo?

Ramondo What you doing here?

Del *(Snarling like a little Rottweiler who is about to defend his territory)* What am *I* doing here?

Rodney *(Trying to relieve the situation, he speaks incredibly quickly)* Um ... We was locked out of our digs and Raquel said we could spend the night here but we're gonna go soon!

Ramondo Oh did she? Well, we'll see about that! *(Exiting to kitchen)* Raquel. What's the idea of letting strangers into the flat without even asking me?

Ramondo closes the kitchen door behind him.

Del I'm gonna kill him! Gonna kill him!

Rodney No, stay calm, Derek!

Del It's gonna take a bloody good surgeon three or four hours to get his magic wand back!

Rodney Oi, oi, oi, oi, oi! Now come on, calm down!

Del I wanna know what the hell is going on here.

Rodney Look, sit down!

Del Look, I'm not having any magician ...

Rodney Sit down!

Reluctantly Del forces himself to sit on settee, but all the time he is straining at the leash.

Rodney Now, look, there's probably a pefectly simple explanation to this.

Del Like what?

Rodney Well, how the hell should I know?

Del There is a simple explanation, Rodney. The Great Ramondo's a bleeding bully boy! Raquel told me. He's got her trapped here. If she don't play ball with him not only has she lost her job but she's lost her home as well! That's blackmail and I don't like that sorta thing! I'm gonna sort it out right now.

Rodney Oi, oi! You're not certain of anything! Don't jump to conclusions. Look, for all you know them two might be ... well, you know.

Del What?

Rodney Well, I don't know ... look, just find out what the situation is first, right? Nice 'n' easy, Del? Right? Nice 'n' easy.

Del Alright! Alright, Rodney. I'm just gonna go in there and just gonna ask a few questions and, you know, like ... and that's all.

Rodney And what happens if you don't like the answers?

Del Well, that's life, innit, eh? Just I'll know where I stand then, won't I, eh?

Rodney Alright.

Del opens the kitchen door.

Del *(Into kitchen)* Alright. Excuse me ... I'm terribly sorry to bother you. I just wondered if we could have a little chat? See if we could come to some sort of a ... an understanding.

Del enters kitchen and leaves door open behind him.

Rodney lays back on settee and sighs heavily. He is feeling tremendous and desperate sympathy for his brother. Now the Great Ramondo re-enters lounge backwards and through the open kitchen door. He finishes his journey crumpled up against a wall. We see Rodney. He is unmoved by this. He half-expected it and blokes being punched through doors have been part of his life for as long as he can remember. Del now appears at the open door.

Rodney That's the way, Del, nice 'n' easy.

Del walks across the fallen Ramondo.

Del *(To Ramondo)* Now do you understand what I was trying to say, eh?

Raquel enters from kitchen.

Raquel Why the hell did you do that?

Del It's alright, it's alright Raquel. It's alright. You don't have to be frightened of the Great Ramondo no more – Del Boy's here?

Rodney whistles the opening bar of the theme from 'The Good, the Bad and the Ugly'.

Del Rodney? *(To Ramondo)* Right, Ramondo – or can I just call you Great, eh? Do you understand what I've been subtley trying to indicate? You are *out*, pal! Your lease has expired! This is nature's little way of trying to tell you to get your arse down the road apiece!

Moves to first bedroom door and exits to first bedroom.

Ramondo *(Pleading with Raquel)* Why don't you explain to him?

Raquel He hasn't given me the chance!

Ramondo *(To Rodney)* You'd better warn him I was in the Territorials!

Rodney I don't think that's gonna cut a lot of ice with him, somehow.

Del enters from first bedroom. He is carrying the jacket of Ramondo's costume and a suitcase. Ramondo flinches away from Del.

Del Alright! There's your coat!

As Del hands Ramondo the jacket so playing

cards fall from the sleeves. Del opens the window and throws suitcase out.

Del There's your case and … and there's the front door! *(Indicates window)* Or would you prefer to take the more direct route?

Ramondo Can I just say something?

Del Yes alright. You can say something. You better make it quick and you better make it polite – there is a lady present!

Ramondo There is nothing going on between Raquel and me!

Del Nothing going on between you two? A fella and a bird sharing a flat, there's nothing going on! What d'you take me for?

Ramondo Look, I assure you it's the truth! You see … I'm … I'm … Raquel is not my type!

Raquel lowers her eyes. She knows it was tough for Ramondo to make this confession in front of total strangers. We see that Rodney has caught on.

Del What d'you mean she's not your type? *(Indicates Raquel)* You could do a lot worse than that.

Raquel *(Opens first bedroom door)* This is Ray's room… *(Opens second bedroom door)* This is my bedroom … Do you see what Ray's saying? If I was the last woman on God's earth I *still* wouldn't be his type!

Del is totally bewildered. He turns to Rodney.

Rodney Take your time, Del.

Ramondo You see, it's purely a financial situation – it's cheaper than us paying for separate flats.

Del *(Finally twigs)* Oh! You mean you're …

Ramondo *(He's not ashamed)* Yes.

Del Well, why didn't you say?

Ramondo It's not the sort of thing one drops into an introduction.

Del now feels genuinely wretched and embarrassed about the whole thing.

Del God – I'm terribly sorry! What must you think of me?

Ramondo No need, really. Over and done with.

Del *(To Raquel)* Well you see I … I didn't know.

Raquel *(Angry with him)* You didn't ask, did you???

Del No, you see I thought … well, I thought that … you see I thought … I mean I … you see … I s … I … didn't I, Rodney?

Rodney Yeah, yeah he did.

Del *(To Ramondo)* You see … ooh … oh dear, I do believe I may have dropped your suitcase out of the window.

Ramondo I'll fetch it. I could do with the air.

Ramondo exits to hallway.

Del *(To Raquel)* No, you see, I'm … you see I thought …

Raquel No, no, no, Del, you didn't *think*! You never think! You don't look, you don't listen, you don't notice any of the signs! You just go at it like a mad bull!

Del I only did it for you!

Raquel Well, if that's supposed to make me feel better, it doesn't!

Raquel storms into second bedroom and slams door behind her.

Pause.

Rodney They might publish your diaries one day, Del. I reckon that could be a winner. I don't believe you sometimes! Why did you do that?

Del He Who Dares Wins, I've always been the same!

Rodney Well, this time I reckon that He Who Dared cocked it right up!

Pause.

Raquel exits from second bedroom carrying pillows and blankets. She hurls them down on settee.

Rodney *(Politely)* Thank you.

Del looks at her like a little lost puppy lost in a storm.

Raquel *(Still angry with him)* I know you did it for me but you were stupid and you were embarrassing!

Del just nods.

Raquel *(Without weakening her hard look she kisses him on the forehead)* Thank you.

As Raquel exits to second bedroom Rodney is left open-mouthed. Del has a grin that could light London.

Del turns to Rodney.

Del *(Thumbs up)* Mag-ic!

EXT. DAY. RODNEY AND CASSANDRA'S BLOCK OF FLATS.

The replacement coach pulls up outside the flats (the windows of the coach are covered in condensation suggesting a long and uncomfortable journey). The coach doors open and a tired, unshaven Rodney alights.

Rodney *(Calls back into coach)* Right then, I'll see you.

We hear a few tired voices call their goodbyes.

As the goodbyes finish we hear Trigger's voice from somewhere deep in the coach.

Trigger *(OOV)* See you, Dave.

Now, at one of the windows, we see a very tired looking Del wipe the condensation away as if he has just woken and is trying to find

The Jolly Boys' Outing

his bearings.

Del Oi oi! Rodders! Rodney! Here! Oi, here a minute! Come here a minute! Listen. You are master of your own flat.

Rodney *(Bored with all the advice)* Yeah, okay.

Del You're a man. Don't want any rules, no collars and lead.

Rodney Alright, Del, alright!

Del Right then. You've gonna go in there, put your foot down with a firm hand and let her know where she stands. Right? You've just … you just gotta sort it out, alright? Just, you know sort it out.

Rodney Alright. I'll see you.

Del Yeah, I'll see you then. Ta ta.

Rodney walks off towards block.

INT. DAY. RODNEY AND CASSANDRA'S LOUNGE/DINER.

At this point no one is in room.

The door to the bedroom is open and reveals an unmade bed. The door to the kitchen is open slightly.

Rodney enters through the main door and surveys the room. Del's 'bubbles' print is on the floor and propped against the wall ready to be returned to the cupboard. Cassandra now enters from the bedroom. She is buttoning her blouse or putting earrings on – enough to suggest she is still getting dressed.

She seems surprised to see him – not panicked – just surprised.

Cassandra *(Unsmiling – she's still got the hump with him)* Oh – I didn't expect you back this early.

Rodney No … well, here I am. Cass, can we have a talk?

Cassandra I don't think this is an appropriate time, Roddy. Maybe later.

Rodney Look, I really think we ought to sit down and discuss …

His speech is cut short by Stephen's entry from the kitchen. Stephen is smartly but casually dressed.

Stephen *(Also seems surprised to see Rodney)* Oh! Hi, buddy, how's it going?

Rodney *(A controlled anger)* What are you doing here?

Stephen Oh, I was just passing. So how was Margate?

Rodney Forget Margate! What are you doing in *my* flat?

Stephen Hey, back off, Rod! I mean, what's the problem?

Cassandra Roddy, what's wrong?

Rodney Well, I'll tell you the problem, shall I? There's something I've really wanted to do for a long time but I've … I've never got round to it! *(To Stephen)* So let me run this past you, Stephen. Try and get your head round this.

*Rodney now belts Stephen right on the nose.
Rodney is not a violent man and chances are
this is the first fight he's had since school. He
wouldn't have the style of a street fighter but
he jabs out a pretty good and powerful
straight right.*

*It knocks Stephen onto the armchair which
topples over with his weight. Stephen is not
hurt badly by the punch, it's more a case of
shock.*

Cassandra *(Horrified by it)* Rodney!

Rodney *(Points a warning finger at his fallen
rival)* Now you know where I'm coming from!
Okay? *Buddy!*

*Rodney now turns slightly and catches sight
of Joanne who has just entered from the
kitchen carrying a tray with three cups of
coffee.*

Rodney *(Casually)* Alright, Joanne? *(Reacts)*
Joanne!

Joanne What have you done to Stephen?
*She places the tray down and rushes to her
husband.*

Stephen *(A very slight smudge of blood on
nose. He speaks with that pinched, nasal sound
of someone with an injured nose)* He punched
me on the nose!

Rodney *(To Cassandra)* Well, what's she doing
here? I thought she was going away for the
weekend to her parents!

Cassandra She was but there was a rail strike!
*(Produces a holiday brochure – safari picture on
front)* Joanne brought this holiday brochure
round for us!

Rodney *(To Cassandra)* D'you see anything in it
you like?

INT. DAY. TROTTERS' LOUNGE.

*This is an hour later. Del is now showered and
shaved. He wears a lairy, towelling dressing-
gown.*

He is talking to Raquel on his cordless phone.

Del *(On phone)* Hello sweetheart? How are you
today? Oh good. How's the Great Ramondo…
Oh yeah … Well, I'm sure in his heart of hearts
he understood … Oh, we've been back about an
hour … Yeah. Mm? No, everyone's alright. Mm-
hmm … We dropped … uh … Rodney off at his
house, yeah … Cassandra? No, she'll be alright,
she'll be as good as gold. Rodney's a bit of a
charmer on the quiet – no, he knows how to
handle situations … Yes I know, sometimes I
wish I was a bit more like him as well … Yeah.

Old, uh … Albert. He's feeling much better now,
yeah … Oh, didn't you hear? He got a whack on
the head.

*Albert enters from kitchen carrying a mug of
tea and a plate of toast. He has a large plaster
stuck on his forehead.*

Del *(cont)* I dunno, I dunno. The strangest thing.
He was lying in bed last night when all of a
sudden a rock came flying through the window,
and it caught him a glancing blow on the head
… Dunno, it's a mystery!

Albert It's no mystery to me! Bloody yobbos
done it! They should be locked up!

Del That's right, Unc. That is absolutely right,
yeah.

Albert Tell her what happened to Boycie and
Mike when they was walking home from the
nightclub.

Del What? What was that?

Albert Someone chucked a suitcase through a
window. Caught Mike right on the shoulder –
fortunately Boycie's head broke its fall.

Albert exits to kitchen.

Del *(On phone)* It's a terrible old world, innit, eh
sweetheart? Listen Raquel. Raquel, you have …
you have forgiven me now, haven't you
sweetheart? Oh good. You know it makes sense.
(Picks up Albert's mug of tea) … Uh, listen, I was
thinking about taking the van out for a test drive
next Saturday, well I'm fitting a new radio, yeah.

*Albert now enters from kitchen with a boiled
egg. He looks for his tea.*

Del I was … uh … thinking I might go down to
Margate. I wouldn't be in a hurry to get home …
I was just wondering uh … if you could get the
Great Ramondo to do a disappearing act? Oh
cushty! Yeah. Oh that's great. Yeah … Alright
darling, I'll see you next uh … next Saturday
sweetheart…. Yeah, alright. Bye for now. Bye.

*Del switches phone off and rubs his hands
together.*

Del Lovely Jubbly!

Albert goes to pick up the mug of tea.

Del Oi! What's your game? If you wanna cup of
tea go an' make one, you lazy old sod, go on.

*We hear front door close. Rodney now enters
from the hall. He is wearing the same clothes
and in the same condition as previous scene.
He remains close to the door. Rodney now
drags his suitcase in from the hall (a new
suitcase).*

Del looks at the suitcase then up to Rodney.

Del Alright bruv? Sort it all out?

The Jolly Boys' Outing

Rodney Come Home

INT. DAY. AN ARNDALE CENTRE.

We hear Del and Albert (OOV)

Albert This is no life for an old war hero.

Del *(Couldn't give a toss)* No, I know.

Albert I fought for this country.

Del Yeah? How did you get on?

Albert I wish Rodney was still working with you.

Del I never thought I'd hear myself say it, but so do I. Listen to me Albert, I don't ask much of you, do I? Cook a little bit of grub. Sweep up my apartment and occasionally, just occasionally, act as my lookout.

Albert It's alright for you. I ain't had no lunch and your suitcase is giving me backache.

Del I ain't had no lunch either and your moaning's giving me heartache. Now shut up and get over there.

We see Del and Albert coming up the escalator, inside the shopping mall. Del is wearing his green trenchcoat, and has the suitcase by his side. Albert is wearing his duffle coat.

Albert What are we waiting for?

Del What do you mean? I'll tell you what we're waiting for. The security people change shifts at midday and the new lot always start on the bottom floor, which gives me time to sell on the top floor. Now come on, come on. Let's go.

They move off.

Albert What you got in that suitcase, then? Hooky gear?

Del *(Deeply offended)* How dare you! I don't deal in that sort of stuff – least not since Raquel's been with me – I can't get her involved in anything like that.

Albert So what you worried about?

Del I am an unlicensed trader. Many moons ago I had an unfortunate misunderstanding with a magistrate who took the law into his own hands and banned every council in London from issuing me with a licence. So I've gotta flog where and when I can.

Albert Well can I go an' get something to eat?

Del No you can't, you're my lookout! Anyway, Raquel's making us something when we get back later.

Albert But I'm hungry now!

Del *(Hands him a fiver)* Go on then, go an' get us a couple of hamburgers.

Albert I'm taking no chances. Say I caught mad cow disease!

Del Don't worry about that! I mean, who the hell would notice?

Albert reacts.

INT. DAY. RODNEY'S OFFICE.

Rodney is seated at his desk punching something out on his computer keyboard. He leans back in his chair and rubs his stomach as he suffers hunger pains. He opens his briefcase, produces a paper bag and pulls out a couple of limp sandwiches. He looks at the sad sandwiches and then throws them in the bin.

He looks out through the glass partition to where his secretary, Michelle, is seated. He presses button on his intercom. We cut to Michelle's desk. We hear the intercom buzz. We now see Michelle is wearing walkman headphones and is listening to music as she busily files her long nails. The intercom buzzes again. Finally, through the glass partition we see Rodney leave his desk, exit from office and approach Michelle.

Rodney Michelle … Michelle! *(He switches the walkman off)* Are you going to the hamburger bar in the precinct during your lunch hour?

Michelle No.

Rodney You're new here and I don't think you've caught the gist of my question. You see, I'm the head of the computer section and you are the secretary to the head of the computer section. And when the head of the computer

section asks the secretary to the head of the computer section whether she's going to the hamburger bar in the precinct, the head of the computer section means, 'Go to the hamburger bar in the precinct because the head of the computer section is starving bloody hungry!'

Michelle You want me to go to the hamburger bar?

Rodney If it's not too much trouble. I'd like the juiciest, greasiest hamburger they have on offer.

Michelle But you've got Mr Coleman from Classic Curtains coming to see you in a little while.

Rodney Yes, I know. That's why I can't get out to lunch and need something bringing in.

Michelle No, what I'm trying to say is, do you want to invite Mr Coleman, an important client, into an office that stinks to high heaven of fried onions and grease?

Rodney's mouth attempts an answer but his brain stops it.

Rodney Michelle, it's my office ... Thank you very much, Michelle. You carry on with what you were doing. *(Indicating her long nails)* They look very nice. You'd make Freddy Kruger dead jealous.

Rodney moves to the window. Rodney looks from his window and reacts.
From his POV we see Raquel approach and stop at a bus stop which is close to the office window. She carries two heavy bags of groceries. Rodney opens the window and calls.

Rodney Raquel! How you doing?

Raquel Hi, Rodney!

Rodney D'you fancy a coffee?

Raquel *(She indicates groceries)* I've got to get this stuff home.

Rodney Come in, I'll get one of the drivers to give you a lift.

Raquel You sure?

Rodney Of course. I'll put the kettle on. *(He pulls window to and then mumbles to himself)* She's got bags of *food*! I'll mug her.

INT. DAY. ARNDALE CENTRE.

We come up on Del biting into a big greasy hamburger. Albert is seated next to him, just finishing his hamburger.

Albert You ready then?

Del No, no, no, not yet! Selling is all about timing. You ever seen one of them nature programmes on the DDC, with Richard Attenborough, where a lion is lying in the undergrowth, watching a flock of antelopes?

Well they ...

Cut to shot of hundreds of shoppers passing through the centre.

Del ...they are my antelopes. And just like the lion, I know when the time is right. I instinctively know when the optimum moment arrives and only then, will I strike.

Albert *(Nods understandingly)* Yeah ... During the war ...

Del *(Cuts straight in. Throwing hamburger inn litter bin)* Right, here we go then! You get to your lookout position over there.

Albert And what d'you want me to do?

Del What d'you mean, 'What do I want you to do?' I want you to get over there in your lookout position and lookout!

Albert I meant, if I see the security blokes coming what shall I say?

Del I don't particularly care. Shout, 'There she blows, ship ahoy, man overboard' for all I care. As long as I don't get my collar felt. Blimey, this 'hands-on management' gives me the right 'ump sometimes! *(Indicating case)* Here, get that up here. Look, we should do well with this stuff. They'll be falling over themselves to get their hands on this top quality gear.

Del opens his suitcase. We see it is filled with seven or eight children's dolls. Albert moves to his lookout position.

INT. DAY. RODNEY'S OFFICE.

Raquel is seated at desk, drinking coffee.
Rodney is talking on phone.

Rodney *(On phone)* Yeah, thanks a lot. She's just finishing her coffee. Give us ten minutes. *(Replaces receiver)* Your van awaits.

Raquel Oh thanks.

Rodney So you and Del are still coming round for dinner next week?

Raquel So long as it's still alright with you and Cassandra.

Rodney Oh yeah, we're looking forward to it. Sorry it's taken so long to invite you. We kept meaning to pop in and say hello. Del phoned me to say you were back in town and liv ... liv ... em ... st ... staying at the flat with him ... *and* Albert. When'd you get back?

Raquel A couple of weeks ago. I was over in America, having a great time when suddenly I thought ...

Rodney *(Cuts in)* Hold on a minute, you were in America?

Raquel Didn't Del say?

Rodney No.

Raquel Oh it was wonderful. We were doing

Rodney Come Home

this tour of *My Fair Lady* down the East coast. I was the flower-seller.

Rodney *(Hides his smile)* Cosmic!

Raquel Yeah, alright – it was very cheap and cheerful but I was seeing the world and getting paid. We did Atlantic City, Miami, New Orleans. Then suddenly I get this sort of urge to come home.

(All the references to Del are said in jokey but loving way)

Rodney What, to *Del*?

Raquel Yes, to Del.

Rodney I wouldn't come home from New Orleans to see Del! I wouldn't come home from the New Forest to see Del!

Raquel Oh, you don't see him the way I do. He's lovely.

Rodney There are many words I could use to describe Derek Trotter but lovely is not one of them … How's the old sod keeping?

Raquel He's fine. He seems – I don't know – quieter than when I first met him.

Rodney Del? Raquel, some years ago Del joined a monastery and took a vow of loudness!

Raquel Oh that's not fair. He *has* changed. He's not so loud and brash as he used to be.

INT. DAY. ARNDALE CENTRE.

We come up on Del who is holding up a child's doll and spieling as he demonstrates its various functions.

Del *(Loud and brash)* Right. Gather round. You all know me, ladies, the crusader against inflation, here to offer you yet *another* bargain of a lifetime! These beautifully manufactured little toys retail around the thirty-six quid mark up Oxford Street, but you all know my motto: 'West End goods at Southend prices'. Now normally I'd ask you ten pounds for one of these exquisite, little toys, and you'd tear me arm off at the elbow to get it – but I'm not asking ten pounds, I'm not asking eight pounds! Seeing as I'm in a festive mood I'm letting 'em go at the rock-bottom, never to be repeated price of seven pounds fifty. Give the chavvies a Christmas to remember. This is none of your foreign junk, these are hand-made in Britain and recognised by the toy industry as being the most life-like dolls ever seen. *(Feeds doll with tiny bottle and teat)* They are so life-like they drink from a bottle, they wet themselves, they speak, they cry and if you keep 'em 'till they're thirteen they break out in acne and wanna go to Bros concerts! Would I lie to you? I'll tell you another feature of this doll. They even sing themselves to

sleep with a bedtime lullaby. Listen.

Del presses an unseen button on doll's back. We now hear one of those robotic voice-boxes. It sounds like a small child singing a Chinese lullaby. Del reacts to the Chinese lullaby – this is something he hadn't reckoned on.

We see some of the women laughing and turning away from Del.

Del *(Switches doll off. Thinking on his feet)* And they can help your child learn a foreign language. Very important with 1992 approaching! *(Desperate as the crowd disperses)* Alright, a fiver! Come on, gimme a fiver! *(To the doll)* Big mouth!

INT. DAY. RODNEY'S OFFICE.

Rodney and Raquel continue their conversation and coffee.

Raquel *(Half-laughing at Del's problems)* He's having a lot of trouble with the exhaust pipe on the van. It's got a hole in it.

Rodney Oh that's a shame. The exhaust was the only decent thing on it.

They laugh at this.

Raquel So how are things with you and Cassandra?

Rodney *(His laughter dies. Now on his guard)* How d'you mean?

Raquel I mean are you both well?

Rodney Oh, yeah, great!

Raquel Is Cassandra still studying hard for promotion?

Rodney Yes – she's still a very ambitious lady.

Raquel So married life suits you?

Rodney Yep … Come on then, what's Del been saying?

Raquel He hasn't said anything, honest! Well, alright, he mentioned that you'd had a couple of rows. Once when you upset Cassandra's boss and his wife.

Rodney That was *nothing*! It was a misunderstanding, that's all. Three minutes after it happened we were all laughing at it!

Raquel Del said she chucked you out.

Rodney Only for a couple of days.

Raquel Then another time Cassandra went back to her parents.

Rodney Yes. But that was nothing either! We're happy.

Raquel That's what I wanted to say to you. I know it's none of my business, Rodney – it's just that I've had a marriage break up and I know how these things can start. A lot of people think a marriage comes complete with gift-wrapping.

But it doesn't – it comes in kit-form – you've got to work at it.

> *Before Rodney can answer Alan enters brandishing a file of papers.*

Alan Excuse me, Rodney, I've just noticed we're doing *more* of this cheap printing for Del! We are not running a charity organisation. *(Notices Raquel)* Excuse me ...

Rodney No, no, Alan. Let me introduce you. Raquel, this is Alan, my boss and father-in-law ... He's Cassy's Dad.

Raquel Yeah, I figured that out, Rodney.

Rodney Yeah, of course. Alan, this is Raquel. Her and Del liv ... her and Del ... her and Del are friends.

Alan Yes, he's told me all about you. You're an actress, aren't you?

Raquel Well, some people say that, others tell the truth.

Alan Oh come on, Del speaks very highly of your talents. We'll have to go out to dinner one night – all of us.

Raquel Look forward to it.

Alan So do I. You'll have to excuse me, I've got to meet someone for lunch. *(To Rodney)* We're going to that new Chinese place down by the arches, they say the food's out of this world.

Rodney *(His stomach rumbling)* good!

Alan *(Pats the file he has just brought in)* Just keep a closer eye on ... 'things', Rodney. This cheap-printing is very good for some people – unfortunately it's not for us! See you again, Raquel.

Raquel Yes, bye.

> *Alan exits.*

Raquel I'd better be going too.

INT. DAY. PRINT WORKS.

Raquel Why don't you pop in on your way home from work this evening? Del hasn't seen you for ages. I'm doing roast chicken, jacket potatoes, and all the trimmings, there'll be plenty there if you're peckish.

Rodney *(Tempted)* Na. I'll take a raincheck on it. I've just got my timings and route figured out to avoid the traffic jam on the one-way system. Some other time, eh? The driver's waiting for you outside.

Raquel Okay. Give my love to Cassy. Bye.

> *Raquel exits.*

Rodney *(Mumbles)* Roast chicken and all the trimmings!

INT. DAY. RODNEY'S OFFICE.

> *Rodney plunges into the bin and retrieves one*

of his discarded sandwiches. We see the sandwich is dotted and smeared with various coloured inks. There is a clean section at the top. Rodney gingerly bites into the clean section.
> At this very moment Michelle opens the door and enters, followed by a businessman.

Michelle It's Mr Coleman from Classic Curt ...
> *Michelle and Mr Coleman react to Rodney and the sandwich. Rodney sheepishly throws the sandwich in bin.*

Rodney *(As much confidence as he can muster in the circumstances)* Hi.

INT. NIGHT. RODNEY AND CASSANDRA'S LOUNGE/KITCHEN.

> *This is five hours later.*
> *Music is coming from the record-player. Cassandra exits from the bedroom. She is wearing casual clothes. She carries a sports bag which has the head of a badminton racquet sticking out of it.*
> *She places the bag on the settee and goes to record player. She removes record and places it in LP cover. (We see the LP cover and the name – Fergal Sharkey)*
> *Rodney enters from front door.*

Rodney Hi-ee.

Cassandra Hi ... *(They kiss)* You're late this evening.

Rodney Yeah, I got stuck in a traffic jam on the one-way system. *(Removing overcoat and sniffing air)* That smells good. I'm starving.

Cassandra I just did myself one of those ready-made meals in the microwave.

Rodney *(Uncertain whether this means she hasn't cooked for him)* Oh! Well, I'm starving.

> *Rodney exits to kitchen. Rodney enters and pulls down door on eye-level oven. It is dark and empty inside.*

Cassandra *(Calls OOV)* There's plenty in the freezer.

Rodney Good! *(Pointedly)* What a very clean oven we've got!

Cassandra *(OOV, hasn't quite heard)* Sorry?

Rodney I was just remarking how amazingly clean one can keep these modern ovens! *(Mumbles to himself)* Especially when one never bloody cooks in it!

> *Rodney exits. Rodney enters from kitchen and reacts as he sees Cassandra buttoning or zipping up her coat.*

Rodney You off out somewhere?

Cassandra Yeah.

Rodney *(Quietly)* Good, it'll make a nice change

Rodney Come Home

for you. So what's it tonight? The *bank's* final exams? The *bank's* annual wine and cheese orgy. The *bank's* yoga and target practise course?

Cassandra I'm playing badminton!

Rodney Oh, I see. Where?

Cassandra The bank's sports club.

Rodney Great. You go an' enjoy yourself, Cassandra. I've got a busy evening ahead as well. I'm gonna sit in and read the *bank's* pamphlet on our joint pension policy!

Cassandra Oh, God! Here we go again! Alright, what's wrong this time?

Rodney With me? What could possibly be wrong with me?

Cassandra If you don't stop being so childish, I swear one of these days I'll smother you with your comfort blanket!

Rodney Me – childish? You're the one who's got to start growing up a bit, Cassandra! When are you gonna realise that you've got a marriage – you've got a home – and you've got *me*!

Cassandra Oh, I never forget that, Roddy!

Rodney I never see you. You just use this flat like a base-camp! You zoom in and out of here like a bluebottle with the runs! I've had double-glazing salesmen spend more time in here than you!

Cassandra Well, whatever turns you on!

Rodney And what's that supposed to mean?

Cassandra Look, Rodney, I like to keep myself occupied!

Rodney But you're always out – on your own!

Cassandra Because you never want to go anywhere with me! I've asked you before to come to badminton but you always refuse.

Rodney Because I don't relish the idea of spending an entire evening whacking a dead budgie over a net! Besides, all our social occasions are in some way tied up with the bank!

Cassandra You resent me pursuing a career, don't you?

Rodney No, I admire anyone who tries to advance themselves. But your ideas on advancement come straight out of Rommel's 'A Thousand and One Things Every Good Panzer General Should Know'! It's relentless! It's Blitzkrieg!

Cassandra Roddy, I am not trying to *advance* my career. I am still trying to make up lost ground! *You* of all people should know that!

Rodney I have in some way interrupted Operation Cassandra? And what exactly is it I'm supposed to have done?

Cassandra Oh, it's just little things. Like that

day my boss, Stephen, and his wife came round here and you punched him in the face!

Rodney Oh, we're still on about that, are we?

Cassandra You *broke* his nose!

Rodney Broke it! I didn't break it! Alright, a *tiny*, hairline fracture, that's all! Anyway, it was a long time ago and I've apologised a thousand times for it.

Cassandra I know you have and I'm perfectly willing to be understanding – as long as you are.

Rodney How can I put this, Cass? This seems a ridiculous thing for a husband to say to his wife, but I'd like to see more of you. The only time we're really together is when we're lying in bed.

Cassandra With our backs to each other!

Rodney That's only because you turn your back on me!

Cassandra You started it!

Rodney Did not! And why is it whenever we have a dinner party we always invite *your* family or *your* friends?

Cassandra We invite your friends as well!

Rodney Name me *one* occasion, just one, when my friends have been round here?

Cassandra Last month Mickey Pearce and Jevon *and* their girlfriends came round for the evening.

Rodney I apologised for that.

Cassandra And next week you've invited your brother and Raquel round for dinner.

Rodney I've apologised for that as well. Look, we always promised each other that if a problem arose in our marriage we would sit down and discuss it in a mature and adult way.

Cassandra Fine. Let's sit down and discuss it in a mature and adult way.

They sit.

Rodney You can go first.

Cassandra No, you carry on.

Rodney No, I'd like to hear what you have to say.

Cassandra You started it, Roddy, so you go …

Rodney *(Cuts in quickly)* I didn't *start* anything!

Cassandra You're the one who came home in a mood!

Rodney I didn't have a mood until I came home and realised there was nothing for me to eat. Again!

Cassandra Oh I see! That's what it's *really* all about! I'm supposed to be the little wife who has the dinner on the table waiting for Rodney to come back from the time-warp! This is not 1933, and the sooner you realise that the sooner you'll stop being so bloody childish!

Rodney Cassandra, if you could avert your gaze from the exotica of the banking world for just

one minute, you would realise, as so many women in Peckham realise, that there is *nothing* childish about Rodney Trotter! And *they* would appreciate having a young, successful and vibrant man like me around! *And* they'd most probably do me pie and chips if I fancied it!

Cassandra Well why don't you go and find one of these women?

Rodney (*A pause as he is put on the spot. It's do something or surrender time*) Alright, I will!

Cassandra Well, go on then!

Rodney I will!

Cassandra And take a bottle of ketchup for your pie and chips!

Rodney I will!

Cassandra reacts.

EXT. NIGHT. FORECOURT AND ENTRANCE DOOR TO RODNEY AND CASSANDRA'S FLATS.

The entrance door is wrenched open and a seething Rodney exits. He is wearing his baggy overcoat and carrying a leather flight-bag which contains a few hastily-packed clothes. His expression is that of a volcano about to erupt. He strides away from the door in a very determined manner. Here is a trendy executive childishly leaving his wife.

EXT. NIGHT. GARAGE BLOCK TO RODNEY AND CASSANDRA'S FLATS.

Rodney strides towards the garage door and pulls it up and open. He enters the garage to the right of car (as if going to driver's side). We have a slight pause during which, any second, we expect the engine to start and the car to reverse out. Now Rodney comes riding out on a bike (his flight bag balanced or attached in some way to crossbar). He doesn't push the bike out and then start riding it – he literally rides straight out of the garage and off into the night.

INT. NIGHT. TROTTERS' LOUNGE.

Thirty minutes later.

Del and Raquel are finishing their dinners. The table is covered in a fine tablecloth, they have a bottle of wine and a candle burns in a silver candlestick. There is subdued lighting (just side lights) and it looks romantic – well, as romantic as you can get in Nelson Mandela House.

Del (*Enjoying the meal*) Mmmh! What a meal! 'Je suis, je reste' as they say in Montpellier.

Raquel Does that mean good?

Del Superb! Haven't eaten food this good since my old Mum was alive. What is it again?

Raquel It's chicken!

Del I know it's chicken! I mean what's the dish called?

Raquel It's called Petti di Pollo Trifolati.

Del Say what you like about the French but they're magic with a saucepan and a bit of salt.

Raquel It's Italian.

Del Yeah, I know it's Italian, I was just saying the French are good cooks as well.

Del Raises his glass.

To … the future.

Raquel smiles and they chink glasses.

Del (*Now changing to a more serious and romantic mood. He takes her hand*) Raquel.

Raquel Mmmh?

Del You've been here a couple of weeks or so now, and … well … you know how I feel about you.

Raquel Do I? You've never said.

Del I thought it was obvious … I … I really like you … And … you don't have to answer this right now, but I was wondering whether you would … whether you would …

Suddenly the main lights are switched on, thus ruining the mood. We see an agitated Albert has entered from the bedrooms area. He is rubbing his beard.

Raquel I've kept your dinner warm in the oven, Albert. Is everything alright now?

Albert (*Referring to beard*) I've cut the singed bits off. You should never light a candle when you've got a man with a beard in the house!

Del You shouldn't have leant across the table to reach the bread! I've a good mind to report your beard to the council! If I hadn't been a bit lively with me Liebfraumilch we could have had a towering inferno on the rates.

Albert (*Indicating candle*) I'll eat my dinner in the kitchen, away from that fire hazard!

Albert exits to kitchen.

Del (*Calls*) And be careful when you get the plate out the oven, the gas is still on!

Raquel You were saying?

Del Eh? Oh yeah.

Del moves to light switch by door and switches main lights off, returns to table, taken Raquel's hand and then tries to rekindle the original atmosphere.

Del You see – you're a woman …

Raquel Thank you.

Del And I'm a man. And – let's be honest – No Man's an Island. D'you see what I'm getting at?

Raquel … No.

Del Well, I don't wanna rush things, but would

Rodney Come Home

you … I mean, would you …

The main lights are switched on as a fuming Rodney enters from hall. He is wearing his overcoat and carrying his flight bag and has obviously come straight here after storming out of his own flat.

Rodney That's it – all over – kaput! That was her last chance!

Raquel Good evening, Rodney!

Rodney I have never been so insulted in all my life!

Del Sit down, bruv, and let me have a try!

Albert enters from kitchen.

Albert What's happening?

Raquel Rodney's left Cassandra.

Albert Not again! This is the third time in eighteen months you two have broken up for good!

Rodney This time it's for *good*!

Del Does this mean our invitation to dinner's off?

Rodney *(Pouring a glass of scotch)* Well of course it does!

Raquel What's brought all this about?

Rodney *(Struggling to screw the top back on bottle)* You'll never believe this. She accused me of being childish!

Del *(Mock horror)* No?

Rodney True!

Rodney hurls the screwtop away in frustration.

Stupid thing!

Del Oi! That's my top!

Rodney Tonight was the last straw!

Del What's she do? Step on your Scalextrix?

Rodney Derek, my marriage has broken up! This is no time for sarcasm!

Rodney begins removing things from his flight bag.

Del Yeah, alright, bruv. Listen, calm down, finish your drink then I'll drive you home and we'll sort it all out.

Rodney You don't seem to understand, I'm not going back. Me and Cassandra have finished – for *good*!

Del Albert, Brandy?

Raquel Rodney, you'll have to at least talk to her sooner or later. There'll be things to be discussed.

Del Yeah, like who gets custody of Barbie and Ken.

Rodney It's all a big joke to you, innit, Del?

Del I just think that you and Cassandra are *both* behaving like a couple of ten-year-olds! You've broken up and gone back together more times

than JR and Sue Ellen.

Rodney Well, this time it's for *good*! I'm staying here.

At this point Rodney removes a bottle of tomato ketchup from his bag. He reacts and quickly puts it back again.

Del Albert, you'd better fetch a blanket and a pillow, make a bed for Rodney on the settee.

Rodney Settee? No, I'll kip in me old room.

Del You can't, Rodney. Raquel sleeps in there.

Raquel *(An embarrassed shrug)* Sorry.

Rodney Why's Raquel in my room? I thought you two were …

Del *(Cuts in quickly)* Rodders! Can I have a word with you in the boardroom?

Rodney moves across and joins Del in a hushed and private conversation.

Rodney I thought you and Raquel …

Del *(Cuts in)* No.

Rodney You mean you're not ..?

Del *(Cuts in)* No.

Rodney But she's been here over a fortnight.

Del *(Drops the 'l' in 'I know')* 'know.

Rodney Must be a record.

Del Yeah … *(Indicating dining table and referring to the romantic conversation)* I was just on the point of asking her whether she'd be so kind as to consider stamping me card when you came storming in.

Rodney Well, just tell her I'm back so, like it or lump it, she's gotta kip with you.

Del *(Deeply offended)* Listen to me, Rodney! Raquel is a lady. And when a lady is ready to … Well, when she's ready she'll let me know.

Rodney How?

Del I dunno! A sign or something.

Rodney Like what?

Del I don't know!

Rodney Maybe she'll put an announcement in the *Sunday Sport*.

Del Look, all I know is she'll let me know! And until that happens you're kipping on the settee, and think yourself lucky!

Rodney Yeah, I don't mind. *(Moving to bar to pour himself another drink)* Anything's better than laying next to a cold pair of shoulders.

Raquel You going to let him stay?

Del I dunno what to do for the best.

Albert Let the boy stay for a few days.

Rodney enters, eating Albert's chicken.

Rodney Cor, I was starving.

Albert Tell him to go back to his wife, Del.

Albert exits.

Albert *(As he leaves)* I fought in the war for you.

INT. NIGHT. DISCO/NIGHTCLUB.

A week later.
This could be the same place where Rodney first danced with Cassandra in series 6, only now we have a few tables round the edge of dance floor. The dance floor is crowded with mainly twenty- to-thirty-year-old people. The hour is late and the lights are low. The music is slow, smooch, romantic. We see Rodney, Chris and Mickey Pearce standing at the bar. The three have had a little too much to drink (not staggering drunk, just a bit too merry for comfort, laughing and giggling at some now forgotten joke).
We see Del and Raquel on the dance floor. As they circle slowly the mood of the music is broken by the giggling from bar.
Del isn't concentrating on the dance, he is looking in Rodney's direction and becoming more annoyed with Rodney's antics.

Del Look at that dipstick! What's he think he's playing at?
Raquel He's had a little too much to drink, that's all.
Del He walked out on Cassandra over a week ago and every night since he's been out on the p ... booze!
Raquel Are you worried about him?
Del Course I am. I've had to look after him most of me life. Michael Jackson's got Bubbles, I've got Rodney!

We cut to bar. Mickey, Chris and Rodney drink tequilla slammers.

Mickey *(Calls to barman)* Can we have ... Excuse me ... Oi! Can we have the same again? This time make 'em large ones.
Rodney and Chris *(Like a cheer)* Yeah!
Mickey It's your round, Rodney.
Rodney Is it? Oh yeah, I suppose it is.

Seated just along from the chaps are two attractive women. They are in their early-to-mid-thirties but very pokeable.

Mickey *(Notices the women)* Christopher, I spy with my little eye two women of the more mature variety.
Chris Lonely housewives out on the pull.
Rodney Leave me out of this.
Mickey Yeah, we intended to.
Chris *(To one of the women)* I know you from somewhere, don't I.
1st Woman *(Obviously not interested and wants to get rid of him)* I wouldn't have thought so!
Mickey He never forgets a face.
1st Woman Neither do I and I'd *certainly*

remember you two!

Chris and Mickey glance at each other.

Chris *(To woman)* Did you go to the Dockside Junior school?
1st Woman Certainly not!
Mickey *(To Chris)* Told you! *(To woman)* He thought you was our old headmistress!

The woman looks offended. Mickey, Chris and Rodney roar with laughter, then join Rodney at the bar. We cut to see Del and Raquel leaving dance floor. Del hears the peals of laughter and looks towards bar. They sit at table.

Del He's already missed a couple of days work 'cos of hangovers!
Raquel I know. I've tried phoning Cassandra but she's just never in.
Del Well, she's busy, ain't she? What with evening school and bank seminars.
Raquel Can't you have a word with Rodney?
Del What can I say? I can't go interfering in his life, he's a married man!
Raquel Mmmh! If my experience is anything to go by, he won't be for long.

Del, now deeply worried, looks towards Rodney. We cut to bar.

Chris What d'you mean you're sleeping on the settee?
Rodney S'true. Del's in his room and Raquel's in my old room.
Mickey I thought Del Boy and her were living together?
Rodney They are ... sort of. But they're not co-habiting – at least they're not co-habiting a bed. Del said as soon as he's – you know – cracked the case, I can have me old room back.
Chris Rodney, let me give you some advice. I am a ladies hairstylist and know intimately the working of the female mind.
Mickey Yeah, 'cos he's a woofter! *(Laughs)*
Chris Please be serious, Mickey! I hate it when you do your Timmy Mallet impersonation! Rodney, why don't you go home to Cassandra? You had a nice flat, a good bird and you've given it all up 'cos of some stupid row!
Rodney If she wants to 'phone me and apologise then I might consider it. But she started it so she's gotta 'phone me first.

As Mickey Pearce begins speaking, so Del appears behind him at the bar. (Del is served with his two drinks – A G&T and a cocktail – almost immediately.)

Mickey What you've gotta do, Rodney, is make Cassandra jealous.
Rodney Yeah ... Why?

Rodney Come Home

Mickey Make her think other women find you desirable.

Rodney (*Likes the sound of this*) Yeah!

Chris Don't encourage Rodney to tell her lies!

Rodney (*Now in agreement with Chris*) That's right ... What d'you mean 'lies'?

Mickey Listen to me, Rodney. I always make a point of making women jealous.

Del The only time you ever made women jealous was the night you won the last house at bingo.

Mickey Oh it's you, Derek! Tell me, how you getting on with Raquel?

Del (*Suspicious of the question. His answer is guarded*) T'riffic! Thank you very much Mickey. What the bleedin hell it's gotta do with you, though, I don't know.

Mickey Just concerned.

Mickey turns to Rodney and Chris and muffles a laugh.

Chris You gonna buy us a drink, Del?

Del Yeah of course. (*Calls to barman and lays a couple of pound coins on bar*) Three coca-colas. (*To Rodney*) Can I have a word, Rodney?

Del turns from bar and makes his way back to table. Rodney leaves bar and follows Del. We cut to the table and Del arrives back with drinks.

Del There you go.

Raquel Thanks.

Rodney, carrying a glass of scotch and dry, arrives at the table. Occasionally he slurs his words.

Rodney Alright?

Del Go on Rodney. Yeah, sit yourself down.

Raquel (*Realising this should be a private conversation, indicates the ladies*) I'll just ... em ... won't be long.

Raquel exits. Del just looks at him as if he seeks an explanation. Rodney senses the look and tries to hide his mild feelings of shame.

Rodney So, you got the exhaust on the van sorted out yet?

Del It's booked in for tomorrow. You can drive it down there for me.

Rodney Me?

Del Well, you won't be going a work, will you? Not after what you've shoved down tonight. So when your hangover's cleared up you can drive the van down there for me.

Rodney I will be going a work in the morning! You can bet your last penny on that! Okay?

Del What are you doing to yourself, Rodney? Every night for the last week you've been out on the booze!

Rodney I'm just seeing my mates, that's all.

Del Yeah, but why's it always Johnny Walker and Ron Bacardi? Rodney – Rodders – you walked out on Cassandra eight days ago. You've made your point bruv. It's time to go home.

Rodney I already went home.

Del No you didn't, you came to my flat.

Rodney Yeah, and I was born there so it's my home! Look, you've never been married so you don't know what it's like.

Del No, but I've mucked about enough to have a fair idea.

Rodney moves away.

Del Rodney ... Rodders.

Del follows him.

Rodney See, to Cassandra life is all drive and ambition. I think she wants to rule the world.

Del No, she don't. She just wants promotion at the bank.

Rodney Zakly! And her determination has made her so blinkered she doesn't notice all the beautiful things that are around her.

Del What, you?

Rodney Well ... if you like! The other month it was her birthday. So I bought her a pair of earrings and a Shergal Farkey LP.

Del A Shergal what?

Rodney Sherkal Fargey ... Fergal Sharkey, the singer.

Del Oh him!

Rodney And a pair of earrings. They were nice earrings, but *little*. There were very *little* earrings. Nice, but ...

Del Little!

Rodney Yes – little. Cassy looked at 'em and said, 'Thank you, Rodney. Aren't they little.'

Del No??

Rodney True as I stand here ... sit here. I suppose *Mummy* and *Daddy* used to buy her *big* presents! I wish I could meet another girl!

Del In your present condition your best bet's to join a Lonely Kidney's Club!

Rodney (*Hasn't heard Del's last remark*) I think married life's been a bit of a let down for young Cassandra!e But I don't care! It's no skin off my nose. Couldn't give a monkey's toss! (*Now, with the combination of booze and emotion, he breaks down*) I love her, Del!!

Del (*Worried that people might see*) Shut up, you tart! Wipe your nose.

Rodney I haven't come up to her high expectations!

Del I'm gonna have a word with your wife, Rodney! I'm gonna tell her that size isn't everything, it's the thought that counts!

Rodney If you get involved, Del … What d'you mean, 'size isn't everything'?

Del Well, those earrings!

Rodney Oh sod the earrings! God, it makes me so angry! Right now I'd like to go out and find a little bloke to have a fight with!

Del Oi, oi, you can cut all that sorta talk out!

Rodney She hardly ever cooked for me! Too busy!

Del You can cook.

Rodney Yeah, but I wanted her to do it.

Del (Now sensing he's getting to the truth) What, you wanted Cassandra to make a fuss of you?

Rodney Yes!

Del She ain't your mum, Rodney.

Rodney What d'you mean?

Del Well – you never really knew the joy of having a mum, did you? You'd only been on solids a while when the angels come and took her away.

Rodney Yeah. I can sort of remember her – but it's … misty. A blonde lady … She was there … then she was gone! Bit like the SDP really! (Giggles at this)

Del (Deeply offended) D'you wanna right-hander for a nightcap, Rodney? You have some respect!

Rodney Sorry, Del! I was just … sorry! What a life, eh? My wife doesn't love me, I ain't got me Mum and some bastard's nicked me bike!

Del I told you not to leave it out on the landing, didn't I?

Rodney Yeah!

Del Don't be defeatist, bruv. These things are sent to test us. Why don't you take a leaf out of my book, eh? Happy go lucky – never let life get me down. Use me as your role model if you like.

Rodney You? You must be joking! Anyway, I don't need a mole-rodel! (Realises he's said it wrong. Tries again) A mole-rodel …

As Rodney tries again Del mouths the words to help him.

Del (Mouths the words) Role … rodel.

Rodney Mole … rod … I don't want one of them! I'm happy as I am! (Notices Raquel returning) … See you later.

Rodney moves back to the bar as Raquel returns.

Raquel Any luck?

Del No. I tried.

Raquel (Kisses him) You're a very nice person, Derek Trotter.

Del Yeah, I know. It's always been me weakness.

Raquel I think Rodney's a very confused young man. Confused and maybe a bit frightened.

Del Frightened? He's a bloke!

Raquel I know. And even 'blokes' get frightened! Everyone's frightened of something!

Del Are they? What you frightened of?

Raquel Shut up, you'll make me feel silly.

Del Go on, what you frightened of? I won't laugh.

Raquel The dark!

Del roars with laughter.

Del What, even now you're frightened of the dark?

Raquel Yeah … Sometimes I lay in bed and the dark seems … well, seems to be touching me … Stupid, eh?

Del Yeah. (Now he becomes very serious. He's going for it, but he knows he could easily blow it) If you like, tonight when you're in bed … in the dark … I'll hold your hand.

Raquel (Smiles at him) Okay. Thank you.

Del smiles – not licentiously – it's a mixture of relief and love. Now he spoils it all.

Del (On the hurry-up) Come on then, drink up. They stand up.

Raquel Listen, Del. My reputation in this area isn't as good as I'd like it to be. So please don't tell anyone about this! About us!

Del Course, I won't tell anyone Raquel. Cor blimey! What sorta bloke d'you think I am? This kind of thing's private! It's between you and me, Raquel – it's us!

Raquel Thanks.

They stand and head towards the exit. They pass the bar where Rodney, Chris and Mickey are still standing.

Rodney Oi, Del. You going? I'll see you later.

Del Righto. And, Rodney, you can sleep in your old room tonight.

Rodney (Realising this means Del has cracked the case, punches the air) Nice one, Derek!

The three celebrate. The following lines are spoken virtually together – just a wall of drunken sound/celebration.

Chris (Applauding) Let's hear it for my man!

Mickey Right-on, Del Boy!

Rodney Let's drink to it!

Del reacts with a 'me and my mouth' expression. Raquel closes her eyes and wishes the ground would open up and swallow her.

INT. DAY. TROTTERS' LOUNGE.

Albert is laying asleep in armchair.
The TV is on and we hear the signature tune to BBC News at six.

Rodney Come Home

TV Announcer This is the six o'clock news from the BBC.

The door from bedrooms area opens and Rodney enters. He is wearing a towelling dressing gown. His hair is wet and he has shaved. He is carrying a radio.

He turns TV off and switches his radio on which immediately blares pop music. He goes to mirror and brushes hair.

The noise from the radio rouses Albert from his slumber.

Albert What's that horrible racket?

Rodney I'm listening to me radio.

Albert I can't sleep with all that noise going on!

Rodney That's an amazing statement coming from a man who slept through two world wars!

Albert I didn't do any sleeping in the war, Rodney! I was out there on the big waves. Shell and fire, that was me. They could make a film about my life story.

Rodney Yeah, Three Men in a Dinghy!

Albert So how you feeling now? Has your hangover cleared up?

Rodney I didn't have a hangover!

Albert So why didn't you go a work this morning?

Rodney None of your business! You ain't half a nosey git, ain't you! It's no wonder they used to chuck you out of the lifeboat!

Albert Yeah, and if that's the sort of rubbish you listened to it's no wonder your wife chucked you out your house!

Rodney *(Seething at this insult)* Cassandra did not chuck me out! I left of my own accord. She's praying for me to go back!

Albert Oh, spending a lot of time at church, is she? Maybe that's why she's never in when Raquel phones her.

Rodney You're just tryin' to wind me up, ain't you?

Albert No I'm not, son, honest ... They found your bike yet?

Rodney Just get off my case, Albert! I'm gonna get dressed!

Rodney exits to bedrooms area taking portable radio with him. Albert goes behind cocktail bar and pours himself a brandy. He is just about to drink when Raquel enters from bedrooms area, looking behind her as if concerned about Rodney. Albert quickly puts brandy down and begins scouring floor behind bar for some imaginary missing article.

Albert You seen my slippers, Raquel?

Raquel *(No hesitation in her reply – she's more concerned with Rodney)* You're wearing them,

Albert. What's wrong with Rodney? He's slamming drawers and banging things around in there!

Albert I think he's still upset about him and Cassandra. I've just tried to give him a few words of encouragement, but nothing seems to work.

Raquel At least you're trying.

Del, wearing a green trenchcoat and carrying an aluminium briefcase, enters from front door and hall. He is in an agitated mood.

Del Where's that idiot?

Albert He's getting dressed.

Raquel Are you alright, love?

Del Eh? Yeah, I'm alright, darling. I think I've got a little touch of that executive burn-out. I could murder a drink.

Raquel Go on, sit down, I'll do it.

Raquel moves to bar.

Del *(Quietly to Albert)* You and me have gotta have a little talk – in private.

Albert Yeah, alright, son. *(Referring to Raquel)* What about her?

Del Leave it to me.

Raquel *(Mystified to find a freshly poured brandy already on bar)* Will a brandy do, Del?

Del Cushty! *(Now a bright idea)* On second thoughts, could you do me a nice decaffeinated coffee? In the percolator, eh?

Raquel But that takes ages!

Del Yeah, I know! But it's much healthier.

Raquel Yeah, alright then. D'you want a coffee, Albert?

Albert I'll have that brandy – save wasting it.

Raquel exits to kitchen.

Albert So what d'you wanna talk about then?

Del Well first of all I'd like to know where my bottle of Courvoesire learnt to pour itself! But that can wait. There are more important things to discuss. I've just been talking to one of the mechanics from the Peckham Exhaust Centre. Rodney took my van down there today. They've got a young receptionist working there, Tania, and that dipstick only asked her out on a date!

Albert You're kidding!

Del I wish I was, Unc, I wish I was! I am disgusted with him!

Albert What's this Tania girl like?

Del Well I wouldn't say no! What I mean, is, she's an attractive girl and nice with it. But that's not the point, is it? What happens if Rodney's seen out with this Tania sort? It'll break poor Cassandra's heart and Rodney'll end up with the sack!

Albert Yeah! And Alan won't do you anymore of that cheap printing you flog to all your mates.

Del *(Emphatically)* No! That's got *nothing* to do with it!

Albert You said that's the only money we've got coming into the flat!

Del I'm only concerned for the future happiness of Rodney and Cassandra. Although that printing does bring a few bob in. I've gotta find a way of putting Rodney off this bird!

Albert So what you telling me for?

Del Well I was hoping you might come up with an idea. Then again I was hoping Millwall might win the UEFA cup! Listen, when Rodney tells us about his date you and me have got to look *horrified*! As if he's going against the Trotter family's moral code.

Albert Oh, he'll never fall for that!

Del Yes, he will!

We hear the sound of pop music approaching from bedrooms area.

Del He's coming. Now don't forget, look horrified! As if you've just seen a U-boat off the starboard bow.

Rodney, now wearing suit and tie, etc. enters from bedrooms area, carrying the radio. Albert immediately looks horrified.

Del *(From corner of mouth to Albert)* Not yet! Not yet!

Rodney *(Switches radio off, referring to Albert)* What's up with him?

Del Gawd knows. Look, he's at the brandy.

Raquel enters from kitchen.

Raquel *(To Del)* Percolator's bubbling. Fancy a coffee, Rodney?

Rodney No thanks, Raquel, I'm going out.

Albert gasps in horror.

Del *(Desperately to Albert)* No! No! *(Now to Rodney)* Going anywhere nice?

Rodney To the pictures.

Del Oh cushty! That's the way to do it, Rodders. Your marriage is going down the Swannee so let's bugger off to the flicks.

Rodney *(Angrily)* Why don't you just butt out, Del?

Del You please yourself, bruv.

Rodney now carefully rubs after-shave onto his face, brushes his hair back and then studies the results in mirror.

Del *(Cont)* Going on your own?

Rodney No, I'm going with – someone.

Albert gasps.

Del *(Spits a hushed warning at him)* One more time and I'll whack you!

Raquel *(Innocently – hasn't caught on to Del and Albert's act)* Who are you taking? Cassandra?

Rodney No, not Cassandra. If you must know it's a girl.

Raquel *(Incredulously)* A girl?

Del *(Horrified)* A girl?

Albert is sipping his brandy and misses his cue.

Del *(Hisses at Albert)* Oi!

Albert Oh! *(Horrified)* A girl?

Rodney Why d'you all keep repeating it? You sound like Jive Bunny! I met a girl called Tania and I asked her to the pictures. What's wrong with that?

Del I don't believe I'm hearing this! You're a happily married man, Rodney!

Rodney *Was* a happily married man, Derek! Then we left the registry office and the magic seemed to go! A happily married man would be taking his *wife* to the pictures!

Del Well, why don't you?

Rodney What?

Del Take Cassandra. Give her a bell, she might fancy going.

Albert There wouldn't be room in the van for Tania *and* Cassandra.

Del I mean give this Tania sort the elbow and take … Just stay out of this, Albert!

Rodney It's no good. Even our tastes in films differ. Cassy used to like heavy dramas and foreign films; *The Grapes of Wrath* and Fellini classics, that sort of thing.

Raquel What are you going to see?

Rodney *Honey I Shrunk the Kids.* Well, that's not my choice. Tania wants to see it.

Del Tania – Tania? Wait a minute. Not that old bow-wow from the exhaust centre?

Rodney *(Happily surprised that Del knows her)* Yeah! *(Now reacts)* What do you mean 'bow-wow'? She's not a 'bow-wow'!

Del Oh do me a favour, Rodney, it's like a Rottweiler with a wig!

Rodney Del, the Tania I'm talking about is very pretty.

Del Have you clocked the hooter on it? Me and Boycie had a bet once whether it was her real nose or she'd had silicone injections.

Rodney Have you ever actually spoken to this person?

Del I said good morning to her once but she was busy gnawing a bone.

Raquel *(Getting slightly miffed over Del's apparent sexism)* I think what Rodney's trying to say, Derek, is that maybe, *just* maybe, this girl might have a nice personality. *(To Rodney)* Has she?

Rodney *(Without hesitation)* No, not really.

Rodney Come Home

Albert Then why you going out with her?

Del He's heard of her reputation, ain't he?

Rodney I don't care about her rep …
(Optimistically) Has she got a reputation?

Del In the past she lived with a few blokes. A darts team I heard.

Raquel *(Angrily at Del)* That is just the kind of old-fashioned, chauvinistic attitude that keeps women second-class citizens in this country!

Del No, no, I'm doing this for a reason, Raquel.

Raquel Sometimes you can be such a sexist! You're not satisfied with tearing the poor girl to shreds because she doesn't look like Kim Basinger! Oh no, you've got to do a character assassination because, in the past, she's done exactly the same as you!

Albert Del's never lived with a darts team!

Del *(Quietly to Raquel)* No, no, you don't understand what I'm doing, darling. I'll explain to you later, alright?

Raquel *(Has no intentions of letting this go)* It's all very well for young men to sow their wild oats. The more the merrier – shows they're red-blooded! But if a girl does the same thing she's a slut!

Del That's where you're wrong, Raquel! Nowadays young men can't sow their wild oats either. We've all seen the film for AIDS on the telly. That's my point, Rodders. These days women are very dodgy. One wrong move and you could be shaking hands with Princess Di!

Raquel '*Women are dodgy*'!

Del Eh? No, no, not you, sweetheart! I meant the others.

Raquel How *dare* you lay the blame for a worldwide epidemic at the feet of womankind!

Del Raquel, if feet were the problem Doctor Scholl could find the cure!

Raquel I have never heard such stupid, pig-ignorant views as yours!

Rodney *(Has been enjoying the row)* Get him on to politics, Raquel, it'll blow your mind!

Raquel Derek, for your information there is a rather ugly rumour going around.

Del Yeah, well introduce it to Rodney, he'll take it to the pictures!

Raquel The rumour is that *man* is the guilty party!

Del On the telly you see this young bloke meet some bird at a disco and …

Raquel To hell with the telly! Let's get one thing clear, Derek! – *Women* played no part in the creation of this *plague*! Aids is like nylon – man-made!

Raquel exits to bedrooms area.

Del *(To Rodney)* See, you've upset her now!

Rodney *I've* upset her? That's it, I'm outta here!
Rodney is about to exit to hall.

Del Listen, Rodney, one little row and you two think your marriage is dead. But it's not, bruv. You could rekindle the flame of passion. Take her a bunch of flowers and a bottle of champagne.

Rodney That's a bit corny, innit?

Del No, that's what I'd do.

Rodney Na, she goes to the evening school tonight.

Del She might cancel it for you.

Rodney You're joking, nothing comes before her stupid, rotten career! Tryin' to rekindle the flame in my marriage is like giving the kiss of life to a rasher of bacon.

Del He who dares wins, Rodney. Just tell her you're sorry and then she'll say she's sorry as well. Before you know it you've made up, you're more in love than ever *and* you might get a little bit! Everyone's a winner! Tête de veau!

Rodney *(Disdainfully)* You might get a little bit! Good God, it's like living with a Big Mac!

Del Right, just for that you can't borrow my van!

Rodney Stuff your van, I'll bus it!

Del *(To Albert)* Good. That's the thanks I get!
Del opens door to bedrooms area.

Del *(Calls)* D'you fancy popping out for a drink, sweetheart?

Raquel *(OOV)* With a creep like you?

Del Yeah.

Raquel *(OOV)* No thank you very much.

Del What a life, eh? What a life!
Del is now struck by a disturbing thought.

Del Wait a minute. That film *Honey I Shrunk the Kids* – what cinema's it on at?

Albert The ABC in the high street.

Del *(Knowingly)* And what's right next door to the cinema? Cassandra's evening school! And tonight's the night she goes.

Albert But she might see Rodney and this Tania girl queuing outside!

Del That's the idea, innit? Dippy Rodney's tryin' to make Cassandra jealous. He's taken Mickey Pearce's advice – and that boy's had about as much luck with women as you had with boats. I've gotta stop Cassandra going to that evening school! I'll see you later, Unc.
Del rushes towards front door.
Raquel now appears at door to bedrooms area.

Raquel *(Now in a softer, let's make up mood)* Del.

Del Yeah, what is it, darling?

Raquel I'm sorry.

Del So am I.

Albert Oh Gawd.

Raquel *(She gestures with her head towards bedroom)* Can we – you know – 'talk'?

Del *(Reacts – what a time to get a promise)* Yeah, of course. I'll be as quick as I can, I promise.

Raquel *(Misunderstanding)* Well, you don't have to be!

Del No, no, see I've gotta pop out somewhere.

Raquel But I wanted to 'talk'!

Del Yeah, but this is important!

Raquel *(In a huff)* Oh well, please yourself!
She exits to bedrooms, slamming door behind her.

Albert Rodney's really upset her, ain't he?
Del lets out a confused sigh and exits.

EXT. NIGHT. FORECOURT AND ENTRANCE DOOR TO RODNEY'S BLOCK OF FLATS.

The van pulls into forecourt and parks. Del alights wearing same clothes as previous scene. He walks across to entrance door. On the wall we have an intercom security device. Del takes a deep breath as he prepares himself for his ordeal. He presses button to flat 16.
After a slight pause we hear Cassandra's voice.

Cassandra *(OOV, distort)* Hello?

Del Hello, Cassandra? It's Del Boy.

Cassandra *(OOV, distort)* Oh, hi Del. Push the door.
We hear buzzer on entrance door. Del steels himself again and enters.

INT. NIGHT. RODNEY AND CASSANDRA'S LOUNGE.

Cassandra is placing a couple of text books in her bag as Del enters through the already open front door.

Del Hello, darling. I was just passing, thought I'd pop in and see how you were.

Cassandra I'm fine. How are you?

Del Couldn't be better, sweetheart. Well, a bit choked about you and Rodders of course.

Cassandra Yeah, well – one of those things, eh?

Del Yeah, one of them things. You off to evening school?

Cassandra Mmmh. Final exams in three weeks.

Del Cushty!

Cassandra How's Rodney?

Del Bearing up.

Cassandra Have the police found his bike yet?

Del No. He's toying with the idea of getting another one.

Cassandra Where's he tonight?

Del Oh, er, he popped out earlier.

Cassandra Oh, well, I hope he has a good time.

Del *(A false chuckle at the irony of this statement)* Yeah!

Cassandra I mean, that's what he wants from life, isn't it?

Del I know what he *really* wants, Cassandra, and I think, in your heart, you do as well.

Cassandra Well, he's only got to swallow his stupid pride and ask.

Del I know. I've tried talking to him but I just can't get through. As my Mum used to say, 'There's none so blind as them what won't listen.'

Cassandra *(A confused, slightly glazed expression)* Very true!

Del Can't the two of you sort it out someway?

Cassandra Oh it's impossible, Del. Rodney won't budge an inch on any given subject. He just fights me all the way. He doesn't like going to the bank's social evenings, he gets bored with my friends – *and* he shows it! The other week I invited some colleagues round. I cooked a lovely meal – I mean, I really tried hard, Del.

Del You're a smashing cook, Cassandra. I remember that Moules Marinier you made us last year. I can still taste it now.

Cassandra Anyway, one hour after we'd finished eating Rodney decided it was time they all went home. So he started giving them subtle little hints like yawning and checking his watch every three minutes. Finally he started whistling the national anthem.

Del Well, Rodney's never been one for staying up late.

Cassandra This was Sunday lunch! Rodney's idea of socialising is a night out at the pub with his mates. What sort of idiot wants to spend his evenings down the Nag's Head?

Del Oh yeah, I mean who would?

Cassandra Rodney's so immature. It's never going to work between us until he learns to grow up.

Del Is it just him?

Cassandra I'm not behaving childishly if that's what you're suggesting.

Del You haven't phoned him though.

Cassandra I'm not phoning him first! He started it!

Del Must have taken years of experience to reach that decision. *(Notices she is wearing a*

Rodney Come Home

small pair of diamond earrings) They're nice earrings, Cassandra.

Cassandra They're lovely, aren't they? Rodney gave them to me for my birthday.

Del They're very, er, *little* aren't they?

Cassandra That's what I like. I don't want a pair of chandeliers hanging from my ears. These are ... these are perfect.

Del But Rodney said ...

Cassandra Rodney said what?

Del Don't matter. *(Mumbles to himself)* I don't believe these two! I'd get more sense out of a crossed line with the Krankies! *(Desperate to stop her)* Listen, sweetheart, I tell you what, give the evening school a miss for once, eh? Come out with me and Raquel. You Dad told me about this great Chinese place, they do a blinding Won Ton on all accounts.

Cassandra Maybe some other time, eh? I really *must* go tonight.

Del Well, I'll tell you what, I'll give you a lift, drop you right outside the school.

Cassandra But it's only fifty yards from the car park.

Del You don't wanna go past that cinema queue!

Cassandra Why not?

Del Er ... there might be yobs there! *(We sense the tremendous struggle he is having with his conscience. He doesn't want to grass on his brother but he doesn't want to see Cassandra hurt)* Oh God! Cassandra, let me ask you a question. Have you ever had a nightmare where you've seen Rodney with another girl?

Cassandra *(Half-laugh)* No!

Del I have! Well, what would your reaction be if you did?

Cassandra What, Rodney with another girl? *(Dismissive shrug)* Wouldn't bother me.

Del Oh good, 'cos Rodney's taken another girl to the pictures tonight.

Cassandra *(Immediate anger and hurt)* He's done what? He's taken another ...! No! Not Rodney, he wouldn't do that!

Del He's tryin' to make you jealous! He wants you to see him and Tania standing in the cinema queue. I said to him, Cassandra's *far* too intelligent to ...

Cassandra *(Cuts straight in)* Who the hell's Tania?

Del She's from the exhaust centre. See, Mickey Pearce said ...

Cassandra *(Cuts in)* It was just a silly disagreement, that's all!

Del doesn't know what to do.

Del You said it wouldn't bother you!

Cassandra It doesn't! The bastard! I love him! *Cassandra starts crying.*

Del Yeah, well he loves you an' all.

Cassandra Oh it looks like it! We only had a row about badminton and he's started an affair with another woman!

Del No, he's just taking some tart to see *Honey I Shrunk the Kids*!

Cassandra *(Cries even more)* I wanted to see that! *(Now crying uncontrollably)*

Del But Rodney said! Oh Gawd!

Del just doesn't know how to handle the situation.
Pause.

Del You're taking this very well, Cassandra.

Cassandra *(Wiping the tears away)* Thanks for telling me, Del.

Del I couldn't stand by and see you walk into an ambush. It's just Rodney's silly way of getting you back.

Cassandra Getting me back for what?

Del No, not getting you back for something! I mean getting you back with him.

Cassandra But *I* haven't gone anywhere! *I'm* still here!

Del Yeah, of course you are, sweetheart, course you are ... Don't go to the evening school, eh?

Cassandra No, I'm not. I'll go round to my friend Emma's house.

Del Good idea. We'll keep this whole thing to ourselves, eh? We don't want the neighbours or – your *Dad* finding out, do we?

Cassandra No, you're right, Del.

Del *(A visible sigh of relief)* Yeah, you know it makes sense. What time will you be back tonight?

Cassandra I don't know. Late. Why?

Del I'll get Raquel to phone you, cheer you up a bit. Her marriage broke up as ... Well, what I mean is, she'll understand what you're going through. You all right?

Cassandra Yes, I'm fine.

Del I'll see you later then.

Cassandra Yeah, bye ... and thanks, Del.

Del walks to door. Cassandra starts removing the books from her bag. Now she loses her temper and empties the books straight onto the floor. She starts jumping up and down on the books and hurls the bag across room (in other words, being very silly).

Del *(Witnessing this display)* You won't do anything silly, will you?

Cassandra *(Sobbing)* No, I'm fine!

Del Lovely jubbly.

INT. NIGHT. TROTTERS' LOUNGE/RODNEY AND CASSANDRA'S HALL.

Midnight.

Raquel is now wearing nightclothes and dressing gown. Del is seated at table and is prising the voice boxes out of the dolls he had been trying to sell earlier on. Albert, also in pyjamas and dressing gown, is watching TV.

Raquel I didn't know what you were doing.

Del *(Moaning about the dolls)* Bloody Korean rubbish! I wish I hadn't put these 'made in Britain' stickers on 'em now! Sorry, sweetheart, what was you saying?

Raquel Earlier this evening, when you were saying those horrible things about women. I didn't realise you were trying to frighten Rodney out of his date.

Del Oh yeah. Didn't work though, did it?

Raquel I couldn't see Rodney being unfaithful, could you?

Del No!

Raquel He's not that stupid, is he?

Del Oh he's stupid enough, he just never gets anywhere with birds! That boy's been blown out more times than a wind sock!

Albert During the war.

Del *(Checks watch)* Cor, look at the time.

Raquel Midnight already.

Albert A crewmate of mine, Sky Piggot, died of a sexually related condition.

Del Yeah?

Albert Yeah, his girlfriend's husband shot him! *(Laughs)*

Del and Raquel laugh along with him. The phone begins ringing.

Del *(Answers phone)* Trotters Independent Traders.

We now intercut between Del and Rodney. The background behind Rodney gives us no indication of where he is phoning from.

Rodney *(On phone)* Del Boy? It's me.

Del *(On phone, still annoyed with him)* Yeah, what d'you want, Rodney?

Rodney *(On phone)* I've been thinking.

Del *(On phone)* I'll call a press conference first thing in the morning.

Rodney *(On phone)* Listen to me, Del. I haven't been drinking. *(Breathes down phone)* See. I've been doing a bit of growing up. And I've realised that you were right and I was wrong.

Del *(On phone)* I know I was right! I told you I was right, but you wouldn't listen.

Rodney *(On phone)* I did listen! I've bought some champagne and roses for Cassy.

Del *(On phone)* That's very corny and a bit too late! You've taken that Tania sort to the pictures now. You can't turn the clock back, Rodders.

Rodney *(On phone)* No, I didn't take Tania out.

Del *(On phone)* It doesn't really matter where … *(Reacts)* You didn't take Tania out?

Rodney *(On phone)* No. I thought of all the things you said, Del. So I phoned her and told her I was a married man. And I told her I was still very much in love with my wife … Does that sound a bit yukky?

Del *(On phone, fearful of all the damage he may have done)* It sounds horrible, Rodney!

Rodney *(On phone)* Then I thought, why am I telling a total stranger this? I should be telling my *wife!* So that's what I'm gonna do. I'm gonna have a little heart to heart with Cassy – try an' put everything right between us.

Del *(On phone)* Yeah, t'riffic! Look, don't go round to your flat just yet, Rodney – Cassandra's not in.

Now we have a different shot of Rodney to show that he is in fact in the hall of his and Cassandra's flat.

Rodney *(On phone)* I know, I'm at the flat at the moment. I'll wait for her. I mean, who's hurrying?

Del *(On phone)* You're at the flat? Oh God! Rodney, there's something I've gotta say to you …

Rodney *(On phone)* Del, you've done enough for me tonight.

Del *(On phone)* Rodders, earlier this evening …

Rodney *(On phone)* There's something I want to say to you, Del.

Del *(On phone)* What?

Rodney *(On phone, becoming emotional)* Love you, Del Boy!

With tears welling in his eyes Rodney slams the receiver down as he is too choked up to talk anymore.

Del *(Reacts to phone being cut off)* Dipstick! *Rodney wipes the tears from his eyes. We see a bottle of champagne and a bunch of roses on the telephone table. Rodney smiles, his expectations for the next few hours are high. To avoid any interruptions he takes the phone off the hook. Del is punching numbers out on his phone.*

Raquel What's happened?

Del Rodney's only back at his flat!

Raquel Well that's good – isn't it?

Del No, it is not good, Raquel – it is very ungood! *(Reacts to engaged signal)* I can't get through. I bet he's taken the phone off the hook!

Albert Perhaps the line's engaged.

Del The only thing that's engaged is Rodney's

Rodney Come Home

hormones!

Raquel Look, I don't understand this. You've been telling Rodney to go back to Cassandra for ages.

Del Yes, but that was before he took Tania to see *Honey I Shrunk the Bloody Kids*!

Albert But you just said Rodney *didn't* take Tania out!

Del Yes – he didn't! But Cassandra – you see – Cassandra thinks he did!

Albert What makes her think that?

Del *(A big innocent shrug)* Someone must have told her!

Raquel *(Sensing the truth)* Oh, Del, you didn't?

Del I only did it for her! I didn't want the poor little mare walking past the cinema queue and seeing her husband having a grope with Miss Kwik-Fit! I didn't want Cassy getting hurt – she's family. I've gotta get round their flat and persuade Cassandra I made a mistake before she sets eyes on that wally!

Del exits to hall and front door.

Raquel Why does he have to interfere?

Albert It's just his nature. Still, it proves his heart's in the right place.

Raquel Mmmmh … Pity about his brain.

INT. NIGHT. RODNEY AND CASSANDRA'S FLAT.

We can hear soft music playing in background. The front door opens and Cassandra enters.
She starts to remove her coat and then reacts as she becomes aware of the music.
The music is coming from their record player. The lights are seductively low.
On the coffee table stands an ice bucket holding the bottle of champagne. Beside this are two champagne glasses and the roses in a crystal vase. Cassandra takes the scene in with an expression that tells us nothing of her true feelings. She turns as we hear the click of a door opening. At the bedroom door we see Rodney.
Rodney smiles at her – a warm, loving smile.

Rodney Cass … I've come home!

Cassandra's eyes widen with anger and hate (her thoughts are simply 'You dirty bastard') We see Rodney's reaction to this.

Cassandra *(Seething, set to kill)* You ..!

EXT. NIGHT. FORECOURT OF RODNEY AN CASSANDRA'S FLATS.

We see the van screech to a halt close to the entrance door. Del alights and hurries towards entrance door. As he approaches the entrance door we see a young couple already entering. Now, from a flat above, we hear the sound of breaking glass and a heated exchange between Rodney and Cassandra. Del and the young couple look up towards the flat and listen to the row.

Rodney *(OOV)* Tania? I don't know anyone called Tania! Is it a man or a woman?

Cassandra *(OOV)* Oh, don't try and deny it Rodney – Del told me all about the two of you.

Rodney *(OOV)* Well he was lying!

Cassandra *(OOV)* She works for the Peckham Exhaust Centre! *(Pause)*

Rodney *(OOV)* *(Quickly changing the subject)* Shall I get a vase for them roses?

Cassandra *(OOV)* Stuff the roses!

Rodney *(OOV)* Oh come on, Cass – you shouldn't believe anything Del Boy tells you.

We see Del's fearful reaction to all this.

Del *(To the young couple)* Lovely evening, isn't it?

Del walks in through the door which is being held open by the man.

INT. NIGHT. FOYER OUTSIDE RODNEY AND CASSANDRA'S FRONT DOOR.

The foyer is on the first floor. We have a couple of front doors. From inside one flat we can hear the heated exchange continuing.

Rodney *(OOV)* If you could just calm down for ten seconds you'd realise this was all a big mistake!

Cassandra *(OOV)* Our marriage was a big mistake!

Rodney *(OOV)* Cassandra, we always said we would discuss our differences in a mature and …

Cassandra *(OOV)* Just bugger off, Rodney!

Rodney *(OOV, a yelp of pain)* Ooohhh!

The front door is wrenched open and Rodney is propelled out of the flat by some unseen force. Stuck in his hair are rose petals, leaves and bits of flower stalks. He is limping and seems in a state of shock. As he turns to appeal the door is slammed in his face. Rodney now sees Del standing at the top of the stairs.

Del She's back, is she?

Rodney Why, Del? Why did you tell her?

Del I'm sorry, Rodders. I *had* to tell her to save her from any pain.

Rodney And what about me? She's just whacked me in the shin with her badminton racquet!

The door to number 14 opens and Rodney's

*neighbour (Frank) appears. He is about 35
and wears just pyjamas.*

Frank It's gone midnight!

Del Well, go to bed then!

Rodney Sorry about this, Frank! *(To Del)* Don't
you dare insult my neighbours! *(Pushes Del
towards stairs)* Get outside!!

EXT. NIGHT. FORECOURT & MAIN ENTRANCE DOOR TO RODNEY/CASSANDRA'S FLATS.

*Del is forced out and followed by Rodney.
They move a few yards away from the door.
(This is so we don't hear or see the door
closing.)*

Del Alright Rodney, alright!

Rodney You! You of all people grassed me up!
You grassed me for something I didn't *do!*

Del Rodney, have you any idea what
Cassandra's reaction would have been if she'd
seen you with Tania?

Rodney Yes, she's just given me a bloody good
example of it! I wasn't gonna take Tania out! I'd
changed me mind before I got to the bottom of
the lifts! I made a stupid threat out of anger and
frustration!

Del But you said …

Rodney I know what I said! But there's a world of
difference between saying and doing! If I'd gone
to the police every time you said you were gonna
kill me you'd still be slopping out in Parkhurst!
Thanks to you my wife now thinks I'm having a
passionate affair with the siren of the exhaust
centre *and* you've offended my neighbours!

*A woman's voice calls out from the darkness
above them.*

2nd Woman *(OOV)* People are trying to sleep!

Rodney *(Total frustration)* Oh shuddup!

Del Alright, alright! Now calm down, Rodney,
calm down. Alright, fair enough. I'm sorry.

Rodney Sorry?

Del Yes, sorry! Is there anything I can do to
help?

Rodney Yes, piss off!

Del Listen to me, you ungrateful little dipstick!
I've dragged myself out in the middle of the
night to help you – and I was on a promise!

Rodney And you listen to me, Del. I don't want
your help! I don't want your favours, assistance
or advice! I don't want nothing off you for the
rest of my life!

Del I was only tryin' to do me best for
Cassandra and you.

Rodney Yeah, and make sure you still got all
that printing done on the cheap!

Del is genuinely hurt by this.

Del You don't really think that, do you, Rodney?

Rodney … Probably not … See you.

*Rodney turns and walks away. Del, defeated
and dejected, turns and walks back towards
van. Rodney watches him go. He now turns
to go back into flats only to find the main
door is locked. He instinctively reaches for his
pocket and suddenly realises he hasn't got
the key. He reaches towards the security
intercom buttons and then realises that is
pointless. He walks back to the top of the
steps.*

Rodney *(Calls)* Del!

Del What?

Rodney I've locked myself out!

Del You've done what?

Rodney I've left the key upstairs!

Del Well, press the intercom button and tell
Cassandra.

Rodney She won't let me in!

Del Yeah, I know, but it might cheer her up a
bit!

*Del walks back to join Rodney.
Rodney now accepts his defeat. He walks
sadly and slowly across to Del.*

Rodney This whole thing hasn't gone quite as
well as I hoped it would.

Del That's jealousy for you, bruv! A dangerous
thing.

Rodney We've naused it right up, ain't we?

Del What's new?

Rodney now feels the cold chill of fear.

Rodney *(Frightened and desperate)* What am I
gonna do, Del?

Del shakes his head – he doesn't know either.

Del Come on, Rodney. Let's go home.

They walk off and both climb into van.

Rodney Come Home

Miami Twice (Part One)
The American Dream

EXT. DAY. CAR PARK AT BACK OF DILAPI-DATED LONDON CHURCH.

We see some of the familiar cars of the regulars. The Trotters' three wheeled van, Del's Capri Ghia, Boycie's Mercedes, Alan's Jaguar, Cassandra's Escort and Denzil's transit bearing the hand-painted legend 'Transworld Express'. Over this we hear the vicar's words from inside the church.

Vicar *(OOV)* Almighty and everlasting God, we give thee humble thanks, for thou hast vouchsafed to call us to the knowledge of thy grace, and faith in thee: Increase this knowledge, and confirm this faith in us evermore.

INT. DAY. THE NAVE OF CHURCH.

The interior is also old and slightly dilapidated. Del and Raquel, who is holding the eight-month old Damien, stand close to the font as the 35-year-old vicar performs the baptism ceremony.

Rodney and Cassandra stand a few yards back from the font. There is obviously an atmosphere between them. We shall discover their fragile marriage has developed a major and mysterious problem. Rodney's eyes flicker uncertainly in her direction. During the vicar's speech we pan across the congregation.

Vicar Give thy holy spirit to this infant, that he may be born again, and be made an heir of everlasting salvation; through our Lord Jesus Christ, who liveth and reigneth with thee and the Holy Spirit, now and for ever, Amen.

During this we see Boycie, Marlene and Tyler (who is now about three). Tyler is wearing a suit and tie and dressed like a little Boycie. Marlene is close to tears as she watches the christening. Boycie is bored and irritable – he has better things to do. We see Denzil and Mickey Pearce watching the proceedings. Mickey is placing film in his camera. Alan and Pam smile benignly – Pam's smile slightly forced – she doesn't mind slumming it once in a while but this is too far down the social ladder for comfort. Trigger is surveying the roof and walls of church – he can't remember ever being in one of these things before. Mike

checks his watch – he's got a pub to open. Albert, in full medals, smiles proudly.

Vicar *(Quietly to Rodney and Cassandra)* Godparents, please. *(Gestures them closer).*

Cassandra *(Quietly to Rodney)* D'you remember what you've got to say?

Rodney *(Quietly)* Yes.

Cassandra steps forward, Rodney is a hesitant step behind her. Rodney still hasn't quite got over his 'Damien, the Antichrist' phase. The vicar takes Damien from Raquel and hands him to Rodney.

Del *(Whispers)* Be careful, Rodney. You drop him, and I'll drop you.

Raquel *(Hisses a warning)* Del!

Del *(Whispers)* Well, he dropped a whole Royal Doulton dinner service once – nearly ruined it!

Raquel *(Whispers)* Shut up!

Del Well!

Cassandra Oh, look at his little face.

Rodney *(Non-commital)* Mmmh!

Vicar *(To Rodney and Cassandra)* Dearly beloved, ye have brought this child here to be baptised, you have prayed that our Lord Jesus Christ would vouchsafe to receive him, to release him of his sins … *(etc)*

We cut away to Alan and Pam as the vicar continues. Trigger is standing directly behind them. Trigger leans forward to Alan. All this in hushed tones:

Trigger Going down the pub, Alan?

Alan Oh yeah, we'll be there.

Pam We're going down the pub, are we?

Alan Got to be polite to Raquel and Del. We've gotta wet the baby's head.

Pam Roughly translated, that means, 'I can't wait to get down the Nag's Head and get legless with Del!'

Trigger *(Leans in to Pam)* Take your time, Pam, we've gotta christen the baby first.

Pam *(Deeply offended, to Alan)* Did you hear that?

Alan Yes! Why you always on about me getting drunk? When was the last time that happened?

Pam The last time you went down the Nag's Head with Del!

Alan I didn't!

Vicar *(In mid-sentence)* … and constantly believe God's holy word and obediently keep His commandments. *(To Rodney and Cassandra)* Dost thou renounce the devil and all his works?

Rodney shoots a fearful glare at Damien. We see Damien looking back at Rodney.

Cassandra I renounce them all.

Vicar Dost thou renounce the vain pomp and glory and the carnal desires of the flesh?

Del shoots a questioning/suspicious glance at Rodney.

Rodney *(To vicar. Embarrassed by Del's glance)* Yes.

Cassandra *(Embarrassed because Rodney has given the wrong answer. Quietly to Rodney)* No!

Rodney *(Quietly)* We do!

Cassandra *(With the correct response)* I renounce them all.

Rodney *(Now remembering the instructions)* Oh yeah, me too.

Cut away to Boycie and Marlene.

Marlene It's lovely, innit?

Boycie Stunning.

Marlene Don't you feel anything?

Boycie Yes, I feel a great urgency to get out of here as soon as possible and finish my packing. You do realise we're going on holiday tomorrow?

Marlene I've finished all the packing! Stop moaning, Boycie, or I'm gonna get annoyed … D'you remember Tyler's christening?

Boycie Yeah. Better church than this though, weren't it?

Vicar *(To Rodney and Cassandra)* Godparents, will you please name this child.

Rodney Yes. it's Damien Derek Trotter.

Vicar *(Questions name)* Damien *Derek*?

Cassandra Yes.

The vicar looks to Del and Raquel.

Del *(Confirms)* Damien Derek.

Vicar Fine. *(He takes Damien and places water on the baby's forehead)* I baptise thee Damien Derek in the name of the Father and of the Son and of the Holy Spirit.

We see Rodney's eyes widening with fear as the Antichrist is christened.

Vicar We receive this child into the congregation of Christ's flock and do sign him with the sign of the cross. *(Makes the sign of the cross on Damien's forehead).*

We see Rodney's fearful reaction to the sign of the cross. He has a great dread that something terrible's about to happen as it did in the film. There is a sudden flash of light across Rodney's face. He whimpers with fear.

We now see it was Mickey Pearce, who is standing close to Rodney, taking a photo of the baptism.

Mickey *(To Rodney)* What is wrong with you, Rodney?

Rodney Nothing!

EXT. DAY. THE FRONT OF THE CHURCH.

The front of the church is even more decrepit than the back or interior. A couple of the windows are boarded up and someone has sprayed 'Free Nelson Mandela' across a wall. There is scaffolding in front of the main doors. The whole group, including the vicar, are on the front steps as Mickey Pearce prepares to take a snap with his Cannon sureshot. He places it on the roof of Del's car.

Del Oi, oi, oi, oi, mind the paintwork, will you?

Denzil Come on, Mickey, get a move on!

Mickey I'm just setting the automatic timer.

Rodney *(To Del)* He's no David Bailey, is he?

Del David Bailey? More like Bathe-it-Daily.

Mickey Ready. Everybody smile.

Everyone smiles.

Mickey Smile, Trigger!

Trigger I am smiling.

Mickey clicks auto-timer on then runs round to get in shot. We see Pam and Alan smiling. Mickey runs round and stands directly in front of Pam. The camera clicks. Mickey moves back towards camera revealing a fuming Pam. The group now breaks up into smaller groups. We see Del and Raquel, who is holding Damien, shaking hands with the vicar.

Del Ah! Thank you very much, reverend, that was a cracking display.

Raquel *(Correcting Del)* It was a beautiful ceremony, thank you.

Vicar Oh, my pleasure. Perhaps I'll be seeing you two again in the near future?

Del What, us two? What, you mean the wedding? Don't hold your breath on it son, she's still married. *(Laughs)*

Raquel *(Gets in quickly) (To Vicar)* I'm legally separated – I'm waiting for my divorce to come through.

Del Yeah, almost pukka.

Vicar When, or if, you need me, I'll be here. God bless you both.

Del Yeah.

Raquel Thank you, Reverend.

Del Thanks very much, Reverend. Oh by the way Reverend. I'll be in to see you in a minute. I've got something I want to talk to you about.

Vicar Yes of course. I'll be inside.

Miami Twice The American Dream

Del Good.

Vicar exits to church, struggling through the scaffolding. We see Mickey Pearce ear-wigging the next few speeches.

Raquel *(Thinking this could be about their future wedding)* What do you want to see him about?

Del Just a bit of business, sweetheart, bit of business.

Raquel *(Angry through disappointment)* Business? How can you discuss business here? This is a church!

Del Ah come on, Raquel, even churches have got to make a profits! Have you read your Bible recently?

Raquel Have you?

Del No, but I remember our RE teacher reading it to us once, and there is a chapter in the Bible actually called the Book of Profits! So don't tell me that God doesn't know a bit of bunce when He sees it!

Raquel No, it … it doesn't mean profit.

Marlene *(Cuts in)* A lovely christening, Raquel, one of the nicest I've been to.

Raquel Oh thanks, Marlene.

Marlene *(Produces a present)* Here, I've bought you a little present. it's one of them baby intercoms. You know, so as you can hear Damien if he cries at night. You can even talk back to him from your living room – let him hear Mummy's voice, you know. You'll be able to fix it up, won't you, Del?

Del Mmh? Oh yeah, no problem, I'll get Rodney to do it tomorrow. Listen, I'll leave you two girls to have a chinwag. See you later, alright. *(He is gone)*

Del moves through the crowd and bumps into Mike.

Mike Er, listen Del, I'm gonna shoot off now, mate, and open up the pub. Listen, about this christening do I'm putting on for you, I'm a bit concerned, mate.

Del Don't be, Michael. I've got every faith in you. *(Tries to get away)*

Mike No, no, no, no I'm concerned about the money! You wouldn't like to actually pay me now? Or at least gimme a deposit.

Del How dare you, Michael, talk business here? Outside a church, this is a church! Cor blimey!

Del exits to church. Mike now considers the strong probability that he's about to be had. Cut to Raquel and Marlene.

Raquel So you're off on holiday tomorrow?

Marlene Yeah, we're going to the States. We fly to Washington, then down to Atlantic City for a week and then on to Florida.

Raquel Stop it, you're making me jealous.

Marlene Well, it's not gonna be *that* good. Boycie's going with me! *(Laughs)*

Marlene now spots Rodney standing alone a few yards behind them.

Marlene Look at poor little Rodney! Is he still living at your flat?

Raquel Well, he stays with me and Del from Monday to Friday then he spends the weekends with Cassandra.

Marlene He only sees her at weekends?

Raquel Yeah.

Marlene Oh well, I suppose it's more fun than fishing!

Raquel and Marlene laugh at this as they walk out of shot to reveal Rodney in background. Rodney is standing alone and looking in direction of car park. We see Cassandra going to her car. Rodney watches her. He wants to call out to her but pride prevents him from doing so. Finally he cracks. He opens his mouth and is about to call when:

Alan *(OOV)* Rodney.

Rodney Hi, Alan.

Alan joins Rodney.

Alan So, how's the new job?

Rodney What new job?

Alan Working for Del.

Rodney Oh *that*? Oh … fine. We've gone international now. Del's very big in Eastern Europe.

Alan Oh that's right. Yeah, he was telling me. He's got contacts in Warsaw.

Rodney No, Walsall.

Alan Walsall?

Rodney Yeah, but this bloke's cousin is an exporter in Romania.

Alan Oh Romania? … Good! Look, er how are you getting on with … er ..?

He sees Cassandra driving away in her car.

Alan *(Cont)* *(Doesn't bother finishing the sentence. Slightly embarrassed)* Oh …

Rodney *(Trying to save the situation)* Oh no, she … she's just going down the pub. I said I'd see her there later. You going down for one?

Alan Yeah, oh yeah, just for a quick one.

Rodney *(Laughs at him)* Just for a quick one! I know you too well!

Alan No, no honestly, it will be just a quick one, I've had my orders! Oh, by the way, I've got something for you.

Alan produces an average size envelope. He doesn't hand it to Rodney at this point.

Rodney What's that?

Alan It's a cheque. D'you remember when you

first started to work for me you joined the firm's pension scheme? Well they finally came up with your repayments. Now I've had a talk to the insurance company and, they say, if you like, you can keep the policy open. I mean, in the long term it might prove to be the basis of a nice little nest egg for later years.

Rodney Well, that's really nice of you, Alan. Yeah, I'm gonna take you up on that offer.

Alan I knew you'd say that.

Rodney Well, you know, I'm not one of these grab the money and run merchants. My philosophy's always been: look after the future *now*!

Alan My sentiments exactly. *(Opens envelope and looks at cheque)* So let's see, nine hundred and thirty five pounds invested in a policy attracting a gross annual interest of what …

Rodney *(Cuts in)* Nine hundred and thirty five pound! Oh I'll take that now, Alan!

Alan But what about the future?

Rodney What future? I work for *Del*!

Rodney snatches the cheque and exits shot.

EXT. DAY. THE CHURCH NAVE.

We see Del walking to a door.

INT. DAY. VESTRY.

Vicar I don't quite understand what you mean, Mr Trotter.

Del Let me try to explain, shall I. Err … let me see, yes … What would you do if you had an extra ten or twenty thousand pounds a year coming in?

Vicar Well … build a new youth club, buy a mini-bus for the old-folks' outings. I'm afraid I'm not used to making decisions of that magnitude.

Del Oh well, I can change all that, Reverend. I have come up with an idea that can revolutionise your fund-raising mechanism. *(Points to silver chalice)* What do you put in there?

Vicar Communion wine.

Del Yeah, I know. but before you pour it in it's not communion wine, is it?

Vicar Well, no, it's ordinary wine until I bless it.

Del 'Til you bless it, exactly! Now then, tell me how long does that take to bless it?

Vicar Two or three minutes.

Del Two or three minutes, right, well let's call it what – say three minutes, that's three minutes, three times a day, that's three three's are nine, nine minutes a day, seven days a week, 'cos I know you blokes, you work on Sundays, an' all don't you? That works out about one hour a week – times fifty two – that works out to about

two days a year you lose just blessing wine. And that's not including the trip down to Oddbins to pick it up. So I reckon that you lose about, what say – one week every year just blessing wine.

Vicar Well, possibly.

Del No possibly, no. Positively. You just think about it – think of all the other clergymen all over the country who are also losing one week every year, eh? Cor dear, we must be losing months and months of vicar-hours! Just … just think of all the good works that you could do with all them lost months.

Vicar Well , I never thought of it like that before.

Del Well I have, I have! And I tell you it has been bothering me. Come and sit down here, sit down, your Reverence. Just a minute. *(Del fetches chair)*

Vicar Well …

Del No, it's alright you just sit down for a second and let me explain. *(Del sits the Vicar in the chair)* 'Cos I have worked out a way in which I can give you back that precious, quality time.

Vicar How?

Del Are you ready for this? Trotter's pre-blessed wine!

Vicar Trotters' Pre-blessed wine?

Del Yes, it's like the holy version of sliced bread. Right, hang on a minute, see, look, I've got this mate of mine, right. I have this mate of mine, he's a vintner up North and he's shipping in this new range of Romanian wine.

Vicar *Romanian* wine?

Del Yeah, it's gonna be all the rage, don't you worry about it. And the idea is this, they drive it straight up from Tilbury to here, where you will bless it by the lorryload, right? Then we'll ship it out to all the churches and all the cathedrals all over the country. I mean once we're up and running there'll be no stopping us. Where are we now? What? It's nearly 1992, I mean this time next year we'll be exporting all over Europe. And here is the brick on top of the chimney, right. We get it at one thirty nine a bottle, we knock it out at two pound fifty! The church'll be rejoicing, the flock'll be redeemed and you and I'll be a nicker and a bit in front – everyone's a winner. Rein a dire, rein a faire as they say in Lourdes.

Vicar *(Is totally fazed out by Del's speed)* Yes, I could see how it could save time, but …

Del Time, yes, of course it can save time. And time is money, money that is much better spent on roof and orphans and organs, that is my motto.

Miami Twice The American Dream

Vicar It's very commendable of you, Mr Trotter, but ... I'm slightly, ... stunned!

Del Yes, of course you are, course you are. Now you know how the people felt when they saw the burning bush or the first Pot Noodle. I mean this time next year, Thora Hird will be asking for *your* autograph! Yeah, I know, it knocks you sideways dunnit? I dunno, it must be a sign or something like that. Anyway, listen, I'll let you think about it, alright. In the meantime what I'll do is, I'll send in the first lorryload so you can have a bit of a practice. See if you can interest your other colleagues you know, square it with the bishops ...

Vicar Well ...

Del That sorta thing. You know it makes sense!

Vicar Yes. Er, Mr ...

Del Oh, by the way, listen, I just wanted to slip you this *(Lays a few notes on table)* that is for the christening – it was a belter. Bonjour for now.

Del exits leaving the Vicar totally confused.
Cut to:

INT. DAY. NAVE. LOBBY LEADING TO MAIN DOORS.

Del walks through the church, he semi-bows awkwardly to the altar. Mickey Pearce is waiting as Del exits.

Mickey Del boy!

Del Sshh, please. *(Indicating surroundings)* What d'you want?

Mickey I've heard there's some business going down, I was just wondering if there was something in it for me. I'm the managing director of me own firm now.

Del Oh yeah? I'm very impressed, Mickey, no, there's nothing in it for you. I'm doing this for charity.

Mickey Oh well, if ... if you, hear of something, let us know, eh? I mean, I've always done you a good turn.

Del When have you ever done anything for me?

Mickey Er ... Well, will do you turns in future then ... Look just remember, if you need any help.

Del Alright, thank you very much, Mickey, I'll bear it in mind, alright ... *(Now thinks)* Wait a minute, wait a minute ... I was wondering ...

Mickey What?

Del No, I don't think you can handle it.

Mickey I can handle it, no sweat. What is it?

Del Well, little bit out of your normal area this, Mickey, as long as you're not frightened of a challenge?

Mickey There's nothing I like better than a challenge. I'm your man.

Del Alright, put it there.

Del spits on the palm of his right hand.
Mickey does likewise. They slap hands.

Del Good, that is a deal. You come with me and I'll tell you what I want you to do.

They walk away from camera.

Mickey My firm is in a phase of expansion. I was computerised three months ago.

Del Yeah? I thought you had a bit of a limp.

EXT. DAY. THE NAG'S HEAD CAR PARK.

Same day, same clothes. We see parked there the three wheel van, Boycie's Merc, Alan's Jag, Cassandra's Escort and Denzil's van. Del now pulls in his Capri Ghia. He alights and makes his way towards the back door to pub. As he does so, the door opens and Cassandra exits, hitting Del with the door as she rushes past. She is upset at something.

Del Oh Gordon Bennett! Oh sweetheart, what's the matter?

Cassandra I've never been so embarrassed. I just wish you could choose your parents!

Del *(Alan's done it again tone)* Oh not! It's not Alan again, is it?

Cassandra It's always the same when we have family parties. A couple of drinks, that's all it takes.

We see Alan appear at door. He appears exactly the same as previous scene. He leans against the wall.

Del You ought to stay off the scotch.

Alan I haven't been on the scotch, I've been on the shandies.

Now Pam appears. She is slurringly drunk. This is a Pam we haven't seen before, with all her working class roots showing.

Pam Hello Del. Issa smashing do!

Alan Yeah, co ... come on, love.

Pam Kissey, kissey Del.

Del begins to comply.

Alan Del!

Del Sorry!

Cassandra Just take her home, daddy!

Alan Oh yeah, what do I do with her then?

Del Well, I've got a length of rope in the back of the van.

Alan gives him a serious looking at.

Alan Don't, Del. Come on, Pam.

Del Ooh! *(Chuckles)*

Alan helps Pam into the back seat of the Jag.

Cassandra *(To Del)* How am I gonna live the embarrassment down?

Del Well, you'd better have a word with

Rodney, he's had years of experience. *(Laughs)* No, sorry, anyway talking about Rodney. What is it between you two. He's well gutted about this Saturday and Sunday arrangement. I mean, what's happened between you two?

Cassandra It's private, Del.

Del Alright, well I won't stick me nose in. But if you wanna talk, either of you, I'm here. And you know me, I'm straight down the line, no old bull and no porkies.

Cassandra Thanks, Del.

Del Alright.

Cassandra Is Damien back at the flat?

Del Oh yeah, yeah.

Cassandra Who's baby-sitting?

Del Mickey Pearce.
They exit to pub.

INT. NIGHT. THE NAGS HEAD.

The christening party is in full swing and Albert is singing and playing the piano. He continues playing for a minute or so and then returns to bar. The juke box then takes over. Del is in background with Raquel.
We see Cassandra standing alone. Rodney appears a few yards behind her so she is unaware of his presence. Rodney is now in shirtsleeves, his suit jacket hanging on a nearby chair. Rodney is unsure whether to approach her: can he risk a row at Damien's christening party? Finally he steels himself, puts on a brave smile and steps towards her. At this point Cassandra's attention is drawn to the bar where Marlene is showing Raquel the holiday brochure.
Cassandra moves towards bar.

Cassandra Oh, is that the holiday brochure?
Rodney is left in mid-approach.

Marlene Yeah, look these are all the hotels we're staying at.
Cut away to bar where we find Boycie and Mike. Halfway through their conversation Rodney appears at bar close to them.

Boycie I don't believe that woman! How many times have I got to tell her to keep quiet about this holiday?

Mike Why's that then, Boyce?

Boycie Well, I don't want every cat burglar in Peckham to know that my house is going to be empty for three weeks, do I? I'm security conscious these days. That's why I haven't ordered a mini-cab to take us to the airport. Del-boy's doing it. I wanted a close and trusted friend to take us.

Mike Yeah, but they were all busy, were they?

Boycie That's right, so I had to ask Del.
Mike and Boycie laugh.

Boycie Mind you, I've gotta hand it to him, he's put on a good spread here today.

Mike What d'you mean *he's* put on a good spread? This is all on the slate. I've got so many of his slates under here I could re-tile me bloody roof.

Rodney Oi, Del'll pay you, no worries.

Boycie Yeah, Del's had a big cheque arrive.

Rodney *(To Mike)* There, what about that, mouthy?

Boycie Nine hundred and thirty five quid!

Rodney *(To Mike)* See?
Rodney now reacts to this familiar figure. Mike and Boycie continue over Rodney's reaction.

Boycie I saw the cheque!

Mike Yeah, I saw an advert for the RAC but I still broke down!
Rodney now dashes across to his jacket hanging on chair. He feels inside pockets but the cheque is missing. Del appears behind him.

Del *(Brandishing the cheque)* Gotcha! You looking for that, are you? What d'you leave this in your jacket for? Someone could have taken it!

Rodney Somebody did bloody take it!

Del This could have been nicked, forged and cashed before you could say Marriage Guidance Council.

Rodney *(Reacts to these words)* Shuddup about that!

Del Well, that's it, listen, I'm taking this down, and I'm paying this into your account, next week, alright?

Rodney Yes, alright.

Del Right. How are things between you and Cassandra?

Rodney Why?

Del Well, you don't seem to be talking to her very much.

Rodney Well, we ain't got much to say to each other.

Del What's the matter Rodney? What's the problem between you two?

Rodney It's private, alright?

Del Look, you used to confide in me. Now you tell me nothing! Look, I might be able to help you.

Rodney Del, watch my lips. It is *private*, alright? I'll sort it out in my own way.

Del Alright! You watch my lips. You'll sort nothing out without talking about it!

Rodney *(Angrily)* Alright!

Miami Twice The American Dream

Del Alright! Go on, go away and enjoy yourself.
Rodney I will!
Del Good!
Del joins Boycie and Mike at the bar.
Rodney moves a bit further down the bar to
where Trigger is standing.
Del Gawd! Mike, give me a Piña Colada, I could
strangle one, will you?
Cut away to Rodney and Trigger.
Rodney *(To himself)* Bloody women!
Trigger Problems, Dave?
Rodney I don't wanna talk about it, Trig. You
ever been wrongly accused of something?
Trigger Yeah, once.
Rodney *(Sensing Trig is a soul-mate)* Yeah?
How d'you get out of it?
Trigger Well, I didn't, I was guilty.
Rodney just stares at him for a few seconds
then turns away. Cut away to Del, Boycie and
Mike.
Del Right then Boycie, now listen to me, I'm
gonna take you down to the airport in style.
You'll go in me Capri Ghia. What time d'you
want me to pick you up?
Boycie About eleven o'clock. The plane leaves
at one thirty.
Mike I don't think I'd go to America.
Boycie And what's wrong with America?
Mike It's violent, innit?
Boycie *(Laughs)* You've been watching too
much telly.
Del Yeah.
Mike I'm telling you, they're on the verge of a
drugs war over there.
Del Oh get out, who told you that?
Mike *(Sheepishly)* Well, I saw a programme on
the telly.
Del On the telly!
Del and Boycie laugh at this.
Boycie See what I mean? Soppy as a sack. I'll
bet he sent a note of sympathy to Rita Fairclough
when old Len snuffed it.
Del You know what, he closed the pub for a
week when Daphne in *Neighbours* died!
Del and Boycie laugh even louder.
Mike When I say a programme on telly …
Trigger *(Cuts in)* I don't think you should laugh
about things like that.
Del Eh?
Trigger The dead can't defend themselves.
Del No, no. You see Trig, the thing was …
Trigger *(Cuts in)* She had a three month old
baby.
Mike Who did, Rita Fairclough?
Trigger I'm talking about Daphne.

Del Yeah, yeah, I'm sorry Trig. No, no, it was …
it was tragic.
Trigger Well, I've made my point.
Trigger moves from bar.
Boycie Yeah … Er … sorry about that, Trig.
Del You've gotta be very careful. I mean Trig
gets very emotional. He's Italian on his dad's
friend's side.
Mike When I say … listen fellas.
Del What?
Mike When I say a programme on the telly, I'm
not talking about *Hill Street Blues* or *Magnum*.
This was *Panorama*!
Del and Boycie *Panarama*!
Mike Yeah, listen, they've got contract killers on
the loose over there.
Del Well how's that gonna affect Boycie? He's
going with Thomas Cook!
Boycie Michael, I hardly think some hit man's
gonna have a pop at two British tourists.
Del Yeah, and if he does he'd better do it in the
evening. I mean, one look at Marlene when she
gets outta bed's enough to make anyone run a
mile! That woman could put the frights up
Hannibal Lecter.
Del, Mike and Boycie laugh at this.
Mike I like that Del.
Now Boycie's laughter slowly dies.
Boycie Here, how'd you know what Marlene
looks like when she gets out of bed?
Del Your milkman told me.
Boycie *(Accepts this as a fair explanation)* Oh!

EXT. NIGHT. THE NAG'S HEAD CAR PARK.
Cassandra is sitting on the wall.
Rodney appears behind her.
Rodney Hi.
Cassandra Hi.
Rodney Lovely evening.
Cassandra Mmmh.
Rodney You got time for a chat?
Cassandra If it's got anything to do with
uniforms the answer's no!
Rodney Ssshh! No, it's got nothing to do with
uniforms!
Cassandra I'm not dressing up as a Victorian
maid for anyone.
Rodney Will you keep your voice down? Look,
I'd had a few drinks, and I said something stupid.
That's no reason to kick me out the flat! I mean,
haven't you ever said something stupid?
Cassandra Yeah, a couple of years ago I said, 'I
do!'
Rodney That's not fair, Cass.
Cassandra I didn't mean it, I'm sorry.

Rodney Look, I won't mention uniforms again – promise.

Cassandra Alright then.

Rodney Well, glad the christening went off alright.

Cassandra I thought it was very really moving. He's such a lovely baby.

Rodney Lovely? He's always biting me. He takes great chunks of flesh out me arms.

Cassandra You liar. He smiled when he saw you.

Rodney Yeah, 'cos he thought here comes elevenses!

They laugh.

Cassandra Oh shut up, he's a beautiful little thing.

Rodney Well, yeah that's easy for you to say innit? You haven't got to live in the same flat as h … *(Realises he's touched on a sore subject)* … Look, I'm sorry, I wasn't tryin' to … well, you know.

Cassandra You don't live at Del's *all* the time. We spend the weekends together.

Rodney Oh yeah, yeah, we spend *weekends* together.

Cassandra Don't start, Roddy. We discussed all our problems with the Relate counsellor. And d'you remember what she said? After she stopped laughing. She advised us to try and get back together gradually by just spending the weekends together at first.

Rodney You must be joking.

Cassandra Well the offer still holds. It's up to you, Roddy. Now, d'you think we could change the subject.

Rodney Yes, sorry! How are things at the bank? Heard anything about your promotion?

Cassandra Not yet. But I'm definitely on the short list. I've been invited to the company's seminar in Eastbourne.

Rodney *(Sarcastically)* Ooh! A seminar in Eastbourne! Oooh! Sorry! Well, it's important then is it, this seminar?

Cassandra It's where the final interviews will be held.

Rodney Well, here's to your future.

Cassandra Ours.

Rodney *(Unconvinced)* Yeah.

Cassandra Don't look like that! Please? This is supposed to be a happy occasion.

Rodney Well, that's just it! Everybody is celebrating. Boycie and Marlene are off to the States, Del and Raquel have just christened the chavvie.

Cassandra Well, that could be us in a while.

Rodney What?… A baby?

Cassandra No, I meant we could go to America. It's always been an ambition of mine. Once I get my promotion we could put some money aside and we could have a holiday in California or Florida.

Rodney Yeah! When?

Cassandra I don't know! A couple of years.

Rodney *(He smiles but his eyes show the disappointment)* Cosmic!

INT. DAY. SID'S CAFE.

Ten days later.

Rodney, suitcase by his side, is seated at a table with Albert, Trigger and Denzil. They all wear their working clothes and Trigger's broom is resting against wall.

Sid, with the obligatory cigarette in corner of mouth, is behind the counter. The other tables are taken by market and building site workers some of whom look very tough characters. Behind him we can hear a slightly heated discussion.

Trigger But it's only a bunch of trees, Dave. There must be thousands of trees in the world.

Rodney It is not just a bunch of trees, Trig! It is the Brazilian rain forest, the lungs of the world! And they are destroying it at the rate of twenty five acres a day!

Trigger Where is that then exactly?

Rodney Huh?

Trigger Where is the Brazilian rain forest?

Rodney It's on the outskirts of Luton! Where d'you think it is, Trig? It's in Brazil!

Del, wearing his yuppie gear, enters in a buoyant mood. As he passes Albert he drops a bag of laundry by his side.

Del Ah, Albert there you are! Listen I've booked you a front row seat at the Launderama Go on, away you go. 'Ere, Rodney, I want a word with you. Ah, giss a decaffeinated Cappuccino and a jam doughnut, will you Sid?

The conversation at Rodney's table continues under this exchange.

Sid He's on about that bleedin' rain forest again! That's the fourth time this week, Rodney's given a lecture in my caff.

Del Well, that's alright, he's worried about our world, ain't he? It wouldn't do you any harm to show a bit more care an' all, look at that.

Rodney You see, it's fossil fuels! People do not realise the damage they are doing to this planet.

Trigger I don't have none of them in my house. I use gas and oil.

Rodney Trig, they *are* fossil fuels!

Miami Twice The American Dream

Trigger Are they? Well, I'll switch to coal in future.

Rodney No! No! Coal is the same!

Denzil I had a coal burner fitted in my place, it's not as dear as you think, you know Rodney.

Albert exits.

Del Put it on Rodney's slate, will you?

Rodney I don't know how many bloody trees there are Trig, they're just cutting 'em down …

Del Rodney, Rodders, Leave it out! You'll never turn this lot Green as long as you've got an 'ole in your ozone! Yep. I've got some exciting news to tell you in private. Come on down here. Private, please, do you mind? Thank you.

Del and Rodney move to an empty table.

Rodney I give up on you two. God! It's so frustrating tryin' to make people understand what is happening on our planet.

Del Yeah, I know, it gives me the right 'ump an' all.

Rodney D'you know, they are more concerned with a postcard from Boycie and Marlene!

Del Gawd, dear, 'ere we had one of those this morning. 'Ere look at that. It's a lovely hotel, innit eh?

Rodney *(Totally exasperated)* Del! Alright, so what's this exciting news, then?

Del Oh yes! Well I went down the bank this morning, right to pay in your cheque. I would have done it earlier but you know, I've been having trouble with me wine deal and what have you.

Sid gives Del a bun.

Del Thank you very much, Sid.

Rodney So *you* have paid it in?

Del Yeah. Of course I have. You've gotta look after that money, Rodney, I don't want you sending it all off to Sting, do I? Anyway, when I was down there I bumped into Cassandra, she was just going to lunch, so I joined her. While I was having lunch I had this great idea on your behalf. Because I know how much you like to travel.

Rodney I am *not* going to Romania! I know your wine shipment's developed problems.

Del Who told you that?

Rodney Raquel said you had a call from Bucharest last night and when you come off the 'phone you was all pale and sweaty.

Del *(Nervous of this news leaking)* Yep, it's alright, it's alright. It's nothing I can't handle – it's just a little hiccup with the old translation that's all. Anyway, listen, this idea was for you and Cassandra. We got talking, we was talking about Boycie and Marlene's holiday, now it

worked out that Cassandra would love to go to America.

Rodney nods.

Del On the way down here, right, I called into Alex's, you know, the travel agent in the High Street. He has got a once in a lifetime offer, never to be repeated, right? It's practically almost a give away, Rodney! Return tickets to *Miami*, two hundred and fifty smackeroonies.

Rodney Yeah, well that's a monkey before you got a bed for the night, innit?

Del No, no, no, no it ain't! You see, because, here's the cherry on top of the cake … two go for the price of one! Think about it, Rodney. You and Cassandra spending a week on Miami Beach!

Rodney *(Smiles at the prospect – he is nibbling the bait)* Miami … Na, I could never afford it!

Del Course you can afford it, what are you talking about, you've got your Maxwell money, haven't you?

Rodney Me what?

Del Maxwell, your pension money!

Rodney *(Has obviously taken the bait)* Miami?

Del Mmmh.

Rodney Two for the price of one?

Del Oh Rodney, just think about it, I mean, she'll love it, she will, I know that. Just imagine how old Cassandra's gonna feel when you announce your holiday of a lifetime! She'll be all over you like a rash! *(Laughs)* I mean, is that a brilliant idea or is it just, like, wonderful, or what?

Rodney Bloody 'ell, Del, it's a cosmic idea!

Del Yeah.

Rodney Would you let me have the time off?

Del Of course you can have the time off!

Rodney Oh, ace. Oh but what about Cassy?

Del No, it's alright, don't worry about her, because the bank like they owe her a couple or three weeks holiday, she told me. You're off and running, bruv!

Rodney Yeah?

Del Yeah.

Rodney I'd better go and 'phone her, just make sure it's alright.

Del No, no!! Don't 'phone her.

Rodney No?

Del No, don't phone her, no, no, no. Sit down there. You take her out to dinner, right and, then when you get to the old coffee and the Gran' Marnier stakes you throw the tickets down on to the table and say; Darling, I'm taking you to Miami. You'll knock her bandy!

Rodney *Yeah!* Right, I'd better get down that

travel agents a bit sharpish.

Del No, no, don't go down there, no, no, no, no, no, no. Stay there. Save the shoe-leather, Rodney. *(Lays two airline tickets on table)* 'Cos you see, I got 'em for you.

Rodney Derek, you are a diamond ... I How did d'you know I wanted 'em?

Del Mmh? Well I just thought to myself, even a plonker like you wouldn't turn your nose up at a deal like this.

Rodney I don't know what I'd do without you sometimes! I wouldn't have thought of that in a million years ... How did you afford it? I thought you were skint.

Del I am. I took your cheque down the bank and cashed it.

Rodney You took one of money out of *my* account ... you ...

Del *(Mistaking this for gratitude)* Don't you dare thank me! It was nothing, it's no big deal, I can forge your signature as easy as that.

INT. NIGHT. THE TROTTERS' LOUNGE.

This is a few days later. Albert is watching TV. Del, in his yuppy clothes and carrying all the yuppy paraphernalia, enters from hall/front door. He appears harassed and hunted. Upon seeing Albert he changes to casual mode.

Del Alright, Unc'?

Albert Yeah, lovely, son.

Del Where is everyone?

Albert Little 'un's in his cot, Raquel's cooking the tea, Rodney's taken Cassandra out to dinner. 'Ere, he's gonna tell her about Miami. Coo, I'd love to be there and see her face.

Del *(A little edge to his tone)* Yeah! So would I. 'Ere look, alright, oi, oi, oi, oi, *(Turns TV off)* now just ... Any calls for me?

Albert Calls?

Del Yes, you know has the telephone rung and a voice asked to speak to me?

Albert Not that I'm aware of.

Del Right, good. Thank God for that!

Albert Talking about God, I saw a funny thing today. I was walking past the church, you know, the one where we held the christening, and there was a big, articulated lorry parked in the grounds. There was some sorta German writing on the side and the back doors were open – full up with cases of wine, it was.

Del looks fearful

Albert And that vicar, the one what christened Damien, he was making the sign of the cross and saying a prayer to this lorry.

Del *(Cringes)* Funny old world, innit, eh? Listen to me. *Anyone* 'phones or calls round here, and asks for me, I'm not in! Alright?

Raquel, unseen by Del, has entered from the kitchen.

Raquel When you say, 'anyone' do you mean particularly people with Romanian accents?

Del No! Hello, sweetheart, didn't hear you creep in. No, I didn't mean people with Romanian accents. I just thought I ought to maintain a bit of a low profile for a while. So anyway, I think I'll go and take a look at Damien.

Raquel You dare! It's taken me over an hour to get him to sleep.

Del Oh, alright, alright. Well, I think I'll make myself a Singapore Sling to er, unwind and then I'll take a nice hot bath.

We hear front door slam.

Albert *(Excited)* Rodney's back!

Rodney enters from hall. He is wearing his best suit and is fuming.

Del Alright, Rodders?

Raquel Come on then. What's Cassandra say?

Rodney *(Slams the hall door)* I'm going to bed!

Del Everything all right, bruv?

Rodney Oh *brilliant*, Del! Bloody brilliant! Cassandra can not come to Miami with me!

Del Eh?

Albert Why not?

Rodney Because she is busy that week!

Raquel Doing what?

Rodney Oh she has to attend the *bank's* seminar in bloody Eastbourne! Can you believe that? She is giving up a trip to Miami for some crappy interviews so as she can become an executive!

Del That girl ought to get her priorities right!

Raquel Now hold on a moment. Let's be fair about this.

Del Now, hold on, let's be fair about this, Rodney.

Raquel Cassandra's told me about these interviews. They're very important to her. She's been going to college and evening school for five years now and it's all been leading to this seminar. You can't expect her to risk her future for seven days in the sun.

Rodney It's not that, Raquel. It's ... well it's just my luck, innit? *Any other* week of the year would have been fine. But, no, it had to be *that* week!

Raquel I know it's tough, Rodney, but ... well ... it's just the way it goes.

Rodney Well for me it is, yeah ... See you in the morning.

Rodney exits to bedrooms area.

Miami Twice The American Dream

Del Yeah. goodnight bruv. Dear, oh dear, oh Lord. That's a body-blow, innit? There you are.
Del hands Albert a drink.
Albert Yeah. He was really looking forward to that as well.
Raquel It's a pity he didn't 'phone Cassandra first to make sure everything was alright.
Del Yeah. Well, of course, I said to him, I told him to, 'Phone her! I said, 'You 'phone her – make sure that she can make that week.' But you know he wouldn't listen, you know what he's like, don't you?
Raquel Mmmh. It's a shame.
Del Yeah.

INT. NIGHT. RODNEY AND DAMIEN'S BEDROOM.

We have never seen Rodney's bedroom before so, regardless of what it may have looked like prior to this, it is now Damien's nursery. It is a smallish room. In one corner is the baby's cot, opposite is Rodney's bed with a very plain, old-fashioned mahogany headboard. We have Rodney's old and slightly battered wardrobe and Damien's brand new set of white chest-of-drawers covered with little transfers of fairy tale characters and a little baby lamp on top. The wallpaper is Thomas the Tank Engine with Smurf curtains. On Damien's side of the room we have a couple of wall pictures of The Shoe People and the Magic Roundabout. On Rodney's wall there is a large poster of ZZ Top.
We see Damien lying fast asleep in his cot. All is warmth and peace – like a scene from a Carvel ad.
We now pan to Rodney's side and find his suit and shirt thrown in a heap on the end of bed. We find Rodney sitting on the bed and just removing and chucking his last sock.
Rodney *(Mumbles very quietly to himself)* Stupid bank! Stupid, stupid bank!
He falls back onto bed and pulls the comforting covers up around his neck. He lays his weary head on the pillow and closes his eyes.
We stay with him for a couple of seconds. All is silent – not even the sound of breathing. Now something makes Rodney half-open his eyes. We cut to a shot from Rodney's POV. We see Damien standing in his cot and staring at Rodney.
Music over:
A quick burst of the Omen theme.
Kill music and cut back to Rodney whose eyes

are also wide open – but with fear. Rodney lifts himself up onto his elbow and tries to regain his composure.
Rodney Go to sleep, Damien! Otherwise Uncle Rodney will get angry, and you wouldn't like me when I'm angry!
As Rodney speaks his next line we pan up to the baby lamp atop the chest-of-drawers. Next to the lamp we see the baby intercom box (Marlene's present).
Rodney *(OOV)* Look just pack it in, will you?

INT. NIGHT. THE LOUNGE.

We find Del and Albert looking curiously towards the other baby intercom box. We hear Rodney from the box.
Rodney *(OOV) (Distort)* You don't frighten me. So just go to sleep, you little sod!
Albert What's he doing in there?
Del Dunno, it sounds like he's having a row with Damien! *(Del moves to intercom box)* How d'you work this thing? *(Del switches his intercom box on)*

INT. NIGHT. RODNEY AND DAMIEN'S BEDROOM.

Rodney lays back in bed and closes his eyes. Now we hear Del speaking through the baby intercom box.
Del *(OOV, distorted)* Who'd you think you're talking to, Rodney?
Rodney opens his eyes in alarm believing that the eight-month-old Damien has just had a pop at him.
Rodney Jesus on a bike!
He leaps out of bed.

INT. NIGHT. THE LOUNGE.

Del is standing by the intercom box as Raquel enters from kitchen.
Raquel What's happened?
Now Rodney, in dressing gown and being pursued by devils, flies in from bedrooms area. He stops and tries to appear normal.
Del You alright, bruv?
Rodney Yeah … yeah, fine.
Raquel You look pale.
Rodney No, um, oh I was just thinking, oh what I, I'll probably won't sleep in here with Damien, no more, 'cos, I … I keep snoring, and waking him up, bless him. I'll, I'll kip down here on the sofa if that's alright?
Del Yeah, anything you like, bruv.
Rodney Right, well, I'll just have a quick shower then I'll hit the sack.

We now hear Damien crying.

Rodney *(To Raquel)* Sorry.

Raquel That's alright, I'm used to it.

Raquel exits to bedrooms area.

Del You going, are you, love, yeah? Alright. You was really looking forward to going to Miami, weren't you?

Rodney I had, dreams, you know, of what it would be like.

Albert You'll get your money back, though son.

Rodney No I won't. The tickets are non-refundable.

Del Still going though, aren't you?

Rodney Well, of course I ain't!

Del Of course you are, Rodney. You've gotta go! Otherwise Cassandra'll think you're nothing but a ... a little puppet who can't do anything unless she, she pulls your strings!

Rodney Yeah, but I'll be all on me own!

Del All on your own! You're only going for a week, ain't you! You ought to to think about him *(Indicating Albert)* He was all on his own once for three months on an uninhabited island. Of course it wasn't uninhabited when he arrived but that's another story! Now listen, Rodney, now you've gotta go. You've gotta prove to Cassandra that you're a man! And you're not frightened to stand on your own two feet in the big world!

Rodney D'you know, you're right!

Del Yeah.

Albert So, are you going, son?

Rodney *(With emphatic, masculine determination)* Possibly!!

Rodney exits to bedrooms area.

Albert He won't go, will he?

Del Yeah course he'll go, Unc'. And d'you know why? 'Cos I'm going with him!

INT. NIGHT. RODNEY AND DAMIEN'S BEDROOM.

Raquel is putting Damien in his cot.

Raquel There you are. You've got a lovely cot, haven't you? You're all warm and happy. We wish poor Uncle Rodney was, don't we? He can't go to Miami now. It's a shame. Shall I put your mobile on for you, the one Daddy bought you? Yeah. *(She winds mobile up)* You've got a lovely Daddy, haven't you? Buying you all these nice presents. *(Now a pause for thought)* Maybe Daddy could go with Uncle Rodney. You wouldn't mind, would you? He'll only be gone for a week. *(She switches mobile on. Nothing. She waits for it to spring into life. Still nothing)* *(Baby talk)* I wonder where Daddy got that from?

Yeah, it's a mystery, like so many things.

INT. NIGHT. THE LOUNGE.

Albert What about Raquel? Can you persuade her?

Del Can Fergie ski? I only wanna go for a week in Miami. It's not like I'm taking a six month exhibition up the jungle, is it?

Albert My Ada weren't too happy when I told her I was going abroad.

Del No, that was 'cos you joined the navy and went round the world seven bloody times. No wonder the poor old cow got the needle.

INT. NIGHT RODNEY AND DAMIEN'S BEDROOM.

Raquel Na-nite, baby. Mummy's just outside. I'll switch your little box on case you need me.

She switches on intercom. We hear Del and Albert speaking.

Del *(Distort)* All I wanna do is go to Miami with Rodney for seven days. I mean, he's got a ticket going begging. Raquel has been to America ain't she? What about me? Nowhere, Benidorm and Bognor, that's me! Na, she'll be alright, Raquel'll be OK, you see. Yeah, I'll work her, everything'll be cushty.

Raquel smiles to herself.

INT. NIGHT. THE LOUNGE.

Albert I wouldn't be surprised if she puts the block on you.

Del Leave it out, Uncle, I'm the guv'nor in this house, ain't I? I shall just tell her, I shall just say, I shall say, 'Raquel, I'll say I'm going to go to Miami with my brother. Like it or lump it.' Yeah, that's what I'll say. Pick the bones out of that, darling!

Raquel enters from bedrooms area.

Del You alright, sweetheart?

Raquel Yeah, he's settled down.

Albert Del's got something to tell you, love.

Raquel Oh yeah, what's that?

Del *(Right on the spot)* That programme you want to watch on the television, the film is just about to start in a minute innit? Come on, come on, come on, sit down on your chaise-longue, that's right.

Raquel But your dinner's in the oven.

Raquel sits on settee.

Del Don't worry about that. I like it all baked up.

Del gets up and turns lights down.

Del There we go. Can I get you a drink?

Raquel No thanks.

Miami Twice The American Dream

Del Oh alright then, now there you go. Are you nice and comfy there?

Raquel Mmmh.

Del sits next to her. Pause.

Del There you are darling, yes, cushty. Come on then, come to your lover, that's it … Oh it's a shame, innit?

Raquel *(Allows herself a little smile as she feigns interest in TV)* Mmmhh!

Del *(Frustrated)* Yeah, it's a *crying* bloody shame.

Raquel What is?

Del Poor little Rodney.

Albert You mean those tickets to Miami, son?

Del Yes, that's right Unc'. 'Cos Cassandra she can't go with him now, so he won't be able to go.

Raquel Couldn't Rodney go on his own?

Del No, definitely not!

Raquel I went to America on my own.

Del Yeah, I know that, but that's 'cos you've got a bit of savvy, haven't you. You couldn't have Rodney Trotter and Dan Quayle on the same continent! No, he needs someone to look after him. Yeah, trouble is, that's it innit? But what can you do, you know.

Raquel Mmmh.

Pause.

Del Poor little Rodney.

Albert Here, I've got an idea.

Del *(Snatches at it)* What's that, Unc'?

Albert Why don't he take someone with him?

Raquel That's a good idea. I'm surprised you didn't think of that, Del.

Del Yeah, well, so am I. Yeah, yeah of course, trouble is … ummm …

Raquel Who?

Del Who?

Albert What about … Mickey Pearce?

Del reacts.

Del That's a, that's a great idea, it's brilliant, it's a brilliant idea, Unc', but the trouble is, the trouble is, the, the tickets you see are made out in the name of Trotter. And they're not transferable.

Raquel You mean, he's got to go with someone named Trotter?

Del Exactly, exactly … Oh dear. *Poor – little – Rodney!*

Raquel *(Can hardly stop from laughing)* Why don't you go with him, Del?

Del *Meeee?*

Albert Yeah! Your name's Trotter.

Del Yes, yes, that's great, yeah. But …

Raquel But what?

Del No I, no I, I couldn't go and leave you and little Damien on your own.

Albert I'd be here.

Del Yeah, that's like asking Macdonalds to look after your cow innit?

Raquel But it's only for a week. I think Damien and I could *just* about manage to survive.

Del Yeah, no, no, I couldn't do that, darling, no because I'm not that sort of bloke, you see. I mean I'd be worried sick.

Raquel Oh, alright then, don't wanna make you ill.

Del *(Reacts, 'shit, I've lost my chance')* On the other hand, I don't wanna be selfish.

Raquel I couldn't imagine you doing that, Del.

Del No, no, no you see, the thing is, the thing is. This is a chance of a lifetime for little Rodney, the poor little cock, you know. And well, as it was my idea I feel partly to blame.

Raquel *(Kisses Del)* Go to Miami, Del.

Del Oh, really?

Raquel Really. You'll love it!

Del T'riffic! Of course, I'm not really looking forward to it, no, I'm only doing it for …

Raquel Poor little Rodney.

Del *(Together)* Poor little Rodney. Yeah, oh darling, you know what Raquel, you've got a heart like a diamond, you have, you have. You know what you remind me of, you remind me so much of my Mum.

Raquel Thanks.

Del And I'll bring you back a blinding present.

Rodney enters from bedrooms area. He is wearing towelling dressing gown and is showered.

Albert Here Rodney, Del's got some good news for you.

Del Yeah!

Rodney Oh yeah, what's that then?

Del I'm coming to Miami with you!

Rodney No you bloody ain't!

Del Eh?

Rodney I ain't going on holiday with you!

Del *(Embarrassed and desperate. To Raquel)* Excuse me. *(To Albert)* Excuse me a moment, would you. *(indicates bedrooms area)* Rodney, can I have a word with you in the executive boardroom, please?

Rodney Yeah, wherever you want.

Rodney exits to bedrooms area.

Del Thank you very much, *(To Albert and Raquel)* sorry about this it's err, he's just a little mixed up! I'll soon straighten him out. Thank you.

Del exits to bedrooms area.

INT. NIGHT. HALLWAY IN BEDROOM AREA.

Rodney is waiting as Del enters from lounge.

Rodney You've got a bloody nerve, ain't you!

Del Ssh, Damien! *(Rodney reacts)* In here. *Opens door to Del and Raquel's bedroom.*

INT. NIGHT. DEL AND RAQUEL'S BEDROOM.

Del and Rodney enter.

Del What's the matter with you, Rodney? What is your problem?

Rodney Del, I'm not flying four thousand miles across the Atlantic Ocean with you in me earhole all day and all night. I was hoping for a break from all that! You seem to forget, I've been on holiday with you before.

Del That's charming, that is, isn't it eh? Absolutely charming! After all that I have done for you. Oh dear what thanks do I get, eh? No bloody thanks, that's the thanks I get! *(We hear Damien crying)* An' I ... an' I ... Now look what you've done! *(Calls from door)* Sshh, sshh, Damien sshh it's alright, Daddy's here. *(Calls louder)* Raquel *(To Rodney)* Of course we've been on holiday before, Rodney, and we had a bloody good time, didn't we?

Rodney No. *You* had a good time, Del, everybody else within a radius of three hundred yards was praying their spleen would burst! You got drunk, you shouted things at women, you got us into fights.

Del We were on holiday!

Rodney Well, this time I'm looking for a more *relaxing* holiday.

Del Relaxing ho ... Oh, I see, so what you are trying to say that I'm not relaxing co ... that I'm not relaxing company, is that, is that ... *(Shouts from door)* Raquel, the baby's crying! *(Closes door)* Look Rodney, that's all different now, that, that was in the past, you see, 'cos I am a changed man, see? The reason why I am changed, I'm telling you, look, I'm a married man with a baby. Well, I mean, I've got a baby. *(Referring to the sound of Damien)* You see, and that's the reason why I've changed. Because I have got a son whom I cherish.

Raquel *(OOV)* Alright, darling, I'm coming.

Del And there is the mother of my son who cherishes me.

Raquel *(OOV, angrily)* Don't break your back, Trotter, I'll deal with him!

Del Thank you, sweetheart, thank you. You're judging me by a few what, misguided incidents, that's all, I've told you, I'm changed now! Rodney, come on, you wanna go to Miami, don't you?

Rodney Well, of course I wanna go! But, well, this time I want it to be – sensible.

Del Sense ... Sensible, course you do! I'm sensible. Sensible's my middle name.

Raquel *(OOV)* Del, will you bring me a nappy?

Del Yes, of course I will sweetheart. See, see that? Look Rodney, look, look, I mean look, all that I wanna do, is just sit on a beach and relax.

Rodney Well, same here.

Del Well, there you are. They've got some blinding beaches in Miami.

Rodney Mmm ...

Del Yeah ... and they've got umm ... some fantastic art museums in Miami.

Rodney Yeah?

Del Oh yeah, yeah.

Rodney I wouldn't mind some of that myself.

Del Well, of course you would and of course you can have it, Cinders, all you've got to do, is to say the magic words.

Rodney Yeah, but how you gonna swing it with Raquel?

Del Oh that, swing it, I've already done it. I told, I tol, I tol, sshh. I, I told her straight. I said I wanna go to Miami with Rodney on holiday, that's what I said and I said like it or lump it. You pick the bones out of that, darling, that's what I said.

Raquel *(OOV)* Derek!

Del Coming, sweetheart! Come on, eh? You and me, eh? What d'you say, yeah, yeah?

Rodney *(A little smile as he weakens)* Well ...

Del *(Yoking him on)* Eh? Yeah, come on! Say the magic words, Rodney!

Rodney Yeah alright then!

Del Yeah! Good boy, that's it, you see you know it makes sense! Right, where's that nappy? *Stretches to top of the cupboards.*

Rodney Well, you see, Del, we're older now, ain't we?

Del Eh?

Rodney We can appreciate the finer things of life, eh?

Del What? Not half!

Rodney *(Reaching up for nappy)* D'you want it?

Del Yeah, yeah gimme *(Catches nappy)* Thanks.

Rodney So this time let's be more – well, what's the word – sophisticated.

Del Yeah, that's a great word. I've got another word as well I was thinking of, like: debonair.

Rodney Yeah, yes yeah. That's a good word.

Del You see what I mean? We're beginning to think alike, bruv.

Raquel Derek!

Del Coming, sweetheart! I'm coming, I'm on

me way. *(Remembers)* Oh yes. *(Del produces his leopard-skin swimming trunks from the cupboard and hands them to Rodney)* Just a minute, I'm coming. Look, good job I kept them?

Del exits with a clean nappy.
Rodney holds up the trunks and stares at them.
Rodney mouths:

Oh, dear God!

We hear the whine of a jet engine over Rodney's face and mixing through into following scene:

EXT. DAY. AIRPORT.

We see a jumbo jet of Virgin Airlines parked at the boarding gate – the mobile walkway is connected to the plane and ready to receive it's passengers. We pan up to window of departure lounge where we see Del looking down at plane.

INT. DAY. DEPARTURE LOUNGE.

The lounge is crowded with holiday makers, etc. Del is looking from the window. He and Rodney are wearing their holiday clothes – Del's are, naturally, brighter than Rodney's. Del moves excitedly to Rodney who is seated.

Del 'Ere, have you seen it, Rodders?
Rodney Seen what?
Del You know, our plane! It's only a Jumbo Jet!
Rodney Yeah, well they usually are. I mean, this is transatlantic, innit?
Del Yeah. *(Savours the word)* Transatlantic!

A member of the Virgin ground staff makes announcement over mike.

GS Thank you for waiting, ladies and Gentlemen. Would all passengers seated in rows 19 through to 40 please come forward to board now? Thank you.
Del Come on, Rodders! That's us!
Rodney Wait, wait.
Del Let's go.
Rodney There's no hurry, Del.
Del Yes, yes there is, there is Rodney. Come on, the sooner we're on the plane, the sooner old Biggles can take off!

Del and Rodney pick up their hand luggage and approach boarding gate where a member of ground staff is checking ticket numbers. There is a small crowd of people here and Del elbows his way through. He bumps into and then elbows one man.

Del *(To man)* Eh! Excuse me, what's your game pal, eh? Come on, there's no rush. *(To Rodney)* Blimey, anybody would think he owned the plane!

Rodney looks at the man and does a double take. We see the man is Richard Branson. Richard smiles politely. Rodney cringes with embarrassment. Shot of Del and Rodney walking down walkway towards plane.

Del Hey, hey come on! Come on, Rodders! *(Singing)* Everything's free in America, kippers for tea in America. *(To stewardess)* Have a nice day.
Rodney Oi! Pack it in, get on that aeroplane!
Del Alright, alright.

Miami Twice (Part Two) Oh To Be In England

EXT. DAY.

Shot of jet airliner flying through sky.

INT. DAY. AIRLINER CABIN.

We track along the cabin taking in a number of average British holiday-makers and a few business-people (not every seat is taken) until we find the Trotters. Del is at window seat and wearing flashy summer shirt, a colourful sun hat and a pair of thick gold-framed, Benidorm-specials sunglasses (often referred to as 'bingo glasses'). He is excited by the whole event – looking from the window and around the cabin – like a kid trying to absorb every second of this adventure. He has a pair of in-flight earphones on. Rodney is in the middle seat (the aisle seat is empty). He is casually reading a book.

Del *(Still with headphones on and so speaking too loudly)* Hey hey hey – we've done it, Rodders!

Rodney Done what?

Del Eh?

Rodney *(A little louder)* Done what?

Del Done it – joined the glitterati!

Rodney The glitterati?

Del Eh?

Rodney Take the headphones off!

Del Eh? Oh. Sorry *(Takes the headphones off)* Do what?

Rodney What do you mean, we've joined the Glitterati?

Del Well we have, ain't we? We're transatlantic people now ain't we, eh? No more of that Costa Del Sewage for us, bruv. We're in the big time now.

Rodney Yeah, I suppose so. Oi, Del, when we land in Miami, right, before we go to any bars or anything like that, the first thing we gotta do is sort ourselves out some transport and accommodation.

Del It's all taken care of, bruv. You know Alex, the travel agent, he faxed one of his people in the States.

Rodney So we're all fixed up? Ace! Oh well, I'll pay Alex when I get back. I'll do it on me credit card, eh?

Del No, there's no need – I've already done it.

Rodney Good!… What, on *my* credit card?

Del Well, yeah. That's what you were gonna do, weren't it?

Rodney Yeah.

Del Well, that's it, I've saved you the bother. 'Cos this is your holiday, and I don't want nothing to mar it.

Rodney *(Politely uncertain)* Thanks.

Del We're gonna live it up a little, ain't we?

Rodney Well … yes! But there are two kinds of living it up, Del. You know – enjoying the freedom from the stresses of work, filling the mind with new sights and sounds, experiencing local cuisine and culture, even indulging in the gifts of nature such as the sea and sun. And then there's *your* kind!

Del What exactly do …

Rodney *(Interrupts him)* There will be no women on this trip! Right?

Del … Can you be more pacific?

Rodney This holiday is not gonna be another Benidorm revisited. And I'm warning you, if I see one, just *one* bra hanging off our car aerial – I'm outta there!

Del I'm not gonna do anything like that. And I would never of even thought of it if you hadn't just brought it up. I don't know what goes on in that little mind of yours. You dirty little devil. Here look – I'm gonna have a little nap. Give us a nudge when the old drinks arrive, will you? Now then how d'you get this chair to go back then?

Del pulls the chair-lever up and his chair disappears from frame in a flash. We stay on Rodney.

As Del's chair whizzes back we hear a thump and the sound of a plastic plate and glass breaking. The woman sitting behind Del yelps in alarm.

Woman *(OOV)* Look what you've done!

Del *(OOV)* Oh, er, sorry about that.

Woman *(OOV)* You've ruined it!

Del *(OOV)* No no no no – that's alright. That'll clean off. Ask the stewardess for a cloth.

Woman *(OOV)* It's dry clean only!

Del No, they put that on the label to impress you.

Rodney puts headphones on in an attempt to block out the row going on around him.

Rodney Bloody 'ell.

We hear (distorted, as if from head-phones) the opening bars of 'Summer in the City'

Del I'll tell you what, give me a serviette and I'll do it. That's right. Hitch your skirt up a bit, gel. That's it. Go on, give us it here. What, on your own, are you?

EXT. DAY. MIAMI AIRPORT (MAIN BUILDING).

Del and Rodney exit the building lugging their suitcases, etc. They hire a taxi. Del shows the driver a piece of paper (obviously contains an address).

The taxi pulls away. Del is wearing the summer hat and sunglasses and continues to wear them until the evening.

EXT. DAY.

Aerial shot of Miami coastline. Sunny day.

EXT. DAY. MIAMI MONTAGE.

Various shots of Miami from taxi window. Shots of Del and Rodney in back of cab enjoying the views and the excitement of the city.

EXT. DAY. CAUSEWAY WITH BAYSIDE VIEW (MIAMI SKYLINE IN BACKGROUND).

The taxi pulls to a halt. Del and Rodney alight. Del takes a photo of Rodney with the Miami skyline in background. Rodney now takes the same photo of Del. A young guy passes by, with sports camera round his neck. Del asks him to take a photo of him and Rodney. Del and Rodney stand with skyline in background. The young guy takes the photo. Now he runs off with their camera. Del gives chase.

DAY. QUIET HIGHWAY ON THE OUTSKIRTS OF THE CITY.

We see a small, rather tacky looking car rental lot: 'Mac's Auto-Rentals'. We see a number of cars of various ages and conditions. In the centre of the lot is a mobile home or shack which houses the office.

The taxi pulls up and Del and Rodney alight

DAY. CAR RENTAL OFFICE.

It's a very untidy and cramped office. Mac, the owner (45, unshaven and doesn't care) is seated behind counter reading a newspaper. Del and Rodney enter.

Del Hello, anybody here?

Mac I'm in here!

Del Oh, right. *(They go through to back office)*

Mac Oh hi, how ya doing?

Del Yeah, listen – our travel agent reckons he's booked a car for us with you. *(Hands Mac paperwork)*

Mac Okay. *(Checks Del's paperwork against his own)* You guys on vacation?

Rodney Yeah, a week's holiday.

Mac No kidding? You come all the way from Australia for a week?

Del No no no – we're not from Australia! No, we are English.

Mac Oh, well you could have fooled me. Well, I won't hold you up. I'll just bring it right around the front.

Mac exits. Del notices an advertisement on wall concerning the 'Star Tours' trip around Biscayne Bay.

Del Hey – look at this! We'll have some of that, eh, Rodders?

Rodney What? Yeah, a nice little boat trip do us the world of good.

Del Yeah.

EXT. DAY. THE CAR LOT.

Del and Rodney out of office.

They place their luggage down.

Rodney Oh wotchya America … Oh, this is gonna be a holiday to remember, innit?

Del Ha ha ha – You said it, bruv.

Rodney is now drawn from his reverie by a sense of curiosity as we hear the low throbbing sound of an approaching vehicle which would appear to have serious exhaust problems.

Rodney turns and reacts. We see Mac at the wheel of a large and old camper.

Del Here we go, Rodders!

Rodney *(Horrified)* What the hell is this, Del?

Mac *(Calls to them)* Alright, you gents have a nice day, now!

Del And you, pal.

Rodney Yeah, thank you.

Mac exits to office.

Rodney What are we gonna do with that?

Del That? That is where we're gonna live. Alex recommended it. See, the advantage is we don't have to stay in one spot, do we? You know, we can move about a bit and it's cheap.

Rodney Del, there is no way I am gonna spend any time in this mobile ghetto with you!

Del Eh, what do you mean you're not gonna spend any time… Look Rodney, I was only tryin'

to save you money. And we won't be trapped, will we? Eh? Because when we get to a campsite we can dump this, then we can go walkies, right?

Rodney Del, we could have booked a ho … Oh, bloody 'ell!! I don't believe that I've got … Alright, on one condition.

Del Alright, sir, what is the condition?

Rodney No curries!

Del Alright, no curries son. Come on then. Let's go'n see America! Hey, hey!

INT. DAY. MAC'S OFFICE.

Mac looks from his window and laughs.

EXT. DAY. CAR LOT.

Del pulls the camper onto the empty highway but he is driving on the left-hand side of the road.

Del Here we go, Rodders!

He is driving away from camera and towards the brow of a hill.
We hear Del singing.

Del (OS) 'Oh the Yellow Rose of Texas is the one I'm gonna see. The Yellow Rose of Texas is the only girl for me.'

Rodney (OS) (Screams in alarm) Deeelll!

A car appears from over the hill on the same side of the road as the Trotters. Del's camper is still on left-hand side of road.
The other car is passing on opposite side.
We hear the driver call out to Del.

Man (OS) You jerk!

Del (OS) Get over, you dipstick!

Rodney (OS) You're on the wrong side of the road!

Del (OS) Eh?

Rodney (OS) They drive on the *right-hand* side of the road over here!

Del (OS) Oh yeah! That's right, yeah.

The camper pulls away and moves to right-hand side of road. Del, completely dismissing the fact that only three seconds ago he almost wiped himself and Rodney off the face of the earth, begins singing again.

Del 'Oh the Yellow Rose of Texas is the one I'm gonna see. The Yellow Rose of Texas is the only girl for me.'

The camper disappears over the brow of the hill.

INT. DAY. MAC'S OFFICE.

Mac is now sitting at his desk reading his newspaper. He laughs as he hears screech of tyres.
On the front page we see the headlines:

'MAFIA TRIAL. VINNY "THE CHAIN" OCCHETTI PLEADS FOR BAIL'
Music under: *A tune very much on the lines of 'The Godfather' theme. We are talking serious Mafiosi.*

EXT. DAY. THE OCCHETTI MANSION.

The white painted mansion is surrounded by finely manicured lawns. A long, sweeping drive leads up to the front steps of the house. The vision suggests tennis courts, swimming pool and twenty or so bedrooms.
The property is protected by a high wall and shrubs. A large set of electronically operated wrought iron gates guard the entrance to drive and property. This is the home of Don Vincenzo 'Vinny the Chain' Occhetti, the 45-year old head of the most powerful Mafia family. He is the Don of Dons – Marlon Brando would call him sir. The Occhetti family and their soldiers are all third and fourth generation Italian-Americans and so, despite their Italian names, speak pure American.
We see the magnificent house which is bathed in Florida sunshine. We see four of the Don's soldiers sitting and lounging around on the steps or walls of house. Three of them are jacketless and are wearing shoulder holsters. (All the soldiers wear dark suits and sunglasses.)
One of the soldiers (Pauly) who is wearing his jacket and appears to be in a position of authority is standing a distance away from the others. His two-way radio crackles into life. He then calls to the other three, one of whom is a tall, thin man and is always referred to as 'Lurch'.

Pauly (Answers radio) Yeah, what is it? Right. (Calls to the other three) Hey, Lurch, Tony, Gino. Smarten up. The Don's left the courthouse.

The other two men put their jackets on and tighten their ties. They now produce pump-action shotguns from behind walls. We see the electronic gates opening and two other soldiers standing guard.
Now a cavalcade of five black limousines glides through the gates. It is made up of two sedans at front and two sedans at rear. In centre is a black stretch-limo with darkened windows.
The cavalcade purrs up the driveway and stops in front of house. Armed soldiers alight from cars and assume guard positions.
Rico Occhetti, the Don's 24-year old son, alights from the front passenger seat of the

stretch-limo.

He opens the back door of the car.

Don Vincenzo Occhetti alights. He wears a light coloured three-piece suit with two thick gold chains hanging across the waistcoat (his trade mark). He now straightens and we see that Don Occhetti bears a striking resemblance to Derek Trotter. This man though, has a dark and sinister soul. His hard unsmiling face holds a menace. He is used to getting his own way and is given to thumping tables and issuing contracts on people's lives when refused.

We shall discover that he is also a desperate man after being trapped by the law for his immoral business activities and violent excesses. He is the kind of man who can turn from the benign calm of your favourite uncle to the screaming tantrums of your worst brat nephew in the click of a switchblade.

His voice is pitched at about the same level as Del's but bears strong Chicago overtones. His skin is more tanned than Del's thanks to the Florida sunshine.

Don Occhetti surveys his kingdom and then reacts.

We see an unmarked car parked outside the main gates. Two men are standing by the car.

Don Rico.

Rico Yeah, pop?

Don Who are those goons in the car?

Rico Police surveillance, Pop, nothing to worry about.

Don Nothing to worry about? I got cops sitting outside my front gate and there's nothing to worry about! What's happened to my civil rights?

Rico *(Quietly)* Well, they kinda diminished after they arrested you, Pop, but you've been released on bail so be happy.

Don Be happy! Be happy, huh? In one week from now I got a jury sitting in judgment on me, looks like I might spend the rest of my life in San Quentin and my son wants to throw a party! Whaddaya, huh, whaddaya? I wanna speak to my lawyer, now!

As Don Occhetti moves towards the house, Rico calls to the family lawyer Salvatore, a dark-suited man of about 40 who is standing a respectful distance away, armed with nothing more than a briefcase.

Rico *(Calls)* Salvatore.

He gestures towards the house. Rico and Sal follow the Don across the courtyard to the house.

INT. DAY. THE LARGE HALL OF MANSION.

The interior of the house is decorated mainly with white or light colours and with the finest wallpapers, rugs, paintings, gold light-fittings and furnished with fine antiques.

It is the very height of opulence. The shutters are closed against the searing sunshine and so the house is darkened – like the souls of those who inhabit it.

Don Occhetti enters through the front doors followed by Rico and Salvatore.

Don *(The kind uncle)* Salvatore ...

Sal Don Occhetti.

Don Ah, Salvatore, haven't I always been good to you?

Sal Yes, Don Occhetti.

Don Haven't I always done favours for your family?

Sal Yes, Don Occhetti.

Don Have I ever done you any harm?

Sal Well, there was that time when ...

A look from Rico stops Sal's speech.

Sal No, Don Occhetti.

Don Hmm, so maybe this time, er, Salvatore you can help me because, erm, I'm a little confused. This is the way I read the situation. You are my lawyer. Correct?

Sal Yes, Don Occhetti.

Don Yet, here I am looking at three to four life sentences in the slammer. *(Now the brat)* So why in hell don't you get off your ass and bury this rap?

Sal *(Gulps back his fear)* Well, you see, we're having problems proving your innocence.

Don Why?

Sal 'Cos you're guilty. *(Realises what he has said and tries to correct)* Oh no, when I say guilty what I mean is ...

Don *(Interrupts)* Guilty of what?

Rico Kidnapping, drug-smuggling, accessory to three counts of murder. Gossip, Pop, just gossip.

Don Hmm, so ... so I made a few mistakes in the past, you know, I mean to say – nobody's perfect.

Rico and Sal nod in agreement.

Don Now you listen to me – when my father, *(Does the sign of the cross)* God bless that man's spirit, when he arrived on these shores from Sicily in 1930, this was a land of democracy and law and order. Now he fought to change all that, but look at us now, huh? What have all his efforts amounted to, huh? Zilch, that's what. Zilch! Salvatore – you call yourself a lawyer? You're a schmuck! And that goes for you too, Rico.

Don Occhetti now begins moving up the stairs with Rico and Sal in pursuit.

Don If your mother was alive today, *(Does the sign of the cross)* God bless that woman's soul, she would disown you.

Rico Come on, Pop!

They move along corridor towards the Don's suite of rooms.

Don *(On the move)* I tell you this, Rico, huh. I never thought I'd see the day when a son of mine would be willing to stand back and watch his own father spend the rest of his life in the state pen sharing meatloaves with the faggots, huh!

They enter Don's suite.

INT. DAY. DON OCCHETTI'S SUITE.

We are in a sumptuously decorated office with an antique desk and a leather Chesterfield suite. To the left two doors lead off. One leads to his bedroom. The second door leads to a bathroom/gymnasium. Hanging on the walls and standing on pieces of furniture are various photos. There is also a large oil portrait in a gilt frame of Don Occhetti. There is a large antique globe of the world which has been converted into a cocktail cabinet. Again, the room is shaded. Don Occhetti enters, continuing his speech from landing.

Don Shall I tell you what'll happen if I go down? All the families'll be carving up our empire like dogs fighting over a weenie-roast. Every Marielito-punk from Little Havana will be tryin' to get a slice of the action! And what about the Colombian, uh?

Sal What Colombian?

Don What Colombian he says!

Rico What are you a jerk, Salvatore?

Don Just sit down, will ya? Sit down. Next week Señor Vasquez arrives here from Colombia to settle our little deal. What d'you think he's gonna do if he thinks I've gone down the tube? I'm getting very worried, Salvatore, I'm getting very nervous about the future. *(Now does an enormous burp)* D'you hear that?

Rico and Sal nod.

Don *(Cont)* That's peptic gas that's caused by nervous exhaustion! What ever happened to the ancient Sicilian traditions of bribery, blackmail, and intimidation? Huh?

The Don opens the globe cocktail cabinet and pours himself a spoonful of medicine. He reacts to the vile taste.

Sal This is not a local police investigation. This is the FBI and we can't pay those guys off.

Rico The jury is locked up in a guarded hotel, the witnesses got round the clock protection, we just can't reach anybody.

Don Then maybe I ought to do something about it myself, then, huh?

Rico You can't, Pop. The police surveillance team is watching every move you make, they even got a TV camera crew filming you for a documentary.

Don They're filming me? What d'they think I am, a common criminal or something?

Rico and Sal shrug.

Don Now you listen to me. Rico, I want you to take some money from the family account and I want you to buy me a DA – you buy me the the the judge – you buy me the senator. A lot of people in this town owe me favours. I want these favours returned.

Rico We've tried, but so far there have been no takers. It looks like people are turning their backs on you.

Don That is a very impolite and highly dangerous thing to do! Now, what I want you to do – I want you to keep searching and I want you to keep thinking. Because somewhere – somewhere out there – lies the answer to my problems.

EXT. DAY. A SIGHTSEEING BOAT IN BISCAYNE BAY

From the Don's last words we cut to Del laughing uproariously. He is now wearing a 'Miami Heats' basketball cap. Rodney is next to Del and is also laughing but in a more self-conscious way. In the background we see a sign which reads:
'Star Tours. See the stars' homes. Julio Iglesias. The Bee Gees. Gloria Estefan.'
We see the object of their merriment is a buxom young girl.

Del Ha ha – look at the state of that! You wouldn't go near that unless you had all your own teeth, would you, Rodders, eh?

Rodney *(Laughing)* Shuddup, you'll get us nicked!

The girl lights a cigarette.

Del Look! Look at her now, look – they say smoking's bad for your chest!

Skipper *(On tannoy)* Biscayne Bay is the centre of the Florida Coast Guards Service. As you may know, Miami has been nicknamed Cocainesville and the officers of Biscayne Bay fight an all year round battle with the drug-runners. And coming up on your left, you will see the home of Barry

151

Gibb, the lead singer of the Bee Gees.
From our boat we see a figure hosing the garden.
Del Look! Look there, look! Look, Rodders, there's a real-live Bee Gee.
Rodney Course it ain't! He's most probably the gardener!
Del No, no, it's him, it's him, it's Barry Gibbs. It is! *(Shouts)* Alright Bazza? Eh?
Rodney Shuddup, will you! That's not him!
Del It is!

EXT. DAY. JETTY.

The figure has his back to us and in background, we can hear Del singing loudly.
Del *(OOV)* 'How deep is your love, is your love, how deep is your love …'
Barry Gibb turns into shot.
Barry Gibb *(Mumbles to himself)* I need all this! *B.G. walks out of shot.*

EXT. DAY. SIGHTSEEING BOAT.

Del No, I reckon you was right, Rodders. It weren't him, most probably the gardener!
Rodney Yeah, what did I say?

EXT. NIGHT. NIGHTCLUB PARKING LOT.

The lot is filled with Mercs and Cadillacs etc, and also two black sedans which should look familiar.
The camper pulls in next to the sedan and Del and Rodney alight. (By now they have managed to wash and put on a change of clothes – Del no longer wears hat or glasses . They get out and check the doors are locked.
Del *(Facing the nightclub as if it's a personal challenge)* That's it. Come on, Rodney, bellies in.
Rodney Del, I still think it would be a better idea if we were to drive to the camper site now and book in first.
Del Rodney, look – it's only quarter to eight, there's plenty of time to get in the old camp-site.
Rodney Yeah, there's also plenty of time for you to get drunk *after* we've booked in.
Del Get drunk? Get drunk? You enjoy putting me down, don't you, eh? You think that I'm just a one-dimensional sort of person, don't you? Well you're wrong! The only reason I want to go in to that club is to make a telephone call because I promised Raquel that I'd phone her as soon as we arrived.
Rodney *(Indicating across road)* And what's wrong with the public call box over there?
Del Well, you can't get a drink in there, can you! Come on!

Rodney Oh – what we gonna do with our luggage?
Del Well, I'll tell you what – why don't we bring it with us and we can put it in the middle of the dance floor and boogy round it like them sorts do at the Nag's Head when they have a disco with their handbags!
Rodney No need to be sarky about it! *(They walk on before Rodney reacts)* Oi – what are you talking about 'disco' and 'boogying?' Del, I am *not* boogying!
Del *(Shouts from entrance of club)* Rodney, please keep your voice down! Remember we're supposed to be ambassadors for our country! Don't want these people thinking we're lager louts, do we? *(To a couple passing by)* Excuse me – mais oui, mais oui.

INT. NIGHT. THE NIGHTCLUB.

It is quite crowded, people drinking at bar, others eating at tables, two couples smooch on dance floor. We see Del and Rodney enter and push their way through to bar.
Del *(Calling barman)* Eh, Juan! Over here, Juan! When you're ready, son.
Francisco, the club owner approaches.
Del has his back to him at this moment and so the only face he can see is that of Rodney.
Francisco Excuse me, gentlemen. I'm sorry but this club is for members only.
Del turns to face him.
Del You what?
Francisco reacts, believing he has just insulted Don Vincenzo Occhetti.
Francisco I am so sorry, Señor, I did not realise it was you!
Del and Rodney look behind them to see who he is talking to.
Francisco Please accept my deepest and sincerest apologies. *(Kisses Del's hand)*
Del and Rodney look at each other.
Del clenches his fist – Rodney restrains him.
Francisco I am honoured that you should choose to visit my humble nightclub. Please, may I offer you a drink?
Del Yes, yeah, we'll have a cubre libra and something non-alcoholic.
Francisco Of course.
Del Yeah and we'll be sitting over there, alright?
Francisco I will be with you immediately!
Del and Rodney move to table as Francisco goes to get their drinks.
Del What was all that about then?
Rodney God knows! Friendly sort of bloke, weren't he?

Miami Twice Oh To Be In England

Del Oh, yeah.

We cut away to table on the far side of club. Here we find Rico, Salvatore, Pauly, Lurch and Tony. They are finishing a meal and involved in a dark and brooding conversation.

Rico There's gonna be a war!

Sal Maybe not.

Rico The only thing that can prevent it is for you to find an alibi for my father.

Sal I don't have to find your father an alibi! I have to find him *nine* alibis! How the hell am I supposed to do that in a week?

Rico How can the justice department can treat him like this. Don't they know who he is?

Sal Yeah, that's the problem!

Rico You mark my words, Salvatore, the moment the jury foreman says, 'Guilty' the war begins.

Sal Maybe not.

Rico Why d'you keep saying 'maybe not'? What d'you think the rest of the Families are gonna sit back on their butts and pretend the old man is still in control? They're gonna go to war! Am I right, Pauly?

Pauly You're right, Rico.

Rico Am I right, Tony?

Tony You're right, Rico.

Rico Am I right, Lurch?

Lurch Maybe not.

Rico *(To Sal)* You see? *(Reacts to Lurch)* There's gonna be a war!

Francisco arrives at table. He is carrying tray with Del and Rodney's drinks.

Francisco Señor Ricardo.

Rico Francisco, can't you see I'm in a meeting here?

Francisco I am sorry to interrupt, Señor but I would like to explain if I'd known *he* was coming here tonight I would have arranged a private room.

Rico If you'd known *who* was coming here tonight?

Francisco Your father!

Rico My father?

Pauly Is this some kind of joke, Frankie? Don Occhetti is under virtual house arrest. He can't get to the john without the police tailing him.

Francisco But he is here! See for yourself. *(Gestures towards corner table)*

Rico, Sal, Pauly, Lurch and Tony rise from table and peer over and through the crowd towards corner table. We have a shot from their POV of Del sitting at table lighting a cigar. We see the Mafia's reaction to this mirage.

They now lower themselves and disappear from view behind the crowd. Cut away to corner table.

Francisco arrives with drinks.

Del Oh, lovely jubbly. How much do we owe you?

Francisco *Please*, it is on the house, you are my guests. Would you like to eat?

Rodney Oh, no thanks, we had something earlier.

Francisco I see. If there is anything that you should require, as always, I am at your service. *Exits.*

Del Big mouth! I expect the grubs most probably been free an' all!

Rodney Course it wouldn't!

Del Listen, Rodney, d'you know what we're dealing with here?

Rodney What?

Del American hospitality! They're famous for it, they are. The most friendliest people in the entire world.

We cut away to the Mafia table.

Tony is listening on mobile phone.

Tony *(Eagerly awaiting the phone to be answered)* Come on, come on. *(The phone is answered)* Yo, Gino! It's Tony … Yeah – is the Don there? *(Pause. To Rico)* He's in the pool.

Rico snatches the phone.

Rico Can you actually *see* him? Good! *(To the others)* Dad's at home, the guy over there ain't him! *(On phone)* Listen carefully. Tell my father to stay in his room till I get back tonight … Just tell him I may have a surprise for him. *(Switches phone off and smiles smugly)*

We cut away to corner table.

Del has finished his drink.

Del I tell you what – I'm boiling!

Rodney That's strange, that. I mean, here you are in a tropical climate, wearing a worsted polyester blue serge suit and you feel hot?

Del *(Uncertain)* Yeah.

Rodney Weird …

He is interrupted by the arrival of the Mafia. They smile benignly at Del and Rodney except for Sal who appears nervous and reluctant to be party to this.

Rico Hi, how you guys doing?

Del Yeah, alright. Yeah – a great time. Thank you.

Rico Good. Let me guess. You're not local people.

Rodney No, no we're here on holiday.

Rico looks at Sal.

Sal Vacation.

Rico Oh, vacation! Yeah, yeah, I thought as

much. Well, welcome to America.

Del Yeah, well, thanks very much, son.

Tony We don't get many Australians round here.

Del Look, we are not *Australian*, right?

Rodney We are British.

Rico British! We love the British! Are you, erm, living locally?

Del Well, no. No, we've got one of them camper things out there in the street, you know. We just whack our bags and what have you in the back and off we go.

> *During the next exchange we see Tony talking quietly to Lurch. Lurch leaves the club.*

Pauly It's the best way to see the country.

Del Yeah, well, I mean – you can't whack it, can you?

Rico *(Confused)* No, like you say, you can't whack it. So can I get you guys a drink?

Del Er, well, er, no …

Sal *(Quietly)* I don't think this is wise, Rico.

Rodney You see the thing is, we've gotta drive over to the camping-site … sorry, the camper-park, before it closes, you see.

Pauly Oh come on, you must have time for one!

Del Well, we can have one, Rodney, what do you reckon, eh?

Rodney Yeah, go on then.

Del Yeah, we'll have a drink with you – let's introduce ourselves. This is my brother Rodney, and my name's Del – that's er, short for Derek.

Rico Hi, Rodney … Derek. I'm Rico. This is my cousin Salvatore and our friend Pauly.

> *Greetings and handshakes all round.*

Sal Are you enjoying your stay so far?

Del Oh yes, er, great. No, we're having a blinding time.

Rico Why don't you join us?

EXT. NIGHT. NIGHTCLUB PARKING LOT.

> *We see the black sedan's trunk is open. Lurch, with a jemmy, leaves the back doors of camper open. He now takes the Trotters' suitcases and hand-luggage from camper and places them in trunk of sedan. He closes trunk and, leaving camper doors open, returns to nightclub.*

INT. NIGHT. THE NIGHTCLUB.

> *It is an hour and something later.*
> *Del, who has had slightly too much to drink, and Rodney are standing and about to leave. Lurch is now part of the group again.*

Rico Come on, come on, you've got time for one more! One more …

Rodney *(Checking watch)* No, no, really. We're pushing our luck as it is.

Del No, he's right, Rico. He's right.

Pauly Come on, one for the road.

Tony Yeah, guys, come one, you got time for one more …

Del Alright, go on then, have one for the road.

Rodney No, no, Del. No, come on mate, cos that campsite's gonna be shut and we're gonna be locked out for the night.

Rico I didn't realise it was so late. We've gotta be going soon. *(They all stand)* Well, Rodney – Del Boy!

Del Rico! Well, thanks very much! It's been really really great meeting you guys, it really has. Thanks a lot and er we've enjoyed your company and everything. Now we gotta go – we'll see you later then, yeah? Thanks a lot – yeah it's been great.

> *General goodbyes from everyone.*
> *Del and Rodney exit.*

EXT. NIGHT. NIGHTCLUB PARKING LOT.

> *Del and Rodney exit from club.*

Del What a blinding night, eh, Rodders? Eh?

Rodney Nice bunch of blokes weren't they?

Del Well, they were diamonds, weren't they. I mean they were absolute forty two carat diamonds. I mean, there we was drinking with them all night, never had to put our hands in our pockets, did we?

> *Rodney sees the camper and runs to it. Del follows.*

Del What's the matter, Rodders? Rodney, what's happened? What's the matter?

> *Rodney emerges from the back of the van.*

Rodney It's all gone!

Del What?

Rodney They've nicked everything! Our suitcases, our flight bags, the duty frees, the lot!

Del Oh, no! I don't believe it! just do not believe it! I mean, we was only in there half an hour! Well, four hours! I mean … Oh, I mean, what's gonna happen, eh? I mean, how we gonna get home?

Rodney Now, Del, don't panic!

Del Eh?

Rodney *(Gestures to inside pocket)* Listen, I took the passports, the flight tickets – I took 'em in there with us.

Del Rodney, Oh Rodney – you are a saint, mate, you are a saint! Well done! Where's the money?

Rodney I left that in the van.

Del You plonker, Rodney!

Miami Twice Oh To Be In England

Rodney *You* told me to leave it!

Del Me?

Rodney Yes! And you told me to leave the luggage in the back!

Del Yeah, well … why didn't you use your own initiative, then, eh?

Rodney 'Cos I didn't even wanna go in to that bloody club!

Del Yeah, alright, alright then! Calm down, just calm down then will you? Cor, stone me! I don't know … How much money we got then between us?

They both search their pockets and produce a few dollars.

What's that?

Rodney *(Counts the combined amount)* Right – thirty two dollars! Right, now what can we get for thirty two dollars?

Del Mugged!

Rico, Sal, Pauly, Tony and Lurch exit from club and approach Del and Rodney.

Rico Hey, you guys still here? Let me guess, you decided to come back and have that one for the road! You son …

Del No, I wish we had, Rico, I wish we had. No, we're thinking of going to the police!

Rico Why? You gotta problem?

Rodney Yeah, we've been robbed.

Pauly You're kidding!

Del No, I wish we was, Pauly! I wish we was …

Rodney They broke into the van while we were in the club. They've taken everything!

Lurch Oh gee, that is just too bad!

Rodney Yeah …

Rico God, I feel so embarrassed. You've just arrived in this country and this happens! What a welcome.

Del Oh don't worry – it's just one of them things, ain't it, son?

Tony So what are you guys gonna do?

Del I don't know what we're gonna do. I mean, you know, we got no money, we got no clothes, we got no duty frees, we got nothing.

Rodney We're just gonna have to go down to the police and get them to sort it out.

Rico Oh, save your breath, Rodney. The cops'll do diddly squat! They don't know their ass from first base. But Salvatore here's a lawyer. *(To Sal)* Maybe you could talk to some of your friends in the DA's office.

Sal *(Still reluctant)* Yeah, first thing in the morning.

Del Could you do that, Salvatore? That would be very very nice of you, wouldn't it, Rodders, eh?

Rodney Yeah.

Rico And in the meantime you two guys are coming home with me.

EXT. NIGHT. OCCHETTI MANSION.

We see two sedans containing Del, Rodney, Rico, Sal, Pauly, Tony and Lurch screech past the gates and up towards the house.
We see the guards at the gate. Del and Rodney stare in awe at the property.
They look at each other in silent disbelief.
The cars pulls up at the front doors of the house and everyone alights.

Rodney Is this your place, Rico?

Rico It belongs to my family.

Inside his suite, the Don watches them arrive on the security monitor.

Del Very nice.

Del and Rodney follow Rico across courtyard, past the swimming pool.

Del What line of business you in?

Rico We're in … er … insurance. And imports.

Del Oh, what imports and exports?

Rico No, just imports.

INT. NIGHT. THE HALL OF MANSION.

Rico leads Del and Rodney in.
Gino is in the hall.

Rico Well, this is it! Welcome!

An intercom rings and Rico answers.

Rico Yo?

Don *(Distort)* Rico, I want you up here – fast!

Rico I'll be right up. *(Replaces receiver. To Del and Rodney)* I'll show you to your guest suite.

Del *(Quietly to Rodney)* Guest suite! We've fallen on our feet here, bruv.

INT. NIGHT. DON OCCHETTI'S SUITE/STUDY.

Don Occhetti is angrily pacing the floor.
Rico and Sal enter.

Rico You see 'em?

Don Yeah, course I saw them and I heard them! What are you doing bringing Australians home, huh?

Sal No, they're not Australian. They're a couple of English guys, over here on vacation. We've put 'em in the guest suite.

Don Limeys? What are you doing bringing Limeys in to my house? You know that I *hate* Limeys.

Rico We met 'em at the club on Coco Walk.

Don Now, wait a minute. What are you doing picking up guys in bars? Huh? What is it with you two? Are you getting light on your feet? Is it too much air in your Nikes, or what?

Rico Listen to me, Pop. These two bozos could be the answer to your prayers. One of them is a dead-ringer for you. Even Francisco at the club thought he was serving you.

Don Look, I saw them here on the security monitor – I saw no similarity whatsoever. He's much taller than me – he's a thinner guy altogether.

Sal No, the other one.

Don You mean … you mean the squirty little dude with the polecat face?

Sal Yeah.

Don Ah, I see, Salvatore. Salvatore, this is your lucky day. 'Cos I'm in a good mood I'm only gonna break *one* of your legs! And because you're a member of the family I'm gonna do it *slowly*!

Rico Come on, Pop, it was dark outside – you couldn't see them clearly. Tell him … *(Gestures to Sal)*

Sal It's true, Don Occhetti, this guy looks just like you.

Don You know, last year I went to the zoo and I saw a camel that looked just like your mother but I didn't invite it home and put it in the guest suite! So, there's a guy who looks like me! What's the big deal?

Rico I'll tell you what the big deal is. Imagine this guy dressed up in your clothes.

Don In my clothes ! What's the matter with you – are you outta your mind, or what?

Rico We dress the limey up in your clothes and we take him out to eat at a nice restaurant. Now, while he's having lunch, in full public view, somebody blows him away. *(Mimes gun to head)*

Sal This is something I do not advise!

Rico Everybody will think that the other Families have had *you* killed! Even the police surveillance-team would be a witness. Don't you see what this means, pop?

Don What?

Rico *(To Sal)* Tell him, Sal …

Sal In the eyes of America there will be no more Don Occhetti! No more Don Occhetti equals no more trial. No more trial equals no more prison sentence.

Rico And while we mourn your passing you sneak off to Rio for a couple of years. Long enough for your plastic surgery to heal and come back as Uncle …

Sal Carlo.

Rico Carlo from New Jersey and take over the family business.

Don Occhetti becomes emotional.

Don Rico, sometimes during my life I have doubted that you were my child. Sometimes I thought that maybe the hospital had screwed-up and given us the baby of a family from Pittsburgh. But I take it all back. You are definitely my son! *(He hugs Rico)* It's brilliant – It's wonderful! It also means one less Limey in the world.

Rico Two, Pop. We're giving his brother a one-way ticket also.

INT. NIGHT. DEL AND RODNEY'S SUITE.

This is a luxurious twin-bedded room with en suite bathroom. Rodney is alone in room, seated on bed, watching TV and pressing remote control button so we continually get the sound and pictures of various American channels. Rodney is like a kid with a new toy. Del enters from the en suite bathroom

Del Rodney – have you had a butchers at the bog? It's solid marble, it is, Rodney. None of that stick-on gear that you get down at the DIY. No, this is the real McCoy. Oh, someone up there loves us.

Rodney Sssh. I'm up to channel forty-nine.

Del Yeah, how many channels are there then?

Rodney I don't know, that's what I'm researching.

Del Good boy, I always said you should be a scientist. Oh look at this! *(Referring to room)* Can't be bad, can it, eh? Look at this!

He jumps on the bed.

INT. NIGHT. DON'S SUITE.

Don Don't let these Limeys call home. I don't want anybody knowing about this address.

Sal Lurch's cutting all the phones, except our business line.

Rico So, as far as everyone in jolly old England is concerned, those two guys have vanished off the face of the earth.

Don They can blame it on the Bermuda Triangle! *Laughter.*

Rico Or the Twilight Zone! *Uproarious laughter.*

INT. NIGHT. DEL AND RODNEY'S ROOM.

Del We have struck gold here, bruv.

Rodney Oh, not many. We'll have to show Rico our gratitude you know. Get him a little present or something.

Del Yeah, yeah, we'll do that. We've got no money. Never mind, I'll nip him for a few quid. Uh, blimey! Eh – we'd better phone in to HQ. Raquel'll be going spare! *(Picks up telephone receiver)* Oh, the line's dead.

Miami Twice Oh To Be In England

Rodney Well, do that. *(Rodney rattles the phone's on/off button rapidly)*
Del Why?
Rodney 'Cos, that's what they do in American films.
Del Oh yes. *(Rattles the on/off button)* No, still dead look.

Rico enters carrying a bundle of clothing.
Rico *(Still wiping tears of laughter from his eyes)* There you go, Derek. These are my … er … uncle's clothes, I think they'll fit you, he's about the same size as you.
Del Yes, well, thanks. Very nice. Oh er, Rico I don't wanna be a pain, but, Rodney's – he's got nothing to wear.
Rico That's okay, we got a guy works here who's about Rodney's build, he'll lend you some of his clothes. *(Picks up intercom)* Lurch?
Rodney Lurch! Saucy berk!
Del Rodney, don't be so ungrateful!
Rico *(Into intercom)* Tell … er … Gino to bring up some of his clothes. *(To Rodney)* Piece of cake.
Del Oh, by the way, the old dog's knackered.
Rico What?
Rodney The telephone's not working.
Rico Oh … Yeah, the telephone. A couple of days ago we had a tropical storm, the whole area's out. Don't worry though, they'll be back soon. Listen, you guys get some sleep because what say tomorrow I take you out to my favourite restaurant? A day on the town.
Del Lovely jubbly.
Rico *(Confused by 'lovely jubbly')* … Yeah. It's a nice little Italian joint. The food is out of this world. Believe me, Del, this place will kill you. *(Referring to clothes)* Oh by the way, wear this suit and the chains. *(Referring to Don O's thick gold chain)* It'll make you look real business-like.
Del Oh yes, yeah, course. This is very me, this, Rico. 'Cos back home in England I am a yuppy. Ain't I, Rodney?
Rodney Er … yeah.
Rico That's cool. Well, nighty-night.
Del Yeah, nighty-night.
Rodney Night.
Rico exits.
Del He is such a nice bloke, ain't he? They broke the mould when they made him, you know.
Rodney *(Now a worry)* Yeah! Look, Del, don't think I'm getting paranoid or nothing, but … Well, did you notice them really tough couple of tough looking blokes down by the gate when we drove in?
Del Yeah.

Rodney And then there was that one downstairs an all?
Del Well, yeah, so what?
Rodney Well … it's most probably ridiculous, but, you don't think that Rico might be …
Del What?
Rodney A noofter!
Del A noofter …! No, he's Italian, ain't he? You can't have an Italian noofter, it's a well known medical fact!
Rodney But they're all blokes!
Del Well, I know that, that's because he's like … he's a man's man, ain't he, eh? I'll tell you what else he is, Rodney. He's a little gold nugget. Yeah, that's what he is, Rodney. A little gold nugget!

EXT. DAY. PECKHAM. THE CHURCH (ST MARK'S).

We see Raquel pushing Damien in his pram past the church. She stops and looks in bewilderment to something happening within the church grounds. We cut to show an articulated lorry with Romanian number plates and lettering parked in grounds. The vicar who christened Damien is standing by the lorry and blessing it. The Romanian lorry driver lounges against lorry cab smoking a cigarette.
Vicar In the name of the Father, the Son and the Holy Spirit, Bless you …
Raquel Reverend?
Vicar Amen. Raquel. I'm glad I've met you. I was going to phone Derek as soon as the lorry had gone.
Raquel Del? But Del's in Miami.
Vicar Miami? Oh dear!
Raquel Reverend, excuse me for asking, but why are you blessing a Romanian lorry?
Vicar I'm not blessing the lorry, it's the contents. Didn't Derek mention it to you?
Raquel No, he didn't sa … Just a minute. Has this got something to do with Derek?
Vicar Well, yes. He did a time and motion study of the blessing of the wine and came up with the novel idea of doing it en-masse, as it were. Then I distribute it to other churches throughout England.
Raquel Oh hell! Oh, I'm sorry!
Vicar It's been a real money saver, especially as Del sells it to us so cheap. There's just one rather major problem. It's turned out to be Romanian Reisling.
Raquel Romanian Reisling!
Vicar Yes. *White* wine. The communion wine is

supposed to be red. It represents the …

Raquel *(Cuts in)* The blood of Christ!

Vicar Exactly! The other churches are returning their cases – daily! I don't want to alarm you, Raquel, but you may be getting a call from the Archbishop of Canterbury's office.

Raquel Oh God!

Vicar That's what I keep saying.

EXT. DAY. BOULEVARD/EXT. MANSION GROUNDS.

Parked in the boulevard is a van bearing the insignia of a local TV news company.

One of the two camera crew is standing on a set of step ladders and looking over the wall of mansion through a pair of binoculars.

The second is seated on sidewalk holding a professional video camera.

1st news person *(On ladders)* Hey, we got some action – gimme that camera.

The 2nd one hands camera up.

2nd news person Is it Occhetti?

1st news No, it's his son and one of the gorillas … Wait a minute!

EXT. DAY. OCCHETTI MANSION.

Pauly and Rico exit. Pauly with a black bag, goes towards a boat.

We see Del, Rodney and Sal exit from the mansion followed by three of the soldiers (Tony, Lurch and Gino). Rodney is now wearing some of Lurch's clothes. Del is wearing the same light coloured, three piece suit, complete with the thick gold chain that we saw Don Occhetti wearing when we first became acquainted with him.

Del Here … *(Referring to suit)* What d'you reckon, then, Rico? Eh? Eh, look at that – it fits like a dream, don't it?

Rico *(Studies Del critically, assuring himself that Del will pass as his father)* Perfect, Del, just perfect.

Rodney Hey, there's a bloke over there with a camera.

From Rodney's POV we see the cameraperson filming them from over the wall.

Del and Rodney both smile towards camera.

Del Oh yeah! *(Gives camera the thumbs up)* Alright, pal? Who's that then, Rico?

RICO *(Pleased that Don Occhetti's last movements are being recorded)* Who knows? Tourists maybe. I'm starving, let's eat.

Del Yeah, and me. Lovely jubbly.

Rico reacts to 'Lovely jubbly'.

They move off towards the cars.

EXT. DAY. STREET OPPOSITE RESTAURANT.

We now see the unmarked police car.

One of the policemen takes a camera and runs off a couple of shots. The other officer is in radio-contact with the station.

1st officer *(On radio)* Twenty-nine thirty.

Radio response Twenty-nine thirty Q-S-K.

1st officer We're on South Bay and Fairisle. Occhetti and the boys have stopped off for lunch at Carlotti's restaurant.

Radio response One-three-two-five. Miami Q-S-L.

INT. DAY. THE RESTAURANT.

It is quite busy with lunchtime diners. The chairs are high-backed and padded leather. There is a table by the edge of the water. Six people are at this table and in the middle of their lunch.

Del and Rodney enter with Rico and boys. The owner, Señor Carlotti, sees what he believes is Don Occhetti. He approaches Del with great respect and fear.

Señor C Don Occhetti.

Del and Rodney think this is a greeting.

Del Don Occhetti to you too.

Rodney Don Occhetti.

Señor C *(Slightly fazed)* I am so happy you have honoured me with your presence here today. On behalf of my family and myself I thank you deeply. *(Kisses Del's hand)*

Rodney and Del look at each other. They assume this is another example of American hospitality.

Del S'alright. Oh, s'alright, you know. Puscas, Puscas.

Señor C *(Doesn't understand this but is too frightened to ask)* I'll prepare for you a table. Would you like to have a drink at the bar?

Del Yes, yes, thank you very much, Señor – I've got a diabolical thirst.

Señor C Excuse me …

Señor Carlotti moves away to bar. We see Rico has moved into the restaurant to look for the boat.

INT. DAY. THE RESTAURANT.

The Trotters and the Mafia are seated at table by the water (Del at head of table, Rodney opposite him). They are halfway through their first course. The previous diners are now at another table.

Del is eating an Italian dish called Gnocchi which contains potato dumplings.

Señor C arrives with a bottle of wine which he

proceeds to uncork as he speaks.

Señor C *(Respectfully to Del)* Is everything to your satisfaction, Señor?

Del It's lovely, Juan. Blinding dumplings.

Señor C Grazi. *(He now hands the cork to Del)* Señor?

Del *(Doesn't know what to do with the cork)* Yeah, that's a lovely-looking cork, innit?

Rodney *(Whispers)* You're supposed to test the bouquet!

Del Oh! *(Still not sure what to do. Finally he sucks the cork)* Thank you.

We see Rodney's reaction. Then we see the reaction of Rico and Sal. They are fearful that Del will blow the scam.

Del *(Reacts to corky taste, but out of politeness)* Oh yes, lovely jubbly. Pour on, Macduff.

Señor C *(Slightly fazed by the experience)* Grazi, Señor.

INT. DAY. BOAT.

This boat is approaching the restaurant. We see Pauly on board. He starts to assemble his gun.

INT. DAY. RESTAURANT.

Knowing that the assassination is about to take place and not wishing to be in the vicinity of any ricochets, Rico and the others have to make their excuses and get the hell out.

Rico Excuse me, Del … I gotta go to the john.

Del Do one for me, son, will you? *(Laughs)*

Tony I've gotta go check the plumbing as well.

Sal I gotta go too.

Lurch And me.

Del and Rodney are mystified as Rico, Sal and the three soldiers exit like a swarm towards the men's room.

Rodney I hope it ain't catching!

Del Must have been them enchiladas they had last night. *(Raises his glass)* Cheers, bruv.

Rodney Cheers, Del.

EXT. BOAT.

We see Pauly still assembling his high power rifle.

INT. DAY. MEN'S ROOM (RESTAURANT).

We find the five mafiosi huddled by the entrance door checking their watches and waiting for the sound of gunfire and screams, etc.

Rico Any time now …

The door now opens and thumps into the mafia. The 1st diner (one of those who had to move to another table) enters and reacts to finding these strange men in the toilet.

Rico *(Embarrassed)* How ya doing?

1st diner *(Worried)* Fine, thank you, fine.

Sal We're just talking.

1st diner Er, sorry to interrupt.

Sal Oh no, no – you're not interrupting.

Lurch *(Referring to urinals – a gruff order)* Well hurry up, just do it!

1st diner Oh.

EXT. DAY. BOAT.

During Del's next speech we see Pauly bringing the telescopic sight up to his eye. We see a shot through the sight.

INT. DAY. RESTAURANT.

Del has moved forward to pick up another dumpling on his spoon.

Rodney *(Embarrassed. A quiet warning)* Don't pick it up with your spoon! Use a fork!

Del Don't be stupid, Rodney, it'd roll off a fork, wouldn't it? No, as I was saying, I've always had this gift. Wherever I go in the world people have always just taken to me.

Rodney What d'you mean, wherever you go in the world? You ain't been nowhere!

Del No, fair enough, I ain't been nowhere. But, I mean, wherever I *have* been people have *always* taken to me.

EXT. DAY. BOAT.

The crossed hairs are centred on Del's forehead again. The finger depresses the trigger.

INT. DAY. THE RESTAURANT.

Del I mean, you take this holiday, for example. I mean, alright, the first night we arrived we was ripped off – we lost everything. But then I bumped into young Rico and he immediately took to me. I don't know what it is – people always seem to like me, I just don't know why.

Rodney No, it's got me bewildered an' all.

Del *(Angrily)* Rodney! *(At this moment the dumpling falls off his spoon and onto floor)*

Del ducks down to pick it up, immediately his head has cleared shot the padded leather back of the chair, directly where his head had been, explodes, accompanied by a very dull thud. Del immediately reappears holding the dumpling and none the wiser.

The only person in the entire restaurant who sees this is Rodney whose mouth drops open

in disbelief.

Del Look at that! I was saving this dumpling to last an all! Blimey, I don't know. *(Is about to eat the dumpling when he notices Rodney's expression)* What's the matter with you? It's hardly touched the ground, did it? Anyway, the floor was clean! Honestly, you and your hygiene!

Rodney Del Boy.

Del What?

Rodney Somebody just shot you.

Del Shot me? Well don't worry, Rodders, I'm feeling much better now.

Rodney Del. *(Referring to back of chair)* Look.

Del What's the matter with you ...?

Del gets up to see the torn and blackened leather back.

Del Gordon Bennett!

In doing so bumps into Giulio, the waiter, knocking him over, dropping trays etc. A female diner screams in alarm as the plates and trays hit the floor.

INT. DAY. MEN'S ROOM (RESTAURANT).

Rico, Sal and the boys smile as they hear the commotion from the restaurant.

Rico Bingo.

1st diner *(Just zipping up, jokes)* Gee, I hope that wasn't my dessert.

Lurch How can you joke at a time like this? *(Referring to Rico)* His father's just been shot.

Rico *(Reacts)* Shuddup, Lurch!

The four exit.

INT. DAY. THE RESTAURANT.

Señor C and Giulio are clearing away the mess and masking Del. Rico and the boys enter.

Rico Oh my God! Somebody call an ambulance. Is he dead?

Del stands.

Del No, but it was bloody close, Rico!

Rico stares incredulously at this resurrection.

Rodney A bullet, right, come out of nowhere and ... if he knew how to use a knife and fork he'd be a gonner!

Del That's right. That's true. Absolutely. Look, there I was – I was just sitting there quietly eating me dumplings, right, and then suddenly, whack! Look, a bullet hits the back of me chair. I mean, you don't need it, Rico, do you? I mean, you don't need it, son!

Rico *(Fazed by the whole thing)* No, no you certainly do not!

INT. NIGHT. PECKHAM. TROTTERS' LOUNGE AND EASTBOURNE/CASS'S HOTEL ROOM.

Raquel and Albert sit staring at the TV which isn't switched on. There is a mood of almost mourning in the flat. The phone rings. It alarms the both of them.

Albert Shall I get it, love?

Raquel Please! If it's anyone from the Church of England, tell 'em I'm out.

Albert *(Answers phone)* Trotters Independent Traders PLC? *(Pleased to hear the voice)* Yeah, it's me! Where are you?

Raquel Is it Del?

Albert No, Cassandra.

We now intercut between the Trotters' lounge and Cassandra's hotel room in Eastbourne.

Cassandra *(On phone)* I'm at my hotel in Eastbourne. Have you heard from them yet?

Albert *(On phone)* No, not yet, love.

Cassandra *(On phone)* Oh, Albert, I'm so worried! We don't even know where they're staying!

Albert *(On phone)* Yes we do. Raquel phoned the travel agent. They hired a camper.

Cassandra *(On phone)* A camper? But that means they could be anywhere!

Albert *(On phone and trying to allay her fears)* No, they found the camper.

Cassandra *(On phone)* Oh thank God! Where?

Albert *(On phone)* It was abandoned in a car park. Everything was gone. Their luggage, passports, money, everything.

Cassandra *(On phone)* Oh God!

Raquel Give me the phone! You'll worry the poor girl to death, you morbid old goat! *(Snatches phone from Albert. On phone)* Hello, Cassandra, it's me.

Cassandra D'you think Rodney's been hurt, Raquel?

Raquel *(On phone)* Of course not. Del's with him.

Cassandra *(On phone)* You don't think he's been arrested, do you? Oh no, Del's with him!

Raquel *(On phone)* Look, don't worry. There's bound to be a simple explanation for Rodney not calling.

Cassandra *(On phone)* Like what?

Raquel *(On phone)* Well.... Del's with him!

EXT. DAY. MIAMI BEACH.

Del and Rico are laid out on beach beds wearing swimming costumes. Behind them stand Sal, Pauly, Tony, Lurch and Gino, all wearing dark suits, collar and ties and sunglasses. We see Rodney approaching carrying a tray of drinks. He is wearing a very

Miami Twice Oh To Be In England

touristy vest and shorts.

Rodney Here you are, chaps.
Hands beers around.

Del Oh well done. Is this mine, Rodders?

Rodney *(To Del)* Oh by the way, the bloke who owns the bar said he offers his deepest respect and his loyalty is beyond question.

Del Oh, that's very nice of him. Have I met him?

Rodney No.

Del Everywhere I go, people seem to be offering me their deepest respect and kissing me 'and and what have you.

Rico They're nice people, Del. Hospitable, salt of the earth.

Del They certainly seem that way, Rico.

Pauly Derek, you ever had a go on one of those? *(Indicates further along beach)*
We see, a few yards away, a number of ski-jets parked on sand and a few people whizzing across the waves on them.

Del Have I ever had a go on one of those, Rodney?

Rodney Course you ain't!

Del No, no, I ain't.

Rico You'd like to try? It's no sweat, I know the owner.

Del What, me? Have a go on one of those things? Oh dear. No way, Pedro!

Rico Come on, Del, there's a first time for ... *(Reacts)* No way, *Pedro?*

Del No, you won't catch me going out on one of them things!

Tony And I was always led to believe that you Brits were a seafaring race.

Del We are! We gave you the world's greatest sailors, pal. Remember that we gave you Nelson, we gave you Drake, we gave you Columbus.
Rodney reacts to last name.

Rico But you're afraid of a few itsy bitsy little waves.

Del No, no, I'm not afraid, Rico. No, no, listen, don't get me wrong. You see, I got no reason to be afraid 'cos I've got a hundred yards swimming certificate back at home, haven't I, Rodders?

Rodney Yeah, he has.

Del Alright, Ok then. Come on. Let's have a go. Away we go. Come on, then.
They all stand.

Rodney *(Quietly to Del)* You sure about this?

Del He who dares, Rodney, he who dares. We don't want them thinking that us Brits are chicken, do we?

Rodney We certainly do not!
They are now amongst the ski-jets.

Del *(Referring to a ski-jet)* 'ere are, this one

looks alright, Rico, don't it?
Rico is at another jet ski near the water.

Rico No, Del, this is the best one.
Del walks towards the water.

Del Oh yeah, course. That one is better than that, innit? Yeah, right.
Del climbs on board.

Rico Come on then. Alright, come on up there. Don't be shy. Now straddle your weight evenly. This is your start button and this *(Indicates right hand grip)* is the throttle.

Del The throttle, right.

Rico Now just remember the faster you go the easier it is to stay up. Way to go, fella!

Del Yes. Cushty! Here we go....
Del revs the throttle and the ski-jet zooms away.
Rodney, Rico, Sal and the soldiers are watching Del from shore.

Lurch Look at that baby go!

EXT. DAY. DEL ON JET-SKI.
He wears a terrified expression but he hides his fear behind macho 'I'm enjoying this' type sounds.

Del *(Shouts)* Lovely, yes! *(Under breath)* Lovely jubbly. This is about far enough now.

EXT. DAY. MIAMI BEACH/SHORE.
Rodney Did he say something then?

Pauly I didn't hear a thing, Rodney.

EXT. DAY. OCEAN.
We now see Del trying to turn the handles to return to shore. We see that the handles won't budge.

Del *(Calls)* Rico, the steering wheel's stuck! The steering wheel's stuck!

EXT. DAY. SHORE.
Rico and the others continue to watch Del go further out.

EXT. DAY. DEL ON SKI-JET.
Del *(Still struggling with handles and calling)* Now the throttle's stuck – Rico! Ri ... co!
We see Del turning the throttle down but this makes no difference to the engine which continues to rev high.

Del I've got an iffy throttle!

EXT. DAY. MIAMI BEACH/SHORE.
From Rodney's POV we can see Del is a few hundred yards off shore and heading directly away towards horizon.

Rodney *(Trying not to let his concern show)* He's going a long way out, ain't he?
Rico Yeah, he's enjoying himself.
Rodney Oh yeah, I know! I'm just saying – he's a long way out.

EXT. DAY. DEL ON SKI-JET.

Del *(Screaming back towards the shore)* Where are the brakes on this bloody thing? Gordon Bennett!

EXT. DAY. MIAMI BEACH/SHORE.

Del is now a speck in the distance.
Pauly *(To Rodney)* What a guy, huh?
Rodney Yeah. He's certainly surprised me.
Rico Why's that?
Rodney Well, he can't even swim!
Rico and Pauly and Tony look at each other with hidden delight.
Sal *(Alarmed at this news)* But I thought he said he had a certificate for swimming.
Rodney Oh yeah, he has, but it ain't his!

EXT. DAY. OCEAN.

Del on jet ski, going further out, screaming.
Del Help! Help!

INT. DAY. AN AEROPLANE CABIN.

We now pan along the seats and passengers as we hear an announcement from the captain.
Captain *(OS) (American accent)* We've begun our descent into Miami and are about twenty-five miles off the coast.
We finish our pan and find Boycie at window seat, Marlene in aisle seat and Tyler in middle seat. A stewardess removes his glass.
Boycie Thank you. Well, Tyler, soon be in Miami. Let's hope it's better than Washington.
Marlene I liked Washington.
Boycie Not much of a beach though, was there!
Marlene In the last fortnight we've been all down the east coast of America and you've done nothing but moan!
Boycie I didn't moan in Atlantic City.
Marlene That's 'cos you was too busy gambling in the casino!
Boycie *(Looks down from window)* That's funny!
Marlene What is?
Boycie There's a bloke down there on one of them ski jet things.
Marlene So what?
Boycie So what? We're *twenty-five miles* off

the coast!
Marlene Well, he must know what he's doing.

EXT. DAY. THE ATLANTIC OCEAN.

We are looking out at nothing but ocean as far as the eye can see. All we can hear over the sound of the waves is the noise of a jet aeroplane somewhere above. Now we hear the sound of a fast approaching engine and Del's voice shouting for help.
Del and the ski-jet now appear from behind camera and rush away from us.

EXT. NIGHT. THE OCCHETTI MANSION. (RAIN).

A worried Rodney descends stairs.
From one of the rooms he hears Rico speaking. The door to the room is slightly open and he can see Rico speaking on the telephone via the reflection in a mirror.
Rico Señor Vasquez? This is Don Occhetti's son, Ricardo. I'm calling to say that our meeting can go ahead as scheduled … Yes, Señor, I understand that your English is not good. *(Now speaks slowly)* Your – meeting – with my – father – can go ahead – as planned … planned … Si … Gracias. I look forward to meeting you … Right. Lovely Jubbly *(Puts phone down then reacts: why did I say that?)* Lovely jubbly?.
Rico exits and comes face to face with Rodney.
Rico *(Slightly thrown by this – wondering what Rodney has heard)* Hi, how you doing?
Rodney Fine. I just thought that might be news of Del.
Rico No. I'll let you know if I hear anything. You're not worried, are you?
Rodney *No!* It's just that he left the beach eleven o'clock this morning and it's now eight-thirty at night, you know.
Rico Your brother's one hell of a fun guy.
Rodney Oh, I know but can you have fun on a ski-jet for nine and a half hours?
Rico Del can! I'll bet he's in a nightclub on Key West with some señorita.
Rodney He's wearing swimming trunks!
Rico They all do on Key West!
Rodney Oh I see. It's like that, is it? I see the phones are working again then?
Rico No.
Rodney But I thought I saw …
Rico That's a private line, purely for business.
Rodney Oh, I see. So, how come that one's working when all the others in the area are out?
Rico *(A big shrug)* Search me.

Miami Twice Oh To Be In England

Rodney I couldn't just use that phone for a minute, could I?

Rico No. I'm expecting a very important business call.

Rodney Right. I just wanted to phone home, you know, tell 'em where we are in case they're worried.

Rico There's nothing for them to worry about, Rodney. You're with us.

Rodney Yeah, yeah, I suppose you're right. Well, I'll be in my room. Well, if you hear anything …

Rico You'll be the first to know. Night.

Rodney ascends stairs. Pauly and Tony appears from rear of house (kitchen or somewhere).

Pauly Lurch is bringing the car round the front.

Rico The tall one's starting to ask questions. Looks like tomorrow we take him for a drive and put him out of his misery.

Tony One down, one to go.

There is a ring at front door bell. Rico opens it. We now see one of the detectives who have been on surveillance duty.

1st officer Evening, Sir.

Rico *(False concern)* Officer! Is there any news of my father?

1st officer Yes, sir, and I'm afraid it's bad news.

Rico Oh God! Good God, no!

1st officer We fished him out three hours ago.

Rico *(Mock tears)* He's dead?

1st officer No, he's alive and well.

Rico What?

1st officer That's what I mean by bad news. See, we know what the plan was, Rico. Daddy doesn't cherish spending the rest of his life in the pen, so he takes a little joyride on a ski-jet, meets up with a friendly yacht and sails off into the sunset? Only it couldn't work, Rico, for two reasons. One: we're watching his every move. We saw him leave, then the coast guards had him on radar. And two: he ran out of gas thirty five miles off Cuba.

The 2nd officer appears with Del who is wrapped in a blanket. His face (eyebrows, eyelashes, lips, hair) is covered with the white stain of dried salt. His skin is sunburnt.

Del Am I glad to be back, Rico. It was 'orrible out there, really 'orrible! I thought I was a gonner, I really did. I don't know what would have happened to me if that police helicopter hadn't found me.

Rico Why don't you, er, go to the kitchen and get yourself something to eat.

Del Thanks. I could murder a piña colada …

2nd officer *(To Rico as Del exits)* Oh, by the way, something's happened to his voice – he sounds Australian. We think it might be salt on the vocal cords.

Rico Oh, rest assured, Officer, I've got something for his throat. Night.

The policemen turn away.

Rico *(To himself)* You Limey turkey! What have we gotta do to get rid of you?

INT. NIGHT. PECKHAM. THE NAG'S HEAD.

We come up on TV on bar – about to show 9 o'clock news. Mike serves drinks to Alan.

Mike There you go, Alan.

Alan Oh, right. How much do I owe you?

Mike No, no, they're with Mickey Pearce – on the last round.

Alan You're joking?

Mike No.

Alan Cheers.

Alan walks towards table where Raquel, Albert, Denzil, Trig and Mickey Pearce are seated.

Mike turns to Sid.

Mike Right, Sid, I'll top you up.

Denzil Come on, Raquel, you're worrying about nothing.

Raquel Nothing? They've been gone for five days and we haven't heard a word from them! And you call that nothing?

Denzil Well, what I mean is, there's probably a simple explanation for it.

Trigger Maybe Dave's gone down to Brazil to have a look at the forest!

Alan *(To Raquel, trying to make her laugh)* There you are, you can't get more simple than that!

Mike Yeah! I mean, look at that telly, Sid. It's all bad news.

Sid You're right, nothing but bad news.

Mike It's all tragedies and disasters.

Sid Yeah, it's all gloom and doom.

Mike I shouldn't have it on during happy hour really. *(Sid reacts)* It's a funny old business with old Del Boy and Rodney, innit?

Sid They'll turn up sooner or later.

Mike Yeah.

Sid I just hope the police catch who ever did it! Right, I must be off. Cheers, Mike.

Mike Cheers, mate. Stay lucky.

Sid exits.

Cut back to table.

Raquel Have you heard from Cassandra?

Alan Yeah. Yeah, she called from the hotel. She's as worried as you are.

Mickey There's nothing to worry about! A few years back my brother went to Portugal on a golfing holiday. No-one heard from him for three months! His wife was phoning Interpol, my Mum was going mad – but he turned up safe and sound.

Raquel Where had he been?

Mickey He'd shacked up with some German tart.

Alan Shuddup, there's a good boy!!

Mickey Alright, so he was bang out of order, but at least he weren't injured.

Denzil Which is more than people'll say about you if you don't shut it! *(To Raq)* Listen, I've known Del a lot longer than you, and sometimes he can be a bit forgetful, *especially* when he's enjoying himself, I mean, he's most probably out there having the time of his life and … I'm not saying the right things, am I?

Raquel No, you're not!

Albert Young Mickey was more comforting than you!

Mike *(Calls from bar)* Here – Raquel! *(He directs her attention towards TV screen)* Look!

We see on TV the footage shot by the two cameramen outside the Occhetti mansion. We see Del and Rodney exit the mansion and talk to Rico.

Mike Hang on – I'll turn the sound up!

Mike increases the sound.

We see Del, in Don Occhetti's suit and chains (with a smiling Rodney right behind him) give the thumbs up to camera.

American commentator The Miami District Attorney's office have named this man. Public enemy number one! His web of vice and corruption has spread throughout the western hemisphere and many consider him to be the most dangerous criminal since Al Capone.

After 'public enemy number one' we cut to Raquel. The rest of the TV commentary is under her words. All eyes turn on Raquel.

Trigger *(To Raquel)* There they are! There's Del and Dave!

Raquel Public Enemy Number One? But he only left Tuesday!

EXT. DAY. MIAMI. THE OCCHETTI MANSION.

We are outside the mansion. Rico joins Pauly from the house.

Pauly What's happening?

Rico I got a call from the airport. The Colombians have landed, they'll be here any minute. I want everyone, and I mean *everyone*, down here to greet them. We need a show of strength, let 'em know they're not dealing with the Boy Scouts.

Pauly No problem.

Rico Hey, where's the Limeys?

Pauly Don't worry, I've taken care of them. They're busy.

EXT. DAY. TENNIS COURTS IN MANSION GROUNDS.

We see Del and Rodney trying to play tennis. Del is wearing tennis whites including long white trousers. Rodney is still wearing tracksuit, trainers and T-shirt.

By now Del is looking quite tanned and more like Don Occhetti by the day.

Del God! Whack it back to me, for God's sake, Rodney!

Rodney I'm tryin' to whack it back! I'm not very good at tennis!

Del No! Really? Anyway, what's the score? I'm six sets up, ain't I?

Rodney No you are not! You're about two games up and it's my serve!

Del No, no, no, it's my serve!

Rodney How can it be? You served during the last game!

Del Yeah I know, and I won! So it's my serve again, innit?

Rodney No, it don't … *(Gives up)* Oh I've had enough of this! I'm going in!

Picks up his jacket from side of court.

Del Oh, just cause you're losing!

Rodney walks off in sulk.

INT. DAY. DON'S SUITE.

The Don is working out in bathroom/gym.

INT. DAY. HALL OF MANSION.

Rodney enters from tennis court. He looks around for someone to give his racquet to.

Rodney *(Calls)* You there, Rico? Lurch? Tony? Anybody about?

Rodney realises he is alone.

Now his eyes wander to the telephone which he had seen Rico using in earlier scene.

Rodney creeps into the room and closes door.

INT. DAY. MANSION. DON OCCHETTI'S SUITE.

Don Occhetti, wearing a pink and green shell-suit, exits from bathroom/gym. He is sweating and has obviously been working out (we see the gym equipment through the open bathroom door). Because of his self-imposed incarnation he is now looking paler and more like Del originally looked.

Miami Twice Oh To Be In England

INT. DAY. ROOM OFF HALL.
Rodney produces a piece of paper from jacket and starts to dial number which is written on paper.

INT. DAY. DON'S SUITE.
The Don gets the medicine bottle out of the globe and goes to intercom. He picks up receiver, dials and takes a swig of medicine, leaving bottle on desk.

INT. NIGHT. EASTBOURNE HOTEL RECEPTION.
The receptionist calls to Cassandra.
Receptionist Mrs Trotter! Mrs Trotter!

INT. DAY. MANSION. TELEPHONE ROOM (OFF HALL).
Rodney *(On phone)* Hello? Cass? It's me. Rodney!

INT. NIGHT. EASTBOURNE. HOTEL RECEPTION.
Cassandra *(On phone. Highly excited)* Where are you? What's happened? Are you alright?
Rodney Yeah, now steady on! No, listen, we're both fine, right!

INT. DAY. DON'S SUITE.
The Don is still waiting.
Don Come on, one of you jerks, hurry up and answer the phone!

INT. DAY. THE HALL OF MANSION.
The intercom phone is ringing as Del enters from tennis courts.
Del *(Answers intercom)* Hello – Battersea Dog's Home? *(He does a dog impression)*

INT. DAY. MANSION. DON OCHETTI'S SUITE.
The Don reacts to Del's voice on intercom. He slams receiver down.

INT. DAY. HALL OF MANSION.
Del smiles to himself as the receiver is slammed down. He makes his way upstairs.

INT. DAY. INTERCUT BETWEEN MANSION TELEPHONE ROOM AND EASTBOURNE HOTEL RECEPTION.
We intercut between Rodney and Cassandra.
Cassandra I've been so worried about you!
Rodney Have you?
Cassandra Yes. I didn't take the interview. They let me off on compassionate grounds.

Rodney What – so you could have come with me after all?
Cassandra Well not without the help of a fortune teller! I didn't know you were going to go missing for the week.
Rodney No, I suppose not.

INT. DAY. THE MANSION. LANDING.
Del, still in tennis whites, exits from his and Rodney's room. Unable to find Rodney, Del believes his brother is playing a sulky game of hide and seek.
Del Rodney, where are you? You're not in our room …

INT. DAY/NIGHT. TELEPHONE ROOM/ EASTBOURNE HOTEL.
Intercut Rodney and Cassandra.
Rodney Oh, I wish you could have come, Cass, you would have loved it. They're such nice people.
Cassandra Well, if you hadn't booked that particular week I would have been with you.
Rodney Yeah, well, I didn't actually book the tickets. Del did.
Cassandra Del? No, he couldn't. He knew I was in Eastbourne that week.
Rodney Well I suppose he thought you … He *knew*? What d'you mean he knew?
Cassandra Yes, I told him over lunch when the seminar was. So why did he book that particular week?
Rodney Isn't it obvious why? So he could get a free bloody holiday!

INT. DAY. DON'S SUITE.
The Don paces angrily.

INT. DAY. MANSION. LANDING.
Del continues looking for Rodney.
Del Rodney. Come on. Come out, come out wherever you are.
He comes to Don Ochetti's door.
Rodney!

INT. DAY. DON O'S SUITE. STUDY.
The Don is standing as he hears Del from outside.
Del *(OOV)* Are you there, Roddy woddy?
The Don quickly sits in a high backed chair with back to door. We see Del enter. The Don and Del are both in same frame. Del surveys the room without moving into it, therefore not seeing the painting and photos.
Del Oh yes, this is very nice. This is a bit of me

this is 'cos I'm a Byzantine sort of bloke.

Del exits. The Don gets up and follows.

Del *(OOV)* Where are you hiding, you little scallywag?

INT. DAY. MANSION. LANDING.

Del is on landing once again. Don Occhetti peers down landing at Del (merely trying to get a better look at his doppelganger). Again, we see Del and Don Occhetti in same frame. Del exits to his room. Don Occhetti steps out onto the landing and considers the likeness. Now, a movement on the stairs draws his attention.

We see Rodney, half-way up the stairs and fuming from what Cassandra has just told him.

Rodney *(To Don Occhetti, believing it is Del)* You git!

We see Don Occhetti's reaction.

Rodney *(Approaching menacingly)* You rotten, conniving, git!

Rodney now grabs the Don of Dons, the most powerful figure in the entire Cosa Nostra, by the throat. Don Occhetti has no choice but to take this treatment. If he speaks or protests in any way he will give the game away.

Rodney You are the most selfish bastard I've ever come across! Do you know who I've been talking to?

Don Occhetti shakes his head.

Rodney Cassandra! Ah, that's shaken you innit? *Don Occhetti nods.*

Rodney You knew all along she wouldn't be able to make this trip, didn't you?

Don Occhetti shrugs innocently.

Rodney You *knew* she had to go to the bank's seminar in Eastbourne! But you didn't tell me that, did you?

Don Occhetti shrugs again.

Rodney No, no, you kept that well quiet, so as *you* could come on this bloody holiday! And where'd you get that stupid track suit from?

Don Occhetti opens his mouth as if about to say something.

Rodney Don't talk to me! I don't wanna hear none of your excuses! Just do not talk to me, alright?

Don Occhetti nods obediently.

Rodney shoves Don Occhetti up against the wall and then moves down landing to his and Del's room. As he is about to enter room Rodney turns and lets the Don of Dons have one more volley.

Rodney Git!!

Rodney exits to room slamming door behind him.

Don Occhetti's look of feigned innocence now changes to one of burning anger and vengeance.

INT. DAY. DEL AND RODNEY'S SUITE.

Rodney has just entered from his confrontation with Don Occhetti and is still in a flaming mood.

He locks the door with a key and then slips the bolts across.

Rodney *(Mumbles angrily to himself)* That's it, you ain't sleeping in here tonight. Rico's gonna have to find you somewhere else for you to sleep!

We now see that Del is standing in the doorway to the en-suite bathroom listening to Rodney.

Del What's up with you, Soppy?

Rodney You know full well what's up with me! You *knew* Cassandra couldn't come away with me on this trip and you knew because *she* told you!!

Del Ah, now you come to mention it she did say something …

Rodney But you planned it! You went to the travel agents and you booked it just so as you could come with me on this holiday!!…

Del Shh. Now listen, calm down, please, Rodders. Just calm down a minute, will you. I'll try and explain everything to you. You see the thing is that erm well … look … That wine deal of mine has gone right up the pictures! I had this phone call from Bucharest – the first lorryload they delivered was *white* wine! So anyway, I … I just didn't know what to do! And you know me, don't you? There are only two things in the world that worry me and that is doctors, you know, Gods! And, well, I was frightened of being cursed! So I thought, well, you know, if I came over here, like, to Miami – he won't find me and that's the only reason I did it, Rodney. Honest, I just, you know, wanted to lay low for a spell!

Rodney Oh yeah, on my pension money! I swear, Del, you are the most 'orrible, dirty little … *(Reacts)* How d'you get in here?

Del What d'you mean, how did I get in here?

Rodney How d'you get in this room?

Del Well, I came through that door, it's a blinding invention!

Rodney No you didn't 'cos I locked that door and the only … How d'you get changed so quickly?

Miami Twice Oh To Be In England

Del What do you mean, 'How did I get changed?' I haven't got changed, have I? I've been wearing this all morning.

Rodney No, I don't understand this. I was just talking to you outside.

Del You were just talking to me outside? You couldn't have done, could you, 'cos I've been in the khazi on suite.

Rodney Derek, I've just been having a row with you out on that landing! You were wearing a pink and green track-suit!

Del *(Worried but calm)* A pink and gre ...

Rodney ... Now I want you to tell me the truth, I won't be angry. Have you ... erm ... taken anything? Have you smoked one of them Jamaican Woodbines?

Rodney The only thing I have taken is a load of cobblers from you! Now, I was talking to you on that landing. Or ...

Del Or what?

Rodney Or someone who looks ... like you.

Del *(Apparently takes this seriously)* Someone who looks like me? What you mean – like what, like a double?

Rodney Yeah.

Del Oh dear, I see. You know what this means, Rodney, don't you?

Rodney What?

Del It means you're a bigger plonker than I thought you were. *(Laughs)*

Rodney Alright. Well, you go and have a look for yourself, he's out there on the landing.

Del Alright, I will if it'll shut you up – you little dipstick.

INT. DAY. DON OCHETTI'S SUITE.

Don Occhetti takes a walkman and earphones from his desk and storms towards bathroom/gym, mumbling as he does so.

Don I don't know what the world is coming to? I'm a prisoner in my own home and all because of those goddamn, sorry-assed, Limeys.

Exits to bathroom and closes door heavily behind him.

INT. DAY. MANSION. LANDING

Del and Rodney walk down corridor. At the end of the landing, close to Don Ochetti's room is the large mirror.
Del and Rodney see their reflections in the mirror.

Del Boo! Oh look – dippy, that's what it was, look – your reflection!

Rodney How can I have a row with a bloody reflection?

Del Well, that's easily done! I've had a barney with myself many a night when I've come home from a party!

INT. DAY. DON OCHETTI'S SUITE. BATHROOM/GYM.

Don Occhetti is now pedalling furiously on exercise bike and is wearing the earphones of walkman which is playing.

Don *(Mumbling)* I'm closing your account, you lime-sucking bozos!

INT. DAY. LANDING.

Del So what d'you want to do – go and check it out then?

Rodney Eh? Erm. Well, I'll go down there and keep a look-out.

Del Oh I see. So you wanna go up there and keep a look out and you want me to go into that room and check it out. Right?

Rodney Yeah.

Del Oh, cushty! *(Mumbles)* Do it yourself Del! Go on then.

Rodney goes up landing.

INT. DAY. DON O'S SUITE. STUDY.

The door opens and Del peers in. He can hear nothing from the bathroom and, as far as he is concerned, is completely alone in suite.

INT. DAY. BATHROOM/GYM.

The Don pedalling away.

Don I hate Limeys! I hate Limeys!

INT. DAY. DON'S STUDY.

Del steps further into the room and cautiously begins to check it out. At this point he doesn't notice painting and photos.
Del picks up a few small antique items and studies them with a few 'Mmhhs' of appreciation.
He goes to desk, picks up a piece and drops it with a crash.

INT. DAY. BATHROOM/GYM.

The Don pedalling away.

Don I hate Limeys! I hate 'em! I hate 'em!

INT. DAY. DON OCHETTI'S SUITE.

Del is now a bit more relaxed. He wanders over towards some book shelves and passes the antique globe cocktail cabinet. He gives it a quick spin and we hear the terrible sound of shattering glass from inside.
Del reacts horrified at this.

INT. DAY. BATHROOM/GYM.

The Don, pedalling, still hasn't heard anything from the study.

INT. DAY. DON'S SUITE.

As Del backs away from the globe his hand reaches out behind him and he knocks the open bottle of medicine over. The medicine spills over Del's right hand. He wipes the medicine from his hand and reacts to the vile smell. As he heads for the door he glances in the direction of the painting. He doesn't take the vision in immediately and now opens door. He is about to leave when he pauses. He now moves back into room and stares, open-mouthed, at the large oil portrait of Don Occhetti.
Del just stares, trance-like, at this vision. He now studies the smaller framed photos. We see a recent picture of Don Occhetti with Frank Sinatra, Don Occhetti with Castro and Don Occhetti with the Pope.
Del passes another photo, then goes back to look again.

INT. DAY. MANSION. HALL.

Rico starts upstairs with Colombian drug baron, Señor Alberto Vasquez and his tough-looking assistant, Jorge Herrera.
Both men are smartly dressed in lightweight suits and carry brief cases.

Rico I'm so pleased you could make it, Señor Vasquez. My father has been so looking forward to meeting you.

Vasquez *(Struggles with English)* And so it is with me, too. Si?

INT. DAY. MANSION. LANDING.

Rodney hears voices from hall and knocks on Don's door.

Rodney Del! Hurry up, somebody's coming!

INT. DAY. DON'S SUITE.

Del moves towards door and sees a newspaper. The main headline reads: 'Mafia Boss Faces Life In Jail'
In smaller print:
'Don of Dons released on bail' Beneath this is a black and white photo of Don Occhetti

Rodney *(OOV)* Del!

Del is now considering the events leading up to this discovery. On Del's face we see other photos. 1. The restaurant. Del turns down to get dumpling and the bullet zaps into back of chair. 2. The ski-jet ride. Del miles out to sea

and screaming 'Help'.

Del *(Now everything fits)* They were tryin' to … kill me! Fromage frais!

INT. DAY. MANSION: LANDING.

We see Rodney at Don's door.
He hears Rico and Colombians coming up stairs.

Rico *(OOV)* After your meeting you must stay for lunch.

Vasquez *(OOV)* Graçias.
Rodney at door, cringing with fear knowing that Del will be caught for sure.

Rodney *(Mouths)* Oh shit …
He runs back to his and Del's room.

INT. DAY. DON O'S SUITE. STUDY.

Del hears Rico and the Colombians.

Rico *(OOV)* You had a good flight?

Vasquez Yes, it's good.
Del looks round for a place to escape but Rico enters. Rico simply assumes Del to be his father.

Rico Pop, the Colombians have arrived.
Del, realising that his voice and accent will give the game away, just smiles and makes noises to all of Rico's questions and statements.

Del Oh …

Rico This is Señor Vasquez and his associate Señor Herrera.

Del Mmmh.

Rico I'll be in the other room if you need me.

Del Ah, mmmh.
Rico exits.

Vasquez *(An obviously practised speech in which he puts too much emphasis on the 'H')* Don Hocchetti, hi ham honoured to meet you, sir.
Vasquez kisses Del's hand and then reacts to the vile, medicine-type taste.

Vasquez Forgive me, Señor, my Engleesh – no good.

Del *(Gesturing for them to sit and trying to say something Italian)* Bonnetti, bonnetti.
Herrera and Vasquez sit.

Vasquez Bonnetti, bonnetti. We bring the final, erm … *(To Herrera)* firmation er …

Herrera Eenformation.

Vasquez *(To Del)* Eenformation, eenformation concerning … concerning our buseeness transaction.

Del Business. *(Because of their lack of English, Del feels confident enough to speak in his normal voice)* Oh, cushty … PA.

Miami Twice Oh To Be In England

Herrera *(Passing papers across desk)* You will read, please?

INT. DAY. BATHROOM/GYM.
The Don still pedalling on the bike.

INT. DAY. STUDY.
Del *(Studies papers briefly)* What – what is this exactly?
Vasquez It is the firmation …
Herrera Confirmatieeon.
Vasquez Confirmateeon. Confirmateeon regarding delivery of merchandise.
Del Oh, er, smashing. Smashing … Er, what sort of merchandise is it then?
Herrera and Vasquez look at each other.
Vasquez Señor, it is the finest, the purest the very best cocaine.
Del reacts.
Del Cocai … *(Coughs)*
Herrera Seventeen tonnes. It is on a yacht anchored offshore.
Vasquez We wait – we await you eenstruction. Don Occhetti, where – where … delivery of merchandise in the boat – you know – where? Where?
Del Em … Deliver, delivery, yes … *(Now remembers his sight-seeing boat trip and the coast guard centre at Biscayne Bay)* I tell you what, yeah, why don't you deliver it then tonight about midnight. You know Biscayne Bay at all? Deliver the merchandise to Biscayne Bay. Biscayne Bay.
Herrera *(Writing this down)* Beescayne …
Vasquez Cayne …
Del Cayne, cayne.
Vasquez Cayne.
Herrera Biscayne …
Vasquez Bay.
Del Bay.
Herrera Bay.
Vasquez It is safe, er, safe?
Del Oh, don't you worry. Yes, oh, the cocaine'll be safe there, all right.
Vasquez Someone there to meet us? To meet us?
Del Oh, I'm sure. Yeah, don't worry, there'll be someone there to meet you alright, yeah.
Vasquez Good. Good. *(OOV)* It ees good to do buseenes with you, señor.

INT. DAY. DON OCHETTI'S SUITE. BATHROOM/ GYM.
We see Don Occhetti still pedalling on the bike and listening to walkman. He is sweating
profusely. He disappears into the inner room and switches the cold tap on.

INT. DAY. DON OCCHETTI'S SUITE. STUDY.
Vasquez and Herrera reacts to the sound of running water coming from the bathroom. Del reacts, suddenly realising that someone has been in there all the time.
Vasquez Er room … Who?
Del Whoom … whom …
Vasquez Whoom? Room? *(Concerned or suspicious)*
Del Er – whom in the room? Yeah … That's a good question – erm whom is in there? That is erm, the bathroom and that is my … girlfriend in there!
Vasquez *(To Herrera in Spanish)* What does he mean?
Herrera Don Occhetti's señorita.
Vasquez Ah, yes, yes, yes, the señorita!
Macho sounds from all of them. From inside the bathroom we hear Don Occhetti do a mighty burp. They all look toward bathroom.
Del Yes, yes, the señorita … *(Del hurrying nervously)* She had a double helping of chilli con carne last night. I told her not to, I mean, I told her!… But you know what they're like, don't you? Well – cor, look at the time then – I think that will conclude our business then, gentlemen.

INT. DAY. MANSION. LANDING.
Del Yes, alright then. Well, thanks very much.
Vasquez Adiós.
Del Adgegos.
Vasquez We will be speeaking soon.
Del Yeah OK, speaky soon. *(As goodbye)* Bonnetti, Bonnetti.
Vasquez Bonetti!
Vasquez and Herrera start to descend stairs. Del runs to his and Rodney's room, still holding paperwork which Vasquez gave him earlier.

INT. DAY. DEL AND RODNEY'S ROOM.
Rodney is pacing in the room as Del bursts in.
Rodney Didn't you hear me knocking? Rico brought two blokes up to that room.
Del Listen to me, Rodney. We are in deep, deep schtuck. This is Mafia country.
Rodney Mafia?
Del Yes! Shh, listen. Come over here. Sit down there. Just listen to me. You know that Rico, Salvatore and all the other guys? They're Mafioso! And you remember that you said to me that you thought you saw a bloke what looked

like me, well, there is one. He's got a room down there – his name's Don Occhetti and he is the boss. I'm telling you, Rodney, this is Marlon Brando time!

Rodney *(Considers it all)* Nah!

Del Yes! I've just read the newspaper down there. It's all about him. You see, this Don, this Don, he's up for trial and it looks like he's well in the frame and he's gonna go down the Kermit and spend the rest of his life in the nick!

Rodney What for?

Del Drug-running, kidnapping and three, you count them, three murders! Right, now that is what all this has been about, Rodney. Don't you understand? Eh? They've been trying to kill me! Think about it! That accidental stray bullet that just whacked into the back of that chair. The iffy ski-boat ride, eh? Don't you see, look if I go for a Burton that means that this Donald – whatever his name is – doesn't have to stand trial and he goes free!

Rodney Look, Del. Don't you think you might be letting your imagination run away with you?

Del I wish I was, Rodney, I wish I was! You take a look at that, pal – go on! *(Hands Rodney the paperwork)* I've been down there and I ... I've just had a little tête-a-tête with two Colombian drug barons.

Rodney Bloody 'ell, Del! He's a Mafia boss!

Del What do you think I've been trying to tell you? Course he is! Look at it – look!

Rodney Oh cosmic!

Del Eh?

Rodney Cos-bloody-mic! I just roughed him up!

Del What?

Rodney *I* have just roughed up a Mafia boss! I called him a git! I just called a *Mafia boss* ...

Del Rodney, just pull yourself together!

Rodney ... a git!!

Del I tell you – these are not the sort of people that you wanna spend your holidays with. I'll tell you another thing, too. That Rico, he can forget that present we was gonna buy him!

Rodney Oh, let's get outta here!

Del How can we, eh? We can't go downstairs 'cos they're all there!

Rodney Let's get out the window then! Let's just get out before I wake up with a bloody 'orse's 'ead on me pillow!

EXT. DAY. MANSION.

We see the back of the house. The walls up to the first floor window are covered with a thick climbing plant (creepers).
Del and Rodney appear on balcony.

Del You go first, Rodney. Go on, go on!
Rodney climbs out gingerly and gets a grip on the creepers. Del follows. Half way down we see the leg of his tennis trousers snag on something and rip from the bottom of the leg up to the knee.

Del Oh, look at this – look!!
Rodney is now on the ground. Del eventually joins him. They run off.

EXT. DAY. FRONT OF MANSION.

As Rico sees Colombians into a taxi we see Rodney and Del peer round edge of house in background.

Rico Mucho ... very much ...

Vasquez Hasta la vista ...
The Don exits from bathroom sweating from his exercise. He move to intercom, close to window. The Don has his back to the window as he talks on intercom.

Don Yeah er ... send Rico up to me. Er, tell him I want to talk to him.

EXT. DAY. MANSION.

Del and Rodney run across lawn to wall.

INT. DAY. DON'S SUITE.

The Don switches intercom off and moves to globe cocktail cabinet. He opens the top of the globe and broken glass and liquid spill out onto floor. The Don stares incredulously at this destruction.

EXT. DAY. GARDENS OF MANSION.

Del and Rodney reach the wall.
Rodney climbs up a bush near the wall and sits astride wall. Del climbs up and grabs top of wall and reacts with pain.

Rodney Careful, Del, there's something sharp up there.
Del is stuck. Rodney pulls him off.

Del Rodney!
They fall back out of frame.

INT. DAY. DON OCCHETTI'S SUITE. STUDY.

The Don is kneeling by the antique globe cocktail cabinet picking up pieces of glass from carpet. Rico enters.

Don How the hell did this happen?

Rico I don't know, Pop. The last time I saw it it was fine. Leave it, I'll get Lurch to do it. Well, the Colombians seem happy.

Don Yeah, well, maybe they won't be so happy after we've had our meeting. So, er, show 'em up, Rico.

Miami Twice Oh To Be In England

Rico Show 'em up? They've just left.

Don Left? What the hell did they come all this way for and then leave without talking to me?

Rico But you had your meeting with them, Pop. I brought 'em in and introduced them … how did you change into that track-suit so quickly?

Don I've been in this all morning, I've been working out!

Rico Oh god! The Limey!

DAY. EXT. MANSION.

Del and Rodney run off.

INT. DAY. MANSION. LANDING.

Rico rushes towards Del and Rodney's room followed by Don Occhetti.

Don I'm in court tomorrow morning! Rico!

INT. DAY. DEL AND RODNEY'S ROOM.

The door bursts open and Rico and Don Occhetti enter.

Rico throws open the bathroom door in his search for Del and Rodney.

Don Do something you stupid jerk!

Rico Don't worry, Pop, we'll get 'em back.

Rico rushes out of room.

We stay on Don O's vengeful face as we hear Rico calling in background.

EXT. DAY. LONG COUNTRY HIGHWAY.

We see a few cars racing past.

We pan back to see an old American convertible driving towards us at about 20mph.

Seated in the front bench seat are Del and Rodney and a little old lady who is so small she has to peer between the top of the steering wheel and dashboard.

Del can't believe the speed they are doing. He looks at the lady then turns to Rodney, begging an explanation.

Old lady Are you enjoying the ride, boys?

Del Oh yes, lovely, Miss Daisy. *(To Rodney)* I don't believe this!

Rodney *(To Del)* It's supposed to be a get-away, at this rate we'll be done for kerb-crawling.

We see the car pull into a roadside cafe/shop. Old lady produces a shopping bag.

Old lady Well, this is about as far as I go, boys.

Del Yeah, well thanks for the lift.

Old lady Have a nice trip back to Australia.

Del We're not Australian! We're English, aren't we?

Rodney Just leave it – come on! She's old!

Del and Rodney run off towards some woods.

As they disappear into the trees so the Mafia's sedan screeches to a halt and reverses. The Mafia alight and collect their guns from trunk.

Rico Are you sure it was them?

Pauly How many guys are running round the Everglades dressed like Jimmy Connors?

EXT. DAY. FOREST.

We see Del and Rodney struggling through the undergrowth.

PECKHAM. INT. NIGHT. TROTTERS' LOUNGE.

Albert paces the floor.

Raquel now enters from hall/front door loaded down with two large shopping bags filled with groceries.

Albert Raquel! Where have you been?

Raquel *(Indicating bags)* I've been to Royal Ascot for the day! Where'd you think I've been?

Albert Cassandra phoned about an hour ago. She's spoken with Rodney.

Raquel She spoke to him? Well, where are they? What's happened?

Albert They've been staying at some millionaire's mansion. A tropical storm knocked all the phones out, that's why they couldn't call.

Raquel Well when are they coming home?

Albert They catch their plane tomorrow. The main thing is, you can stop worrying. They're both safe and sound.

EXT. DAY. MIAMI: THE EVERGLADES.

We see Del and Rodney struggling through the undergrowth.

EXT. DAY. EVERGLADES.

We see the Mafia and their guns struggling through another part of undergrowth.

EXT. DAY. THE EVERGLADES.

In the background we see the forest leading down to what appears to be a grassy clearing. The camera is positioned low and the foreground appears to be solid ground. This is in fact the everglades flora which grows on the water.

We see Del and Rodney running out of the forest towards the clearing.

As Del steps onto the 'solid' flora he sinks into water up to his waist.

Del Come on, Rodney. Where's your stamina? *(Del into water)*

Bloody hell! Help me out of here, Rodney.

Rodney Come here!

Rodney helps Del out.

Del I can't!

Rodney Careful!

Del Gordon Bennett! *(Referring to the flora)* What the 'ell is this stuff anyway?

Rodney I think it's water hyacinth. I've just been reading about it in my Greenpeace magazine.

Del Well, what's it doing there – floating about on the water?

Rodney That's what it does. It grows on the water. Here, we must be in the Everglades.

Del Everglades? Looks more like a swamp to me!

Rodney Well it is a s ... don't matter.

Del Oh Rodney, just get me home, will you? Back to England's green and pleasant land and those dark volcanic mills.

Rodney *(Reacts to 'volcanic mills')* Yeah! Oh, look, Del, let's have a rest, eh? I think we're safe enough. Nobody could find us in here ... *(A fearful reaction)*

Del Look at me. Look! My hands are all bleeding – me clothes are torn, me arse is soaking wet!

Rodney And you're still whining!

Del Yes, it's alright for you, innit, eh? If I get piles you can have half of 'em!

> *There is now a sulky silence. As we watch them sulking we see an alligator crawling past about twelve feet behind them.*
> *Rodney, hearing a rustling behind him, turns and faces the gator. Rodney is frozen.*
> *He now slowly turns back to face the water. He considers his next move for a couple of seconds.*

Rodney *(Quietly)* Del Boy.

Del Oh, shuddup, Rodney, you're getting on my nerves.

Rodney I want you to do something for me, Derek. I want you to stand up and *very slowly* walk away.

Del What is this? Simple Simon Says?

Rodney Very slowly walk away, Del. We don't want to alarm it.

Del Alarm what?

Rodney That thing behind us.

> *Del looks behind and reacts.*

Del That thing? Get out of here!

> *Del leaps and runs for his life. Rodney follows.*

EXT. DAY. ANOTHER PART OF THE EVERGLADES.

> *Del and Rodney run into shot and stop.*

Del *(Fighting for breath)* That was a bloody crocodile, Rodney!

Rodney No, it weren't a crocodile!

Del I know a crocodile when I come face to face with one! I've seen enough Tarzan films.

Rodney That was an alligator!

Del It's the same thing, innit?

Rodney No, no it's not! I mean, they may look alike and they are from the same family, but biologically ...

Del *(Cuts in)* Do they eat you?

Rodney Yeah.

Del Well it's the same thing then, innit? I mean, who the hell let it out?

Rodney No, no, they live here in the Everglades.

Del They? D'you mean to say there's more than one of em?

Rodney Yeah! But don't panic. It's very rare to see them during the daylight 'cos they're normally a nocturnal animal.

Del Nocturnal! Are you tryin' to tell me that come teatime there'll be millions of the gits?

Rodney Yeah.

Del I don't believe this! I just don't believe it! I've gotta be honest with you, Rodney. All in all I'm beginning to wish that I hadn't come on this holiday with you!

Rodney Well, don't you blame me! I did not invite you, Derek – you invited yourself!

Del *(Hearing something)* Listen! Listen to that!

> *We hear the sound of a distant boat engine.*

Rodney It's a boat! It's a boat, my son! We're saved.

> *Rodney is about to move forward when Del drags him down.*

Del Get down, Rodney, get down! It could be the Mafia!

Rodney What would they be doing on a boat?

Del Water skiing! What d'you think?

> *We now see a hire-boat appear.*

EXT. DAY. HIREBOAT/EVERGLADES.

> *Now we hear a familiar voice.*

Boycie Look, Marlene, an eagle!

Marlene It's not an eagle, it's a heron.

Boycie Well, it's a big bird anyway!

> *Tyler now points into undergrowth.*

Tyler Look, it's Uncle Rodney!

Marlene Listen to him. Uncle Rodney. The imagination these kids have.

Boycie Yeah. Right, let's take some photographs

> *Boycie begins snapping away. We see his shots (frozen as in photograph) and hear the camera shutter.*

An alligator.

A turtle.

*Del's face looking through the undergrowth.
A heron.*

Now Boycie reacts.

Boycie Marlene … You know just *(Now chuckles at the silliness of his next statement)* for a moment there I thought I saw … Gordon Bennett!

We see Del and Rodney standing in the undergrowth.

Marlene It's Del and Rodney! Ooo ooh, Del!

Del *(Calls)* Boycie!

Rodney Get over here! Quick!

Boycie What, in God's name, are you doing here?

Del I forgot to kiss you goodbye at Gatwick! Get that boat over here. Quick!

Boycie Wayne – get over there.

The boat crosses the water.

Marlene You alright, Del?

Del T'riffic, sweetheart.

Del and Rodney clamber aboard.

Del Come on, Rodders! Let's go, let's go!

Boycie *(To Del)* Good God, you smell like a vegetarian's fart!

Del At least my house hasn't been burgled!

Boycie *(His smile wiped from his face)* What??

Rodney It's a joke, a joke!! Right, now let's get going!

Boycie Right, Wayne. Let's go!

*The boat begins to roar away from us.
Now we see the Mafia on the shore line.
Rico grabs a gun (a hunting rifle) from someone.*

Sal Rico, as your lawyer I am asking you to consider your actions carefully before you do anything you may regret.

Rico Ok, I'll consider it! *(Brings gun up to eyeline)*

Del Everyone, duck!

Boycie Why?

We hear a gunshot and a bullet whistles over their heads.

Del That!

Boycie Get a bloody move on, Wayne!

EXT. DAY. EVERGLADES. JETTY AND TOURIST AREA OF PARK.

We see two armed rangers step out of their office upon hearing the gunshot.

1st Ranger Did you hear that, Curtis? There's some jerk out there loosing off lead! Come on.

*The two rangers run to their boat.
As they do so we see Del, Rodney, Boycie and Marlene pulling into shore in their boat.
They climb ashore obviously shaken by their experience.*

Boycie *(Moaning as they walk towards shops, etc)* Everything was going well! We were having a lovely holiday …

Marlene *(Cuts in)* Shuddup moaning.

Boycie And then they turn up! And within fifteen seconds some sod's shooting at us!

Marlene You've done nothing but moan ever since we left Washington!

Boycie Get that bloody boat in for God's sake!

As Del passes the empty ranger's office he remembers the paperwork Vasquez gave him.

Del Rodney, hang about a minute.

He takes the crumpled and wet paperwork from his back pocket and places it on the door.

Del Rodney, let's go home.

Rodney Del, our plane don't leave till tomorrow night.

Del I know but we can sleep at the airport. At least we'll be that much closer to dear old England. Give us a lift to the airport, will you, Boycie?

INT. NIGHT. AN AIRLINE CABIN.

The film/video screen is down and the passengers are watching news from America.

Newsreader Last night coast guards from Biscayne Cove boarded a Colombian yacht and discovered seventeen tons of cocaine. Also on board the yacht was the wanted drug baron, Alberto Vasquez. He was taken to Miami police central where he is being questioned by FBI agents. The tip-off for the drug bust came when details of the delivery were left in the Florida park ranger's office. But the big story today – in Miami Superior Court Don Vincenzo Occhetti, *(Picture of the Don)* head of the most powerful Mafia family in America, was found guilty of kidnap, drug-running and three counts of conspiring to commit murder. He was given six life sentences to run concurrently. His son, Ricardo Occhetti, was arrested yesterday for illegal hunting in the Everglade National Park and for possessing an unlicensed firearm. Police are now looking for two Australians who may be able to assist them in this matter.

*During all this news we pan down the aisle of plane. As we near the end we can see some of the passengers reacting to a violent smell.
We now find Del and Rodney fast asleep and snoring and still wearing the ripped and dirty clothes of yesterday.*

INT. DAY. PECKHAM. THE TROTTERS' FLAT.

We are in the hall and facing the front door.
The door bell rings.
Raquel opens door to Del and Rodney, who
are unshaven and filthy.
Nothing is said.
Del and Rodney force painful smiles and
Raquel gestures them inside.

INT. DAY. TROTTERS' LOUNGE.

Raquel enters followed by Del and Rodney.
Del and Rodney stop and react horrified.

We now see that the lounge is filled to the
brim with what looks like seven hundred
cases of Romanian reisling. The vicar is sitting
on the cases.

Albert *(Glad to see them back)* Welcome home,
boys!

Del and Rodney look at each other with a
'and we thought things couldn't get worse'
expression.

PHOTOGRAPHS © DAVID EDWARDS

WANTED BY THE FBI

PHOTO EARLY 1991

CASE: Kiddnapping, drug-smuggling, accessory to three counts of murder.

NAME: Don Vincenzo Occhetti

AGE: 45   **DOB:** 1946

HEIGHT: 5" 5" approx   **WEIGHT:** 151 approx

NATIONALITY: Italian/American

COMMENTS: Subject is very dangerous - approach with extreme caution!

Mother Nature's Son

INT. NIGHT. NAG'S HEAD PUB.

*This, as we shall soon discover, is a dream
sequence, although the audience should not
be aware of this.*
*The greatest party in the world is taking place
in the Nag's Head pub (could even be a
christmas party – christmas tree, cards,
decorations, etc). Everyone is there. 'Merry
Christmas' by Slade is playing loudly.*
*There is so much food, so much booze, so
much fun, so much love that everyone in the
country should wish they were at this
wonderful party. Everyone is smiling, you can
hardly see what's happening for glinting
teeth.*
*Some people are behaving uncharacter-
istically. Boycie and Marlene are jiving,
Rodney and Cassandra are smooching and
kissing quite passionately.*
*At this point Raquel is holding the twenty-
two-month-old Damien who wears a T-shirt
with his name emblazoned across the front
and is holding a helium inflated balloon.*
*With hand-held camera we mingle through
the happy crowd.*
*A happy Raquel hands the baby to Del whilst
she refills her glass with champagne.*
*Del dances with Damien for a while until,
surprisingly, Rodney opens his arms wishing
to take Damien. Del hands Damien to Rodney
and Rodney continues the dance. Rodney
behaves in a very affectionate uncle way to
Damien, tickling the child and making him
laugh as he dances round the room.*
*Now Rodney comes to the mirror on wall, he
looks in mirror and is mystified.*
*We now see from Rodney's POV that Damien
is missing from the reflection – it is simply
Rodney, with his arm in the pose of holding
the child, and a disembodied balloon floating
in the air.*
*Away from mirror, Rodney double checks and
we see he is still holding Damien. He looks
back at mirror and again Damien is missing.
Rodney is totally horrified, and opens his
mouth to let out a cry.*

**INT. NIGHT. RODNEY AND CASSANDRA'S
BEDROOM.**

*Rodney and Cassandra are in bed. Cassandra
is fast asleep.*
*From the dream/nightmare Rodney lets out a
cry of alarm, there are beads of sweat on his
brow. He wakes from the nightmare and
sucks in air in rapid breaths. He checks
radio/alarm clock. it stands at 6.59am*

Rodney *(Deeply depressed)* Oh, God! not
another day!
*Rodney lays for awhile, calms himself and
regains some of his lost composure.*
*The radio/alarm clock now switches to
7.00am and 'Merry Christmas' by Slade
begins playing from radio-alarm.*
Rodney switches it off quickly.

Cassandra *(Without opening her eyes)*
(mumbles) What's the time?

Rodney It's time for us to emigrate or at least
discuss the advantages of a suicide pact.

Cassandra And how are we feeling this
morning?

Rodney *Great!* How else could I feel? I'm thirty
one years of age and I work for Trotter's
Independent Traders.

Cassandra There are lots of people who'd give
their right arm to be in your position.

Rodney I know, but they're all tucked up safe
and sound in their padded-cells.

Cassandra Well, at least you seem a bit more
cheerful than yesterday.

Rodney You should come round to Trotter
Towers with me one morning, Cass. It would
give Terry Waite the shakes. You can't move for
teething rings and Farley rusks and funny smells.
It's like nightmare on Sesame Street. Raquel's
got post-natal depression, Albert's got post-naval
depression and Damien keeps chucking toys at
my head.

Cassandra Oh you big baby, they're only fluffy
dolls.

Rodney I know, but Del's bought him a Tonka
toy for Christmas.

Cassandra How is Del now?

Rodney Still putting on a brave face. Laughing
and joking his way all the time. He's worrying
the life out of me. We haven't bought or sold a
thing in months and there he is running round
like Ken Dodd on ecstasy. And there's something
else bothering him. I've see it in his eyes before.
It's either when he's bottling up some terrible
secret or he's had a really iffy pork pie … oh,

maybe it's just the recession. We're broke and he won't admit it.

Cassandra There are a lot of people in the same boat.

Rodney You're doing alright.

Cassandra And what does that mean?

Rodney Well, you've just been promoted at the bank. Don't get me wrong, you worked hard for it and I'm proud of you. What I mean is, you've succeeded, you've made it to the top.

Cassandra I'm in charge of small business investment at our Peckham branch, it's hardly the House of Elliot, is it?

Rodney At least you've done *something*. I'm just me.

Cassandra *(Kisses him on cheek)* You'll do for me, big boy.

Rodney *(Seems concerned at this potential sexual advance)* I'd better make the coffee.

Cassandra No, stay here awhile. You know what I'd like to do?

Rodney *(Worried)* No.

Cassandra I'd like us to go away for a weekend. Just you and me, somewhere really nice. I know we can't afford it at the moment, but I get a bonus at the end of the year, so maybe then, eh?

Rodney *(A tiny glimmer of hope)* Yeah?
She kisses him.

Rodney I'm sorry, Cass. I've been feeling down – a bit pressurised. That's why I've been, you know ... a bit lacking in certain areas recently.

Cassandra *(Massages his neck)* I understand. That's why I want us to go away, so you can relax. Is that nice?

Rodney *(Enjoying the massage)* Yeah, that's really good.
The bedside phone rings loudly.

Rodney *(Panicked)* Don't answer it!

Cassandra Why not?

Rodney It'll be Del!

Cassandra How d'you know?

Rodney It's his ring.

Cassandra It's seven in the morning!

Rodney That doesn't bother him. Sleep is for wimps, remember?

Cassandra It might be mummy! For all we know she could be ill!

Rodney Still don't answer it!

Cassandra Don't be ridiculous! *(Answers phone)* Hello? Morning, Del.

Rodney *(Whispers)* I left five minutes ago.

Cassandra *(On phone)* No, he left about five minutes ago ... mmh ... yeah ... I know he's your brother ... well, I know that Rodney's

worried about you as well ... *(Now angrily)* Look, it happens to a lot of men when they're under stress!

Rodney *(Under his embarrassed breath)* Jeez! I don't believe him!

Cassandra *(On phone)* ... Well aren't you the lucky one!... *(Shocked)* That's private and personal! ... Have I got a what? No I haven't and I wouldn't know where to get one!

Rodney *(Shouts)* Tell him to mind his own bloody business! *(Reacts as he realises he's been heard)*

Cassandra *(On phone)* Oh, Roddy's just popped back!

Rodney *(Quietly)* No I haven't!

Cassandra *(On phone)* Oh, he's left again! Yeah, thanks a lot, Del. Bonj ... *(Corrects herself)* Bye. *(Replaces receiver)*
Rodney and Cassandra look at each other.

Rodney Toast and marmalade?

INT. DAY. TROTTERS' LOUNGE.

It is 7.00 in the morning. The dirty breakfast crockery, etc, is still on the dining table. Next to table, seated in his high chair and still wearing his jim-jams, is Damien, eating toast and jam. His high-chair tray is littered with soft vinyl toys which he often hurls to the ground or at Rodney or Albert's head. As the scene progresses, due to Damien's uncanny accuracy, Rodney and Albert get whacked on the head by one or two of Damien's toys but they are so accustomed to this they never react. Rodney is seated at table reading one of Damien's Mr Men books. Albert is having a snooze in the armchair. We cut away to Rodney whereupon a green vinyl toy elephant hits him squarely on the back of the head. Rodney takes absolutely no notice – it's as if it hasn't happened. Raquel enters from bedrooms area carrying a basket of washing. Rodney hides the Mr Man book and starts reading the Independent.

Raquel Any tea in the pot, Rodney?

Rodney *(Feels tea pot but more interested in newspaper article)* Yeah, plenty.
Rodney makes no effort to pour her a cup.

Raquel Oh good
Raquel awaits – or hopes – for an offer. It is not forthcoming.

Raquel *(Sarcastically)* Would you like me to pour you a cup, Rodney?

Rodney *(Considers offer)* Erm ... na, I had breakfast earlier. Anyway, don't you worry about

Mother Nature's Son

me, Raquel, you've got enough on your hands.

Raquel Thank you. *(She picks up the green elephant and places it back on Damien's tray)* There you are, darling.

Raquel exits to kitchen.

Slight pause.

The green elephant whacks Rodney on the head again. Rodney continues reading newspaper without a blink of an eye. We see the morning mail (one single brown envelope) drop through the letter box.

Rodney collects the mail and then places green elephant back on Damien's tray.

He now switches radio on which is playing 'Crocodile Rock' by Elton John.

The radio wakes Albert.

Albert Is that the radio?

Rodney No, Elton John popped in, he's rehearsing in the kitchen. It's eight bells in the morning, Albert – what are you doing asleep?

Albert *(Referring to Damien)* That little sod had me awake half the night.

Raquel has entered at this point to clear some stuff from the table.

Raquel He's teething, Albert. Can't you remember when you had teeth?

Rodney He can't remember when he had gums!

Raquel exits to kitchen.

Albert Any tea in the pot, Rodney?

Rodney No, it's empty.

Albert Call that music? it's a bloody racket. That's all you youngsters are interested in, noise, noise, noise!

Rodney Didn't your generation ever enjoy itself, Albert?

Albert When I was your age I was fighting a war!

Rodney Well, you must have made more bloody noise than me, then, mustn't you?

With a sneer Albert picks up the Daily Mirror and starts reading. A pink, vinyl toy pig hits Albert firmly in the back of the head. He takes absolutely no notice. Del enters from bedroom, all fresh and wearing his Gordon Gekko gear. He switches radio off and then ruffles Damien's hair.

Del Wotchyer, soldier. You're a cracker. Can't imagine what this flat would be like without Damien, can you Rodders?

Rodney No … little devil.

Del You alright, Rodney?

Rodney Yeah, t'riffic.

Del No, I mean, are you *alright*, Rodney? *(Nods head in that 'you know what I mean' manner)*

Rodney *(Quietly seething)* Yes! everything's alright!

Raquel has entered with the baby's breakfast (a bowl of mushy Weetabix).

Raquel Why, what's wrong then?

Del Nothing, sweetheart! Everything's cushty between Rodney and Cassandra, ain't it, Rodders? Just a bit of stress, that's all. Can happen to any man, I've just been lucky. Do us a bit of breakfast, sweetheart.

Raquel Do you a …! don't you think I've got enough to do? I've got the baby to feed and clean, I've got the old man of the sea there moaning 'cos his egg was runny, I've got washing and ironing to do, beds to make and hoovering to do. And I finish all that just in time to cook dinner! Do it yourself, Trotter! Albert, you can feed the baby. *(Hands Albert the bowl and spoon)*

Raquel exits to bedrooms area.

Del I don't know what's wrong with her. I keep asking but she won't tell me.

Del exits to kitchen followed by Rodney.

INT. DAY. TROTTERS' KITCHEN/LOUNGE.

Del and Rodney enter. During speech Del takes bacon from fridge, etc.

Del What more does she want? I mean, she's got a nice home, a lovely little baby, and she couldn't ask for a better bloke than me, could she?

Rodney No.

Del But is she happy? No she is not. I mean, I'm down that casino nearly every night till the early hours of the morning tryin' to win us a few bob. She should see how much I owe 'em then she might realise how hard I've been trying. But she don't seem to appreciate a thing these days.

Rodney Del, maybe it is 'these days' that's getting her down. None of us have got any money, there's nothing for her to look forward to. Just a daily round of washing and ironing and toil and boredom.

Del Well, we've all gotta take the rough with the smooth, ain't we? And I tell you one thing, bruv, it's gonna get a lot rougher before the year's out.

Rodney Righto, Derek, let's have it out in the open. I want the truth this time. Something's happening and I've got a right to know.

Del No, everything's alright, Rodders, I mean, we got no money and no business and our future's about as bright as a Yugoslavian tour operator's, but other than that everything's cushty.

Rodney No, there's something else, Del. I noticed a little while ago, you've lost that kind of – zip. The old Derek Trotter could smell a fiver in a force nine gale. They used to say if Del Boy fell into a viper's pit he'd come out wearing snakeskin shoes. But you seem to have lost something. It's like you're carrying some burden. Maybe that's affecting Raquel, it's certainly affecting me.

Del *(Indicates Rodney's groin)* Oi, I ain't taking the blame for that thing!

Rodney Shuddup! Now if you don't tell me what it is I'll … well, I don't know what I'll do. I just think it's fair I should know.

Del Yeah, you're right, Rodders. I could never hide anything from you could I? D'you remember a couple of years ago I applied to the council to buy this flat? Then they ummmed and aahed about it.

Rodney I thought they laughed.

Del That was the first time. I applied again after that. What with the local elections and strike, everything got held up. Well, I sort of forgot about it. A couple of days ago, right out the blue, the papers finally come through. I own this flat.

Rodney Bloody 'ell!

Del I've worked it out – the mortgage repayments are two and a half times the rent – and I can't afford that!

Rodney And that's what's upset Raquel?

Del No, I ain't told her about it yet. Guess what else comes with the flat? D'you remember Grandad's old allotment?

Rodney Not that?

Del Yeah? No-one's been even near it for yonks. In the last thirty years more people have walked on the moon than that allotment. What the hell do I want with an allotment? it's just my luck, innit. I feel like a mosquito who's caught malaria.

Albert now enters, holding bowl and spoon. His beard is covered with the mushy Weetabix.

Albert Little sod threw his breakfast all over me!

Del *(Revolted)* Oh my God. Giss the spoon, I'll feed him.

Albert Raquel's taken him to have a nap.

Del It puts you right off.

Rodney There's nothing worse than Weetabix in a beard, is there?

Del and Rodney exit to lounge. Del re-enters kitchen with sauce bottle. Albert is eating the sandwich.

Del *(To Albert)* Sauce?

Del goes into lounge.

Del It's all going down the tube, Rodney. I've gotta get some money from somewhere, bruv. It's getting on top of me. I can feel myself cracking.

Rodney Listen to me. There was this guy I used to know a few years back at my evening school. He reminded me of you in many ways. He was a really bright, dynamic, go ahead sort of guy – but like I say, in other ways he reminded me of you. He was the kind who'd take a gamble, wasn't frightened of living on the edge. Well, a couple of years back he found the thing you've always been looking for – a gap in the market.

Del A gap in a warehouse door'd suit me at the moment.

Rodney Myles was a bit of a friend of the earth.

Del Myles?

Rodney He liked all that natural food, even grew his own vegetables.

Del Well, he certainly *sounds* the dynamic type.

Rodney Don't put it down, it's a massive market, Del, more and more people are turning to health foods for, well, for their health. Anyway, what Myles noticed was; if he wanted to buy a bag of natural fertiliser he had to go to a specialist garden centre or smallholding. Then, if he wanted some organic vegetables he had to go to a health food shop. So he came up with the idea of combining the two entities. *One* centre where you can buy all your organic fertilizers and your health foods. He now owns four of these places and he's opening a new one next month in Maidenhead. In two and a half years he's become a millionaire!

Del A millionaire?

Rodney At least.

Del is now waiting for the sting. What's in for us Trotters?

Del *(Optimism and greed)* And?

Rodney And what?

Del Where do we come into it?

Rodney Oh. Well, me and Cassy shop there sometimes, she likes all that organic food.

Del Yes, I know that! What I'm saying is, what's in it for us?

Rodney Well … nothing.

Del Nothing?

Rodney No.

Del So what d'you tell me for?

Rodney I was trying to point out that even in these dark days of recession some people are doing well.

Del Oh I see! It was just a nice little story? The

Mother Nature's Son

parable of the lucky git! Yes, well, that has cheered me right up. Oh, I've gotta tell Raquel.

Del moves to door to bedrooms area.

Del *(Calls from door)* Raquel, you've gotta come and hear Rodney's story about some mush who's doing *really* well. made a couple of million apparently. It's warmed the cockles of my heart, it really has. Anyway, I'm just gonna punch Rodney on the nose then I'm off out.

Rodney I wish I'd kept my mouth shut now!

Raquel enters from bedrooms area. She is now smiling, it's a menacing friendliness.

Raquel Where you going today – darling?

Del *(Fazed by her attitude)* Em … I'm not sure at the moment. I'll mooch about, see if I can make us a bit of poppy.

Raquel I've got a much better idea. Why don't you go down and clear up your allotment?

Del Allotment?

Raquel Mmmh. *(Produces the brown envelope and takes paper from inside)* This arrived this morning from the council. It's a summons.

Del Yeah?

Raquel Mmmh. Apparently people have been dumping rubbish on *your* allotment! It's now considered to be an environmental health hazard. They're giving you two weeks to clear it up or you've got to appear in court! They even mention the possibility of a custodial sentence.

Del Well. There's a thing, ain't it?

Raquel Are you gonna tell me what the hell's happening or have I got to starve it out of you?

Del Tch, this has spoiled the moment, sweetheart. I was gonna tell you all about it tonight.

Raquel Tell me what?

Del It'll be much better tonight.

Raquel *Now*!

Del Well … this flat.

Raquel What about this flat?

Del I've bought it! – it's *ours*!

Raquel moves across to Rodney. Rodney nods.

Raquel Oh, good!

Del I'll get a couple of bottles of champagne, shall I?

Raquel Not for me, Derek, I feel light-headed already.

Del We own our own home now. This is all ours! We can do what we want with it.

Raquel Like what? Add a conservatory or a nice patio?

Del At least we got a roof over our heads.

Raquel And fourteen other families! I'm gonna change the baby's nappy. *(Exits to bedrooms area)*

Del *(To Rodney)* I think she's excited really – you know, inside.

Rodney Yeah, you could tell.

Del I think she was a bit choked.

Rodney Well, who wouldn't be?

Del I'll go and calm her down.

Del exits to bedrooms area.

INT. DAY. TROTTERS' FLAT. HALLWAY/ BEDROOMS AREA.

Raquel is taking a fresh nappy from a cupboard or somewhere. Del enters from lounge.

Del Look, sweetheart, I don't blame you for having the rats. The way things are it's enough to give Harry Seacombe the 'ump. But you know me, I'll bounce back, we'll soon have some cash on the hip again.

Raquel Is that what you think this is all about, Del? Money?

Del Well, what then?

Raquel God! haven't you noticed, Derek that I haven't been out of this flat for months?

Del You go shopping three times a week

Raquel I'm not talking about shopping! I mean going *out*! There's another thing, Del. *(Indicates Damien's room)* Last year I decorated our baby's room.

Del I know, and you made a blinding job of it.

Raquel Thank you. You went out and got a piece of carpet. It didn't fit, but … *(A 'who cares' shrug)*.

Del I'm still on the look-out.

Raquel And our baby had his own little room. Warm, cosy, safe. Then three months ago you evicted Damien, moved him in with us and filled his lovely little room up with all your old junk!

Del Old junk! That's not old junk. That's my stock.

Raquel Your stock, old junk, same thing!

Del Raquel, you seem to be forgetting what happened to the rest of my stock. Someone broke into the garage and nicked it. I had to bring the rest of it up here to protect it.

Raquel Oh, Del, hasn't it dawned on you yet? All you have in that room is what the thieves left behind! How the hell do you hope to *sell* it when the burglars wouldn't take it for free?

Raquel exits to Damien's room leaving Del pondering her words.

INT. DAY. DAMIEN'S BEDROOM.

The walls are covered in baby wallpaper but that is about the only sign that this was ever a baby's room. It is now a store room and full

*of cardboard boxes of various sizes and other
bits of junk that Del has been unable to sell.
One of the larger boxes has the words:
'Crowning Glory'. This contains the remainder
of the wigs that Del bought in the final
episode of series 7 ('Three Men, A Woman
and A Baby').
Five or six other large boxes contain the
remainder of the 'Romanian Rheisling' which
Del sold to the church in 'Miami Twice'
A few of the smaller boxes have printed
across them: 'Video Classics'
Hanging from the picture rail on one wall is a
deep-sea divers suit complete with weighted
boots and brass helmet.
Del enters.
From one box Raquel produces a Bros LP.*

Raquel A hundred and fifty Bros LPs!

Del Fashions change so fast in the pop world, I
was caught unawares. They could be back in
fashion next month.

*From another box Raquel produces a 'Free
Nelson Mandela' T-shirt.*

Raquel Two hundred and seventy five 'Free
Nelson Mandela' T-shirts.

Del I bought 'em on a Thursday evening and
Saturday morning he was out on parole. I mean,
how was I supposed to know?

*Raquel has opened another box and
produced a few Charles and Di
commemorative wedding plates and cups.*

Raquel Charles and Di wedding plates.

Del Nothing that a good sorting out couldn't
cure.

*She opens a small jewellery box which
contains a man's chunky gold identity
bracelet.*

Raquel A nine carat identity bracelet inscribed
with name 'Gary'. We've got a boxful of men's
wigs you bought before Damien was born! Fifty
pirated versions of The Poseidon Adventure – all
on Betamax! 200 litres of Romanian Rheisling.

*Raquel now gestures to the diver's suit but
can find no words to say about it.*

Raquel Clear it out, Del. Dump it with the rest
of the rubbish on your allotment! Just clear the
room out and give it back to our baby.

Del And what's to say tomorrow I won't find a
buyer for all of this stuff?

Raquel What are the chances of you bumping
into a bald-headed, anti-apartheid, deep-sea
diving Bros fan who has a betamax video
recorder, likes Romanian Rheisling and whose
name's Gary?

Del Alright, I'll get shot of it all.

Raquel That will cheer me up, Del. Really. I'll be
a happy woman again. Promise.

She exits.

Del *(To himself)* Wait 'til you see our mortgage!

*Del looks around sadly at his only stock in the
world.*

Del *(A quiet prayer)* Dear lord, *please* let me
prove to you that wealth won't spoil me.

Rodney and Albert enter.

Rodney Raquel said we had to help you clear
this room out.

Del Yeah, I've decided to get rid of it, have a
clean start.

Rodney You're not dumping the wine, are you?
Couldn't you sell it to Mike at the Nag's Head?

Del No I couldn't, Rodney! He's a very good
friend.

Albert And he's tasted it. *(Referring to diver's
suit)* What d'you buy that thing for?

Del It was supposed to be a surprise present for
you, so that you could go and have a look at all
the ships you sailed on. ... No, I read in one of
the colour supplements that diving was all the go
with the yuppies.

Rodney reacts.

Rodney But they meant scub ...

Del Eh?

Rodney Don't matter.

Albert Seems a shame to throw it all away.

Del I've got nowhere else to store it. I mean, the
garage ain't safe anymore.

Rodney What about Grandad's shed?

Del What shed?

Rodney The one on his allotment. Well, your
allotment now.

Del Yeah. I forgot he had a shed! We'll pug it
away in there. Good thinking, Rodney. Come on
then. You two bring all this stuff down and I'll
go open the van door.

Del exits.

Rodney and Albert look at each other.

EXT. DAY. THE ALLOTMENT.

*We see a large expanse of average to shabby
council-run allotments. The three-wheeled
van and the green Capri are parked close-by,
both packed with boxes, etc, from Damien's
room.*

*We now zoom in to the allotments and find
Del, standing in the furthest, most overgrown
allotment of them all.*

*At the back of the allotment we see a
dilapidated old shed. Dumped in amongst the
grass and weeds are parts of a car's engine,
the rusted front wing of a car, a few old*

Mother Nature's Son

wooden crates, piles of rocks and masonry and four large aging and rusting industrial drums (the sort of thing that could contain chemicals.)

We find Del and Rodney standing in grass and weeds which reach almost up to their chins. Del appears stunned.

Rodney Well, what d'you reckon then?

Del What do I reckon? the last time I saw anything like this was in that film *Gorillas in the mist*. It's a jungle! God knows what lives in here.

Albert suddenly appears from out of nowhere.

Albert Del!

Del *(Jumps with fear)* Gordon Bennett! Don't *do* that, Albert! You nearly gave me a connery then! *(To Rodney)* I could have sworn I saw the blowpipe and poison dart.

Albert You seen all that rubbish that's been dumped over here?

They move off.

Del Dear oh dear. This is ruining my shoes, you know. *(Referring to the drums)* Look at all this stuff. What're those drums doing here?

Rodney Dunno, but they're full. I wonder what's in 'em?

One of the drums is lying on its side and some of the liquid has leaked out. It is a bright yellow liquid.

Albert There's one open here. Some sort of yellow stuff.

Rodney *(Peers in and then reels away from the acrid odour)* Blimey! Smell that!

Del *(Sniffs)* What is that?

Rodney I don't know, but it could be toxic.

Del It could be bloody poisonous an' all!

Rodney Yeah.

Del wanders off towards the shed. He opens the shed door and surveys the inside. His eyes finally move to the shed floor. He sees something on the floor that revolts him.

Del Eeuurgh, the dirty, rotten filth … Rodney!

Del exits shed.

Del I tell you what we'll do. Me and Albert'll get the gear from the van, Rodney, you clear the shed out.

Rodney Righto.

At this point we see Trigger approaching with his dust cart and broom. He wears a 'Peckham cleansing department' donkey jacket.

Trigger Del boy, Dave.

Del Alright, Trig? Don't fancy sweeping all this stuff up for us, do you?

Trigger I'm not a road sweeper anymore.

Rodney No? What are you now, a piano tuner?

Trigger I'm an environmental hygienist.

Albert And what do they do when they're at home?

Trigger Well, sweep the roads. but the council have upgraded me.

Albert *(Referring to the spilt liquid)* Perhaps Trigger knows what this is. It's his game, ain't it?

Del Oh, Albert! Trigger can't find his way out of a telephone box.

Albert He may have come across it on his rounds. Have a look, Trig.

Trigger peers into one of the drums with the eye of an expert.

Trigger It's some sort of yellow stuff.

Del Bloody 'ell, you were right, Albert. He got it spot on.

Rodney No hesitation either, was there? You've gotta get rid of this stuff and fast. *This* is the environmental health hazard the council are talking about.

Del How d'you know? I mean look, there's a lot of old crap round here.

Albert They're just rocks and lumps of metal. you can cut your finger or scratch your knee, but this stuff – who knows what it is.

Del We'll pour it down the drain then.

Rodney You can't pour it into the public sewers, it could be volatile, you could end up with sh – we could create a disaster area. I tell you one thing, Del Boy, either these things go away or you do!

Del Where am I gonna get rid of them?

Trigger There's a 24 hour waste disposal depot down Stamford Road. Drop 'em off down there.

Del That's a good idea, Trig. We'll get these barrels in the back of the van, won't we, Rodney?

Rodney No.

Del Well how are we gonna get rid of them then?

We now hear the blast of a van's horn. We see Denzil momentarily in his 'Transworld Courier Service' transit. Cut to see Del's reaction. Cut to Denzil driving along in his van.

Denzil Oi! Del Boy!

Back to our group. See idea form in Del's brain.

Del/Albert/Rodney Denzil.

EXT. NIGHT. THE ALLOTMENTS.

Denzil's van is parked close by with the back doors open. Del, Trigger and Denzil, dressed in their everyday clothes, are studying the barrels.

Denzil appears very dubious.

Del *(Cheerfully)* Righto. Come on then, Denzil. Let's get these barrels on the back of your van, Denzil.

Trig immediately takes hold of barrel and prepares to lift.

Denzil Hey hang on, hang on. not so fast! What are these things?

Trigger They're barrels!

Denzil I can see they're barrels! I mean, what's in 'em?

Del Nothing to worry about, just some gunge.

Denzil Gunge? What sort of gunge?

Del What d'you mean, what sort of gunge? Gunge is gunge, innit?

Denzil No, it isn't! There's harmless gunge, the sort you can give kids for Christmas and they make models out of – and then there's killer gunge! One sniff and you're down the co-op collecting your divi's!

Del This is not killer gunge! What sort of bloke d'you think I am?

Denzil This could be anything, Trig! For all we know this could be ... Well, could be bloody Concorde fuel!

Del No, honest, it's not Concorde fuel, it's anti-freeze from the Starship Enterprise! Bloody Concorde fuel! *(Moving to shed)* It'll be battery acid for Thunderbird Three next! You wally! Look, d'you want the contract or not? I'm a busy man, I've got things to do.

Del enters the shed which is dimly lit by a small gas lamp.

Denzil How can you be certain this stuff isn't dangerous?

Del *(Emerges)* Because it's not – and that's the truth! *(Goes back inside shed)*

Trigger *(To Denzil)* There you are, you've heard it from the horse's mouth. Now, you get that end ...

Denzil *(Cuts in)* What d'you mean, I've heard it from the horse's mouth? That's Derek Trotter in there, not bloody Einstein!

Trigger Del knows what he's talking about! and I don't see what the Beatles manager's got to do with it anyway!

Denzil Look, Trig ... What?

Trigger When we was at school Del Boy was the best in our class at chemistry. He used to sell home-made fireworks. He even blew the science lab up once.

Denzil I remember, I was doing detention in there at the time!

Trigger And you say he don't know what he's talking about!

Del (OOV) Denzil, believe me it's harmless – and to prove it I'm gonna help you carry it. I can't say fairer than that, can I?

Denzil unscrews the lid of one barrel and smells contents.

Denzil *(Reacts to acidic smell)* Jeez! It doesn't smell harmless!

Del (OOV – shed) Nor does my Uncle Albert but he wouldn't hurt a fly. Look, trust me, will you? I am your friend! You know it makes sense.

Trigger They can't be dangerous, Denzil.

Denzil But how do you know?

Trigger Because Del has offered to help us carry 'em!

Denzil Yeah, but ... *(Finally concedes the point)* Yeah, okay, Trig, I suppose you've got a point. *(Calls to shed)* You gonna help us lift these barrels onto the van, then?

Del (OOV – shed) Just coming.

Del now exits from shed wearing the deep-sea diver's suit (complete with brass helmet) we had seen earlier hanging in the lock-up. Denzil reacts to the vision. After a cursory glance, Trigger doesn't appear that surprised. Denzil just stares at Del.

Del Come on, Denzil, we ain't got all night!

They just stare at him.

Del That's the way. Lovely jubbly.

EXT. NIGHT. COUNCIL TIP.

The tip is protected by a chain-link fence and gates. A sign is revealed in the headlights of Denzil's van. Sign reads: 'Peckham Borough Council Environmental Waste Processing Plant.'

The van – with Denzil driving, Trigger seated next to passenger door and Del (still wearing the full diver's suit) seated in between them – pulls to a halt. We see that the gates are locked and the plant is closed and in complete darkness.

Denzil It's closed!

Trigger *(Checks watch)* Well, it's a bit late, innit?

Del What d'you mean 'a bit late?' You said it was open twenty four hours a day!

Trigger Yeah, but not at night!

Denzil and Del look at each other.

A man, out walking his dog, passes by in front of the van. We see his reaction as he spots a man in diver's suit sitting in the front of a transit van.

Denzil So what do we do now? We've got six thousand gallons of – something in the back of my van!

Mother Nature's Son

Trigger We could take it to the other council place I used to work at!

Del Is it open?
Trigger No.
Denzil *(Screaming in frustration)* Well, what's the point in taking it to your depot if that's not open either?
Trigger It soon will be open – I've got a spare set of keys. *(Produces bunch of keys)*
Denzil You sure it'll be alright?
Del Who cares?
Trigger Yeah, no problems. Back up, you're alright behind, Denzil.
Denzil I mean, is it legal?
Del *Yes!* Now back up, Denzil! I'm getting bloody hot in here. I don't see what the fascination is in this diving lark.

EXT. NIGHT. NAG'S HEAD CAR PARK.

We see the diver's suit laying on the passenger seat of Del's Capri. Del, Trigger and Denzil exit from pub.

Del *(To Denzil)* Here you are then. Now ain't you glad you listened to me? These are austere times, Denzil, and if it hadn't been for my persuasion you'd have turned a contract down tonight.
Denzil Yeah, I suppose you're right.
Del No suppose about it. Right, that's fifty quid I owe you.
Denzil You *owe* me?
Del *Yes!* I'm not having you do this for me as a favour, no matter how much you'd like to.
Denzil Yeah, but I thought …
Del You can't persuade me, Denzil, so don't waste your breath. I'll see you for the money – and no argument! *(To Trig, referring to Denzil)* He'd do anything for anyone wouldn't he?
Trigger That's what mates are all about, innit.
Del Course it is. Gets you right there sometimes. Your name's in me book, Denzil, I won't forget tonight.
Denzil Same here!

Denzil and Trigger move towards Denzil's van.

Del Thanks for everything, lads. See you Denzil.

Denzil turns and raises his hand, the palm of which glows an eerie radio-active yellow.

Denzil See you, Del.
Del *(Notices the glow. Calls to Trigger)* See you, Trig.

Trigger turns and raises his hand, the palm of which glows an eerie radioactive yellow.

Trigger See you.

Del is the only one to notice this. He is slightly bemused by the strange sight but just shrugs it off as an optical illusion. He climbs into Capri.

EXT. DAY. THE GARDEN AND ORGANIC FOOD CENTRE.

The sign above the centre's main doors reads: 'Nature's Way'
We see the van pull into the parking area.
Rodney is driving, Del is reading the Financial Times and so doesn't realise where they are.

Del What's this?

Rodney Oh, d'you remember that bloke I told you about? Myles.

Del *(Jealousy showing)* What, the one who's done *really* well, a millionaire in two and a half poxy years?

Rodney Yeah. Well, this is one of his places.

Del So what we doing here?

Rodney *(Has produced a small slip of paper)* Well, Cassy asked me to pop in there and get a bit of shopping.

Del Shopping?

Rodney For dinner tonight.

Del Oi! what's the point in getting married and then doing the bloody shopping yourself? No wonder you've got … problems.

Rodney Oi! you just keep your nose out of my business! Alright?

Del I tell you something. I bet I know what Cassandra's thinking when you're laying under the duvet at night

Rodney Yeah?

Del I bet she's thinking, 'I wonder how many tangerines Rodney could get for a pound.'

Rodney You keep on like that, Derek, and you'll be sorry!

INT. DAY. NATURE'S WAY.

To one side we see bags of natural fertilizers, peat and mulch, etc, plus gardening tools and equipment.
To the other side lies the organic foods centre which is like a small self-service mart. The shelves are filled with pre-weighed and packed vegetables and fruit, etc. There is also a vast range of natural fruit and health drinks plus a massive display of mineral waters from Britain and the continent. Signs everywhere tell of the fresh, organic and natural emphasis of the establishment.
Del and Rodney enter the food department with Rodney checking his shopping list.

Del *(Too loud for Rodney's liking)* Cor, don't half pen and ink in here, dunnit?

Rodney Ssshh! it's all the fertilizers and manu and other things. every single item in here has been grown the way nature intended.

Del Oh yeah? it must be nice for you and Cassandra to sit down to dinner knowing that everything on your plate was once under a pile of horseshit.

Rodney I'll get my shopping then we'll be off.

Del Oh good.

Del follows Rodney around the store. Rodney places a bag of potatoes in his trolley.

Del Look at the price of these spuds!

Rodney You pay extra because they're organic. I tell you, there are no E120 additives in these foods.

Del No E120s? Before you met Cassandra you thought an E120 was a bus. What's this, sprout tops? Twenty-eight pence a pound? Look at these carrots. I mean, it's …

Rodney places two litres of mineral water in trolley.

Del *Sixty five pence* for a bottle of water?

Rodney Will you mind your own business! Cassandra and I happen to like this water!

Del studies all the other brands of mineral water. Not being a regular shopper, he is astounded at the price labels.

Del *(Another bottle)* Why don't you have this one then, it's only seventy-two pence a bottle … blimey! And this is what people are spending their money on nowadays?

Rodney Yes, it's one of the few remaining growth industries.

Del *(A plan is obviously brewing)* Is it really?

Rodney's attention is drawn by the sound of Myles's voice.

Myles Rodney!

Rodney Myles!

Del *(To another customer)* Black eye beans?

We cut away to find Myles.
Myles is 31 and an earnest person in a corduroy kind of way. He is a friend of the earth and a successful businessman – a cross between Richard Branson and David Bellamy. He wears a sports coat with leather elbow patches and sports a 'save the whales' badge. Myles can adopt a superior attitude with those he considers to be his inferiors.

Rodney Hey, Myles, how you doing?

Myles Pretty good. yourself?

Rodney Fine. Oh, by the way – Myles, this is my brother, Derek – Del, this is Myles.

Del Nice to meet you, son

Myles *(Barely looking at Del)* You too.
(Referring to his shop) So, what d'you think?

Rodney In one word 'impressed'.

Del In one word 'bloody expensive'.

Myles Expensive?

Del Look at the price of the spuds and carrots

Mother Nature's Son

and your brussel sprout tops, twenty-eight pence a pound! Water, seventy-two pence a bottle.

Myles That water happens to come from the most natural sources in Britain – and France and Switzerland and Italy, I might add. I'm a founder member of the SWANS committee.

Del *(Genuinely confused)* SWANS? What, you mean the big white duck things?

Myles looks to Rodney.

Rodney No, Del. It's an acronym.

Del Oh well, that's what I thought. I was just about to say that's an anacronym. You can bet your life. I'd have put money on it.

Myles And you'd have been right.

Del What d'you feed 'em on?

Myles What do I feed what on?

Del Your acronyms.

Rodney No, no. It's not a duck or a goose or anything. An acronym is a word made up of the initials of another set of words.

Del Oh *that* sort of acronym?

Myles Gotta rush, Rodney. It's been, er … It's been real.

Myles exits.

Rodney Big bloody ducks!

Del You what?

Rodney SWANS are the initials of the Spa Water and Natural Springs committee and Myles is the vice-president … he's the one who hands out the certificates of purity. Without his signature none of these companies can sell their goods. I can't help but admire him. I tell you, that bloke is going places.

Del Yeah, well, with a name like Myles he's bound to.

Rodney *(Remembering)* Cabbage.

Rodney moves off to finish his shopping. Del stares back at the shelves of potatoes, water and carrots. We're not sure exactly which one has drawn his interest.

EXT. DAY. THE ALLOTMENT.

The part of the allotment we can actually see is now cleared of the rubbish that had been dumped there, including the rocks and rubble and, obviously, the drums of gunge. The long grass and weeds, except for a couple of thick bushes, have been cut down and part of the ground has been dug-over.
The green Capri is parked close by.
We see Del and Albert sitting in deck chairs close to the shed. They are both wearing wellies and gardening gear and look like a couple of extras from Emmerdale Farm. Del's Dan Archer image is ruined slightly by his

aluminium Arnie Becker briefcase.
Albert is cleaning out and sucking on his old pipe as if preparing it for filling. He keeps the pipe in evidence.

Albert It just shows you what a little bit of hard work can achieve.

Del Yep. Gives you a sort of warm feeling, don't it? I mean, what's a few aching muscles and blisters on the hands compared with this vision in front of us.

Albert I know what you mean, Del.

Del *(Looks at watch)* Oh, look at that. It's twelve o'clock. *(Calls off camera)* Oi, you two.

We see Trigger and Denzil. One of them is holding a garden fork, the other a shovel. They are both dirty and sweating.

Del You go an' get a bite to eat, you deserve it, you've worked hard.

Trigger and Denzil walk towards Del and Albert.

Trigger See you in an hour, Del Boy.

Del No hurry, Trig.

Denzil We're never gonna get this finished today, you know.

Del There's always tomorrow, Denzil, that's my motto. I'll see you in an hour.

Denzil and Trigger move off towards Denzil's van.
Now the three wheeled van screeches to a halt and an irate Rodney alights and approaches Del and Albert.

Trigger *(To Rodney)* Dave!

Rodney What's your bloody game, Del?

Del Something wrong, bruv?

Rodney Myles has just phoned the flat. He wanted to confirm his appointment with you.

Del Oh good, he's on his way then.

Rodney What are you playing at, Del?

Del After our visit to Myles' place last week something happened to me, Rodney. It was like a blinding flash of light – like St Paul on the road to Tabascus. I went green, Rodney. I realised that what I had here was not just an allotment – it was God's good earth in which I could grow vegetables and … things. These rough hands are gonna feed my woman and child. I'm a born-again gardener, Rodders.

Rodney But you've never done gardening in all your life.

Del Well, it's been a bit difficult, innit living on the twelfth floor of a tower block? But now I've got a chance.

Rodney But, Del, to you a King Edward is something you smoke. *(Referring to Albert)* And the only thing he's ever grown is a beard! You

don't know anything about gardening.

Del No, but I know a man who does. That's why I gave good old Myles a bell. He didn't seem to mind.

Rodney Well … no, I suppose not. I mean, it's in his interest, ain't it? He could sell you some of his fertilizer and what 'ave you.

Del Exactly. He helps me, I help him, 'conseil d'etat' as they say in Grenobles. Hold up, here he comes now.

> *We see Myles' car, a Citroën 2CV, approaching. Rodney moves away to greet Myles.*

Del Ship ahoy, Albert. Now you know what you've gotta do and say, don't you?

Albert Leave it to me, son.

Del Don't go overboard! Nice and easy, alright? Off you go then.

> *Myles alights from his car and studies the allotment with a somewhat confused expression.*

Del Myles, nice to see you again. Beautiful day for sowing a turnip, eh?

Myles *(Referring to the allotment)* Is this it?

Del Well … yes!

Myles You told me you had 'land!' You were even talking about leaving one area to lay fallow.

Rodney *(Embarrassed)* It's just an allotment.

Myles I know it's an allotment! I can see it's an allotment!

Del Well, I'm new to all this gardening malarky. I just thought that you, being a friend, would be willing to advise. And Rodney said that you are the kiddy when it comes to an organic swede.

> *Myles accepts the compliment with a modest smile.*

Del And of course, anything I need will be bought from your organic garden centre.

Myles *(A heavy, reluctant sigh)* Yes, okay, fine. Are you working with compost?

Del *(Indicating Albert walking behind him with a lit pipe)* No, it's most probably his pipe.

Myles I mean, do you have a compost heap?

Del No, but I'm keeping an eye out for one.

Myles First things first. We have to ascertain what kind of soil you have.

Del Well, it's this – earthy sort.

Rodney There are many varieties of soil. There's, er … well, there's all sorts, ain't there, Myles?

> *Myles picks up a small handful of soil and rubs in between his fingers. He considers the texture of soil whilst making those expert doctor type sounds; 'mmmh' … 'hmmm'*

Del *(To Rodney)* What's he doing?

Rodney *(Embarrassed by Del's naivete)* Tch! He's a gardener. He's … well, … what are you actually doing, Myles?

Myles I'm testing the soil for texture and structure. *(Still rubbing soil between fingers)*

Del *(To Myles)* I'd have a care, son, there's a lot of cats round here.

Rodney Just leave him alone, Del.

> *Myles, with bits of earth remaining on fingers from his texture testing, now wets his fingers with his lips.*

Del *(Horrified, thinks Myles is eating the soil)* What's the weirdo up to now?

Rodney He's testing the structure!

Del He'll be testing the hospital's stomach pump if he ain't careful!

Myles It's slightly alkaline.

> *Myles hands Del a few small crumbs of earth to test for himself.*

Del No thanks, son, I had a fry-up 'fore I come out.

> *Rodney turns away from Del and Myles in embarrassment. We hear Myles talking in background as we stay on Rodney.*

Myles You realise, Derek, this could take up to five years of drainage and care to achieve the best crops.

> *Rodney now does a double-take on something he has seen towards the back of allotment. He moves towards it. Whatever it is confuses and bemuses him. He is totally mystified by the vision.*

Del *(Optimistically)* Five years? I thought it'd take a long time.

> *We cut away to show for the first time 'the Peckham Spring' in all its glory.*
>
> *Many of the old rocks that had been dumped on the allotment are now piled in a circle with grass and plants growing between and around them to give the impression of age. Water bubbles out of a pool set within the rocks and runs away through a drain away.*

Rodney *(Incredulously to himself)* What the ..?

> *We see Albert digging in background. He sees Rodney's reaction to the 'spring'. Albert places his finger over his lips in a 'keep quiet' gesture to Rodney. A horrified Rodney now realises that this is what Del was up to. He moves closer to the spring. We see Del and Myles continuing in the background.*

Myles I think we'll try a cocktail of fishmeal and dry-blood, mushroom compost and horse and raw manure.

Del *(Rubbing hands together in delight)* Lovely jubbly!

Mother Nature's Son

We cut away to Rodney who is still studying the Peckham Spring. Now, with his suspicions on red alert, Rodney begins moving away from the spring and towards the longer grass that leads round the back of the allotments. He is obviously seeking the source of the spring.

Myles Blood, fish and bone, that's what we need here, Derek.

Del Just what the doctor ordered. *(Del is suddenly alarmed to see Rodney searching through the long grass).*

Myles If that doesn't work we'll try a touch of hoof and horn.

We cut back to Rodney and his search. He is Now some thirty yards or so away from the spring. now, partially, hidden in the grass, we see a hosepipe. Rodney follows the hosepipe to a communal water tap hidden behind some heavy bushes or some kind of structure. He turns and looks in Del's direction with a bemused, begging look in his eyes. Del returns a fierce warning look.

Myles is waffling on in background.

Myles We'll have to talk about crop-rotation, Derek. but the first thing is a good old-fashioned digging over. I'll get my soil-testing kit from the car.

As Myles turns he catches sight for the first time of the spring.

Del No, no, Albert'll run to the car for you, Myles.

Myles What's that?

Del What's what?

Myles That! the water.

Del Oh *that*? That's the old Peckham Spring. Rodney, go an' fetch Myles's soil-testing kit.

Rodney has joined them.

Myles No, no, wait a moment. The Peckham Spring? I never realised there was a spring in Peckham!

Del Oh yes. That's why it's called the Peckham Spring – it's in the doomsday book.

Del It's been there for well, centuries. We don't actually know where the spring comes from, do we, Rodney?

Rodney No, but it's certainly 'sprung' up from somewhere, innit, Del Boy?

Del Yeah. Our old Grandad tried to block it off but it kept bubbling up somewhere else, so in the end we just left it. Now, where'd you leave your kit, Myles?

Myles No, that can wait. This is fascinating. A natural urban spring! This is a real discovery! Is it pure?

Rodney *(Grabs the opportunity to kill the scam)* I wouldn't have thought so, Myles, not with this alkaline soil.

Albert Pure? I've been drinking that water since I was a little nipper and it never done me no harm.

Albert now digs, but with great energy and gusto.

Del *(To Myles)* Take no notice of him. He's 98, a bit ... you know ... *(Del taps temple to suggest senility)*

Myles He's 98?

Del Yeah. Ain't he, Rodney ... *bruv*?

Rodney *(Sheepishly)* ... Yeah!... but only recently.

Albert I've drunk from the finest wells and rivers on this planet and there is nothing to touch the Peckham Spring.

Myles Derek, I wonder if you'd mind me taking a sample of this water away for analysis?

Del What for?

Myles To test its purity.

Rodney It's not pure, Myles! Take my word for it, it's not pure!

Del Rodney's right, Myles, of course it ain't pure. It's coming up from the centre of the earth through all them 'orrible rocks and things.

Myles Yes! And it's those 'rocks and things' that filter the water of impurities and give it its life-preserving qualities. *Minerals*, Derek, minerals! You may remember I told you that I was the vice president of the SWANS? *(Now a friendly laugh at the memory)* And you thought I meant 'big white ducks'.

Del Oh yeah!

Del and Myles laugh at this.

Myles Well, what SWANS actually stands for is: the Spa Water and Natural Springs Committee. We test the waters of all the springs and spas in Britain and give certificates verifying the quality and contents.

Del Sorry, Myles, you've lost me.

Rodney I've got a feeling it won't take you long to catch up, Del.

Myles D'you remember last week when you and Rodney were at my garden centre? Did you notice all the various mineral waters I sell. Waters from all over Britain and indeed Europe.

Rodney You remember, Del, you checked the prices on about nine or ten of 'em.

Del Oh *them*?

Myles Yes, them! Now what I'm saying, Derek – may I call you, Del?

Del Oh mai oui, mon pleasure.

Myles *If*, and I do emphasise the word 'if' – if this water should pass our laboratory tests there is a strong possibility that we could actually bottle it.

Del What d'you mean 'bottle it'?

Rodney *(Becoming bored with Del's game)* He means put it in bottles, Del.

Myles I am a conservationist, a friend of the earth and *deeply* concerned with our planet's future. But I am also a businessman. Now I don't for one moment expect someone like you to see the potential of this water, so let me explain in simple terms. *You* have the source, ie, the Peckham Spring, I have the means of selling it through my natural food centres – and, if successful we could even expand to supermarkets and other outlets.

Del Wait a minute, wait a minute. Let me get this straight. Are you saying that we can *sell* this water?

Rodney By George I think he's got it!

Myles I'm saying there's a *possibility*. It all depends on the laboratory report. Now I need something to take a sample with.

Albert There's a bucket here.

Myles No, it must be a sterilised container. I'll just drive back to the centre. I'll only be a short while.

Del No need, Myles. I think I've got the very thing in my briefcase. Albert! Come here! *(Leads them over to shed to open his Arnie Becker briefcase)* I've been down Mothercare this morning, got my little boy a bottle. *(Produces film-wrapped baby-bottle)* A 'sterilised', bottle. Will that do?

Myles That's just the job. How old's the baby?

Rodney Nearly two.

Del Yeah! He's a bit slow going on to solids. Still, we're not worried, Rodney was on the breast till he was three and a half. Albert, go an' fill this up from the Peckham Spring. And don't get any dirt on that bottle.

Albert Leave it to me, son.

Myles *(Myles feels he should do this himself)* Well, I think maybe I should ...

Del *(Cuts his thought off)* Now, there's something I wanted to ask you Myles, when you talk about 'crop rotation' do you mean that every so often I've gotta dig the potatoes and sprouts up and turn 'em over?

Myles What? No, no. Let's say for instance one season you grow potatoes in this area of the allotment, well, next season you should grow some other root vegetable in that area.

Del Oh right. Like rotate it? Makes sense.

Rodney arrives at spring to join Albert.

Albert What d'you want, Rodney?

Rodney I've just gotta see how you get out of this one.

Mother Nature's Son

Albert bends down as if about to fill the baby-bottle from the spring. Now, from underneath his coat, he produces a canvas knapsack and opens it. Inside we see a half-empty bottle of Buxton or Malvern water (still) and an identical baby-bottle already filled with the mineral water. Albert removes the full baby-bottle and hides the empty baby-bottle in knapsack.

Rodney I just don't believe this. We'll all end up in nick!

Albert Not me, Rodney, I'm an old man.
Albert now approaches Del and Myles, shaking the baby-bottle as if shaking off water drops.

Del *(To Myles)* So we'd rotate them as well. Ah, here it is.

Albert *(to Myles)* Is that alright, son?

Myles That's wonderful, thank you so much. I'll get that off to the laboratory this afternoon. *(Places bottle in pocket)* Now – beans and carrots.

Del Eh?

Myles We were discussing the growing of beans and carrots.

Del Oh that? Na, don't worry about that. I've gone off the idea of growing vegetables now. Come on, let's go an' get a drink. Come on, Albert.
Del walks off towards the green Capri, his scam having worked and no longer having any interest whatsoever in the allotment. He leaves behind a slightly bewildered Myles and a deeply embarrassed Rodney.

INT. DAY. TROTTERS' LOUNGE/KITCHEN.
The lounge and kitchen have been transformed into a bottling plant. We see cardboard boxes bearing the name and logo of 'the Peckham Spring'. There are piles of sticky-back Peckham Spring labels. Del is in the kitchen filling bottles straight from the tap (with the aid of a funnel). He hands the bottles to Rodney who takes them to Raquel who puts the tops on them and Albert then puts them into boxes.

Rodney I think it's a miracle.

Del It's a miracle alright, Rodney. It's dear old mum smiling down on us and making sure her little boys don't starve.

Rodney No, I mean I think it's a miracle we've been doing this for three weeks now and we're not banged up in nick.

Del The reason we're not banged up is because we're not doing anything illegal.

Rodney Not doing anything ill ... we're selling public water to the public!

Del That's where you're wrong, Rodders. This stuff used to belong to the public but Maggie privatised it. It now belongs to a board of directors and a load of investors. They sell it to us, we sell it on. All we're doing is repackaging it. It's like Esso buys oil from Kuwait and repackages it as petrol. Is that illegal?

Rodney They could have us under the trade descriptions act. You call it Peckham Spring but it's not a spring.

Del Sainsburys sell french beans but do they come from France?

Rodney Alright, what about this claim on the label: 'From an ancient and natural source'?

Del Yeah, the Thames. You can't get more ancient and natural than that! We've got a certificate from the SWANS committee to prove that this is the finest water they've ever analysed.

Rodney Yes, because what they analysed wasn't this. It was Malvern or Buxton water.

Del Oh shuddup splitting hairs! Over the last fortnight Peckham Spring has becomes Myles' biggest seller. He's doubled his order twice now. Just go and see how Raquel's getting on!
Rodney carries a few bottles in for Raquel to pack.

Rodney *(To Raquel)* I'm surprised you'd be a party to all this.

Raquel I'm doing it purely for the man I love, Rodney. I'll claim a crime of passion – or insanity. Anyway, I haven't noticed you turning any of the money down, Rodney.

Rodney Raquel, I'm only tryin' to make it easier on Del when his case comes to court. The less Del makes out of this scam the lighter his sentence will be. To you it may look as if I'm sharing the profits, but in my heart I'm simply halving the guilt.

Raquel That is true brotherly love and courage, Rodney.

Albert If they didn't mean so much to me I'd give you one of my medals.
Del enters from kitchen.

Del I think we all deserve a little break.

Albert Yeah, this water's making my skin go funny.

Rodney That's saying something from an old sailor, innit?
The phone rings.

Del *(Answers)* Peckham Spring, PLC ... Myles, nice to hear from you, son ... mmmmh ... really ... no?

Rodney *(Assumes they've been caught)* Oh God!

Del *(On phone)* No, we can up production. We are in a go position, Myles, give us the word and we will not be found wanting ... bonjour for now. *(Switches phone off)* He's got meetings arranged for next week. Some supermarket conglomerates are showing an interest and a chain of hotels and restaurants are very keen.

Albert We'll have to take on extra staff.

Del We'll cross that bridge when we come to it, Unc. Right, back to work, the people of this wonderful country are thirsty – God, it makes me feel so proud! I wouldn't be surprised if the queen gave me an award for this.

Rodney About two and a half years, I reckon.

INT. NIGHT. RODNEY AND CASSANDRA'S BEDROOM.

Cassandra lays in bed reading a magazine.
Rodney enters and prepares to get undressed.

Cassandra I see Peckham Spring's really selling well.

Rodney *(Every mention of the word panics him)* What d'you mean?

Cassandra I had lunch at the local wine bar today and they're selling it. The waiter said it was their most popular brand. I must admit it has got a taste of its own.

Rodney *(Quietly)* It's called fluoride.

Cassandra Sorry?

Rodney I say it's gotta be tried.

Cassandra Oh yeah, everyone's buying it. It's on trial.

Rodney *(Panic)* Trial? What d'you mean trial? What trial?

Cassandra Myles was saying a major supermarket chain are giving it a two week trial.

Rodney Oh! Oh yeah, that's right.

Cassandra You okay?

Rodney Yeah, I'm fine.

Cassandra Look, if you're still worried about ... well, just remember what the doctor said, don't be uptight.

Rodney It's nothing to do with that ... Cass ... if I tell you a secret d'you promise not to tell a soul.

Cassandra *(Hoping for something juicy)* Cross my heart. Go on, what is it?

Rodney You know Peckham Spring?

Cassandra Mmmh, what about it?

Rodney It's ... it's tap water.

Cassandra Tap water?

Rodney Yeah ... it's tap water.

Cassandra What d'you mean, 'tap water'?

Rodney Well ... water from a tap.

Cassandra From a tap? What tap?

Rodney The one in Del's kitchen.

Cassandra You are kidding, aren't you? Tell me you're joking, Roddy.

Rodney No, really. He just puts a bottle under the tap, fills it up and sells it for 45 pence.

Cassandra Oh my God! Oh God help us!!

Rodney It's alright, calm down, it's nothing to do with you.

Cassandra Nothing to do with me? Where do you think he got the capital to buy all those bottle and boxes and equipment and the money to pay daddy for printing his labels?

Rodney Well, I never really gave it that much ... from you?

Cassandra Yes. He came to the bank and asked for a loan.

Rodney And you gave it to him?

Cassandra I'm in charge of small business investment and this seemed to be a small business investment with a future. I mean, someone had discovered a natural spring that had received a certificate of purity from Myles.

Rodney And you believed Del?

Cassandra No Roddy, I believed you!

Rodney Yeah, well, Del said I mustn't tell anyone. Why didn't you tell me you'd loaned him the money?

Cassandra Because that is confidential information between the bank and its client!

Rodney Well, now you know. What are you gonna do?

Cassandra I've got no choice, Roddy. I'm going to have to keep quiet about it.

Rodney Really?

Cassandra Well, I just crossed my heart and promised you I wouldn't tell a soul. And if I was to tell the bank I'd most probably lose my promotion – and I don't really fancy driving out to Wormwood Scrubs every Sunday to see my husband ... on the other hand is selling water illegal? I was charged 20 pence last week in a garage just to fill my radiator up ... Del's kept up all the repayments – and you're earning lots of money out of it.

Rodney I've never been so well off. But you see, Cass, there are geological aspects coming into play. We are taking thousands and thousands of gallons every week. The water board have got workmen on the estate, they think they've got a major underground leak! Here we are in the middle of winter and the local papers are issuing drought warnings. So people are going out and panic buying Peckham bloody spring! Which means we've got to take more water to stay up with the demand.

TITco Presents:

PECKHAM
SPRING WATER

So pure it's blasphemous

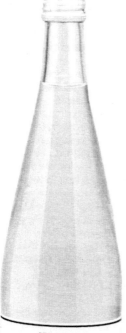

With the purest water, hand extracted from the crystal (palace) springs beneath South London's metropolis, we guarantee that with a daily dose of 150ml, you can:

-Reduce Gluttony!*
-Be More Attractive!*
-Lose Weight!*
-Replenish Hair Loss!*
-Increase Your IQ!*

"The purest water I have ever come across"
– Nikolas Vristozny of the Chenobyl Water Company

"It's better than oranges at half-time"
– Paul Slater Manager of Peckham United U13

*"Nicer than that French c**p"*
– Lord Harris Department of Foreign Affairs

"It's my favourite tipple, when at meetings with John Paul."
– Mother Theresa (Peckham Trinity Hall)

The perfect drink for today's stressed out yuppies.

* We at TITco do not accept responsibilty for weight gain, hair loss, retardation, plain old ugliness or any other symptoms of contaminated water.

Cassandra is now rubbing his neck to relax him.

Cassandra *(Whispering in his ear)* Ssshhhh.

Rodney And to top it all some prat's advised him to advertise on local radio.

Cassandra turns away sheepishly.

Rodney No. You? why?

Cassandra Del's my client, Roddy. It's my job to advise him.

Rodney But you're not dealing with a normal person. This is Derek Trotter! Don't you understand, he's sucking the land dry. I'm worried we're going to get a visit from Bob Geldof and Lenny Henry any minute!

INT. NIGHT. NAG'S HEAD PUB.

Raquel, Cassandra, Albert and Rodney are seated at table. Boycie and Marlene are also at the bar.

Boycie I've always believed in powdered rhino horn.

Marlene breaks away to speak to Raquel.

Marlene *(To Raquel)* I was ever so happy to hear your good news. It must be lovely to suddenly come into money after all these years.

Raquel Well, we're enjoying it.

Marlene I bet you are. You can come to my coffee mornings now.

Raquel Thanks.

Marlene I'll see you in a minute, I'm bursting. *(Exits frame)*

Raquel *(Seething)* You're not the only one.

Cassandra *(To Raquel)* It'll be a garden party next.

We cut to bar where Rodney is just about to take another round of drinks to the table.

Boycie I hear business is booming, Rodney.

Rodney Yeah, couldn't be better. The old Peckham Spring is selling hand over foot.

Boycie I just find it hard to believe that someone with Del Boy's attitude could suddenly become so professional in his business approach.

Rodney He's just never had the chance to prove it before, that's all. I mean, if he hadn't cleared that allotment up so well he'd have never discovered the spring in the first place.

Mike What made him clear it up? I mean, I've never seen Del as an Alan Titmarsh. A tit, maybe ...

Rodney During our lifetime, Mike, we all go through many changes. Del suddenly became very ecologically aware, aware of the damage we were doing to mother earth.

Mike Yeah, and I suppose that summons from the council made him even more ecologically

aware.

Rodney Erm, well, it might have helped. but at least he brought in a firm of experts to get rid of those drums of chemicals.

Boycie A team of experts? How long have Denzil and Trigger been experts??

Rodney *(This is news)* Denzil and Tri ... he told me he used specialists!

Boycie and Mike laugh.

Rodney *(Now on the defence)* On the other hand, Trigger *could* be considered to be a specialist.

Mike Trigger still ain't sure what end of the dart to throw!

Rodney I mean, he works for the council so he could dispose of them drums at the environmental waste unit.

Boycie According to Denzil they chucked 'em in a pond!

Rodney *(Horrified)* In a pond? They threw 'em in a pond? You wait till I see, Del!

Rodney moves to table.

Boycie What d'you reckon to all this Peckham Spring lark, Mike? Knowing Del I wouldn't be surprised if it ain't coming out of a tap.

Mike Don't be silly, Boyce. I've seen the certificate, signed, sealed, the works. I mean, look, I'm buying the stuff, d'you think I'm stupid?

Del appears at bar.

Del Michael, my usual, one for your good self and whatever Boycie's having.

Boycie Cheers, Del Boy. I've been hearing so much about your success. Couldn't have happened to a nicer fella.

Mike That's what I keep saying.

Del And me.

Boycie I hear expansion is on the cards?

Del You wouldn't believe, Boyce. Looks like we've gotta get a couple of extra delivery vans.

Boycie Cost money, Del.

Del I'll get a loan from Cassandra and the bank, won't I?

Mike Yeah, but you've gotta pay interest, ain't you?

Boycie And I've heard the interest rate's going up.

Mike So have I.

Boycie Plus, everything that goes through the bank is recorded on computers and may come to the attention of our hard working friends at customs and excise. What you need is a silent partner. Someone who's willing to put, say, five grand in for a small annual dividend – three percent at a guess. No questions asked.

Del What a good idea. Someone who'll put in

Mother Nature's Son

ten grand for a three percent dividend.

Boycie Ten gr ... alright, Del, I'll take a flyer on that one.

Del You're in, Boyce.

Mike Well, if the traps are open I'll take the five grandsworth.

Del One and a half percent annual?

Mike Do me.

Del Cushty! And, of course, silent partners keep their mouths shut, don't they?

They all spit on palms and smack hands to seal the arrangement.

Mike Tell you what, why don't we toast the deal with Peckham Spring?

Del Na, let's have something else.

We cut away to table.

Cassandra In a pond?

Rodney That's what Boycie said! You wait till he gets back to the table.

Cassandra No, Roddy, no arguments tonight, please ... I want this to be a nice celebration – it's the first time we've all been happy for ages.

Rodney Yeah, alright I'll have him tomorrow.

Del arrives back.

Del First thing in the morning, Rodders, we'll go down to the allotment and clear all the rubbish out of the shed. I mean, what do we need with Bros LPs and Rumanian Rheisling.

Raquel Or them wigs.

Del (Laughing) Those wigs! I don't know why I ever bought them.

Albert A wig saved my life once.

Del We'll take it out and dump it all somewhere.

Rodney Yeah, so long as it's not in a pond, eh, Del?

Del (Innocence) A pond? What's he on about?

Cassandra Don't know.

Marlene How could a wig save your life?

Boycie You've got a mouth and a half on you, Marlene!

Marlene Well, I'm interested.

Boycie It's bound to be something that happened 'during the war.'

Marlene It might not have happened during the war!

Albert During the war ... *(Del and Boycie move away)* ... during the war I was on a corvette out in the Pacific fighting the Japs. now, my old skipper, Captain Kenworthy, he used to wear a wig. You couldn't tell though – except in rough seas when it used to slide to one side. Anyway, one day we were attacked by a kamikaze pilot. He came zooming in towards us – I remember saying to the skipper, 'the way he's carrying on he'll kill himself'. Anyway, he's crashed right into

us. So there we were, nine of us and the skipper marooned at sea with our lifeboats smashed to pieces.

Mike Wait a minute, you're not tryin' to tell us that ten of you got on the captain's wig?

Albert Don't be facetious, Michael, I'm talking about heroes.

Mike Oops, sorry!

Albert Finally we got washed up on this island where the natives had never seen a white man before. They were waggling their spears and looking very angry. Then Captain Kenworthy said, leave this to me lads. He stepped forward, brave as a lion, and whipped his wig off. You should have seen their faces. See, the skipper knew they'd never seen a wig before.

Marlene So what did they do? Make him a God?

Albert No, they killed him. They wanted the wig, see, thought it had magic powers. So they all ran off to have a ceremony and we had it away on our toes. Got picked up by an Australian frigate.

Rodney Well, we're off home now.

General goodbyes. Rodney and Cassandra pause before leaving.

Cassandra Roddy. D'you remember we said that when we could afford it we'd have a weekend away somewhere?

Rodney Yeah.

Cassandra Well, we can afford it now, can't we? So why don't we go? Tomorrow night. Just us two.

Rodney All alone.

Cassandra You and me in a lovely hotel overlooking the sea.

Rodney With a king-size bed! You can do a lot of rolling round in a king-size bed.

Cassandra Hmmm!

Del/Boycie/Mike (Together) Oysters.

Rodney (Quietly) Del, I won't be in tomorrow.

Del Why?

Rodney Tomorrow night me and Cass are gonna go down to the seaside – just to be on our own for a while. You don't mind?

Del Course not, bruv. (What a wonderful idea) I tell you what. We'll come with you. Raquel, fancy a weekend by the sea?

Raquel Take me home, I'll pack the bags!

A look is shared between Rodney and Raquel. Rodney crosses to Cassandra.

Del (OOV) This calls for a celebration.

Boycie (OOV) Definitely.

Raquel (OOV) Not another celebration.

Mike (OOV) Why not? This is my living.

Rodney *(To Cassandra)* Guess what?
See Cassandra's reaction.

EXT. NIGHT. THE M23.

We see signpost to 'Brighton'
The green Capri passes with Del driving,
Rodney in front passenger seat, Raquel and
Cassandra in back seat with Damien between
them strapped in a baby chair. (Or it could be
funnier if Raquel was in passenger seat and
Rodney was scrunched up in back seat with
Cassandra and Damien who is eating a
wagon wheel.)
Music over:
The Beatles 'Money'

EXT. NIGHT. THE GRAND HOTEL, BRIGHTON.

The Capri pulls into parkway amongst a Roller
and a couple of Mercs. Music continues over.
The Trotters alight and the doorman takes
their luggage from boot (Del's leopard-skin
suitcase, etc). Del hands a twenty pound note
to the valet who opens the car door for him.
Del goes round to the front entrance. He
peels a twenty pound note from a massive
wad he is holding and hands it to doorman.

INT. NIGHT. THE FOYER. GRAND HOTEL.

Music continues over. We see the Trotters
enter, Raquel carrying Damien who is holding
his plastic pig toy. Rodney, Cassandra and
Raquel are feeling a little queasy about Del's
ostentatious display.
They approach the reception desk.
Del tucks a twenty pound note under the
bellboy's lapel. Bellboy exits.
See Raquel's reaction.
See Rodney and Cassandra's reaction. Del fills
in the registration form. Damien's toy flies
into shot and hits the receptionist. We see
Del's reaction.
We see Damien's face. We see Rodney and
Cassandra's reaction. Del hands the card to
the receptionist. Receptionist asks how he'll
pay. Del produces a wad of notes. We see
Cassandra's reaction. We see Rodney's
reaction. We see the Trotters and several
members of staff carrying their cases start to
go up the stairs. Del appears on the balcony.

INT. NIGHT. PRESIDENTIAL SUITE.

Music stops. This is an hour or so later. On
table stands the half finished silver platter of
light refreshments including a bottle of
Peckham Spring. Raquel is laid out on the

bed, a glass of champagne in hand. Del
saunters round the room, taking in and
enjoying every item of his new found luxury.
Del Another glass of champagne, sweetheart?
Raquel Oh, I think you could persuade me.
Del *(Refills her glass)* This is in our blood, innit,
darling?
Raquel Well the champagne certainly is.
Del No, I mean this lifestyle. I always promised
you this kind of life. Didn't I always promise you
this kind of life?
Raquel Yes, you did. And I'm gonna make the
most of it before they put you in prison.
Del Raquel, they can't put me in prison. You've
gotta do something illegal to go to prison. I am
merely selling a very popular product. Look, even
the finest hotels in the world are buying
Peckham Spring. No, we're on a winner. This is
just the beginning. *(To Damien)* You won't know
any other life, will you, champ? You'll grow up
with Mercedes, Cecil Gee suits, Lanzarotte.
You'll take it all in your stride. And good luck to
you.
Raquel I think it's time I put him down
Del Yeah. I'll go an' see how Rodney's doing.
(He moves towards connecting door.)
Raquel Leave 'em alone. They're … well,
they're trying to sort their lives out.
Del But it's nine o'clock. We're in Brighton.
Blimey, they should show some more decorum!
Del exits through connecting door.

INT. NIGHT. AMBASSADOR SUITE.

The TV is on and we can hear a news report.
Rodney is wearing his pyjama top and is just
tying the cord on pyjama trousers as Del
enters through connecting door.
Del Oi up!
Rodney turns away in embarrassment.
Rodney What are you doing?
Del I just popped in to see how are you are.
Don't get embarrassed, you've got nothing in
there to frighten me.
Rodney Why have we got an interconnecting
door?
Del Ah, that was my idea. I asked for that so
that we could all mingle like a family – that's
what families do.
Rodney I know, but you're popping in and out
like a gas meter reader.
Del Oh shuddup, you tart. Where's Cassandra?
Rodney She went in the bathroom about half
an hour ago.
Del *(Worried)* Them sandwiches were alright,
weren't they?

Mother Nature's Son

Rodney Yes. She's gone to … you know, slip into something.

Del Half an hour? What's she slipped into, a coma?

Rodney No. She's *(mimes spraying perfume)* and what 'ave you.

Del You'll be alright, bruv. The sea air does something to a woman.

Rodney Yeah?

Del Yeah. I remember a bird I had years ago, Gloria something or another. Cold woman, she could freeze for Birdseye. Then one weekend I took her to a caravan site in Herne Bay – she become a wild thing. It went from *Mary Poppins* to *Debbie Does Dallas* before the lids come off the take away. It's the ozones, makes them all sensual … d'you want any Brut?

Rodney No.

Del You'll be alright, bruv. Just relax, okay? Don't be taut and rigid – well not all of you, anyway.

Rodney Will you just get out of here … and don't you listen!

Del And don't you make any noise, Damien's asleep in there. See you in the morning.
Del exits.

INT. NIGHT. PRESIDENTIAL SUITE.

Del enters from Rodney's room. Raquel is not in room. Del goes over to the sleeping Damien.

Del That's it, babe, you have a lovely warm sleep and dream some lovely dreams. Dream about Christmas and about all the lovely presents Santa Claus is gonna bring you – 'cos a little baby like you has gotta be right at the top of his VIP list. When I was a little ankle-biter like you all I had for Christmas was an orange and a clump round the earhole. Still, the orange was nice … I wish I knew what you was dreaming … still, long as it's a lovely one … and I'm in it.
The door from bathroom opens and we see Raquel wearing a long, silk nightdress. Del tries hard to control his feelings of excitement.

Del Raquel!
He moves towards her.

Del You look … you look really nice, Raquel.

Raquel Thank you.
Del hands her glass of champagne. They look at each other for this moment.

Del I love you.

Raquel I love you, Trotter.
Del now takes off his braces with great urgency.

Del *(With a 'let's get at it' attitude)* Right!
Del goes to side of bed, leaving a slightly disappointed Raquel.

INT. NIGHT. AMBASSADOR SUITE.

A now very relaxed Rodney is seated on the bed wearing a towelling dressing gown, watching the news on TV.
We almost repeat the previous scene.
The bathroom door opens and Cassandra appears wearing a very expensive and slinky nightdress.

Cassandra Sorry I've been so long.
He stands. They move towards each other.

Rodney They say the best things take time.
They kiss and then fall onto bed.
As they kiss we hear the newscaster on TV. Rodney and Cassandra are so engrossed in each other they hear none of this broadcast.

Newsreader *(OOV)* And a late news item. The London Borough of Peckham is tonight without water after a local reservoir was found to be contaminated by an unknown chemical.
Cut to TV. We see news film of frogmen in a reservoir and a crane hauling one of the drums from Del's allotment, the logo clearly showing. The drum is spilling yellow liquid into the water.

Newscaster *(continues over film)* The drum of chemicals, which is still to be identified, was discovered late this afternoon and appears to have been dumped in the reservoir up to a month ago. A spokesperson for the Peckham water board has emphasised that the cutting of water supplies is purely a precautionary measure and there is no need for alarm.
Cassandra, who hasn't heard a word of this, switches TV off by remote control.

INT. NIGHT. PRESIDENTIAL SUITE.

The lights are low.
Del and Raquel lay in bed looking at each other.

Del Everything's coming up roses for us, innit, sweetheart?

Raquel Getting better every day.

Del And it's all thanks to the Peckham Spring. You know, I wouldn't mind betting that this time next week my name'll be in all the papers.
Del switches the bedside lamp off.
The room is now in darkness except for a strange eerie green glow from the bottle of Peckham Spring.

Fatal Extraction

INT. DAY. TROTTERS' LOUNGE.

There is a Christmas tree and a few decorations in background. The table is laid for breakfast with all the usual condiments plus a half-full plastic bottle of tomato ketchup.

Damien, in his jim-jams, is seated in high-chair eating scrambled eggs and beans.

Albert is seated at table reading the Daily Mirror – headlines read: 'Peckham Riots!' sub-headline; 'an excuse for looting, say police'.

An icy Raquel enters from kitchen carrying two plates of sausage, egg and baked beans. She slams the plates down on the table which makes Albert jump in fear of this angry woman.

She opens the door to bedrooms area and calls.

Raquel *(Angrily)* Derek! Your breakfast has been on the table for the last fifteen minutes!
Raquel returns to table.

Raquel *(Sweetly to Damien)* Is that nice?

Albert Yes, thank you.

Raquel I was talking to Damien!
Albert squeezes some ketchup onto his plate and the plastic bottle makes that awful, squelchy farting sound.

Raquel Next time you do the shopping buy the ketchup in a *glass* bottle! And another thing, Albert. Will you please stop boiling your old vests and pants out on our cooker? This is almost the twenty-first century and we have washing machines for that sort of thing!

Albert Look, Raquel, why are you angry at me? I'm not the one who's been coming home late every night! I'm *always* here in the flat.

Raquel *(Icily)* Yes! Aren't you just?
Exits to kitchen. Del enters from bedrooms area.

Del *(Yawns and then holds his aching jaw)* Morning Unc.

Albert Morning.

Del Bloody tooth! *(To Damien)* Hello, Champ! Good morning. How are you this morning? This looks really good, dunnit eh?

Albert You're in trouble, son. Raquel's on the warpath.

Del Oh, she don't frighten me, Albert. I've handled much more violent women than her.
Raquel enters from kitchen.

Del Good morning, sweetheart. Any calls for me last night, was there?

Raquel I haven't a clue, I went to bed early! Why don't you get yourself an answering machine, Derek?

Del An answering machine, good idea darling, yes, just what the business needs is an ansaphone. Especially seeing as you're too exhausted to do it these days. *(Before Raquel can answer)* I tell you what, Damien's getting a bit big for that high-chair – look at him, he'll be starting work soon.

Raquel There's nothing wrong with the high-chair.

Del Exactly! No, that is in very good nick. I might get a few quid for that. I think I'll put an ad in the local newsagents.

Raquel What time d'you get in last night?

Del Me, ooh, er, 'bout quarter past twelve.

Raquel It was twenty to two!

Del Was it? The battery's going in this watch.

Raquel So where were you?

Del I went down the Nag's Head and had a swift half, and then I had to go and meet someone in the casino.

Raquel Oh? that's a relief. For a minute there I was worried you might be squandering our money.

Albert How much d'you win, son?

Del *(Quietly)* Shuddup!

Raquel Don't be silly, Albert. Del doesn't know what winning is! Eat your breakfast, Del.

Del I thought you said all this fried stuff was bad for my veins.

Raquel Eat your breakfast, Del! *(Exits to kitchen)*

Albert She's not happy, son!

Del Well, she's a woman, isn't she? Anyway, it takes my mind off me tooth.

Albert I don't know! What with you and poor Rodney. He's started to look ashen-faced, ain't he?

Del Yeah, he does looked a bit cream-crackered of late. Don't worry, I'll have a word with him, I usually manage to sort out his problems.
Del squeezes ketchup onto plate accompanied by the farting sound. There is no reaction from Albert.

INT. DAY. RODNEY AND CASSANDRA'S LOUNGE.

Phone conversation intercut with Trotters'

kitchen at same time. *The phone rings.*

Cassandra *(On phone)* Hello?

We intercut between Raquel (on cordless phone in the Trotters' kitchen) and Cassandra.

Raquel *(On phone)* Cassandra? It's Raquel. Can you talk? Rodney's not there, is he?

Cassandra *(On phone)* No, he's left for work.

Raquel *(On phone)* I just phoned to see what the doctor said last night?

Cassandra *(On phone)* Oh, she was ever so nice. Basically she said not to worry. She's got three couples on her books who've been trying for babies for over a year, so Rodney and I are almost rookies. I've got to take my temperature hourly, keep a chart, all the usual stuff. Oh and she's given me some exercises that are supposed to strengthen the muscles.

Raquel Have you abandoned that, erm 'schedule' thing she worked out for you? I don't know how either of you kept up the pace! It sounded excessive for Mel Gibson and his wife let alone you and Rodney!

Cassandra No, I've decided to continue with that. I know it hasn't worked but Rodney's enjoyed himself trying!

They both laugh.

EXT. DAY. LONDON STREET/BUS PASSING/BUS INTERIOR.

We cut inside bus where we see Rodney wearing working clothes. He appears depressed, put upon and almost asleep. Behind him we see Mickey Pearce stand and move up aisle to alight from bus.

Mickey Alright, Rodney?

Rodney Yeah alright, Mick.

Mickey What you been up to? You look like some vampire's been having a go at you!

Rodney I'm fine, thank you very much!

Mickey You weren't involved in that riot on the estate the other night, were you?

Rodney No, I was not! As if I'd get involved in a riot!

Mickey Well, you don't look well! *(To an old lady behind him – everyone's aunt)* he looks shagged out, don't he, love?

Lady *(To Rodney)* You don't look well, dear.

Rodney There's nothing wrong with me, alright?

INT. DAY. RODNEY AND CASSANDRA'S BEDROOM/TROTTERS' FLAT.

Continuation of phone conversation.

Cassandra Raquel, you haven't mentioned this baby business to Del, have you?

Raquel *(On phone)* Of course not!

Cassandra *(On phone)* Rodney thinks we ought to choose the right time to tell him.

Raquel *(On phone)* I'll leave it to you.

Cassandra *(On phone)* How are things with you and Del?

Raquel Much the same. He didn't get in 'til twenty to two this morning.

Cassandra Why don't you ask Rodney to find out what's happening?

Raquel Because I'm a bit frightened of what the answer might be. I think the first flush of fatherhood and domesticity has cooled and he's gone back to his old ways – down the pubs and casino with his stupid mates!

Raquel *(On phone)* I'll have to go, someone's coming. Talk to you soon. Bye.

Switches phone off.

Del enters kitchen.

Del He's dropped a load of beans on the carpet.

Raquel Well, why don't *you* wipe them up?

Del Me? Let the old git wipe 'em up himself!

Raquel Oh, Albert!

Del Have you spoken to Cassandra recently?

Raquel No.

Del Well, when you do can you find out if there's anything wrong between her and Rodders.

Raquel Don't go interfering in their lives, Del!

Del Eh? He's my kid brother, I've got a right to interfere. If they've got a problem I just wanna help out.

Raquel *(Laughs at the irony of his statement)* Oh God! That is the best yet!

Raquel exits to lounge.

Cut to lounge:

Raquel enters. She picks up Damien from chair.

Raquel Come on, time for your wash.

Albert starts to exit.

Raquel Not you, Albert. If you're doing this to annoy me, it's not working!

Albert returns. Del enters from kitchen.

Del Makes you wonder if it's all worth while, don't it, Unc?

Albert If you say …

Albert exits to hall. Del now reacts as his bare foot lands in the small pile of baked beans.

Del *(To himself)* Oh, you mucky old sod!

Albert enters from hall carrying a small leaflet.

Albert I picked this up at the library yesterday. *We see the front page of leaflet bears the single word 'Relate'.*

Del Relate?

Albert It's the new word for marriage guidance.

Fatal Extraction

I didn't know if it'd be any good to you.

Del Yeah. Oh, thanks very much Unc. Actually it's just the sort of thing I'm looking for, this.

Albert turns his back and moves to armchair and so doesn't see Del using the leaflet to wipe the beans from his foot.

Del I'm just gonna make a private phone call. *Del exits to kitchen and closes door behind him.*

EXT. DAY. THE LIFT FOYER. NELSON MANDELA HOUSE.

A sign tells us this is the Nelson Mandela House, 12th Floor. We are looking at the outer lift door. We see the light from the lift car appear at the door window. The doors open and we see Rodney standing inside the lift, asleep. The doors now start to close. Rodney wakes and makes a grab for the doors. He is too late and the lift descends with Rodney's face at the window.

INT. DAY. RODNEY AND CASSANDRA'S BEDROOM/TROTTERS FLAT.

Cassandra on bed, doing exercises. The phone rings. We intercut between Del (in kitchen) and Cassandra.

Cassandra *(On phone)* Hello?

Del *(On phone)* Oh, hello Cassandra, it's Del Boy. How are you, sweetheart?

Cassandra *(On phone)* Oh fine thanks.

Del *(On phone)* Cushty. Look, Cassandra, I don't want to interfere or anything like that, but I'm a bit worried about young Rodders. Well, he seems a bit worried – he's not his old self. And I just wondered if there was anything I could do to help?

Cassandra *(On phone)* Look, if you must know, Del, Rodney and I are trying for a baby.

Del *(On phone)* Yeah alright, I'll get off the phone then, alright!

Cassandra *(On phone)* No, not right now! Rodney's not even here, he left half an hour ago!

Del *(On phone)* Blimey, he left half an hour ago and you're still panting?

Cassandra *(On phone)* I'm in the middle of my exercises!

Del *(On phone)* Oh your exercises? I see what you mean! I though that you … well never mind what I thought. But look, I can't help you unless you let me know what's happening.

Cassandra *(Hand over mouthpiece)* Oh God!

Cut to Trotters' lounge. Rodney enters from front door.

Rodney Alright? *(Flops down on settee)* Where is everyone?

Albert Raquel's seeing to the little 'un and Del's in the kitchen making a private phone call.

Rodney Who to?

Albert I think it's the marriage guidance people.

Rodney But him and Raquel aren't married!

Albert I know but they row, don't they? I'll make you a new pot of tea, son.

Rodney Oh yeah, cheers.

Albert exits to kitchen. He leaves the kitchen door open. We see Del in kitchen talking on phone. He has his back to us. He wanders in and out of shot but never sees that Rodney is present.

Del *(On phone)* No, you see the thing is, you know that a man, well a man, any man can lose his … his drive.

Cassandra *(On phone)* Rodney hasn't lost his drive!

Rodney, believing Del is talking to a Relate counsellor, can't believe what he's hearing. He gets up and moves nearer kitchen door.

Del *(On phone)* No, no, no, I'm not saying that is happening, no. But what I'm saying is that, you know, a man, can, well you know, lose his oomph! *(Rodney is silently laughing)* And naturally the woman, you see, she becomes disappointed and frustrated. But that's not necessarily the man's fault, is it eh?

He closes door.

Raquel enters from bedrooms area.

Rodney Morning, Raquel.

Raquel Oh morning, Rodney. Where's Del?

Rodney He's on the phone.

Raquel Who to?

Rodney Dunno! So how's life treating you?

Raquel How's life treating me? D'you mean besides him coming in at all hours of the morning, spending every spare hour with his mates down the pub and wasting our money in that casino?

Rodney Yeah.

Raquel Well, I'll give you an example of how life's treating me, Rodney. Have you seen what's inside my wardrobe?

Rodney No.

Raquel Well, not to put too fine a point on it, the only times my clothes look fashionable is when I'm watching UK Gold! Now, a short while ago Del happened to mention that he had a contact in the rag trade. This fella could get the very latest in fashion *and* all the top designer-labels. Christmas was approaching, Del asked me what I'd like. 'Anything you want, sweetheart, just name it.' So I said I wouldn't mind a little

number by Bruce Oldfield. *(Holds up LP cover)* He got me *Tubular Bells*!
Rodney That's *Mike* Oldfield!
Raquel I know!
Cut to kitchen.
Del *(On phone)* Yeah, now all you've got to do sweetheart, is you just take your time and you'll have a lovely healthy baby. Just like my Damien, nine pounds he was, yeah. I remember the day he was born. Yeah, of course me and Raquel, you know, haven't given up hope of doing it again sometime.
Albert exits kitchen and leaves door open.
Cassandra *(On phone)* What's the baby's weight got to do with it?
Del *(On phone – loud enough for Rodney to hear)* No, no, no, it doesn't matter how big it is, does it?
Rodney turns away to hide his laughter from Raquel.
Raquel *(Calls)* Who you talking to?
Del Cassandra!
Rodney Get off that phone!
Del Morning, Rodders!
Rodney grabs phone away from Del.
Rodney *(On phone)* Cassandra, why are you discussing our private life with ? I don't care. This'll be all over the Nag's Head by dinner time!
Del has exited to lounge.
Del *(To Raquel)* That's the thanks I get!
Raquel I thought you'd have been used to it by now!

EXT. DAY. THE COUNCIL ESTATE. FILM.
Thirty minutes later.
All around we have evidence of the recent riot. The shells of burnt out cars still smouldering, rocks and broken glass are strewn across the roads, some of the ground floor flats have their windows boarded and somewhere we see the sad remains of a large communal Christmas tree now black and burnt. The three wheel van passes us and bumps over the stones, etc.
Del They still ain't cleared this place up, have they?
Rodney Not a lot of point. I've heard they're expecting another riot. They reckon anything could set it off.
Del I've heard they're thinking of twinning this estate with Jurassic Park!
Del and Rodney laugh.
Del *(A sudden tooth pain)* Cow, bloody hell!
Rodney You wanna go somewhere with that tooth.

Del I go everywhere with it, don't I? It's stuck in me bloody head!
Rodney I meant the dentist!
Del Yes, I will.
Rodney Can I switch the radio on?
Del Yeah go on then, alright.
Rodney switches radio on. We hear the song 'One Voice'. Del sings along for a couple of bars.
Del Do you know, this is Raquel's most favourite number.
Rodney Yeah, can I switch it off?
Del No, leave it … Every time I hear this number you know it always reminds me of my Raquel. Yeah, go on switch it off.

INT. DAY. SID'S CAFE.
The last verse or so of 'One Voice' is playing on Sid's radio. Denzil and Trigger, in working clothes, are at counter talking to Sid. Sid hands Denzil a bowl of porridge.
Sid There you go, Denzil, one bowl of piping hot porridge. That'll warm you up on a cold morning.
Denzil Cheers, Sid. *(Hands Sid money)* There's a hair in this.
Pulls hair out.
Sid Giss it here.
Takes hair and flicks it on floor behind counter.
Denzil There's another one!
Sid Hang on.
Sid removes hair from porridge and flicks it on the floor behind counter.
Denzil That's disgusting that is, Sid. If the health authorities saw this they'd close you down!
Sid *(Proudly)* I've been closed down for a lot worse than that, Denzil! *(To Trigger)* I hate these politically correct people!
Trigger Yeah.
Sid What you having, Trig?
Trigger I'll try some of that porridge.
Del and Rodney enter.
Del Just a cup of tea, for me, Rodney.
Rodney moves to counter.
Rodney Two teas, Sid.
Trigger Alright, Dave?
Rodney Yeah, alright, Trig.
Del sits with Denzil.
Denzil Don't have the porridge, Rodney. I've just found hairs in mine.
Sid It was only two hairs!
Denzil That's enough, isn't it?
Del Maybe there's a sporran in it!
Denzil So how's it going, Del? You got all your

Fatal Extraction

Christmas presents?

Del No, not yet. Damien wants a pet.

Denzil I didn't think the council allowed pets.

Del No, a little one, you know like a rabbit or a guinea-pig, something like that.

Trigger and Rodney join them.

Trigger How's it going, Del?

Del Don't ask, Trig.

Denzil Things still the same then, eh?

Del Yeah, still giving me strife.

Trigger Yeah, it's a bitch, innit?

Del *(Surprised at Trigger's tone)* Well, that's stronging it a bit? Trig!

Trigger No, you're too soft, Del! I've been in exactly the same boat as you. D'you know what I done? I got shot of it!

Denzil Look? Trig, it's not as simple as just get shot of 'it'!

Rodney No. Del loves ... Well, a strong bond exists, doesn't it Del?

Del Yeah. We've been together a long time!

Trigger And you're just gonna get more and more aggro! I know how you feel. You, become attached to em, give 'em little pet names. I've done it. But take my advice, Del, get down the dentist and have it out.

Del Oh! My tooth?

Trigger It's best in the long run, Del. Try my dentist, he's good, I've been going to him for years.

Del Yeah alright, I might try that, Trig.

Denzil Trig, we were talking about Del and Raquel! *(To Del)* Are you having rows?

Rodney He's never there to find out, are you?

Del No. She's talking to me – unfortunately! I'll never understand the workings of a woman's mind. I suppose that's why I gave up trying in the end. *(To Rodney)* 'Ere, who was that bird I used to go out with?

Rodney Which one?

Del Cor, what was her name?

Trigger What's she look like?

Del She was a redhead.

Denzil One of the redheads ... Pauline?

Del No.

Rodney Veronique from Woolworths?

Del No.

Trigger Janine?

Del Her?

Rodney Marian?

Del Who's Marian?

Rodney I don't know. You met her at Catford Dog Track, you bought her a ring.

Del Oh yeah. No, not her! No, no, who am I thinking about? Was her name? Her dad was a tattooist. She had this tattoo of a heart with a dagger going through it on her thigh.

Rodney Don't ring a bell.

Del Well, you would have only been about two. What was her name? She worked in a betting shop down Lewisham Grove.

Trigger A betting shop ...

Denzil Down Lewisham Grove.

Del Look, it don't matter. I went out with her for – it must have been a *month*! Actually she was going steady with another bloke at the time, but it didn't worry me! Made it more exciting. Well, she was a sporting girl – a good all-rounder, you know what I mean? Well, I'd saved up all me money to take her on holiday – it was gonna be really exotic. You know, the holiday of a lifetime. When all of a sudden, right out of the blue, for no reason, she packed me in. And yet the night before I'd taken her home to meet me Mum and Dad for the first time.

Rodney Yeah?

Del So the next day I went to the betting shop, you know to have a chat, take her out for lunch and all that. And they said that she weren't there, but I knew she was 'cos her crash helmet was hanging up on the hook. You know where I found her? She was hiding up on the roof. She said she was sunbathing.

Denzil Well, maybe she was sunbathing.

Del Na, it was a sloping roof. I mean, there she was, with her laying back against the tiles with her stilettos jammed in the gutter. She nearly fell off twice. Anyway, that was that. Cor, blimey, what was her name?

Trigger D'you get your money back on the holiday?

Del No. You know what these caravan sites are like, don't you?

INT. NIGHT THE ONE ELEVEN CLUB/CASINO.

Averagely crowded. We see the various card games, roulette, etc in action. Del, in evening suit, is standing at bar drinking a scotch. We see Rodney, suited up, approaching bar.

Rodney Del Boy.

Del Rodders! What you doing here?

Rodney Well, I had a couple of hours to kill. So I said to Cass I'll pop down the club and see Del.

Del Good. *(Calls)* 'Ere Miguel, there you are look, a lager-top, please.

Rodney You're drinking a lot of scotch these days.

Del Yeah, well, it's the only thing that dulls the pain, innit?

Rodney Talk to her, Del. There's nothing that

can't be sorted by talking it out.

Del I'm not talking about Raquel, I'm talking about my tooth.

Rodney Go to the dentist then!

Del I don't like dentists!

Rodney Well, let it go rotten and get septicaemia.

Del Look, shuddup moaning, will you? I've come here to psych myself up for the game and you do nothing but lecture me! It's like trying to play poker with Neil Kinnock!

Boycie, in evening suit, joins them.

Boycie Del Boy, Rodney.

Del How's it going, Boycie?

Boycie Life's one long uphill struggle at the moment, Derek. The second-hand car business is in the biggest slump since – well, since the last one. Me and Marlene could only afford one week's holiday in Barbados this year.

Del Oh that's terrible, innit? Please don't go on about it, you know how easy I cry. *(To Rodney)* We'll have to hold a whip for him.

Rodney Yeah, can I count the lashes?

Boycie Look, I happen to believe that everyone has the right to expect a certain standard of living. I mean, it's alright for you coming from that council estate – sometimes I almost envy you. Not often, I must admit. Especially with all the problems you've got.

Del We ain't got no problems. Raquel and I are just going through a sticky patch, that's all!

Boycie When I mentioned 'problems' I was referring to that riot the other night. I hear they went through the whole estate looking for any half-decent vehicle and then setting fire to it! Your three-wheeled van alright was it, Del Boy? *(A big grin)*

Del Yes, thank you, Boycie, they didn't lay a finger on it.

Boycie Well that's a Godsend, at least.

Del Yeah, that's only 'cos I know the leader of the rioters! Terrible though, innit eh? The way they set fire to their own people's property when there's a very big car site just up the road!

Rodney But that's Boycie's car site, Derek.

Del Oh, it is Rodney! Well, let's hope someone does not suggest that to the rioters – eh, Boycie?

Boycie *(Calls)* Miguel, can you get my friends a drink? Same again please and put it on my account. Well, I must be off. Lots of luck, eh?

Del Yeah cheers, Boycie.

Boycie exits. Del and Rodney laugh to each other.

A very voluptuous and attractive young girl is now behind Del. She wears a low-cut dress

and a wonderbra (or uplift-bra) so breasts are propped high and round. She should be a tall girl so that Del stands almost eyeball to boob with her. Del turns and reacts as if slightly dizzy.

Del Miguel! Cor, blimey! I don't know about my teeth! I think my eyes need testing. I turned round a bit quick just then and I thought Right Said Fred had just walked in. *(Laughs)*

Rodney laughs. His laugh now dies as the girl's large and tough looking boyfriend stares at him.

INT. NIGHT. TROTTERS' LOUNGE.

Raquel is ironing. Albert is asleep in chair. We can hear and see TV (Crimewatch).

Sue Cook Good night.

Nick Ross Good night.

Raquel looks at the clock.

INT. NIGHT. ONE TO ELEVEN CLUB.

This is a few hours later. Ties have been loosened, etc. Smoky atmosphere.

Del and Rodney are seated at the roulette table.

Del Ain't you gonna have a bet?

Rodney No I'm not. It's a mug's game. Hasn't it dawned on you yet the only one who wins is the casino owner?

The croupier pushes a bundle of chips to Del.

Del Sorry, what were you saying?

Rodney Yeah, alright, so you were lucky. Well, you've won now so let's go home.

Del Don't talk wet, I'm on a roll! We'll play the evens.

Del places all his chips in the appropriate square.

Rodney Del, will you spare one moment's thought for Raquel?

Del Who d'you think I'm doing this for, Rodney? I'm doing this for her and Damien! Rodney, I couldn't say anything before – because I didn't want word to get out – it's been very delicate. But I'm tryin' to put down a big deal with Ronnie Nelson.

Rodney So what are you doing down here at the One to One Club most nights?

Del Because he owns it, don't he? He don't come in before one o'clock in the morning, so I've gotta hang have a word with him. I can't let this deal slip through me fingers, Rodney! I'll tell you what it is, it's six hundred and fifty hand-held camcorders. Made in Russia.

Rodney Russian camcorders? I didn't think they went in for all that *You've Been Framed* cobblers.

Fatal Extraction

Del No, these are ex-military. They've got night-vision on them and everything.

Rodney So, we're gonna buy six hundred and fifty Russian Army camcorders?

Del Yeah, with a bit of luck … Eight hundred and ninety five quid.

Rodney You're gonna pay eight hundred and ninety five quid for a camera?

Del No, eight hundred and ninety five quid for the lot!

Rodney They sound very classy!

Del State of the art!

Croupier Thirty red.

> *The croupier pushes a larger pile of chips to Del. Del places them all back on evens.*

Del *(Smiles smugly at Rodney)* Aren't you gonna have a bet?

Rodney No! Look, try an' look at it from Raquel's point of view, Del. She's in that flat night after night with Horatio and his tales of the sea and you're down here drinking and gambling.

Del I know! But does she appreciate it?

Rodney No.

Del No, she does not! She thinks I'm out every night enjoying myself! *(Finishes scotch. To waitress:)* Excuse me darling, same again, please? That's the trouble with women, Rodney, they change – and they expect you to change with 'em. She wanted me to become a pipe and slippers man, you know, having a cup of tea and a biscuit and watching *Family Fortunes*. Well, stuff that for a game of toy soldiers! Don't get me wrong, I'm not averse to a cup of Darjeeling and an 'obnob, but there's a time and a place for everything. I like life on the tightrope and I enjoy the company of me mates and I don't see why I should change just 'cos I've met Raquel?

Rodney And who are your mates, Del? Boycie the freemason, a total snob who thinks anyone who's got a pound less than him's a peasant! Denzil's a man who eats porridge with a wig in it! And what about Trigger, a roadsweeper who gives pet names to his teeth!

Del They're still me mates! I'm not like you, Rodders, Del Boy's not for turning!

Rodney What's that supposed to mean? Marriage hasn't changed me!

Del Oh it has, Rodney! I've seen you and that Cassandra – she's into all this conservation malarkey, and so Rodney is as well.

Rodney Look, I have not changed, Del. When I make up my mind about something, *nothing* can alter it! Alright?

Croupier 140 pieces sir, thank you.

> *The croupier pushes a massive pile of chips to Del.*

Del We'll stick with evens, shall we?

Rodney *(Produces some money)* I'm gonna go and get some chips!

> *Del laughs as Rodney moves towards cashier.*

INT. NIGHT. RODNEY AND CASSANDRA'S BEDROOM.

> *Cassandra is in bed with a thermometer in her mouth. She looks at the clock and turns the light off angrily.*

INT. NIGHT. THE ONE ELEVEN CLUB.

> *The club is less crowded now. Del and Rodney are still at the roulette table but now Del only has one chip left. He and Rodney both look desperate.*

Rodney *(Appealing to the ball)* Come on! Reds! Reds! Reds!

> *The waitress approaches Del.*

Waitress Excuse me, Del, I'm afraid Ronnie won't be here now – I'll leave a message for him.

Del Yeah, alright … Thanks!… Come on, Rodney, let's go home.

Rodney No, hang on. The ball ain't landed yet!

Croupier Seventeen, black.

Rodney Shit!

> *They stand. Del flips his last chip to the croupier and they walk towards the entrance.*

Del Rodney, how much d'you lose?

Rodney Fifty.

Del You plonker.

Rodney I wouldn't have gambled at all if you hadn't encouraged me!

Del Oi, oi, oi, don't blame me! What d'you come in here for if you didn't want a flutter?

Rodney I'll tell you why, shall I? Cassandra suggested I come down here!

Del Oh yeah, why?

Rodney So as we could get you home at a decent hour. We are trying to save your relationship with Raquel! You've been falling in half past one and two o'clock in the morning! And it is not on Del!

> *They arrive at exit door.*

EXT. DAY. ONE ELEVEN CLUB/LONDON STREET.

> *A milk float is passing. Del and Rodney exit and stare incredulously at the daylight.*

Rodney It's daytime!

Del It's eight o'clock in the morning! This is all your fault, dopey!

Rodney Me?

Del Yes! You you you kept me talking in there!

Rodney Oh yeah? And who was doing all the gambling?

Del Well, you were doing your fair share! Cor blimey, I could have been home *hours* ago if it weren't for you! You've really dropped me in it this time, Rodney!

They are walking away from camera.

Del Look, we've gotta be down the market in half an hour!

EXT. DAY. MARKET. FILM.

At this point we just see Del and a small crowd. Behind Del there are a few cardboard boxes declaring the name of some Mickey Mouse ski-equipment company.

Laying on the boxes are a couple of gaudily-coloured ski jackets, etc.

Del *(Talking to crowd)* Right, listen, I know what you're thinking, I know what you're thinking, because I can read your minds. You're thinking, what do I want with all this skiing equipment? There ain't no mountains in Peckham. Absolutely true. In a few months time *you* yourself may decide to take an Alpine holiday. Now, due to my unique style of bulk-buying, you can go togged out in the latest up-to-the-minute fashion at bargain basement prices. Now I'm gonna show you how stylish this gear is because it is being modelled now by my younger brother, Rodney.

We now see Rodney standing close by. He wears the complete skiing outfit save for skis. He wears a ski mask, tinted goggles and a woollen hat. A pink, purple, yellow and green ski-jacket and gloves. A pair of moa-trousers (they're heavily padded and quilted type normally worn in arctic conditions). But instead of ski-boots he wears a pair of old trainers.

Del Now, the jacket is padded in pure fibre-glass and quilted in natural nylon. Now this jacket alone would set you back about a hundred and twenty quid at Lillywhites – but this can be yours for a mere thirty five pounds and it comes in all sizes. Now *all* this equipment here is manufactured by the one country that leads the world in Alpine clothing – namely, Fiji *(Del's mobile phone starts ringing)* Just a moment please, this is probably the Austrian Olympic squad wanting to increase their order.

(On phone) Hello, Trotter Independent Traders, PLC, Arctic-clothing department

We see Trigger moving past Rodney, sweeping the gutter and pushing his barrow.

Rodney remains motionless.

Trigger *(No reaction to Rodney's appearance)* Alright, Dave?

Trigger goes on his way.

Del Rodney, it's Cassandra! *(Hands phone to Rodney)*

Rodney *(On phone)* Cass, I've told you never to phone me at work! What? What now? Cass, I can't ... I'm in the middle ... Yes, alright! *(Switches phone off)* Del, I've gotta shoot off. Cassy needs me at home.

Del What for?

Rodney Well, it's probably the right time.

Del Oh come on, Rodney, she'll keep till this evening.

Rodney No, it's ... Well, you know! She's most probably at the right temperature!

Del Stone me, Rodney. What are you two trying for, a baby or a barbecue? Go on, go on, hurry up!

Rodney dashes off still in the ski gear.

Del indicated Rodney's jeans, etc, which are in a pile on one of the boxes.

Del *(Calls)* 'Ere, don't you wanna change your clo ... *(We now see the crowd has dispersed)* Oh, look at that!

INT. DAY. RODNEY AND CASSANDRA'S HALL/FRONT DOOR/LIVING ROOM.

We hear key in lock. The door opens and Rodney bursts in, exhausted from running and still wearing the skiing clothing.

Rodney *(Calls)* Cass, I'm home.

Cassandra *(OOV)* I'm in here, Roddy.

Rodney Right, won't be a minute.

Rodney strips off down to T-shirt and striped underpants and then exits to living room. Cuts to living room: Rodney bursts in. We see Cassandra seated in armchair. Also in room are Raquel and Damien and their suitcases.

Rodney Sorry about that Raquel, I was ... I was hot. What you doing here?

Cassandra She's left Del.

Rodney Left him? Why?

Raquel D'you know what time he got in this morning?

Rodney *(Guiltily)* No!

Raquel Quarter past eight!

Rodney Geddaway!

Raquel He just changed into his working clothes and went straight down the market. He didn't even stop for a cup of tea. Well, that was the last straw. He's not treating me like that anymore!

Rodney Look, you've gotta try an' look at it

Fatal Extraction

from his point of view, Raquel. There are extenuating circumstances.

Raquel Like what?

Rodney Well … He's having a lot of trouble with his teeth.

Cassandra That's no excuse.

Rodney No, I know. But he is in pain!

Raquel So am I, Rodney, so am I!

Rodney Well, where you gonna go?

Cassandra I said they could stay here.

Rodney Here? But this is a one-bedroom flat!

Cassandra This is a sofa bed.

Raquel I won't be here for long. A couple of nights, that's all. Is that OK with you?

Rodney Yeah, yeah, of course.

Cassandra Good. I'll make us a cup of something.

Raquel I'll help.

> *Cassandra and Raquel exit to kitchen. Rodney remains pondering and worrying about this turn of events. Now he becomes aware of something. He looks up and we see Damien staring at him. We see Rodney's reaction. Damien now smiles at Rodney. We see Rodney's face and, this time, we hear the zing, zing of violin strings a la Psycho.*

INT. DAY. NAG'S HEAD. STUDIO.

> *This is lunchtime, same day.*
> *Del, Trigger, Denzil and Boycie are seated at table. Mike brings a tray of drinks across.*

Mike Here we go, gentlemen. Drinks. Is that right, Del, just a lemonade for you?

Del Yeah, that's right, yeah. I'm going down to visit Trig's dentist this afternoon, I don't want to smell of booze.

Mike So how's things on the home front? You and Raquel still at pistols drawn, are you?

Del Yeah, still involved in the cold war. But I'm gonna live my life the way I wanna live it. Give her time and she'll learn.

Denzil That's exactly the attitude I took with my Corinne. Even when she left me I refused to change – seven years ago but I haven't changed.

Del Yeah, but there's a difference though, ain't there Denzil? Raquel would never leave me because it's the real deep love thing!

Mike Women are a mystery, though, ain't they?

Del What? Here's a mystery for you. Here's a … Answer me this. Why is it that women always wanna know what time you got in? Right, they say to you, 'What time d'you get in last night?' And you say; 'Oh I don't know, about quarter past twelve.' And they say; 'No you didn't, it was twenty to two!' And I think to myself, well why bloody ask?

Mike Yeah, he's right, he's right. Why ask? It's like saying to you, 'What's that on the telly, *Coronation Street* or *Eastenders*.' And you say, 'It's *Eastenders*,' and they say, 'No it ain't, it's *Coronation Street*!' I mean, why ask?

Del Why ask?

Boycie Beats me!

Mike You know, I came home one night and my missus said to me, 'Where are you living now?' And I said, 'Here!' And she said, 'No you ain't!' And threw me suitcase at me! I mean, why ask?

> *Pause, then:*

All Why ask?

Trigger Why ask?

Boycie Well, I mean that's women for you, innit? I mean, they're a different breed. Take my Marlene, she's always moaning on and on that I don't respect her. I mean, me! Don't respect me own wife! Daft old mare! I mean I love her, don't get me wrong. But sometimes I think getting married was the worst mistake I ever made in my life. I sometimes think back to when we first met in Lewisham Grove. I wish I'd never ever walked into that betting shop now.

> *Del looks at Denzil. Denzil and Del look at Boycie.*

Trigger Oh, so that's who you …

Del and Denzil Trigger!

Trigger What?

Denzil I've just remembered something very important I meant to tell you.

Trigger What's that?

Denzil … It's gone now!

Trigger Oh, that's alright, Denzil, that happens to me all the time. *(Pause)* See, I was just gonna say something important to Del and now it's gone now. So how'd it turn out then, Mike?

Mike Eh?

Trigger *Coronation Street* or *Eastenders*?

Boycie As long as it weren't *El Dorado* we can all sleep easy, eh?

> *Albert enters.*

Del Alright, Unc? Any messages?

Albert That bloke phoned about the video cameras. And er, someone come round moaning about, er, a pair of ski pants. Oh, and Raquel's left you.

EXT. DAY. LONDON BACKSTREET/DENTAL SURGERY.

> *We see the van (Del driving) pull up outside the surgery. They get out and walk towards the surgery.*

Del I don't believe it, Rodders, I just don't believe it! I've never, *never* had a woman walk out on me like that.

Rodney Yes you have.

Del Who?

Rodney All of 'em!

Del Yeah, but they didn't have my child with them, did they?

Rodney Look Del, I feel a bit embarrassed, about Raquel staying at the flat and that. But what could I do? Couldn't refuse, could I?

Del No, of course not, bruv. No, you couldn't see 'em turned out on the street, could you? No, you look after 'em, I'll see you're alright for some money.

Rodney Oh, don't be silly.

Del No, no, no, come on, straight up. I appreciate what you're doing.

Rodney Look, Del, I reckon all it would take is one phone call and you two'd be back together in no time. It would take just one word – 'sorry'.

Del No, I think you're right, Rodney. Alright, get her to phone and apologise and I'll forget it.

Rodney I'm talking about you!

Del Me? What have I done?

Rodney Raquel hardly ever sees you! You treat that flat like a lodging house. She told me you walked in the bedroom one night and Damien screamed – thought you was an intruder!

Del That is rubbish, that is! Look, I've been under a lot of stress lately, what with business deals and all that.

Rodney Well, I explained to her. I said Del's been under a lot of pressure, what with business and his teeth going manky.

Del Exactly. What with … My teeth are not going manky! They just need looking at, that's all!

Rodney Well, get in there and have 'em looked at then!

Del I don't like dentists!

Rodney It's like the Milky Bar Kid!

Del I'll tell you what we'll do, right? Look, we'll go down to Ronnie Nelson and pick up the cameras, then we'll come back here and I'll go to the dentist.

Rodney No! You go to the dentists now, and then we'll pick the cameras up! Oh go on, get in there!

Del Are you coming in with me?

Rodney No. I'm gonna have a kip in the van.

Del Hey! Oi! Rodney, I'm gonna get yo …
He winces and puts his hand to his cheek.

INT. DAY. DENTAL SURGERY.
Del is in chair as the dentist (Mr Ellis) probes

about in his mouth. The receptionist (Beverley) enters. Beverley is in her late thirties, attractive and has a pleasant nature. She speaks with a working to middle-class accent.

Beverley I'm sorry to interrupt. Mrs Patel just rang to cancel her four o'clock appointment.

Dentist Thank you, Beverley.
Beverley exits.
The dentist hits one of Del's back teeth and he cries out in pain.

Del Aaaagh!

Dentist That's the one!

Del Well I know that!

Dentist Help yourself to the, erm … *(Points to mouthwash)*

Del Mmmm? Oh, cheers. *(He drinks it)*. Thank you.

Dentist *(Making a few notes)* D'you have regular dental checks, Mr Trotter?

Del Oh yes, doctor. You can't be too careful where the old choppers are concerned, can you.

Dentist And who was the last dentist you saw?

Del The last one … that would be Mr Owens, had the surgery down Gandhi Avenue.

Dentist Mr Owens? He died on the night of the Queen's Silver Jubilee, 1977.

Del I know, it was tragic, weren't it?

Dentist So you have a regular check-up every sixteen years?

Del I think it's better in the long run, don't you?

Dentist Yeah, yeah, I'm afraid this tooth of yours is beyond repair, Mr Trotter. It'll have to come out.

Del Oh, it's gotta come out. Well, I'll make an appointment to see you next week.

Dentist No, no, I'll do it now.

Del Now?

Dentist Don't worry, you won't feel a thing. *(Produces a syringe and hypodermic needle)* This'll just make one side of your face a bit numb.
Del studies the needle with growing alarm.

Del Ah you see, but the thing is, you know, er, I'm in a bit of a hurry, see.
He is approaching Del with needle.

Dentist It'll only take five minutes.

Del My brother's out there in the van.

Dentist Just a little prick.

Del Oh, do you know him then, do you?

INT. DAY. THE VAN.
Same time. Rodney is sitting in the passenger seat. His eyelids are slowly closing as the excesses of the last week take their toll.

Fatal Extraction

He folds his coat into a make-shift pillow, lays it between the two seats and lays his head down on it.

INT. DAY. DENTAL SURGERY.

The dentist slowly removes the syringe and needle from Del's mouth.

Del Aaaaagh!

Dentist There we are. Now, if you'd like to sit in the waiting room for a while, just leave the anaesthetic time to work. I'll call you in five minutes.

Del Thank you, doctor.

Del exits to waiting room. Four patients are seated here. Beverley is behind the reception counter. Del enters from surgery. A buzzer sounds.

Beverley *(Calls next patient)* Mrs Marshall. You can go through now.

A patient enters surgery.

Del *(To Beverley)* I've just gotta wait for this jollop to work.

Beverley It doesn't take too long. Perhaps we could complete this form while you're waiting. It's just for new patients. I've got most of your details … Now then, let me see. Next of kin.

Del Next of kin? Blimey, I'm only having a tooth out!

Beverley It's just local health authority procedure.

Del I haven't got no next of kin.

Beverley What, no-one?

Del Well, there's me brother.

Beverley Have you got any dependants?

Del Yeah, my brother.

INT. DAY. THE VAN.

Rodney is sleeping on his make-shift pillow. Now behind him, in back of van, we see a movement. A small rodent is scuffling around. It approaches Rodney's head and we see it is a gerbil. Rodney opens his eyes as he hears, or becomes aware, of movement. He turns and looks at the creature. He looks back to camera. His eyes widen in fear.

INT. DAY. THE WAITING ROOM. FILM.

Del Yeah, I've got a son.

Beverley Ah, that's better.

Del It's Damien. Damien Derek Trotter.

Beverley Oh, my daughter's got a little boy called that.

Del What, Damien Derek Trotter?

Beverley No! just Damien.

Del You're having me on. You've got a grandson?

Beverley Yeah!

Del Never! You must have had your daughter very, very young. I'd put you down as, well, you know, late twenties.

Beverley Oh, get off!

Del No honest, straight up. *(Gesturing into surgery)* Is he your husband, is he?

Beverley Mr Ellis? No, I just work here.

Del I see. I thought it might be, you know, like a family business, something like that.

Beverley No. I'm divorced. We broke up about, well, nine years ago.

Del Oh really. My wife … er partner … well, she, you know, she left me.

Beverley Oh I'm sorry. You know, people say time's a great healer but I'm not so sure. Even now I sometimes think about those days and … well, it still hurts you know.

Del Yes, I know the feeling. I still get these little pangs.

Beverley When did your relationship break up?

Del This morning.

Beverley This morning?

Del Perhaps you and me ought to go out with each other you know, and cry on each other's shoulders.

The entrance door bursts open and Rodney enters.

Rodney Del! There is a rat in the van!

Del You what?

Rodney In the van! There's a rat!

Del A rat?

Rodney In the van!

Del What you on about?

Rodney I'm trying to inform you that there is a rat in the van!!

Del It's not a rat! It's a gerbil.

Rodney Alright, so it's a gerbil.

Del I know, I got it for Christmas.

Rodney For Chris … For Damien?

Del Yeah, it's one of his presents, Gerry the Gerbil. I had it in a cage in the back of the van. The door must have come open or something, I dunno. Go and put it back in the cage.

Rodney *(Obviously not relishing the thought of touching Gerry)* Eh?

Del Go and put the gerbil back in the cage.

Rodney exits.

Del *(To Beverley)* Dependants! No, my boy wanted a pet for Christmas, so I went down the shop and got him Gerry the gerbil. So, what about it Beverley?

Beverley Sorry?

Del You and me … having a date.

Beverley Oh, it's very nice of you, but … you see, the thing is, your relationship's only just broken up. In a couple of days' time you could both be back together again.

Del No, no, I won't. It's finished! Kaput. There's no going back. I'm a free agent – I'll go where I want, and with whom I want.

Beverley Ok then. *(Writes on notepaper)*

Del Lovely jubbly! You know it makes sense. Well, I'll see you this evening then, about eight o'clock? I'll take you out for a slap up meal, you know, steak, onion rings …

Beverley Fine. *(Hands Del the note)* That's where I live. And that's the phone number in case anything goes wrong.

Del *(Slurring)* She y'sheeving.

Beverley What?

Del *(Gesturing to jaw)* Oh, sorry, der anshe'ic's beginnin' to work.

Beverley He'll be with you in a minute.

Del Oh right. I'll jusht, er, shit 'ere.

INT. NIGHT. THE TROTTERS' LOUNGE.

Somewhere in room we see Gerry the gerbil in his cage. There are four or five large cardboard boxes which are covered in Russian writing. A couple of the video cameras are on display. They are very large and very heavy. They are painted in khaki and olive green camouflage colours and have Russian writing on them. Rodney goes to pick one up and realises it is heavier than he imagined. He puts more effort into it and manages to lift the camera.

Albert enters from his bedroom.

Albert Are they the Russian cameras Del was telling me about?

Rodney No, this is a pair of Chelsea boots with an elasticated gusset! Of course it's a bloody Russian camera!

Del, dressed to kill, enters from bedrooms area and proceeds to splash himself with Brut whilst giving the mirror a severe hammering.

Del Alright then?

Albert How's your mouth, Del?

Del Oh, can't feel a thing. Brilliant dentist.

Rodney These camcorders are bigger than I imagined.

Del Yeah, they are a bit on the wide side, aren't they, eh?

Rodney You said they were hand-held?

Del Well, you're holding 'em in your hands, ain't you?

Rodney Only just! How are you supposed carry one of these round Eurodisney on your shoulder? You'll do your back in!

Del Well, that's good for you Rodney, good for your strength, you see, build your strength up won't it, eh? Save you a fortune on all them weights and rowing machines, and all that sort of stuff. I wonder what this writing says on the side there?

Rodney Reject, most probably!

Del These are not rejects. Rodney these are top of the range, these are. look at them, look how solid they are, no bits of plastic to break off. The cassette, look at that, is inside the camera, don't muck about with them soppy little things. No, this was designed for tank warfare, this you know. *(Looking through eyepiece)* Yes, look at that. I can just see 'em now … alright Number One, fire a shot across his bow.

Rodney places camera on table and removes the cassette. We see it is three inches longer than British cassettes. Rodney takes it to the VCR and tries to force it into slot.

Rodney Del …

Del Yeah?

Rodney They don't fit the machine!

Del Yeah, I know that. I know they are a different size. But it's no problem. 'Cos Ronnie Nelson, he's got a consignment of Russian VCRs coming over next Tuesday from Volgograd.

Rodney Oh right. So, if we actually do find a mercenary who wants to tape his next tank battle to show the wife and kids, he's gotta buy a Russian VCR off us an' all? I can't see 'em queuing for this one, Del!

Del Ninety five quid the set, can't be bad, can it, Eh? Think about it Rodney, you'll make your money on this and *more*! All you gotta do is fall on your arse and old Jeremy Beadle'll give you a grand!

Albert You going out, Del?

Del Yes! yes, I'm going out. I've got a date.

Rodney A date?

Del Uhuh.

Rodney What d'you mean you've got a date?

Del I've got a date. I met this woman down at the dentist's. I'm taking her out for dinner.

Rodney I don't believe I'm hearing this!

Albert Well you've surprised me, Del. Raquel and your baby are only just round the corner and you're going out with some young bird!

Del She is not a young bird! She happens to be a grandmother!

Rodney A grandmother? Well, perhaps she could bring her sister along for him! *(Indicates Albert)*

Del She's a very young grandmother! Sister

Fatal Extraction

along …! And don't look at me like that, Rodney! Raquel was the one who walked out on me! You don't know what it's like. I'm not an island, Rodney – a man gets lonely.

Albert But Raquel only left this morning!

Rodney Del, she's left you for longer periods when she's been out shopping.

Del Yeah, I know. But it's horrible here now.

Rodney You've got Albert.

Del That's what I mean.

Rodney Could you honestly *cheat* on Raquel?? Two-time the mother of your baby?

Del Oh bonnet de douche! I'm only taking her to a Berni Inn!

Rodney Yeah, but that can lead to other things, can't it?

Del Yeah, like next week I'll take her to a Spudulike.

Rodney You know what I mean! Did you know Raquel was crying this afternoon!

Del Crying?

Rodney Yeah. Sat on our sofa crying her eyes out – because of you!

Del Poor cow!

Rodney That's what I thought! Well, I'll see you later. Do enjoy your steak, Derek.

Del Rodney, Rodney, alright. Alright, alright, you've made your point. I was only tryin' to see, you know, if I could still pull. *(Picks up phone)* I'll call her and break off the date.

Rodney Good. And while you've got the phone in your hand give Raquel a call and ask her to come home.

Del No way, Pedro! If she wants to come back to this flat she's gotta call me.

Rodney Oh you kill me, Derek. I'll see you tomorrow.

Rodney exits to hall. Del punches numbers on phone.

Albert You're doing the right thing, Del … It was a bad move.

Del Yeah … *(We hear ringing tone)* Perhaps you're right. Pity, really, she fancied one of these cameras an all!

We hear phone being answered by Beverley's ansaphone.

Beverley *(Ansaphone)* Hi, this is Beverley. I can't come to the phone right now but if you'd like to leave a message after the tone I'll get back to you.

Del Ah yeah, hello Beverley. *(We hear beep tone)* This is Del Boy. Erm, the thing is, I can't make our date tonight. Erm, you know, I'm sorry … I'll give you a call another time. Alright? Yeah. Bonjour.

Albert I'll pour us a drink, Del.

Del Yeah, I wish I had a dog or a cat.

Albert You've got that gerbil.

Del Yeah, but I feel like kicking something up the arse.

INT. NIGHT. RODNEY AND CASSANDRA'S BEDROOM.

A few hours later.
Rodney and Cassandra are lying in bed.
The bedroom door is closed.

Cassandra He was doing what?

Rodney Ssshhh! Raquel's in there!

Cassandra *(Quieter)* He was going out with another woman.

Rodney He was threatening to. He was all dressed up, he looked like a heart-throb out of *Crossroads.*

Cassandra D'you think he's going through a mid-life crisis? You know, dressing up, trying to attract young girls?

Rodney No. If that was the case then Del's male menopause started when he was fourteen! Anyway, she's not a young girl, she's a grand-mother.

Cassandra A grandmother?

Rodney Sshh. He met her at the dentist's. I don't think much would have happened on their date anyway. they'd have most probably sat in a Berni Inn counting her teeth!

Cassandra Why doesn't he just phone Raquel? They're obviously both missing each other.

Rodney Well, it's his pride, isn't it? He's the man who must be seen to be the man. He's never had a very modern attitude towards women and relationships. When he was younger Del's idea of safe sex was not telling a girl where he lived. S'funny, but, in them days, Del used to be my hero.

Cassandra Del? You're joking.

Rodney No – I could tell you things about Del Boy that would amaze you.

Cassandra Go on then, amaze me.

Rodney Well … *(Thinking hard of something to surprise her)* There yeah there was the time he took his O Levels. I was only a little sprog, but I can still remember the night Del brought his results home. He had got eight As.

Cassandra Eight As? Del?

Rodney Yeah! A for English, A for maths, the list just went on.

Cassandra Wait a minute. they were someone else's results weren't they?

Rodney No, no. They were Del's results. I can remember Mum and Dad were all excited. We had a big family celebration, aunties, uncles, the

lot. Del was tossing up where to go, you know, Oxford or Cambridge. He phoned up both universities, made a few enquiries – what the pubs are like, that sort of thing.

Cassandra I can't imagine Del getting eight As.

Rodney No! He surprised everyone! Then a couple of days later we go a letter from the school. turned out the As all stood for Absent.

Cassandra *(Laughing)* He hadn't turned up for *any* of the exams?

Rodney No, not one. He'd been down the market flogging some hooky Tom Jones LPs. Mind you, you wouldn't have laughed if you'd been there at the time. My dad went potty! He was shouting at Del, calling him names. Del was ducking round the room tryin' to escape. Then it all turned violent – he'd been out drinking you see. He took his belt off, he started whacking him – punching him and everything! That's what he was like. Me mum was screaming, 'Don't hit him, don't hit him!' And I was crying.

Cassandra God, poor Rodney! Was he hurt?

Rodney Not too bad, he was in hospital for a couple of days. Me mum took me up to visit him.

Cassandra And what happened to your father?

Rodney I'm talking about my father!

Cassandra Oh, I thought you meant Del!

Rodney Oh no! He was alright. He was a dirty little fighter. He used to go in low and grabbing! I've seen him in so many fights over the years. I've heard sounds that only a white hunter could make sense of. I suppose that's why he was my hero. 'Cos from that day onwards my dad never whacked me again. He was too frightened of what Del Boy would do to him if he found out. So that's how my life went on. As long as Del was around no one could do me any harm. Of course, he made up for that in later life, but …

Rodney turns to Cassandra.
We see Cassandra is removing a thermometer from her mouth. She studies the temperature and nods to Rodney.

Rodney *(Almost fearfully)* Is it time again?

Cassandra Mmmh. How you feeling?

Rodney Well … You know, I'll give it a go.

She smiles and starts kissing Rodney's neck.

Rodney Oh, that's nice. Don't bite me, you know how easily I bruise.

They lay back on pillows kissing.
Cassandra closes her eyes in pleasure. She now opens her eyes and reacts. We cut to see Damien in his little pyjamas standing at the bottom of bed and looking at her.
The bedroom door is still closed.

Cassandra *(Nudges Rodney)* Rodney.

Rodney Mmmh?

Rodney sees Damien and reacts, pushing himself further back against pillow and uttering a small cry of alarm.

Rodney Aaaaagh!

Cassandra It's alright! He's just wandered in.

Rodney Wandered in? Cassandra, I *locked* the bedroom door!

Cassandra looks at Damien. We now hear a burst of the theme from The Omen over Cassandra's face. There is a knock on the bedroom door. The door opens as Raquel speaks.

Raquel *(OOV)* Alright if I come in?

Rodney *(Great relief)* I didn't lock the door!

Cassandra Rodney! *(Pushes him)*

Raquel *(To Damien)* There you are! Mummy's been looking everywhere for you. Sorry about this.

Cassandra S'alright.

Raquel I don't know. He sleeps all day and only comes alive at night.

Rodney and Cassandra look at each other.

Raquel *(To Damien)* Say, 'Na-nite' to Uncle Rodney and Auntie Cassandra.

Damien Night.

Cassandra Night, Damien.

Rodney Night.

Raquel and Damien exit. Rodney and Cassandra look at each other.

Cassandra What d'you think then?

Rodney Leave it to tomorrow, shall we?

Cassandra Yeah.

They switch lights off.

INT. NIGHT. THE NAG'S HEAD AND RODNEY AND CASSANDRA'S BEDROOM.

It's a packed pub. The usual crowd are there. Rodney, Albert and Trigger are sitting at a table. Rodney has a collection tin with the logo of a whale on it. As Rodney talks so Mike passes.

Rodney Look, it's for an endangered species! Do you realise what's happening to … *(Turns to Mike)* Listen, er, Del's been hitting the sauce a bit heavy lately. Just keep an eye on him, would you?

Mike Yes, I understand, leave it to me, Rodney.

Rodney Cheers. *(To Albert and Trigger)* Look, all I'm asking for is fifty pence.

Albert What happens when you save all these whales? They'll start breeding won't they?

Rodney Well, I wouldn't be surprised.

Trigger I don't know how anyone could fancy a whale.

Fatal Extraction

Albert No, I don't. Big ugly things ain't they?

Rodney No, look … you haven't got to breed with them, they can sort that sort of thing out for themselves.

Albert I know a lot more about the sea than you do Rodney.

Rodney Oh God, here we go …

Albert You'd be surprised how quickly these whales breed.

Rodney Three …

Albert And they're not always as gentle as some people imagine.

Rodney Two …

Albert You get quite a lot of 'em together and they can be quite dangerous.

Rodney One.

Albert During the war …

Rodney We have lift off.

Albert I was in a submarine in the Barents sea and we got attacked by a whale.

Rodney It was probably trying to protect its young Albert.

Albert No it wasn't. It fancied us!

Rodney A whale got the hots for your submarine?

Albert Yeah, it was horrible. We were shaking all over the place.

Trigger It's like your worst nightmare, innit Dave?

Rodney No. My worst nightmare is sitting in a pub having a conversation with you two!

Trigger Mmmh.

Albert It went on for about half an hour. The skipper told us to hang on for dear life and don't do anything to annoy it. He put the periscope up at one point.

Trigger Up where?

Albert He looked through the viewfinder and went white as a sheet. God knows what he saw but that man never ate halibut again.

Rodney So what d'you do when it was over? All lie back and had a cigarette?

Albert Don't take the mickey out of me, Rodney. Have you ever tried to lay an underwater telephone line during the mating season?

Rodney No, no, I haven't.

Albert Well my advice to you, son, is don't ever attempt it! *(Stands and moves to bar)*.

Trigger You wanna listen to him, Dave, he knows what he's talking about.

Del enters.

Del Alright, Rodders!

Rodney I never thought I'd hear myself say this, but, here comes a man with some intelligence.

'Ere listen, you gonna give a couple of bob for charity.

Del Yeah, you know me, I'd' do anything for a good cause. What's this?

Trigger He's tryin' to save whales.

Del Oh no no no no, that don't get nothing – not after the way they beat us at rugby last year.

Rodney Yeah, fair enough.

Del So how's Cassandra? She pregnant yet?

Rodney No. Ain't likely to be either with that little git standing at the bottom of the bed!

Del What little git's that?

Rodney Erm. Oh, it's erm, yeah it's Cassandra, she's got this big teddy bear, she's had it since a kid, you know, and it sort of sits at the bottom of the bed – and puts me off.

Del Silly mare! How would she like it if you had your Meccano set at the bottom of the bed, eh?

Rodney Yeah, alright. Well, don't go on about it! It's personal, it's summat that you …

Pause. Both stand to move away from Trigger.

Del See you later, Trig. *(On move)* Alright, how's Damien and Raquel?

Rodney Alright. She's taking Damien up London tomorrow to show him the sights. Apparently his Daddy's always been a bit too busy to do it himself.

Del Yes, he is too busy. He's too busy out there earning the poppy to pay for the grub and the underfloor heating! Still crying is she?

Rodney Yes! All through yesterday afternoon, and then all through tea time.

Del Is it getting on your nerves?

Rodney I'll tell you what's getting on my nerves, shall I? You are missing Raquel and Damien and Raquel and Damien are missing you, but nobody it seems – nobody, has the intelligence to sort out the situation.

Del All she's got to do is phone me.

Rodney But she doesn't know how you feel. She thinks you want a life of living it up with your mates and going to casinos. She doesn't realise it was just a phase while you were putting a deal together because you never told her.

Del Well I had to play it close to my chest didn't I? I didn't want word slipping out.

Rodney But she don't know that.

Del Yeah. What with that and my tooth …

Rodney Now you've had that out! Del, phone her and tell her.

Del What, that I've had my tooth out?

Rodney No! Phone her and tell her that you … Oh tell her what you bloody like, just phone her!

Del Alright, alright Rodney. I'll give her a bell.

Del moves across to public phone. He places money in machine and dials number.
Mike approaches and places a large scotch on telephone box.

Mike There you are, Del, a large scotch on the house.

Del Oh cheers.

Rodney Mike, what are you doing? Don't go giving him large scotches on the house!

Mike Oh Rodney, I'm sorry, I forgot. *(Calls)* Del, that's one eighty-five, son.

Del I didn't even ask for it!

We hear money drop into box as call is answered.

Del *(On phone)* Hello, hello, sweetheart, listen – don't say a word, just don't say anything. Just, just listen to me while I'm in this mood. right now I'm missing you darling and I want you to come home. Now I know I haven't been very fair to you, look, in the past but I can explain if you'll just give me the chance I still love you and that will never change. Things'll be different in the future. So what d'you say, eh? Oh, sorry Cassandra – yeah I wanna speak to Raquel. She's in the where? Oh alright, I'll hang on.

Boycie enters.

Boycie Del Boy?

Del Oh hello, Boycie.

They both see Beverley, stand from a table in background. She sees Del and smiles to him. Del returns a nervous grin. Beverley exits the pub.

Boycie Who was that woman?

Del Mmmm? What woman? I didn't see no woman.

Boycie That one that just smiled at you.

Del I didn't see anybody smile at me. No one's smiled at me all evening.

Boycie Where do I know her face from? *(Pause)* Oh yeah, I remember, Bronco, Marlene's brother. He was in hospital last year and we went up to see him. That's where I saw her.

Del Oh, that's cleared that mystery up then.

Boycie moves away.

Del Wait a minute. Bronco, wasn't he in a psychiatric hospital?

Boycie Yeah.

Del reacts.

Cut to Rodney and Cassandra's bedroom: Cassandra hands phone to Raquel. We intercut between Del and Raquel.

Raquel *(On phone)* Thanks. Hello? Hello? Hello?

Del *(On phone)* Hello? Hello, Raquel. *(Sits)* How are you?

Raquel *(On phone)* Fine. You?

Del *(On phone)* Yeah, lovely … I'm missing you, darling.

Raquel *(On phone)* I'm missing you as well, you rotten sod!

Del *(On phone)* Come on then, why don't you come home, eh?

Raquel *(On phone)* It's not as simple as that!

Del Sweetheart. Don't take too much notice of me in the last month. It's been a one-off, that's all.

Raquel *(On phone)* What about the month before that?

Del *(On phone)* Yeah, well that was a one-off an' all.

Raquel *(On phone)* Well, I didn't like your attitude. You were willing to gamble with our housekeeping money, with our future in some grotty little South London casino!

Del *(On phone)* Look sweetheart, that's all in the past I tell you. No more casinos, no pubs.

Trigger *(Calls)* Same again, Del?

Del Yeah, alright Trig, thanks. Yeah, *(Now for Raquel's sake)* just a, you know, a lemonade and a lime.

We see Raquel smiling at this.

Raquel *(On phone)* Listen to me, stupid. I don't mind you going down the Nag's Head so long as it's not *every* night! And when you do go down there I wouldn't mind going as well!

Del *(On phone)* Yeah, well, that's my thoughts entirely sweetheart! Exactly. We'll just go down, go down at weekends, you know, to be sociable. Listen, I'll tell you what sweetheart, if you're gonna go out shopping you get me a pair of those chequered slippers and a hundredweight of 'obnobs! I'm a changed man. I am, I'll even take little Damien out, you know, no excuses! So what do you reckon, sweetheart, can I come and pick you up?

Raquel *(On phone)* Not right now. Damien's fast asleep.

Del *(On phone)* Alright, what about first thing in the morning?

Raquel *(On phone)* I promised to take him up London, Madame Tussauds. Unless you'd like to come with us.

Del *(On phone)* Oh no, no I can't darling, I'm going to pick up all them Russian VCRs. Erm, look. I'll pick you up tomorrow night, yeah?

Raquel *(On phone)* Alright then.

Del *(On phone)* Alright. Raquel say the magic words.

Del *(On phone)* Go on, go on Raquel, say the magic words.

Raquel *(On phone)* Tch! I love you, Trotter.

Fatal Extraction

Del *(The winning goal)* Yes! Alright, darling, I'll pick you up tomorrow, alright? Ta ta. *(To himself)* That is it, Del Boy, you're a changed man – this is the first day of the rest of your life. *(Calls)* Michael. A bottle of your finest champagne, please. thank you.

EXT. NIGHT. THE COUNCIL ESTATE.

We are in high position (As if looking down from the rooftop of one of the tower blocks). Below us is the pedestrian concourse between other tower blocks. It's 2 am and all is in darkness save for a couple of street lamps. The world is silent, not even a dog barks in this quiet slumberworld.

We now see Del moving unsteadily through the concourse. He knocks a dustbin over and its rattle echoes through the night air. In the distance a dog barks. We cut to: ground level where we find Del shooshing the rattling dustbin lid. Del is drunk but not paralytic. It is a mix of champagne and euphoria. He feels happy and at one with his world.

Del *(To the rattling dustbin lid)* Sssshhh! Ssssshhh! Sssshhh! Ssssshhh!

Del smiles to the world. He is happy and loved.

Del *(Sings, slowly getting louder)* 'One voice, singing in the darkness'

We hear the dog start barking.

Del 'All it takes is one voice, singing so they hear what's on your mind, *(We see a light come on in one of the flats)* And when you look around you'll find there's more than one voice, *(We see another two lights switch on in different flats)* singing in the darkness. Joining with your one voice, *(Now another dog joins in the barking)* Each and every note another octave.'

Arthur What's going on down there?

Del Hands are joined and fears unlocked, if only one voice …

A man (Arthur) appears on one of the balconies. He is in pyjamas and dressing gown.

Del *(Sings)* would start on its own. We need just one voice

We now see seven or eight flats are lit. A woman (Vi), also in night attire, appears on balcony in opposite block. A baby starts crying.

Vi What's all the racket?

Del 'Facing the unknown – and then that one voice would never be alone.'

Arthur It's Trotter! He's drunk again!

Vi Why don't you go off home to bed, Derek?

INT. NIGHT. THE TROTTERS FLAT. ALBERT'S BEDROOM.

Albert is woken up by Del's singing. He turns on his bedside lamp and moves towards window. Cut to

EXT. NIGHT. THE COUNCIL ESTATE.

Now half the lights in the immediate vicinity are on. More people are out on balconies shouting at Del and each other. A man (Mick) in his mid-forties appears on a balcony wearing just a vest and underpants. He has obviously been drinking.

Mick *(Begins singing along with Del)* 'Pack up all your cares and woes, Here I go, singing low, Bye-bye blackbird.'

Del 'It takes that one voice, Singing in the darkness, All it takes it one voice, Shout it out and let it ring, Just one voice, It takes that one voice, And every never be alone, It takes one voice, just one voice…'

Arthur *(Calls across to Mick)* Why don't you shut up, Mick! You're making him worse!

Mick You want me to shut up? Why don't you make me shut up?

Arthur Right, I'll shut that big mouth of yours! Downstairs!

Mick It's a fight you want? Right, I'm in for some of that! *(Mick exits into flat)*

Vi Oh no, that's all we need.

Del One voice …

We see Albert appear on the Trotters' balcony.

Albert *(Calls)* Del Boy! Del! Come in here!

We now see a 30-year old rastafarian (Texo) appear on his balcony. He looks down to see what all the fuss is about. He now smiles widely and chuckles to himself.

INT. NIGHT. RODNEY AND CASSANDRA'S BEDROOM.

Darkness. All is quiet. Rodney and Cassandra sound asleep. Now the bedside phone rings.

Cassandra *(Mumbles sleepily)* Oh no!

Without opening his eyes or moving his head from the pillow, Rodney reaches out and fumbles for receiver.

Rodney *(On phone. Clinically asleep)* Hello? Yeah … Alright. Bye bye.

He replaces receiver.

Pause. Rodney and Cassandra continue sleeping peacefully. Now one of Rodney's eyes opens slightly as the message begins to register. Now both eyes.

Rodney Del Boy's singing in the precinct!
Cassandra What?
Rodney Del's singing in the precinct.
Cassandra I can't hear anything.
Rodney No. that was Albert on the phone.
Del's singing on the estate. It's quarter past two
in the morning and Del's singing.
Cassandra Why?
Rodney *(Punching numbers on phone)* I don't
know!
Cassandra Has he woken anyone up?
Rodney Yeah, you and me for a start! *(On
phone)* Albert. Why is Del singing ? Yeah …
Mmmmm. Right … *(To Cassandra)* No, he don't
know either. *(On phone)* What d'you mean,
come round? What d'you want me to do –
harmonise with him? Albert, there's not a song
in the world Del knows all the words to, so he'll
be finished in a minute, won't he? No, I am not
coming round! I'll see you tomorrow. *(Replaces
receiver and lays back on bed)* I don't believe it!
(Pause) I'd better go round and see what's
happening!

EXT. NIGHT. THE COUNCIL ESTATE.

*Now virtually all the lights are on. There is
mayhem. Mick and Arthur, who have both
donned trousers, are squaring up to each
other in the precinct. Del is in background still
singing. Babies are crying, dogs barking.*

Del 'Ba da da da da … Just once voice singing
in the darkness, all it takes is one voice, Shout it
out and let it ring, Just one voice, it takes that
one voice, and everyone will sing.'
*We hear the distant sound of police sirens.
Mix to:*

INT. NIGHT. TROTTERS' LOUNGE.

*An hour later. Albert enters from kitchen
carrying two mugs of coffee. Rodney is
looking from the window and down at the
riot which is now taking place outside.
Reflection of flames flit across the window
and Rodney's face. We can hear the sound of
breaking glass, police sirens, shouting crowds,
burglar alarms and minor explosions.
Rodney looks up as we hear the heavy
thudding sound of helicopter rotor blades
passing overhead. We see the beam of its
searchlight pass across the window.
He looks back to the precinct.*
Albert What's happening now, Rodney?
Rodney What's happening? They're rioting
again, that's what's happening! Why don't you

go and look for yourself?
Albert You're joking! I might get a brick come
through the window!
Rodney We're on the twelfth bloody floor,
Albert. What d'you think they've done, invited
Geoff Capes along?
Albert Mrs Murphy said they've brought the
horses out.
Rodney Yeah. The police have gone to get
theirs now.
*Del enters from bedrooms area wearing his
silk dressing gown.*
Del Oi, oi, oi oi oi, can't you turn that telly
down – I'm in here trying to get some sleep ain't
I, eh?
Rodney I don't believe it! Eh! Would you go
and look out that window and see what's
happening!
Del Why, what's the matter now?
Rodney It's a full-scale inner-city riot going on
downstairs! They're all there, Del Boy. The SPG,
snatch squads, looters, people who wanna get
on telly and, unless I'm very much mistaken, Kate
Adie!
Del Oh, oh, well, what started them all off
again then?
Rodney You!
Del Me? what have I done? *(Sits)*
Albert You were singing, Del.
Del Singing? Me!
Albert Now don't try an' deny it, son, 'cos I
heard you.
Del Singing? Oh, yeah, that's … no, wait a
minute, I remember now, that's right. I was
celebrating, Rodney. Raquel and Damien are
coming home.
Rodney Oh, that's a good reason for a civil war,
innit?
Del I was feeling a bit euphoric. *(Takes Albert's
sandwich)* What's more natural than to give vent
to your joy with a little song, eh?
Albert It was, 'One Voice Singing In The
Darkness'.
Rodney Yeah. Hark at them now, there's
bloody thousands of 'em!
Del Alright, OK! *(To Rodney)* I'm sorry.
Rodney Oh well, that's alright then, innit,
Albert?
Del Alright, what do you want me to do? Tell
me what I should do and I'll do it.
Rodney Oh well, why don't you just stand out
on the balcony and shout 'Stop it!'?
Del Oh, don't be ridiculous, they won't take no
notice of that will they? *(Up)* I tell you what I'm
gonna do. I'm gonna get dressed and I'm gonna

Fatal Extraction

go down there.

Rodney Eh? 'Ere listen, what you gonna do? You gonna try an' talk some sense to 'em?

Del No, I'm gonna flog 'em some of this ski gear.

Del exits to bedroom area.

EXT. DAY. THE MARKET.

The following day. The back doors of the three wheel van are open. Rodney is in back of a larger van which has some insignia that tells us this is: 'Nelson's TV and Video'. Rodney is handing Del flat packed cardboard boxes with Russian writing on them. These are the VCRs Del spoke about. Del is packing them into the back of the three wheeler.

Del There we are. Lovely jubbly. Come on then, off we go.

Rodney Aren't you gonna check 'em?

Del Mmmm? I don't have to – I know what's in them. they're Russian video recorders.

Rodney No, I mean, aren't you gonna check they're OK?

Del Yeah, I've had a look at one. They've got buttons and lights, they seem kosher to me. Go on, get it in there.

Del looks up and reacts. We see Beverley passing through the crowd. She sees Del and smiles. This time Del doesn't return the smile. He stares back, frightened.
Del turns to Rodney.

Del Rodney! come here quick, Rodney. Look at that woman, that woman.

Rodney Who?

Del There!

We see Beverley is no longer there.

Rodney What's the matter with you?

Del Don't matter, Rodney, forget it! Come on, hurry up, Rodney. Let's get all this stuff down to the garage, then I've gotta pick up Raquel and Damien from your place.

Del now scans the area searching for Beverley.

Rodney You alright?

Del Yes! yes. Come on, just …

EXT. DAY. LONDON ROADS (INT. CAPRI).

We see the green Capri pass us, Del driving, Raquel and Damien in back seat and lots of baby paraphernalia piled into the passenger seat.

Raquel I saw the riot on TV this morning. What started it this time?

Del I dunno. Seems to be the slightest little thing starts it off these days. Still, it was all nice and quiet when I left this evening.

EXT. DAY. THE COUNCIL ESTATE AND INT. CAPRI.

We see the riot has started again. We are at a stand off stage. The police and the rioters are about thirty yards apart. (Mike, Arthur and Vi are among rioters) The police are banging their riot shields with truncheons in a threatening rhythm. The rioters are jeering and egging the police to come forward. A few sticks are being thrown towards the police. In background a few fires can be seen burning. We see the Capri pull up on the periphery of the riot area. Del and Raquel stare horrified at the scene in front of them.

Raquel I thought you said it had all quietened down! We'll have to turn round and go back to Rodney and Cassandra's.

Del But we live here!

Raquel How the hell are we gonna get through that lot in one piece?

Del Well, I'm not turning round.

Del starts blasting on the car horn. We see the officer in charge of the riot squad. He hears the car horn and looks in direction of the little Capri. We see a couple of the leaders of rioters do likewise.

Police officer *(To his men)* Hold it, hold it, hold it. It's Del Boy.

Arthur *(To others)* It's Del Boy!

The cry goes up from another couple of the rioters as they appeal for a moment's truce. Now the thumping of shields stops. The jeering and throwing of stones, etc, stops.

Police officer *(Gestures to Del)* Come through, Del.

The Capri now drives slowly down the avenue between the opposing forces, bumping over the rock strewn road. Raquel stares disbelievingly at this miracle. The Capri pulls to a halt. Del calls out to one of the rioters, a young black guy.

Del Oi, Texo! I've got that VCR that goes with your camera.

Texo Nice one, Del. Be round tomorrow.

Del winds down passenger window. Calls to a young PC.

Del Oi, Alex! Tell your sister I've got her video recorder.

PC Righto, Del, I'll tell her Tuesday when I go round for tea.

Del Lovely jubbly.

The Capri drives on until it is clear of the

fighting. All remains calm still. Del now gives a toot on the horn (like the kick-off whistle). The police immediately start thumping their shields, the rioters start jeering and throwing things – the riot is on again.

INT. DAY. THE LIFT FOYER/12TH FLOOR, NELSON MANDELA HOUSE.

The following day. Del, in working clothes, exits the lift. Standing by slatted-window we see a middle-aged Asian man. He has one of Del's Russian cameras and is trying to film the estate. The camera obviously isn't working and he thumps it to try and make the motor work. Del quietly unlocks door to his flat and sneaks in before the man can see him.

INT. DAY. THE TROTTERS' FLAT. STUDIO.

Del closes front door and breathes a sigh of relief. Now he hears two female voices from the living room. He slowly moves towards the living room door, fear growing inside. Here we find Raquel chatting away to Beverley. Del enters and tries desperately to hide his shock.

Raquel Oh, Del, this is Beverley. Beverley, this is my ... well, this is Del.

Beverley Hi.

Del Er, wotchyer.

Raquel Beverley's interested in Damien's high-chair.

Del How'd she find out about that?

Beverley I saw an ad in the newsagents' window – I was out the other night on my own, you know, nothing to do ...

Del Oh, yeah.

Beverley (To Del) It's for my daughter's baby.

Raquel His name's Damien as well.

Del Oh, cushty!

Raquel Could you deliver it later today?

Del Yeah, I suppose so, yeah.

Raquel Del. Beverley might not be able to afford the full amount. D'you think we could come to some arrangement with her?

Del Yeah, yeah, well yeah. I'll leave that up to you, sweetheart. Look I've just remembered, I've gotta go out and meet someone. Yeah.

Beverley Nice meeting you.

Del Yeah, bye.

Del exits to hall.

Raquel He's not usually like that. Must be pressure of business.

Beverley Mmmh!

INT. DAY. THE NAG'S HEAD.

Rodney is seated at table eating lunch.

Del joins him.

Del Rodney. Rodney, Rodders. I've got a problem. I've got a big problem. Do you know that woman we saw in the market the other day?

Rodney What, the one who wasn't there?

Del Yes, that one! She's only haunting me, Rodney, she's only bloody haunting me!

Rodney Haunting? What d'you mean, haunting you?

Del She's haunting me. She ... She's the one I made the date with and then gave her the elbow! And, ever since then, she's everywhere that I look! I mean the other night she was here in the pub and then this morning I was driving down the road and she was standing there by a bus stop, and then she was in the market the other day – you saw her!

Rodney No, I didn't.

Del Yeah, see what I mean? And today, to top it all, today I went home and she's in *my* flat!

Rodney What was she doing in your flat?

Del Oh she *said* that she'd come to buy Damien's high-chair! If she thinks I'm gonna believe that she's got another thing coming!

Rodney How'd she know it was for sale?

Del She *said* she saw the ad that I placed in the local newsagents!

Rodney Oh, that is a bit far fetched, innit?

Del Exactly!

Rodney Oh, you crack me up, you do! Let's have a look at the facts, shall we? So she was in this pub! Now maybe, just maybe she was having a *drink*! And then you saw her in the market lunchtime – do you reckon she might have been shopping?

Del Bit of a coincidence, though that, innit?

Rodney And then you saw her waiting at a bus stop! Now this is just a hunch, Del – but do you reckon there is an outside chance that she might have been waiting for a bus?

Del Well, I don't know, do I! I'll tell you what I *do* know, though. She's an ex-psychiatric patient!

Rodney So?

Del So! She is a jealous woman Rodney! A woman scorned! Now, jealous women are no problem to me normally, you know, I mean I can handle all that, but this one is a jealous woman who's an olive short of a pizza! And she knows where we live!! We could all wake up one morning and find we was killed while we was asleep!

Rodney You're letting your imagination run away with you. Does she seem odd in any way?

Fatal Extraction

Del I don't know! You can judge for yourself, you've gotta deliver the high-chair (*Throws scrap of paper with address on table.*)

Rodney Why have I got to go?

Del Because I've got a wife and kid.

Rodney Yeah, but I've got a wife and a … thermometer.

INT. DAY. THE TROTTERS' LOUNGE.

One hour later. Nobody is in lounge at this moment. Del (same clothes as previous scene) enters from hall/front door.

Del (*Calls*) Raquel! Raquel! Where are … Raquel!

There is no reply. Now Del senses something is wrong. He scans the room trying to find a clue to his intuitive reaction. Now he finds Gerry the gerbil's cage. The door to cage is open and it is empty. Something draws his attention towards the kitchen. Cut to kitchen: Del enters. On stove we see a large aluminium cooking pot which is bubbling and steaming.
Del, terrified of what he might find, approaches the pot. He removes the lid and peers in. He reels back in horror.

Del Oh no, oh my God!

Raquel rushes into kitchen.

Raquel What's happened?

Del Look!

He takes a pair of wooden tongs and pulls a pair of white long-johns from pot.

Raquel What's wrong, Del?

Del Albert's boiling his pants again! Where's the gerbil?

Raquel In Damien's room, he's playing with it. Del, what is wrong with you?

Del I've got to sort this all out. I've got to sort it all out. I've gotta go out, darling. I've gotta meet someone.

Del exits.

EXT. DAY. LONDON STREET/DENTAL SURGERY.

Fifteen minutes later.
The Capri screeches to a halt outside the surgery. Del alights and rushes into the surgery.

INT. DAY. DENTIST'S WAITING ROOM.

Three or four patients are waiting. Beverley is behind counter. Del rushes in.

Del (*To Bev*) Right, now you listen to what I've got to say! You leave me and my family alone! You don't frighten me. I'm not scared of you.

The deep-toned buzzer goes.

Beverley (*To one of the patients*) Mr James.

Mr James enters surgery as Trigger exits.

Beverley (*To Del*) What's wrong with you, you moron?

Trigger Oh, just a couple of fillings. Alright, Del?

Del Yeah, yeah. See you later, Trig.

Trigger exits.

Del You were following me!

Beverley *I've* been following *you*?

Del Yes.

Beverley I thought it was the other way round! Everywhere I go I see you! I go in a pub with my daughter and son-in-law and you're there. I'm waiting for a bus and *you* drive by! I go and do a bit of lunchtime shopping in the market and surprise, surprise, there you are again! I even went to buy a second-hand high-chair and you walked in!

Del I live there!

Beverley Ok, I'll let you off that one!

Del Right.

Beverley Listen, I think, *Mr Trotter*, our wires have become crossed somewhere along the line.

Del But *you* were in a psychiatric hospital!

Beverley Yes.

Del Oh ho ho, don't try an' deny it! A friend of mine was visiting a relative there and he *saw* you!

Beverley Yes. I worked there as a receptionist.

Del Sorry?

Beverley I'm a medical receptionist! (*Gestures to counter and appointments books*) It's what I do, see?

Del So you, you weren't following me?

Beverley Good God! D'you think I'm hard up? Now understand this, Mr Trotter. If you follow me or come to my place of work and pester me again, I'm going to court and take out an injunction against you.

Del Don't you worry, darling, this is the last we'll hear of each other.

Beverley Good! Oh and by the way, I suppose I should have expected as much, but that high-chair's got a screw loose.

Del Well, tighten it!

Del exits.

INT. NIGHT. TROTTERS' LOUNGE. STUDIO.

This is Christmas day. All the family are there.

Del (*Pours a drink*) There we are sweetheart, go on, get that down you.

Rodney That was a lovely dinner, Raquel.

Raquel Thanks. Another drink, Cassandra?

Cassandra Better not, I'm doing the driving.
Del No, no, no, no, come on, you can stay over tonight. We've got plenty of room, we can all mix in, can't we?
Cassandra *(To Rodney)* Shall we?
Rodney Yeah, let's enjoy ourselves, eh?
Del Yes, that's it, you know it makes sense! Oh darling, shall I put your *Tubular Bells* on?
Raquel No, no! Er, not yet, Del.
Del Alright. She loves that *Tubular Bells. (Picks Damien up)* Hey, come on champ. It's bedtime for you. Come along, that's it. Let's go to bed, that's it, good boy, off we go.
Everyone Good night.
Del Say goodnight.
Damien Na-night.
Del Look, isn't he lovely? He's only ten. Here we go. Which is your room then?
Del and Damien exit to bedrooms area.
Cassandra So what d'you get Del for Christmas?
Raquel I got him one of those answering machines he's always on about.
Albert That'll save me getting any more rollickings for forgetting messages.
Rodney Yeah. You know, this is quite a good one. How much did this cost you? *(Plugs phone into wall)*
Raquel Sssh. It didn't actually cost anything. I swapped it for Damien's high-chair.
Rodney Yeah, well you know I reckon you got a good deal there. Does it work?
We hear a beep from machine.
Now we hear Del's voice.
Del *(On machine)* Oh hello, Beverley, this is Del Boy. Erm listen, I'm sorry, I've got to cancel our date tonight. Erm, yeah, I'll, er, I'll give you a call.

Alright? Bonjour.
The line goes dead. We see Raquel's reaction and Rodney's, Cassandra's and Albert's. Del enters from bedrooms area with one of his Russian cameras on his shoulders filming the family.
Del *(Singing)* Watch out, Trotter's about. Hey, watch out, Trotter's about! Hey hey hey hey watch out now Trotter's about . Hey, come on, what's the matter with you, eh? Eh? Well come on, smile!
V/O continues over cut to:

EXT. NIGHT. TROTTERS' FLAT.
Crane down from ext. balcony to see new tree and children looking up at it.
Del What's wrong, sweetheart?
Raquel Don't touch me, Trotter! Don't come near me, don't even look at me!
We hear door slam.
Del What have you said to her, Rodney?
Rodney Me? *I* haven't said anything!
Cassandra Don't try and blame Rodney, it's nothing to do with him!
Albert Don't look at me either, son. I'm keeping out of this.
Del Look, ah, there you are, Raquel. You feeling better now, darling?
We hear a china ornament smash against wall.
Del Eh? Raquel, that could have hit me!
Raquel It was meant to hit you!
Del Will someone tell me what have I done! What have I done?
The singing ('Silent Night') now takes over from the row.

Fatal Extraction

Heroes and Villains

EXT. NIGHT. STREET. LONDON – THE NIGHTMARE.

It is a disturbing and desolate scene of poverty, neglect and suffering. Toxic steam from the poisoned sewers wafts up from the drains. Litter blows down the darkened street and past starving people who lay on the pavements wrapped in rags. A digital wall-clock juts out above a darkened jewellers shop. It tells us this is: '2nd November. 2026'.

A tall, white-haired, man in his mid-sixties walks along the pavement with the help of a stick. He has his back to camera. He is smartly dressed but in a futuristic fashion. The starving throng hold its hands out to him. Without breaking step he distributes a few coins amongst them. We now see the man from the front and realise it is Rodney but now aged 64.

He pauses and looks around at his world. On a corner we see a couple of futuristic policemen who wear black SWAT type uniforms and are armed with metal batons, sub-machine guns and military style metal helmets upon which is printed 'state police'.

A large advertising billboard depicts a futuristic concorde type jumbo-jet with a tail logo which reads; 'Trotter Air.' The legend beneath informs us: 'Trotter Air gets you there.'

Another advertising sign shows a smiling and happy thirteen year old girl seated at a table upon which is what appears to be a plate of golden fish fingers. The teenager is holding a fork upon which is what seems to be half a fish finger. But instead of the inside of the finger being white and fresh it is a brown, gooey substance. The legend tells us this is: 'Trotter's meat fingers – guaranteed to contain no natural ingredients'.

Another advertising sign depicts two young lovers looking romantically into each other's eyes. To one side of their faces is a cardboard packet (like a pack of Durex.) The legend tells us this is: 'Trotterex. Family Planning – Go Equipped'.

Old Rodney now looks up to the sky. From his POV we see the top of a massive skyscraper. A brilliantly lit sign on top of building tells us this is: 'Trotter Tower'. The skyscraper is very futuristic and is covered in gold and silver cladding which sparkles in the moonlight. We pan down the skyscraper to the large main doors at ground level. A sign above main doors reads: 'Trotters Independent Traders Company (TITco Global PLC)'.

Rodney studies the signs and adverts in that manner of his which suggests that everything in life still stuns him.
Old Rodney enters the building.

INT. NIGHT. TOP FLOOR OFFICE SUITE.

We are in a futuristic foyer with various office doors leading off. The 'TITco' logo is everywhere. On the wall we find two large portraits in gold frames.

The first portrait is of Damien, now aged 35. A gold nameplate in frame reads: 'Sir Damien Trotter'.

The second portrait is of Del, now aged 78. A gold nameplate in frame reads: 'Lord Trotter of Peckham'.

From the floor to ceiling windows we have a panoramic view of London. Outside we see a helicopter-type machine approaching the tower before drifting up and out of sight as it prepares to land on roof. It has no rotor blades and makes the sound of a jet. On its side is the 'TITco' logo.

A puff of smoke drifts up and across lens. We pull back to find Del, now aged 78, and still smoking a big cigar. Del is dressed in the finest of futuristic clothes.

Del Our jetcopter arrived, Raquel. I'll ring for the maid.

Del presses a wall button. We find Raquel, now aged 67 and also draped in the finest of clothes, seated in a chair and sipping champagne.

Raquel I'll say bye-bye to Damien first, darling. How long's he going to be in there?.

Del You can't rush him, sweetheart, he's putting a very important deal together. He's talking to President Reeves in Washington.

Raquel (*Impressed*) President Reeves! Really?

The lift door opens and Rodney alights.

Del There you are Rodney, where you been? Damien phoned you over an hour ago.

Rodney I know, but the state transportation

workers have gone on strike.

Raquel On strike? I thought Damien had made strikes illegal.

Rodney Yes, the police were shooting them as I left. Damien said he wanted to see me urgently.

Del Come on. I'll take you through.

Del leads Rodney towards the office door. Raquel follows.

INT. NIGHT. ULTRA-FUTURISTIC OFFICE.

As Lord Derek, Lady Raquel and Rodney enter office we find Damien, now 35, black hair, piercing brown eyes and dressed in the finest clothes, is talking on a futuristic phone.

Damien *(On phone)* Listen to me, Keanu. You just sit there in the White House all day twiddling your thumbs and just playing at leadership! People are beginning to see through you. I mean, you still allow that old-fashioned system to operate – what was it called … democracy! I got rid of it in Europe years ago.

See Rodney's reaction. Del and Raquel are beaming proudly.

Del What a boy eh? What a boy.

Damien What's wrong with going to war with China? War is good! Well, of course, millions will be killed. A war without death is like a salad without watercress! You worry too much … I've got a busy night so make the declaration tomorrow.

Slams phone down.

Sound: From outside we hear the sound of a short burst of machine gun fire.

Damien looks from his window and down into the street below.

Damien *(Cont)* Last time she jumps a red light.

Damien now becomes aware of Rodney's presence. He smiles at Rodney and stares with deep piercing eyes.

Uncle Rodney.

We hear a brief two-bar piece of the Damien theme.

Rodney Damien.

Damien *(Hands Rodney a piece of paper)* Take this round to the Chinese embassy. It's your visa application. I want you in Beijing for the war – you report back to me.

Rodney War! I don't wanna go to war!

Raquel What's wrong with you, Rodney?!

Rodney I don't wanna go to war!

Del Rodney, it's for the company.

Damien War is good!

Del You know it makes sense.

Rodney It doesn't make sense!

Raquel What would your Uncle Albert say?

Rodney *(Becoming increasingly confused)* I don't know!

Del Let's find out.

Del presses a button. A large wall panel slides away to reveal a large glass case. Inside the case is a 100 year old Albert. His beard is longer than ever and he is connected to wires and cables and intravenous tubes. He doesn't move, he just stares ahead blankly. Rodney stares at this vision in horror. Without Albert's lips moving we hear a loop–tape begin.

Albert *(On tape)* During the war – During the war – During the war…

The "during the war" continues throughout. Cassandra, now aged 55 enters dressed in a maid's costume.

Cassandra *(To Del)* You rang, your Lordship?

Del Yes, fetch our coats, dear, we're going out.

Rodney *(Horrified)* Cassandra! What are you doing here?

Cassandra Damien took over my bank and fired me. I'm the maid.

Del *(Shrugs)* It's a job, Rodney.

Rodney *(Now becoming emotionally excited)* No, this isn't fair!

Del *(Trying to calm him)* Rodney!

Rodney It's not right, you shouldn't be doing this!

Del Rodney!

Rodney Everything was nice and now you've messed it all up!

Del Rodney!

Del and Rodney's voices begin to echo. We see Del's face as the picture slowly goes out of focus and into mist.

Rodney *(Echo)* I wanna go back to how it used to be!

Del *(Echo)* Rodney … Rodney!

Now slowly we come back to today and Del's face. He is wearing his market cap and market clothes and is talking straight into camera.

Rodney! Rodney! Rodney!

We now dissolve through to:

INT. DAY. THE TROTTERS' FLAT.

Rodney is seated on one of the latest 'armchairs' and is slowly coming out of his nightmare.

Del Rodney! Rodney, Rodney! Wake up you dipstick!

Rodney *(Half-asleep)* Why couldn't you have left things alone Del?

Looks around room.

Oh God, it was a dream.

Heroes and Villains

Del What's the matter with you? You been on that Rastafarian Old Holborn again?

Rodney No, no, I just drifted off there for a while. Oh man, I had the wildest dream!

Del What was it all about? Aah! Was it all sunny and little birdies going tweet tweet tweet?

Rodney Alright, sorry! So what's happening?

Del *(As he opens and reads an official-looking letter)* What's happening? I'll tell you what's happening. Rodders, we have bought a hundred and twenty five Latvian radio alarm clocks that go off anytime they bloody want. We've got two hundred aerodynamic cycling helmets that turn out to be horse-riding crash helmets that some git sprayed red. We've got a box of baseball caps that even E17 fans won't buy, there's a gang of hoodlums mugging anyone who dares to put their head outside the front door … *(Waves letter)* And the council have turned down my application for a home-improvement grant! Other than that – all is well.

Del moves to door to bedrooms area.

Rodney *(Closes his eyes in luxurious security)* Thank God! Everything's normal.

Del *(Calls)* Raquel, there's a letter here for you. What's all this falling akip at ten to eight in the morning? Don't you sleep at home?

Rodney You know my situation!

Checks no-one else in the flat can hear. It's Cassandra and this baby thing, innit? The hospital's worked out another schedule for us. I'm at it like a rattlesnake! It's horrible.

Del But that was always your ambition!

Rodney Yes, but some people dream of singing *La Traviata* at the Royal Opera House, but they don't wanna sing it three bloody times a night.

Del Make your throat sore, wouldn't it?

Rodney Yes. They've put her on a special diet an all that. The gynaecologist reckons it's just a matter of time – but Cass keeps getting broody … I got her a rabbit.

Del A rabbit … What, that's in her diet?

Rodney No, a pet rabbit! Something she can make a fuss over. I know it was a stupid idea. I wish I hadn't bothered now …

Del So the hospital's done all the tests and everything?

Rodney Yes. Look, this is personal. I don't want this being broadcast!

Del Who's gonna listen? You've had her tubes looked at?

Rodney Yes! God! Everything's fine but we just can't crack the case …Every day I'm taking specimens to the clinic and God knows what else. It's all to do with ovums and … things. The hospital keep showing me films of inside the human body. Cor, it don't half put you off, Del.

Del I can imagine. Gimme *Debbie Does Dallas* any day. Right, we'll have a spot of breakfast and then get down the market. You wanna boiled egg?

Del exits to kitchen. Rodney follows.

Rodney *(Sharply)* No!

Del Alright, alright.

Rodney Del, d'you mind if I ask a favour? Could I have this afternoon off?

Del Why? She ain't booked you in for another seeing to, has she?

Rodney No! it's erm … It's me birthday today.

Del Is it your birthday? Blimey, it's your birthday! I completely forgot! Well, in that case Rodney, the answer's no. D'you think Richard Branson would have the afternoon off?

Rodney Doubt it, he doesn't even know it's my birthday.

Del I mean, would he have the afternoon off for his own birthday? Of course he wouldn't. He's out there in the financial fast lane – no time for jollying it up 'cos it's his birthday.

Rodney *(Disappointed)* Alright then.

Del *(Lets him suffer – now a big grin)* Course you can have this afternoon off. You can go home now if you want.

Rodney No, this afternoon'll do. Cass has got a half day and we're gonna go shopping.

Del hands Rodney three birthday cards.

I didn't forget, did I? There's your cards, birthday boy.

Rodney Cheers, Del.

Rodney looks at one card

Del That's from Damien.

Rodney's hands shake.

Rodney Oh … Bless him.

Del hands Rodney a small wrapped present.

Del And that's from me and Raquel.

Rodney unwraps the present which reveals a small jewellery box. He opens box and produces a chunky, gold identity bracelet. He stares at it. It is the worst present he could imagine.

Del It's a chunky, gold identity bracelet.

Rodney Yeah, I can see that.

Del It's just like mine Rodney, look at that – 24 carat that is Rodney, no old rubbish. See, it's got your name on it.

Rodney studies the engraving.

Rodney 'Rooney'?

Del No, that's Rodney.

Rodney But it says 'Rooney'. There's an 'O' where the 'D' should be.

Del No, that is a D. It's that copperplate lettering. So, what do you think?

Rodney You shouldn't have.

Rodney goes to put the bracelet in his pocket

Well, put it on then.

Rodney Eh? Right. Thanks Del.

Rodney slips bracelet on.

Del Oi! Don't you go getting all emotional on me.

Rodney Alright then.

Del exits to kitchen. Raquel, in dressing gown, enters from bedrooms area.

Raquel Morning, Rodney.

Rodney Hiya, Raquel.

Raquel *(Points to bracelet)* What's that?

Rodney It's a chunky gold ID bracelet.

Raquel *(Studies it)* 'Rooney'?

Rodney No, that's 'Rodney'.

Raquel Looks like 'Rooney.' That's an 'O', isn't it?

Rodney No it's a 'D'. It's copperplate writing.

Raquel *(Laughing)* Well, it looks like 'Rooney' from where I'm standing. Where d'you get it from?

Rodney It's your birthday present to me.

Raquel Oh! It's your birthday! Sorry. Happy birthday, Rodney.

Rodney Thanks.

Raquel Del chose the present. I didn't even know what he'd got you. Where is he?

Rodney In the kitchen. He's a bit disappointed, the council have just turned down his application for a home improvement grant.

Raquel *(Surveys flat)* I suppose they didn't have half a million pounds handy.

Rodney What did he want to do then?

Raquel Who knows! Put an extension on the balcony and build a double garage, knowing him.

Del enters from kitchen with tea pot and mugs.

Del I wanted a mere five thousand pounds to put new kitchen units in.

Rodney Well that sounds fair enough.

Raquel Oh get real, Rodney. There's no way he was gonna put new units in. He just wanted five grand.

Rodney But the council would have checked to see you'd had the work carried out.

Del Leave off, Rodders. You give 'em an nightmon month aa story and they forget all about it. They're all busy organising carnivals and things. Anyway, they've turned me down, so I don't know why we're discussing it, it's all epidemic. Who's the letter from?

Raquel Don't know yet.

Raq exits to kitchen with mug of tea

Del sits at table and reads council's rejection letter.

Del Gits.

INT. DAY. TROTTERS' LOUNGE.

Rodney reads a newspaper. As he does so a football suddenly bounces off his head.

Rodney *(Without turning round)* Morning, Damien.

We now find Damien standing by the door to bedrooms area. He is wearing pyjamas and dressing gown and one of the baseball caps (back to front).

Del It's a cracker, innit, son?

Damien My Dad gets me everything … *(To Rodney)* D'you want to play war?

A flashback to the nightmare. Damien (35) straight into camera.

Damien War is good.

Rodney No! Bit busy.

Del Go on, you've got time for a little battle.

Rodney No. I'm alright, honest.

Del *(To Damien)* I'll get you your cereal.

Del exits to kitchen.

Damien When I'm older will people still wear baseball caps?

Rodney When you're older, Damien, people will wear whatever you tell them to wear.

Damien Oh cool! If you get a birthday cake, Uncle Rodney, can I have some?

Rodney Yeah, of course you can.

Damien has retrieved his football. He opens door to Albert's room and throws the ball in and runs away to bedroom.

Albert *(OS) (Shouts)* Little git!

Albert enters with the ball wearing a dressing gown but is bare-legged except for a pair of scrunched up socks, one of which reveals a big-toe and carrying slippers. Rodney, hardly reacts to any of it, he just allows Trotter-life to wash over him.

Albert Ain't it bloody fair, eh?

Rodney Oh my God, Albert! Your socks look like the bomb-squad's been having a go at 'em!

Albert All I need now is that hospital to get you and Cassandra pregnant, then I'd have two of the little sods bouncing things off me head and sticking marmalade in me slippers.

Rodney *(Sudden panic)* What do you know about me and Cassandra and the hospital?

Albert *(As he pours tea)* Nothing, son, nothing at all … What's an ovum?

Rodney I don't belie … Were you listening to me and Del's conversation?

Heroes and Villains

Albert I wasn't listening, I just heard. Don't worry, you know me, son, I'm saying nothing.

Del enters from kitchen.

Del Morning, Unc. Oi, you be careful when you collect your pension today. There's a gang of muggers operating round this area.

Albert They don't worry me, son. I boxed for the navy. They called my left hand 'Trotter's Trembler'.

Del I won't ask what they called your right hand.

Del and Rodney laugh.

Rodney If all else fails Albert, you could always chuck your socks at 'em.

Del checks his watch, which reads 8 o'clock, and a sudden panic sets in.

Del *(Urgency)* Come on, Rodders, let's go.

Rodney What's the hurry?

Del Come on, quick!

Rodney Shall I load the van up?

Del No. I've got to get the Capri in for a tune up first. Come on, hurry up!

(Calls)

See you, sweetheart! Come on, Rodney.

Del and Rodney exit and we hear front door slam. Raquel enters from kitchen still with letter in hand.

Albert What's he in such a hurry for?

Raquel Don't know

Raquel, with a sudden fear, looks up at the wall clock which reads 8 o'clock

Oh no, not again!

Now, from inside the 'betatime radio/alarm' clock boxes we hear a cacophony of 125 alarms and radios begin playing. We have all different sounds – digital buzzers and beepers and warblers and bells of different pitch – radio stations playing different records – chat shows – news items.

EXT. DAY. FRONT OF NELSON MANDELA HOUSE.

We see a gang hanging around somewhere. The gang consists of:
Gary: The leader: A strapping, tough looking six footer of about 19.
Scott and Kevin: Two other lads about the same age but not as big.
Dawn: A 17 year girl.
They are watching a young mother pushing her baby in a pram passing by. Their eyes firmly on her handbag. Gary gives a nod and the gang begins to move towards the mother. At this point Del and Rodney exit the front doors in a hurry.

Del You take the van, Rodney, I'll follow you in the Capri Ghia.

The sudden arrival of Del and Rodney force the gang to abort their action. Gary gestures to the gang to move off in the opposite direction.

Rodney What's the big hurry?

Del Eh? Erm, I've booked the Capri in for half eight.

Rodney Oh right. *(Looks up at flats)* What's that racket? Sounds like someone's having a rave.

Del Tch! Some people, eh?

They climb into vehicles.

INT. DAY. SID'S CAFE.

Sid is behind the counter with his customary cigarette between his lips. In the background in kitchen area is Sid's assistant cook. Trigger, in working clothes and Boycie, in suit and tie and reading a car-dealer's magazine, are seated at a table. Trigger is sporting a small, silver medal on his chest. Trigger's broom is leaning against wall.

Trigger Did I tell you what Councillor Murray said to me when she gave me this medal?

Boycie Yes! Trigger, you are boring the pants off me with this bloody medal!

Trigger No. She said, 'I thank you on behalf of the council and the people of Peckham!'

Del and Rodney enter.

Del Morning, Sid. What d'you fancy, Rodney?

Rodney I'll have a cheese roll.

Sid *(Calls to cook)* One cheese roll.

Cut to table.

Trigger I still find it hard to believe!

Boycie So do I! Medals for road sweepers! They'll be giving Del Boy an award for good taste next!

Del and Rodney join them at table.

Del Morning all.

Boycie Thank God you've arrived! He can bore you two with it now!

Rodney What's that then?

Boycie Trigger's got a medal.

Del Oh yeah. Where'd you find that, Trig?

Trigger I was awarded it. Look

(Shows them a photo).

It's a picture of me receiving my medal from Councillor Murray.

We see it is a photograph of Trigger, in uniform, with broom held proudly in hand, receiving an award from Councillor Murray in the town hall.

See, that's me.

Rodney Oh that's you, is it? I'm glad you

cleared up, Trig.

Del Let me have a look at that. So that's Councillor Murray, is it? That's the cow that refused my application for a council grant. I've never been treated so badly in all me life.

Boycie Derek, when you have the time you'll have to tell me all about it.

Del Hey, d'you reckon your friends at the masonic lodge might have some influence at the town hall?

Boycie No. I've just often wondered what it must be like to apply for a council grant.
    (His laugh)

Del And the day started out so well, didn't it?

Trigger It's Councillor Murray's idea. She's head of Finance and Facilities at the Town Hall and she says local people should be rewarded for services to the community. A proud moment in my family's history.

Boycie Trigger, you haven't got a family history. You were created by a chemical spillage at a germ warfare plant somewhere off Deptford High Street.

Trigger Maybe. But I still feel proud.

Rodney So what exactly is the award for?

Trigger For saving the council money. I happened to mention to her one day that I've had the same broom for the last twenty years. She was very impressed and said have a medal. Twenty years. Long time, Dave.

Rodney Yeah, I know. It's two decades innit?

Trigger I wouldn't go that far, but it's a long time.
    Sid arrives with teas and things.

Del If you've had that broom for 20 years d'you ever actually sweep the roads with it?

Trigger Well of course! But I look after it well. We have an old saying that's been handed down by generations of road sweepers: 'Look after your broom ...'

Rodney *(Finishes saying for him)*
And your broom will look after you.

Trigger ... No Dave. It's just: 'Look after your broom'.

Rodney Oh, that old saying!

Trigger Yeah. And that's what I've done. Maintained it for twenty years. This old broom's had seventeen new heads and fourteen new handles in its time.

Sid Well, how the hell can it be the same bloody broom then?

Trigger There's the picture of it! What more proof d'you need?

Boycie Did you tell this Councillor Murray bint about the seventeen new heads and fourteen

new handles?

Trigger No. I didn't get technical with her. Anyway, I'll see you around.

Sid Bon appetite.

INT. DAY. THE TROTTERS' FLAT.

Two hours later.
We come up on Raquel's letter which has been opened and read. Raquel, now dressed, is talking on the phone. This is obviously quite an emotional conversation for Raquel.

Raquel *(On phone)* Yeah ... I know ... This has come as a bit of a shock to me.
    Cut to hall. Del enters from front door. Begins unbuttoning his coat when he becomes aware of Raquel's voice. He listens to conversation. We cut between the lounge and the hall.

Raquel *(On the phone)* I haven't heard from you for years. Last time we met I got the impression that I wasn't important in your life any more.
    We see Del's reaction to this. He is angry, hurt and afraid.
(On phone) Yeah, I understand OK, let's meet ... *(Emphatically)* No! I'll come to you ... This weekend? I'm not sure ... Del? I don't know really. I suppose I'll have to tell him the truth. I'll give you a call ... OK ... I know you do ... Of course I still love you.
    Now becomes tearful.
Bye.
    She replaces receiver. We see Del. This is his nightmare coming true.
    Cut to lounge. Raquel is wiping her eyes. She looks vengefully at the ansaphone. She switches a button on ansaphone.
    We hear Del's voice coming from machine. He speaks in a false, posh and slightly nervous tone that so many people do when confronted with recording the outgoing message. Del enters from hall.

Del *(All false happiness)*
Alright, sweetheart?

Raquel Yeah. What you been up to?

Del *(Nerves beginning to show)* Oh, I met a bloke down the market. I've ordered a consignment of electric doughnut makers ... I bumped into Boycie. He said that Mike at the Nag's Head is selling tickets for some party this weekend. Fancy going?

Raquel This weekend? No, not really.

Del OK ... Any phone calls?

Raquel Erm, no ... Del, can we talk?

Del Yeah, course we can.

Heroes and Villains

Raquel There's something I've gotta tell you. I'd like to sit down.

Del Go on then.

Raquel I mean both of us.

They sit.

That letter I got this morning.

Del Yeah.

Raquel It was from my Mum and Dad. I've just got off the phone to them.

Del gives an audible sigh of incredible relief.

Raquel You OK?

Del T'riffic. Your Mum and Dad? I didn't know you had a Mum and Dad. No, what I meant was you never mentioned them. Every time I've brought the subject up you said you stopped talking to 'em and you don't know where they are.

Raquel Years ago we had a big bust up when I told them I wanted to go into show business. My Dad – he's a bit old-fashioned – he said some nasty things – you can imagine.

We see that Del can't imagine.

So I stormed out, went into digs and that was the last contact I had with them – until now. They got my address from the landlord at my old flat. They've been phoning for the last couple of weeks but just kept getting the answer-machine.

Del Yeah, a lot of people get nervous about leaving messages on them machines.

Raquel No, they left lots of messages but the rotten machine didn't record them.

Del I wonder what the bloody hell's wrong with this thing. I'll have a butcher's at it – bound to be a button or something on it.

Del moves to ansaphone and gives it a whack.

Raquel So I phoned 'em … We had a nice chat … They seemed different – sort of, understanding.

Now slightly weepy.

I cried.

Del *(Hugs her)* You silly old thing.

Raquel My Mum said they'd missed me. *(Now breaks down completely)* And my Dad said he loved me!

Del *(Kisses her on forehead)* Well, ain't that nice, eh? Lovely jubbly.

Raquel *(Drying her eyes)* I told them about Damien.

Del And?

Raquel They were pleased. They seemed really excited they had a grandson. I told them all about him. All the little things he does. They even wanted to know what he liked to eat.

Del D'you tell 'em about me?

Raquel I mentioned you.

Del D'you tell 'em what I did?

Raquel No. There wasn't time. They just wanted to know about Damien … They mentioned going up there at the weekend – they want to meet him.

Del Well, that'll be nice for Damien as well.

Del now busies himself trying to repair ansaphone.

Raquel Yeah … *(Now broaching a difficult subject)* The thing is. Well, see, my Dad's a bit of an old fuddy-duddy and he hasn't been well recently …

Del *(About machine)* Bloody thing!

Raquel And I think meeting you might be a bit too much for him. So, I don't want to offend you, but d'you mind if just me and Damien went?

Del That's the last time I buy anything off Ronnie Nelson!

Now a terrible thought.

Oh, Mon Dieu! I've just remembered, darling. I won't be able to come with you. I've gotta go to Covent Garden and pick up a van load of vegetables Saturday morning.

Raquel Ah, they were really looking forward to meeting you as well, never mind.

Del Alright sweetheart, you take Damien and have a nice time. I tell you what, take the Capri Ghia, let 'em see their little girl's done alright for herself.

Raquel Ok. Thanks, Del. *(Kisses him)* I do love you.

Del Well of course you do, I'm that sort of bloke. What's your dad do?

Raquel He's an antique dealer.

Del Is he? I tell you what, down in the garage I've got a lovely …

Raquel I'm not taking anything with me!

Del Alright then, fair enough, just a thought. You go on – build a few bridges.

Raquel I'll try. I'll make you a coffee.

Raq exits to kitchen.

Damien enters from bedrooms area.

Del Here, Damien, guess who you're gonna see on Saturday? Your Nan and your Grandad.

Damien Have I got a Nan and Grandad?

Del You have now.

Damien Did you get 'em for me?

Del No, they belong to your Mum. They're lovely, and they love you. You wait and see, they'll make a right fuss of you. Yeah, they're really nice people.

Damien What are they called'?

Del *(Hasn't got a clue)* What are they called? Eh? Em … Nan and Grandad.

INT. NIGHT. RODNEY AND CASSANDRA'S LOUNGE.

There are birthday cards in evidence.
On sideboard we see a cage which contains a small white rabbit. Rodney and Cassandra are relaxing on settee, drinking champagne whilst listening to music.

Cassandra Did you feed the rabbit?

Rodney Yeah, I chucked a carrot in earlier.

Cassandra Good.

At this point Rodney is at ease. Cassandra now checks her watch. We see Rodney's expression change as a cold fear grips him. Cassandra notices his expression.

Don't worry.

Rodney I'm not.

Cassandra It's only once tonight.

Rodney Right.

Cassandra Least I think it is.

From the side of settee she produces a large graph-type piece of cardboard. It is covered in dates and red and yellow dots and crosses.

Yeah, just the once. Happy birthday again.

Rodney Look at Tuesday.

Cassandra Happy birthday again.

Rodney Thank you.

They chink glasses. In so doing Rodney's bracelet is revealed. Cassandra starts laughing at it.

Oh leave off, Cass.

Cassandra Sorry, Rooney.

Rodney Del's gotta be the only bloke who could buy a gold identity bracelet and take it to a dyslexic engraver.

Cassandra You got lots of nice presents as well.

Rodney Yeah, I did.

Cassandra I was talking to Mummy today and she said, as a special birthday present to you, why don't we fly over to the villa next week. I'm owed some time off and Del hasn't given you a holiday since ... well, he hasn't given you a holiday! I thought it might help. You and me down there on the Costa Del Sol, sangria and warm evenings – we might be able to relax, and Doctor Carr said relaxation is very important in our case.

Rodney Yeah, sounds good, don't it? Wait a minute. What about the rabbit?

Cassandra Couldn't we give it to Del?

Rodney No, he'd eat it!

Cassandra Aren't there any sort of kennels? You know a place that looks after rabbits. Like a cattery but – well a rabbitry

Rodney A rabbitry? That's a Chinese toilet! Maybe your Mum and Dad could look after it.

Cassandra Hardly, they'll be at the villa with us.

Rodney They'll be there as well? How are we supposed to relax and – sort of – stick with the schedule with your Mum and Dad there?

Cassandra I've figured it all out. Rodney. We won't do it in front of them! When we want to, you know, relax, we'll go to our bedroom! What d'you think?

Rodney But they'll be in the room next to us! I mean, what about the panting and screaming and 'Yes, yes, yes!'

Cassandra You'll just have to control yourself.

Rodney No, it'll never work. Besides I can't leave Del now, business ain't going too well.

Cassandra I know, I looked at your account.

Rodney But we feel we're on the verge of something.

Cassandra Yeah, that's what I thought! Oh come on Rodney, I was really looking forward to getting away for a few days. I've checked the flights and there are seats available Thursday morning.

Rodney I can't, Cass. You go.

Cassandra You don't mind?

Rodney Of course I don't. Go on, a rest'll do you good.

Cassandra kisses him.

Cassandra You won't go to this party Mike's organising, will you?

Rodney Of course not! What party?

Cassandra I don't know, Raquel mentioned it when she phoned earlier. I don't want other women throwing themselves at you.

Rodney Cassandra, that is something you're gonna have to put up with!

Cassandra But it'll mean putting our schedule on ice for a week.

Rodney looks disappointed.

Rodney 'Fraid so ... Tch!

We see a look of great relief on his face.

INT. DAY. NAG'S HEAD.

Three days later.
Mike is behind bar reading the Daily Mirror It is a quiet lunch time. The only customers in bar are Denzil in working clothes and Boycie in suit and overcoat who are seated at table reading newspapers.
Marlene is seated at bar reading a magazine. She is in full make-up.
Trigger's broom is leaning against the table.

Mike You both got tickets for Saturday's party?

Boycie and Denzil Mmmhh.

Mike I can tell you're looking forward to it!

Mike looks to his hot'n'cold food cabinet

Heroes and Villains

which is filled with sausages, chips, pies, slightly curled sandwiches, etc. He shakes his head sadly at the waste.

Marlene, fancy something nice to eat?

Marlene I do as it happens, Mike. *(To Boycie)* Boycie, shall we pop down The Harvester in a minute?

Boycie, Marlene and Denzil laugh.

Mike *(A false laugh)* I don't get much trade but I do have a good laugh! Bloody 'ell.

Trigger, in road sweeper's uniform, passes on the way to the table. We should notice he also sports a small silver medal on his chest. Mike produces a handful of tickets.

Trigger. D'you fancy a ticket? Tenner each.

Trigger Righto, Mike.

Mike What d'you mean, 'Righto, Mike?' You don't even know what they're for.

Trigger *(As if Mike is stupid)* Tch! It's bound to tell you on the ticket, innit?

Mike Oh yeah, I didn't think of that. Every year us local publicans organise a fancy dress ball. Prizes, the lot. This year it's old Harry Malcolm's turn – he's the landlord at the Crown and Anchor. He's holding the party at his house – he's got a great big place over Dulwich way.

Indicating ticket.

See? It's got spot prizes, everything. Look, top prize is a brand new stereo system worth over a thousand pound.

Trigger Fancy dress! I've only got my mohair suit and my best jumper.

Mike Perfect!

(Takes money)

Trigger Did I tell you about my medal?

Mike Yes, you told me a couple of times yesterday and three times this morning.

Trigger Did I tell you, Marlene?

Marlene Yes, love. You sent us a fax last night.

Trigger moves to Boycie and Denzil. Boycie and Denzil see Trigger coming and try to hide behind their newspapers. Del and Rodney enter.

Greetings are exchanged as Del and Rodney move to bar.

Del Alright Mike

Del turns to Marlene.

Wotchyer, sweetheart.

He touches her up. Boycie reacts.

Marlene Stop it! Honestly. Cassandra get off alright?

Rodney Yeah, I've just come from the airport.

Marlene And Raquel's away too, ain't she? I bet you two'll be out galavanting Saturday night.

Del Ooh no, we're not like that anymore. A cup

of Bournvita, plate of toast and *Match Of The Day*, that's us, eh, Rodders?

Rodney Heaven!

Marlene *(Spots Rodney's ID bracelet)* That's nice … 'Rooney?'

Del No, it's 'Rodney'.

Rodney It's not an O – it looks like an O but it's not! Quiet today, innit?

Del Yeah, there's more life in one of his pork pies. Come on Michael. A pint of your finest lager-top for Rodney and a Manhattan for moi.

Mike Fancy something to eat, Del. How about a nice beef stew?

Rodney looks at the unappetising fare.

Del Yeah, that'll keep the cold out.

Rodney You should be careful with the old beef, Del.

Del Oh leave off, you brass.

Trigger, broom in hand, is passing on way to exit.

Trigger I don't know what you are worried about. I've been eating British beef all my life.

Del Sauasge and chips, please, Mike. Rodney?

Rodney Something that was fresh this morning.

Rodney moves away

Del And a *Daily Mirror* for Rodney.

Del and Rodney join Boycie and Denzil. Greetings are exchanged.

Denzil Any luck, Del?

Del Loads of it, all bad! Just had a word with Paddy the Greek. You know them 9 carat gold bracel *(Corrects himself in Rodney's presence)* 24 carat gold bracelets I was selling? I've just found out they've all been deported along with Ugandan Maurice.

Denzil Why did you trust him with all that gold in the first place?

Del Because he told me he was an exporter.

Rodney Yeah, an ex-porter, he just got the sack from British Rail.

Del Life's one long struggle.

Moans of agreement from the others.

Sometimes I feel like King Farouk holding back the tide. I've got a kid tothink of now.

Denzil I've got bills coming out of me ears.

Boycie I've got Marlene.

Rodney It's Canute

Del You can say that again.

Denzil, Mike and Boycie all agree. Rodney just looks on as if to say, 'Why do I bother?' Mike crosses over with food. Marlene follows.

Mike *(Trying to cheer Del)* D'you wanna buy a ticket for a publican's ball?

Del Only if it's a raffle.

Everyone except Mike laughs.

Mike Your loss.
Returns to bar.
Denzil You're right, Del, it sounds boring.
Rodney Anyone going?
Denzil Me.
Boycie I've got to go, the host is a fellow mason. Last year's do was a real good laugh.
Denzil I heard it all ended in a big punch up.
Boycie Yes it did. But during the struggle Marlene got a whack on the nose.
Marlene And you did nothing about it, did you?
Boycie What could I do? You threw the first punch.
Denzil *(To Marlene)* Were you injured?
Boycie No, fortunately her make-up cushioned the blow. *(His laugh)*
Rodney picks up his pint of lager and examines it.
Rodney *(Panic)* I've just remembered! I was supposed to take Cassie's specimen into the clinic this morning! I've left it in your kitchen on your work top.
Del Well that's alright, take it tomorrow.
Rodney No you don't understand. It's not supposed to be left in direct sunlight. You're supposed to find a cool, dark spot where it won't be disturbed.
Marlene How about Boycie's pants?
Everyone laughs, including Boycie – now his laugh dies as he realises the joke is on him.

INT. DAY. TROTTERS' LOUNGE.

One hour later.
Albert is on phone to Raquel.
Albert *(On phone)* Yes, everything's fine, Raquel – although there's no food in the fridge – but I'm not complaining. You just have a nice time, gel …
We hear front door slam.
Hold on, I think Del's back.
Del and Rodney enter – returning from the pub.
Del Boy, Raquel's on the phone.
Del Right, thanks, Albert. I'll take it in the bedroom.
Del exits to bedrooms area.
Albert *(On the phone)* He's gonna take it in the bedroom, love. See you soon, bye.
Hangs up.
I suppose your Cassandra'll be there by now.
Rodney checks his watch on same wrist as ID bracelet.
Rodney She should have landed by now. Bloody 'Rooney!'

Albert I don't know why you wear an ID bracelet. Men – real men – didn't wear them in my day.
Rodney You used to wear dog-tags round your neck.
Albert They were ID necklaces! Completely different.
Rodney To be honest, Unc, I don't wanna wear this thing but I don't wanna hurt Del's feelings.
Albert I understand, boy … During the war.
Rodney God!
Albert I had a mate who had exactly the same problem. His Mum had bought him a gold watch which he hated. But he didn't wanna hurt her feelings. So he had to find a solution to the problem.
Rodney So what's he do?
Albert One night he went round all the pubs in Portsmouth flashing his gold watch about. On the way back to ship he got mugged … Problem over.
Rodney That was a good idea, weren't it?
Albert There's a lot of mugging going on round here, Rodney.
Rodney Albert, I'm not seriously considering it as a viable option! God Almighty! I'll just have to tell him the truth.
Albert Be gentle though.
Albert exits to kitchen. Rodney begins practising breaking the news.
Rodney Del, about this thing you gave me for me birthday.
Del It's a beauty, innit?
We see Del has entered from bedrooms area. He takes coat off.
Rodney Eh? Yeah … Em, thing is …
Del I tell you what Raquel and Damien are having a nice time. Getting on really well with her Mum and Dad.
Rodney Yeah? I didn't know Raquel had any parents.
Del Nor did I. They turned up out of the blue. There was a bit of a family barney in the past and now we're trying to patch things up. A kiss and a cuddle's all it takes.
Rodney Oh, well that's good, innit? Didn't you want to go and meet your common-law in-laws then?
Del Well, I would have gone but, to be honest, Raquel didn't want me to go.
Rodney What, she told you?
Del She was having a difficult time in telling me so I made an excuse to let her off the hook. I think she thought I might embarrass her.
Rodney *(Nods in thoughtless agreement)*

Heroes and Villains

Mmmh ..! *(Now corrects it)* What d'you mean? That's silly! How could you possibly embarrass her?

Del Well, that's what I thought! Her old man's an antique dealer. I was gonna let him have a look at the Jacobean cine-camera ... She most probably wants to save me for later. So, what was you gonna say about the bracelet?

Rodney Eh? Erm, nothing. I'm well pleased with it.

Del And you'll never forget your name will you?
Albert enters from kitchen.

Albert *(Moaning)* Raquel goes away for a few days and this flat becomes a shambles. There's no food in the fridge, the veg is on the turn and that apple-juice is 'orrible. I've eaten better on a life-raft.
Exits to his bedroom.

Del Shuddup moaning, you old git! Don't he go on? Apple juice, what apple juice?
Rodney shrugs. Now a cold fear. Rodney rushes to kitchen. He now enters from kitchen.

Rodney *(Horrified)* It's Cassandra's specimen! It's gone!

Del You mean? I don't believe him!

Rodney What am I gonna tell Cassandra?

Del Tell her it spilt in the van as you went round a corner.

Rodney I can't lie to her, Del.

Del Alright, tell her Albert drunk it.

Rodney I can't tell her that, can I? It's just one thing after another.

Del Yeah, same here. We need to get out, bruv.

Rodney How d'you mean?

Del Well, I've been thinking. Cassandra's away in foreign climes and now Raquel's had it away on her toes to Milton Keynes. And what's happening tomorrow night? It's the big party, innit? The publican's ball. So I was thinking, so while the mice are away why don't us cats go out and play. It'll be like the old days, Rodney.

Rodney We're not gonna be pulling birds, are we?

Del We never pulled birds in the old days so what chance we got now? Come on, what d'you say?

Rodney Well, it's only harmless fun, innit?

Del We'll go for a couple of hours. A sausage roll, bit of a grin, that's all. The top prize this year is a stereo system worth over a grand.

Rodney What'd they give prizes for?

Del The best fancy dress.

Rodney Fancy dress! I'm not going up like some zoom!

Del It's only a laugh! We'll pop down the fancy-dress shop in the High Street and pick something out. I need you to choose the right costumes and win us that top prize. 'Cos you've got a GCE in art. I need your creative input. You're the one with the flair and the imagination.

Rodney I suppose so. Shall I tell you what I'm imagining right now? I imagine you've been planning the whole thing, ain't you? I bet that since you knew Raquel was going away, you've been planning to go to that party and try and win that prize!

Del If your mother could hear you now! Is that what you really think of me? The woman and child that I love have gone away for what will obviously be a very emotional and draining weekend – and all Del Boy can think is, 'Let's go an' jolly it up and try and win a prize!' Oh yeah, that's Del Boy, shallow as a worm's grave.

Rodney No, what I meant was ... Well, it just seemed a bit ... Alright, I'm sorry.

Del That's alright then, apology accepted.

Rodney Hang on, I've just remembered. It's an all-ticket affair.

Del Don't worry, I bought a couple as we were leaving.
Produces two tickets.

Rodney Ace!

EXT. NIGHT. PECKHAM BACK STREETS.
Del and Rodney are on their way to Harry's fancy-dress party. We see the three wheeled van pass us – at this point we don't know what they are going to the party as. The van backfires loudly.
We hear conversation from inside van.

Rodney *(OS)* I feel stupid! I don't know how we got out of the estate without being seen.

Del *(OS)* Don't worry, we'll be there in a minute.

Rodney *(OS)* Yes, but then we've got to get home dressed like this!

Del *(OS)* Who's gonna see us at five in the morning?

Rodney *(OS)* Yeah, suppose so. Five in the morning? You said we're only going for a couple of hours.

Del *(OS)* Yes, but you get involved, don't you?
The van coughs and farts a few times and splutters to a halt.

Rodney *(OS)* What's happening?

Del *(OS)* There must be something wrong.

Rodney *(OS)* I wish I was mechanically minded like you.

Del *(OS)* I'll open the bonnet, you go an' have a look at the engine.

Rodney *(OS)* Go an' have a look at the ... I'm not getting out the van dressed like this!

Del *(OS)* No one'll see you. Look, the street's empty.

Rodney *(OS)* At the moment! But I'll guarantee you the minute we step out of this van a thousand people'll pour out of a ... of a ... of a place where a thousand people are! You have a look, it's your van!

Del *(OS)* You tart, Rodney.

We see the driver's door open and Del's foot is covered in a suede, elf-like bootie. As Del approaches the bonnet of van we now see him in all his glory. He is dressed as Batman, complete with hood and cape. He checks the street and then opens bonnet.

Rodney pops his head out of the open window of passenger side. He is dressed as Robin, with eye-mask, etc.

Rodney See anything?

Del Gimme a chance. Can't see a thing here in the dark.

Rodney alights from passenger side and joins Del, cautiously checking that no passer-by will see him dressed as Robin. Del has removed something from the top of the engine. He now produces a lighter and snaps the flame on to give him some light.

Rodney *(Innocently at this point)* What you looking for?

Del I'm tryin' to see if the petrol's getting through to the carburettor.

We have a few beats before Rodney's eyes widen in horror. He leaps back.

Rodney You idiot! You could blow us to kingdom come!

Del Don't be daft! There's no petrol coming through, is there. There's a blockage, that's why we've broken down. Quick. Back in the van, I don't want people seeing you dressed like that – you look like a right plonker.

They both scamper back into the van.

INT. NIGHT. VAN.

Del *(Almost as if it's Rodney's fault)* What are we gonna do now, eh?

Rodney I don't know, Derek! We are sat in the middle of Peckham at 10.30 at night dressed up as Batman and Robin! You – you chose these costumes! I wanted to go as The Blues Brothers!

Del Rodney, we'd have still broken down and been in this embarrassing situation, wouldn't we?

Rodney Oh yeah! We'd have both been wearing suits and ties – right couple of zooms

we'd have looked!

Del But we'd never have won first prize as The Blues Brothers!

Rodney At least we could have walked home!

Del Stop moaning. We've got to think of a way out of this.

Rodney Alright, let's think about it.
Produces mobile phone.
We phone the RAC.

Del Yes, ask to be put through to their 'Broken Down Whilst Dressed As A Couple Of Prats' department?

Rodney Alright then, the police?

Del The police? We'd never live it down, Rodney. Our lives would be hell! We'd have to emigrate.

Rodney At this particular moment in time, that doesn't sound a bad alternative.

Del There's always a way, Rodney. Let's sit here and think.

Rodney The pubs'll be chucking out soon. They'll tear us to shreds.

Del Tell you what, old Harry's house is nearer then any other place. If we run we could be there in five minutes.

Rodney But we'll be seen! People on buses, people in restaurant windows.

Del No. Not if we go through the back streets and the alleys. All you got down there are winos and crackheads and let's face it, they see Batman and Robin every night of the week. Come on, we can do it.

Rodney Five minutes?

Del Five minutes if we hurry.

Rodney Oh jeez!

EXT. NIGHT. BACK STREETS/TOWNHALL.

This is a street that runs along the back of the town hall. Parked opposite, and close to the corner of an alley is a modern car. The back door to the town hall is opened by a commissionaire and Councillor Murray exits, carrying handbag and briefcase.

Cllr Murray I'm going now Tom.

Commissionaire I'll see you out. Goodnight, Councillor Murray.

Cllr Murray Good night, Tom.
The door closes and Councillor Murray makes her way across the road to the car.
She stops at the driver's door and opens her handbag for the car keys. At this point Dawn (the girl member of mugging gang) rushes round the corner, apparently in a wild panic.

Dawn Sorry, Miss, you seen a policeman round here?

Heroes and Villains

Murray No, I haven't!

Immediately Gary (the leader) steps out from behind the corner.

Gary Good! Giss your money!

Cllr Murray What are you doing? *(Calls)* Tom!

The other members of the gang, Scott and Kevin, have now appeared and the mugging begins.

Cllr Murray Help!

Scott Someone shut her up!

Gary Get her handbag!

Dawn puts her hand round Murray's mouth. Scott now sees something up the road that makes him freeze in incredulity. He nudges Gary.

Scott Gary!

He gestures up road.

Gary looks and freezes. Dawn and Kevin and now Murray all do likewise. We see from their POV: two hundred yards away, Batman and Robin are running towards them.

Gary *(Incredulously)* What's happening?

Cllr Murray *(Equally incredulously)* I haven't the faintest idea!

Gary *(Terrified, to rest of gang)* Go!

The gang run off leaving Murray open-mouthed in disbelief.

Batman and Robin now run past her.

Batman now stops – Robin stops a bit further on.

Del Councillor Murray?

Cllr Murray *(Frightened)* Yes.

Del I recognise you from your photograph. Derek Trotter. You may remember I wrote to you sometime ago about a …

Rodney Del, let's go!

Del Yes. Well, sorry, must dash. Maybe another time?

Batman and Robin rush off.

Murray watches them, still in total shock.

INT. NIGHT. HALLWAY OF BIG HOUSE.

The door to the main room is closed. All we can hear is the sound of polite, muted conversation. The front door bell rings. Boycie exits from the main room. He is dressed in a black two-piece suit, white shirt and a black kipper tie.

He opens front door and Del and Rodney enter.

At first Boycie is surprised, but he now allows himself a little smile.

Del Oh Boycie, let us in, will you?

Boycie What have you two come as then?

Rodney *(Innocently)* Batman and Robin.

Del Ignore him, Rodders. Just ignore him. Where is everyone?

Boycie *(Points to main room)* Straight through there, Caped Crusader.

Del You ain't gonna win nothing dressed like that. *(To Rodney)* Amazing, innit? We've come as Batman and Robin and Boycie's come as the Penguin …

Del and Rodney move towards door (checking themselves in mirror first)

Boycie *(Quietly)* Oh no, Del Boy – not the Penguin – more like the Joker.

INT. NIGHT. MAIN ROOM OF BIG HOUSE.

We find a crowd of people of various ages and colours sipping drinks and engaged in polite conversation. They are all dressed in black – this is in fact a wake.

Mike approaches Kenny, Harry (the host's) son. Kenny is 50.

Mike Kenny. Mike from the Nag's Head. I was really cut-up yesterday when I heard about your Dad. Still, at least he didn't suffer.

Kenny No. He had a good innings and he'd have been well chuffed to see all his family and friends turn up for his wake like this.

Now the double doors from the hall open and Del and Rodney enter.

Del and Rodney Da da da da da da da da

Rodney stops singing as he sees the crowd.

Del Da da da Batman! Da da da … *(The song dies on his lips)*

Boycie has followed them in.

Boycie Derek. Harry died yesterday.

Del He di ..! Why didn't you tell us that out there in the hall instead of letting us run in here like that?

Rodney Yeah. We were going da da da da and all that!

Boycie It completely slipped my mind completely. Strange what grief can do.

Now laughs his laugh but realises it is out of place.

Boycie exits into the crowd. Del and Rodney remain for a moment looking and feeling very silly. Now Kenny approaches.

Kenny Del. I don't know if you remember me. I'm Kenny, Harry's son.

Del Yeah, course I remember you.

Ken I phoned round everyone to tell 'em the party was off. I left four or five messages on your answer machine. Obviously you didn't get 'em.

Rodney No, the machine's been playing up.

Del I'm gonna get shot of that bloody machine. Look, Kenny, I'm sorry about all this.

Kenny Don't be silly. The old man's most probably up there now having a bloody good laugh at you all. You'll stay, won't you?

Del Oh yeah, of course.

Kenny Grab yourself a drink and something to eat.

Del Alright, cheers

Kenny moves Into crowd. Denzil appears.

Denzil Didn't you know Harry had died?

Del Of course we knew Harry had died! That's why we've come dressed as Batman and Thingy!

Rodney Robin.

Del Yeah! I suppose the prize-giving's off now?

Rodney I love him. Bloody love him.

Trigger arrives wearing a black suit, white shirt and a black tie. He approaches Del and Rodney and makes no reaction to the way they are dressed.

Trigger Alright Del, Dave. Bit of a choker innit old Harry popping off like that?

Rodney Yeah. We didn't know the fancy dress party had been cancelled.

Trigger Me neither.

Rodney You mean, that's your costume?

Trigger Yeah, I come as a chauffeur. I feel a bit

stupid now.

Del Yeah, you do stand out a bit. I'll get us a drink.

Trigger I don't think you and Del would have won first prize.

Rodney No?

Trigger No. You're alright, but Del don't look nothing like Tonto.

EXT. DAY. THE MARKET. LOCATION.

A week later.

Del has the suitcase open on the ground We see it is full of the red riding helmets and the baseball caps. Rodney is close by leaning against frame of one of the stalls and reading the Peckham Echo. The headline reads: 'Councillor Murray Breathalised After Mugging Claim'

Sub headline reads: 'Batman and Robin saved me, claims town hall chief' Del is already bored with the rejection of his wares and it tells in his voice.

Del *(Fed up)* Aerodynamic cycling helmets. *(Taps one for us to hear a metallic sound).* As worn by Chris Boardman – and his cousin Stan … Baseball caps. Look at that, beautiful.

Heroes and Villains

Straight from LA, as worn by MC Hammer ... Buy the kid one for Christmas. Unisex baseball caps, designed especially for your sons or daughters – or your Rottweiler goldfish. Baseball caps. I can't see us doing a lot of business today. Let's sling it all in the van and go home.

As Del turns back to suitcase, etc, we see four lads (about 16-17 years of age) are studying the baseball caps. The four lads all wear back-to-front baseball caps.

Del D'you wanna buy one?

1st lad We've already got baseball caps.

Del Not like this these you ain't. These are a brand new design straight from Los Angeles.

2nd lad (*Studies inside of a cap*) It says here 'Made in Taiwan'.

Del Yes, made in Taiwan but designed in America. The Bloods and the Cripps are wearing these, they're all the go over there.

1st lad Yeah? What's so special about 'em? They don't look any different.

Del Haute Couture is obviously not your strong point, is it. I'll show you.

He directs first lad to a small mirror which is hanging on end of stall. Del removes lad's back-to-front baseball cap and places the new one on his head – but he places it with the peak at front.

Del See, with these one's the peak is at the front!

We see Rodney has now noticed something in another part of market. We see an elderly lady standing close to a stall and putting her purse back into her handbag. We also see the three men and a girl mugging team are close by and eyeing her.

Dawn moves in and asks the old lady the time. The boys move in closer.

Rodney Del! Have a look.

Del What's up?

We now see Scott and Kevin crowd the old lady, Gary (the leader) grabs the old lady's handbag and pulls it from her. In the struggle the old lady falls to the ground. The gang disperse. We concentrate on Gary with the handbag.

Del Get after him, Rodney!

Rodney Right!

Rodney dashes off in pursuit.
Del closes his suitcase and chases after Rodney. We see the old lady on the ground and in shock, being comforted by some women shoppers.
Rodney dashes past. Del now arrives with his suitcase and stops.

Del (*To old lady*) You alright, darling?

Old lady Little buggers have nicked me handbag, son. My bloody arse is hurting as well.

Del You just take it easy. Call the police and an ambulance for her.

Del dashes off.

EXT. DAY. LONDON STREETS.

We have two streets running parallel with each other; between them are three smaller streets which join both main streets.
We see Rodney is chasing Gary (with the handbag) towards the upper of the two main streets. Gary turns left and now begins to run along upper main street with Rodney in pursuit.
We find Del, with the suitcase, at the lower main street. He looks up along the first adjoining street and, at top of street, he sees Gary rush across the street and out of sight, immediately followed by Rodney. Del runs along to the next adjoining street and, at the top of street, he witnesses the same scene. We now cut to upper street where we see Rodney in pursuit.
Gary turns off street and Rodney follows.

EXT. DAY. AN ENCLOSED GARAGE BLOCK OR FACTORY YARD.

The now exhausted Gary runs into a garage block or factory yard and finds all escapes routes are cut off.
An exhausted Rodney now appears at entrance. Rodney smiles confidently knowing Gary is cornered. A 'gotcha' smile. The trapped Gary looks around him desperately. He now looks at Rodney and his confidence begins growing. His face becomes more aggressive. Rodney's smile dies as he realises Gary is a lot tougher than him. Gary steps towards Rodney. Rodney takes a step back. Gary starts to move forward. Rodney runs. We cut to Del still at lower street. He looks up adjoining street and is amazed to see the whole scene reversed. Rodney dashes across street being pursued by Gary.
Del runs back to second adjoining street and sees the scene repeated. We now see Rodney running along upper main street and turning right whilst being pursued by Gary. We see Rodney hurtling back towards market with Gary in pursuit.
In distance we can hear a police siren.
We come to a corner which is angled by solid and high brick walls. Rodney rushes past the

corner. *As Gary is about to run past corner so Del's suitcase appears at head height.*
Gary runs headfirst into it and collapses in an unconscious heap. (We hear a metallic crash as his head hits the suitcase – the riding helmets)
Del now appears from behind corner of wall.
Del *(To Gary)* Whoops-a-daisy.
Rodney Right, you've had your fun and games sunshine! Consider yourself nicked.
A young policeman appears on scene.
Del It's alright, officer. I caught him, he's over there.
PC Thank you, sir. *(Out of the frame)* Come on, you 'orrible little sod.
We now hear and then see (as they come into frame) that the PC has grabbed Rodney.
Rodney *(OOV)* No, no! *(In vision)* Not me!
Del No, it's the other one!
PC Sorry!
The PC grabs Gary and searches him. From out of Gary's pocket he pulls three watches.
Ooh, you can tell the time can you? *(produces a purse)* You don't look like the type of person to carry a purse! *(From the other pocket he produces a gold ID bracelet)* God, no taste! And is your name 'Rooney?'
Del No, hang on, that's my brother's. *(To Rodney)* How's it get in there?
Rodney It must have slipped off during the struggle.
PC I'll have to take statements from you two. If you wouldn't mind following me down to the station.
Del Of course, officer.
The PC leads Gary off to the police car.
Rodney Well, what about that! We're a couple of fine upstanding citizens, Derek.
Del Catalogue raisonne as they say in Beritz. Better leave your bracelet in the van, Rodney. Don't wanna be seen in a police-station wearing that!

INT. DAY. TOWN HALL. LOCATION.
Three weeks later.
A small crowd of people including Raquel, Cassandra, Albert and a disgruntled Rodney are witnessing Del's medal ceremony. Rodney is unhappy that Del is getting all the praise. There you a coming towards the end of his speech.
Mayor We read and we hear about so-called have-a-go-heroes, but we very rarely have the honour of meeting one. Well, I'm proud to say that here, in Peckham, we have our very own

have-a-go-hero.
At this point we see Councillor Murray enter the hall late. She begins a whispered conversation with one of her aides.
Mayor And so it is my greatest honour and privilege to present this medal for bravery to Derek Trotter.
Applause.
Councillor Murray reacts upon hearing Del's name.
Cllr Murray *(To aide)* That's Batman!
She moves out of shot leaving a bewildered aide. A press photographer appears.
Press Mr Trotter, could I have a couple of pictures?
Del Mange oui, of course.
As Del is having his pictures taken, Rodney appears next to him.
Rodney How comes I didn't get a medal? I did all the running.
Del Yes, but you were running away from him!
Rodney I wasn't 'running away' from him actually. I was just luring him.
Del Well you weren't half luring him fast! You came past me like Linford Christie – minus the poodle he keeps down his shorts.
Press *(To Rodney)* Could you mind out the way please, sir …
Del Yes. Mind out of the way. You're casting a shadow.
Rodney returns to the family.
Cassandra Why didn't you get a medal, Rodney?
Rodney They offered me one but I said I wanted to remain anonymous.
Cassandra *(Impressed)* Ohh.
She kisses Rodney. As she does so Rodney catches Raquel's eyes. Raquel just smiles knowingly.
As Del is about to join the family, Councillor Murray arrives.
Cllr Murray Mr Trotter. Councillor Murray. We met, the night you were dressed as Batman.
Del *(Terrified Raquel might hear)* Oh yes, that's right.
Cllr Murray I've never been so frightened in my life.
Del It was only a costume.
Cllr Murray No, I mean terrified of that awful gang of muggers. At least they're all behind bars now, thanks to you. If ever there's anything I can do for you, please don't hesitate to call.
Del Oh really, it was nothing.
Murray walks away. Del suddenly realises there is something she can do for him.
Oh, Councillor Murray. As a matter of fact there

Heroes and Villains

may be a little something you could help me with. Can we talk?
Cllr Murray Of course.
Del Cushty!

INT. NIGHT. TROTTERS' LOUNGE.

Rodney, Cassandra, Raquel and Alb are dressed up in their finest for the family celebration. Albert wears all his medals. They all have glasses of champagne except for Cassandra who has a glass of orange juice. Rodney is reading the front page of the Peckham Echo. The headline reads: 'Local Man's Award For Bravery' Sub-headline reads: 'The Hero Who Fought Crime – And Won!'
Beneath this is a picture of Del receiving his medal from the Mayor and Councillor Murray.

Rodney We'd better cut this one out for the family album. A Trotter's never won a medal before ... Well, Albert's won three or four dozen.
Cassandra Why'd they use the word 'man'? They could have mentioned Rodney.
Rodney looks at her, injured by this slight upon his masculinity.
Cassandra I mean, why didn't they say 'men'?
Raquel Yeah, Rodney was there as well.
Albert They do mention him. Here you are, 'Mr Trotter was aided in the capture of the muggers by his younger brother, Rooney.'
Rodney *(Reacts)* Bloody Rooney!
We hear a champagne cork pop in kitchen. Del, wearing the medal, enters with another bottle of champagne.
Del Here we go, fill your glasses, I'd just like to say a little something on this auspicious occasion. We are not just celebrating me becoming the first Trotter to win a medal without getting wet. This is in fact a double celebration.
Cassandra *(To Rodney)* You told them!
Rodney I didn't honest! I swear! How d'you lot find out?
Raquel Find out what?

Cassandra You mean you don't know?
Raquel No, but I'm starting to put two and two together.
Rodney Alright. Let me just say that if, in the near future, anyone wants to buy Cassandra and I some Mothercare vouchers, they will come in bloody handy!
Del punches the air.
Del Yes my son, we have scored!
Rodney also punches the air.
Rodney And it was a beauty!
Raquel I don't believe ... When d'you find out?
Cassandra We had it confirmed this afternoon!
Del and Rodney are now dancing an impromptu knees up and singing.
Del and Rodney 'Three lions on his shirt, Jules Rimet still gleaming...' (etc)
Albert *(Shakes Rodney's hand)* I'm really pleased for you, son. I know you've been through hell to get there.
Rodney Sssh shhh shhh!
Del Oh, a little cousin for Damien to play with.
Rodney Yeah!
Raquel Wait a minute. You said this was a double celebration before you found out about Cassandra being pregnant. So what else were we celebrating?
Del That's right. This is now a treble celebration. You know I was turned down by the council on my home improvement grant? Well, they changed their minds.
Produces a cheque.
Look, they sent me a cheque for five grand.
Raquel They gave you five thousand pounds.
Del Yep, what can't speak can't lie.
Rodney *(Is studying the cheque. Knowingly)* Signed by Councillor Murray.
Del That's right. *(A big grin)* Not a bad old world is it, bruv?
Rodney *(A big grin)* Getting better all the time, Del Boy.
They clink glasses.
Del Lovely jubbly.

PECKHAM
Echo

WEDNESDAY, DEC 18, 1996   YOUR FAVOURITE LONDON LOCAL SINCE 1888   15p

WIN 12 BOTTLES
OF PECKHAM SPRING WATER

ALSO INSIDE

10 MEDAL FOR LOCAL ROAD SWEEPER

14 LOCAL MAN 'HARRY' REMEMBERED

18 125 LATVIAN RADIO ALARMS TO BE WON

LOCAL MAN'S AWARD FOR BRAVERY

The Hero Who Fought Crime – And Won

Local Hero Derek Trotter was awarded a medal yesterday by the Mayor and Councillor Murray, for his outstanding bravery and courageousness. He was aided in the capture of the muggers by his younger brother, Rooney.

Derek said, "Yeah, we were on our way to Harry's fancy dress party dressed as Batman and Robin - my brother wanted us to go as the Blues Brothers! We wouldn't have won first prize if we went as the Blues Brothers! Anyway it was 10.30 and our motor packed in right in the middle of Peckham we didn't know whether to phone the RAC or the police."

Modern Men

INT. NIGHT. TROTTERS' FLAT.

Rodney, in his best suit is seated reading woman's magazine. Albert, dressed in his best clothes enters from the kitchen with crisps.

Albert You alright, son? Looking forward to tonight down the pub?

Rodney Yeah. I don't want a big thing made of it, you know. I mean, me and Cassandra are having a baby, that's all.

Albert Yeah, but you know what Del's like. Any excuse for a celebration. You don't think Del'd mind if I borrowed some of his after-shave, do you?

Rodney What do you want to use after-shave for? You've got Epping bloody Forest growing round your chops!

Albert I just wanted to smell nice, that's all.

Rodney Well in that case, don't use Del's after-shave!

Del in best suit enters from kitchen carrying a bowl of crisps and one of nuts.

Del Oh, there you are Rodders, I didn't hear you arrive. Go on, help yourself to a dry roasted. Where's Cassandra then?

Rodney Raquel wanted to show her something in the bedroom.

Albert It's them baby-clothes she's got for you.

Rodney Oh, she shouldn't have done that.

Del No, it's alright, they're some of Damien's old clothes.

Rodney *(Mild alarm)* What?

Del Suit your nipper a treat they will.

Rodney Yeah ... I'm gonna get a beer.

Rodney moves towards kitchen.

Albert If it's a boy d'you reckon it'll look like Rodney?

Del It don't matter as long as it's healthy.

Rodney stops in doorway and reacts. He exits to kitchen.

No, I know what Raquel's doing, she's showing Cassandra some of them new clothes I bought her today.

Albert New clothes? It's not her birthday, is it?

Del No, it's not her birthday. Well, they're not 'new' clothes, they're as good as.

Del picks up his book.

And it means I done my bit for charity.

Rodney enters from kitchen with a beer.

Ah, Rodders there you are, you seen this?

Modern Man, brilliant it is. It says here: 'You shouldn't wait for special occasions to give your loved one a present. Arrive home with a little surprise any day of the week and help keep your relationship exciting'. I done that, it says: 'Your partner should never have to seek attention from you. A compliment is the easiest thing to give and the nicest thing to receive.' It's obvious when you come to think about it, it's far easier to say something nice than something nasty.

Raquel and Cassandra enter from the bedrooms area. She is dressed in her best frock. She opens her arms in a 'well what do you think' gesture.

Raquel Well?

Busy reading his book.

Del Yes, very well, thank you darling!

Raquel *(Deflated)* Oh! Good.

Albert You look lovely, Raquel.

Raquel Thank you very much, Albert.

Rodney Yes, you look very nice, Raquel.

Raquel Thank you. Wait till you see this.

Raquel exits to bedrooms.

Albert And you look lovely, Cassandra.

Cassandra Thank you, Albert.

Del Oh, there you are, sweetheart.

Feels her belly.

How's my little nephew?

Cassandra Get off!

Raquel returns wearing a fur jacket.

Raquel Well. What d'you think?

Rodney and Cassandra look at each other uncertain of how to react.

Cassandra Well, this is difficult, Raquel. You see, Rodney and I are both opposed to the fur trade.

Rodney What Cass is trying to say is, we both think it looked better on the animal. Whatever that was.

Albert Innit marvellous? Del buys Raquel a coat and you two have a pop at her!

Rodney Del bought it? Oh, I'm sorry, Raquel, I thought it was real!

Del No, dopey, no, it's stimulated fur!

Rodney Sorry, didn't realise.

Del I tell you what we are going to do then. 'Cos little Damien's downstairs with the baby sitter, so let's have a couple of glasses of champagne and then get down the Nag's Head for some decent celebrations.

We see a worried Rodney draw a twenty pound note from his pocket. He quickly replaces it.
(To Cassandra) And oi, you're on orange juice, alright.

Cassandra Yes, thank you, doctor.

Del All part of the service.

Del and Rodney exit to kitchen

Rodney Del. I feel a bit embarrassed.

Del You don't need to. I mean you got a tie, and suit, the full Monty.

Rodney No, no. I didn't mean that, I've only got twenty quid on me.

Del What happened to your wages?

Rodney That is me wages.

Del Oh yeah. I remember we had a bit of a hard week, bruv.

Rodney I know. I was there!

Del Well, I'm even worse off than you. I spent all my money on Raquel's dress. Don't worry about tonight's festivities, we'll put it on the slate.

Rodney D'you reckon Mike'll stand it?

Del Course he will. He's a diamond that man, absolute diamond.

Rodney Well I hope you're right … And oi, why don't you say something nice to Raquel? She's got herself all done up and you ain't said a word.

Del I was busy reading me book, weren't I?

Del and Rodney exit to lounge.
By now Raquel and Cassandra are seated on settee, Raquel reading her magazine.

Alright, alright, don't worry, I'll think of something nice to say. Lets go. Come on then girls, ladies and gentlemen, time to celebrate, go on Rodney, you got the girls, Albert this is yours.

Raquel *(Sees something in magazine)* I don't believe it!

Cassandra What's that?

Raquel You see this girl here. I worked with years ago when I was in show business. She was just a kid then! Look at her now, she's about to appear in the new James Bond film!

Cassandra Ooh, Piers Bronson.

Rodney Now you don't need Piers Bronson dear, you've got me.

Cassandra Yes, haven't I just?

Del *(Looking over Raquel's shoulder)* Well, I tell you what, Raquel. If she can be in a James Bond film, so could you.

Raquel *(Laughing but complimented)* Oh shut up.

Del No, you could.

Raquel Don't be silly.

Del I'm serious. I mean, look at her, she's a dog.

Raquel reacts. Cassandra closes her eyes and turns away. We see Rodney's reaction.
Del gives Rodney the thumbs up as he sips the champagne.

INT. NIGHT. NAG'S HEAD.

It is Saturday night and a packed bar is celebrating Rodney and Cassandra's good news. We find Rodney, Cassandra, Raquel, Denzil, Boycie and Marlene seated at table close to bar. Rodney, Boycie and Marlene appear to have had one too many. Albert is at the piano playing and singing 'You must have been a beautiful baby'.
Trigger is at another table chatting with a few of the regulars. Mickey Pearce is at the bar chatting with a few younger guys. Del is at the bar with Mike who is placing drinks on a tray and other drinks on counter.

Mike So that's a G&T for Raquel, a Tequila Slammer for Rodney, orange juice for Cassandra. Oh by the way, that Doctor Singh, the Indian bloke was in here this afternoon asking about you! Something to do with some paint you sold him.

Del *(Hides his momentary panic)* Was he?

Mike He seemed rather anxious to talk to you. Problems?

Del No, no, no! A simple misunderstanding. Nothing that can't be sorted out with a civilized chat. If he calls in again, Mike, will you tell him I've gone to live in New Zealand.

Mike I think I can remember that. Here, have Rodney and Cassandra thought of a name for the baby yet?

Del No, not yet, Mike. It's early days, she's only just a little bit pregnant, ain't she? Long way to go.

Mike Still, shows Rodney got the hang of it in the end.

Del Oh yes! He's a Trotter, Michael. We don't stop till the job's finished. Right, so that's a Singapore Sling for me, a cognac for Boycie, vodka and lime for Marlene, a Cubre Libre for Denzil, *(Indicates Albert)* a rum and blackcurrant for Bobby Crush, scotches for the market lads, a pint of diesel for Trigger…

Calls over to Mickey.

Mickey, what you and your mates having?

Mickey Canadian Clubs all round, Del. Cheers.

Del And have one yourself, Mike.

Mike Thanks, Del. Right, that's, er call it twenty five pound for cash.

Del Put it on the slate, Michael.

Mike There's no more slate, Del. I've had a visit

Modern Men

from the brewery.

Del Right.

Produces a fiver.

There's a fiver, and, erm …

Patting clothes in search for wallet.

Would you Adam and Eve it? I've only gone and left me wallet at home. I remember now Damien was playing with it earlier. I was teaching him on financial management – you know, avoiding expensive pubs, that sort of thing.

Mike starts to take drinks back.

Mike That's alright, I'll sell 'em to someone else.

Del What d'you mean, you'll sell 'em to someone else? They'll be second-hand.

Mike I'll sell 'em cheap then!

Del Well, I'll give you a fiver for 'em now.

Mike Look Del, it's not my fault, it's the brewery! They've brought in this revolutionary new rule; from now on customers have to pay for their drinks.

Del I hate all these newfangled ideas! I tell you what I'll do for you. Wait there.

Del produces a bag. From his bag Del produces a hair-dryer. It is a different shape from the normal hair-dryer.

Del I've just laid me hands on these brand new, radically-designed hair-dryers. They retail at sixty nine pounds ninety nine in Regents Street, it's yours for fifteen nicker.

Mike Del, look at my hair. What do I need one of them? I've only gotta stick me head out the window for ten seconds and I'm bone dry!

Del produces a jagged ended attachment.

Del But this comes complete with a volumiser. Gives your hair lots of body.

Mike So I could end up looking like Lilly Savage? Very tempting.

Del I'm giving it you for fifteen quid, Mike!

Mike Alright, giss it here.

Puts dryer behind bar.

You still owe me a tenner!

Del I tell you what. You are a bit of a gambling man. We'll have a bet, double or quits. If I win I give you a fiver for this round. You win, I owe you a tenner.

Mike But you already owe me a tenner!

Del You've nothing to lose then, have you?

Trigger approaches at this point and observes Del and Mike.

Hold your hands out in front of you and I bet I can make you turn them over without touching you.

Mike You can make me turn my hands over without touching me?

Del Yeah. It's called 'The Power of Positive Thought'. Go'n, hold 'em out.

Mike holds his hands out in front of him palms down.

No, the other way.

Mike turns his hands, palms up.

There you go, see.

Places the fiver in Mike's upturned palm.

Thank you, Michael.

Del takes tray and returns to table. Mike, holding the fiver, is despondent at losing so easily. Trigger is smiling in wonderment at the trick.

Trigger That's good, innit?

Mike Oh brilliant, Trig, bloody brilliant.

We cut to the table where Del has handed drinks out (or everyone's helping themselves from the tray).

Boycie *(Had one too many)* I have been a motor-dealer for many years now, but, until recently, I never thought of the damage exhaust emig … emiti….

Denzil Fumes.

Boycie Yes. Never thought of the damage fumes did to our world. Let me explain my theory. *(To Rodney)* And the girl Cassandra will bear me out, she works in a bank.

Rodney I know, we're married.

Boycie Precisely.

Del Same again, Mike.

Boycie Now, allow me to continue. My theory is: the future holds the key to all our success.

Del Don't tell Raquel's Dad that, he's an antique dealer.

Boycie We must support the future! By that I mean our world and children. Now I've recently invested a lot of money in electric cars.

Marlene Yeah, he bought Tyler a Scalelectrix set.

Boycie I'm not talking about model bloody racing cars, for Gawd's sake!

Everyone laughs.

Rodney No, he means electric engines. And he's right, Cassandra will bear him out. My wife I'm proud to say, has just got another promotion.

Raquel Oh. Congratulations

Del Well done darling.

Cassandra I haven't been promoted, Rodney. I've just been moved to a new department. My banks has instigated this kind of 'Save the World' programme. We're investing capital in companies involved in recycling and conservation initiatives.

Del She could be talking about us, couldn't she?

Rodney Could she?

Del We have always been very environmentally conceptual.

Raquel Well, I've discovered a new use for old clothes – I wear 'em.

Everyone laughs.

Del It's your round, Rodders.

Rodney Right.

Rodney moves to bar. Mike is placing drinks on counter.

Mike If it's the same as the last round it'll be twenty five pounds.

Rodney Twenty five quid! Erm, Mike?

Mike *(With his back to Rodney)* No!

Rodney produces two tenners and ponders his predicament Trigger approaches.

Trigger Alright, Dave.

Rodney 'Ello Trig

Trigger I can make you turn your hands over without touching you.

Rodney Eh?

Trigger I can make you turn your hands over without touching you. Hold 'em out.

Rodney, with a heavy sigh, paces the tenners in his pocket and holds his hands out palms up.

No, the other way.

Rodney turns his hands over, palms down.

Trigger See?

Hands Rodney a fiver.

There you go, Dave.

Trigger walks away leaving a totally bewildered Rodney with a fiver. At this point Albert finishes his song to much applause. He makes his way to the table.

Denzil Well done, Albert, very nice.

Boycie Yes, it reminded me of the theme track from Noddy – the Movie.

Rodney returns with tray of drinks

Denzil Boycie's right about one thing. You and Rodney should be investing in your children's future. Things like schooling.

Boycie You gotta send 'em to a private school.

Del I'd love to, but I haven't got that sort of money to throw around.

Calls over to bar.

Set 'em up again, Mike.

Marlene Our Tyler's been private since he was three. He's seven now and he can almost write his name.

Del *(Impressed)* Really? We'll have to scrimp and save and send Damien private.

Rodney Well, I'm not sending my child private. There's nothing wrong with state education.

Del I'm not seeing Damien end up in our old school, the Dockside Secondary Modern.

Albert Ooh, that was a tough old place.

Del Tough? We had the only school magazine with an obituary column.

Denzil See, Rodney, we didn't stand a chance of getting a decent education 'cos of the size of the classes.

Boycie Fifty, sixty to a class.

Cassandra Oh you're exaggerating, your classes weren't that big!

Denzil It's the truth, Cassandra. By the time the teacher'd finished reading the morning register it was dinner time.

Del You could tell the calibre of the school by the head boy.

Marlene Who was it?

Del Trigger.

Trigger hears his name and joins them.

Trigger D'you·call, Del?

Del Ah, there you are, Trig. We were just talking old school.

Rodney Alright, let's ask Trig. And you lot stay quiet, no prompting! Trigger, did you have big classes at your old school?

Trigger No, not very big.

Rodney *(At Del)* See!

Trigger High ceilings though.

Boycie And a few low ones. Remember your accident?

Trigger Oh yeah.

Raquel Why? What happened?

Denzil Trig was walking through one of the corridors and he smacked right into a Mind Your Head sign.

Boycie Gave him a right clout. His family sued the education authorities for brain-damage.

Del The judge awarded him seven pound fifty compensations.

Albert *(Confused)* How d'you walk into a 'Mind Your Head' sign? Didn't you see it?

Trigger Of course I saw it, but in those days I couldn't read.

Trigger returns to bar. We see the reactions of Albert, Cassandra, Rodney, Raquel, Marlene and finally Del – it' the first time he's heard the truth about the incident.

Rodney Perhaps it would be best to go private.

Cassandra Yeah, maybe.

Mike *(Calls)* Is someone gonna collect these drinks or what?

Rodney I'll get 'em.

Rodney moves to bar. Mickey Pearce approaches.

Mickey Rodney, congratulations.

Rodney Thanks, Mickey.

Mickey Here, I was down Sid's Caff yesterday and

Modern Men

that Doctor Singh came in looking for Del Boy.

Rodney *(Worried)* Did he?

Mickey He struck me as an angry man. What's it all about?

Rodney Oh, it's something to do with some paint and his surgery. I mean, at the end of the day it's not my problem, is it? I just work for Del.

Mickey Yeah. That's just it. You're just an employee. You just follow orders. Pick things up put things down and then pick 'em up again.

Rodney *(Senses an insult)* Yeah. But I do think for myself.

Mickey But it's not really a job requirement, is it? I start a new job next month. Good money, prospects, company car, the lot.

Rodney Yeah? What are you, a double-glazing salesman?

Mickey No I'm not! Although it is to do with glass.

Rodney What, windows?

Mickey It's a brand new company. They've invented these new solar windows.

Rodney It's double-glazing, innit?

Mickey No, no, no. I mean, fair enough, It does involve two panes of glass, but it's not double-glazing.

Raquel appears behind Rodney.

This company is very profile-conscious and customer-driven. I'm gonna be executive of area perspective and overview, combined with an aggressive targeting strategy.

Rodney You're a salesman.

Mickey No, I'm almost a scientist! It's a whole new concept in user-friendly heating.

Rodney You're a double-glazing salesman, ain't you?

Mickey Yeah. It's better than working for Del, innit? I mean, you're like a 34 year old paper-boy.

Rodney I might not be working for him much longer. I'm on the look-out for something decent ... Oh, Raquel!

Raquel I just came up to give you a hand with the drinks.

Raquel takes a couple of drinks and returns to table.

Rodney Listen to me. There are a few up and coming young firms who are after me.

Mickey Oh yeah, I bet you're being head-hunted by Ian Beale. Well, you'd better do something quick, Rodney, you've got a kid on the way.

Mike *(Calls)* Ladies and gentlemen, will you please raise your glasses to our future Mum and Dad, Rodney and Cassandra.

Locals Rodney and Cassandra.

INT. NIGHT. DEL AND RAQUEL'S BEDROOM.

Same night. Raquel is lying in bed reading a book. Del enters dressed in lime green silk pyjamas with his book.

Raquel *(Quietly)* Oh my God!

Del Well what d'you think?

Raquel Very nice, Del. They're very ... nice.

Del Got 'em off Paddy the Greek, seven pound fifty, can't be bad, eh?

Raquel Lovely.

Del climbs into bed. Del reads a few lines.

Del It says here a bloke's supposed to make contact with his feminine side. Don't mean you've gotta wear a blouse or something does it?

Raquel No, I don't think so.

Del Did you know geezers had feminine sides?

Raquel Well, I've read about it. Look, I wouldn't worry, I don't think it applies to you.

Del Thank God for that. Brilliant book. Did you know that women need to know that they are not taken for granted?

Raquel Really?

Del Yeah, there's some real eye-openers in here.

Raquel Del, can we talk for a minute?

Del *(Engrossed in book)* Eh?

Raquel I heard Rodney and his mate, Mickey Pearce talking tonight. He's starting a new job.

Del Mickey Pearce, you must be joking! That bloke's been on the dole so long he gets invited to the staff dance.

Raquel I heard him telling Rodney about it.

Del The last job Mickey Pearce had was over the East End as a trainee jury-nobbler.

Raquel Del, will you do something for me? Give Rodney a proper job.

Del He's got a proper job.

Raquel No he hasn't, he works for you.

Del Well that's a proper job.

Raquel Alright, what does he do?

Del Well, he, sort of ... well ... lifts things, and ... keeps an eye out ... and, er ... drives.

Raquel And how would you describe his job? Give it a name, a title.

Del Well, he's a ... erm ... He's a ... a Rodney.

Raquel That's not a proper job!

Del It is! There are a lot of people around who are ... 'Rodneys'.

Raquel Give him a job and a title he can be proud of. In seven months he'll be a proud father.

Del Listen Raquel, Look, you don't know him like I do. Rodney's never been what you'd call

247

astute. If I'd left him in charge we wouldn't be where we are today.

Raquel No?

Del No. He hasn't got a business brain. If Rodney owned a flower shop he'd close on Valentines Day.

Raquel Make him feel important. Do something to help him.

Del I'm in the process of doing that very thing. I'm trying to get Rodney some part-time help. With Cassandra the way she is, you never know when he's gonna get a call and have to dash off. So I've let it be known I'm looking for an assistant for Rodney. Someone to take the weight off his shoulders

Raquel Aaah, that's nice of you.

Del I know, I'm a nice fella … This thing with Cassandra.

Raquel You mean her pregnancy?

Del Yeah. Not making you broody, is it?

Raquel No! I never want to go through a pregnancy again.

This is all serious/jokey.

Del Hurt, did it?

Raquel Stung a bit.

Del Yeah, I could tell.

Raquel What gave it away? All that screaming?

Del Yeah, that was the main clue. Still, he was worth it in the end, weren't he?

Raquel Yeah, of course he was. It's not just that. There's the financial side as well. I mean, we can barely afford to pay the mortgage on this place let alone feed another mouth. And then there's the age thing to be taken into account.

Del True. You ain't getting any younger, are you?

Just a look over her book from Raquel.

INT. NIGHT. RODNEY AND CASSANDRA'S BEDROOM.

Same time. Rodney and Cassandra are lying in bed.

Rodney is deep in depressing thought.

Rodney I've been thinking. One day they might make a musical about the history of the Trotter family. Then as a sequel they could do *Schindlers List On Ice.*

Cassandra Correct me if I'm wrong but are you feeling slightly under-motivated tonight?

Rodney There are people on death row with more motivation than me. I've got to get another job, Cass! I get so frustrated working for Del. I just wish he'd present me with a challenge every now and then, like … I don't know … giving someone their change. Tomorrow we are trying

to sell these Mickey Mouse hair-dryers and some aerodynamic cycling hats which are really horse riding helmets that have been sprayed red – and we've got a very angry Sikh after our blood. This is not what you'd call job satisfaction.

Cassandra Rodney, you're the only one who can change Del's attitude. Just going out in the morning hoping for the best is not good enough. At the bank we always advise small businesses to target specifics to achieve maximum market penetration.

Rodney Cassandra, we're talking about Derek Trotter! To Del, 'Market Penetration' means sex under a barrow!

Cassandra But at least you can try to influence him I mean, you're involved in decision-making now, aren't you?

Rodney Oh yeah, sometimes he lets me toss the coin. Decision-making! He's just bought himself a book.

Cassandra Del has?

Rodney Oh yeah. All words, no pictures. It's called *Modem Man* and, according to the author, modern men are decisive, positive decision-makers and Del is making decisions all over the shop! It's thanks to some of Del's decisive, positive decision-making that we have got the consignment of Mickey Mouse hair-dryers and a load of cycling hats that are horse riding helmets sprayed red!

Cassandra Look, why don't you talk to him? I know he jumps the gun a lot, but he does listen to you.

Rodney Yeah, I suppose you're right. Actually I had a word with him this morning and told him he should stop making these on the spot decisions. I said to think things through, consider it, look at all the angles and weigh up the pros and cons. And I think it hit home. Yeah, I'm sure he took my words on board.

INT. NIGHT. TROTTERS' FLAT. DEL AND RAQUEL'S BEDROOM.

Same time. Del and Raquel in bed reading their books.

Del I'm gonna have a vasectomy!

Raquel bursts out laughing.

Did I say something?

Raquel What's brought this on?

Del It says in my book that modern men take the responsibility when it comes to family planning. Millions of men all over the world are having the snip – they do it while you wait.

Raquel Del, why don't you think about it for a while?

Modern Men

Del What's to think about, sweetheart? We can't afford to have another chavvie so I'm a modern man making a positive decision.

Raquel But you've got to consider the future. I mean, I don't want to be a prophet of doom, but what would happen if say in ten years time things didn't work out between us and we broke up. Then you met someone else and wanted to raise another family?

Del Oh, don't be silly, sweetheart.

Kisses her.

Ten years from now I won't be able to raise a smile let alone anything else!

INT. DAY. TROTTERS' LOUNGE. INTERCUT WITH DEL AND RAQUEL'S BEDROOM.

Following day. Rodney, in working clothes, is seated at the table with a cup of tea and looking very down in the mouth.

Rodney *(Calls to kitchen)* I can remember when we set off on the road to our horizon! It was bloody years ago! We had a Labour government, you could eat beef. Des O'Connor was white. And look at us now!

Del *(OS)* How can I put this, Rodney? Shuddup!

Rodney sips his tea. He now becomes aware of something. He turns and finds Damien is standing behind the cocktail cabinet and staring, unsmiling at him.

Rodney flinches as a cold chill runs down his spine.

Rodney Morning, Damien.

Damien I can make you turn your hands over without touching you.

Rodney Yeah?

Damien Hold your hands out.

Rodney holds his hands out as if hypnotised. Turn them over.

Rodney turns his hands over. Damien smiles victoriously.

See!

Damien exits to bedrooms area calling as he does so.

Mummy. I made Uncle Rodney turn his hands over.

Rodney sighs in relief. Del, dressed in suit but minus shoes, enters from kitchen.

Del Alright, I grant you things are a bit bleak at the moment.

Rodney That's like saying the Antarctic's a bit nippy.

Del Our fortune lies just around the next corner. In fact, I'd go so far as to say, this time next year, we'll be millionaires. I mean, we're there where the big opportunities happen. We are in the very forefront of the enterprise-cultured.

Rodney Enterprise cul ... You're so enterprising you bought a load of horse-riding crash helmets! Didn't you stop to think for one moment that Peckham is not big show-jumping country?

Del We'll sell 'em, don't worry. I don't know what's the matter with you. You seemed to have stopped believing. Mum said to me on her deathbed ...

Rodney Oh no!

Del She said, 'Del Boy, never stop believing. Cos if you stop believing you've nothing left to hope for.'

Rodney You've got to have a dream, if you don't have a dream, then how you gonna have a dream come true?

Del That's exactly what she said Mum – she never stopped believing – even after you were born.

Rodney Yeah, well that's all very well, but when ... What's that supposed to mean? 'Even after I was born'?

Del Don't get me wrong, it weren't your fault and none of us blamed you.

Rodney What wasn't my fault?

Del Well, you being a problem child.

Rodney I wasn't a problem child! I was a good boy.

Del Yes, but you did have a problem – you kept getting taller.

Rodney What did you want me to do, stay at two foot four the rest of me life?

Del See, most boys could wear the same trousers for a year and a half, but after a couple of months they'd look like bermuda shorts on you.

Rodney Well most of the pictures I've got of me as a schoolboy I was wearing short trousers anyway.

Del No, Rodney, they might have looked like short trousers but they weren't short trousers. If you look very carefully at the bottoms of the legs you'll find that they are all fraying. That's where two months earlier they'd been rubbing on your shoes. Never stop believing Rodders. Right, I've gotta make a phone call then we'll get going

Del exits to bedrooms area.

Albert enters from kitchen carrying a cup of tea.

Rodney This is difficult.

Albert What's wrong?

Rodney Well, I've got a bit of good news and a bit of bad news for Del ... I'm applying for another job.

Albert Yeah? What's the bad news?

249

Rodney That is the bad news! The good news is I'll stay on with Del until he finds someone suitable to replace me.

Albert Well, that should take him about half an hour.

Rodney Yeah, you won't be saying that when I'm the managing director of something, will you?

Albert You got something lined up then?

Rodney produces the Peckham Echo.

Rodney There's a job advertised in the paper. Listen to this:

He reads from newspaper.

'Local company seeks ambitious, energetic and creative young person to join its successful sales force.' Well, who they describing?

Albert No, go on.

Rodney It's me!

Albert Is it?

Rodney Yes!

He reads on.

'Experience with computers an advantage but not essential. Successful applicant will receive full training, good salary and company vehicle.' Well, I'm experienced with computers.

Albert I know. But you've never got one to work yet.

Rodney Oh, shuddup!

Albert exits to his bedroom laughing.

INT. DAY. DEL AND RAQUEL'S BEDROOM

Raquel is in dressing gown and putting clothes on hangers and back in wardrobe. Del is dressed, minus shoes, and is talking on his new mobile phone.

Del *(On phone)* Yes … I'll call in this afternoon and sign all the forms. Yes, thank you. Bonjour.

He switches phone off.

Look at that, me new digital phone, clear as a bell.

Raquel Was that the clinic you were talking to?

Del Yeah. I'm having it done next Tuesday.

Raquel You're serious about this, aren't you?

Del Oh yeah, never been more serious.

Raquel Look, Del, volunteering for this vasectomy is very brave and thoughtful of you, and I'm flattered that you're doing it for me. But you don't have to do it.

Del No, I think it's for the best, sweetheart.

Raquel But if you get … you know, sore – I don't want you coming back to me and saying, 'It's all your fault, Raquel!'

Del As if I would do that!

Del is now putting his shoes on and is some distance from his mobile phone. The mobile phone begins ringing.

Del That's the first call on me new phone. Answer it darling, will you? And be posh!

Raquel What?

Del Be posh.

Raquel Yes, sir!

On phone in very exaggerated posh voice.

Hello, how may I help you?

Smiles at Del.

We now intercut with lounge.

Rodney *(On BT phone)* Oh hello. I'm phoning about the job advertised in the *Peckham Echo*.

Cut to bedroom.

Raquel reacts as she recognises Rodney's voice.

Raquel *(Very posh)* Hold the line, caller. *(To Del)* Have you put an ad in the *Peckham Echo*?

Del Yeah, help for Rodney. Who's that?

Raquel Rodney.

Del Rodney? What's he phoning me for? He's only in the bloody living room.

Raquel No, he's applying for the job.

Del What? He's applying to assist himself!

Smiles.

I gotta think about this. Press hold, it plays music.

Raquel *(On phone)* I'll put you on hold whilst I connect you with our marketing department.

Cut to living room.

Rodney *(On phone)* Thank you.

From Rodney's phone we hear a click and then "Old Shep" begins playing.

Rodney looks at the phone and thinks, 'Old Shep'? It is a strong clue, but he doesn't get it.

Cut to bedroom.

Del Treacherous little git! I'm gonna wind him right up.

Raquel No, Del, don't. He'll feel embarrassed.

Del With any luck.

Del takes phone. Now on the phone in strong Welsh accent.

'Allo, this is the Marketing Manager, sorry to have kept you, My name is Ivor Hardy …

Rodney *(On phone)* Oh hello Mr Hardy.

Del *(On phone)* And you are?

Rodney *(On phone)* My name's Rodney Trotter.

Del *(On phone)* Trotter you say? You're not related to the Trotter brothers, are you?

Rodney *(On phone)* No, I've never heard of them.

Del *(On phone)* Oh well, you're lucky. I've heard rumours about them. Right couple of scallywags so I hear! Well, mind you the elder one's OK. A very good businessman and intelligent with it, so

Modern Men

I'm told. It's his dippy young brother who's the problem.

Rodney *(On phone)* Oh really? Like I say I've never heard of them. So, you mention a good salary and company vehicle – could you tell me a little more about that, please? ... Mmmh ...Yes, I can ride a bike.

> *Del, with phone concealed in pocket, enters from bedrooms area.*

Del Alright, Rodders?

Rodney *(On phone)* Just one moment please. Yeah. T'riffic.

Del *(Scanning room)* I wanna make a call.

Where's the phone?

Rodney Erm – I'm using it, talking with Cassandra.

Del She alright is she?

Rodney Yeah, great.

Del Give her my love.

Rodney Will do.

Del And give her yours as well.

Rodney Eh?

Del In my *Modern Man* book it says it's very important to tell the lady in your life that you love her, especially when she's pregnant. Go on, tell her.

Rodney What? No, I feel embarrassed.

Del There's only you and me here and I suggested it. Go on, tell her.

Rodney Later.

Del No, go on, tell her.

Rodney *(Quietly)* God! *(On phone. Very quickly so it's almost indiscernible)* I love you.

> *Del, about to enter kitchen, produces his phone and cups his hands round mouthpiece.*

Del *(On phone)* Sorry, what was that?

Rodney *(On phone)* Nothing. I coughed.

Del *(On phone)* Oh, for a moment I thought you said you loved me.

Rodney *(On phone)* No, I just coughed. So what exactly do you sell and what would be the successful applicants duties?

> *Now Del enters from kitchen. Rodney has his back to Del. Del slowly moves forward until, for the final lines, he standing next to Rodney.*

Del *(On phone as Hardy)* Well we buy and sell anything we can lay our hands on, isn't it? And you will be expected to go down the market and sell the old crap from a suitcase. You could be just the man for the job, Mr Trotter. We're always on the lookout for ...

> *Now adopts his normal voice.*

... devious little plonkers like you!

> *Rodney looks at Del – now down at Del's phone. He now looks at his own phone.*

Rodney *(On phone)* Did you put that ad in the paper, Derek?

Del *(On phone)* Yes I did, Rodney!

> *Rodney hangs up.*

Rodney I don't believe it! The one job in the paper I really fancied and it was mine! So what's going on then? Were you gonna find someone else and then get rid of me?

Del No, Rodney. You were trying to get rid of me! I was looking for someone to help you, in case you have to get away quickly because of Cassandra. I was just tryin' to help you, Rodney, that's all.

Rodney *(Touched by Del's thoughtfulness)* I didn't realise. Thanks, Del – and I'm sorry.

Del So what's all this new job lark?

Rodney It really hit home the other day. When the baby's born we gotta fill in the birth certificate. There's a section there that says; 'Father's Occupation' And I thought, what do I put? A gofer!

Del No. You put 'Sales Director.' I'm going to expand, Rodney. From now on, Rodders, you are in charge of sales and I'm in charge of purchasing. You'll be in the marketplace, you'll be selling. I'll be up there in the factories and the warehouses buying it. If one line is selling particularly well, you get on the blower to me and say, buy more of them Del.

Rodney Yes! We should have done this ages ago.

Del Expansion.

> *Rodney follows Del into kitchen.*

Rodney And streamline the business.

Del Yes. We'll expand by streamlining! So, what d'you say?

Rodney I assume I'll receive an increase in salary commensurable with my extra responsibility and workload?

Del Yes. Say fifteen per cent.

Rodney But you don't pay me regularly now.

Del Well, I'll have to owe you more ... Rodders, I feel as if we have just taken the first step on the road to our horizon

Rodney Yeah, me too

Del Come on. Let's go down Sid's caff. Historic moments always make me fancy a bacon roll.

INT. DAY. SID'S CAFE. LOCATION.

> *Rodney is seated at table eating a bun. Del is sitting opposite finishing a fry-up. Del sees something at cafe window and panics.*

Del Quick Rodney! Get down!

> *Del and Rodney hide beneath the table.*

Rodney What's happening?

Del It's that Doctor Singh!

> *We see a tall, well-built Sikh man looking through cafe window. Satisfied that Del is not there, he leaves.*
> *Rodney and Del clamber out from beneath table and sit back in seats.*

That was a close one.

Rodney He's gonna catch us eventually.

Del Yeah, well we'll cross that bridge when we come to it ... Rodney, I've been thinking.

Rodney What about?

Del A vasectomy.

> *Rodney chokes on his bun. Del pats him on back.*

Gone down the wrong hole, has it?

Rodney Yeah. A vasectomy??

Del Keep the noise down!

Rodney How does Raquel feel about it?

Del No, I'm gonna have it done!

Rodney I know that! Bloody hell! I meant, have you discussed it with Raquel?

Del Yeah, last night I said to her 'Sweetheart, I'm gonna have a vasectomy.'

Rodney So it was quite an in-depth discussion?

Modern Men

Del You can't make these decisions lightly.

Rodney And what was her reaction?

Del Well, she was quiet for a while – then she started laughing again. See, we can't really afford another nipper and we ain't got room in the flat anyway. And I don't think Raquel fancies having another baby, not after Damien.

Rodney Can't blame her.

Del How d'you mean?

Rodney Well, it was a long labour, weren't it? She had a bad time

Del That's right. So in the end we both agreed it was for the best. And what do we want with another baby? We've got Damien and he's like two kids rolled into one, ain't he?

Rodney At least ... Del, there are other ways of not having a child. Couldn't you, you know, wear something in bed?

Del Wear something – I've got me new pyjamas ... Oh gotchyer! No, too risky!

Rodney What about a cap?

Del A cap?

Rodney I don't mean go to bed in a beret. I mean a medical sort of thing.

Del No, don't fancy that. Lennie Norris's missus used one of those and she still fell for a kid. You know him, that boy down the market with the flat head. See, me and Raquel have only gotta look at each other and she's three months gone. I must be full of hormones.

Rodney I'm full of hormones as well! You can't get any more hormones into me. Doctor said.

Del Yeah, but I think I must have loads of, you know ... tadpoles.

Rodney Tadpoles?

Del Those things you see on the telly under the microscope.

Rodney I've got loads of them as well!

Del Yeah, but I must have more tadpoles than the Serpentine!

Rodney Funny innit? I'm just starting off and you're putting a stop to it.

Del Yeah, it's a funny old world.

Rodney You gonna have it done at the hospital?

Del Well, I ain't letting Trigger do with his Black and Decker, am I?

Rodney I mean, are you going to the hospital or the local clinic?

Del The clinic. I want your advice. Before I have it you know – done ...

Rodney Yeah?

Del Well, a lot of these rich and successful go to one of these banks and leave their – tadpoles.

Rodney Do they?

Del Yeah, I read it in my book. D'you think I should do that?

Rodney You could. I don't know how Nat West'll feel about it.

Del No, special banks that freeze things. Then, when I'm rich and famous, future generations will be able to use it. There could be lots of little Damiens everywhere.

Rodney No! What I mean is, it could upset Raquel. Psychologically, she might think you were being unfaithful. You know how a woman's mind works.

Del I never thought of that. Well done, bruv. Come on then, onwards and upwards. Rodney, don't tell anyone about this, will you?.

Rodney Of course not.

They move towards door.

Del *(Cheerfully)* Thank you very much, Sid, that was horrible as usual.

Sid *(Equally cheerful)* All the best, Del.

Del exits. Rodney is about to exit.

Rodney Sid. Del's having a vasectomy.

Sid A vasectomy? *To other diners.* Del Boy's having a vasectomy.

Rodney exits leaving the entire cafe discussing Del's vasectomy.

INT. DAY. SURGICAL THEATRE. DREAM SEQUENCE.

A frightened Del is laid on a surgical bed. He is wearing a surgical gown which is done up down to the thighs. We see his bare legs. A white-coated middle-aged nurse is exiting the room.

Nurse The doctor will be with you in a moment.

Del Thank you, nurse.

Del looks at the instruments tray. He sees a scalpel which twinkles with razor-sharpness. The door opens and Doctor Singh enters. He smiles at Del.

Dr Singh Mr Trotter.

Del *(Terrified)* Doctor Singh. Em, about that paint I sold you for your surgery.

Dr Singh Oh, let's not worry about that, I have work to do.

He picks up the scalpel.

Not nervous are you?

Del Just a tad you know. It's my first time.

Dr Singh *(Laughs almost evilly)* Mine too!

Del visibly gulps. Dr Singh pulls Del's gown open in a brusque manner.

Del flinches.

Dr Singh *(Apparently examining vitals)* Mmh mmh ... Mmmh ... You're a big man, Mr Trotter.

Del Oh, thank you doctor.

Dr Singh pats Del's stomach.

Dr Singh You should go on a diet.

Laughs.

I always say that, just to relax the patient.

Del Yeah, I've got to remember that one next time I've got some bloke's vitals in me hand.

Dr Singh I'll give you a small injection just to numb the area.

Del Oh thank you.

The Doctor now produces a large hypodermic syringe with a long needle.

He approaches Del.

Dr Singh This might sting a bit.

Del opens his mouth to cry out in fear.

INT. NIGHT. DEL AND RAQUEL'S BEDROOM.

Del is in bed asleep. He wakes from his nightmare and cries out.

Del Aaarghhh!

Raquel What's wrong?

Del Eh? Oh, nothing! Bad dream. Can't remember what it was about now. This, em, this vasectomy idea. What d'you really think about it?

Raquel I don't mind, honest.

Del Alright, Raquel, you win! I won't have it done.

EXT. DAY. NELSON MANDELA HOUSE.

The three-wheeled van pulls up and Del and Rodney alight. Del opens the back of the van and takes his suitcase out.

Rodney So what finally put you off the vasectomy then? Didn't have the balls?

Laughs.

Del No, I wasn't frightened! It was a medical reason. See, I kept thinking about the tadpoles.

Rodney What about 'em?

Del Well ... where do they go?

Rodney How d'you mean?

Del Well when you have the operation it stops 'em going, well, their normal route so where do they go?

Rodney Were you worried about 'em hanging round on street comers?

Del All I'm saying is they've gotta go somewhere. It got to such a point I thought I'd be frightened to sneeze.

Now Doctor Singh appears as if from nowhere.

Dr Singh Aah! Caught you at last, Mr Trotter.

Del Doctor Singh, how nice to see you again.

Dr Singh Have you seen my surgery recently? That paint you sold me is peeling off in great chunks. It's a medical practice, Mr Trotter, and it looks as if my walls have got scabies! Patients are leaving me.

Del Yes. The thing is, Dr Singh, we didn't realise until some time after that the paint was ever so slightly out of date, did we, Rodney?

Rodney No. We spotted a tin and noticed it said: 'Use By June 1983'.

Dr Singh Well I want something done about it and fast!

Del Yes of course, Doctor Singh. I'll have a member of my painting and decorating department call on you tomorrow.

Dr Singh If you don't, Mr Trotter ...

Points a threatening finger at Del.

I'll be back!

Singh moves away towards a small pop-pop motorbike.

Del Yes thank you, Doctor Singh. Missing you already ...'I'll be back'! He always says that. Did you know that's why they've nicknamed him the Turbanator? The Turban-ator. Geddit?

Rodney I don't believe you sometimes! Doctor Singh is an honest and law-abiding man. You knew that paint was iffy.

Del How was I supposed to know? What am I, some sort of paint expert?

We see Doctor Singh driving off on his small motorbike ...

Don't give me all that rubbish about him being a law-abiding man! Look, riding that bike without wearing a crash helmet.

Rodney He is a Sikh! Under the law Sikhs are excused crash hats! I mean, how's he gonna get a helmet over that turban?

Del Yeah, I didn't think of that. I suppose that's why you never see a Sikh astronaut.

Rodney *(Sighs)* More than likely, Del.

Rodney enters the flats. Del watches Mr Singh driving away.

INT. DAY. TROTTERS' LOUNGE.

Wall clock stands at 5.30. Albert is reading a newspaper.

We hear Rodney and Del's raised voices from the open door to bedrooms area.

Rodney *(OS)* I am not wearing it, OK? It's half past five and that's my going home time!

Del *(OS)* Rodney, opportunities don't stop presenting themselves just 'cos Cassandra's put the sprout out. At least you know it looks so you can get an overview.

Rodney *(OS)* This is bloody stupid, Del and I'm not doing it!

Del *(OS)* Since when has a safety-device been stupid? This little invention of mine could help

Modern Men

prevent serious injury. I mean just imagine, there are millions of Sikhs all over the world driving motor-cycles who are completely unprotected.

Rodney enters from bedrooms area. He is wearing his normal clothes but strapped to his head is one of Del's horse-riding protective helmets with a turban wrapped round it. Del opens his arms expansively as if to say: look how wonderful Rodney looks. Albert looks at Rodney, shakes his head sadly, and returns to his paper.

Del And the answer to all their problems is my new company – TCT!

Albert TCT?

Del Trotters Crash Turbans. This is our opportunity to do something for our fellow man.

Rodney It's also an opportunity for you to get rid of them horse-riding crash-hats you got lumbered with.

Del Hang about, this is a stereototype, Rodney.

Rodney It's not even a prototype! It's a show-jumping helmet with one of Raquel's old scarfs glued on top!

Del Exactly! That's because Raquel is one hundred percent behind this project! She said, 'Take whatever you need Del, I wanna do my bit for mankind'.

Rodney sees himself in the mirror.

Rodney Look! Look! I mean … Look!

Del I think you look rather dashing.

Rodney I look like a human-cannonball who's crashed into someone's washing-line.

Del God, I hate vanity! Rodney, think of this in humanitarian terms. Every time a Sikh bloke gets on a motorbike, like our friend Mr Singh, he is taking his life in his hands. That's why you never see gangs of Sikh Hell's Angels. But once these come on the market they'll all be dashing around like Barry Sheen. As soon as you've taken this over to Southall and Wembley and shown the Sikh community in all its glory …

Rodney *(Cuts in)* Take it over and show 'em?

Del They will be buying these by the thousand. Then we'll be selling throughout Asia and America and Australia.

Rodney You expect me to go over and sell it?

Del You are my new director of sales aren't you?

Rodney They'll smash my head in!

Del Of course they won't, they're peaceful loving people. Anyway even if they do, you'll be wearing a Trotter Crash Turban! A perfect opportunity to prove how effective it is! You know it makes sense.

Rodney All I know is I am not stepping outside this door dressed like this!

Raquel enters from kitchen carrying cutlery and dinner things which she takes to table.

Raquel *(No reaction to Rodney's condition)* Alright, Rodney.

Rodney Hiya, Raquel.

Albert During the war.

Del Will you shut up? Can't you see that Rodney and I are in the middle of a very important board meeting and we are not interested in U-Boats or giant squids!

Albert I was just gonna say that during the war I spent some time in India and I got to know a little about the Sikh religion. And what I discovered was; to a Sikh the turban has supposed to enter the body. In other words it has to be in contact with the head.

Rodney Yeah, see this thing doesn't touch the head 'cos there's a bloody horse riding helmet in between!

Del Alright, I'll stick a bit underneath so it is touching the head! I haven't finalised the design yet! What d'you think of it, Raquel?

Raquel I can't see it catching on, Del. I mean, what would you wear with it?

Raquel laughs. Now spots something.

Is that my scarf?

Del I'll get you another one, don't worry.

Raquel You've got a nerve, Trotter!

Del Look at it again, Raquel and realise this is not a fashion statement.

Raquel I guessed that, Derek. I guessed that!

Del It's a safety device.

Rodney Del, people'd rather be critically injured than wear this!

The phone rings and Albert moves to answer it.

Del Answer that will you? You take my word for it. Three months from now you'll see that thing on *Tomorrow's World*.

Raquel More like *Wayne's World*.

Rodney I am not going on *Tomorrow's World* looking like this.

Albert Rodney, it's Cassandra's bank for you.

Rodney Oh Gawd, I suppose she's got another late meeting. Hello … When?

Del People laughed when they invented air bags.

Raquel No they didn't, it was a good invention.

Del Alright, tell me one invention that was laughed at when it was first seen.

Raquel *(Points to Rodney's head)* That!

Rodney *(On phone)* Yeah, I'm on my way, thank you.

Replaces receiver.

Del What's up, Rodders?

Rodney *(Too shocked for tears or emotion)* They rushed Cassandra to hospital. She's had a miscarriage.

Del, Raquel and Albert just stare blankly at this news.

INT. NIGHT. HOSPITAL/A&E WAITING AREA.

It should look over-crowded, under staffed and under-funded.

The waiting area is crowded.

In the background people are queuing to register at admin' counter. Nurses and doctors are rushing to and fro.

Hospital staff are carrying more seriously ill patients on stretchers.

There are parents with crying children and babies, someone with their arm in a make-shift sling, someone in a track-suit, their broken ankle heavily bandaged, someone with blood over their eyes and nose where they have taken a fall or been beaten up and elderly couples, frightened and just waiting patiently.

Walking around and through the seated patients is a young man who is generally being a pain in the arse to everyone.

He is six feet tall and well-built. He wears scruffy jeans and an equally scruffy T-shirt. He is unshaven and you would guess, in his private life, is a drunkard and a bully. He is used to shouting and frightening people and therefore getting his own way. He's the kind of guy you would love to see someone beat up.

Man *(Shouting at passing staff)* Are you lot having a laugh with me or something? I've been here nearly twenty minutes already and the only person in this poxy hospital who's spoken to me is that old cow.

Indicates registration clerk.

Receptionist I'm sorry sir, but we're very busy, we'll attend to you as soon as we can. Now, if you'd like to take a seat.

Man I'll tell you what I'd like to do darling. I'd like to take a seat and chuck it through that bleedin' window.

During this Del and Rodney have entered through main doors. Rodney is in a state of shock and fear.

Del Take it easy, Rodney, everything's gonna be alright.

Del approaches a sister

Excuse me, nurse. D'you know which ward Mrs Trotter is in?

Sister Are you Mr Trotter?

Del Yes, I am.

Sister This way.

Del Come on, Rodders.

INT. NIGHT. HOSPITAL CORRIDOR.

The sister, followed by Del who is followed by Rodney, move down the corridor until they come to a gown room.

The sister produces a theatre gown and hat.

Sister *(To Del)* Put these on. It's just a precaution.

Del puts gown, etc, on.

Rodney is just standing in background like a spare one. The sister indicates down corridor.

Mrs Trotter is in a single room, number 46, on the right. Please remember she is, naturally, still very upset and we don't want her being excited in any way.

Del Thanks.

Del moves off.

Rodney Can I put one of them on?

Sister *(For the first time becomes aware of Rodney)* Who are you?

Rodney I'm her husband.

Sister *(Refferring to the fast disappearing Del)* Who the hell's that then?

Rodney He's my bruvver.

INT. NIGHT. OUTSIDE ROOM 46.

Del arrives at room 46. He pauses at the door as he awaits Rodney's arrival. Rodney, with gown on and just placing hat on head, arrives.

Rodney *(Looks at the door with trepidation)* What the bloody hell am I supposed to say to her?

Del You'll say something, Rodney. Don't worry, it'll just come. Now listen to me, Rodney, at this pacific moment in time, Cassandra she don't need doom and gloom. She needs you to be optimistic.

Rodney Oh yeah, I feel optimistic, right now don't I?

Del It doesn't matter how you feel, Rodney you have got to …

Rodney *(Cuts in)* It doesn't matter how I feel?

Del No. You do your crying in the van on our way home! Right now you've got to be her rock. Talk about the future, not the past or the present, just the future. But cause you two, you two have got so many good times to come. Things are gonna get better and better.

Rodney Ain't it strange how I find that hard to believe right now?

Del Well you believe it 'cos it's true. Right now

Modern Men

she needs your strength. So no booing or sobbing, just be comforting and understanding. It's time to be a man, Rodney. A real man. Right?

Rodney Right.

Del OK. Good boy.

Del opens the door.

INT. NIGHT. SINGLE WARD/ROOM 46.

Cassandra is seated in the bed propped up by pillows. She is just staring blankly at the wall in front of her. The door opens and Rodney and Del enter.

Rodney smiles to her.

Rodney The bank phoned and told me.

Cassandra smiles back to him and then breaks down.

Cassandra *(Tearfully, almost like a child)* I'm sorry, Rodney!

Del breaks down crying. After his big corridor speech, Rodney allows himself a glance at the sobbing Del. He now moves to Cassandra.

Rodney What are you saying sorry for? Don't be silly.

Cassandra I let you down! I let everyone down!

Rodney Of course you didn't! It happens, Cass, it just happens. There was nothing you or I could do.

Del You didn't let anyone down sweetheart. And don't blame yourself. You tell her, Rodney. This time next year – go on, tell her.

Rodney Yeah I will. *(Joins Del)* Look, I think maybe this'd be a good time for us to be on our own to discuss a few things.

Del Yeah, I think you're right, bruv. Cassandra, me and Rodney are gonna pop outside for a little chat.

Rodney No, I meant me and Cassandra should be on our own.

Del Of course! Yes, right! *(To Cassandra)* I'll see you later, Cassandra. And …

Doesn't know what to say.

You know I'll wait for you outside, Rodders.

Del exits and closes door. Rodney sits by bed and takes Cassandra's hand.

Cassandra looks into his eyes but cannot find any words.

Cassandra *(Cries)* I lost our baby.

Rodney I know. I can't leave you alone with anything, can I?

He smiles at her.

She smiles back through her tears. They hug each other.

We're gonna get over this, Cass, and we're gonna win. And d'you know why? It's because we are strong – very strong. Things are gonna

get better and better and better for us. Or as Del would say, betterer.

Cassandra *(Smiles)* I love you, Rodney.

Rodney And I love you, Cass. I love you so much.

INT. NIGHT. A&E WAITING ROOM.

The scruffy bully boy is still walking round and complaining loudly.

We now see Mike talking to a doctor. He has a bandage on his forehead.

Mike It sort of burnt me right across the forehead here.

He produces Del's hair-dryer.

See, the bloke what sold it to me said it was a hair-dryer. It turns out to be an electric paint-stripper.

Doctor Come with me, Mr Fisher.

The Doctor and Mike move off.

Man Why's he getting seen before me?

Del, in gown and cap, enters.

I don't know why people bother paying their national health stamps. If I'd ever had a job I wouldn't have paid for 'em.

Receptionist Would you please keep your voice down?

Man No. It's a free country and I'll shout as much as I want! Well, like you're looking after all these bloody malingerers – I should be top of your list.

We see Del eyeing the man. There is a vengeful look on Del's face.

I took some pills earlier, now I've no idea what they are 'cos I was drunk, but they're starting to upset me! You nurses are always whinging about getting poor wages. You don't deserve anything better 'cos do you hear that, you're all sodding useless.

Del approaches.

Del Excuse me, sir.

The man turns.

Man What?

Del now chins him with a crisp right-hander. The man is catapulted backwards by the force of the blow. The back of his legs hit a low table and he somersaults on to his back. He ends up sprawled on the floor with his head resting up against a wall. Del approaches.

Del Feeling any better?

Man *(Glassy-eyed and frightened)* Yes, thank you, doctor.

Del All part of the service. Bonjour.

As Del passes an elderly couple who have witnessed the incident in wide-eyed surprise:

I bet you wish you'd gone private, don't you?

257

Time On Our Hands

TROTTER FLAT. INT. STUDIO. NIGHT.

It is 6.30am. A worried, pressurised Raquel is seated at the pub-bench table. She is studying a recipe book and making notes for a shopping list.
On the table is a tea pot and cornflakes, etc.

Raquel Potatoes … garlic … lemon grass. Lemon grass! Where the hell am I gonna get lemon grass from? Oh to hell with it, we'll have it without lemon grass.

Del in dressing gown and just woke up, enters from bedrooms area

Del It's six thirty, what are you doing up?
Raquel I couldn't sleep. I'm worried about tonight.
Del Raquel, it's only your Mum and Dad coming for dinner.
Raquel It's not only my Mum and Dad coming for dinner.
Del What, are they bringing some neighbours or something?
Raquel I mean, it's not that simple! My parents and I didn't see each other for years – didn't even talk.
Del I know. But you've kissed and made up now, ain't you? You and Damien, spent the weekend at their house.
Raquel I know. But now they're coming here! They've never been to the flat before. I've never cooked for them before … They've never met you before.
Del Exactly! I'll be right by your side. What have you told them about me?
Raquel Well … I said your name was Derek …That's about it really.
Del Well, with someone like me that's all you need to know. What you gonna do us to eat?
Raquel Noisettes of lamb in red wine and cognac.
Del You don't need to go to that trouble, Sweetheart, a bacon sandwich'll do … Oh you mean tonight! Lamb in red wine and cognac. Lovely jubbly. It's gonna be a great evening.

Albert enters from bedroom and crosses to hall.

Del Morning, Unc.
Albert Morning all.
Raquel And another thing. You promised you'd get another table and some proper chairs! We can't eat at this thing.

Del It's all taken care of, sweetheart. Denzil' s coming round later to take all this gear away and deliver our new stuff. I don't know why you're going to all this bother. I did say we could take 'em out for dinner. I'm really well in with the manager at the local restaurant.
Raquel No, this is my home now and if my parents want me back in their lives they'd better get used to it. Besides, Spudulike's always full on a Friday.
Del Have it your way, I'll do us a bit of breakfast, shall I?
Raquel OK. Will you check behind the bar and see if we've got any cognac?
Del There's loads. Albert, what d'you want?
Albert Well, if we're starting early I'll have a cognac as well.
Del That's for tonight's meal! I'll pour you a cup of tea. Albert, tell Raquel to stop worrying and fussing about this meal tonight will you?
Albert You've got nothing to worry about, love. We'll all lend a hand. You do the meat and I'll do the gravy.
Del See, I'll do the veg, I'm a dab hand with a pint of water and a bucket of cabbage.
Albert The only thing we've gotta worry about is whether those bloody lifts are working – they broke down twice this week. We can't have Cassandra climbing up all those stairs, not after what she's been through. Are her and Rodney coming to dinner?
Rodney Well, I invited them. But the way they are at the moment, who knows.
Del I hope they do – they need to get out.
Raquel What d'you mean? Rodney's out every night!
Del He's going through a very bad time, Raquel.
Raquel He's going through a very bad time? How d'you think Cassandra feels? She's the one who had the miscarriage! She needs her husband by her side, not out drinking in some pub or club.
Del I know that! But she's a woman, isn't she? She's stronger than Rodney. I've known him all his life. He's always found it difficult to face up to things that hurt him. He tends to to walk away and pretend it isn't happening. That's what he's doing now. But once he gets it off his chest he'll be fine.

The phone rings.

(On phone) Trotters Independent Traders … Hello, Cassandra, what are you doing up early?… Was he? *(To Raquel)* Rodney was only out again last night till the early hours.

Raquel I know, you were with him!

Del Eh? Oh yeah!

Hands Raquel phone.

Here are, you talk to Cassandra.

Raquel I'll take it in the kitchen.

Raquel exits to kitchen.

Albert What Rodney needs is a counter-worry.

Del You what?

Albert During the …

Del If you say during the war, I'll pour this cup of tea over your head!

Albert I wasn't gonna say during the war!

Del Alright then.

Albert Bloody little know all!

Del Sorry.

Albert That's alright. During the 1939-1945 conflict with Germany – I was sailing on a frigate, HMS *Spinx*, in the Adriatic. Now in those days a ship's crew was full of stress and fear.

Del Especially when they saw you walking up the gangplank!

Albert So our old skipper, Captain Kenworthy, used to allay all those fears by creating a counter-worry. Like one day he announced there was a cholera epidemic on the ship.

Del I bet that cheered you all up, didn't it?

Albert It took their minds off the U-Boats and sharks.

Del Well, thanks for that, Unc. It's lucky your Captain Kenworthy never became a Samaritan. You wouldn't be able to get a tug under Chelsea Bridge for falling bodies!

Raquel enters from kitchen.

Raquel He's still the same. Cassandra said he's even stopped going to see the counsellor at the hospital.

Del Well, Albert reckons that we ought to tell Rodney there's a cholera epidemic in Peckham and that should get him out of his mood.

Albert I said give him a counter-worry. Look, If Rodney thought a close friend or a relative was ill he'd start worrying about them and stop worrying about himself.

Raquel Yeah, I see. So when that person becomes better Rodney would have forgotten what he was worried about in the first place.

Albert Exactly.

Raquel It's worth a try. It's got to be someone he really cares for.

Del Damien.

Raquel How can you ask a five year old to act ill?

Albert I could pretend to be ill.

Del Yeah, but how can he notice the difference? It's gotta be me, innit?

We hear front door slam.

Del Listen to me, I'm ill alright?

Del lays on settee and begins coughing and wheezing. Rodney enters wearing his working clothes.

Rodney Morning.

Albert Morning, son. How's Cassandra?

Rodney Fine, thank you.

Del *(Pained and ill)* Morning, Rodney.

Coughs.

How are you?

Coughs.

Rodney Alright.

Sits and reads his paper.

Raquel Del's not very well, Rodney.

Rodney Oh, I'll go home then.

Del No, I might make a recovery.

Albert We called the doctor in last night.

Rodney *(Couldn't care less)* Yeah.

Del I suppose you're wondering what he said?

Rodney *(Concentrating on paper)* What?

Del He said I would live – but he doesn't recommend it.

Rodney Right.

Raquel *(Quietly)* I'm worried about him, Rodney. Has he ever suffered with pleurisy?

Rodney Only when he's tried to spell it.

Raquel I'll make a pot of tea.

Raquel exits to kitchen.

There is a pause while Rodney continues reading the newspaper apparently oblivious of the other two. Del looks to Albert. Albert shrugs.

Del, forgetting himself, calls out.

Del Raquel.

Now he remembers he is ill and coughs.

(Weakly) Could I have a cup of tea too, please?

Rodney It's alright. I'll get it.

Del Thank you Rodney.

Rodney exits to kitchen. Del sits up.

You uncaring little git! I could be on me last knockings here and you don't give a toss if I've got yellow fever or foot-fungus!

Cut to kitchen. Raquel is pouring boiling water into teapot.

Rodney Del wants a cup as well. What's wrong!

Raquel I'm just worried, that's all. A man can't keep on drinking and smoking and staying out late without it having some effect!

Rodney There's no need to worry, Raquel. Del's one of them people who survive everything.

Time On Our Hands

They're a sort of tribe. You find members of 'em in every country in the world. Their entire lifestyles and philosophies fly in the face of medical science. They drink too much, eat greasy food and smoke cigars and cigarettes, but nothing ever happens to them. Anyone else tried it and they'd be dead by forty, but this tribe just goes on. They usually pass away peacefully in their sleep aged ninety – next to 'em is a burnt-out roll-up, an untouched sausage sandwich and a half-finished guinness. And don't ask whether Del's one of them Raquel, 'cos he is! He is.

Raquel Actually Rodney, I was talking about you.

Rodney Me? There's nothing wrong with me!

Raquel Rodney, you've been banned from The Nag's Head. Serial killers don't get barred from that pub! I know what's happened and I can only try to imagine how you and Cassy must be feeling. But you're out almost every night at the pub, leaving her alone in the flat.

Rodney Cass wants to be on her own.

Raquel No, she doesn't. She wants support. She wants you ... I'm not stupid enough to say forget what's happened – you never can. What I'm saying is; get back to basics, to all the everyday things that have to be taken care of. You've got to do it for Cassandra and for you and for the baby you will one day have.

Raquel smiles reassuringly at him but Rodney turns away, refusing to discuss the matter. Raquel shrugs and exits to lounge.

EXT. DAY. DEL'S GARAGE/GARAGE BLOCK.

Five hours later. Rodney is working in the garage trying to itemise all the various bits and pieces that TITco has acquired over the years. Scattered around the many shelves in the garage are various boxes of batteries, electrical plugs, smoke detectors, sunglasses, superglue, frying pans, ladies tights, etc. Hanging on one wall is Del's old diving suit. On the garage floor (and outside the garage) we see a pile of cobweb covered briefcases, bits of cars, a couple of bicycle frames, two or three tea chests full of gold toot and against one wall an ancient gas stove. Rodney, still in his depressed, distant mood, is checking through the items and making notes in a small pad. He is throwing himself into work in an almost obsessional way.

Del Alright, Rodders? What you up to?

Rodney Cataloguing our stock. I'm gonna put all of this on computer.

Del Computer? Rodney, we've had this discussion before. It's dangerous. Someone could hack in and find what we've got.

Rodney Hack into our computer?! Del, if we found someone was hacking into our computer all the police would have to do is go an' arrest Mr Bean! We need to record it on floppy disk, Del, so we know exactly what we've got.

Rodney pulls open the drawer on a small, old, cardboard filing box which contains a few ancient pieces of paper.

Rodney Look, these are the records for ... Trotters Independent Traders. I began filing 'em when I first started working for you sixteen years ago. But you told me to stop it.

Del Because we don't need them, do we?

Taps temple.

It's all up here, Rodney. Squirrels don't have computers but they know where their nuts are.

Rodney But where d'you get it all from?

Del How should I know? It's like a verruca – you know you've got it, but you don't know where it come from.

Rodney Well, I'm gonna make a note of everything. And I'm gonna chuck a lot of this junk out.

Del Now you be careful, Rodney. Remember, one man's junk is another man's treasures.

Rodney Derek, we have got a pile of Shawaddywaddy LPs in the corner under a tyre for a Triumph Herald and an artificial limb. These are not gonna make big news on *The Antiques Roadshow*!

Del Those LPs are collectors items.

Rodney Well let's find a one-legged Shawaddywaddy freak and flog 'em to him! And if he turns up in a Triumph Herald we've had a result!

Del What is the matter with you, Rodney?

The moment the words leave his lips, Del closes his eyes and silently curses himself.

Rodney What's the matter with me? Didn't anyone tell you?

Del Rodney, I didn't mean it like that!

Rodney My wife was rushed to hospital a fortnight ago and we lost ... There's nothing wrong with me, Del Boy. Everything's hunky dory.

Del Rodney, I'm sorry! What I meant was ...

Rodney I had a dream a few weeks ago. In this dream you and Damien ruled the world.

Del *(pleased with the prospect)* Oh yeah?

Rodney Yeah. You owned companies, corporations, conglomerates everywhere ... It was horrible!

Del What d'you mean?

Rodney You know what I was? I was the messenger! I mean, you and Damien were presidents and chairmen and I was a bloody messenger! And then I started thinking, maybe it wasn't a dream, maybe it's a prophecy. You know, like in the Bible when King David saw seven fat cows and seven skinny ones.

Del No, that sounds more like he's come out of the Nag's Head disco!

Del laughs, Rodney doesn't.

Rodney Perhaps it was a prophecy that I would always be the messenger! The messenger of bloody doom! I mean, nothing has ever gone right for me, has it? I mean, am I being punished for something I did in a previous life? If I am I wish to God I knew what I'd done 'cos I might have enjoyed it!

Del I know how you feel, Rodders.

Rodney I don't think you do, Del! All my life I've tried to do the right thing.

Del So have I, Rodney.

Rodney I've been kind to people.

Del Me too.

Rodney I've never hurt anyone.

Del Nor have I.

Rodney I've paid my taxes.

Del We all do our bit.

Rodney And what's been my rewards? Knock-backs, put-downs and sand in me face. I'd love a bit of good luck, Del. Not just for me, for all of us. For me and Cassandra, for you and Raquel, for Damien and Albert. I just wish something good would turn up.

Del is standing by an old tea chest filled with bits and pieces of old rubbish.

Del Everyone feels the same, Rodney. That's why everyone's doing the Lottery! *(Referring to tea chest)* If this was life's lucky dip, I'd like to put my hand in and go, da daaa. *(Lifts out a pocket-watch)* Bing! There you are, Rodney, I've changed our lives. But ain't that easy is it?

Rodney No.

Del throws the watch carelessly away. We see it land on the top grill of the old gas stove.

Del I tell you what, why don't you and Cassandra come round for dinner tonight?

Rodney I don't fancy it, Del.

Del I've got Raquel's Mum and Dad coming round.

Rodney That's why I don't fancy it!

Del Come on, Rodders! I'm a bit nervous. Raquel's old man's a successful antiques dealer. I don't know what we're gonna talk about. I mean the only antique I've got is Albert. You and Cassie are bright! So when I cock up, which I'm

bound to, you and her can keep the conversation bubbling along … Come on Rodney – for me.

Rodney I'm not in the mood, I've got other things on me mind.

Del Yeah, I understand. Why don't we go up to the flat and talk about those other things?

Rodney I don't wanna – why does everyone want me to talk about it?

Del You've gotta talk about it!

Rodney Got to? What is this, some new law Brussels have introduced? Your wife's had a mis – bad turn, so you've got to talk about it?

Del Alright, alright. Let's just go up to the flat and have a cup of tea.

They both wander away.

INT. DAY. NELSON MANDELA HOUSE/LIFT FOYER.

Three minutes later. One of the lift doors has got an 'out of order' sign on it. Del and Rodney enter and Rodney presses for second lift.

Del Have you made any attempt to discuss this with Cassandra?

Rodney Del, will you just leave it alone!

Del I'm only tryin' to help, Rodney. You can't just keep walking away from it!

Rodney I am not walking away from it! Look, you get the lift, I'll take the stairs.

The lift doors open.

Del Look, hang about. It's here now … Come on, I won't mention it again.

Del and Rodney enter lift.

INT. DAY. THE LIFT.

The lift walls are covered in graffiti. 'Chelsea FC' 'Millwall FC', a few graffiti tags. Del presses the button for floor 12. The lift door closes and we hear the hum of the motor.

Rodney Look at the state of these lifts! What's going on in their brains?

Del Bunch of half-heads, aren't they?

Rodney spots a small piece of graffiti which reads: 'Del Boy is a sex machine'

Rodney Look! 'Del Boy is a sex-machine'. Who'd write something like that?

Del *(Guilty)* Dunno!

Rodney now spots another small piece of graffiti (which we don't see). At this point we concentrate on Rodney and cannot see what Del is doing.

Rodney *(reads)* 'Rodney Trotter …'… The lying gits!

Now the hum of the lift motor stops. We hear

Time On Our Hands

a metallic shaking as if the car has shuddered
to a halt. Rodney looks up to ceiling and then
around him.

What's happened?

Del *(Immediately an uneasiness)* It's broken
down. They're always breaking down! Poxy
bloody council.

Rodney What's the matter with you?

Del Nothing's the matter with me! Just take it
easy, Rodders.

Rodney I'll press the alarm button.

Del I'll do it! Good thinking Rodney! Alarm
button.

*Del, apparently, presses the alarm, but
because the button is masked by his body, we
don't actually see him do it.*
There is no response from button.

Del It's broken! I don't believe it, even the
alarm's broken!

Del starts kicking the metal walls.

Del *(Shouting)* Help! Help. Two men are
trapped in the lift!

Rodney Alright, alright! There's no need to get
in a lather about it. Someone will press for the
lift in a minute, realise it's not working and call
the engineers. We'll be out soon.

Del I just don't like being all closed in like this.

Rodney I never knew you were claustrophobic.

Del I'm not! I just don't like being closed in like
this!

Rodney Look, let's just sit down on the floor
and relax. They'll be here in a minute.

Del Yeah, yeah, that's the way bruv, nice and
easy, nice and easy does it.

They sit with backs to wall.

Rodney The oxygen right falls down to the
bottom, this way we get cleaner air.

Del Good, good!

*We stay on Rodney as he notices another
piece of graffiti. Now Rodney becomes aware
of smoke drifting across his face. We see Del
has lit a cigar.*

INT. DAY. TROTTER HALL.

*Thirty minutes later. Denzil and his assistant
are manoeuvering the last of the furniture out
of the front door.*
They are both absolutely exhausted.
Raquel is in a state of shock.
Denzil wipes sweat from his brow.

Denzil Your lifts have broken again! We had to
carry that stuff up twelve flights of stairs. Del
said him and Rodney'd be here to help. Where
are they?

Raquel *(Numbly)* Dunno.

Denzil Look, it's not my fault, Raquel. Del asked
me to deliver that table and to store this patio
stuff in my lock-up.

Raquel Yes.

Denzil *(Gesturing to lounge)* And the table
and chairs are only on hire, they've gotta go
back by Monday, they're having a big do at the
town hall.

Raquel Yes.

Denzil And then I'll be bringing all this stuff
back.

Raquel Oh good!

Denzil Yeah. *(To assistant)* Come on then!

INT. DAY. THE LIFT.

*Thirty minutes later. Del and Rodney have
both removed their coats and unbuttoned
their shirts. They are both sweating. Del
paces, his claustrophobia reaching breaking
point.*

Del They're not here yet, are they?

Rodney Give 'em time. Sit down, take it easy.

Del sits next to Rodney.

Rodney Let's play a game.

Del A game? You got a ball on you then?

Rodney No. A different sort of game. I Spy.

Del I Spy?

Rodney Yeah. Go on, you can go first.

Del Alright, dopey! I spy with my little eye
something beginning with W.

Rodney Er... walls?

Del Walls. Yes, that's right. Well, that's the end
of that game then, innit?

Rodney Well, you choose the game.

Del How about hide'n'seek?

Del now stands and paces again

Rodney I never thought I'd see you like this!
You're acting like a big kid just 'cos we're stuck
in a lift for awhile.

Del Yes, well you don't know how I feel!

Kicks the lift doors a couple of times.

I feel ... I feel sort of frightened! You don't know
what that's like!

Rodney I don't know what it's like! How d'you
think I've felt for the last couple of weeks since
Cassie ... since what happened ?

Del I don't know, Rodney, I don't know how
you've felt!

Rodney Well, I'll tell you, frightened ain't the
word! D'you know what I did last night?

Del No, but I bet it was depressing!

Rodney I sat and read my diaries from when I
was a school kid.

Del See, I was right!

Rodney No, not quite. I actually noticed

263

moments of hope inside those pages – I mean there weren't many – just the occasional oasis of promise in a desert of pessimism. They were simple hopes, as you'd expect for someone of my age. I hoped for – hairs, hoped I'd do well in my exams, I even hoped for a good job when I left school.

Del Well, you got hairs, didn't you? Think how Right Said Fred must feel.

Rodney Me and Cass were so happy, Del. We were looking forward and all we could see in front of us was a big wide highway and we were just cruising like we were in a Rolls-Royce. And suddenly it came to a shuddering halt – just like this poxy lift. Suddenly 'Happy Families' became 'Dungeon and Dragons'. And I've never felt sodding pain like that in all my life.

Del Is Cassandra hurting?

Rodney Well, of course she is!

Del How d'you know? You haven't talked to her about it.

Rodney No, and d'you know why? Because … it's because … It's almost like if I don't talk about it, it might not be true.

Del But it is.

Rodney I know! I know. But if I don't say it …

Del If you don't say what?

Rodney We lost our baby!

Del But you did – and now you've said it.

Rodney Yeah. I've said it! You just shield yourself from it, you know. I've just been lying, ain't I?

Del In a way. And what about Cassandra?

Rodney Not her. Cassandra can't tell a lie.

Del Raquel can, the moment one leaves my lips.
They both laugh.

INT. DAY. TROTTERS' HALL/LOUNGE.

Albert enters carrying a 'wine rack' shopping bag that tinkles with bottles. He too is exhausted.

Albert *(Calls)* Both those lifts have broken down again!

Albert opens door to lounge. Albert opens door from hall. The bench-type pub table and all the patio furniture has been replaced by a long, twelve seater dining table and 12 chairs – the kind you might find in a manor house. There is no three piece suite for anyone to sit on. Raquel is just standing and staring at the furniture.

Is this the stuff Del was talking about?

Raquel Yes.

INT. DAY. THE LIFT.

Rodney Cassie seemed so fragile. I wanted to cuddle her and talk to her about it – but I was frightened I might – sort of break her.

Del No. She's strong, Rodney. It's a dropped stitch in life's tapestry. That's what mum used to say when things went wrong.

Rodney Yeah, I suppose that's about the strength of it when you think about it.

Del Of course it is. You two'll pick up the bits and pieces and be cruising down that big highway again. Cassandra wants to talk about it, she told Raquel.

Rodney What do I say to her?

Del All the things you just told me – well, you can leave the bit about the hairs out. You go home and have a heart to heart with her right now. And while you're there, you ask her if she fancies coming round for dinner tonight.

Rodney Yeah, I'd love to Del, but there is the little matter that I'm stuck in a lift.

Del Oh yeah.
Del now moves to the lift's control panel and opens it.
Let's have a look in here.

Rodney *(It suddenly dawns on him)* Your claustrophobia cleared up quick, didn't it?

Del Yeah, I seem to be over the worst.

Rodney Almost as quick as that flu you had this morning.
Rodney stands.

Del Well, these things come and go don't they? Oh look, there's a little switch in here.
Del turns a switch and we hear the hum of the lift motor and the metallic shuddering as the lift begins moving again.
There you go.

Rodney You git! You stopped it!

Del It was the only way I could get you talking! You can't run away in a broken lift.

Rodney You git!
Del is laughing.
Now Rodney is laughing too.
You! You git!

INT. NIGHT. TROTTERS' LOUNGE/HALL.

The big table is laid for dinner. It's busy and eday, everyone rushing in and out of the kitchen trying to help. Rodney is opening a bottle of sherry. Cassandra is placing wine glasses on table. Del is behind cocktail bar pouring himself a Tia Maria and Lucozade. Raquel enters from kitchen and checks table.

Raquel What else, what else? I'm bound to

Time On Our Hands

have forgotten something.

Cassandra Everything's fine. Calm down. You'll have a hot flush in a minute.

Raquel I'm just so nervous something will go wrong … Del, please don't use any of your French phrases to my parents.

Del Right you are sweetheart. Aren't they up on the old French then?

Raquel No … The meat!
Raquel rushes to kitchen.

Rodney I'll get some wine, put it in the cooler.

Del *(To Cassandra)* Well, we seem to have everything under control.
Damien is seated at the end of the table playing with a Star Wars type space rocket. He lands it on and across the table.
Damien! Don't do that!
Takes rocket from Damien.
It's only plastic, you'll break it.

Cassandra What did you say to Rodney?

Del Me? Nothing.

Cassandra He came home and he was – I don't know – kind of different. We sat down and talked about what happened and he accepts it now. He seems ready to get on with things.

Del It was nothing to do with me Cassandra. I told you, give Rodney time and he'll come round all on his own.

Cassandra Yeah …
She kisses Del on the cheek.
Thank you.

Del That's what I'm here for.
Rodney, with wine, and Albert, in best suit and rows of medals, enters from kitchen followed by Raquel.

Albert I've made the gravy and put it in the oven.

Raquel Thank you, Albert.

Rodney Where we gonna sit once dinner's finished?

Del *(Indicating the same places.)* You'll sit there, Cassandra'll sit there, Raquel …
At this point the front door bell rings.
Everyone freezes and looks towards hall.

Raquel Oh God!

Albert Calm down the lot of you. I'll answer the door. Lot of good you'd have been on the Russian convoys.
Cut to Trotters' hall. Albert enters from lounge and opens front door to James and Audrey, Raquel's parents. James is in his early 60s, well-spoken and smartly dressed. He is an ex-navy man who enjoys a laugh and a drink. He is carrying a bottle wrapped in paper. Audrey is in her mid 50s, middle class,

well meaning but lacking in sense of humour – not a fierce person – just doesn't get jokes..

Albert Good evening. You must be be Raquel's parents.

James Yes. My wife, Audrey, and I'm James.

Albert Lovely to meet you. Please follow me.
Albert exits to lounge. James is looking at Audrey questionably.

Audrey *(Whispers)* She did say he was older than her.

James I know, but …
Cut to lounge. James and Audrey enter.

Raquel Hi Mum, Dad.

James Hello, darling.

Audrey Darling.
Damien rushes at them.

Damien Nanny, Grandad!
James picks Damien up.

James Hello, champ, how are you?.

Raquel Mum, Dad, this is Derek's brother. Rodney, and his wife, Cassandra. James and Audrey.

Rodney and Cassandra Pleased to meet you.

James Pleasure.

Audrey Lovely to meet you

Raquel And this is my … this is Derek.

Del Au revoir.

Audrey Oh you're Derek.
About to indicate Albert.
We thought …

James *(A false cough)* We thought … we thought you were busy working this evening.

Del Oh no, not on a special occasion like this.

James As it is a special occasion I've bought this rather nice bottle of port. It's 15 years old.

Del 15. We'll have to be careful with that, it might have acne! *(Laughs)* Please, Jim, Audrey take a seat and I will fetch us an aperitif.
As Del passes Rodney and Cassandra and winks at them.
I'm knocking 'em bandy!
We see Rodney and Cassandra look at each – Del's going OTT already.

INT. NIGHT. TROTTERS' FLAT. LOUNGE/ KITCHEN.

The first course is finished and cleared from the table. Now the table is loaded down with tureens of vegetables and a covered silver salver containing the noisettes of lamb. Del is dishing the lamb onto plates as Raquel brings another tureen in. Albert enters from kitchen with the gravy boat. Albert then returns to kitchen.

Del Rodney, would you fill the glasses, please?

Rodney Yes of course. More wine Audrey … James?

James No, I don't think I should. I've got to drive back to the hotel tonight.

Raquel Why don't you get a cab back, pick the car up in the morning?

James What d'you think?

Audrey It's your decision.

James What the hell. Pour away, Rodney.

Del Yes, that's the spirit, you know it makes sense. You can always leave your car outside …

Reacts.

On second thoughts we'd better put his car in my garage.

James Is it not safe outside?

Del Well, not if you've become attached to your wheels it's not.

Hands last plate out.

There we go, look, s'cuse fingers. I'll just get another bottle of wine.

Del exits to kitchen.

James So Albert was in the navy?

Raquel Very much so.

James I was in the Royal Navy myself, twelve years, first officer.

Cassandra You and Albert'll have to have a chat.

Rodney *(Under his breath)* After we've gone home!

Cut to kitchen. Albert is making the coffee, pouring boiling water into a glass coffee pot. Del is uncorking another bottle of wine.

Del The old wine's going down well, we need another bottle. What are you doing?

Albert I've made the coffee.

Del It's too early! They 've only just got their main course.

Albert It don't usually take us that long to finish our dinner.

Del But we're not galloping down a Big Mac and chips, are we? We've got guests, we're taking our time savouring the food and the ambience, we're sipping the wine and we're conversing. They're having a chat between each mouthful. It's sophisticated, it's civilised …

Picks up coffee pot.

I'll stick it in the microwave.

He now gets a whiff of the coffee – he smells it again.

What coffee d'you make this with?

Albert That jar over there.

We see a jar of coffee and next to it a jar of gravy granules.

Del This ain't coffee, smell it! It's bloody gravy!

Albert *(Smells it)* Yeah, that's gravy. It's not my

fault, it's them jars! Look at 'em! How am I supposed to tell the difference?

Del It's easy! One's got Nescafé Coffee on the label and the other's got Bisto granules!

Albert Well, I was in a hurry and I got 'em mixed up.

Del Wait a minute. If you've made gravy in the coffee pot, what are they pouring over their dinners?

Cut to lounge. Rodney, Cassandra, Raquel, James, Audrey and Damien are all at table with their dinners in front of them. James is pouring gravy on his dinner.

James This looks lovely darling.

Rodney Yeah looks great, Raquel.

Raquel Thank you.

The door to kitchen opens and Del pops his head out.

Del Alright?

Audrey *(Pouring 'gravy' on dinner)* Wonderful.

Del Cushty.

Del closes door. Cut to kitchen

Del They've done it. They're doing it now. They're pouring Maxwell bleedin' House over their lamb noisettes and veg. I don't believe you! Not only have you managed to sink every aircraft carrier and battleship that you ever sailed on, now you've gone and knackered a gravy boat! What are we gonna do?

Albert Well, I ain't having any of it!

Albert exits to lounge leaving a worried Del in kitchen. Cut to lounge.

Albert enters and takes his place at table. Damien is about to eat some of the food.

Raquel Not yet, darling, wait for Daddy.

James So, how long were you in the navy, Albert?

Albert Over fifty years, man and boy. Started in the merchant, went on to the Royal then back to the merchant.

Audrey Amazing. You must have some stories to tell.

Rodney Oh God yes.

Del enters from kitchen with open bottle of wine.

Del Sorry to have kept you, bit of trouble with the cork.

Del takes place at table.

Cassandra *(Offers gravy boat)* Del?

Del NO! I mean I'm tryin' to give it up. *(Offers boat to Albert)* Uncle?

Albert Not for me, son.

Del Go on, have some! *(Quietly)* You git!

James Are you a naval man, Derek?

Del Me? Not really James, I'm more of a leg

Time On Our Hands

man myself.

Raquel No, Dad meant were you in the navy!

Del Oh I see. No, although when I was younger I toyed with the idea of a career in the services.

Audrey has just taken a mouthful of food. She reacts to the coffee and lamb flavour.

Raquel Everything alright, Mum?

Audrey *(With a mouthful of food)* Mmmhh!

Damien This is horrible!

Raquel eats some food and reacts. She looks to Del who shrugs.

We now see Rodney and Cassandra reacting to the vile taste.

James I hope you won't be offended darling, but I'm rather full up.

Rodney, Cassandra and Audrey Same here!

Del We've got a lovely sweet out there, apple, everything.

Audrey I'm not really that hungry.

Rodney, Cassandra and James Me neither.

Raquel Alright … Well, I'll fetch the coffee.

Del Right.

As Raquel enters kitchen. Del and Albert look at each other in horror knowing Raquel is about to bring in a pot of gravy.

INT. DAY. DEL'S GARAGE/GARAGE BLOCK.

Following morning. Del has just reversed James's car (small BMW) out of garage and is parking it as James arrives on foot. Rodney, in working clothes, is inside garage continuing his cataloguing of the Trotters' stock.

Del Ahoy there, Jimmy.

James Morning, Derek … Rodney.

Rodney How are you this morning?

James Oh fine. Had a bit of a jippy tummy last night.

Del Must have been something you drank.

James More than likely. Well, thanks for looking after the car.

Del Mais oui, my pleasure.

James So this is your Alladin's cave I've heard so much about?

Del Yes, we are in very much the same business, Jimbo. You're an antiques dealer and I'm … I've got some interesting pieces.

James Yes! Well, must dash, long journey. You'll have to come and visit us sometime.

Del Love to. Drive carefully.

James is now looking round the inside of the garage. James is just about to move to his car when he spots something on top of the old gas stove.

James What's that?

Rodney Em … It's a gas stove.

James No, on top of it.

James picks up the old, tarnished watch.

Del Oh that's just an old watch I got out of a house clearance years ago. I've got a lovely collection of Shawaddywaddy LPs.

James opens the watch and looks inside.

James Good Lord!

Del Yeah, it's dirty, innit? Rodney, you got any of that WD4O there?

James No, I mean, it has the name 'Harrison' engraved in it. You see there? 'Harrison. AD 1774'.

Del Yeah, I never looked inside. Is that good?

James Good? John Harrison was just about the finest watchmaker of his time – of any time. How did you come by this watch, Derek?

Del Well, it was about fifteen, sixteen years ago. There was this old girl down Deptford way. She owned a pawn shop. Anyway she died, no family, so the shop was sold off and the landlord of her house asked me to clear the place out. I found that up in the loft.

James Did the landlord pay you to clear the house?

Del You're joking, the tight old git. No, I was given a score for the privilege. Although I found a lovely little rocking chair that went for fifty sovs, so I was happy.

James Would you have any proof that this watch is your property? A receipt, something like that.

Del No, you see, I don't keep receipts, they just clutter the place up and …

Rodney Hold on. Sixteen years ago? That's when I started working for you.

Del Yes thank you, Rodney, leave *This Is Your Life* to Michael Aspel.

Rodney I mean, I kept files in those days.

Del and Rodney move to the small cardboard cabinet and Rodney begins sifting through the small amount of paperwork. James remains by cooker.

James You see, Derek, I'm something of an amateur horologist.

Del *(Quietly)* I thought it was too good to be true. Now he's gonna tell our bloody fortune.

Rodney No, an horologist. It means an expert in watches.

Del Oh that sort of horologist.

Rodney produces a piece of paper.

Rodney I've got it, I've got it. The receipt from the landlord.

Reads from receipt.

For two paintings, four jugs, one rocking chair – one silver fob watch engraved 'Harrison'.

Del Good boy, Rodney. What have I always told you? Make a note of everything. You never know when you might need it.

Gives receipt to James.

There you go, Jimbo.

James This is marvellous. I've never been so excited.

Del I bet Audrey had a blinding honeymoon!

Rodney What exactly do you think it is then?

James I'm almost too frightened to say it! Let me give you a brief history lesson. Back in the early seventeen hundreds sea captains found it almost impossible to plot their positions once out of sight of land. They could work out their latitude by using the sun or the pole star …

Del Doddle.

James But they couldn't work out their longitude. Until John Harrison invented a clock that could tell them exactly where they were on the globe. In fact, he went on to make many of these marine timekeepers, they're called H one to five and they are all at the Greenwich museum. But it's known he was working on H six or as he called it – 'The Lesser Watch', We have his designs for the piece but the watch itself was never seen. Harrison died in 1766 and nobody knows whether he ever completed his great work. So the lesser watch drifted into the realms of mythology .

Rodney Mythology? What, was he Greek?

James No he was English, he lived not far from here.

Rodney *(Half laughing)* You don't think that's it, do you?

James *(Deadly serious)* If it is, Rodney, it's a major, major discovery.

Rodney Blimey!

James Would you mind if I took this with me Derek? There's some people I'd like to look at it.

Del Could I just have a word with my partner here? One moment. *(To Rodney)* If that watch is worth money, he might half inch it.

Rodney Del, if he rips us off, he's also ripping off Raquel, his only daughter, and Damien, his only grandchild.

Del Yeah, he seems sound as a pound to me. Right Jim, you take it with you.

James Thank you. Have you got some old rags to wrap it? I want to keep it completely safe. Can I use this?

Rodney That's my coat.

James I'm sorry.

Del *(Handing him some old rags)* There you go.

James Thank you. I feel almost faint.

Del Well, you be careful driving that car, Jimmy

– I don't want that watch getting damaged.

INT. DAY. NAG'S HEAD.

Three weeks later. Lunchtime.
Del and Rodney, both dressed smartly, and Denzil and Trigger, in working clothes, are at the table. Boycie is at the bar talking to Mike.

Rodney So next thing, Raquel's old man's on the phone to us.

Del The experts have looked at it and it's kosher.

Denzil This is the watch that's been missing for over three hundred years?

Del Yep. Harrison's Lesser Watch.

Trigger So what is it?

Del It's a watch!

Rodney Its more than that. It lets you know exactly where you are anywhere in the world.

Mike How's it get lost then?

Rodney I don't know how it got lost! It just did.

Del And then I discovered it and realised it's true value. If it hadn't been for me, it could have ended up anywhere.

Rodney Yeah, like chucked on top of an old gas cooker.

Boycie And it's gonna be auctioned?

Del That's right. This afternoon, two thirty at Sothebys.

Denzil How much d'they think it's worth?

Rodney They don't know. Nothing like it's ever come on the market. Could be ten grand.

Del Fifteen at least.

Rodney Twenty maybe.

Boycie Well, on your way back from the auction pop into my showrooms. I've got two lovely Skodas at five grand each

Laughs his laugh.

Del Yeah, you won't be laughing like that when we get back.

Mike So you two could be famous then – well, amongst watchmakers.

Rodney Yes. Yeah, why not. We discovered it. And as Andy Warhol said, 'Everyone will be famous for fifteen minutes'.

Denzil How can everyone be famous for fifteen minutes? There's not enough time in the world?

Rodney No, no. He didn't mean everyone would be famous! You know. He was generalising upon the modern society. You know, people become famous for a little while then they disappear. Like Rene and Renatta, Simon Dee.

Trigger Or Gandhi.

Rodney Yeah. So see maybe this time it's … Gandhi?

Time On Our Hands

Trigger Yeah. I mean, he made one great film and then you never saw him again.

Del *(Taps his watch)* Let's go.

INT. DAY. SOTHEBY'S AUCTION ROOM.

Ninety minutes later.
A packed house. Some people on telephone receiving instructions from abroad.
The auction is already in progress for some other clock or watch.

Auctioneer Thirty five thousand … One more bid. Forty thousand … The bid is forty thousand pounds.

Del and Rodney enter and stand at the back.

Del Is that ours, Rodney?

Rodney Don't be stupid!

Auctioneer Forty five thousand … Forty five thousand. I'm selling at forty five thousand. That was lot 72.

Lot 72 is removed.
Now we see the porter displaying Del and Rodney's watch. The watch has now been cleaned and is gleaming silver.

Rodney Is that our watch?

Del Yeah, They've given it a rub over with Brasso.

Auctioneer Now we come to Lot 73.

We see people sitting up and taking notice, we hear a buzz of expectation and excitement.

This is quite simply the most significant discovery in horological terms of this century. The watch has been authenticated and accepted by all the leading experts as being made in 1774 by John Harrison. It is the, until now, mythical 'Lesser Watch'. I'd like to start the bidding at one hundred and fifty thousand pounds.

Rodney's mouth drops open. We hear a body thud and find Del laying on the ground. Rodney leaves him there.

Auctioneer Thank you …

Takes bid.

Two hundred thousand …

Takes bid.

Two fifty.

INT. DAY. SOTHEBY'S RECEPTION OR ANTE ROOM.

Del is seated on chair still feeling a bit faint, Rodney is next to him.

Del Oh dear. It was when he said a hundred and fifty thousand. That's when I came over bad.

Rodney *(Also in shock)* It went on, Del. Two hundred thousand, two fifty, three. That's when I dragged you out.

Del You mean it ended up at three thousand pounds?

Rodney It's still going on?

Del Well, let's get back up there.

INT. DAY. SOTHEBY'S AUCTION ROOM.

We see Del and Rodney enter.

Auctioneer Three and a quarter. The bid is in the room. Three and a half.

Del It's three hundred and fifty grand!

Auctioneer *(Takes bid)* Three and three quarter. Four, thank you. The bid stands at four million. *Del's mouth drops open. We hear a body thud next to him.*

Four and a quater, the bid is in the room … *(Takes bid)* Four and a half million … *(Indicates someone on phone)* With Dubai … *(Takes bid)* Five million *(Indicates someone on phone)* With New York … *(Takes bid)* Five and a half million – in the room.

Fade out on auctioneer's voice.

EXT. DAY. LONDON STREET.

We see the three wheeled van parked at a meter. A sign in van's window reads: 'midwife on emergency call'.
We see Del and Rodney approaching. They have just left the auction and are in a state of deep shock. They climb into van (Del driving).

TROTTER VAN. INT. DAY.

Del and Rodney just sit quietly for a moment. They are both very calm-shocked.

Del So, what was the final outcome?

Rodney It was bought by an anonymous bidder. He's giving it to the Maritime Museum at Greenwich. So, at least it stays in the country.

Del Oh good. I meant what was the final score? How much exactly did it go for?

Rodney *(Takes some paperwork pocket)* Six point two million.

Del closes his eyes as acid indigestion grabs him.

Rodney Just over three million each

Del Well we've had worse days, ain't we?

Rodney Oh yeah … D'you wanna go first or shall I?

Del How about together?

Rodney Alright then. One, two, three.

Now they both go absolutely potty – screaming, punching the air, hurling themselves about. We see a passerby witness this lunacy.

Right, calm down. We'd better go home and tell the girls, but let's break the news gently, we

don't wanna spoil a nice day like this by taking one of them to the cardiac-arrest unit.

Del No, there's somewhere else I wanna go first.

EXT. DAY. BOYCIE'S CAR SHOWROOMS.

Thirty minutes later. The sign above showrooms tells us this is: 'Boyce Auto's' 'Used Cars of Distinction'. Del and Rodney are looking at a Rolls-Royce.

Boycie Oh no! Talk about the barbarians at the gates. Do you have to leave that van thing outside my showrooms? Customers might think I've been reduced to advertising for the local cinema – they're showing *The Flintstones*.

Del If only you knew, Boycie, if only you knew!

Boycie Gimme the keys

Del chucks him the van keys and moves over to the Rolls-Royce. Boycie calls to his 18-year-old car cleaner.

Boycie Tony, drive that van round the corner, will you?

Tony To the car park?

Boycie Or the scrapyard, which ever comes first

Tony You're not worried it's gonna get nicked are you?

Boycie Nicked? Who's gonna nick that thing? Other than a recently arrived Albanian joyrider. It certainly ain't gonna be used in a ram raid, is it?

Boycie moves off to his office. We now see the object of Del's interest. It is a 3 year old Rolls-Royce. A sign on it reads:
'Car of the Month' It is priced at £80,000

Del Beautiful innit? Luxury and style. Very me don't you think?

Rodney Yeah ..! Buy it.

Del Shall I?

Rodney You like it, buy it.

Del *(Bottle goes)* No. Not until that cheque's cleared. I've got a terrible feeling that this entire deal's gonna go pear-shaped.

Rodney Del, we're dealing with Sotheby's and the Greenwich museum, not Ronnie and Reggie!

Del But in case this goes tits-up! I'll be left with an eighty grand debt.

Rodney Yeah, take your point. Well, you sit in the nice car, see if it suits you.

Rodney looks towards Boycie's office with a vengeful smile. Rodney walks away leaving Del making 'bip bip' noises.

INT. DAY. BOYCIE'S OFFICE.

Boycie is behind desk with paperwork. Rodney enters.

Boycie You'll be bringing the family down next

to have your picture taken next to it. Picnic hampers and God knows what else.

Rodney I wanna buy it.

Boycie bursts out laughing.

Rodney That's a good 'un, Rodney! Tell me, what drugs are you on this week?

Rodney hands Boycie the paperwork. Boycie studies the cheque as his laughter dies. He looks to Rodney for help or an explanation.

Rodney Six million. We were hoping for a bit more, but the market's a bit depressed.

Boycie Sit down please. Sonia, fetch me and Mr Trotter a coffee.

Boycie opens a cocktail cabinet.

Boycie Drink?.

Rodney T'riffic.

INT. DAY. BOYCIE'S CAR SHOWROOMS.

Del is now walking round and admiring – drooling – over every tyre and body contour. Rodney and Boycie approach.

Rodney *(Hands Del keys)* There you go. It's yours.

Del You what?

Rodney The Rolls-Royce. It's yours. I've just bought it for you.

Boycie Soon as the cheque clears Del Boy, it's yours.

Del You bought it for me? Why?

Rodney A little present. Just to say thanks.

Del turns and looks at the car lovingly – emotionally.

INT. DAY. TROTTERS' LOUNGE.

Raquel, Albert and Cassandra wait anxiously for Del and Rodney's return.
Albert is on the phone.

Raquel *(Checking her watch)* Where the hell are they?

Cassandra Perhaps they're in discussion with the directors at Sotheby's.

Raquel gives her a withering look.

Cassandra No, perhaps not.

Raquel Maybe they're talking with the curator at the museum.

Cassandra Maybe.

Albert *(On phone)* Thanks a lot. *(Replaces receiver)* They're not at the Nag's Head

Cassandra I guessed Rodney wouldn't be in the Nag's Head, Albert.

Raquel Has he stopped drinking?

Cassandra No, he's been barred.

We hear front door close and now Del and Rodney enter. Raquel, Cassandra and Alb look

Time On Our Hands

at them expectantly – is it good news or bad news? Del and Rodney don't want to just blurt the news out and cause heart attacks and so we have a kind of Mexican stand-off. Finally …

Raquel Well?

Del Yeah, fine thanks.

Raquel No! I meant, what happened?

Rodney Oh, at the auction?

Cassandra Yes, at the auction! Did it sell?

Rodney Yeah, it sold, didn't it, Del?

Del Yes, we sold it.

Albert I knew it. Beautiful piece of machinery … How much d'you get?

Del Guess.

Raquel Oh come on, just tell us!

Rodney No, go on guess.

Albert Five thousand pounds?

Del No.

Raquel and Cassandra's spirits visibly sag in disappointment.

Albert Six thousand.

Del Close. Add a nought.

Cassandra Sixty thousand pounds?

Del You can tell she works in a bank, can't you?

Rod Hardly any hesitation … No, not sixty thousand. Add another nought.

Albert But that's … what is that, Cassandra?

Cassandra Six hundred thousand pounds?

Del No ..! Will you tell 'em or shall I?

Rodney Erm … You can have the privilege, Derek.

Del Thank you, Rodney. You two girls hold on to your stays … Add one more nought.

Raquel, Cassandra and Albert exchange disbelieving glances. Cassandra just stares wide-eyed at Rodney. Rodney returns a gentle nod. Raquel looks at Del and shakes her head. Del smiles and nods his head. Del hands them the Sotheby's paperwork. Raquel, Cassandra and Albert read the paperwork. They now look up at Del and Rodney.

Del *(To Rodney)* Call intensive care.

Raquel stands.

Raquel Six million pounds?

Del Mmmh.

Pause.

Raquel now bursts into tears, rushes to cocktail bar for a tissue.

(To Rodney) Told you she'd be happy.

Albert and Cassandra sit in stunned silence. We now see Damien staring at Rodney. Rodney reacts. Damien now smiles at Rodney. Rodney's reaction is one of: 'Did Damien turn this thing round for us?'

Del Now we've gotta take things nice and easy – no going mad and splashing it around on anything that grabs our fancies. I know six million sounds a lot but it'll be very easy to blow it on silly luxuries.

Raquel But we can go out in the week and look for a house, can't we?

Del Of course we can, darling. Any day except Wednesday, that's when my Rolls-Royce is being delivered.

EXT. NIGHT. NAG'S HEAD.

Parked here are a few ordinary cars and a couple of builder's vans etc. Now we see Del's Rolls glide in to a space.

INT. NIGHT. NAG'S HEAD.

We hear a buzz of conversation in the bar, it is full of people in deep discussion and the impression is they are all talking about the Trotters' new-found fortune.

We see Trigger and Denzil in conversation at a table. We see Mickey Pearce and mates discussing the situation. We see Mike, Boycie and Marlene at the bar discussing it in bewildered terms. Now everyone becomes aware that the Trotters are in the house. They all look towards entrance door.

Here we find Del, Rodney, Albert, Raquel and Cassandra. They are all dressed in brand new and very fine clothes – even Rodney has a cigar. At first the Trotters are unsure of the welcome and they pause uncertain whether to venture any further.

Now Denzil stands and begins clapping. Now the whole pub rises in applause. It is genuine delight from everyone, except Boycie. The Trotters puff their chests out and meander through the adoring masses. Del returns a small, royal wave and they all accept the handshakes from Trigger and Denzil and pats on backs from Mickey Pearce, etc.

It is a show of real warmth and affection from all the locals and regulars.

The Trotters are proud and dignified and enjoying every bloody second of this public approval. They are not flash or lauding it – just enjoying their fame – Del might even get emotional.

Del and Rodney arrive at bar to receive a reluctant and vinegary handshake from Boycie and Marlene.

Mike *(Grinning proudly at his famous customer)* Yes, sir, what can I get you?

Del Champagne all round, Michael.

Cheers from the crowd

Rodney Whoops. We've only gone and left our wallets at home again.

Mike Please, that is no problem.

Del On the slate, Mike?

Mike On the house!

Del No, we'll pay our way. And while we're at it, let's have all your sandwiches!

Del and Rodney both reach in pockets.

I'll get 'em.

Rodney It's alright. I've got some money here, somewhere.

Del No, no Rodney. I'll get the sandwiches, you bought the Rolls.

Rodney *(Laughing)* You bought the Rolls!

EXT. NIGHT. TROTTER MANOR.

It is a large, imposing detached house somewhere in the home counties which we might guess would have cost a million pounds. An estate agent's sign says the house is sold.

A house sign says this is Trotter Manor.

Parked in the in-and-out gravel drive is the Rolls-Royce, the green Capri and the three wheeled van, all lit by passive-lights.

Virtually every window in the house is lit to give it a warm, glowing feeling.

INT. NIGHT. TROTTER MANOR. DRAWING ROOM.

The furnishings and decor are a mixture of Del and Raquel's tastes. From Raquel we have the more practical and understated, nice three piece suite, etc, coupled with various examples of Del-chic, such as the large, family portrait of Del, Raquel and Damien hanging above the fireplace and the olde English bar complete with repro horsebrasses.

Raquel is seated on the settee reading to a pyjama-clad Damien in front of the crackling log fire.

Del is behind bar smoking an oversized cigar and pouring champagne into three glasses.

Del takes a moment to look proudly around his castle and at his family.

Albert enters wearing an elegant silk smoking jacket over a crisp white shirt and cravat.

Del compliments him on his dress as he hands him a glass of champagne. They are trying desperately to be posh.

Del shows Albert a brochure for a large white motorlaunch (a 250,000 job)

Albert studies the brochure admiringly.

INT. NIGHT. RODNEY AND CASSANDRA'S APT/LOUNGE.

A large, modern and stylish penthouse apartment somewhere in the heart of London.

From the floor to ceiling picture windows we can see the lights of London glittering below like christmas tinsel.

Rodney, dressed the way he now feels – rich, relaxed and confident – looks round his castle.

Rodney *(With a clenched fist victory gesture)* Yeah!

He turns to find Cassandra is watching him. She smiles at him, happy to see him happy.

EXT. DAY. TROTTER MANOR.

A massive back garden, at least two acres. Del and Raquel stand, arms round each other, and look at 'their house'. They turn and smile at each other, still not quite believing their luck.

EXT. DAY. RODNEY AND CASSANDRA'S APT.

Rodney and Cassandra are standing on the roof garden of their penthouse apartment. Stretched out before them is the Thames, the Houses of Parliament, etc.

They also have their arms round each other and, by their expressions, they, too, cannot believe their luck.

Cassandra now notices something below and draws Rodney's attention to it. From Rodney and Cassandra's POV we see a large white motorlaunch gliding along the river with Albert, all done up like a sea captain, at the wheel. Cassandra laughs at the sight. Rodney's reaction is more cautionary – 'Albert's gonna kill someone!'

INT. NIGHT. TROTTER MANOR. LIBRARY.

A few nights later. Del enters and surveys the room. He is wearing a particularly bright pair of slacks (yellow, maybe). He is now beginning to feel like a fish out of water in this large house with so many rooms and so few people to fill them.

He is already starting to miss his old haunts and old mates. He longs for the Nag's Head and the One Eleven Club and The Star of Bengal and the Market and Sid's Caff.

He takes one of the leather bound books from a shelf, opens it and reads for a second. He closes book and replaces it. He literally doesn't know what to do with himself and his time.

Time On Our Hands

INT. NIGHT. TROTTER MANOR. SNOOKER ROOM.

The lights over the table flicker on as Del enters. He takes cueball and rolls it into the pack. He has his snooker table and no-one to play with. He switches lights off as he wanders out of the room.

We get the feeling he is like a big cat trapped in a zoo cage, pacing his alien environment as his frustration and disappointment grows.

EXT. NIGHT. NELSON MANDELA HOUSE.

One hour later. We see Del's Rolls-Royce glide to a halt.

Del alights and surveys the old estate. He is still wearing the bright slacks.

He breathes in a deep lungful of London air and starts coughing. He now smiles in appreciation.

INT. NIGHT. TROTTERS' LOUNGE.

The lounge is in darkness, empty of furniture (except for the old cocktail bar) and bare of pictures and curtains. The front door opens and Del enters.

He switches the light switch on but to no avail and then remembers the power was switched off.

He wanders over to the bar and picks up his old cigar-pot. He discovers just one cigar in pot, removes it, lights it and savours it. He now studies the room and begins remembering some of the events that have taken place here over the years. Del picks up a suitcase and sits on it. We hear voice over.

V/O Del Boy. It's time to get up. It's seven thirty.

Del Yeah, alright mum.

V/O It's your fault if you've got a hangover. You can't have today off. You're taking your eleven plus.

V/O I never raised a hand to your mother Rodney, except in self-defence.

V/O Your dad always said that one day Del Boy would reach the top but then again he used to say that one day Millwall would win the cup.

Rodney now enters.

Rodney Alright?

Del Yeah. What you doing here?

Rodney Raquel phoned, said you'd gone missing. I guessed you'd be here.

Del I'm just taking one last look at the old place.

Rodney You put it on the market yet?

Del No, not yet. It just didn't seem right selling it. You know, all the – Mum and Grandad. I'll feel alright about it next week, put it with an estate agent. Talking of agents, I called into the travel agents in the week. Booked us all a holiday in Barbados. My treat.

Rodney Oh nice. Flying first class?

Del Concorde.

Rodney Even better. Shame about Albert's boat, weren't it?

Del Yeah, what a stupid place to put a bridge, eh?

Rodney Yeah. Right over a river like that. So how are you?

Del Oh, couldn't be better bruv. It's wonderful – everything's coming up roses.

Rodney Alright, what's wrong?

Del It's all so easy now. All my life I've dreamt of becoming a millionaire. Of having a Rolls-Royce and a big house in the country and jetting off to the Caribbean and all that.

Rodney Well, you've got it.

Del I know. But it's not the way I thought it would be. You see, the dreaming and scheming and chasing and trying – that was the fun part, you know. It was dangerous, impossible – it was like Columbo sailing away to find America, not sure whether he was gonna fall off the edge of the world. That's how I used to feel.

Rodney Well, you fell off a couple of times, didn't you?

Del Once a month regular. But now I've found it – I've got what I was searching for – the hunt is over, and what do I do now? Learn to play golf?

Rodney Well, you've got the trousers for it at least. Look, why don't you just enjoy your retirement?

At this point Del is standing close to and has his back to Albert's/Grandad's old bedroom.

Del I don't wanna enjoy my retirement. I wanna feel like I used to feel – all eager and alive. I want something exciting to happen.

The door to Albert's bedroom opens and Albert appears behind Del who reels away in alarm.

Aaargghh! Blimey Albert, you garrity old git! I thought you was a bloody ghost .

Rodney He never got the hang of this haunting, did he?

Albert What you two doing here?

Del Well. Never mind, what us two are doing here. What are you doing here?

Albert Well, I just came back to pick up a few of me belongings.

Produces duffle bag.

Thought I'd have one last look at the old flat before you sell it.

Rodney Yeah, well, we've all had a good look

now. Let's lock it up and go, shall we?

Rodney and Albert exit to hall. Del lingers taking one last look. Now the BT phone starts ringing.

Del We forgot to tell British Telecom that we were moving. *(Answers phone)* Hello?… Watcher Lennie, how you doing, pal?… Yeah? *(To Rodney)* Lennie Norris. He's got four hundred electronic carpet steamers. Retail at hundred and fifteen, he's selling them at twenty five quid each.

Rodney Del, we're not in the business any more.

Del I know Rodney, but we've gotta double our money on the deal, Rodney.

Rodney Derek, can you hear me over those trousers? We are not in the business anymore, mate!

Albert You've got millions in the bank and you still wanna ponce around making twenty five quid on a carpet-steamer. You make me laugh.

Del *(Very reluctantly)* Yeah, he's right. No I'm sorry, Len, we're not interested. Trotters Independent Traders are no longer in business … Bonjour.

INT. NIGHT. NELSON MANDELA HOUSE.

Parked next to Del's Rolls-Royce is Rodney's Jaguar sports car. Del, Rodney and Albert exit the flats. Rodney moves to his jaguar.

Del D'you fancy going down to the Golden Dragon for a Chinese?

Albert Yes. I'm feeling a bit peckish now you mention it.

Rodney Yeah, I could go a sweet and sour something.

Del Leave the cars, we'll have a toby.

Rodney Yeah, alright.

The three of them begin walking away. Del suddenly stops.

Del Mon Dieu, Mon Dieu, what a fool I've been …

Rodney What's wrong now?

Del Well, there's me thinking now we've got all this money it spells like the end. But it don't – it's

the beginning. Don't you see? For the first time in our lives we've got money to invest!

Rodney No!

Albert Dangerous business, investment!

The three begin walking away from camera arguing.

Del Don't you remember all those years you used to say to me 'We should be investing, Del Boy'.

Rodney No I never said that!

Del Well, it must have been me then. I know one of us was right. We can invest big-time in the futures market. Hey, we can get into Hong Kong, Singapore, Peking.

Albert Beijing.

Del There as well, I don't care.

Rodney You're putting me off my crispy duck! I don't want to invest!

Now, slowly, the flats and the estate begins to fade and the road the three are walking on is transformed into the yellow brick road. Del, Rodney and Albert become cartoon silhouettes and still walk away from us arguing.

Del Rodders, have I ever let you down?

Rodney Yes! Like a couple of years ago when you told me I'd won a holiday in a painting competition but forgot to mention that, for an entire week, I would have to pretend to be 14 years old!

Del That's always been your trouble, Rodney, you always dwell on the past. Mum said to me on her deathbed …

Rodney Now don't start on about Mum and her deathbed!

Del She said to me on her deathbed, 'Del Boy, if you and little Rodney become rich, invest in the futures market!'

Rodney You liar! There wasn't a futures market when Mum was alive!

Del Exactly, it just shows you what a visionary she was! This is our big chance, Rodders. He who dares wins! This time next year we'll be billionaires!

Time On Our Hands

TRIGGER'S BRAIN TEASERS

1. What is Uncle Albert's middle name?

2. How many GCEs does Rodney have and what subjects are they in?

3. What was the full name of the Trotter's mother?

4. Who were Erotic Estelle and Lusty Linda?

5. Who became known as a Jaffa?

6. Del once arranged for Rodney and Grandad to paint a Chinese restaurant yellow. Was it:
a) The Golden Chopstick
b) The Golden Dragon
c) The Golden Lotus
d) The Golden Wok?

7. Slater was a much-loathed policeman and was once married to Raquel.
What was his first name?

8. Match the Trotter and their misdemeanour:
Del   gun running
Rodney   theft of a painting
Grandad   possession of
                  cannabis

9. Who is Rodney's mother in law?

The Nags's Head - Pub Quiz

10. Which Hollywood star was going to appear in *Little Problems*?

11. What is the name of Del and Raquel's child?

12. What club was Rodney forced to join in *The Unlucky Winner Is..*?

13. Before joining the cast of *Only Fools and Horses* as Nag's Head landlord Mike Fisher, actor Ken Macdonald starred in another BBC comedy series. What was it?

14. What blew up in *The Jolly Boy's Outing*?

15. What is Rodney's middle name?

16. By what name was *The Singing Dustman* usually known?

17. Who, according to Mickey Pearce were *'The Coachbusters'*?

18. Which tycoon made a guest appearance in *Miami Twice*?

19. What did Rodney think June, Del's date at the opera, was in *A Royal Flush*?

20. Why is Colin Ball known as Trigger?

21. Which *Carry On* film actress played Auntie Reen in *The Frog's Legacy*?

22. How much money was Del and Rodney's H6 Harrison watch sold for at auction?

23. What was *Only Fools and Horses* originally going to be called?

24. Before becoming an actor, Buster Merryfield, who played Uncle Albert, had another job. What was it?

25. Who is convinced Rodney's name is actually Dave?

26. Who made her first appearance in the episode *Sleeping Dogs Lie*?

27. Who had a number one hit with *Boys Will Be Boys*?

28. Where were most of the recent episodes of *Only Fools and Horses* filmed?

29. Who couldn't pronounce his Rs?

30. According to Rodney, what was the big difference between fictional Wall Street high-flyer Gordon Gekko and Del?

DEL'S DUCKERS AND DIVERS

31. Who directed the x-rated film *Night Nurse*?

32. According to Del, who was Entertainments Officer on the *Belgrano*?

4

The Nags's Head - Pub Quiz

33. What is the name of Del and Rodney's father?

34. What is the name of Boycie and Marlene's child?

35. Who was Otto?

36. What was the name of Rodney's literary masterpiece?

37. Who was nicknamed 'The Ferret'?

38. Which one of these is not one of Del's contacts?
a) Sunglasses Ron
b) Monkey Harris
c) Computer Paul
d) Ginger Ted
e) Dirty Barry
f) Ugandan Maurice

39. What was the name of Rodney's secretary when he worked for Alan Parry?

40. According to his military record where did Albert spend most of the war?

41. Match the people and their occupations:

Brendan O'Shaughnessy	restaurateur
Alex	solicitor
Iggy Higgins	travel agent
Mario	bank robber
Solly Atwell	painter and decorator

42. Why did Grandad complain about paying £1,200 for a hotel?

43. Who was sent to a young offenders home after having 3,000 Green Shield stamps planted on him by Roy Slater?

44. Why, according to Trigger, was Gandhi like Simon Dee or Renee and Renarta?

45. What are the name of Raquel's parents?

46. Which star of ITV's The Bill appeared as a customs officer in *It Never Rains*?

47. What did Trigger lose in Margate?

48. What was Elsie Partridge?

49. How much did Rodney pay for the Rolls Royce he bought Del?

50. According to Boycie, who are rumoured to pay Peckham villain Eugene Macarthy protection money?

51. Who was Sylvester?

52. What destination did Rodney win a holiday to?

53. Chrisopher Ryan, who played Tony Driscoll in *Little Problems* starred in another BBC comedy hit. Was it:
a) Porridge
b) The Young Ones
c) The Good Life or
d) The Brittas Empire?

54. Why was Trigger barred from The Nag's Head?

55. Whose middle name is Aubrey?

56. Whose death led to huge embarrassment for Del and Rodney in *Heroes and Villains*?

57. What was Covington House?

58. What role did Raquel once play in an episode of *Doctor Who*?

59. Why did Mike burn his head with a hairdryer in *Modern Men*?

60. Who was Albie Littlewood?

RODNEY'S GCE STANDARD LIST

61. In *A Royal Flush* what relation is Lady Victoria Marsham Hales's father to The Queen?

62. How old was Rodney when his and Del's father walked out on them?

63. According to Del,
a) Which singer's mother wore the brand of tights he once tried to sell, and
b) Whose sister?

64. Which of these is NOT one of Del's cocktail creations?
a) Drambuie with lime and soda.
b) Grand Marnier and orange.
c) Baileys and blackcurrant.
d) Dubonnet and coke.
e) Tia Maria and Lucozade.
f) Malibu and Cherryade.

65. Where were the Trotter family living in 1936?

66. Whose chandelier did the Trotters accidentally destroy in *A Touch of Glass*?

67. What was the total booze bill at Grandad's funeral?

68. Who was Ivor Hardy?

69. What is the main ingredient for one of Del's Tequila Sunsets?

70. According to Del who was a "little fella, one blue eye, one brown eye, talks with a squint, walks with a stutter"?

71. At what club in Margate was Raquel working as a magician's assistant?

72. Del and Rodney's Grandma once stole a painting. Who was it by?

73. What price did Grandad pay for a budgie from Louis Lombardi in the episode *Who's a Pretty Boy?*

74. When Rodney first met Cassandra, where did he tell her he lived?

75. What name did Dockside Secondary Modern School have when it became a comprehensive?

76. What is 94628/A76?

77. Who was the 'Prodigal Plonker', according to Del?

78. What is the name of Marlene's mum?

79. Who does Del ask for directions to Holland in *To Hull and Back*?

80. Where did Mike Fisher's old landlord pal emigrate to?

81. What was the name of the fish stall that Del ran with Jumbo Mills?

82. What is the name of Denzil's courier company?

83. What would you get if you ordered a mashed monkey sandwich at Sid's Café?

84. Why did Trigger tell the Technomatch Friendship and Matrimonial Agency that he was a bus inspector rather than a road sweeper?

85. How was Derek Duval's lunch with Raquel interrupted?

86. In *Mother Nature's Son* what is the SWANS Committee?

87. What comedy show had *Only Fools and Horses* as the title of one of its episodes?

88. Which veteran BBC newsreader appeared in two episodes *Only Fools and Horses*?

89. What was the proposed name of the spin-off series the BBC planned to make, centred around Rodney Trotter if David Jason had left the series in 1986?

90. Who sang the song Uncle Albert used in the episode *He Ain't Heavy, He's My Uncle*?

8. Del – receiving stolen goods
Rodney – possession of cannabis
Grandad – gun running
Grandma – theft of a painting.

9. Pam Parry.

10. Sir Anthony Hopkins.

11. Damien.

12. The Groovy Gang.

13. *It Ain't Half Hot Mum.*

14. A coach.

15. Charlton.

16. Tony Angelino.

17. Del, Rodney and Albert.

18. Richard Branson.

19. A kissagram.

20. Because he looks like
a horse.

ANSWERS

1. Gladstone.

2. Two – maths and art.

3. Joan Mavis Trotter.

4. A pair of inflatable dolls.

5. Boycie.

6. c) The Golden Lotus.

7. Roy.

The Nags's Head - Pub Quiz

21. Joan Sims

22. £6.2 million.

23. Readies.

24. A bank manager with NatWest.

25. Trigger.

26. Marlene.

27. Bunch of Wallies.

28. In Bristol.

29. Tony Angelino in *Stage Fright*.

30. Gordon Gekko had brains.

31. Mickey Pearce.

32. Uncle Albert.

33. Reg Trotter.

34. Tyler.

35. The Doorman at the One Eleven Club.

36. The Indictment.

37. Albert – for falling down pub cellars.

38. c) Computer Paul.

39. Michelle.

40. Stationed at a storage depot on the Isle of Wight.

41. **Brendan** – painter and decorator. **O'Shaughnessy**
    Alex – travel agent.
    Mario – restaurateur.
    Iggy Higgins – bank robber.
    Solly Atwell – solicitor.

42. Because it was next to a smelly waterworks.

43. Trigger.

44. Because he made one great film and was never seen again.

45. James and Audrey Turner.

46. Graham Cole, who plays, PC Tony Stamp.

47. His inflatable dolphin.

48. A spiritualist.

49. £80,000.

50. The SAS.

51. A: Denzil's wife Corinne's budgie.

52. Mallorca.

53. b) *The Young Ones*, in which he played Mike.

54. For stealing a pork pie.

55. Boycie.

56. Harry Malcolm – landlord of The Crown and Anchor.

57. The ancestral home of The Dukes of Malebury.

58. A lizard person – she had one line.

59. Because it was actually an electric paint stripper – and had been sold to him by Del.

60. Del's best friend who was killed in an accident in 1965.

61. Second Cousin.

62. Six.

63. a) Sacha Distel
    b) Charles Aznavour.

64. Baileys and blackcurrent.

65. Peabody Buildings, Peckham Rye.

66. Lord and Lady Ridgemere's.

67. £86.

68. A pseudonym Del used in *Modern Man* to fool Rodney.

69. Gin.

70. Cassandra's dad, Alan Parry.

71. The Mardi Gras Club.

72. Joshua Blythe.

73. £45 – but he told Del he'd paid £50.

74. Kings Avenue.

75. A: The Martin Luther King Comprehensive School.

76. The number of Rodney's criminal record file.

77. Roy Slater.

78. Dora.

79. A man working on an oil rig.

80. The Isle of Wight.

81. Eels on Wheels.

82. Transworld Express.

83. A corned beef sandwich.

84. To add a bit of glamour.

85. By Charles, the restaurant's headwaiter with news of a telephone call from his "New York office".

86. Spa Water And Natural Springs Committee – it hands out certificates of water purity.

87. Citizen Smith, which was also written by John Sullivan.

88. Richard Whitmore.

89. Hot Rod.

90. Paul and Linda McCartney.

date: 1982 page: 1 of 6

Christmas Trees

This short episode was broadcast on Monday December 27th 1982 as part of the BBC Television comedy compilation, The Funny Side of Christmas.

CHRISTMAS TREES

EXTERIOR. IT IS CHRISTMAS. DEL IS AT A STREET MARKET WITH HIS BATTERED SUITCASE RESTING UPON A CARD TABLE. HE'S SURROUNDED BY A GROUP OF POTENTIAL PUNTERS.

DEL:

Now don't muck about. I'm here to sell my wares and they are guaranteed – guaranteed to cure hardcore, softcore and pimples on your tongue. Now look here, look at this. (HE POINTS TO A TACKY PLASTIC CHRISTMAS TREE) That's beautiful innit, eh? Isn't that beautiful? That's *raise de chassie* as they say in Dieppe. Now be honest, have you ever seen a christmas tree like that before? No of course you haven't, and I'll tell you the reason why. Because this is not an ordinary christmas tree. This is a new advanced micro chip christmas tree as advertised on *Tomorrows World*. Now, I would... (DEL'S FLOW IS INTERUPRED WHEN HE SEES A WOMAN LOSE INTEREST AND TURN TO WALK AWAY) Just a sec... excuse me madam, excuse me... don't you know it's rude to walk away when someone's talking to you? Well go on then, if you must – but hurry back. Listen, this christmas tree contains all the traditional Yuletide values plus 21st century technology. Let me give you just two of its manifold advantages. One – you do not have to buy electric lights, baubles, bangles and beads because this tree comes complete. Two – you don't have to struggle with it like you do the old forest type Christmas tree because this tree folds down (DEL DEMONSTRATES HOW THE TREE FOLDS DOWN USING A TELESCOPIC MOTION) and fits neatly... (HE TRIES TO PLACE IT IN HIS CASE BUT IT IS TOO BIG) it fits neatly, very, very neatly... (IT FINALLY FITS WHEN HE BENDS THE TOP AND DEL SNAPS THE CASE SHUT) into the suitcase. Now if you went up Harrods you'd pay 27 quid for one of these and you'd think that you were getting a right result. Well I'm not going to ask you for 27 quid. I'm not even going to ask you for a score. Who said 15? Who said... put your money away love... put your money away... I don't want 15, I don't want 12. I'm not even asking for 10. Right, come on girls – fastest first wins – it's six quid and I'm having bread and cheese for my christmas dinner. (THE CROWD IS UNIMPRESSED AND BEGINS TO DISPERSE) Come on six quid... anybody? The lot's got to go, Six... six. (DEL LOOKS DESPONDENT. AN OLD LADY APPROACHES. DEL IS DELIGHTED) Alright as you are the first you can have it for a fiver darlin'. There you go, that's it. (DEL GIVES THE OLD LADY A HUGE BOX CONTAINING A TREE, RODNEY WANDERS OVER WITH TWO MORE) Mind you don't fall off your bike.

date: 1982   page: 3 of 6

RODNEY:
I've just got these out of the back of the van.

DEL:
Well you can just take them back again can't you? These are going down about well as Union Jacks in Buenos Aires.

RODNEY:
How many have we sold?

DEL:
Well, including hers... er... one.

RODNEY:
One down 149 to go.

DEL:
What do you mean one down?

GRANDAD ARRIVES, CLUTCHING A THERMOS FLASK.

GRANDAD:
Here you go Del Boy, you left your flask of coffee on the sideboard this morning.

DEL:
Thanks very much Grandad, I could just a go a nice hot cup of coffee. You didn't forget my saccharines did you?

GRANDAD:
I got them this morning.

DEL:
Ah good man.

DEL TAKES A MOUTHFUL OF THE COFFEE AND IMMEDIATELY SPRAYS IT BACK OUT.

DEL:
This is stone cold.

GRANDAD:
Well it would be, it's been standing on the sideboard for hours.

DEL:
Couldn't you have made fresh?

GRANDAD:
I didn't have time to make coffee, I had to get your flask down to you.

CHRISTMAS TREES

DEL:
You silly old... Here, Rodney, chuck that away will you? (HE PASSES THE FLASK TO RODNEY WHO THROWS IT ONTO A PASSING COUNCIL DUSTCART) You could have easily have made some fresh couldn't you? (DEL REALISES WHAT HE JUST SAW RODNEY DO) I meant the coffee you plonker! Stone me, I only nicked that flask last week.

DEL AND RODNEY STARE INTO THE DUSTCART, IT IS FULL OF RUBBISH.

DEL:
Go on, get in there and fish it out.

RODNEY:
I'm not getting in there with all that rubbish.

DEL:
What are you talking about? it's tidier than your bedroom.

RODNEY:
I'm not going in there and that's final.

DEL:
How am I ever going to become a millionaire when I'm surrounded by wallies? Go on, pick up that stuff and we'll go and get a cup of tea at Sid's.

AT SID'S BURGER VAN – A TYPICAL GREASY SPOON. SID HAS A FAG HANGING FROM HIS MOUTH, THE ASH PROBABLY ADDS TO THE FLAVOUR OF THE FOOD HE SERVES.

DEL:
Give us three teas will you, Sid?

SID:
How's your luck?

DEL:
Don't ask, just don't ask. I'll have three ham rolls an' all. (TO RODNEY AND GRANDAD) Do you want anything to eat?

GRANDAD:
I'll have a Wagon Wheel, Del Boy.

RODNEY:
Yeah, I'll have one of those monosodium glutamate pies of yours please.

SID:
(ANNOYED) *Steak* pie.

RODNEY:
So what happens if we don't get rid of them trees, eh? We done our money I suppose?

17

date:1982 page: 5 of 6

DEL:
It's the world recession innit? It's effecting everyone. 'Ere Rodney, come here, come here a minute will you? Come here... I've got something to show you. Every year for as long as I can remember the market traders have given a Christmas tree to that church over there, but this year they just can't afford it. It's the little orphans that I feel sorry for. I mean every Christmas they'd come down from the orphanage, they'd hold an open-air carol service round the tree. Looked really lovely it did – I thought about crying once. Still times change don't they? It's not all *san fairy an oy*. Sid, put them ham rolls in a paper bag for me will you? Come on Grandad I'll give you a lift home. Oi, Rodney see if you can do something with them Christmas trees will you? Good lad.

OUTSIDE THE CHURCH DOOR. RODNEY HAS JUST ERECTED ONE OF THE TELESCOPIC TREES.

RODNEY:
(TO VICAR) Right, ready when you are Rev.

VICAR:
Here goes then. (HE TURNS ON THE POWER, THE TREE LIGHTS UP AND START FLASHING) Oh, they flash.

RODNEY:
Yeah. They're not supposed to. I mean it's not much of a tree but it's the only one I could...

VICAR:
No, you're wrong Rodney. This is the finest christmas tree our church has ever had. You know for a growing number of years I have become dismayed, even shocked by the attitude of youth but today you walked into this church and offered us this tree simply because you care. You have rekindled my faith in the human race. It's not nicked is it?

RODNEY:
(APPALLED ANYONE COULD SUGGEST SUCH A THING OF HIM) No, no of course it's not nicked. I mean, who'd nick that?

VICAR:
Well, God bless you my son. They'll be a place waiting for you in heaven.

RODNEY:
Oh good, well tell him I'm in no hurry, won't you? Merry Christmas.

VICAR:
Merry Christmas to you.

AS RODNEY LEAVES THE CHURCH GROUND HE IS PLEASED WITH HIS WORK, BUT HIS FACE DROPS AS HE HEARS DEL'S LATEST LINE IN PATTER WITH A NEW GROUP OF PUNTERS.

CHRISTMAS TREES

DEL:
Look at that, that is beautiful innit, eh? Because this is no ordinary christmas tree. As I was saying this is the only christmas trees as used and recommended by the Church of England. If you'd just like to cast your eyes over there you'll see what I mean. (DEL SPOTS RODNEY, WHO HAS A FACE LIKE THUNDER) (TO RODNEY) Well done Rodney, I knew you wouldn't let me down. Now as I was saying the Archbishop of Canterbury himself actually has one of these Christmas trees in his front room. Now you could too have one in your front room for the ridiculously low price of just £7. That's all I'm... (A WOMAN LEANS FORWARD) £7 you got £7 lady? Thanks very much. That's the right money... take that one there.

RODNEY:
You dirty little mercenary.

DEL:
We needed someone to promote our product...

RODNEY:
But God? You knew I'd give that tree to the vicar didn't you? All that rubbish about them little orphans. You've got no ethics have you? You don't even know what ethics are do you?

DEL:
Yeah, ethics – they make model aeroplanes don't they? (CUSTOMERS APPROACH) Yes sir, certainly. That's it. Just the right money. Thanks you very much. You take that one.

ROD:
That's Airfix... I don't believe you sometimes.

DEL:
(TO RODNEY) Listen Rodney, just a minute, listen to me. The vicar's happy because he's got a Christmas tree right? The punters are happy because they think they're getting something special right? And we're happy because we're making £3.50 on every tree. So everyone's a winner. Now are you gonna sell a tree? You can sell two if you like.

RODNEY:
No way my son. I've heard of the commercialisation of Christmas but this is taking the... (RODNEY PAUSES AS HE SEES DEL WITH A LARGE WAD OF NOTES) £3.50?

DEL:
All in lovely crisp readies

RODNEY:
(RODNEY SUDDENLY FINDS SOME ENTHUSIASM) (TO PUNTERS) All right girls, have your money ready... no don't worry.

date:1986 page: 1 of 4

Royal Variety Performance

The following scene took place during the Royal Variety Show on November 27th 1986. The opening exterior scene was the first time that part of the show had been pre-recorded.

ROYAL VARIETY PERFORMANCE

EXTERIOR: THE ROYAL VARIETY PERFORMANCE IS TAKING PLACE IN A
LONDON STREET DEL, RODNEY AND ALBERT ARE UNLOADING BOXES OF 12-
YEAR-OLD SCOTCH WHISKY FROM THE VAN.

RODNEY:
Del are you sure this is Delaney's Club?

ALBERT:
Course it is Rodney. I ain't been here for years but I'd recognise it anywhere.

DEL:
Come on Rodney, grab hold. (HE GIVES RODNEY A BOX) Here Albert, this is
yours. Take it will you? (THE BOX IS LABELLED GLEN
McDONALD WHISKY – PRODUCT OF MALAYSIA)

RODNEY:
Produce of Malaysia?

DEL:
Don't worry about that.

RODNEY:
I'd check Del – make sure this is the Delaney's Club.

DEL:
Course it is – look at the sign there, Du-lane-e.

A SIGN WHICH NORMALLY READS DRURY LANE THEATRE IS ONLY PARTLY
LIT SO ONLY THE LETTERS D U LANE   E   E ARE SHOWING.

(CONT) He's got two GCES and he still can't read – come on Albert, in you go.
That's it and you Rodney. Listen the first person you see ask for the manager,
Chunky Lewis.

DEL:
(FROM WINGS) Are you there Chunky, Chunky, are you there? Rodney mind
that big thing will you? (RODNEY TRIPS AND FALLS) You Plonker.

RODNEY:
Sorry.

DEL WALKS ONTO THE STAGE.

DEL:
Chunky are you there? He's not here Rodney. There's nobody here. He's
probably popped out for a doner kebab or something. Anyway drop the gear
down here for a minute. We'll hang about for a while. (DEL AND ALBERT
LOOK AROUND) Here, they haven't half done the place up a bit since we was
here last, eh Albert?

ALBERT:
Yeah, it's changed. He's had a roof conversion, hasn't he? I bet this'll be
lovely when it's finished.

DEL:

Rodney, this is a prime example of what's I've been trying to tell you all these years. See from little acorns. This used to be a tiny little dive of a place didn't it Albert?

ALEBRT:

Yeah, just a little strip joint that's all it was.

DEL:

Still you can see what old Chunky's done with it. He's actually opened it up, knocked a few walls down. Spent a bit of money on the old décor. It's like I've been trying to say to you Rodney, it's your little acorns. I mean you've got to remember, Marks and Spencer's started with a barrow didn't they? Henry Ford – he started with a barn. Nissans – they started with a hut. From little acorns, innit eh? And these (THE BOXES OF WHISKY) are our acorns. This time next year we're going to be millionaires.

RODNEY:

Del, this stuff ain't gonna sell. This is not 12-year-old whisky.

DEL:

That's what it says on the box.

RODNEY:

You printed that. This stuff is not 12 years old.

DEL:

Look we've got and import licence for it Rodney, what do you want – a bloody birth certificate?

RODNEY:

A connoisseur would be able to tell...

ALBERT:

A connoisseur might but members of Delaney's club wouldn't. I mean by the time they get in here most of them have got one paddle in the water.

RODNEY:

(RODNEY HAS NOTICED THE AUDIENCE) Del, there's people out there.

DEL:

Oh yes, so there is. It's alright don't worry about it. They are the members – you can tell – look at there eyes. (TO AUDIENCE) All right don't panic. It ain't a raid. Carry on drinking. Course I expect they are waiting for the performance to start. In the old days you know Rodney, the girls would be on now. Where is he? Chunky, Chunky. Gordon Bennett. Come on.

RODNEY SPOTS THE ROYAL BOX AND IT'S OCCUPANT – HER MAJESTY THE QUEEN MOTHER.

RODNEY:

Albert, Del... Del.

ROYAL VARIETY PERFORMANCE

ALBERT:
(ALBERT SEES TOO) Del Boy.

DEL:
What's wrong?

RODNEY:
Look who is sitting in the box to your right.

DEL:
(DEL THINKS HE MEANS ALBERT, WHO IS SITTING ON A BOX OF WHISKY TO DEL'S RIGHT) Well he's sitting on the box to...

RODNEY:
I don't mean Albert.

RODNEY WHISPERS TO DEL. DEL
GOES TO LOOK BUT IS DAZZLED BY
THE THEATRE LIGHTS.

DEL:
Is that you Chunky?

RODNEY:
The other box?

(DEL CAN'T BELIEVE HIS EYES) No no, it is, its... (ALL THREE BEGINS TO BOW AND SCRAPE. ALBERT SALUTES)

RODNEY:
I think we've made a mistake.

DEL:
Well don't panic, don't panic. Just pick up the gear, pick up the gear. It's alright. Pick it up Rodney, move out, move out. (ALL THREE BEGIN BACK OUT TOWARDS THE WINGS) Slowly, slowly, no one will be any the wiser.

RODNEY:
What about that lot?

ALBERT:
I don't think they noticed us.

DEL:
I mean, we don't want the papers getting hold of this do we, eh?

RODNEY:
No, we'd look right dipsticks wouldn't we?

....**DEL:**
I didn't mean that. I mean – what's Her Majesty doing in Delaney's Club?

The Robin Flies At Dawn

THE ROBIN FLIES AT DAWN

THE VAN IS NOW CAMOUFLAGED AND HAS BEEN FITTED WITH A MACHINE GUN (OR WHATEVER). ROD IS AT THE SIDE OF THE VAN HOLDING A PAINTBRUSH. THE WORD PECKHAM HAS A DASH THROUGH IT AND UNDERNEATH, HAND-PAINTED, IS THE WORD KUWAIT. ROD IS PUTTING THE FINAL TOUCHES TO THE 'T' IN KUWAIT. DEL IS WATCHING HIM WITH A CRITICAL EYE.

DEL:
(TO CAMERA) You switched that thing on yet, Albert?

THERE IS A SLIGHT CAMERA WOBBLE, AS IF SOMEONE IS TOUCHING IT.

ALBERT:
(OOV FROM BEHIND CAMERA) I don't know. How d'you know when they're on?

DEL:
Well I don't know, do I?

RODNEY:
(TO DEL, REFERRING TO ALBERT) He's no David Bailey is he?

DEL:
David Bailey? More like bathe-it-daily.

ALBERT:
(OOV) During the war...

DEL:
Shut up! We ain't got all night.

ALBERT:
I think it's working now, Del.

ALBERT NOW APPEARS. HE JUST GRINS AT THE CAMERA.

DEL:
(TO CAMERA) Good evening chaps.

ALBERT SALUTES WITH HIS RIGHT HAND. DEL SALUTES WITH HIS LEFT HAND.

DEL:
(CONTINUED) This is Derek Trotter reporting from a secret location somewhere in southern England.

RODNEY:
(TO DEL) It's High Wycombe.

DEL:
You dipstick Rodney! You don't know who'll get hold of this videotape.

date:1990 page: 3 of 5

ALBERT:
Saddam Hussein could be watching this in his bunker in Bagdhad.

RODNEY:
Well he ain't gonna be able to make head nor tail of what Del says. He can't ask for a vindaloo without major confusion.

ALBERT:
There you go again. Say there's an officer over there called Major Confusion!

RODNEY:
Oh don't be so bloody daft!

DEL:
(TO ALBERT) I think we'll have to put this on micro-film.

ALBERT:
I think you're right son.

DEL:
(TO CAMERA) As I was saying. We're here, with all the wives and girlfriends. (MAYBE THE GIRLS WOULD LIKE TO CHEER AT THIS POINT TO MAKE THEIR PRESENCE KNOWN) That's that horrible noise you can hear. They've all been at the Doobonnay. And we're at this secret location.

ALBERT:
It's not High Wycombe. It just looks like High Wycombe.

DEL:
(EXASPERATED) God! *Lapin saute!* That is top secret, you dozy old git! (TO CAMERA) Sorry about that. So, we're all in High Wycombe... Shit! Now look what you've made me do.

(NB: LAPIN SAUTE MEANS RABBIT STEW)

RODNEY:
What's it matter ? It's a stupid idea anyway! Who ever heard of sending a three-wheeled van to war?

DEL:
But it's nippy Rodders. It can whizz in an' out of them old sand dunes. You can go right underneath a camel in one of these things and it wouldn't even know you'd been there 'til it go a whiff of exhaust.

RODNEY:
Oh, it'll get a whiff of exhaust alright! They think those five hundred burning oil wells are bad – wait until this thing arrives.

DEL:
There is a finely tuned, thoroughbred engine under that bonnet.

THE ROBIN FLIES AT DAWN

RODNEY:
Oh do me a favour! Half the people on our estate are suffering with bronchitis
'cos of this van!

DEL:
It's just burning a bit of carbon, that's all. This is the Concorde of three-
wheelers. It's just that you don't know how to drive it. See, this van is like a
woman... (LOOKS IN THE DIRECTION OF THE WIVES AND GIRLFRIENDS) It
needs caressing... (ANOTHER LOOK IN THEIR DIRECTION) and a bit of gentle
persuasion... (ANOTHER LOOK)

ALBERT:
I'm saying nothing!

RODNEY:
You could be right. It reminds me of some of your ex-birds – it drinks too
much, makes funny noises and is old enough to know better!

DEL:
Thank you Rodney. (TO CAMERA) Now, in the back of my van you'll find a
few goodies that I'm sending over for you.

ALBERT:
Oh, that's a nice gesture.

DEL:
I'm a nice person, Unc. (TO CAMERA) And it's all selling at knock-down prices.

RODNEY:
You're actually selling stuff to our troops in the Gulf?

DEL:
At knock-down prices Rodney. (TO CAMERA) So, General Peter de Billiard
will collect the dosh, he's on ten per cent, you've got the bargain of a
lifetime and I've done me bit for King and country. Everyone's a winner.
Ventre a terre.

(NB: VENTRE A TERRE MEANS AT FULL SPEED.)

(NOW SERIOUS, POSSIBLY BRING THE WIVES AND GIRLFRIENDS IN) Right,
we've done all the silly stuff now, so I'd like to say a few words on behalf of
your wives and families, us Trotters and everyone back here in Britain. We're
all very proud of what you've achieved over there. Proud of your courage,
your efficiency and the way you've carried it out. All we want you to do now is
get home as quick as possible. So from all of us here, God bless you all.

(THEY RAISE THEIR CANS OF NON-ALCOHOLIC LAGER AND TOAST THE
TROOPS)

DEL:
(CONT) And don't worry about the wives and girlfriends. I'll look after them.
They're safe in my hands. You know it makes sense.

SCRIPTS - VOLUME THREE

RODNEY:
Can we finish it like one of them news reports?

DEL:
Go on then.

RODNEY:
(TO CAMERA) This is Rodney Trotter, News at (CHECKS WATCH) Quarter Past Five, (ASIDE TO DEL) this thing still ain't working properly.

DEL:
(SIDE OF MOUTH) Get on with it!

RODNEY:
(TO CAMERA) From fighter command, High Wycombe.

DEL:
And very soon, in the nearest pub.

THEY ALL RAISE THEIR
CANS AGAIN.

WITH THANKS TO:
*THE ONLY FOOLS
AND HORSES*
APPRECIATION
SOCIETY,
PO BOX 92,
ESSEX, RM6 6DN

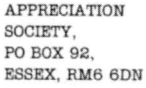

THE ROBIN FLIES AT DAWN

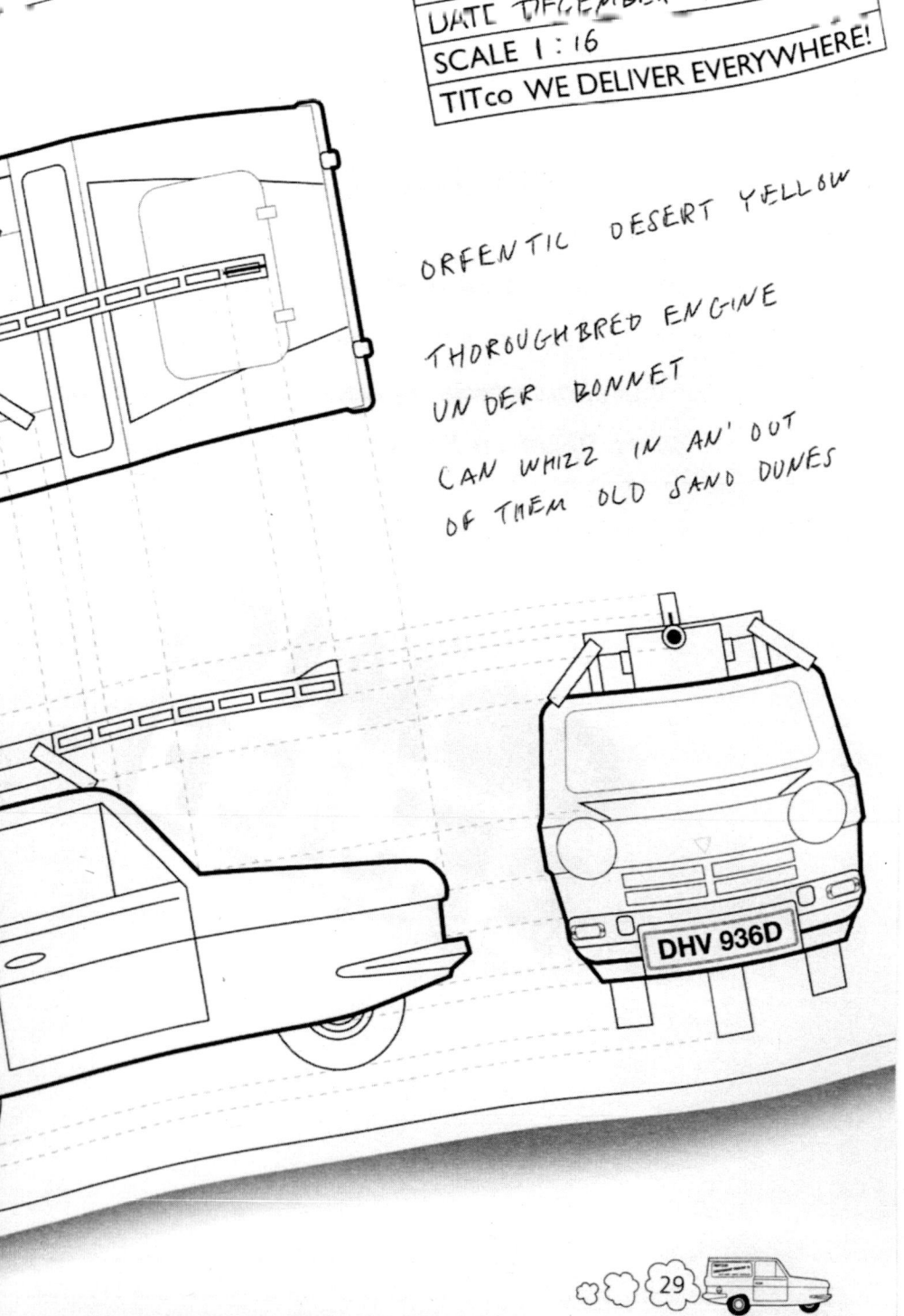

TITLE TROTTER TANK
DATE DECEMBER 1990
SCALE 1:16
TITco WE DELIVER EVERYWHERE!

ORFENTIC DESERT YELLOW

THOROUGHBRED ENGINE
UNDER BONNET

CAN WHIZZ IN AN' OUT
OF THEM OLD SAND DUNES

DHV 936D

Comic Relief Special

The Trotters became millionaires in the christmas episodes in 1996 but were back in the flat as usual for this short special episode broadcast during Comic Relief on Friday 14th March 1997.

COMIC RELIEF

SCENE: THE LIVING ROOM OF THE FLAT AT NELSON MANDELA HOUSE.

RODNEY IS SITTING AT THE TABLE, EATING PIZZA AND READING
A HOLIDAY BROCHURE. DAMIEN IS SITTING NEXT TO ALBERT, ALSO
EATING PIZZA. ALBERT IS SITTING ON HIS CHAIR, LISTENING TO
THE STEREO. DEL ENTERS FROM KITCHEN AND HANDS RODNEY A
CAN OF BEER.

DEL:
Here you go, Rodders. (TURNS TO DAMIEN)
Alright, champ? Oh, thinking of
taking Cassandra away on a little
holiday to Greece, are you?

RODNEY:
Thinking being the operative word.

DEL:
That's very near the place that I went
about four years ago. 'Orrible it was.
Cor dear, yeah. Mosquitoes the size of
sparrows – showed up on radar. And
the place we stayed at – cor, dear – the
room was never swept, the food was
diabolical, and the sheets, they weren't
changed from one week to the next.

RODNEY:
You should have gone self-catering.

DEL:
We did. And then, of course, the
little one, he went and got a
tummy bug, dashing to the khazi
every five minutes.

RODNEY:
Yeah, alright – I get the picture!

DEL:
And then Raquel was frightened
that Damien might catch it.
(RODNEY, PUZZLED LOOKS AT
ALBERT AND DAMIEN) So,
when are you thinking of booking your
holiday then?

date:1997 page: 3 of 8

RODNEY:
Del, we're not going to book the holiday. Me and Cass sat down last night and worked out our finances.

DEL:
Well, what's happened to your wages?

RODNEY:
My wages? I usually blow them on a donor kebab on the way home!

DEL:
No, I meant your combined wages, didn't I? I mean, Cassandra, like, she earns well, doesn't she?

RODNEY:
We've gotta pay the mortgage on our flat, the loan on Cassie's car, rates, life insurance, pensions, heating, food and clothing.

DEL:
That's what I mean – you waste it! Listen to me, though. I had a thought last week.

RODNEY:
Oh, you should have said something – we'd have had a little celebration!

DEL:
Don't you get sarky with me, Rodney! This financial situation ain't all my doing. But I have thought of a way of bringing some serious money in – modelling.

RODNEY:
(SURPRISED) Modelling?

DEL:
Yes, yes! Photographic modelling. Clothes, you know, that sort of thing for magazines and maybe – what – even the telly? (RODNEY POINTS TO HIMSELF AND THEN TO DEL) Hmm? No, not us two, you dipstick! Him! (POINTS OVER TO THE CORNER OF THE ROOM, WHERE ALBERT AND DAMIEN ARE SITTING)

COMIC RELIEF

RODNEY!
Albert?

DEL:
Oh, for god's sake! What could that old duffer be – Captain Birdseye's stunt man?

RODNEY:
Well, who then?

DEL:
Damien!

CUT TO DAMIEN, COVERED IN PIZZA, AND SMILING SWEETLY. CUT BACK TO RODNEY, WITH A WORRIED LOOK ON HIS FACE.

RODNEY:
Oh, I don't think that's a very good idea, Del.

DEL:
Why not? He's a good-looking kid and these model agencies, they're desperate for little chavvies to do adverts like Smarties and all that. Just think Rodders, this time next year... his little face could be on every television set in the country

RODNEY LOOKS AT DAMIEN AGAIN.

RODNEY:
No, no. I don't think it's right, you know, parents pushing kids into show business.

DEL:
No, I would be pushing him, would I? It's in his blood. I mean, you know, look at Raquel.

RODNEY:
What about her?

DEL:
Well, she was in show business, weren't she?

RODNEY:
She was a stripagram!

DEL:
Once, Rodney! Just once.

RODNEY:
What I'm trying to say is, it's unfair to force Damien to do something he might not want to do. I mean, when he's older, he might choose to take up modelling. He might even enjoy it, but it would be his decision.

DEL:
You think the world of that little boy, don't you?

RODNEY:
(WONDERS WHAT TO SAY, AND THEN SMILES) Well.

DEL:
Yeah, I can tell that you do 'cause I can see it in your eyes! Here you are, aren't you lucky, Damie? You've got an uncle that loves you nearly as much as your mummy and daddy.

RODNEY:
So, anyway, we're still stuck in the same potless situation, 'ain't we?

ALBERT:
You two don't know when you're well off.

DEL & RODNEY:
Oh God!

ALBERT:
During the war...

DEL:
Oh God!

ALBERT:
I saw real hardship. Refugees, entire families had lost their homes and didn't know where their baby's next meal was coming from. Same thing's

COMIC RELIEF

happening today. You think you're hard up, Rodney? Well, think about
Africa.

DEL:
What are you talking about? I mean, if he can't afford to go to Greece, he
certainly can't afford to go to Africa!

RODNEY:
No, Del. I think he means, you know, all the starving people in Africa.

DEL:
Oh yeah. Yeah, that's right. We never really think about that, do we?

RODNEY:
No. Well, once a year when it comes on the telly.

DEL:
I mean, well, you know, we think we're hard up but, we've got a roof
over our head, 'ain't we? And we eat every day. It's what I've always
said, Rodney, 'One man's floor is another man's ceiling.'

ALBERT:
We couldn't help them people back in 1941 'cause we didn't have
anything ourselves, but times have changed. I'd love to be able to just
open a door and walk back into 1941.

RODNEY:
How can anyone just walk back to 1941? That's stupid.

RAQUEL:
I'm going to bed, Del.

DEL:
Yeah, alright. Goodnight, Sweetheart.
(RODNEY HAS A LOOK OF DÉJÀ VU
ON HIS FACE) (1) Yeah, don't be so
stupid, Albert. I'm not a Detective
Inspector, but even I can work that
one out! (2)

RODNEY:
To be perfectly honest we don't know
how to end this scene.

DEL:
No, you see we conned you. This

date: 1997   page: 7 of 8

isn't really Only Fools and Horses – we are working for Comic Relief and what we would like to say at this pacific moment in time is, 'Give us some dosh'.

RODNEY:
He means send it to Comic Relief not literally to us...

DEL:
Leave this to me will you Rodney? (AND QUIETLY TO RODNEY) We could start Trotter Relief – everything would go towards charity.

RODNEY:
Yes, but would any of it actually arrive? For the last ten years Comic Relief have been helping the poorest people in Africa but they also support projects all over the UK. They are helping old people who are living below the poverty line.

DEL:
Homeless youngsters who are living on the streets or whose lives have been buggered up by drugs or booze. Women and little 'uns who are being hurt by people who drink too much and loads of other brilliant projects right across the plectrum.

RODNEY:
(WHISPERS TO DEL) Spectrum.

DEL:
Um, mais oui.

RODNEY:
And unlike Del's Ukrainian compact disk player, it works. Tonight we have the chance to improve someone else's life, so please go to your bank or building society.

DEL:
Or give us a bell on 0345 460 460 and...

BOTH:
Give us some dosh.

COMIC RELIEF

DEL:
You know it makes sense.

Notes:
The jokes, of course, are that: (1) Nicholas Lyndhurst plays a character who travels back in time to 1941 in the BBC comedy series *Goodnight Sweetheart* and (2) David Jason plays Detective Inspector Jack Frost in the ITV police drama *A Touch of Frost*.

Del's Cocktail List

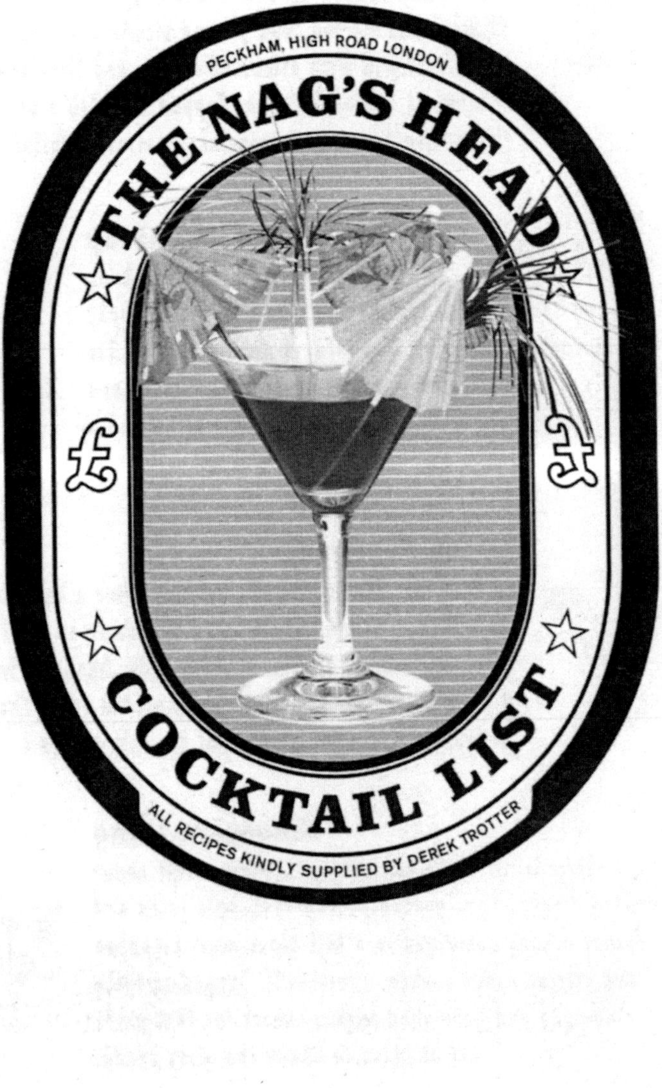
PECKHAM, HIGH ROAD LONDON
THE NAG'S HEAD
COCKTAIL LIST
ALL RECIPES KINDLY SUPPLIED BY DEREK TROTTER

Caribbean Stallion

A shot of tequila and a shot of coconut rum and one of Creme de Menthe, a smidgin' — just a smidgin', of Campari, with the merest suggestion of angostura bitters and topped up with fresh grapefruit juice. Shaken, not stirred, and poured slowly over broken ice. Garnished with slices of orange and lime and your occasional seasonal fruits. Topped off with a decorative umbrella and two translucent straws. Voila!

Peckham Pick-me-up

A wonderful way for high-flying businessman to keep up their energy for those big money deals. Ricky Branson swears by it, I'm told. A double shot of Tia Maria in a small glass, topped up with Lucozade, and served with ice, just one translucent straw and a decorative umbrella. Cushty.

Flying Scotsman

Perfect for relaxing on the balcony after a hard day at the office — or market. A large Drambuie in a tall glass, with lime, topped up with soda, heaps of ice, a slice of lemon and a little cherry on the top. The decorative umbrella is optional for this cocktail.

Singapore Sling

This drink shows those Chinese know a bit about mixing drinks. Gin, grenadine and pineapple juice and cherry brandy combined in a tall glass over ice cubes and stirred - not shaken - very well. Topped up with club soda and garnished with a cherry for that extra bit of class to knock the girls bandy.

Del's Cocktail List

Tequila Sunset

You can almost smell the chilli con carne and sombreros of Mexico when you have this tipple. I actually got the recipe off a Mexican barman who lives in the flat upstairs. Tequila, orange juice combined and poured over broken ice. The decorative umbrella is essential for this one. If I run out of tequila, I use gin.

Lovely Jubbly

Came up with this one myself during a quiet lunchtime at The Nag's Head where my friend Mike makes some wonderful concoctions, which is handy 'cos his beer is like diesel oil. Gran Marnier, angostura bitters, grapefruit juice and hint of Vimto in a tall glass with ice and the umbrella. Too many of these and you can feel a bit Tom Dick, so watch it.

Pina Colada

The creme de la menthe of cocktails. In my game, image is everything and the Pina Colada with all the trimmings sends out all the right signals. Three measures of rum, three tablespoons of coconut milk, the same of pineapple, a few ice cubes, flung in a blender, mixed and poured into a fancy glass. Stick a slice of pineapple on the rim of the glass, a maraschino cherry, a colourful umbrella and a couple of straws and there you have it. Class in a glass.

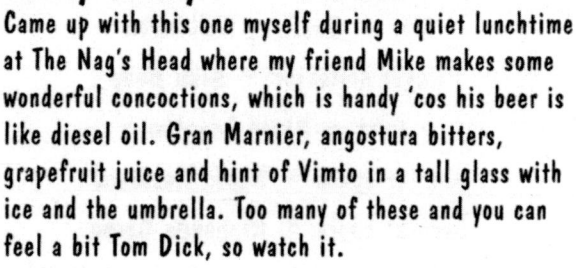

All recipes kindly supplied by Derek Trotter

Derek Trotter ★ David Jason

Rodney Trotter ★ Nicholas Lyndhurst

Uncle Albert ★ Buster Merryfield

Man in market ★ Paul McDowell

Vicky ★ Sarah Duncan

Trigger ★ Roger Lloyd Pack

Policeman ★ Andy Readman

Sid ★ Roy Heather

Dosser ★ Robert Vahey

Eric ★ Geoffrey Wilkinson

Ticket collector ★ Alan Cody

June ★ Diane Langton

Man at opera ★ Robin Hereford

Lady at opera ★ Richenda Carey

St Johns ambulance man ★ Gordon Salkilld

Mr Dow ★ Roger Davidson

Henry ★ Jack Headley

Charles ★ Peter Tuddenham

Patterson ★ Arnold Peters

Carter ★ Ifor Gwynne-Davis

Mrs Miles ★ Kate Williams

Lady at dinner ★ Daphne Goddard

Giles ★ Stephen Riddle

Boycie ★ Jahn Challis

Mr Jahan ★ Adam Hussein

Vicar ★ Angus Mackay

Auntie Renee ★ Joan Sims

Mike ★ Kenneth MacDonald

Cast List

Marlene ★ Sue Holderness

Andy ★ Mark Colleano

Lisa ★ Gerry Cowper

Man in market ★ Duncan Faber

Woman in market ★ Angela Moran

Raquel ★ Tessa Peake-Jones

Mickey Pearce ★ Patrick Murray

Jevon ★ Steven Woodcock

Chris ★ Tony Marshall

Nerys ★ Andree Bernard

Technomatch agent ★ Christopher Stanton

Sonia ★ Jean Warren

Charles ★ Nicholas Courtney

Policeman ★ Paul Beringer

Policewoman ★ Margaret Norris

Naval Officer ★ Martin Cochrane

Mrs Sansom ★ Jean Challis

Cassandra Parry ★ Gwynneth Strong

Denzil ★ Paul Barber

Alan Parry ★ Denis Lill

Pamela Parry ★ Wanda Ventham

Stephen ★ Daniel Hill

Joanne ★ Gail Harrison

Trainee ★ Jake Wood

Harry ★ Roy Evans

Mrs Baker ★ Katherine Page

Helen ★ Dawn Funnell

Mrs Cresswell ★ Rosalind Knight

Inga ★ Bridget Erin Bates

Ramondo ★ Robin Driscoll

Policeman ★ Del Baker

Singer ★ Lee Gibson

Drummer ★ Alf Bigden

Bass player ★ Dave Richmond

Organist ★ Ronnie Price

Eddie ★ Steve Alder

Michelle ★ Paula Ann Bland

Frank ★ Philip Blaine

Chris ★ Tony Marshall

Woman in club ★ Jean Harrington

Neighbour ★ Linda James

TV announcer ★ Patrick Lunt

Vicar ★ Treva Etienne

Baby Tyler ★ Danny Rix

Baby Damien ★ Grant Stevens

Richard Branson ★ Himself

Barry Gibb ★ Himself

Myles ★ Robert Glenister

Damien ★ Robert Liddement

Newscaster ★ Richard Whitmore

Diver ★ Luke Brannigan

Damien ★ Jamie Smith

Beverly ★ Mel Martin

The Dentist ★ Andrew Charleson

Lady on the Bus ★ Kitty Scopes

Arthur ★ Derek Martin

Cast List

Mink ★ Nick Maloney

Vi ★ Lyn Langridge

Policeman ★ Linford Brown

 Texo ★ Bryan Brittain

Casino waitress ★ Lorraine Parsloe

Councillor Murray ★ Angela Bruce

Dream sequence Damien ★ Douglas Hodge

Kenny ★ Steve Weston

Gary ★ Scott Marshall

Scott ★ Dan Clark

Kevin ★ Fuman Dar

Dawn ★ Sheree Murphy

Old lady ★ Bay White

Mayor ★ Robin Meredith

Photographer ★ Richard Hicks

Market lads ★ Lee Barritt/Leonard Kirby

Dr Singh ★ Bhasker Patel

Man in hospital ★ Phil Cornwell

Sister ★ Beverly Hills

Doctor ★ James Oliver

Nurse ★ Corrine Britton

Receptionist ★ Lorraine Ashley

James ★ Michael Jayston

Audrey ★ Ann Lynn

 Auctioneer ★ Seymour Matthews

Tony ★ Jotham Annan